WORKSHOPS IN COMPUTING
Series edited by C. J. van Rijsbergen

Also in this series

ALPUK91, Proceedings of the 3rd UK Annual Conference on Logic Programming, Edinburgh, 10–12 April 1991
Geraint A. Wiggins, Chris Mellish and Tim Duncan (Eds.)

Specifications of Database Systems
International Workshop on Specifications of Database Systems, Glasgow, 3–5 July 1991
David J. Harper and Moira C. Norrie (Eds.)

7th UK Computer and Telecommunications Performance Engineering Workshop
Edinburgh, 22–23 July 1991
J. Hillston, P.J.B. King and R.J. Pooley (Eds.)

Logic Program Synthesis and Transformation
Proceedings of LOPSTR 91, International Workshop on Logic Program Synthesis and Transformation, University of Manchester, 4–5 July 1991
T.P. Clement and K.-K. Lau (Eds.)

Declarative Programming, Sasbachwalden 1991
PHOENIX Seminar and Workshop on Declarative Programming, Sasbachwalden, Black Forest, Germany, 18–22 November 1991
John Darlington and Roland Dietrich (Eds.)

Building Interactive Systems: Architectures and Tools
Philip Gray and Roger Took (Eds.)

Functional Programming, Glasgow 1991
Proceedings of the 1991 Glasgow Workshop on Functional Programming, Portree, Isle of Skye, 12–14 August 1991
Rogardt Heldal, Carsten Kehler Holst and Philip Wadler (Eds.)

Object Orientation in Z
Susan Stepney, Rosalind Barden and David Cooper (Eds.)

Code Generation – Concepts, Tools, Techniques
Proceedings of the International Workshop on Code Generation, Dagstuhl, Germany, 20–24 May 1991
Robert Giegerich and Susan L. Graham (Eds.)

Z User Workshop, York 1991, Proceedings of the Sixth Annual Z User Meeting, York, 16–17 December 1991
J.E. Nicholls (Ed.)

Formal Aspects of Measurement
Proceedings of the BCS-FACS Workshop on Formal Aspects of Measurement, South Bank University, London, 5 May 1991
Tim Denvir, Ros Herman and R.W. Whitty (Eds.)

AI and Cognitive Science '91
University College, Cork, 19–20 September 1991
Humphrey Sorensen (Ed.)

5th Refinement Workshop, Proceedings of the 5th Refinement Workshop, organised by BCS-FACS, London, 8–10 January 1992
Cliff B. Jones, Roger C. Shaw and Tim Denvir (Eds.)

Algebraic Methodology and Software Technology (AMAST'91)
Proceedings of the Second International Conference on Algebraic Methodology and Software Technology, Iowa City, USA, 22–25 May 1991
M. Nivat, C. Rattray, T. Rus and G. Scollo (Eds.)

ALPUK92, Proceedings of the 4th UK Conference on Logic Programming, London, 30 March – 1 April 1992
Krysia Broda (Ed.)

Logic Program Synthesis and Transformation
Proceedings of LOPSTR 92, International Workshop on Logic Program Synthesis and Transformation, University of Manchester, 2–3 July 1992
Kung-Kiu Lau and Tim Clement (Eds.)

NAPAW 92, Proceedings of the First North American Process Algebra Workshop, Stony Brook, New York, USA, 28 August 1992
S. Purushothaman and Amy Zwarico (Eds.)

Formal Methods in Databases and Software Engineering, Proceedings of the Workshop on Formal Methods in Databases and Software Engineering, Montreal, Canada, 15–16 May 1992
V.S. Alagar, Laks V.S. Lakshmanan and F. Sadri (Eds.)

First International Workshop on Larch, Proceedings of the First International Workshop on Larch, Dedham, Massachusetts, USA, 13–15 July 1992
Ursula Martin and Jeannette M. Wing (Eds.)

continued on back page...

Antonio Albano and Ron Morrison (Eds.)

Persistent Object Systems

Proceedings of the Fifth International Workshop on Persistent Object Systems, San Miniato (Pisa), Italy, 1–4 September 1992

Published in collaboration with the British Computer Society

Springer-Verlag
London Berlin Heidelberg New York
Paris Tokyo Hong Kong
Barcelona Budapest

Antonio Albano
Dipartimento di Informatica, Università di Pisa
Corso Italia 40, I-56100 Pisa, Italy

Ron Morrison, BSc, MSc, PhD, CEng
Department of Mathematical and Computational Sciences, University of St Andrews, North Haugh, St Andrews, Fife, KY16 9SS, Scotland

ISBN-13:978-3-540-19800-0 e-ISBN-13:978-1-4471-3209-7
DOI: 10.1007/978-1-4471-3209-7

British Library Cataloguing in Publication Data
Persistent Object Systems: Proceedings of the Fifth International Workshop, San Miniato (Pisa), Italy, 1–4 September 1992. – (Workshops in Computing Series)
I. Albano, Antonio II. Morrison, Ron III. Series
005.1
ISBN-13:978-3-540-19800-0

Library of Congress Cataloging-in-Publication Data
International Workshop on Persistent Object Systems (5th : 1992 : San Miniato, Italy)
Persistent object systems : proceedings of the fifth International Workshop, San Miniato (Pisa), Italy, 1–4 September 1992 / [edited by] Antonio Albano and Ron Morrison.
p. cm. — (Workshops in computing)
"Published in collaboration with the British Computer Society."
Includes bibliographical references and index.
ISBN-13:978-3-540-19800-0
1. Object-oriented data bases—Congresses. 2. Object-oriented programming (Computer science)—Congresses. I. Albano, Antonio. II. Morrison, R. (Ronald), *1946–* . III. British Computer Society. IV. Title. V. Series.
QA76.9.D3I59 1992 92-27164
005.1'1—dc20 CIP

Typesetting: Camera ready by contributors

34/3830-543210 Printed on acid-free paper

Preface

The Fifth International Workshop on Persistent Object Systems took place in the historic setting of Centro Studi "I Cappuccini" della Cassa di Risparmio di San Miniato, San Miniato (Pisa), Italy from 1–4 September 1992. The workshop continued the tradition of the previous four in concentrating on the design, implementation and use of persistent systems. The other workshops in the series are:

	Date	Venue	Organisers
POS1	27–30 August 1985	Appin Scotland	Atkinson, Buneman and Morrison
POS 2	25–28 August 1987	Appin Scotland	Atkinson and Morrison
POS 3	10–13 January 1989	Newcastle Australia	Koch and Rosenberg
POS 4	23–27 September 1990	Marthas Vineyard USA	Dearle, Mitchell and Zdonik

The series of Workshops on Database Programming Languages is closely related to the POS workshops. These have been held every other year out of phase with POS, and tend to concentrate on the design and theory of persistent systems. The workshops in the DBPL series are:

	Date	Venue	Organisers
DBPL 1	7–10 September 1987	Roscoff France	Bancilhon and Buneman
DBPL 2	4–8 June 1989	Salishan USA	Hull, Morrison and Stemple
DBPL 3	27–30 August 1991	Nafplion Greece	Kanellakis and Schmidt

This book follows the format of the workshop. Of the 39 papers submitted for the workshop, 22 were accepted in order to allow plenty of time for discussion. As at POS 4 in Marthas Vineyard each paper was followed by 5 minutes of questions and each session by a 30 minute discussion. The contents of these discussions are summarised by each session chair as an introduction to the papers. An innovation at POS 5 was the introduction of keynote discussion sessions. These were 90 minute directed discussions led by a panel of experts with audience participation. The three subject areas for discussion were operating system support for persistence, persistent type systems, and persistent software environments. The fruits of these keynote discussions were recorded and are contained in this book.

POS 5 was organised by Antonio Albano and Ron Morrison. The superb local arrangements were made by Ettore Ricciardi, Isabella Kardasz and Luigi Mancini. To them we extend our thanks for the excellent food and wine and the general ambience of the peaceful and beautiful surroundings. The picturesque setting of the monastery provided an ideal place to study and relax. The social programme included a visit to Siena on the Wednesday afternoon and evening, and a delightful harpsichord recital by Chiara Tiboni and Annalaura Cavuoto in the old chapel at the monastery on the Tuesday evening.

Each paper was refereed by three members of the programme committee which consisted of:

Antonio Albano (Pisa)
Peter Buneman (Pennsylvania)
Claude Delobel (INRIA)
Gail Mitchell (Brown University)
Marie-Anne Neimat (Hewlett-Packard)
John Rosenberg (Sydney)
Santosh Shrivastava (Newcastle upon Tyne)
Malcolm Atkinson (Glasgow)
Alan Dearle (Adelaide)
Luigi Mancini (Pisa)
Ron Morrison (St Andrews)
Fausto Rabitti (IEI-CNR)
Peter Schwarz (IBM)
David Stemple (Massachusetts)

Fred Brown (St Andrews) and Richard Connor (St Andrews) also helped in the refereeing process.

We would like to thank Helen Bremner for her help in organising the papers at this workshop and Dave Munro, Richard Connor and Graham Kirby for their help in putting the book to bed.

The use of Centro Studi "I Cappuccini" was offered by the Cassa di Risparmio di San Miniato.

Finally, we acknowledge the generous support for POS 5 provided by: Cerved, Consiglio Nazionale delle Ricerche, Università di Pisa, IEI-CNR, Engineering – Ingegneria Informatica S.p.A., Hewlett Packard Italia, Informatica Universitaria s.r.l., Progetto Finalizzato "Sistemi Informatici e Calcolo Parallelo" of CNR and the ESPRIT III BRA 6309 Fide_2.

Antonio Albano
Ron Morrison

Contents

Object Store Addressing

Ron Morrison

Department of Mathematical and Computational Sciences, University of St Andrews
St Andrews, Scotland

Critical to the efficient utilisation of persistent systems are the mechanisms used to position objects in the persistent store and to map them to and from physical store in order that they may be operated on and then made to persist. In the long term, hardware support may be available for these activities but this depends upon the present day object store designers and implementors providing good designs together with experimental evidence of their efficacy. In the short term, persistent object stores have to be constructed using conventional hardware sometimes with some operating system support. Different opportunities for efficient experimentation present themselves with the various combinations of hardware and operating systems available today. It is the role of object store architects to exploit these opportunities to provide the base technology on which persistent systems may be constructed. Evaluation will quickly follow. Presently there are so few working persistent object stores available that each new one is eagerly welcomed into the fold. It is this newness with its innovative technology that makes the area of study so exciting.

Objects in the persistent store reside in the persistent address space (PAS). In order that they may be made available to the ongoing computation they have to be mapped into the virtual memory or physical address space of the machine. During this Workshop session the papers took as background that a paged virtual address space was available and the mapping onto physical addresses was performed by the paging hardware. Two papers, one by Singhal, Kakkad and Wilson, and the other by Vaughan and Dearle concentrated on the mapping of objects between persistent address space and virtual address space (PAS <=> VAS). The components of such a mapping are:

- the nature of PAS addresses,
- the nature of VAS addresses,
- how is the mapping performed, and
- when is the mapping performed.

Both papers made the very pragmatic assumption that the PAS was bounded by the number of bits used to represent a persistent identifier (pid). For Singhal, Kakkad and Wilson this was 32 bits (word) and for Vaughan and Dearle it was 64 bits yielding 2^{32} and 2^{64} byte address spaces respectively. Once an object is allocated a pid in the PAS, it occupies a fixed position and any relocation requires a complete scan of the object store. Furthermore components of objects are also fixed except where an indirection mechanism is used to access them.

The alternative to the above is to use symbolic addressing. This allows for independent relocation of objects but requires a mapping table or set of mapping tables to translate the symbolic address to a fixed address suitable for conversion to a virtual address. This effectively bounds the address space even when the address is two part allowing for the symbolic addressing of object components to accommodate independent relocation of these parts. An example of such a persistent addressing scheme is found in Multics.

Virtual memory systems use an integral number of bits to represent the address and therefore determine the size of the VAS. Most modern machines use a 32 bit word for a virtual address but soon 64 bit virtual address systems will be commercially available. There was some discussion as to whether 64 bits was enough! Hidden drawbacks of some operating systems are that they reduce the effective size of the VAS available to the user and often do not provide support for controlling the paging mechanism.

Where the PAS is smaller or equal to the VAS it is a simple matter to map persistent addresses onto virtual addresses in a 1 to 1 manner. Indeed where this is the case a static mapping is the most efficient. Where the PAS is larger than the VAS only a proportion of the PAS can reside in the VAS at any one time. This implies that translation tables are required to perform the mapping and the reverse mapping of VAS <=> PAS.

The mapping of a persistent address to a virtual address may be performed every time the persistent address is encountered dynamically by inspecting the translation tables. In such cases reverse translation is unnecessary. An alternative is to overwrite the translated persistent address with the virtual address obtained from the translation tables. This technique, known as swizzling, is a relatively simple matter where the addresses are the same size, but more difficult otherwise. Removing an object from the VAS to the PAS now requires the reverse mapping table.

Swizzling can be performed eagerly, lazily or at some point in between. Eager swizzling translates all the persistent address in an object as it is mapped into the VAS. No further address translation from PAS -> VAS for this object will be required as the program executes. Lazy swizzling performs the translation on first encountering the pid. The relative efficiency of these schemes depends on the dynamic load on the system.

In the scheme presented by Singhal, Kakkad and Wilson the swizzling activity is eager. Persistent addresses and virtual addresses are the same size, 32 bits, but the effective VAS is much smaller due to the operating system. Thus the overwriting is simple. In this scheme the PAS is split into contiguous areas equal to the size of a VAS page. The swizzling occurs as the pages are brought into the VAS from the PAS and deswizzling, the reverse activity, takes place on movement from the VAS to the PAS. The cost of performing the swizzling is low compared to the cost of fetching the page. The scheme does however use virtual addresses eagerly. When a page is brought in, the closure of all pages that it refers to are allocated addresses in the VAS. This may cause premature exhaustion of the VAS for which a solution is provided. The system is packaged as a portable C++ library and can be used with any standard C++ compiler.

Vaughan and Dearle begin with a comprehensive survey of existing object store addressing techniques and propose a variation on Wilson's scheme that does not exhaust the VAS so eagerly. The swizzling is neither eager nor lazy but as they describe, a hybrid. Addresses in the current page are swizzled eagerly but others are deferred. By utilising the memory protection mechanism, accesses to PAS addresses can be trapped and resolved on a page by page basis. The authors also allow for a PAS that is twice the size of the VAS and utilise the extra bit effectively in tracing copies of the persistent address.

The third paper in the session by Malhotra and Perry described the use of a workbench for evaluating strategies for allocating objects to pages. An analogous problem of allocating files to nodes in a distributed network is known to be NP complete and therefore some heuristic methods must be used in performing the calculations for even modest numbers of objects.

Allocating Objects to Pages

Ashok Malhotra and Kenneth J. Perry
I.B.M. T.J. Watson Research Center P.O. Box 704,
Yorktown Heights, New York 10598 USA

Abstract

The problem of clustering objects onto units of secondary storage is both important and difficult. It is related to the problem of allocating files to nodes in a network and both problems have been shown to be NP complete. This paper discusses a workbench for evaluating heuristics to solve the object clustering problem and the somewhat surprising result that real problems can sometimes be solved quite easily.

1 Introduction

Several researchers have recognised the importance of storing related objects together and devised various schemes to implement clustering. Some of them [7,9] have observed that clustering can lead to large improvements in performance. The simplest schemes [6,8] allow the programmer to specify which objects should be placed together. The problem with this approach is that while the programmer may have a good idea of local access patterns the global problem is extremely complex and strategies based on local information are likely to be suboptimal, perhaps severely so. A better approach is to use the structure of the object classes to infer access patterns and place objects accordingly [2,9]. Here, again, the information is local, albeit more powerful and pervasive. Both these methods suffer from the shortcoming that access patterns may change as the database evolves and objects are created, deleted, changed in size and are updated to refer to different objects. Thus, even if one of these schemes is used for initial placement, a dynamic algorithm is required to periodically reorganise the database and ensure that good clustering is maintained. Cactis [7] and O_2 [2] incorporate dynamic clustering heuristics.

Our objective is to be able to evaluate heuristics. To do this we devised a workbench that compares the result of a heuristic with the optimal solution obtained by exhaustive enumeration. The algorithm used by Cactis is very similar to a heuristic we evaluated using the workbench. This is discussed later.

2 Model

We model the clustering problem as follows. Assume a database of object instances stored on secondary memory which is divided into pages (or disk cylinders or other physical partitions) of fixed size. The objective is to minimise the cost of some number of queries each of which accesses a set of objects. The cost of a query is directly proportional to the number of pages it accesses.

We formulate the problem over a set of objects O:

$O = \{ o_1 , o_2 , ... , o_n \}$

and a set of queries Q:

$Q = \{ q_1 , q_2 , ... , q_m \}$

such that each query q_i has a probability of occurrence p_i obtained by normalising its frequency (or weight) and contains a set of objects:

$q_i = \{ o_{i,1}, o_{i,2}, ..., o_{i,k} \}$

The database is assumed to contain a number of pages of fixed size. Objects are assumed to have constant size. A solution to the clustering problem is an assignment of each object in O to some page. The cost of a query, given an assignment, is the weight of the query times the number of pages that have to be read to access the objects it references. The cost of a solution is the sum of the costs of queries in Q.

The purpose of this simple model is solely to investigate the effects of clustering. It suffices for deriving lower bounds on the cost of query sets. Other considerations that affect real world performance have been abstracted out.

From the probabilities of the queries and the objects they reference, it is simple to derive the matrix $[p_{i,j}]$ of the conditional probability of accessing object j if object i is accessed. This formulation is similar to the Markov formulation of [10]. This paper also provides a good introduction to the importance as well as the difficulty of the problem and shows that the problem is NP complete. Eswaran [5] shows that the related file allocation problem is NP complete.

That the clustering problem is NP complete means that there are instances of the problem that are very hard to solve. We would hope that the instances that arise in practice, however, are not difficult to solve. Nonetheless, the NP completeness result indicates that the clustering problem is inherently difficult to solve and, most likely, the cost of solving the problem is exponential in the number of objects. The exponential growth is discouraging since for each additional object the cost of solving the problem increases by a multiplicative factor. Thus a problem involving 20 objects is 11 orders of magnitude more expensive than a problem involving 10 objects.

One reason that the cost of solving an instance of the clustering problem is so expensive is that there is a daunting number of possible assignments of objects to pages. Linear or Integer Programming formulations such as the one devised by Chu [4] involve a very large number of variables and become computationally infeasible for relatively modest problems. Existing work on this and similar problems, therefore, tends to focus on developing good heuristics. The purpose of the workbench is to help evaluate candidate heuristics. To test how close a heuristic comes to the optimal, we have to find the optimal and this requires exhaustive enumeration. The following section discusses how the workbench makes exhaustive enumeration feasible.

3 Workbench

A clustering problem of, say, twenty objects gives rise to approximately 10^{24} ways of assigning objects to pages. To make such numbers computationally tractable we first use two observations that are independent of the query set and then use the structure of the queries to further reduce the assignments that are of interest. These techniques are discussed below.

3.1 Canonical Representation

To examine all possible assignments of objects to pages we first generate all the page distributions. A page distribution is a sequence of numbers (the number of objects in each page) each of whose elements is less than or equal to the page size and whose sum is the size of O. Then, for each page distribution, we enumerate all assignments of objects to pages. For a 20 object problem with a page size of 5 there are about 400,000 distinct page distributions and 20! or about 10^{18} assignments per distribution. The first observation we made in an attempt to reduce these numbers is that many of the assignments are permutations of one another. It is possible to avoid permutations by defining a "canonical" representation of each permutation and enumerating only canonical representations instead of all permutations. Given a page distribution, a canonical assignment of objects to these pages is one in which the following properties hold:

1 The objects assigned to each page are arranged in order of increasing object identifier.
2 The pages are arranged so that the identifiers of their first objects are in increasing order.

Given a page distribution the canonical representation reduces the number of assignments that have to be considered for 20 objects from 10^{18} to the order of 10^{10}. This is an improvement of 10^8 but even with this improvement there are a very large number of assignments to consider. Note, that to find the optimal solution, we have to consider page distributions in which all pages are not full. We must consider every page distribution since it is easy to generate examples where the optimal assignment has partially empty pages. To reduce the number of page distributions we made a second observation i.e. the sum of the occupancy of any two pages must be greater than the page size. This restriction arises from the fact that if the objects in any two pages can be completely stored in one page then the one page assignment has a cost that is no greater than the two page assignment. With this restriction the number of distributions that has to be considered for 20 objects with a page size of 5 decreases from around 400,000[1] to 103. This is a great reduction in complexity but there are still 10^{10} assignments to be considered for each distribution!

3.2 Using the Query Set

The canonical representation and the above restrictions limit the enumerations to be considered in a manner independent of the query set. We now discuss reductions that can be achieved by taking into account the particular set of queries.

In searching for a minimum cost solution, we keep track of the current minimum cost. Any assignment with greater cost can obviously be discarded. Moreover, it is possible to determine from a partial assignment that any completion of this assignment to a total assignment will have cost greater than the minimum. Thus, we can use a branch and bound technique to eliminate whole classes of assignments. For example, suppose the query set includes a query with extremely high weight that references exactly two objects. Then any assignment that places these two objects on distinct pages has a cost greater than the weight of the query. If this is greater than the current minimum, there is no need to extend this partial assignment (an assignment of only 2 objects) to the many total assignments that are its completions.

Clearly, for any partial assignment, one cannot determine an exact cost for each of its completions without actually completing the assignment but one can place a lower

---

[1]Note that two page distributions that are permutations of one another are distinct distributions and must both be considered. This is because the canonical representation of an assignment enforces an ordering of objects in the assignment i.e. object 1 is always the first object on the first page.

bound on the cost of the completions. For each query, we can calculate a lower bound on the cost of satisfying this query. This lower bound is just the minimal number of pages required to hold all the objects referred to by the query times the query's weight. The minimal number of pages is calculated as follows:

1 Determine the cost of satisfying the subset of the query involving only the objects assigned in the partial assignment. This simply involves counting how many pages are touched by this subset of the query.
2 Determine by a case analysis whether any pages in addition to those counted in 1. must be touched in accessing the objects of the query not in the subset, i.e., the objects of the query that have not been assigned in the partial assignment:
   - If the number of unassigned objects of the query exceeds the remaining capacity of the page currently being assigned to, then this query must be split across at least one additional page.
   - Even if the remaining capacity of the page is sufficient to hold the unassigned objects of the query, the current page being assigned to must be touched if it was not already touched by the assigned objects of the query.
   - If the page being assigned to has sufficient remaining capacity and was already touched, placing the unassigned objects of this query on the page may not be a canonical representation of an assignment. If so, at least one more page must be touched. By checking whether the object identifiers of the unassigned objects of the query exceed the object identifier of the last object assigned to the page, we can determine whether or not a canonical representation of a completion of the partial assignment is possible.

The net effect of all of the above is to determine as soon as possible whether the splitting of objects into pages induced by the partial assignment causes all of its completions to have cost exceeding the current minimum cost of a total assignment. We will call the set of remaining assignments, i.e. those that have not been eliminated on the basis of any of the above arguments, the set of qualifying assignments. Using lower bound information on partial assignments for the 20 object problem, the set of qualifying assignments included a few hundred elements.

3.3 Exploiting Parallelism

Another technique for attacking computationally large problems is to throw more resource at them. In particular, we use a network of workstations to independently evaluate the assignments. The exhaustive enumeration problem can be easily written to run on such a configuration. Our implementation first generates the page distributions. This is simple and quick. Different distributions are then assigned to different workstations and each workstation exhaustively enumerates the assignments for the distribution as previously described. Because the branch and bound technique uses the current minimum to discard whole sets of assignments, each workstation posts each new minimum it encounters to a shared file so that all workstations can read the latest minimum every few seconds.

3.4 Breaking into Sub-problems

Even with all the previous techniques, there is a limit to the size of problem that can be solved in reasonable time. To go beyond this limit, we break up a problem that involves a large number of objects into several sub-problems that involve fewer objects each.

This is very profitable because of the exponential growth of the problem: the cost of solving 2 problems of 10 objects each is still roughly 10 orders of magnitude less than solving a single problem of 20 objects. The use of this strategy is motivated by the observation that, in practice, most queries access only a small fraction of the total number of objects, and that the sets of objects referenced by many pairs of queries is disjoint. We begin by partitioning the set of queries into "equivalence classes", where the queries in each class reference many common objects. The equivalence classes are selected so that the set of objects referred to by the queries of each class are disjoint. This allows us to consider the queries and objects of each equivalence class as separate, smaller sub-problems that can be solved individually. A heuristic still is necessary because, in actuality, the objects referred to by the queries in two equivalence classes might not be completely disjoint. In practice, two equivalence classes are often joined by only one or two objects whereas the classes themselves contain many more. So the members of the class are "more tightly bound" to each other than to members of other classes.

4 Performance of the Workbench

To gauge the performance of the workbench we ran an experiment assuming an Entity Relationship database [3] and queries that navigate over relationships. We feel that this is a realistic assumption for real world environments. In particular, we took a well known Entity Relationship model and used a set of test cases that were devised as a performance benchmark to generate the queries. We selected several sets of objects and sets of queries from the Entity Relationship database and ran exhaustive enumerations of all qualifying assignments for the sets of objects and queries. In doing the experiment we found something surprising:

- The set of qualifying assignments was very small. For example, a 20 object problem produced a few hundred qualifying assignments out of 20! possible assignments.
- The cost distribution over the qualifying assignments was very flat and at or close to optimal.
- The 20 object problem ran in about an hour on a single moderately powerful workstation, without breaking up the problem into smaller sub-problems.

Thus, exhaustive enumeration can be used to find optimal assignments for problems of moderate size.

The reason for the flat distribution is not difficult to guess. We are looking at the top of a very large distribution and it is not surprising that the few remaining assignments are relatively similar and close to optimal. The low cardinality of the qualifying set is more puzzling. We speculate that this may have to do with the Entity Relationship database and the structure of queries on such a database. In an Entity Relationship database, queries follow predefined paths or Relationships. Often the structure of the database resembles a tree and queries start from the root and navigate different parts of the tree. With such a structure, objects near the root of the tree participate in many queries. Thus these objects must be kept together and this reduces the possibilities enormously.

5 Evaluating Heuristics

The dynamic clustering heuristics mentioned in the introduction [2,7] use reference traces to obtain object reference counts and inter-object reference counts that they use as input. Our approach derives this information from an analysis of the database workload: basically the objects referenced by each transaction. For simplicity, the transactions are assumed to be queries that access the same objects every time they are run. This entails no loss of generality. The advantage of this method is that by keeping statistics on the workload we can tell when the workload changes and the database needs to be reclustered. Also, if the database is used differently during different periods, e.g. predominantly for queries during the week and for batch jobs during the weekend, the database can be reclustered to optimize performance for each type of workload.

We tested several heuristics. The first heuristic (really a class of heuristics) we tested is a greedy algorithm that attempts to place objects with the highest inter-object access probabilities together. This is very similar to the algorithm used by Cactis [7]. The algorithm starts by finding the pair of objects with the highest inter–object probability and putting them in a page. Next, it finds the objects with the highest inter–object access probability to the set already in the page and adds these to the page and so on until the page is full. Several variations of this basic strategy are possible. The problem is that this very reasonable looking heuristic does not work well! This became obvious after comparing the heuristic with the qualifying assignments generated by the workbench. We were then able to construct an example that shows why it runs into problems. Thus, the workbench not only helped us evaluate the heuristic but uncovered its weakness as well.

Consider a simple problem with four objects, a page size of 2 and four queries:

$Q_1 = \{ 1,2,3,4 \}$
$Q_2 = \{1,2,3\}$
$Q_3 = \{1,2,4\}$
$Q_4 = \{2,4\}$

Assuming equal query probabilities, this problem has the inter-object frequency matrix shown below where the entry in row i column j is the number of queries in which object i and object j appear.

-	3	2	2
3	-	2	3
2	2	-	1
2	3	1	-

The heuristic would put objects 1 and 2 in a page as they have the highest inter–object access probability and objects 3 and 4 in the other page. This assignment has a cost of 8 as every query needs both pages. The alternate assignment {1,3}, {2,4} turns out to be better with a weight of 7 as Q_4 can be satisfied with only the second page.

Another problem with this heuristic is that at some stages you end up with a larger set of objects that should be added to a page than can be accommodated in the page. In such a case, the set has to be split in some arbitrary fashion and this can result in poor clustering behavior.

The second heuristic we tested was the graph partitioning algorithm developed by Barnes et al. [1] and is recommended by [10] for the clustering problem. It also does not work well for similar reasons. It, too, looks at arcs which are (weighted) connections between points (objects), similar to our inter–object access probabilities and attempts to minimise the weights of the arcs that are cut. The problem is that it exaggerates the weights of the cut arcs. Consider a single query with many objects. If the objects have to be partitioned into two pages the graph partitioning algorithm computes the cost by adding one for every pair of objects in different pages whereas the true cost is only 2. Using this heuristic on the above example the assignment {1,2}, {3,4} would have a computed cost of 9 while the assignment {1,3}, {2,4} would have a computed cost of 8. These are as opposed to their "real" costs of 8 and 7.

6 Conclusion

This paper has described the construction of a workbench for evaluating heuristics for the object clustering problem. In writing and testing the exhaustive enumeration algorithm we found that in practical cases the set of qualifying assignments for sub-problems was very small, and presented a flat distribution close to optimal. It was also not overly difficult to compute. We intend to continue to use the workbench to evaluate heuristics but even in the absence of a good heuristic the object clustering problem can be solved as follows for many interesting practical cases.

- Break up the problem into sub-problems as discussed earlier.
- Select a best assignment for each sub-problem by enumerating the qualifying set of assignments. Typically, there will be many best assignments.
- Combine the best assignments for the sub-problems to obtain an assignment for the entire problem.

References

[1] Barnes, E.R., Vannelli, A and Walker, J.Q., A New Heuristic For Partitioning the Nodes of a Graph, Siam J. Disc. Math 1988; 1,3

[2] Benzaken, V. and Delobel, C., Enhancing Performance in a Persistent Object Store: Clustering Strategies in O_2, In: Dearle, A., Shaw, G.M., and Zdonik, S.B. (eds), Implementing Persistent Object Bases: Principles and Practice, Morgan Kaufmann, San Mateo, CA, 1991, pp 403-412

[3] Chen, P. P-S., The Entity-Relationship Model - Toward a Unified View of Data, ACM TODS 1976; 1,1:9-36

[4] Chu, W.W., Optimal File Allocation in a Multiple Computer System, IEEE Trans. on Computers 1969; C-18,10

[5] Eswaran, K.P., Placement of Records in a File and File Allocation in a Computer Network, In: Proc. IFIP, North Holland, 1974.

[6] Hornick, M.F. and Zdonik, S.B., A Shared, Segmented Memory System for an Object-Oriented Database, ACM Trans. Office Systems 1987; 5,1

[7] Hudson, S.E. and King R., Cactis: A Self-Adaptive, Concurrent, Implementation of an Object Oriented Database Management System, ACM TODS 1989; 14,3:291-321

[8] Shannon K. and Snodgrass R., Semantic Clustering, In: Dearle, A., Shaw, G.M., and Zdonik, S.B. (eds), Implementing Persistent Object Bases: Principles and Practice, Morgan Kaufmann, San Mateo, CA, 1991, pp 389-402

[9] Stamos, J.W., Static Grouping of Small Objects to Enhance Performance of a Paged Virtual Memory System, ACM Trans. Computer Systems 1984; 2,2:155-180

[10] Tsangaris, M.M. and Naughton, J.F., A Stochastic Approach for Clustering in Object Bases, In: Proc. SIGMOD '91, ACM Press, New York, 1991, pp. 12-21

Texas: An Efficient, Portable Persistent Store

Vivek Singhal, Sheetal V. Kakkad, and Paul R. Wilson
Department of Computer Sciences
The University of Texas at Austin
Austin, Texas USA
oops@cs.utexas.edu

Abstract

Texas is a persistent storage system for C++, providing high performance while emphasizing simplicity, modularity and portability. A key component of the design is the use of *pointer swizzling at page fault time*, which exploits existing virtual memory features to implement large address spaces efficiently on stock hardware, with little or no change to existing compilers. Long pointers are used to implement an enormous address space, but are transparently converted to the hardware-supported pointer format when pages are loaded into virtual memory.

Runtime type descriptors and slightly modified heap allocation routines support pagewise pointer swizzling by allowing objects and their pointer fields to be identified within pages. If compiler support for runtime type identification is not available, a simple preprocessor can be used to generate type descriptors.

This address translation is largely independent of issues of data caching, sharing, and checkpointing; it employs operating systems' existing virtual memories for caching, and a simple and flexible log-structured storage manager to improve checkpointing performance.

Pagewise virtual memory protections are also used to detect writes for logging purposes, without requiring any changes to compiled code. This may degrade checkpointing performance for small transactions with poor locality of writes, but *page diffing* and *sub-page logging* promise to keep performance competitive with finer-grained checkpointing schemes.

Texas presents a simple programming interface; an application creates persistent object by simply allocating them on the persistent heap. In addition, the implementation is relatively small, and is easy to incorporate into existing applications. The log-structured storage module easily supports advanced extensions such as compressed storage, versioning, and adaptive reorganization.

1 Introduction

Texas is an object-oriented persistent storage system implemented as a C++ library. An application linked with the Texas library can create and manipulate two varieties of objects, *transient objects* and *persistent objects*. A transient object's lifetime is bounded by the duration of the program execution in which it was created. That is, when the program terminates, it destroys all transient objects created during that execution. Persistent objects, however, are automatically written to disk so that these objects may be accessed during subsequent program runs; in this respect, persistent objects have properties of file data, while preserving object-and-pointer semantics transparently [1, 2, 3].

In Texas, an object's persistence is orthogonal to its type, in a manner analogous to C or C++ "storage classes." A persistent object is simply one that is allocated in the persistent heap, as opposed to the conventional (transient) heap, or in the activation stack or static area.

For both efficiency and portability, Texas uses a standard C++ compiler; the compiler emits code in the usual way, without distinguishing between transient and persistent objects.

A running program cannot directly manipulate persistent objects on disk; instead, Texas transparently loads objects into virtual memory. Because persistent object storage is intended to replace entire user-level file systems for most purposes, a persistent object can contain references to any of a potentially huge number of other persistent objects. In the current implementation, persistent objects are stored in a single persistent storage file.[1] References between them (*persistent pointers*) are represented as 64-bit file offsets. When persistent objects are loaded into virtual memory, these file offsets are translated into virtual memory addresses (*swizzled pointers*).

This *pointer swizzling at page fault* time efficiently supports very large address spaces on standard hardware; we intend for Texas' addressing scheme to be extensible, and scalable to networked systems where a single address space is used for millions of machines with terabytes of data apiece.[2]

1.1 Features

The Texas persistent store includes the following features:

- *Transparency* A program accesses transient and persistent objects in the same way, because all objects "seem" to reside in virtual memory. If client code doesn't need to distinguish between transient and persistent objects, it is not forced to.

- *Efficiency* In most cases, access to persistent objects is as fast as access to transient objects. The only overhead associated with persistent object access is the initial cost of translating persistent pointers into swizzled pointers when a page is brought into virtual memory.

- *Scalability* Repeated touches to a page incur no extra overhead in address translation; the page fault-time costs should decrease as memory sizes increase and thus the number of instructions between faults increases.

- *Robustness* Texas uses logging techniques to provide checkpointing and crash recovery facilities.

- *Portability* Texas can be used with most C++ compilers and modern operating systems, and does not require any special system privileges or resources.

- *Compatibility* The implementation is compatible with existing code libraries. Recompilation is only necessary if these libraries create persistent objects. Moreover, only minimal source code modifications are necessary for a program to take full advantage of Texas' persistent storage and recovery facilities. (Texas' address translation scheme could also be used to reconcile data formats when sharing data between heterogeneous machines [4] and/or merging previously distinct address spaces.)

---

[1] It would not be difficult to remove this restriction and support a system spread across multiple files and/or devices.

[2] Despite the fact that we actually live in a hilly area, the name "Texas" is intended to suggest a very large, flat space.

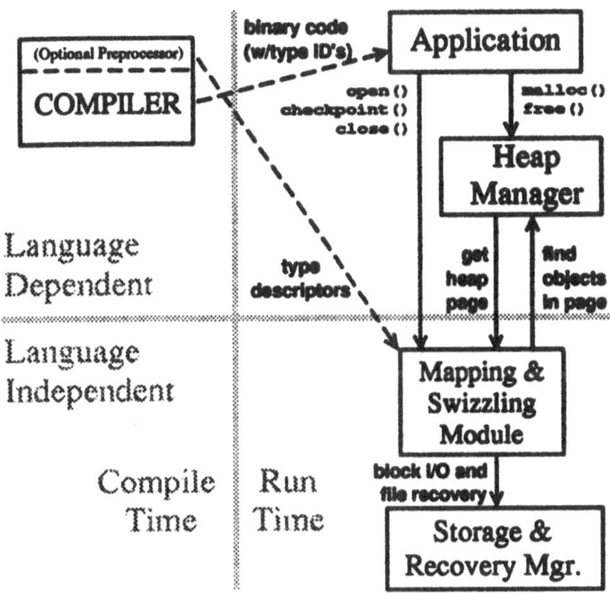

Figure 1: Modular Structure of Texas

- *Pay-as-you-go costs* Texas' pointer swizzling costs are incurred only by programs that need them, rather than by all programs. The costs can be reduced to the vanishing point if the hardware-supported address space approaches (or exceeds) the amount of data in use; it provides efficient backward compatibility with narrow machines and extensibility to very large networks of machines with very large amounts of storage.

- *Modularity* Texas is composed of a set of largely orthogonal modules, with address translation, caching, and checkpointing handled in nearly disjoint code. This has made development easy, and allows experimentation and enhancement by reimplementing small parts of the system.

1.2 Overview

This paper describes the design of Texas, and how its modules implement the above features. Note, however, that several of the algorithms are straightforward, and could be easily replaced with similar algorithms which are better suited to specific applications. Although Texas is currently implemented for C++, it could be used with other languages by replacing the heap manager and type descriptor interface. (see Figure 1).

Several key ideas underlie the design of Texas. The system uses an efficient pagewise address translation technique to provide convenient access to persistent data and to implement huge address spaces. Conventional virtual memory is used in the usual way to cache persistent pages—caching is therefore part of the underlying system, and needn't be implemented for Texas at all.[3] Logging and recovery are implemented separately. Only the pointer swizzling module depends on the format of data objects; caching, disk management, and recovery are done in terms of uninterpreted blocks of data.

1.3 Organization of the Paper

Section 2 discusses pointer swizzling at page fault time, followed by Section 3's discussion of heap management; heap management is implemented on top of the pointer-swizzled memory layer, but provides a hook so that the swizzling code can find pointers within heap objects. Section 4 explains how an existing virtual memory is straightforwardly exploited to provide caching. Section 5 discusses log-structured storage, including its support for pagewise checkpointing and recovery; Section 6 describes several extensions intended to reduce the volume of checkpointing writes. Sections 7 and 8 describe the current status of the system and our plans for future work, and Section 9 concludes the paper.

2 Pointer Swizzling at Page Fault Time

The modular structure of Texas is strongly influenced by the use of pointer swizzling at page fault time. This section describes the algorithm briefly, but see [4] for a more detailed treatment.

Texas uses conventional virtual memory access protections to ensure that the first touch to any page is intercepted. Faulting on a page causes it to be loaded and scanned for pointers, which are then translated into actual addresses. This may require other pages of virtual memory to be reserved for referred-to persistent pages, so that the addresses can be resolved.

2.1 Algorithm Description

When a program gains access to a persistent store, it can request pointers to one or a few special rooted objects, which can be retrieved by name. When a rooted object is requested by name, Texas reserves and access protects a page of virtual memory, which acts as a placeholder for the persistent page containing the object. It then returns an actual virtual memory pointer into that page, i.e., a pointer to the rooted object's position in the page. The persistent page containing the rooted object is not actually loaded into memory until it is actually referenced.

Figure 2 shows the state of the system after traversing a root pointer (to object A) and faulting one page into memory. The page containing object A has already been faulted into virtual memory, had its pointers swizzled, and been made accessible to the program. That page holds pointers into two reserved pages; those pages are reserved for the persistent pages containing objects D and B, respectively, as shown by the dashed double arrows.

If the application program traverses the pointer from object A to object B, it incurs an access protection exception, and the faulting-and-reserving process repeats. The protection fault handler loads the faulted-on page with the corresponding

[3] It would be simple to implement our own caching module, given a facility such as Mach's external pagers. We intend to do just this, to experiment with different caching techniques, but normal virtual memory caching works just fine.

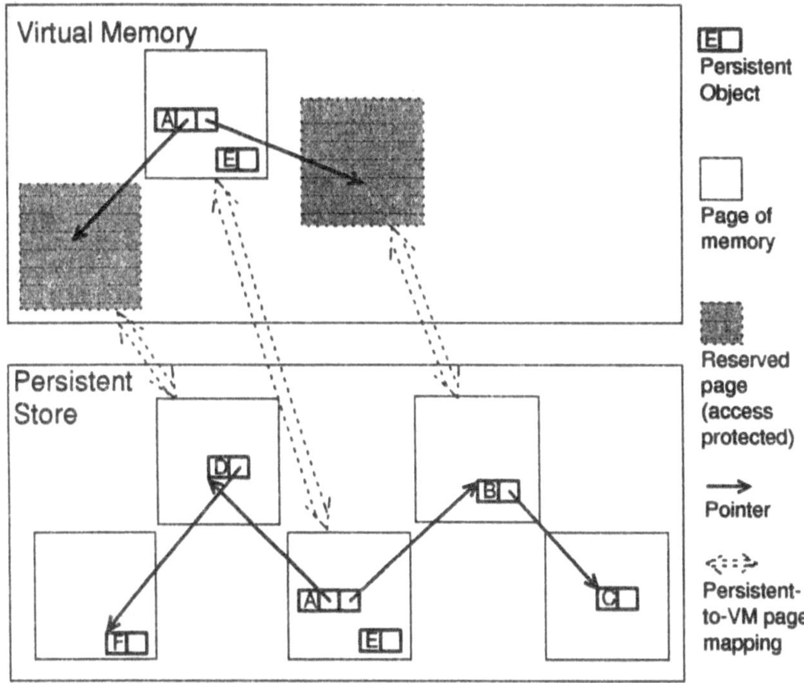

Figure 2: Persistent pages reserved in virtual memory

persistent page, and translates all of the persistent pointers it holds into swizzled pointers.

Even if the object referenced by a persistent pointer does not yet reside in virtual memory, the handler must still provide the eventual address for object. To do this, it reserves (and access protects) another place in virtual memory for the persistent page holding the pointed-to object, C, as shown in Figure 3.

(The mapping between the persistent page and the virtual page is established by recording it in a table. It is then trivial to translate the pointers into the page; it is only necessary to replace the page number bits of the persistent pointer with the (shorter) page number of the reserved virtual memory page.)

Pages of virtual memory are thus reserved "one pointer ahead" of the actual page referencing behavior of the program, in a a pagewise wavefront, just ahead the actual access patterns of the running program. Any page directly reachable from a page that is touched must have space reserved for it in virtual memory. When a reserved page is touched, the wavefront is extended past it, to the pages it holds pointers into.

This wavefront preserves a crucial constraint: the running program is never allowed to see a page containing persistent pointers. It only sees pages containing pointers represented as normal hardware-supported pointers—i.e., actual addresses of objects at particular locations in virtual memory. Pointers to previously-touched pages can be dereferenced in a single load or store machine instruction, just as in a normal virtual memory. This is quite different from conventional pointer swizzling schemes, which require frequent checks to see whether persistent pointers have been

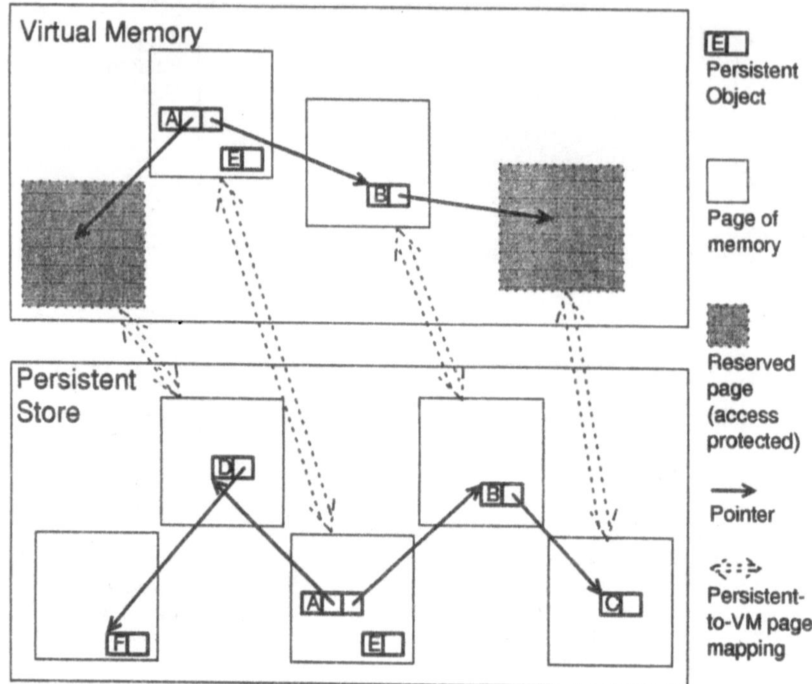

Figure 3: After dereferencing a pointer into a reserved page

converted to actual addresses [5, 6]. The space cost for mapping tables is also small, because pagewise translation requires only an entry per page, rather than an entry per object.

(This incremental process of reserving pages is a variation on Appel, Ellis, and Li's incremental copying garbage collection scheme, which is itself a variant on Baker's incremental copying scheme [7, 8, 9, 4]. The Appel-Ellis-Li system uses page protections to trigger scanning of pages and relocation of referred-to objects, while our system uses them to trigger scanning of pages and relocation of referred-to *pages.*)

Our implementation of pointer swizzling requires no special hardware and no special operating system features to perform well. In modern versions of UNIX, virtual memory pages can be access-protected and protection fault handlers can be set using regular system calls.[4]

We believe page-fault-time swizzling to be especially attractive because it scales well to systems with large main memories. As memories get larger, the average number of instructions executed between page faults goes up; this should make the cost of pointer swizzling proportionally smaller. Conventional pointer swizzling schemes do not have this property, because their checking overheads are directly tied to the rate of program execution.

Another convenient property of our system is that storage and data transfer

[4]We use `mprotect()` to access-protect pages and `signal()` to set protection fault handlers. We do not currently use the `mmap()` system call because its behavior varies significantly between different flavors of UNIX; similarly, we avoided `mlock()` because it requires super-user privileges.

requirements are essentially the same as those of a conventional virtual memory. Pages of data are transferred on demand, and reserved pages do not require any physical storage (neither RAM nor disk) until they are actually used.[5]

2.2 Address Space Reuse

Despite the fact that reserved pages don't require storage, exhausting the virtual memory address space is still a potential problem. If too many pages are reserved, eventually there will be no more uncommitted pages of address space, and pointers to new persistent pages cannot be translated.

Currently, we do not address this issue explicitly; we assume that programs will be broken into individual transactions that do not exhaust the address space. A program that touches and/or reserves gigabytes of pages may have to flush its virtual memory cache back to the persistent store between transactions, and start the faulting-and-reserving wavefront over again for the next transaction.

We intend to address this issue by implementing an incremental *address space reuse* algorithm, which periodically rebuilds the wavefront in a less expensive manner [4]. Rather than actually evicting all pages, only to fault the working set back in immediately, the actual evictions are deferred so that the working set can be kept in transient memory during the rebuilding of the mappings. Incremental address space reuse exploits the fact that caching and address translation are essentially orthogonal—protecting pages and rebuilding address mappings by faulting needn't cause the actual data in the pages to be moved back and forth.

For the present, however, this address space reuse algorithm does not appear to be necessary; we expect that few applications will require it. Even for persistent stores containing many gigabytes of data, few programs are likely to touch (or reserve pages) more than a gigabyte during a run.

2.3 Sharing and Compatibility

In the long run, as computers become more powerful and ever-larger storage is required, we expect the reuse algorithm to deal satisfactorily with most applications. Its performance is dependent on various kinds of locality, however, and it is conceivable that programs with poor locality on a huge scale could suffer significant overhead from rebuilding the wavefront. We believe that such programs will be very unusual for many years, and are likely to be run on very powerful 64-bit machines in any event.

Our pointer swizzling scheme can reconcile 64- and 32-bit addressing, so that most data can be shared between machines with different word sizes.[6] Only programs which actually exercise a 64-bit address space during a run would need to be run on 64-bit hardware. Eventually, it may also be desirable to link many 32-bit and 64-bit machines into a network with a conceptually flat 128-bit address space implemented in software; implementing huge address spaces in software is easy using pointer swizzling at page fault time [4].

---

[5] The current configuration does actually allocate swap disk for pages of virtual memory, but future versions will avoid this by using of `mmap()`.

[6] It is only necessary to use 64-bit pointer fields uniformly. On 32-bit machines, the pointers can be swizzled to 32-bit addresses that actually occupy only half the field. It is even easy to design compatible instruction sets so that binary code can exploit whichever hardware address size is available [4].

In [10], it was claimed that pointer swizzling schemes (including ours) have several drawbacks; we believe these claims to be based on misconceptions, or to be much less troublesome than they seem at first glance. In particular it was claimed that sharing is inhibited by pointer swizzling, and that swizzling costs are unavoidable.

Sharing within a node is not in fact inhibited; it is only necessary for different processes (or protection domains) on the same node to share the same set of persistent page mappings, rather than each process keeping its own set. (The basic protection domain scheme advocated in [10], is entirely compatible with such sharing.)

Sharing pages across nodes in a distributed system would not be costly; in a straightforward scheme, pointers could be unswizzled on transmission and re-swizzled according to the prevailing mappings on the receiving machine. This cost would probably be small relative to the basic trapping and messaging costs in a shared virtual memory.

Equally important, the costs of pointer swizzling could be optimized away in those cases where they are not needed. In a network of 64-bit machines where a larger address space is unnecessary, pages could be permanently assigned to the same virtual addresses on all nodes. Data could then be shared in a "pre-swizzled" format, with no translation costs whatsoever.

One advantage of pointer swizzling in such a network is that it would provide backward compatibility with smaller machines, as well as extensibility for network growth and future machines which might eventually exhaust the 64-bit address space [4]. Small machines would incur costs in swizzling pointers from the globally shared format to their local, narrow format, but this would not affect the performance of the larger-address machines at all. Similarly, the ability to change mappings and swizzle pointers needn't incur any cost until the address space is exhausted remapping actually begins—that is, if you never need it, you never pay for it.

Pointer swizzling at page fault time is thus effectively a "no-cost option," even if one assumes that 64-bit machines will rapidly dominate the market and displace the installed base of 32-bit machines.

In addition, pointer swizzling at page fault time has a large advantage in that it can serve as a reconciliation layer to resolve conflicts between different address spaces. Even in a world of 64-bit hardware, this is highly desirable. For example, consider the case of merging two local-area networks, each with its own flat shared address space (*a la* [10]). Pointer swizzling can be used to resolve conflicts between address spaces without an agonizing renaming process—by its very nature, pointer swizzling at page fault time allows different machines (or subnets) to map the same data to different local virtual addresses. It therefore requires no clairvoyance on the part of system administrators to ensure that no conflicts arise between systems that might eventually be merged, e.g., when an organization is restructured or one company acquires another.

The only remaining concern from [10] is the complexity added by having the memory system rely on pointer-finding within heap data. We believe this to be a very small cost; as the next section will show, our interface to GNU C++ does not require modifying the compiler at all. True "higher-level" languages (e.g., Lisp, Smalltalk, Eiffel, Modula-3) would be even easier to interface with the memory system.

2.4 Type Descriptors

In order to perform pointer swizzling, Texas must be able to accurately locate the pointers within a faulted-on page of data. Although *conservative* pointer identification techniques are usually sufficient for non-copying garbage collection [11], they are unsuitable for pointer swizzling. Pointer swizzling must *accurately* translate between persistent and swizzled pointers; the misidentification of a pointer could result in the erroneous modification of a nonpointer value. (As we describe in [4], conservative techniques *can* deal with pointers from the stack, which is convenient when implementing incremental address space reuse.)

To support identification of objects within a page, we use a slightly modified version of the standard GNU `malloc()` (described more fully in Section 3).

To accurately identify pointers within a page, Texas first finds the objects within the page, and then uses *runtime type identification* information in the objects' header fields to identify the pointer fields. Unfortunately, there is no standard runtime type ID feature in C++ yet. In the meantime, we enhance C++ by defining a *type descriptor* object for every class declared by the program. When a persistent object is created, the memory allocation routine (`malloc()`) augments the object with a type descriptor pointer. This pointer references the type descriptor object that describes the layout of objects of that class.

Type descriptors can be generated automatically by a compiler or by a separate preprocessor. The Free Software Foundation's GNU C++ 2.2 compiler provides a command-line switch to optionally create type-descriptor objects [12]. (Other type descriptor systems have also been proposed and/or implemented, and it is likely that one will eventually become standard for C++. For our purposes, any of them is acceptable.) We are also writing a preprocessor that scans a program's source code for all class declarations and generates corresponding type descriptor definitions; this preprocessor will make Texas independent of any particular C++ compiler.

2.5 Related Work

A commercial object oriented database management system (ObjectStore, from Object Design, Inc.) uses pointer swizzling at page fault time to provide uniform access to transient and persistent objects [13]. Fundamentally, ObjectStore and Texas use similar techniques to implement persistence (developed independently), but few technical details are available about ObjectStore's implementation. The systems probably differ in a variety of ways, not least in their approaches to generating type descriptor information. ObjectStore is closely tied to a proprietary version of AT&T's `cfront` compiler; Texas is compatible with most off-the-shelf C++ compilers through the use of a preprocessor to generate type descriptor information.

Recently, we learned[7] that the basic idea of pointer swizzling at page fault time was apparently discovered and abandoned in the late 1970's, during the development of persistent Algol. A system running under VMS used pointer swizzling at page fault time, but performance was poor, and the technology was never fully developed; the initial disappointing performance was due in part to comparatively high trap overheads and page fault frequencies, given the small memories and slow processors of that time. We also believe that the basic technique may have been devised more

[7] Malcolm Atkinson, personal communication, 1992.

or less independently in several places over the last decade. The Moby address space system for LMI Lisp Machines [14] used pagewise relocation, but pointers were swizzled on discovery (one at a time) using the hardware's support for tagging. (A similar Scheme was later developed for the TI Explorer, and Moby may also have inspired Object Design's system.) A stock-hardware version of a capability-based system [15] developed at Monash University may also use similar techniques, but we have been unable to obtain details as of this writing.[8] A form of pointer swizzling at page fault time was also used in a recent experimental version of the Comandos [16] operating system[9], though apparently it was never fully developed and nothing was published about it.[10] (We welcome correspondence on earlier implementations of pointer swizzling, especially those using pagewise swizzling and/or mapping.)

In any event, simple pointer swizzling has been used in many places; we intend to show in this paper that page fault-time swizzling with pagewise relocation is especially attractive given current hardware and software trends, and that it can be implemented with surprisingly little change to other aspects of a system.

3 Heap Management

Texas lets programs access multiple persistent stores, each with its own heap; programs may also create transient objects on a normal transient heap. A naive memory manager would create separate heap areas for persistent and transient objects. A persistent heap would start at an arbitrary address, and each heap would grow and shrink independently. This design requires an *ad hoc* static partitioning of a process' virtual address space. Our memory manager avoids statically partitioning the address space, and thus unnecessary restrictions on the number of pages used for any particular heap.

To avoid static partitioning limitations, our memory manager manages heap space as non-contiguous sets of pages. A given page holds objects belonging to exactly one heap, but pages belonging to several heaps may be interleaved in any order in memory.

Like any heap allocation system, the Texas memory manager maintains data structures that record free heap space. Because transient and persistent objects cannot reside on the same page, separate *free lists* are maintained for each heap. The free lists are themselves stored as persistent data structures, so that free space within partially-filled persistent pages can be reallocated during subsequent program runs.

The free list for each heap is actually structured as a vector of separate free lists for different *size classes*. A size class is simply a small range of object sizes; objects are allocated in free chunks of memory large enough to hold the actual size of object, but possibly with wasted space if there's not an exact fit.

When an object must be allocated and the free list for the appropriate size class is empty, a new page is allocated to that heap, and it is immediately divided into a page full of uniform-sized chunks, which are linked onto the free list.

---

[8] From [15], it would appear that this system swizzles object identifiers, rather than persistent addresses, requiring per-object translation tables. The version documented in [15] (for specialized hardware) swizzled pointers *on discovery* [6], rather than at page fault time, as our system does.

[9] Pedro Sousa, personal communication, 1992.

[10] Comandos also uses object identifiers rather than persistent addresses, and requires per-object mappings.

Like the standard GNU `malloc()`, our heap allocator expends little effort attempting to coalesce free blocks into larger blocks. (In the case of the GNU malloc, this is because it favors speed over space costs: it is often unnecessary to coalesce blocks, which often end up being split again anyway, wasting time both ways.)

Splitting each page into uniform-sized chunks, makes object identification extremely easy. We only need to examine the header of the first object in the page; its size class—and thus the size class of all the objects on the page—can be determined. The alignment of objects' headers follows trivially.

A special exception is the case of objects that are too large to fit on a single page, and cross page boundaries. Rather than recording the actual size class for such pages, the page is flagged as being part of a large object. Large objects' boundaries are stored in a special table, so that their starting addresses (and type descriptors) can be found.

Using a different heap management algorithm (such as first-fit or best-fit) would complicate the process of finding object's headers and pointer fields, but we believe it could be done with little additional overhead—the necessary techniques are already well-developed for use in garbage collection.

4 Caching

Pointer swizzling at page fault time implements address translation on top of the abstraction of a conventional virtual memory; we exploit this fact to use the underlying virtual memory as a caching mechanism. Once a page has been loaded into virtual memory from the persistent store, it may be paged out to backing store and back in again as necessary. Pages containing swizzled pointers may be paged in and out, independently of the transfer of pages between virtual memory and the persistent store.

(There is no explicit cache module in Figure 1, because virtual memory does the caching in the usual way. While Texas does take advantage of the protection features provided by a modern virtual memory system, it does not look beneath the virtual memory abstraction *per se*—that is, it is not concerned with whether pages are memory resident or not.)

This approach is appropriate for many applications such as typical CAD databases, or simply replacing conventional files in conventional applications. Paging swizzled data locally avoids unnecessary communication with the persistent store, and also avoids the (much smaller) cost of unswizzling and reswizzling pages.

In other applications, it might be preferable to page directly from the persistent store. This would avoid redundant storage of pages in both the persistent storage file and the local backing disk's swap area. It would also reduce the possibility of dirty pages being paged out to swap disk, only to be subsequently paged back in so that they can be written to the persistent store.[11] Naturally, evicting pages directly back to the persistent store would be especially appropriate for diskless clients.

Texas could easily be modified to evict pages back to the persistent store, given control over pageouts. This could be achieved using something like Mach's external pager facility, but it would make the system somewhat more complex and less portable.

[11] We believe this problem can also be addressed satisfactorily by writing dirty pages back to the persistent store early, in effect "cleaning" them, as we will describe in Section 5.

When using the virtual memory system for caching, it is important to avoid caching the persistent storage file in the filesystem cache; once a page has been loaded from the persistent storage file into the virtual memory, it is implicitly cached. Caching it in a file system buffer is a waste of resources, so the persistent storage file should be stored in an uncached area of disk.

5 Disk Storage Management and Recovery

Like any useful persistent store, Texas supports checkpointing and recovery; with a persistent store, the conventional heap/file distinction is lost, and explicit checkpointing must take the place of "saving changes to a file." We have implemented two different checkpointing schemes for Texas. The first was a conventional *write-ahead logging* scheme; that is, changed pages were written "off to the side" in a log. (The persistent storage file itself was only modified after all changes were safely written to the log, so that a crash would not leave the store in an inconsistent state.[12]) We have recently replaced this with a more flexible *log-structured storage module.*

5.1 Log-structured Storage System (LSS)

Rather than refining our crude write-ahead logging scheme, we chose to replace both the log and the persistent storage file with a log-structured storage system which supports checkpointing directly and efficiently. The LSS is essentially the lower levels of a *log structured file system* [17]; and manipulates a single large uncached file (currently, a raw UNIX disk partition).

In a log-structured store, the entire disk is used as a log, and the log itself acts as the final repository of data pages. Rather than "updating" blocks that reside in fixed locations on disk, logical blocks can migrate, with no "home" location. The "current" version of a block is simply the last one written to the log, and changes to a file can be committed by updating indexing information to point to the new versions of changed blocks.

This "write anywhere" property has many advantages for implementing advanced functionality. It has been promoted as a means of increasing effective write bandwidth (by allowing writes to proceed nearly continuously to a contiguous area of disk) [17], but we believe a well-implemented conventional logging scheme can perform similarly.[13]

For our purposes, the real advantages of "write anywhere" disk management lie elsewhere. While we are interested in high write bandwidth, we are equally interested in improving read latency and bandwidth, especially for programs that manipulate very large amounts of data and whose performance may not be dominated by checkpointing writes. As we will discuss in more detail in Section 8, block mobility makes it easy to implement several attractive advanced features: sub-page logging, adaptive disk reorganization, compressed storage, and multi-versioned storage.

---

[12] Once all the writes are on stable storage, they can be safely propagated to the persistent store; a crash during this propagation phase only requires repeating the phase until it succeeds; repeated writes due to retries will have no lasting effect.

[13] Where a conventional logging scheme must reclaim log space by writing changes to the "home" locations of blocks, a log-structured file system must reclaim log space by some form of garbage collection. The efficiency of either scheme depends (at least in part) on the lifetime distribution of block versions. If too many new but long-lived versions of blocks are created, they must be migrated to free log space (in write-ahead logging) or to compact the log (in log-structured storage), and performance may suffer.

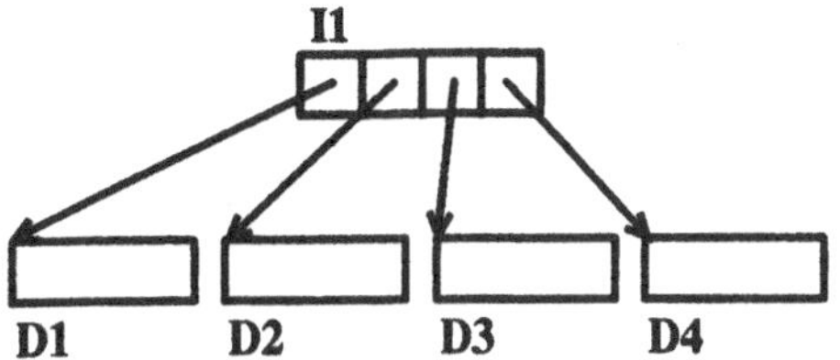

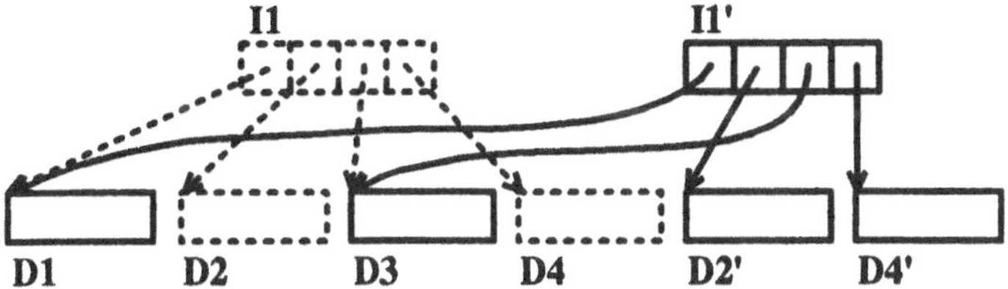

Figure 4: A tree-indexed file

5.2 LSS File Structures

In the LSS, each file is stored as a tree-indexed sequence of data blocks. That is, a file is actually structured as a multiway search tree, somewhat like a B-tree, with the data blocks as the leaves. This structure is shown in the top part of Figure 4. When data blocks are changed, new versions are written. This requires updating their parent (indexing) blocks.

Unfortunately, updating parent blocks in the conventional way would require seeks to write *their* new data, which is precisely what log-structured storage is intended to avoid. Rather than seeking and overwriting parent blocks with updated pointers to moved children, the parent blocks are treated in exactly the same way as the children—new versions are written to the disk as part of the log-writing stream. This problem recurs, because any pointers to the parent node must be written out as well; so each ancestor (all the way up to the file's top-level indexing node) must be written. As shown in the lower part of Figures 4, when data blocks D2′ and D4′ are written, indexing block I1′ is also written. The old versions, (D2, D4, and I1) simply become garbage. Once the new version of the top-level indexing node has been written, the changes to a file (or several files) can be committed atomically by writing a special commit record. The commit record simply signifies that the new top-level indexing node(s) should be used, rather than the old one(s).

This is essentially an application of functional (side-effect free) programming technique to the representation of tree structures on disk. When leaf nodes (data blocks) are replaced with new versions, a new copy of the file's whole indexing tree is made. The copy is optimized by using shared structure—any nodes that aren't changed are simply shared, instead of copied.

Because this copying is nondestructive, it can easily be extended to keep multiple versions of any file or set of files. It is only necessary to retain multiple top-level indexing nodes, and to avoid reclaiming any physical block version that is part of

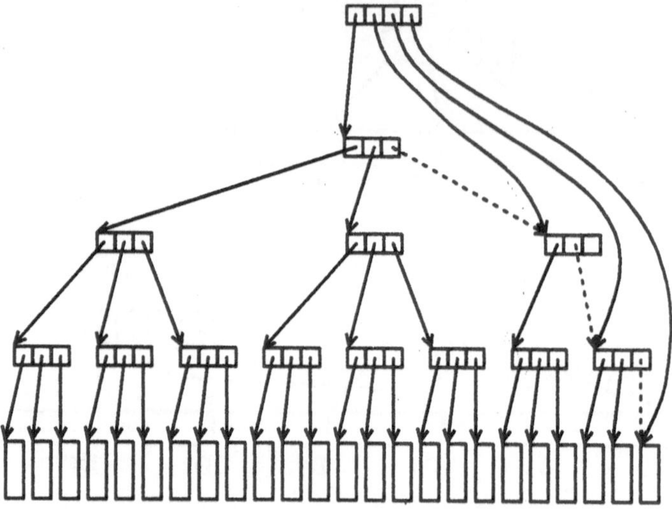

Figure 5: Right-shallow file indexing trees

any valid file version.[14]

In our LSS, the trees are *right shallow*, meaning that incomplete rightmost subtrees of the whole tree hang directly off of the top-level indexing node (see Figure 5). When a subtree fills because of file "appends," the full subtree is pushed down and to the left to become a rightmost subtree of a larger subtree.[15]

The advantage of this structure is that trees are very bushy, because only the rightmost subtrees are ever incomplete, and the tree as a whole is never more than one node deeper than a perfectly symmetrical tree. This minimizes the number of ancestor nodes that must be written when a data block is written, and appends are especially cheap. For small- to medium-sized files, only one or two ancestors must be written for any write to an arbitrarily chosen block. Most append operations only require modifying the top-level indexing node, because the rightmost several data blocks hang directly off of it.[16] This structure is therefore equally suitable for random search and update patterns, and also for serial file construction, e.g., writing event logs.

5.3 Log Reclamation

Log reclamation in a log-structured storage system [17] is essentially a matter of garbage collection [18, 9]. Committing a new version of a file disconnects the top-level indexing node from the current state of the file system; it is therefore garbage (subject to reclamation). Any lower-level indexing and data blocks that are not reachable from a valid top-level node are likewise garbage and may be reclaimed.

[14] This requires only a slight modification to the reference-counting scheme used to keep track of free disk blocks.

[15] This is quite different from conventional UNIX file structures, which are left-shallow and do not require rebalancing as they grow larger.

[16] Occasionally, subtrees must be pushed down, but this rebalancing is infrequent and the more expensive rebalancings are extremely infrequent.

Our log reclamation scheme is quite straightforward, relying on reference counting of data and indexing blocks. A special file (itself stored in the LSS) holds a bitmap of free blocks. The normal checkpointing of the LSS keeps this bitmap consistent with the checkpointing of data files.

Currently, we use a very simple bitmap scanning technique to find mostly-free areas of disk for writing new versions of blocks. This is rather different from the copying compaction employed by the Sprite LFS [17]. Our technique is more akin to the sweep phase of mark-sweep collection, and we believe it may be more appropriate than copying compaction under most circumstances. (We currently have no compactor at all, though we intend to implement one for situations in which fragmentation costs are high.)

It is interesting to note that the *garbage detection* problem is trivially solved using reference counting, and this gives tremendous flexibility in the choice of garbage reclamation and reallocation strategies. Rosenblum and Ousterhout use a technique that is analogous to generational copying collection [17]—that is, they take advantage of the fact that most block versions live only a short while, because they are superseded by subsequent writes of the same logical block. They use a copying compactor to reclaim the space for obsolete versions of logical blocks. While the generational heuristic is likely to be effective in most circumstances, it is unnecessarily indirect and ill-informed.

The information provided by the reference counting garbage detector can easily inform more *opportunistic* strategies, which take advantage of complete information about which blocks are free.[17] This opportunism can avoid expending effort where it is unnecessary, and might be used to dynamically choose between mark-sweep style reuse and copying compaction.

Mark-sweep is advantageous when fragmentation is naturally low, as we expect it to be in most cases, due to locality effects. Rosenblum and Ousterhout have reported [17] that many moderate-sized areas of disk[18] contain no live block versions at all by the time their collector "cleans" (copy collects) them. In those cases, no special effort should be required to find long runs of contiguous or nearly-contiguous disk space. Our bitmap sweeping technique should work well in such situations.

Copying compaction has the advantage of eliminating fragmentation, but incurs additional, less predictable costs in updating younger blocks holding pointers to relocated blocks. In the worst case, it appears to require cleaning *all* segments younger than the oldest segment being cleaned, because creating new versions of indexing blocks may itself cause fragmentation.[19]

6 Sub-page Logging to Reduce Checkpointing Writes

Pagewise pointer swizzling is attractive because it can exploit spatial locality, but pagewise operation also has disadvantages, particularly in checkpointing short transactions. If transactions have poor locality of writes, pagewise checkpointing will save

[17] This is analogous to opportunistic garbage collection for general-purpose systems, as in [19] and especially some proposals by Barry Hayes [20].

[18] I.e., "segments"—the units of contiguous allocation in their system.

[19] This corresponds to the typical approach employed in generational garbage collectors, where some generation is chosen for garbage collection, and all younger generations are also collected during that collection [21, 9]. This is unnecessary with a non-moving collector where liveness is known beforehand.

too much unchanged data; a single write to a page during a transaction will cause the entire page to be written to disk.

For long-running transactions which manipulate considerable quantities of data, this cost is probably not unacceptable; simply reading large amounts of data requires disk seeks which are usually more expensive than the log writes. For small transactions, however, the working set of the program is likely to reside in memory, and the log writes may well be the limiting performance factor. In this case, the actual limitation is likely to be disk *bandwidth* (rather than latency), since log writes can be written as a continuous stream with few seeks.

White and DeWitt have compared ObjectStore (a pagewise scheme similar to ours) and several versions of the E system, using finer-grained (objectwise) swizzling and checkpointing [6]. Their results appear to bear out the thesis that pagewise schemes work best for long transactions—because they can typically exploit spatial locality—but exhibit poorer performance when transactions are short and locality of writes is poor.

While our system is designed primarily for applications with relatively long transactions, such as typical CAD applications, we would like to provide support for small transactions as well. To do this, we are implementing *sub-page logging*, so that we can checkpoint areas of memory that are smaller than pages. Rather than writing out entire dirty pages, we can often write out only those parts of a page that have actually changed. In order to do this, we need the ability to detect which sub-page units have changed and which have not.

We are investigating two possible approaches to this fine-grained checkpointing. One is to keep dirty bits for small areas, either fine-grained hardware dirty bits (as in the ARM 600 [22]), or *card marking* techniques, which maintain dirty bits in software [19, 23]. Another is to use *page diffing* (i.e., word-by-word comparison with a clean copy) to find out which parts of dirty pages have actually changed.

All of these approaches are independent of our pagewise pointer-swizzling scheme, and exploit the orthogonality of address translation and data storage; checkpointing is carried out at a different resolution than address translation.

Currently, we intend to use page diffing, not fine-grained hardware dirty bits or (software) card marking, because it requires no change to the hardware, operating system, or compiler, and we believe it will perform quite well, given current ratios between CPU and disk speeds.

6.1 Page Diffing

Page diffing is also conceptually straightforward—it is only necessary to keep a clean version of each modified page, and compare the modified and unmodified pages at checkpoint time. Only the changed parts need to be written to the log.

We are currently implementing page diffing using write-protection traps to trigger a copy upon the first write to each page; the write protection trap handler copies the page into a *clean version buffer*, unprotects the original, and lets the program resume. This scheme incurs costs proportional to the number of dirtied pages per transaction—each written page causes a trap, a page copy, and a page diffing operation. In addition, there is a space cost of one page of clean version per page written.

It may seem that these costs are quite high—an isolated write to a 4 KB page, for example, will cost several thousand instructions at checkpoint time. We believe this cost is quite acceptable for the majority of applications. The main cost of checkpointing small transactions is not the cost of executing instructions in memory, but the cost of disk operations to commit data to nonvolatile storage. It is attractive to expend thousands of instructions to avoid writing an entire page of data.

Consider a typical high-performance workstation disk with a bandwidth of roughly 4 MB/sec for large writes, e.g., streaming data to a contiguous area with few seeks. Four megabytes per second is 4 KB per millisecond—or roughly a page per millisecond.

On the other hand, consider CPU operations. Common workstation and PC speeds are in the tens of MIPS, soon to be in the hundreds. A 100 MIPS processor can execute 100,000 instructions per millisecond. It will therefore be worthwhile to spend roughly 100,000 instructions to save one page's worth of data writes.

(Because page copying and diffing are memory-intensive, their speed may not scale directly with processor speeds. They have excellent sequential locality, however; they are likely to exploit increases in memory bandwidth quite well, rather than being closely tied to memory latency. It should also be noted that the diffing of pages can be done in a pipelined fashion, in parallel with the writes. If transaction commits are the limiting performance factor, most page diffing can be done in the idle time while other pages are being written. The actual page diffing is therefore likely to be effectively free, though the trapping and copying is not.)

Current operating system implementations incur high trap overheads, usually around 10,000 or 20,000 instruction cycles per trap. Even so, this is only a fraction of the instructions necessary to negate the advantage of page diffing. It appears that page diffing will eliminate most of the cost of worst-case write locality. Improved trap handling performance would naturally increase the attractiveness of this scheme. (We believe that trap handling overheads are amenable to significant reductions, and that operating system implementors are likely to achieve those reductions as more applications exploit virtual memory facilities; see [24, 25, 26] for more detailed discussions of these issues.)

A caveat is in order here: the trade-offs involved are very sensitive to changes in CPU and storage technologies. If, for example, nonvolatile RAM is used for checkpointing, checkpointing writes may become much cheaper, and applications may exploit that by checkpointing more frequently. In that case, the time spent diffing pages may go up significantly, and fine-grained dirty bit schemes will become correspondingly more attractive.[20]

6.2 Limiting the Space Costs of Diffing

Besides the time cost of page diffing, there is a space cost, namely the cost of keeping clean versions of modified pages. For short transactions, where checkpointing writes are the limiting factor, this is not generally a problem—the problem is the time required to commit a moderate number of dirty pages to disk, not the storage required for a large number of dirty pages.

For longer transactions, on the other hand, the sheer volume of dirty pages may be a significant space cost. We have chosen to limit this cost by keeping a relatively

[20] We believe that fine-grained hardware dirty bits are a good idea in general [26], but do not want to depend on them at present for reasons of simplicity and portability.

small buffer of versions of dirty pages, and writing out pages early if the buffer fills. The buffer is managed in roughly least-recently-changed fashion, so that the most stable versions are written first. When a changed page version is written from the buffer, the corresponding page is access protected so that subsequent changes can be detected, and a new copy made.

We believe that this strategy will be good for the performance of both long and short transactions. Writing out changes prematurely may increase disk bandwidth requirements for long transactions, but is likely to increase overall performance by decreasing commit latency—blocks that are written prematurely (and which do *not* change again before the transaction commits) need not be written out commit time. Given some locality of writes, this should increase total traffic somewhat, but make it less bursty.

7 Current Status

Currently, Texas' log-structured storage scheme is still under development, but a version of Texas is up and running using a simple write-ahead logging scheme.

As reported in [4], the swizzling scheme performs as expected: for programs with good locality, the cost is essentially zero, while for programs with poor locality, paging costs dominate address translation costs.

Our type descriptor system requires some hand-coding. This is due to bugs in the GNU C++ compiler, rather than any problem with Texas itself; we hope and expect that these bugs will be fixed soon. We are also developing our preprocessor to make the system compiler-independent. The preprocessor currently parses C++ and recognizes class definitions, but the actual generation of runtime descriptors is not complete.

Checkpointing performance, even without the log-structured file system and sub-page logging, is acceptable. Preliminary benchmarks for short transactions, using code from White and DeWitt's variant of the OO1 benchmark, show performance to be comparable to the systems they measured, on comparable hardware. Exact comparisons are not possible because of differences in hardware configurations.[21]

With a very preliminary version of the log-structured store, performance appears to be significantly better, and in fact our system superficially outperforms most of the systems reported in [6].

These results are hard to interpret, however, both because of the inexact match in hardware used, and because our system is a single-workstation system, while the systems tested in [6] were two-workstation client-server configurations. In addition, our storage system is incomplete (especially in terms of its log-reclamation and compaction strategies), so its eventual performance may be somewhat different. On the other hand, we expect our page diffing techniques to reduce costs further, so we are quite pleased with our preliminary results.

In a test corresponding to White and DeWitt's Figure 7, our system outperformed all of their E variants and ObjectStore (version 1.2) by at least a small margin. In a test corresponding to their Figure 8, with finer-grained transactions, Texas consistently outperformed two E variants by a small margin, while two other E variants consistently outperformed our system, again by a small margin; all of

[21]Like White and Dewitt, we are using SPARCstation ELC's, but with different disk drives; we don't believe the difference in drives would make a major difference to performance, but we can't be certain.

these systems outperformed ObjectStore. Again, we must stress that these are very preliminary results, and the systems are not exactly comparable. (In particular, ObjectStore is a commercial product with many advanced features, rather than a stripped-down minimal system like ours.) Qualitatively, though, our system appears to perform extremely well in terms of address translation costs [4] and to be competitive with other systems in terms of checkpointing.

8 Future Work

In the near term, our main goals are to complete the type descriptor generator and log-structured storage mechanisms so that we can test and benchmark Texas more fully. After a period of debugging and tuning, we will then issue a beta release, probably early in 1993.

After Texas is stable, we intend to release it generally as free software, most likely in the public domain. Soon thereafter, we intend to create a client-server version of Texas, for distributed applications. (We may also try a distributed virtual memory approach.) We are exploring several issues related to distributed systems, including having independently sharable and protectable heap areas within a single store. We are currently leaning toward a scheme that is similar to the protection domain scheme of the Opal operating system [10].[22]

A major goal of this project is to produce a useful, high-performance persistent store and give it away, so that we can develop a significant user base of actual programs that will fully exploit the potential of our pointer swizzling and storage schemes. Our decision to support C++ was largely motivated by the desire to have a significant number of applications that could be easily ported to our system, so that we can properly evaluate it.

Once we have a user base, we also intend to use Texas as a vehicle for basic research in locality of reference in large sets of data. Conventional filesystem traces are difficult to interpret, because the references to file blocks are a very complex function of program's conceptual referencing behavior; domain-level objects may move from file block to file block, perhaps being in multiple places at once, and unrelated objects may map to the same logical or physical file block over time. Because a persistent store preserves object identity, reference behavior should be somewhat easier to interpret and exploit.

After gathering reference traces and running them through simulators we have developed [27], we intend to experiment with actual implementations of novel replacement policies, and prefetching policies exploiting adaptive reorganization. Adaptive replacement will require using an external pager mechanism (or something similar) to override the default caching of the underlying virtual memory. Adaptive reorganization for prefetching [28, 26] can straightforwardly be added to the log-structured store, due to its write-anywhere policies; this will also require an external pager facility to exploit it for the local caching mechanism.

Log-structured storage also lends itself to *compressed* storage of data blocks. Given that blocks can move around on the disk anyway, it is a small step to let them vary in size, depending on how well they happen to compress.[23]

[22] Our subheaps would take the place of their low-level notion of contiguous "segments," and subheaps might act as sets of objects with distinct policies controlling migration, replication, coherence, and garbage collection.

[23] This is particularly easy if copying compaction is used to reclaim log space, because contiguous allocation regions

Previous work in compressed file storage has focused primarily increasing effective disk capacity for typical file data. They therefore focus on byte string-oriented compression techniques such as bytewise Lempel-Ziv variants [29, 30].

Our goals are quite different. We are focusing on decreasing effective memory *latency* for typical *heap* data. Given that we page objects in a heap format, and also store them in an only slightly different format in the persistent store, we are much more interested in heap data layouts than conventional file I/O formats. We would like to add a level of *compressed in-memory storage* to the memory hierarchy, intermediate in performance between normal (non-compressed) RAM and disk [26].[24]

We are developing adaptive compression techniques that exploit the typical low information content and word-wise alignment of heap data fields, and the strong alignment and grouping regularities imposed by typical heap allocation schemes. In our initial tests, we have gotten compression factors for C++ heap data that vary between 30 and 90 percent with fast single-pass algorithms, which can compress a 4 KB page in a very few milliseconds on a relatively slow (Sun SPARC ELC) processor. We are optimistic that for typical programs we will achieve compression factors of two to four, with compression taking a fraction of a millisecond on next-generation processors.

9 Conclusions

Texas provides persistence with good performance for C++ programs running on stock hardware and stock operating systems. It is surprisingly simple and flexible, however, and requires little or no change to existing compilers.

The current version of our persistent store, excluding the log-structured storage module, is less than four thousand lines of C++ code. Log-structured storage adds less than two thousand lines. While we expect these figures to grow somewhat, and we expect to add more modules (e.g., for concurrency control), this is a gratifyingly small amount of code for a persistent storage mechanism with high-performance address translation and checkpointing.

This simplicity and flexibility is largely due to the use of pointer swizzling at page fault time, which lets us treat address translation, caching, and recovery as nearly orthogonal features. Address translation can be performed by access protection trap handlers, with a conventional virtual memory performing data caching. Write protection handlers support logging writes to a modular log-structured storage subsystem.

Page fault-time address translation has essentially zero overhead for programs with good locality, and appears to be competitive with other schemes in general. Likewise, pagewise logging performs very well when write locality is good, and subpage logging promises to keep it competitive when write locality is poor.

Our modular approach appears to work well, allowing us to easily change storage management schemes. Texas and its log-structured storage system are promising

make it easy to allocate variable-sized blocks contiguously. It's not much harder for a non-moving log reuse policy, however, because data blocks don't need to be stored entirely contiguously; this greatly simplifies packing problems.

[24] A similar approach has been taken for compressing compiled code in the Acorn system, though it operates on a program-wise basis rather than a pagewise basis.

both as an easy-to-use, high-performance persistence mechanism and as a flexible testbed for basic research in locality, distributed systems, and storage techniques.

Acknowledgements

We would like to thank the organizers and participants of POS-V, as well as several seminar students who helped design Texas—Roberto Bayardo, Atif Chaudry, Shankar Krishnamoorthy, Rajiv Kumar and Rekha Singhal. Thanks also to Seth White, for sharing the benchmark code from [6]; to Mark Johnstone, for last-minute programming help with the log-structured storage system; and to Janet Swisher for help with the figures and text.

References

[1] M.P. Atkinson, P.J. Bailey, K.J. Chisholm, P. W. Cockshott, and R. Morrison. An approach to persistent programming. *The Computer Journal*, 26(4):360–365, December 1983.

[2] W. Cockshott, M. Atkinson, K. Chisholm, P. Bailey, and R. Morrison. Persistent object management system. *Software Practice and Experience*, 14(1):49–71, January 1984.

[3] Alan Dearle, Gail M. Shaw, and Stanley B. Zdonik, editors. *Implementing Persistent Object Bases: Principles and Practice (Proceedings of the Fourth International Workshop on Persistent Object Systems)*. Morgan Kaufman, Martha's Vineyard, Massachusetts, September 1990.

[4] Paul R. Wilson and Sheetal V. Kakkad. Pointer swizzling at page fault time: Efficiently and compatibly supporting huge addresses on standard hardware. In *International Workshop on Object Orientation in Operating Systems*, pages 364–377, Paris, France, September 1992. IEEE Press.

[5] J. Eliot B. Moss. Working with objects: To swizzle or not to swizzle? Technical Report 90-38, University of Massachusetts, Amherst, Massachusetts, May 1990.

[6] Seth J. White and David J. Dewitt. A performance study of alternative object faulting and pointer swizzling strategies. In *18th International Conference on Very Large Data Bases*, Vancouver, British Columbia, Canada, October 1992. To appear.

[7] Henry G. Baker, Jr. List processing in real time on a serial computer. *Communications of the ACM*, 21(4):280–294, April 1978.

[8] Andrew W. Appel, John R. Ellis, and Kai Li. Real-time concurrent garbage collection on stock multiprocessors. In *Proceedings of SIGPLAN '88 Conference on Programming Language Design and Implementation*, pages 11–20. SIGPLAN ACM Press, June 1988. Atlanta, Georgia.

[9] Paul R. Wilson. Uniprocessor garbage collection techniques. In *International Workshop on Memory Management*, pages 1–42, St. Malo, France, September 1992. Springer-Verlag Lecture Notes in Computer Science vol. 637.

[10] Jeffrey S. Chase, Henry M. Levy, Edward D. Lazowska, and Miche Baker-Harvey. Lightweight shared objects in a 64-bit operating system. In *ACM SIGPLAN 1992 Conference on Object Oriented Programming Systems, Languages and Applications (OOPSLA '92)*, Vancouver, British Columbia, Canada, October 1992.

[11] Hans-Juergen Boehm and Alan Demers. Garbage collection in an uncooperative environment. *Software Practice and Experience*, 18(9):807–820, September 1988.

[12] David Wallace. Runtime type support in C and C++. Technical Report revision 1.1, Cygnus Reports, 1992.

[13] Charles Lamb, Gordon Landis, Jack Orenstein, and Dan Weinreb. The ObjectStore database system. *Communications of the ACM*, 34(10):50–63, October 1991.

[14] Richard Greenblatt. Unpublished technical report on the Moby address space. Technical report, Lisp Machines, Incorporated.

[15] M. Anderson, R. D. Pose, and C. S. Wallace. A password-capability system. *Computer Journal*, 29(1), 1986.

[16] Jose Alves Marques and Paulo Guedes. Extending the operating system to support an object-oriented environment. In *ACM SIGPLAN 1989 Conference on Object Oriented Programming Systems, Languages and Applications (OOPSLA '89)*, pages 113–122, New Orleans, Louisiana, October 1989.

[17] Mendel Rosenblum and John K. Ousterhout. The design and implementation of a log-structured file system. In *Thirteenth ACM Symposium on Operating Systems Principles*, pages 1–15, Pacific Grove, California, October 1991.

[18] Jacques Cohen. Garbage collection of linked data structures. *Computing Surveys*, 13(3):341–367, September 1981.

[19] Paul R. Wilson and Thomas G. Moher. Design of the opportunistic garbage collector. In *ACM SIGPLAN 1989 Conference on Object Oriented Programming Systems, Languages and Applications (OOPSLA '89)*, pages 23–35, New Orleans, Louisiana, October 1989.

[20] Barry Hayes. Using key object opportunism to collect old objects. In *ACM SIGPLAN 1991 Conference on Object Oriented Programming Systems, Languages and Applications (OOPSLA '91)*, pages 33–46, Phoenix, Arizona, October 1991. ACM Press.

[21] Henry Lieberman and Carl Hewitt. A real-time garbage collector based on the lifetimes of objects. *Communications of the ACM*, 26(6):419–429, June 1983.

[22] Walter R. Smith and Robert V. Welland. A model for address-oriented software and hardware. In *Proc. 25th Hawaii Int'l Conference on Systems Sciences*, January 1991.

[23] Craig Chambers. *The Design and Implementation of the SELF Compiler, an Optimizing Compiler for an Object-Oriented Programming Language.* PhD thesis, Stanford University, March 1992.

[24] John Ousterhout. Why aren't operating systems getting faster as fast as hardware? In *USENIX Summer Conference*, pages 247–256, Anaheim, California, June 1990. IEEE Press.

[25] Andrew W. Appel and Kai Li. Virtual memory primitives for user programs. In *Proceedings of the Fourth International Conference on Architectural Support for Programming Languages and Operating Systems (ASPLOS IV)*, pages 96–107, April 1991. Santa Clara, CA.

[26] Paul R. Wilson. Operating system support for small objects. In *International Workshop on Object Orientation in Operating Systems*, Palo Alto, California, October 1991. IEEE Press. Revised version to appear in *Computing Systems.*

[27] Paul R. Wilson, Shubhendu S. Mukherjee, and Sheetal V. Kakkad. Anomalies and adaptation in the analysis and development of prepaging policies. *Journal of Systems and Software*, 1992. Technical Communication, to appear.

[28] Jean-Loup Baer and Gary R. Sager. Dynamic improvement of locality in virtual memory systems. *IEEE Transactions on Software Engineering*, SE-2(1):54–62, March 1976.

[29] Vincent Cate and Thomas Gross. Combining the concepts of compression and caching for a two-level file system. In *Fourth International Conference on Architectural Support for Programming Languages and Operating Systems (ASPLOS IV)*, pages 200–209, Santa Clara, California, April 1991.

[30] Michael Burrows, Charles Jerian, Butler Lampson, and Timothy Mann. Online data compression in a log-structured file system. In *Fifth International Conference on Architectural Support for Programming Languages and Operating Systems (ASPLOS IV)*, September 1992.

Supporting Large Persistent Stores using Conventional Hardware

Francis Vaughan, Alan Dearle

Department of Computer Science, University of Adelaide
Adelaide, Australia

Abstract

Persistent programming systems are generally supported by an object store, a conceptually infinite object repository. Objects in such a repository cannot be directly accessed by user programs; to be manipulated they must be fetched from the object store into virtual memory. Thus in these systems, two different kinds of object addresses may exist: those in the object store and those in virtual memory. The action of changing object store addresses into virtual memory addresses has become known as *pointer swizzling* and is the subject of this paper.

The paper investigates three approaches to pointer swizzling: a typical software address translation scheme, a technique for performing swizzling at page fault time and finally a new hybrid scheme which performs swizzling in two phases. The hybrid scheme supports arbitrarily large pointers and object repositories using conventional hardware. The paper concludes with a comparison of these approaches.

1 Introduction

Most persistent and database programming languages are supported by an object store, a conceptually infinite repository in which objects reside. In order to manipulate these objects, they must be fetched from the object store into directly addressable memory, usually virtual memory. In systems which support orthogonal persistence [3] this is performed transparently. Thus in these systems, two different kinds of object addresses may exist: those in the backing store (persistent identifiers or PIDs) and those in directly addressable memory (virtual addresses).

Many researchers have argued that large pointers (anywhere up to 128 bits) are required to support persistent systems [9, 17]. Persistent pointers need not be the same size as those supported by virtual memory (usually 32 bits); indeed persistent identifiers may be arbitrarily long. This paper presents a new architecture which supports arbitrarily large pointers and persistent stores using conventional hardware.

The persistent address of an object may be mapped onto a virtual address in a number of ways:

- Dynamically translate from a PID to a virtual address on each dereference.
- Make an object's virtual address coincident with its persistent identifier.
- Perform a once only translation from a persistent identifier to virtual address, overwriting the copy of the persistent identifier in the virtual address space with a virtual address so that all subsequent dereferences incur no translation penalty.

This last option has become known as *pointer swizzling* and is the subject of this paper. The first option, dynamic translation, is seldom more efficient than swizzling [16]. The second option is only possible if persistent stores are small enough to be contained within the virtual memory. All these techniques have been used to implement persistent object stores [8, 12, 13].

Pointer swizzling may be performed at a variety of times, the earliest being when objects are loaded or faulted into memory; this is termed *eager pointer swizzling*. The latest time swizzling may be performed is when a pointer is dereferenced, and is termed *lazy pointer swizzling*. When swizzled objects are removed from virtual memory, virtual memory pointers must be replaced by PIDs; this is often referred to as *unswizzling* or *deswizzling*.

Eager pointer swizzling has some advantages; in particular, if a data set may be identified in its entirety, all the pointers may be swizzled at once, avoiding the necessity to test whether a reference is a PID or a virtual address prior to every dereference. However, this approach has the disadvantage that pointers may be swizzled, involving some computational expense, and never used.

Some systems use an *ad hoc* swizzling scheme; in these systems persistent pointers are the same size as VM addresses and may be coincident with the virtual address space. Whenever possible data is simply copied at the appropriate position into the virtual address space from the store. However if the appropriate region has already been allocated, swizzling is employed. Such systems are unable to support persistent stores larger than virtual memory and are not discussed further. It is believed that a variation of this scheme is also used by Object Design [15] .

In persistent systems it is unusual to be able to identify a self contained data set and some lazy swizzling is unavoidable. The first persistent systems to employ swizzling [4] relied upon a software test to distinguish between PIDs and local addresses. Recently, schemes have been described which avoid performing these tests by performing pointer swizzling at page fault time [18]. In this paper we present a new hybrid technique which offers many of the advantages of both these approaches.

The remainder of the paper is structured as follows: firstly we will describe a typical software address translation scheme. This is followed by a discussion of Wilson's scheme: a technique for performing pointer swizzling at page fault time. Next we introduce a new scheme which is a hybrid and performs swizzling in two phases and an analysis of this scheme is made. We also suggest some implementation techniques that may be utilised in conjunction with such a scheme. The paper concludes with a comparison of the three architectures.

2 Software address translation

The first object systems to be called persistent [4, 5] performed lazy pointer swizzling implemented entirely in software. In this section, for illustration purposes, we will concentrate on one of these, the Persistent Object Management System written in C, the CPOMS [7]. The CPOMS is the underlying system used to support implementations of PS-algol [2] under Unix.

The persistent store implemented by the CPOMS is a large heap with objects being addressed using persistent identifiers (PIDs). How PIDs are interpreted is not relevant to this paper and the interested reader is referred to [6] for more details. PIDs may be arbitrarily large but in current implementations PIDs are identical in size to the normal pointers (known as Local Object Numbers or LONs) used by the PS-algol run time system [1] . PIDs are distinguished by having their most significant bit set. Hence it is possible for the PS-algol run time system to distinguish between a LON and a PID.

PIDs are pointers to objects outside of the program's virtual address space, therefore the objects to which they refer cannot be directly addressed by a PS-algol program. To ensure that PIDs are not dereferenced, a test is made prior to the use of any object address;

in the PS-algol system this test is made using in line code. When an attempt to dereference a PID is detected, the referenced object is fetched into memory and the PID is swizzled and replaced with the appropriate LON. This process is shown in Figure 1 below in which objects B, C and E have been fetched into directly addressable memory where they are represented by objects B', C' and E'. Note that some references within virtual memory are virtual memory addresses whereas other are PIDs.

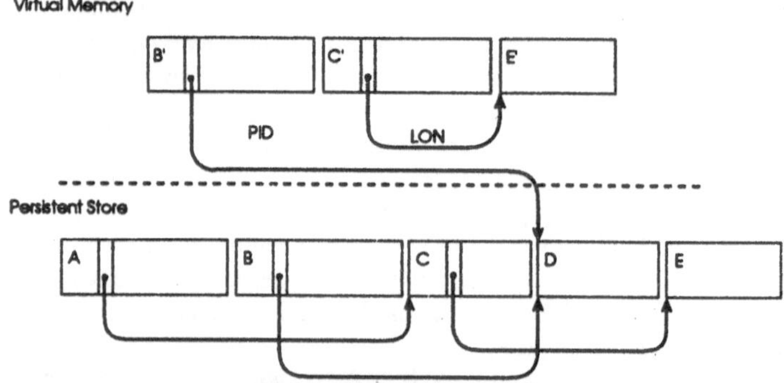

Figure 1: Swizzling in PS-algol

In order to prevent more than one copy of an object being made, a data structure called the PID to Local Address Map (PIDLAM) is kept. When a PID is first used and the object to which it refers is copied into local memory, the PID is entered into the PIDLAM along with the LON of the copy as shown in Figures 2 and 3. Therefore, if another instance of the same PID is encountered, the LON of the copy can be found from the PIDLAM. This is necessary to preserve referential integrity in the running system.

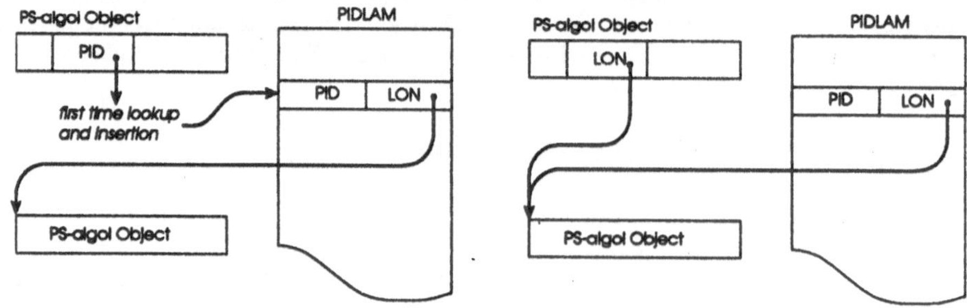

Figure 2: Looking up a PID in the PIDLAM

Figure 3: Overwriting a PID by a LON

Although relatively simple, this mechanism compromises performance in five areas:

- all the address translation is performed in software,
- all pointer dereferences must be checked using software to ensure that the pointer is not a PID,
- disk fetches occur on a per object basis,
- large objects must be copied into virtual memory in their entirety, and
- every unswizzled pointer to an object must be swizzled at the time of dereference, even if the referend is resident in local memory.

The first, fourth and last of these problems may be eliminated if the hardware address translation mechanisms may be exploited. As stated earlier, this is only possible if the persistent identifier of an object is made coincident with its virtual address; clearly this approach may only be used with relatively small stores. The second problem may be eliminated if persistent addresses are illegal virtual memory addresses since an access will cause the hardware to raise an exception. This is only more efficient if the operating system provides a light weight exception mechanism. The CPOMS partially addresses this problem by eagerly swizzling certain pointers and in so doing avoids some checks. For example, pointers loaded onto a stack in the dynamic call chain are eagerly swizzled. The third problem may be overcome by amortising the cost of disk access across many object fetches.

3 Address translation at page fault time

Recently, an approach has been suggested by Wilson [18] that employs both pointer swizzling and page faulting techniques. The basic strategy is to fetch pages of data into virtual memory rather than individual objects. As pages are fetched, they are scanned and all (persistent) pointers are translated into valid virtual memory addresses. References to non-resident objects cause virtual memory to be allocated; these pages are fetched only if the pointers into them are dereferenced. In Wilson's scheme, pages of data in virtual memory only contain valid virtual memory addresses, never persistent identifiers.

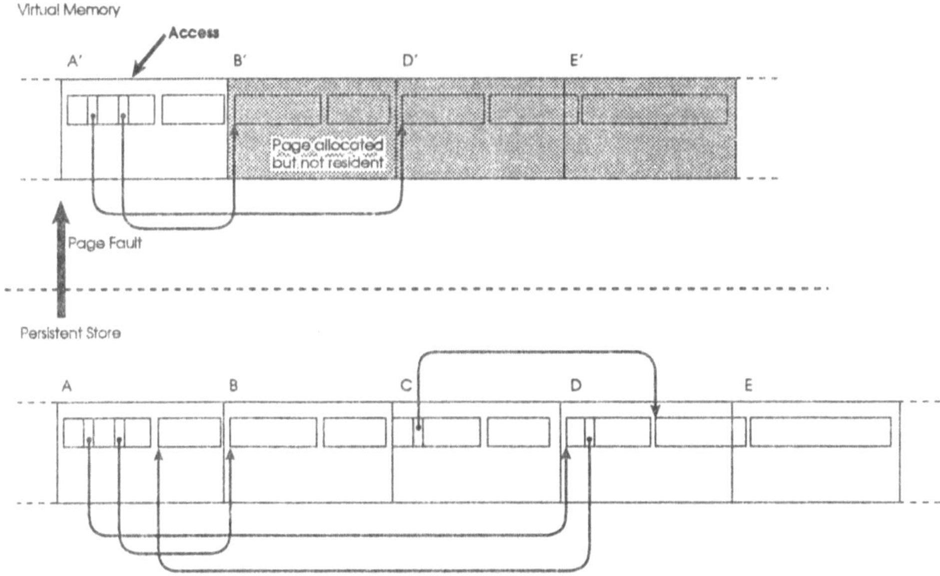

Figure 4: Page faulting and allocation in Wilson's scheme

Figure 4 shows Wilson's scheme in operation; in the diagram, a non-resident persistent object on page A (i.e. an object on a page that has not been fetched into virtual memory) has been accessed. This will cause a copy of page A, denoted A', to be fetched into virtual memory. At this time, the page is scanned and all the pointers in it are swizzled into valid virtual memory addresses. Since page A contains references to objects on pages B and D, locations for pages B' and D' must be allocated in virtual memory and the pointers into those pages swizzled to the addresses of B' and D' with appropriate offsets added. Virtual memory must also be allocated for page E since objects from page D overlap that page. Note that the loading and swizzling of pages B', D' and E' is performed lazily: only space is allocated for them in virtual memory. This mechanism causes virtual memory which may never be used to be allocated. Since pages B, D and E may have already been faulted into virtual memory, a translation table similar to the CPOMS PIDLAM must be maintained to avoid loss of referential integrity.

When a reference to a previously unseen page is encountered whilst scanning an incoming page, three actions are required. Firstly a new translation table entry for the page is allocated. Secondly, the store is interrogated to discover the page's crossing map (described below). Thirdly, virtual memory space is allocated for the page. Interrogation of the store is potentially expensive and since it is performed eagerly, at page fault time, is a potential performance bottleneck.

When a page is scanned, it is necessary to find all the pointers on that page; provided that objects are self describing, this requirement reduces to finding the header of the first object on or overlapping the page boundary. This same requirement is made of object systems by some parallel garbage collection techniques [11, 14] and the solutions are well known. The first solution is to maintain a bitmap known as a *crossing map* which indicates if an object header is coincident with the start of a page.

To find all the pointers on a page, the system has to scan the pages which precede the faulted page starting at the first page which has a object header coincident with the start of the page. This obviously can be expensive if there is a high degree of crossing and the pages are mostly on disk. Another technique is to maintain an array of pointers containing one pointer for each page in the system. Each pointer points to the first object header before or aligned with the start of the page. In this way, at most two pages need to be examined when a page is faulted.

If pointers are stored contiguously in objects a further optimisation is possible. Rather than an array of pointers, an array of tags is maintained, with each tag corresponding to a page in the store. Each tag, which may be encoded into 32 bits, describes any partial object which may overlap the start of the page. The tag consists of the length of the partial object (if any), the offset of the first pointer in the partial object (if any) and the number of pointers in the partial object (if any). This optimisation means that only the faulted page needs to be examined when a page fault occurs.

In Wilson's scheme, page evacuation from virtual memory is convoluted. This problem is exacerbated by the fact that virtual memory is eagerly allocated and hence the need to reuse virtual memory addresses potentially more frequent. If a set of pages is written back to persistent storage, the pointers in those pages must be deswizzled into PIDs by consulting the translation table. However, if virtual memory is exhausted and a virtual memory range is to be reused by another persistent page, all pointers which refer to the old contents must be removed.

A translation table that contains an entry for each instance of a referend object can become very large. Wilson proposes a scheme in which the translation table provides a per page rather than per object mapping. To implement this, PIDs are structured so that the offset within the holding page of an object is encoded into the object's PID. For example, assuming 8k byte pages and word alignment of objects, eleven bits are needed to describe the offset. This leaves 53 bits of a 64 bit PID to identify the page. The structure of PIDs is depicted in Figure 6.

This scheme has two advantages. First, it is only necessary to maintain a mapping from pages within the large persistent address space to pages in the machine virtual address space. This table is relatively small and of fixed size. Secondly, an object's offset is required in the construction of a swizzled pointer. If the offset were not coded into the PID, further interrogation of the store manager would be required, adding extra cost to the swizzling process.

4 A hybrid approach

The CPOMS and systems like it require software tests prior to each object dereference to check if the pointer being dereferenced is a persistent identifier. Wilson suggests that pointer swizzling may be performed at page fault time. This implements a barrier that ensures that a running program may never encounter a PID. However this is not achieved without cost; space must be allocated in virtual memory for every page referred to by data resident in virtual memory. Whilst this does not seem too onerous it has some unfortunate consequences.

Firstly, space in virtual memory is allocated greedily, this may cause virtual memory to become exhausted even although much of it has not been used. The counter argument says that many programs will have a high degree of locality of reference. However consider an array of large objects such as images – whenever the array is faulted into memory, enough virtual memory must be allocated for all the referenced images. It is likely that such an operation would be common in persistent applications although uncommon in traditional database applications.

We now present a hybrid architecture which does not require software checks for pointer validity and does not involve greedy allocation of virtual memory. The architecture is designed to support PIDs which address a space much larger than virtual memory and makes the requirement that PIDs are at least twice as large as virtual memory addresses. From this point on, to ease discussion, we will assume that a PID is 64 bits and virtual memory pointers are 32 bits.

In this architecture, pointers are swizzled in a two phase process: first at page load time to refer to an entry in a translation table and secondly to a virtual address when the referend object is first accessed. When pages are first accessed, they are copied from persistent memory into the virtual address space and scanned to find the pointers contained in them. Rather than allocating virtual memory for every page referenced by the page being faulted in, as happens in Wilson's scheme, the long pointers contained in the page are swizzled to refer to either:

- entries in a translation table if the referend object is not present in virtual memory (*partially swizzled*), or
- a virtual memory pointer (*fully swizzled*) if it is.

This is shown in Figure 5 below.

The translation table used in this scheme may be similar to either the one used by the CPOMS (a per object translation table) or by Wilson (a per page table). The table contains the persistent and virtual address (if any) of all objects (or pages) referred to by objects resident in virtual memory. For the remaining discussion we will assume a per page translation table. Unlike the CPOMS, the table is protected from any access by the user process, thus when a partially swizzled pointer is dereferenced an access fault occurs.

This triggers the second phase of the swizzle in which the pointer (currently containing the table entry address) is overwritten with the virtual address of the referend.

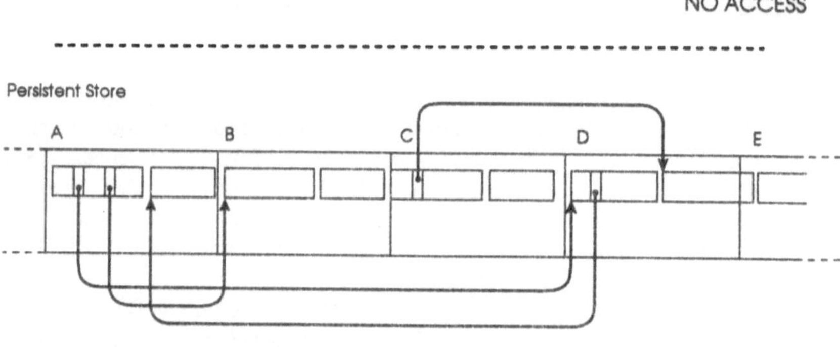

Figure 5: Partially and fully swizzled pointers

If the referend is not resident in virtual memory, the page containing it must be loaded from the persistent store. To do this, the PID, which may be found in the translation table, must be presented to the store manager. Using this the store manager can supply the appropriate page(s) containing the object. Once the page is loaded the partially swizzled pointer is overwritten with the virtual address of the object and the object dereference can proceed. The page load may result in new entries being created in the translation table. In contrast to Wilson's scheme it is only when an object is used that the store is interrogated to discover how much virtual memory must be allocated.

When a persistent pointer is fully swizzled half the space in the pointer is unused – this space is used to store the address of the corresponding translation table entry. This allows the pointer to be easily deswizzled.

In a partially swizzled pointer the space is used to store the offset within the page at which the object begins. This offset, when combined with the address at which the page is placed when it is faulted into virtual memory, forms the object address of a fully swizzled pointer. The store formats for pointers and the translation table entries are shown in Figure 6.

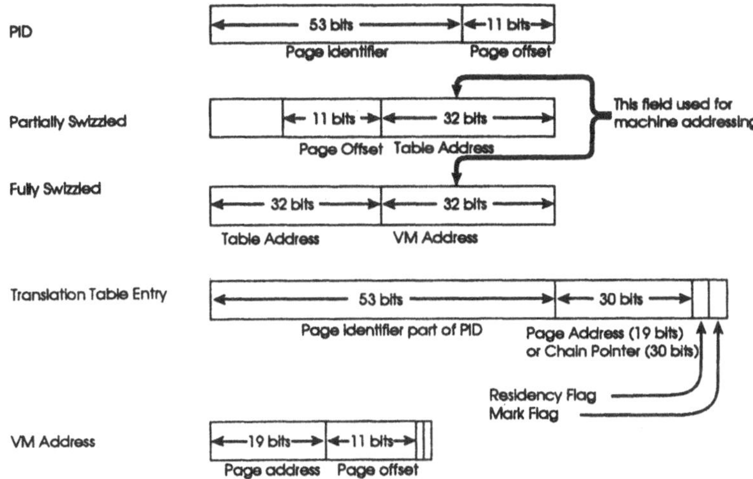

Figure 6: Pointer and translation table formats

The translation table maps from page identifiers in the persistent store to pages within the machines virtual address space. Each translation table entry holds the page identifier field of a persistent identifier, a virtual memory address, a residency bit and a mark bit. If the residency bit is set the virtual memoty address holds the address of the corresponding page in memory, otherwise it may contains the head of a partially swizzled pointer chain which is discussed next. The formats depicted in Figure 6 assume a 32 bit virtual address space and a page size of eight kilobytes.

4.1 Eager Swizzling

The eager swizzling technique described by Wilson has the advantage that when a page is faulted into memory all the pointers which refer to objects on that page are automatically correct (since those pointers already refer to the correct virtual addresses on that page). A late swizzling scheme does not have this advantage, however this may be simulated. A form of eager swizzling can be provided by threading a linked list called the *partially swizzled pointer chain* through of all instances of pointers referencing objects on a page. When an object is faulted into memory the swizzling code not only swizzles the pointer that caused the fault, but follows the chain and swizzles as many other pointers as it can. This is eager pointer swizzling; as discussed earlier, this is only more efficient if some of these pointers are used. This very much depends on the nature of the system, programs and programming languages being used and the marginal costs of creating and following the pointer chains versus the cost of on demand per pointer swizzling.

As described the pointer formats do not provide space for the link field needed to implement the partially swizzled pointer chain. The chain may be implemented by using one of the following:

- Making PIDs large enough to accommodate the link. Expanding PIDs to 96 bits also has the advantage of providing a much larger address space.
- Using a per object translation table. Using this technique the translation table pointer field in a partially swizzled pointer uniquely describes the referend object. The upper half of the pointer does not contain the page

offset and is free to hold the link field. However per object translation tables can become very large.

- By encoding the information. The problem is that 30 bits are required to implement the chain (assuming word alignment.) The table address requires 28 bits (assuming 16 byte table entries), the offset requires 11 bits, leaving only 25 bits free. Therefore another five bits are required. These bits may be stolen from the table address if the translation table is made 32 times as large as normally required.

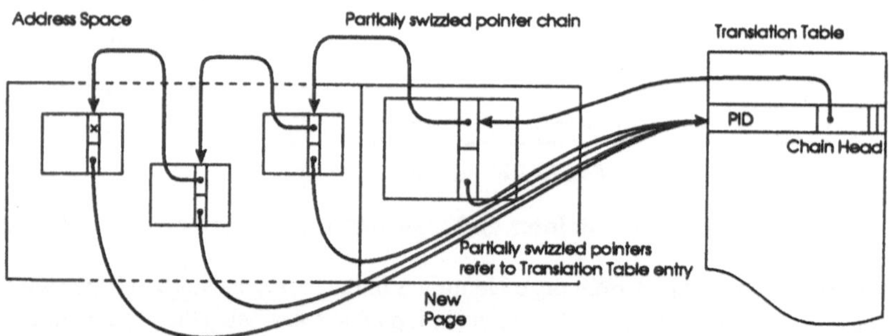

Figure 7: A pointer is inserted into the partially swizzled pointer chain

The partially swizzled pointer chain is formed as pages are loaded into virtual memory. If an instance of a PID is encountered which is already in the translation table, the head of the partially swizzled pointer chain is loaded into the unused space in the partially swizzled pointer and the address of the new instance is copied into the chain pointer head stored in the translation table entry. This process is shown in Figure 7 above.

During the execution of a program, some of the pointers in the partially swizzled pointer chain may have been overwritten by the user making (64 bit) pointer assignments. Such a break is simple to detect when the chain is being scanned since an overwritten pointer will not refer to the expected table entry. If the chains are broken, it is not possible to find all the instances of a partially swizzled pointer. However, the remains of the chain will continue to exist and many of the pointers in it may be still be swizzled through the partial chains referenced by the translation table entry and the pointer being swizzled. Also, future dereferences of pointers in a partial chain will permit yet more pointers to be found and swizzled at low cost. It is possible to maintain intact pointer chains by requiring that code doing pointer assignments perform list insertion and deletion as part of the assignment process. We consider that this would be too expensive for the marginal gains.

4.2 Deswizzling

Virtual memory addresses may only be interpreted inside the address space in which they were created. Therefore the only meaningful addresses that can be used in pages outside of a virtual address space are PIDs. The necessity to make copies of pages outside of a virtual address space arises for two reasons:

- to send pages to a process resident within another virtual address space,
- to send pages back to the persistent store.

This requires the pointers within the page copies to be fully deswizzled (PIDs). This is performed by following the reference to the translation table entry contained within the pointer and overwriting the pointer with the PID found in the table.
The management of pages within the virtual address space involves the allocation and control of two resources:

- physical memory, and
- virtual memory.

Physical memory is a finite resource and will rarely be large enough to hold the working set of pages used by a program. Pages will be removed from physical memory either to make room for another page needed for computation to continue, or when data is shared between separate virtual address spaces. When a page is removed from physical memory, pointers within it must be deswizzled as described above. A page which is not resident in physical memory may still reside within the virtual address space of the process.

In a persistent operating system [10] the integration of swap space and persistent storage may give considerable advantages. We will therefore assume that pages removed from physical memory are either returned to the persistent store or to another persistent application.

Virtual memory is also a finite resource. Programs that use very large data sets or those which are very long lived may eventually exhaust virtual memory. Indeed, the architecture described in this paper is designed to support such programs. When virtual memory is exhausted, virtual address ranges require reuse in a manner analogous to the reuse of physical memory. It should be noted that both Wilson's scheme and the hybrid design require that virtual memory addresses be reallocated in such a way that the reallocated ranges do not divide objects.

When a page is removed from the virtual address space, it must also be removed from physical memory if resident. At this time all references to that page from within virtual memory must also be removed. This involves ensuring that all references to objects in the removed page are partially swizzled pointers by deswizzling the appropriate fully swizzled pointers.

4.2.1 Deswizzling in Wilson's Scheme

Wilson proposes a scheme to reclaim pages of virtual memory that works as follows. Initially all of virtual memory is protected from access. Whenever the mutator attempts to access a page that is protected from access two actions are taken. First, the page protection is removed. Next, the page is scanned to find all pointers on it and any referenced pages are marked. Finally the mutator is resumed. As the mutator executes it constructs a new working set of pages. At some time in the future any page that is neither open for access nor marked as referenced may be reused. Once page reuse has begun it is possible that when a protected page is scanned a pointer to a reused page will be encountered. When this occurs a new range of virtual addresses must be allocated and the pointer changed to refer to this new location. This process is similar to the greedy allocation that occurs when a page is retrieved from the persistent store described earlier.

4.2.2 Deswizzling in the Hybrid Scheme

The hybrid scheme provides greater flexibility in address space reuse. Since partially swizzled pointers do not directly reference virtual addresses, fully swizzled pointers may be replaced with partially swizzled. This allows address ranges within virtual memory to be reused whilst references to objects that once resided within those addresses remain in virtual memory. In the hybrid scheme page reuse occurs as follows.

During normal execution a candidate set of page ranges can be identified for reuse, using conventional LRU techniques. This may be integrated with the LRU scan used to manage allocation and reuse of physical memory. When it becomes necessary to reuse virtual address ranges, access to virtual memory is denied as in Wilson's scheme. However, in the hybrid scheme reuse can proceed immediately. Those address ranges considered as candidates for reuse may be reused as soon as their contents are secure in the stable store. An exception will occur on the first access to a page since reuse started, again the exception handler scans the page in the same manner as Wilson's scheme. However rather than allocating new address ranges for those pointers that reference reused addresses, pointers to objects within reused address ranges may be replaced with their partially swizzled form. Thus partially swizzled pointers serve two purposes: to permit virtual memory to be deallocated at low cost and as a mechanism to avoid greedy allocation of virtual memory.

In addition to the mutator causing pointers on pages to be deswizzled, it is advantageous to provide a parallel sweep of virtual memory that eagerly scans pages and deswizzles pointers. Once all virtual memory has been swept, all allocated pages will be open for access and no direct references to deallocated pages will exist. The mutator can attempt to reference a page that is tagged for reuse by dereferencing through a partially swizzled pointer. If this page has not been reused and is still resident in memory it need only be removed from the reuse set and scanned for pointers. The partially swizzled pointer is fully swizzled and execution continues. It is not necessary to reuse all address ranges tagged for reuse. At any time ranges can be removed from the reuse set and references to objects within them left intact.

The ability to choose the number of pages to be reused ahead of time, which pointers to deswizzle, and the rate of progress of the parallel sweep provide useful tuning parameters to the memory management system. Setting the system to label all pages as reused, and to untag any referenced pages upon page scan effectively reduces to Wilson's scheme. Labelling all pages as reused, and deswizzling all pointers encountered effectively frees the entire virtual address space. A complete spectrum of choices is available within these extremes.

4.3 Elaboration of detail

The above description glosses over a large number of important details namely:

- finding object addresses,
- pointer comparisons,
- large objects,
- management of the translation table,
- creation of new objects,
- exception handlers, and
- access to the translation table.

We will now proceed to describe these implementation details.

4.3.1 Finding object addresses

When an access is attempted through a partially swizzled pointer three actions are required:

1. find the object to which access is being attempted,
2. overwrite the pointer with the virtual address of the referend, and finally,
3. update the saved state of the executing code's register set to refer to the object.

None of these activities is straightforward, and requires detailed study at the basic level of the machine's operation. Consider the code fragment shown in Figure 8 below, a type *tuple* is declared to be a record and an instance of that type is created. Later in the program a field of an instance of type *tuple* is dereferenced.

```
type tuple is record( a,b,c,e,f,g : integer )
let an_instance := tuple( 1,2,3,4,5,6 )
.....
write an_instance.f
```

Figure 8: Dereferencing a field of a record.

Consider the implementation of the program above. The pointer denoted by *an_instance* may be partially or fully swizzled; an aim of the architecture is to avoid user code having to test which of these it is. Fully swizzled pointers do not present a problem: the dereference is performed without incident. A partially swizzled pointer will result in an attempt to access an address within the translation table and this will cause an access fault. However, the address that causes the fault will not be the address of *an_instance*'s translation table entry since an offset will have been added to the object pointer in order to extract the field. Hence, although an access fault will deliver the address of the fault to the exception handler, the address will not directly resolve the identity of the required object. Similar problems occur in the other two phases; the swizzling code must be able to find and swizzle the object pointer, but ordinarily there is no record of the location of that pointer. If this swizzle is not performed, the system reduces to a translation per dereference design.

In the hybrid system, the saved state of the executing thread is repaired by an exception handler which must therefore be able to determine which machine registers contain the addresses requiring change. This can be arbitrarily difficult; to make the problem tractable steps must be taken to ensure that when an object reference is made, it must be performed in such a way that allows the recovery of the information needed to complete the swizzle. This requires a specification of the object access process at the machine code level.

All of the information required will ordinarily pass through the processor during the execution of a dereference sequence. The difficulty is in keeping track of this information and making it available to the exception handler. A similar sequence is executed whether the access is a read or a write. In general a dereference takes place in three steps and is shown in Figure 9 below:

1. The address of the pointer to the head of the object being referenced is loaded into a register.
2. Using that address, the address of the object is loaded into a register.

3. The offset within the object is added to the object address and the result used as the address of the memory access.

For the mechanism described in this paper to work, the only changes required to this sequence are to ensure that the pointer address is not overwritten after the pointer value is loaded (which ordinarily is a legal optimisation) and to ensure that the instruction sequence always uses the same registers for this purpose, allowing the exception handler to find the necessary addresses.

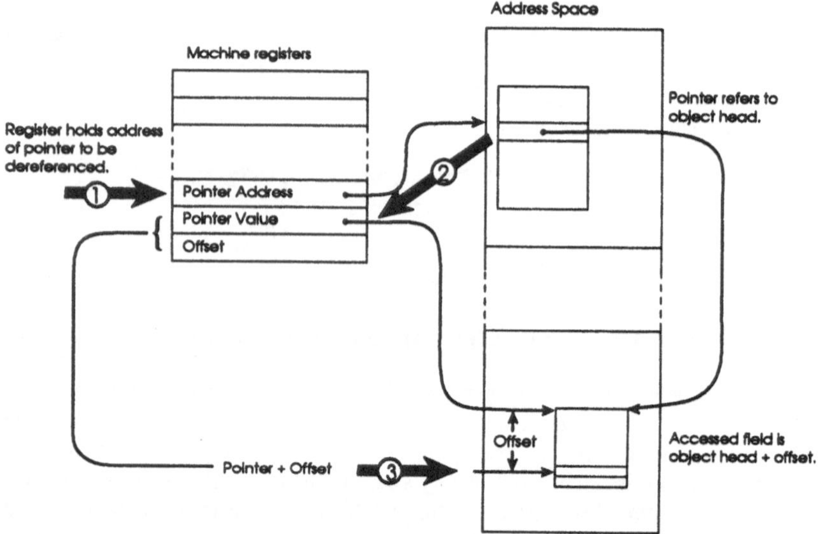

Figure 9: The three steps in pointer dereference

The result of these restrictions is a scheme in which during a dereference operation two registers are reserved for particular purposes. Firstly a *Pointer Pointer* register is loaded with the address of the pointer to the object being dereferenced. Next the *Object Pointer* register is loaded with the value referenced by the Pointer Pointer register. This value is either the address of the head of the object (for fully swizzled pointers) or the address of a translation table entry (for partially swizzled pointers). Finally, the offset is added to the contents of the Object Pointer register (with a single indexed addressing mode instruction) and the result used as an address to effect the dereference. If the pointer is partially swizzled an access exception will occur. The exception handler will receive an address within the translation table, allowing it to distinguish the exception from any others that may occur. In processing the exception the exception handler places the fully swizzled value of the pointer in both the location referred to by the Pointer Pointer register and into the Object Pointer register, then the instruction that caused the exception is restarted. If the pointer is fully swizzled then the instruction will execute without incident and with no extra cost. This process is shown in Figures 10 and 11 below. The Pointer Pointer and Object Pointer registers are only special during the process of a dereference, they are available for general use at other times.

The mechanism relies on the translation table residing in protected memory and an exception being raised when access to that memory is attempted. When the offset is added to the Object Pointer it is possible for a legal memory address to be generated. This may be avoided if the translation table is positioned in high memory and grows downward and that the exception mechanism checks for arithmetic overflow during the addition.

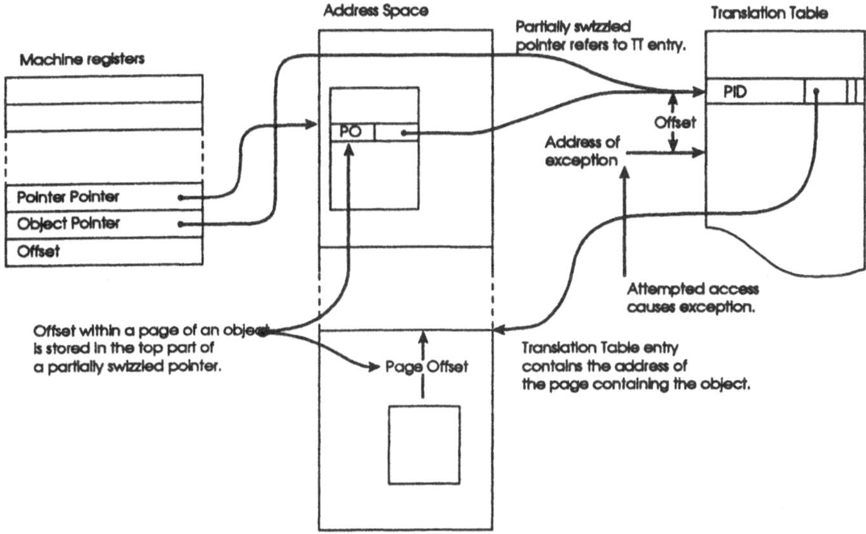

Figure 10: Pointer dereference via a partially swizzled pointer

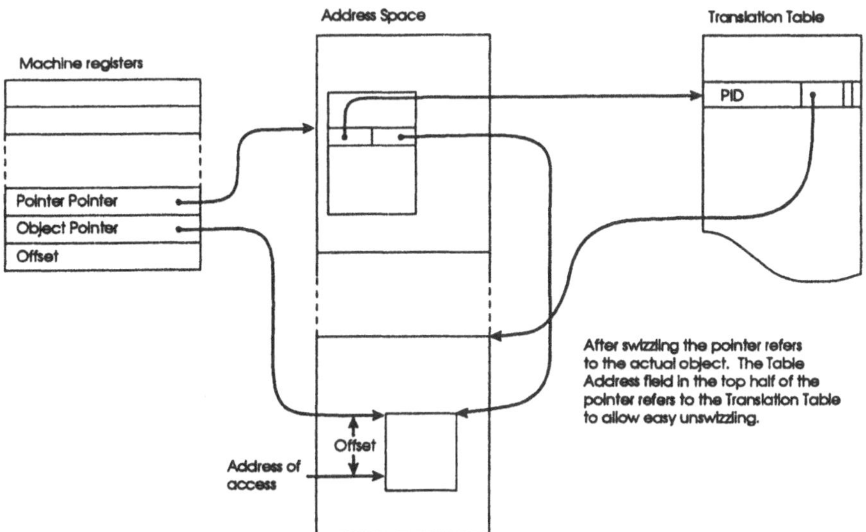

Figure 11: Dereference after the completion of swizzling

The scheme described above is directed at those processor architectures that only support simple addressing modes and require a number of instructions to carry out a dereference. Some processors are capable of executing the sequence described above in a single instruction, on such architectures the exception handler can decode the instruction pointed to by the saved PC. Such a scheme can be more flexible for two reasons. Firstly it may use many different addressing modes and secondly, it is not necessary to designate particular registers since the instruction will indicate unambiguously which registers are being used and for what purpose. However, the complexity of the exception handler is higher.

4.3.2 Pointer comparisons

Since a pointer can exist within the system in one of two forms, care must be taken with pointer comparisons. Pointers can either be partially swizzled in which case they contain an offset and a reference to their translation table entry, or fully swizzled, in which case they contain a translation table reference and a pointer to the actual object. These two forms can be differentiated since the translation table and object area occupy distinct address ranges. In both formats a reference to a translation table entry, and the page offset is present, it is therefore enough to compare these values when performing pointer comparison.

4.3.3 Large Objects

Objects which cross page boundaries and more importantly very large objects which span a large number of pages require no special treatment. When an object spans more than one page it is not necessary for the whole object to be resident at one time. However it is necessary to reserve enough virtual memory to hold the object in a contiguous span so that it is possible to fault the rest of the object into memory as it is required. This preserves all the advantages that a demand paged virtual memory space has for sparse access to large objects.

4.3.4 Management of the translation table

The scheme described uses a translation table similar in format to that used by Wilson. Whereas translation tables in Wilson's scheme are of fixed size, only describing pages in the machine address range, our scheme requires a table that provides entries for every page that is referenced by pointers within virtual memory. Growth of the translation table takes the place of greedy allocation of virtual memory in Wilson's scheme.

The table has two major constraints placed upon its organisation: firstly, translation table entries are referenced directly by objects, therefore table entries may not move. Secondly, the action of swizzling pointers requires that it is possible to find entries from their PID quickly, otherwise the swizzling on page fault becomes a performance bottleneck.

Since pages are removed from the virtual address space, the translation table will eventually contain entries for pages which are no referenced from the virtual address space. By a simple modification to the scan used to deswizzle pointers during reclamation of virtual address ranges, these stale entries can be garbage collected. Any pointers found during the scan may be followed and the mark bit set in the referenced translation table entry. Once the scan has completed, the translation table is scanned and those entries without a mark bit set may be reclaimed. During this scan partially swizzled pointers for which the referend is resident may also be swizzled. Thus the reclamation pass through memory results in all references to resident objects being fully swizzled, stale entries in the translation table being eliminated and the freeing of virtual memory.

4.3.5 Creation of new objects

Many objects are created during the execution of user code; many of those objects will be short lived and therefore not require the allocation of a PID. Objects only require a PID when they become visible outside of the virtual address space in which they were created. In practice, this means an object that already has a PID acquires a reference to them.

We now describe a scheme whereby the allocation of PIDs is performed at the latest possible time. Pointers to new objects only contain the object's address; the field that would ordinarily refer to the translation table address is set to a sentinel value that indicates that the object does not yet have a PID allocated. When a page is deswizzled, pointers to objects without PIDs will be detected. At this time, a PID is allocated and a translation table entry created.

4.3.6 Exception Handlers

Clearly one of the main performance determinants of this scheme will be the performance of the exception handling mechanism. Conventional operating systems can provide a platform with which to prototype a system such as we have described. However they place a large overhead on the user program, typically over 10,000 machine cycles per exception. Where the designer of the system has control of the hardware and is able to define the actions of the exception handler the overhead can be as low as a dozen machine cycles. The architecture described in this paper is of most benefit in an operating system designed from scratch to support it.

4.3.7 Access to the translation table.

In the hybrid architecture described in this paper user code is prohibited access to the translation table whilst the exception handler and page fault handler have full access to it. This situation is also found in some garbage collection schemes [11] and the solutions are the same. If the exception and fault handlers are implemented within the kernel they can make use of the full access accorded the kernel to user address spaces. Alternatively it is possible to place the translation table within the user's virtual address space but to have a protected area of the same size at high memory to which all the partially swizzled pointers refer. When interpreting pointer values during swizzling and deswizzling the offset between the translation table and the protected area is subtracted from the pointers to provide the actual address within the translation table. This allows the system to be implemented without modifying the operating system kernel.

5. Comparison of the schemes

The following table summarises the main design features and costs of each of the three schemes described.

- *Granularity* is the size of the entity which the swizzling scheme manages.
- *Code compatibility* lists those areas in which specific changes to the code running on the system must be made.
- *Dereference overhead* is the extra cost (if any) of performing a dereference operation.
- *Assignment* is the size of the data assigned in pointer assignment.

- *Object fault overhead* lists the main activities that must be performed when a reference to a non-resident object occurs.
- *Recovery of VM* lists what actions are required when virtual memory is exhausted.
- *Recovery of Translation Table* lists what actions are required when space for the Translation Table is exhausted.
- *VM space allocation* lists the entities for which virtual memory must be allocated.
- *VM space used* lists the entities for which virtual memory is used to hold data.
- *Translation Table allocation* lists the objects for which an entry in the *Translation Table* must be made.
- *Deswizzle action* compares the costs of deswizzling a pointer.
- *Stabilisation Action* lists the actions required to stabilise the state of the system to persistent storage.
- *Large object overhead* compares the use of virtual memory to hold large objects.
- *Sensitivity to exception handler speed* compares how performance is affected by the exception handling mechanism.
- *Overall VM space* compares the use of virtual memory of the systems.

Feature/System	CPOMS	Wilson	Hybrid
Granularity	Object	Page	Page
Code compatibility	Software check per dereference	No implications	Use of defined sequence for dereference, and pointer comparison
Dereference overhead	Software check per dereference, possible swizzle	None	Usually none, possible swizzle
Assignment	Virtual address	Virtual address	Twice virtual address
Object fault overhead	Copy single object from store	Copy page from store and swizzle internal pointers. For each new referenced page, interrogate store and allocate memory	Copy page from store, swizzle internal pointers and follow pointer chains if used
Recovery of VM space	Rebuild system if VM exhausted	Invalidate VM and rebuild	Invalidate VM and rebuild
Recovery of translation table	Rebuild system if PIDLAM exhausted	Fixed size table	Garbage collect translation table
VM space allocation	Accessed objects	All referenced pages	Accessed pages
VM space used	Accessed objects	Accessed pages	Accessed pages
Translation table allocation	Accessed objects	Entry per page of VM	Entry per page of VM
Deswizzle action	Follow pointers to PID stored with object	Search translation table for object entry	Follow pointer to translation table
Stabilisation action	Per modified object: Deswizzle pointers, write object to store	Per modified page: Deswizzle pointers, write page to store	Per modified page: Deswizzle pointers, write page to store
Large object overhead	Entire object kept in virtual memory	Accessed pages kept in virtual memory	Accessed pages kept in virtual memory
Sensitivity to exception handler speed	Little impact	Slight impact	High, less when swizzle chain is used
Overall VM space	Lowest	Highest	Low

Each of the three systems described has particular strengths. The CPOMS design is the most parsimonious in the use of virtual memory, but also the one with the highest run time overhead. Wilson's design has the lowest running costs when not page faulting, but the highest page fault costs. If the amount of virtual memory used becomes large Wilson's scheme must incur the cost of rebuilding the working set and expense of an extra translation table. Hence Wilson's design is probably best suited to environments small enough for it never to be necessary to recover allocated virtual memory. Applications with shorter lifetimes and smaller data bases would be most suitable. The hybrid scheme has running costs similar to that of Wilson's design, has lower page fault costs, and is able to recover virtual memory and translation table space more easily. This is at the cost of forcing the use of a special dereference instruction sequence, and double length pointer assignments.

Pointer swizzling may be characterised by the time at which: pointers to be swizzled are encountered, translation table entries are allocated, memory for the object is allocated, an object is loaded from the store, the initial pointer that refers to the object is swizzled. Further characterisations are: whether other instances of the pointer to the same object are swizzled at the same time, and whether pointers within objects newly faulted into memory are swizzled to refer to resident objects. Each of these activities may be performed either eagerly or lazily, the following table summarises the characteristics of the three systems described.

Feature/System	CPOMS	Wilson	Hybrid
Locate pointers	Lazy	Eager	Eager
Translation Table allocation	Lazy	Eager	Eager
Allocation of VM	Lazy	Eager	Lazy
Object Loading	Lazy	Lazy	Lazy
Swizzle to VM Address	Lazy	Eager	Lazy
Swizzle other pointer instances	Lazy	Eager	Eager/Lazy
Swizzle new pointers	Lazy	Eager	Eager

6 Conclusions

This paper describes three architectures capable of supporting arbitrarily large persistent identifiers and large object stores using conventional hardware. Two of these represent opposite ends of a design spectrum; the third is a new hybrid architecture which embodies useful attributes of the other schemes and which has some useful attributes in its own right. The hybrid architecture maintains the advantages of lazy swizzling found in the CPOMS design namely only allocating space for objects, and fetching objects, when they are referenced. The hybrid design also maintains the advantages of page based designs, requiring no runtime checking of pointers and allowing sparse references to large objects without the need to copy entire objects into virtual memory. A design for machine level dereferencing has been presented that allows exception handling code to swizzle pointers on demand without requiring checking by user code. Many of the techniques described in this paper may be of benefit in other designs.

Acknowledgments

This paper benefits from discussions with Malcolm Atkinson, Ron Morrison, John Rosenberg, Sándor (Alex) Farkas and Kevin Maciunas. For those discussions we thank them. We would also like to thank Tracy Lo Basso, Bett Koch and Andrew (Noid) Cagney for their comments on an earlier draft of this paper. This paper was completed despite the arrival of Graham Stewart Dearle on 3/7/92. This work is supported by ARC Grant number A49130439.

References

1. "PS-algol Abstract Machine Manual", Universities of Glasgow and St Andrews, PPRR-11-85, 1985.

2. "PS-algol Reference Manual - fourth edition", University of Glasgow and St Andrews, Persistent Programming Research Report 12/88, 1988.

3. Atkinson, M. P., Bailey, P. J., Chisholm, K. J., Cockshott, W. P. and Morrison, R. "An Approach to Persistent Programming", *The Computer Journal*, vol 26, 4, pp. 360 - 365, 1983.

4. Atkinson, M. P., Bailey, P. J., Cockshott, W. P., Chisholm, K. J. and Morrison, R. "POMS: A Persistent Object Management System", *Software Practice and Experience*, vol 14, 1, pp. 49-71, 1984.

5. Atkinson, M. P., Chisholm, K. J. and Cockshott, W. P. "PS-algol: An Algol with a Persistent Heap", *ACM SIGPLAN Notices*, vol 17, 7, pp. 24-31, 1981.

6. Brown, A. L. "Persistent Object Stores", Ph.D Thesis, Universities of St. Andrews and Glasgow, 1988.

7. Brown, A. L. and Cockshott, W. P. "The CPOMS Persistent Object Management System", Universities of Glasgow and St Andrews, PPRR-13, 1985.

8. Cockshott, W. P., Atkinson, M. P., Chisholm, K. J., Bailey, P. J. and Morrison, R. "POMS: A Persistent Object Management System", *Software Practice and Experience*, vol 14, 1, 1984.

9. Cockshott, W. P. and Foulk, P. W. "Implementing 128 Bit Persistent Addresses on 80x86 Processors", *Proceedings of the International Workshop on Computer Architectures to Support Security and Persistence of Information*, Bremen, West Germany, ed J. Rosenberg and J. L. Keedy, Springer-Verlag and British Computer Society, pp. 123-136, 1990.

10. Dearle, A., Rosenberg, J., Henskens, F. A., Vaughan, F. A. and Maciunas, K. J. "An Examination of Operating System Support for Persistent Object Systems", *25th Hawaii International Conference on System Sciences*, vol 1, IEEE Computer Society Press, Poipu Beach, Kauaii, pp. 779-789, 1992.

11. Ellis, J., Li, K. and Appel, A. "Real-time Concurrent Collection on Stock Multiprocessors", DEC SRC, 25, 1988.

12. Kaehler, T. and Krasner, G. "LOOM – large object-oriented memory for Smalltalk-80", *Smalltalk-80: Bits of History, Words of Advice*, ed G. Krasner, Addison-Wesley, pp. 251-270, 1983.

13. Koch, B., Schunke, T., Dearle, A., Vaughan, F., Marlin, C., Fazakerley, R. and Barter, C. "Cache Coherence and Storage Management in a Persistent Object System", *Proceedings, The Fourth International Workshop on Persistent Object Systems*, Marthas Vineyard, ed A. Dearle, G. Shaw and S. Zdonik, Morgan Kaufmann, pp. 99-109, 1990.

14. Kolodner, E., Liskov, B. and Weihl, W. "Atomic Garbage Collection: Managing a Stable Heap", *Proceedingss of the 1989 ACM SIGMOD International Conference on the Management of Data*, pp. 15-25, 1989.

15. Lamb, C., Landis, G., Orenstein, J. and Weinreb, D. "The Objectstore Database System", *CACM*, vol 34, 10, pp. 50-63, 1991.

16. Moss, J. E. B. "Working with Persistent Objects: To Swizzle or Not to Swizzle", COINS, University of Massachusetts, 90-38, 1990.

17. Rosenberg, J. "Architectural Support for Persistent Object Systems", *International Workshop on Object-Orientation in Operating Systems*, IEEE Computer Society Press, Xerox-Parc, California, 1991.

18. Wilson, P. "Pointer Swizzling at Page Fault Time: Efficiently Supporting Huge Address Spaces on Standard Hardware", *ACM Computer Architecture News*, June, pp. 6-13, 1991.

Keynote Discussion Session on Operating System Support for Persistence

John Rosenberg
Department of Computer Science, University of Sydney, Australia

Alan Dearle
Department of Computer Science, University of Adelaide, Australia

1 Introduction

Three distinct approaches have been adopted by research groups building systems which support orthogonal persistence. The first approach is to build a persistent store which operates above a conventional operating system such as Unix. Examples include PS-algol [1], Napier88 [9], E [10], etc. This approach has the advantage that existing tools and facilities can be used to assist with the development and maintenance of the persistent system. However, it has the disadvantage that the interface provided by conventional operating systems is often inappropriate for supporting persistence and it may not provide enough control over the hardware support for memory management. This makes it difficult to produce scalable and efficient systems.

The second approach is to develop new hardware with explicit support for persistent systems. Examples include Monads [11], Mutabor [6] and the Rekursiv [5]. This approach shows some promise in that it is possible to provide explicit hardware support for objects and relationships between objects, thus improving efficiency. The major problem is that hardware development is expensive and it is currently not feasible for a research group to produce hardware with performance characteristics comparable to commercial systems. It is also difficult to distribute the results of such research. A related approach is to develop hardware to be added on to an existing system (e.g. ACOM [7]). This approach shows some promise, but is yet to be proven in practice.

The third approach is to use conventional hardware, but to develop a new operating system with an interface specifically oriented towards supporting persistence. Examples include Clouds [3] and, to some extent Choices [2]. This approach attempts to remove the impedance mismatch between the requirements of persistent systems and the facilities provided by the operating system. Since the operating system is built directly on top of the raw hardware it is possible to make maximum use of the hardware facilities provided. This approach has the potential advantage that it should be possible to move the operating system to the latest hardware technology as it is developed.

This keynote discussion session examined the issues associated with the design and construction of operating systems specifically oriented towards supporting persistence. The session began with a short introduction by John Rosenberg. He posed the following questions as a starting point for the discussion:

- What are the appropriate abstractions which should be provided by the operating system?
- Is there a minimum set of requirements from the hardware?

- Would it be better to enhance an existing operating system so as to keep a level of compatibility?
- Is it really necessary to develop a whole new operating system or can we build efficient persistent systems by careful use of existing operating systems?
- Are we doomed from the outset without some hardware support?
- At what level is distribution supported?

A panel of five were given an opportunity to present their case and this was followed by general discussion. The panel members were:

- Peter Brössler, a Lecturer in the Faculty of Informatics at the University of Bremen, Germany.
- Alfred Brown, who at the time of workshop was a Lecturer in the Department of Mathematical and Computational Sciences at the University of St Andrews. He has recently taken up a position as a Senior Lecturer at the University of Adelaide, Australia.
- Jörg Kaiser, a Research Scientist at the G.M.D., Bonn, Germany.
- Ashok Malhotra, the Manager of the Persistent Objects Project at IBM T.J. Watson Research Center, Yorktown Heights, U.S.A.
- Francis Vaughan, a PhD student in the Department of Computer Science at the University of Adelaide.

The presentations by the panel members and the discussion are summarised below.

Peter Brössler

Peter argued that operating systems often reflect the state of the art in hardware technology. As a result deficiencies in the hardware tend to cause operational problems, bad performance and security leaks. Conventional hardware is always a compromise between what is desirable from the software point of view (both operating system and applications) and what is cost effective. Related to this is the fact that new developments in hardware design are often triggered by operating system requirements, e.g. memory management.

In the light of the above, Peter listed some of the requirements of persistent object systems. These include:

- very large unique object identifiers
- fast address translation from these object identifiers to main memory addresses and disk addresses, and fast indexing into other structures
- low-level protection mechanisms including object encapsulation
- object sharing between processes and users
- transaction management

Peter pointed out that what is considered to be experimental today, may be part of "conventional" architectures in the future. Given that persistent systems will play a prominent role in future computing, Peter argued that it is sensible to build the next generation of "conventional" computer architectures with appropriate support for persistence built-in. Such support would include:

- a segmented, uniform, persistent and stable virtual memory with mechanisms for sharing, distribution and protection of objects
- transaction management with locking and recovery of logical units (objects)

Peter concluded by suggesting that this level of hardware support was essential if we are to build operating systems on which we can construct efficient and scalable persistent object systems.

Alfred Brown

Fred argued that the hardware and the operating system are not really the problem, provided at least the basic facilities are provided. The real issue is to provide appropriate object caching so as to avoid operating system access as much as possible.

The conventional approach to building persistent systems is to build a persistent store above the operating system (e.g. Unix) and then to provide an object cache above this store. This should allow for efficient object manipulation for those objects in the cache. A two generation garbage collection scheme which usually only examines objects in the cache may be employed. This masks the persistent store performance and appears to work well with small working set sizes. The major disadvantages of this scheme are the address translation costs, the copy/write-back costs between the cache and the store and the difficulties with matching the cache size with the working set size and the available physical resources.

Fred argued that, as the working set sizes grow, most persistent object cache implementations tend to self destruct. This is a result of naive implementations rather than any intrinsic failings. He gave some examples which include:

- large caches are used to overcome the problems but these may not match the available physical resources (e.g. memory)
- non-linear cache management algorithms are used and these become very expensive
- no attempt is made to determine the working set size
- no attempt is made to determine the optimal working set size for the current system load

Fred argued that research into these specific limitations, resulting in the design of efficient object caches, will provide the best chance for wide spread acceptance of persistent object systems. He listed the following as potential approaches:

- design new algorithms which effectively integrate the cache management algorithms, e.g. marking may be overlapped with object purging
- design new algorithms whose cost is related to the amount of data they manipulate, not the cache size
- design a cost model for the new algorithms which allows for overall system performance, e.g. the effect of page faulting
- design heuristics based on cost models to dynamically reconfigure the object cache with respect to size and operation

Jörg Kaiser

Jörg began by pointing out that systems may be considered to consist of four basic layers. These are the application, language environment, operating system and the hardware architecture. The last two provide generic services whereas the layer above the operating system is language specific. The question for system designers is what is the appropriate division of labour?

There are clearly design trade-offs between efficiency, which is usually gained by moving facilities down in the hierarchy towards hardware implementation, and flexibility which is provided by implementations at higher levels in software. An overriding factor in both cases is dependability which includes aspects such as reliability, stability and security.

Jörg argued that existing hardware architectures already provide some support for persistence in the form of large virtual address spaces (up to 64 bit addresses on the latest architectures) and sophisticated access rights on a page basis. Similarly, operating systems such as Mach provide the ability to map secondary storage (disks) onto regions of the virtual address spaces and to control these using mechanisms such as external pagers. What additional hardware support is required?

Jörg suggested that what is missing is fine grain protection on subpage structures. This is essential for the implementation of efficient and reliable persistent systems in which language level objects are supported. He argued that this does not require a completely new machine, rather hardware can be added to existing machines. All that is required is a simple fine grain read/write/execute protection scheme embedded in the memory address path. This can be used to implement more sophisticated protection paradigms in software.

Ashok Malhotra

Ashok argued that there is no need to develop new architectures or low-level software; the appropriate facilities are already available in the IBM AS/400 series of machines. The AS/400 has a capability-based protection system implemented using tagged pointers. The architecture is object-based with the structure of all objects being hidden and only their behaviour is exposed. The architecture supports 96 bit unique object identifiers (OIDs) and detects references beyond the end of objects.

These facilities are used to implement a single level store which encompasses all memory and disk storage. All objects (source code, executables, application data, relational tables, journals, etc.) are held within the one store on which processes may operate. There is no file system. The AS/400 uses a combination of hardware and microcode to provide these facilities.

Ashok argued that this level of support can be used to implement efficient and scalable persistent object systems. This is elaborated in [8]. In addition, it is essential to have hardware support for small object protection so as to guarantee the integrity of pointers and object boundaries.

Francis Vaughan

Francis discussed the virtues of implementing persistent systems above conventional operating systems. He argued that operating systems present a virtual machine for use by higher layers of software. The issue is whether this machine is appropriate for the development of persistent systems. Given that the agent of persistence in conventional operating systems is files, the answer would appear to be no.

It could be argued that by use of memory-mapped files it is possible to provide appropriate support. Francis pointed out that orthogonal persistence requires more than just persistent data. Some systems require that processes are persistent, and what about kernel data structures, asynchronous events and exception handling? All of these issues need to be addressed in order to provide proper support for persistence.

Francis argued that it is possible to implement a system supporting orthogonal persistence above conventional operating systems, but only at considerable cost. A large amount of time and effort must be expended in working around the basic inadequacies of the operating system. The techniques usually exploited are virtual memory protection and various clever exception handling mechanisms. Francis has considerable experience in using such mechanisms to build a Napier system above the Mach kernel. Although they have constructed a working system, they have had to compromise the design on several occasions.

Francis concluded by arguing the case for the design of a new operating system which is specifically designed to support persistent systems [4]. Such an operating system would provide basic abstractions more appropriate for use by persistent environments.

General Discussion

The discussion following the presentations was quite wide ranging. However, one of the major issues was whether it is necessary (or even sensible) to provide hardware support for persistence. Several people argued that hardware support is unnecessary and that it is possible, using techniques such as pointer swizzling, to build efficient and scalable persistent systems above conventional architectures. The analogy of CISC vs RISC was used on several occasions. The RISC proponents have argued that it is better to build an extremely simple but fast machine and then construct more complex operations in software. Is the same true for persistent systems? It was argued that at least until we understand more about the nature of persistent systems we should not build things into the hardware.

At the other end of the spectrum it was suggested that the RISC philosophy does not preclude support for persistence. The basic RISC argument is that only frequent operations should be built into hardware. This would suggest that support for pointer de-referencing and fine-grain protection may be sensible. It is also interesting that these issues only arise on loads and stores in a RISC architecture and so such support should not compromise the speed of other operations.

A second topic of discussion was how to measure the cost of the various proposals. Very few existing persistent systems have any accurate measurements. One of the difficulties is knowing what to measure. However, until we do perform some proper analysis we will not know which areas need to be optimised. For example, it has been argued by several people that large object identifiers (128 bits) are desirable for persistent systems. However, we have seen no comprehensive evaluation of the cost of these.

A third issue discussed was the question of the level at which support should be provided. There is clearly tension between the issues of flexibility versus efficiency. Hardware support improves efficiency, but perhaps with a loss of flexibility. Support at the operating system level may be a good compromise. It was pointed out that Multics provided considerable support for persistence with very little hardware support. Despite this, the system was used for many years in a production environment.

Finally the issue of multiple languages was raised. Several existing persistent systems rely on a single language (or at least a single type system) for protection. It was argued that support for multiple languages and exchange of data between languages is essential. This is clearly an area for future research.

Conclusions

There is no clear agreement on the level at which support for persistence should be provided. However, it appears that most people feel that existing architectures and operating systems as a combination do not provide an ideal environment for experimentation. Although hardware support is appealing in terms of the potential performance improvements, there are major disadvantages. Appropriate operating system support may be able to remove many of the difficulties currently being experienced by system developers. However, concurrently with the development of new operating systems, we must produce performance analysis tools so that we can fully evaluate their effectiveness.

References

[1] Atkinson, M. P., Chisholm, K. J. and Cockshott, W. P. "PS-algol: An Algol with a Persistent Heap", *ACM SIGPLAN Notices*, 17(7), pp. 24-31, 1981.

[2] Campbell, R. H., Johnston, G. M. and Russo, V. F. "Choices (Class Hierarchical Open Interface for Custom Embedded Systems", *ACM Operating Systems Review*, 21(3), pp. 9-17, 1987.

[3] Dasgupta, P., LeBlanc, R. J. and Appelbe, W. F. "The Clouds Distributed Operating System", *Proceedings, 8th International Conference on Distributed Computing Systems*, 1988.

[4] Dearle, A., Rosenberg, J., Henskens, F. A., Vaughan, F. and Maciunas, K. "An Examination of Operating System Support for Persistent Object Systems", *25th Hawaii International Conference on System Sciences*, vol 1, (ed V. Milutinovic and B. D. Shriver), IEEE Computer Society Press, Hawaii, U. S. A., pp. 779-789, 1992.

[5] Harland, D. M. "REKURSIV: Object-oriented Computer Architecture", Ellis-Horwood Limited, 1988.

[6] Kaiser, J. "An Object-Oriented Architecture to Support System Reliability and Security", *International Workshop on Computer Architectures to Support Security and Persistence of Information*, Springer-Verlag, Bremen, Germany, 1990.

[7] Kaiser, J. and Czaja, K. "ACOM: An Access Control Monitor Providing Protection in Persistent Object-Oriented Systems", *Proceedings 5th International Workshop on Persistent Object Systems*, Springer-Verlag, San Miniato, Italy, 1992.

[8] Malhotra, A. and Munroe, S. J. "Support for Persistent Objects: Two Architectures", *Proceedings of the 25th Annual Hawaii International Conference on System Sciences*, vol 1, IEEE Computer Society Press, pp. 737-746, 1991.

[9] Morrison, R., Brown, A. L., Connor, R. C. H. and Dearle, A. "Napier88 Reference Manual", Universities of Glasgow and St. Andrews, Persistent Programming Research Report PPRR-77-89, 1989.

[10] Richardson, J. E. and Carey, M. J. "Implementing Persistence in E", *Proceedings of the Third International Workshop on Persistent Object Systems*, (ed J. Rosenberg and D. M. Koch), Springer-Verlag, pp. 175-199, 1989.

[11] Rosenberg, J. "The MONADS Architecture - A Layered View", *Proceedings of the 4th International Workshop on Persistent Object Systems*, Morgan-Kaufmann, pp. 215-225, 1990.

Selection Box

Chris. J. Barter
Department of Computer Science, University of Adelaide
Adelaide, Australia

This session contained three papers, only loosely related to each other, but addressing important issues in persistent object systems.

The first paper on measuring persistent object stores was presented by Malcolm Atkinson. He argued that the problem of performance measurement needed to be separated into two distinct tasks, that of the gross performance of stores as seen by their users, and that of the mechanisms employed to implement such stores, so as to give store designers better engineering insights into their internal behaviours.

He argued for the criteria to be used in designing benchmark tests for the measurement of external behaviour, produced results for a range of benchmark tests, and gave an interesting analysis of those results. One important result was that persistent stores can exhibit various kinds of overload behaviour, but these are not easily understood in terms of the parameters of external performance measures, but require a study of internal mechanisms.

The second half of the paper was devoted to these internal mechanisms and their measurement. The approach was to develop a theoretical framework within which to postulate laws of persistent store behaviour, and the design of experiments to validate those laws. Those experiments revealed phase changes in the behaviour if internal mechanisms which might explain various kinds of overload behaviour recognised in external performance measurements.

The second paper was presented by Graham Kirby on persistent hyper-programming, a concept developed jointly by researchers at St. Andrews and Adelaide. In this method of programming, values in the persistent environment, including procedures, are used in the composition of new programs. This allows checking to be performed at composition time.

The paper also outlined how hyper-programming facilities may be conveniently provided within the persistent environment.

Giorgio Ghelli presented a paper on the efficient implementation of record sub-types in persistent languages. This was based on the separation of the issue of representation of sub-type values from that of the search method used to extract fields from records. The latter are constructed by the compiler according to criteria based on properties of the sub-type values and their access fields, so as to be most efficient.

Work was also reported on self profiling of these access structures, with a view to dynamic re-configuration according to actual access patterns. A cost model was developed and experimental results presented.

Atkinson was asked by Ashok Malhotra about performance measures in the context of other concurrent users accessing the store. Atkinson replied that it was important to specify the nature and extent of such access as part of the benchmark, which was not the case for example in the OO1 benchmark. Ron Morrison observed that the phenomenon of phase change was likely to prove to be important in understanding store behaviour, and its prediction would be valuable.

Giorgio Ghelli asked how well the measures of performance matched the predictions of the models used. Atkinson replied that they did not match very well due to effects such as cache and virtual memory effects.

Ron Morrison asked if performance measures on cache and virtual memory effects could carry over into store technology, and Atkinson thought that they probably did not do so directly, but should be modelled and measured in a store context.

Antonio Albano asked if the OO1 benchmarks had any relevance to persistent store design, and Atkinson replied that the results were very load dependent, and the behaviour could not be explained at present.

Antonio also asked Graham who was advantaged by the hyper-programming technique, the programmer or the compiler. Graham replied that both were advantaged - the compliler because of the reduced need to generate checks in programs for things that had already been checked at composition time, but the main advantage was to the programmer in the increased ease of program construction. Ron Morrison observed that not only were the ideas an interesting advance in programming and compiler technology, but they were only possible in persistent environments.

After some discussion on record sub-types, Giorgio Ghelli observed that although Dixon and Schweitzer had proposed a scheme for efficient record sub-type access, these relied on having non-conflicting access labels which can be arranged in closed systems, but that is not the situation in persistent systems where new code can be added incrementally.

Measuring Persistent Object Systems

M.P. Atkinson, A. Birnie, N. Jackson and P.C. Philbrow

FIDE Group, Department of Computing Science, University of Glasgow
Glasgow, Scotland

{mpa,birniea,jacksonn,pp}@dcs.glasgow.ac.uk

Abstract

Measurements of persistent systems are reported. A discussion of issues and criteria that should guide measurements and their interpretation is initiated. Measurements which may inform the engineering of persistent object stores are discussed and in particular a proposal is made for the formulation of laws governing the behaviour of persistent object stores. Some initial laws are presented. Experiments examining adherence to these laws are briefly reported.

1 Introduction

This paper is intended to fulfil two goals: to report on recent measurements of persistent systems conducted by the authors and to initiate a discussion of the issues and criteria that should guide measurements and their interpretation. There have been repeated calls for measurement of persistent object stores at the POS workshops [4]. The intuition behind these calls and our measurement work is that measurement is a necessary component of developing well engineered persistent object stores. The measurements are required for two purposes: to validate or refute our theories about the behaviour of persistent object stores and their work loads and to allow better comparison of the effectiveness of various technologies.

There appear to be two quite distinct reasons for measuring the properties of a persistent object store:

1. to establish the gross behaviour of a store implementation for the benefit of consumers; and

2. to better understand mechanisms and hence to conduct more precise engineering.

In the automotive industry the former is typified by figures such as the time to accelerate from 0 to 100 kph and the consumption of fuel in litres per 100 km, while the latter is typified by the brake horse power and torque of the engine at various revolutions per minute or the aerodynamic drag as a function of speed.

The criteria for these two classes of measurement are quite different. For the gross behaviour the principal concern is marketing, whether selling a car or selling the ideas behind a software architecture for a persistent object system at a workshop. Here the measurements have to be understandable, have to bear a reasonable relationship to the way the consumer will use the product and have to be trustworthy in the sense that they are consistently measured.

The criteria for engineering measurements are far more complex. Primarily they should serve the rôle of enabling better engineering. This means that they need to be related to precise and validated models of the system that they are intended to improve. The measurements are used both to establish the validity of the models and to determine parameters. Comparisons are of interest to engineers in their capacity as consumers and generators of designs. In persistent object systems both the models and measures have yet to be established.

The paper consists of two almost independent parts. In Part 2 our initial efforts in establishing gross behavioural measurement techniques are presented. Two benchmarks are described and the results with Napier88 are reported. This leads to questions about what benchmarks and what measures would be regarded as appropriate in this context. It also provides an illustration of how these may be set up without requiring initial bodies of data and of the limitations of the current techniques.

Part 3 discusses the kind of measurements and models which may inform the engineering of persistent object stores. In particular there is an initial proposal about formulating laws governing the behaviour of persistent object stores and some of the experiments examining that behaviour are briefly reported.

Part 4 presents a summary and conclusions. It includes comments on measurement of both external and internal properties and some observations on the difficulty of performing these experiments.

2 Measurements of external behaviour

Measurements produced in this category should meet four criteria: relevance, reliability, feasibility and independence. To be *relevant* the measurement must be one which measures aspects of performance which concern the wider audience of consumers and which is determined under conditions of typical load. For example, the typical metric is elapsed time or response time and the typical load is a complex mixture of operations on large, complex data structures that are intended to be characteristic of real loads. We discuss below how this representative load may be selected. The complexity of any remotely representative load makes these measurements difficult to interpret for engineering purposes and we have therefore concluded that those measurements should be designed and conducted separately. Only if such relevance is achieved will the results be *useful*, otherwise the consumer will say, "But with my work load ...".

To be *reliable* the measurement must be such that if it were repeated by an independent body the result would be the same. This requires that the measurement be well specified so that there is no ambiguity in its parameters that could be interpreted differently on different occasions. For example the precise structure and size of the test data, the sequence of operations, the concurrency, recovery and stabilisation, and the performance characteristics of the supporting machine will all need to be specified. Only if such reliability is achieved will the results be *trustworthy*, otherwise the consumer will suspect that the result was achieved by using an unlikely volume of RAM, or some such trick.

To be *feasible* the measurement must not require excessive resources to set up. For example, it is unlikely that teams will write very large amounts of application code or arrange complex transformations of large volumes of data. To gain confidence in measurements they usually require repetition. The total testing time must therefore be reasonable, both in the labour costs of setting up and running the tests and in the computational costs. This is particularly the case where we are seeking measurements of systems that are being built within research projects and hence this criterion has weighed heavily with us.

To be *independent* the measurement must be re-usable in all the other persistent object stores activated by all conceivable persistent and database languages. This requirement indicates that the measurement will be specified in a language independent form. There are conflicts here between the precision required for reliability and the necessary freedom to allow many different approaches to handling the data and operations.

These four criteria are in mutual conflict, for example the complexity and size of relevant workloads are in conflict with the feasibility requirement. Below we report on two external behaviour measurement attempts. One of these is the Object Operations benchmark and the other is a MAPS benchmark. The experiments are reported first and then an analysis of their performance against the four criteria leads to suggestions about future external behaviour measures.

2.1 Running the Object Operations benchmark

The Object Operations benchmark version 1 (OO1) was defined by Cattell and Skeen [7, 8] and has recently been used to measure a number of OODBMS [6]. It is based on an engineering parts database. There are four tasks:

1. Lookup 1 000 parts from randomly generated integer keys (the part number);

2. Traverse all parts reachable to a particular depth from a randomly selected part;

3. Reverse traversal — as above but finding those parts which connect *to* the selected part; and

4. Insert 100 new parts, each with three connections.

The initial test load comes in two sizes: a collection of 20 000 parts and a collection of 200 000 parts. The implementor is free to choose how the parts are represented though there is a specification of how much scalar data each must contain. The size and performance of the machine on which the test is run is not specified.

2.1.1 The OO1 benchmark in Napier88

We set up this benchmark in Napier88 version 1.1 [12] running on Brown's persistent store [5]. Each part was represented by an instance of a Napier88 **structure** type.

The set of parts was represented using a map [3] which itself is represented as a tree the leaves of which are vectors of vectors containing the map elements [1]. Each part, each list element in a part, each map, each tree node in a map, and each vector is an object[1] in the persistent store.

The results of running these operations for 20 000 parts on various machines and with various store sizes are summarised in Figure 1. The three sets of MAPS results include results from two implementations of the benchmark in Napier88. In interpreting these results the reader should bear in mind that the version of Napier88 used was interpreted, was based on a compiler developed for other research purposes, on a store designed with different workloads in mind and on a prototypical implementation of MAPS[2]. The results for other systems are from [7].

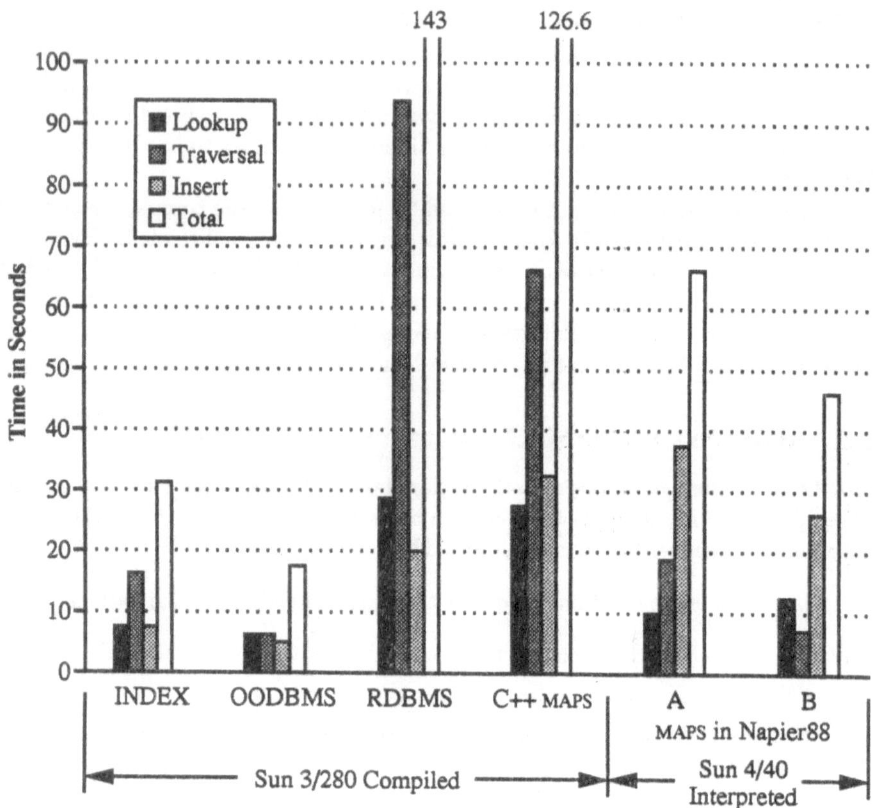

Figure 1: Comparison of external behaviour revealed by the OO1 benchmark (small remote database, cold cache)

The results of running the benchmark using Napier88 for 200 000 parts were not reported due to excessive or erratic execution times which are discussed in Section 2.5.

[1]This is a simplification, these map elements are each two or three Napier88 store objects.

[2]New versions of most of these software components have since been implemented or are under development.

2.2 Running the MAPS benchmark

This benchmark focuses on the use of an associative and set-like structure built out of objects in the persistent store. A sketch of the map data structure was given in Section 2.1.1 and details may be found in the references cited. The principal interest behind these measurements was to investigate the behaviour of the underlying store when the map algorithms were run.

In the interests of relevance the load has two characteristics:

1. There is a mixture of successful operations with unsuccessful ones that is intended to mimic typical loads: 30% successful insertions, 5% failed insertions; 35% successful lookups, 10% failing lookups, 15% successful deletions and 5% unsuccessful deletions[3];
2. There is a simulation of 'hot data', so that 90% of the operations are focused on 10% of the data with a slowly moving focus, e.g. in a bank a small number of accounts are very active, in a CAD system the objects currently displayed are those that receive most operations.

In the interests of reliability the work-load is defined in terms of four parameters:

3. The pseudo-random number generator — which will always be the 32 bit version of a specified random number generator based on shifting and XOR [13][4];
4. The initial seed for this, which is always 13;
5. The batch size, *bs*, which is typically 1 000, and which determines how coherent the operations are; and,
6. The number of batches, *nob*, which was 1 000 or 2 000 in our tests, and which determines both how long the test takes and how large the data collection becomes.

In the interests of feasibility there was no initial data, the database grows as a result of there being more insertions than deletions particularly initially. The code is precisely defined so that another implementation will generate the same load. A pseudo-code description is given below:

```
let m = an empty map
let batches = a vector of 500 places to store a seed each marked unset
let dp = a pointer to the next free space in  batches
initialise random with seed 13
for nob repetitions do
    let r = random()
    !!use r to choose op for the next batch in ratios given above e.g.
    let op = operations[ r rem 100 ] !!operations is pre-populated with procs
```

[3]Unsuccessful insertions occur when the uniqueness constraint is violated, lookups fail when the key they are searching on is not in the data collection, and unsuccessful deletions occur when the item to be removed is already absent.

[4]This random number generator is chosen because we exploit the property that it does not repeat for 2^{32} applications and assume that no measurement run will do 2^{32} test-level operations. This assumes 32 bit integers are always used.

```
if op requires an existing batch e.g. lookup or unsuccessful insert then
  let r = random()
  let rr = if random() rem 100 < 10 then r rem dp else r rem dp div 10
  let savedSeed = seed
  if batches[rr] is set do !!do nothing if no batch
    seed := batches[rr]
    doBatch( op )
    if op is delete then mark batches[rr] unset
    seed := savedSeed
else !!here op does not require an existing batch
  if op is insert do
    batches[dp] := seed !!when dp wraps this changes the focus
    step dp
  doBatch(op)
report time, cpu time etc.
```

The batches are implemented in the following fashion:

```
let nb = random() rem bs
for nb repetitions do op( random() )
```

As well as being feasible this batch organised test load with a precise relationship to a specific random number generator is a valid attempt at independence. This has not been tested outside the confines of MAPS implementations: it has been used for measurements of map structures in Napier88[5] and a separate implementation of MAPS in C++ running on a different store.

2.3 Analysis of external behaviour measurement techniques

The two examples of measurement techniques for persistent object stores will be compared with the four criteria given above. This is followed by an account of the difficulties experienced with measuring the external behaviour and the even greater difficulties interpreting the results.

Considering relevance, the OO1 benchmark exemplifies one particular requirement — the maintenance of directed acyclic graphs and traversals over them — whereas the MAPS benchmark exemplifies the maintenance of set properties together with associative access. Inevitably an external behaviour measurement only identifies a particular workload performance (town-driving) and these may be suitably characteristic. Neither really exploits the ability of persistent stores to hold complex graphs linking objects with wide variations in size. For example, as the OO1 benchmark specifies the number of components this can be held as a vector[6] whereas in any real application it would vary dramatically in size and would be held as a list or set [2]. Perhaps more realism would be obtained if the data associated with the objects were more typical, e.g. an image of size given by some specified random distribution, a matrix of size given by another distribution and a shape representation given by an arbitrary graph again with specified size distribution. But note

[5]The Napier88 code is available for those who wish to repeat the experiment.

[6]We resisted the temptation to use three fields in the part object (*cmpnt1*, *cmpnt2* and *cmpnt3*) which would have eliminated an object per part and an object access (and potentially object fault) per traversal.

how that realism eats into the feasibility criteria. Similarly the MAPS load is atypical as many practitioners would choose (we think wrongly) to make a specialised data structure that was built-in to support associatively accessed sets. Again the potential for variety of objects and traversal patterns is not exploited.

Considering reliability it is useful to divide the parameters between those that specify the work-load and those that specify the measurement context. The workload in the OO1 case is not precisely specified. The implementor of the test is left with many choices, for example how to generate the parts, how to choose their subparts and how to represent the subpart and superpart relationships. It is intended that the MAPS workload be precisely specified to the extent that two implementations would execute exactly the same pattern of operations with exactly the same arguments. With regard to the context neither measurement has fully specified the requirements. For example, the OO1 benchmark requires that the disc storage be held on a different machine (a file server, a database server or an object server?) but does not state whether concurrent access to the data on the server from other clients must be supported and/or must be actually presenting a simultaneous load during the measurements. If concurrency is a requirement in either case then the other loads and/or the granularity of locking would need to be specified. Where the measurements are being used to compare software architectures and algorithms the hardware context should be specified and some scheme should be given for normalising the results against relative hardware performance. There is a major conflict here with the requirement for independence. Fixing the hardware would prevent evaluation of parallel and special purpose hardware architectures and the range of hardware performance even within single processor architectures introduces non-linear effects and makes normalisation almost impossible.

Considering feasibility both benchmarks have demonstrated success. The OO1 benchmark has already been implemented on many stores [6] and the MAPS benchmark was implemented in two contexts. Both avoid the problems of initial data. Both will scale to provide measures appropriate to various scale and size tasks and can be developed using very small test cases.

Considering independence, both can be easily reproduced in a variety of languages with a variety of type systems. Of course, there is a sharp trade off between independence and relevance. If we want to measure the properties of persistent stores that are achieved by the latest type systems it will be difficult to devise equivalent implementations in the traditional technology.

2.4 External behaviour measurement technology proposal

It is believed that the measurement strategy of applying a controlled mixture of reproducible and re-usable batches of operations, developed in the MAPS benchmark are a good foundation both for achieving better reliability while retaining feasibility and for allowing greater relevance to be achieved while allowing controlled erosion of independence. A richer set of operations will be specified which exercise a broader range of data structures hung from the associatively accessed set and possibly interlinked. A given measurement run will then exercise a pattern of these according to an initially specified distribution of usage frequencies, the pseudo-random sequence and the hot-spot algorithm.

The operations can more or less be specified independently of one another and as a result the OO1 case would be a special case where the appropriate operations were run. The strict requirement would be that each application *op*(n) would use a fixed length subsequence, itself a function of n, of the pseudo-random sequence so that in all repeats of runs (potentially using different implementations of the operations) the operations are called with the same sample of random numbers in the same order. For each *op* the framework needs to know whether it needs an existing batch to be applied and in that case whether it destroys the batch, whether it will fail if a batch already exists, whether it requires new territory to succeed and whether if it is then applied it generates a new batch.

This would allow the research and development community to argue separately about the characteristic operations that might run in a persistent object store and consequently develop their specification. A work-load would then be characterised by a distribution of operations to apply (town versus motorway driving) typically not using every operation. A test result would specify this distribution as well as the final measurements. Ultimately we might agree that certain mixtures are particularly useful.

Feasibility is retained since initially a team wishing to measure their store could implement a chosen subset of the operations, either to save work or because those operations were characteristic of their target load. Independence is retained by a similar mechanism. If operations that are not easily reproduced on older technology are introduced, they can be omitted on the older technology and the reported results will show they were omitted.

The problem of specifying the contextual properties is harder to solve. If the system does not offer stability and recovery we would not call it a persistent object store and would not be interested in the measurements. The frequency of stabilisation can be dealt with by making it another of the operations. It should be possible to measure with and without concurrent operation. There are many applications where concurrency is not required just as there are many for which it is important. Any reported measures should say what concurrency was operational. Later we should specify concurrent loads. Any attempt to specify a particular machine configuration for measurement will date rapidly and is too restrictive. Measurements when reported should precisely specify the machine configuration and software used. There is no prospect of normalising measurements taken on different machines until the internal behaviour is better understood.

2.5 Interpreting the external behaviour measurements

The measurements using Napier88 presented above are difficult to interpret. It was apparent that the store we were using was designed to accommodate a different load and so we were unable to complete the measurements up to the scale we would have wished. The results were reproducible[7] with good accuracy provided we stayed below these overload contexts (see below). The measurements were repeated with various size stores on various SUN SPARCstations with different arrangements for accessing disc and with various amounts of RAM. Within one context reproducibility remained good but it was difficult to predict how performance would change as the

[7]Once we overcame the usual experimental problems, for example runs at night avoiding network and machine load would occasionally give anomalous results, which were identified as coincidences with the automatic incremental dumper running.

context changed. In particular it was difficult to explain when overload would set in and prior to full overload why various resonances appeared. New stores were on their way and we wished to be able to better predict and characterise their behaviour. The load in the benchmark cases was so complex that it was difficult to analyse the internal behaviour of the store though we were able to re-perform measurement runs collecting trace data such as summaries of the state before and after garbage collections and information about resource usage such as the number of page faults.

In the figure below (Figure 2), each point corresponds to the execution time for 10 000 operations of a third benchmark where each operation adds data to a map. The behaviour for the first 750 000 operations was acceptable and gave the impression that the measurements were identifying a reproducible property of the system. However, beyond that point, where some form of overload has set in, the erratic behaviour indicated that there were phenomena in the system that we could not sensibly describe with a few parameters and which were difficult to explain. Repeated measurement runs repeated the results up to overload; the instability commenced at the same point each time, but the details of the subsequent fluctuations were markedly different. Each time the store crashed before the target of 1 000 000 insertions was reached.

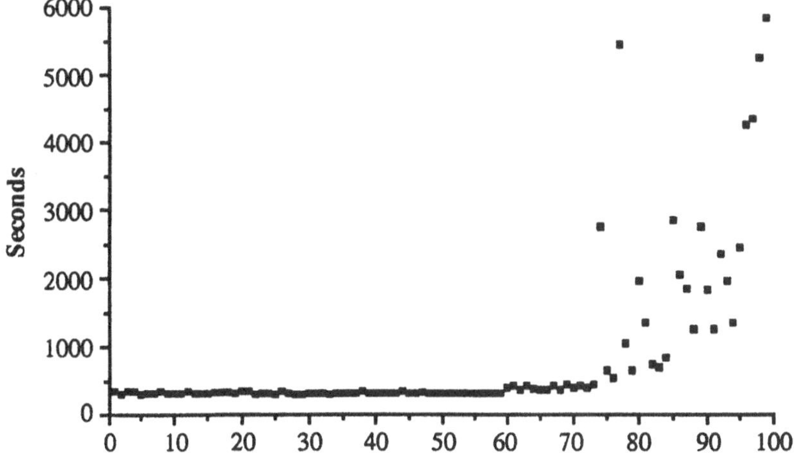

Figure 2: Measurements of elapsed time for successive 10 000 insertions into a Napier88 map

The overload can be postponed by moving to larger machines or sometimes by adjusting system parameters. It is a result of the interaction of the code of the benchmark with the implementation of Napier88 and its store, the filing system, the paging system and the hardware. The complexity of this interaction and the lack of information about the internal behaviour of the interacting components makes predicting the overload, explaining the behaviour and targeting remedial action extremely difficult. Consequently the external measurements are not particularly useful yet. They will give a false impression if measurement stopped just before overload set in. If measurement continued they are almost uninterpretable. Perhaps the most important parameter obtained is the point at which overload sets in, but that isn't often published. We refer to it later as a phase change.

3 Engineering measurements: Internal behaviour

In contrast to the previous group of measurements these measurements are not concerned with being realistic, instead the measurement should select some particular property of the store's behaviour and enable it to be better understood. For this purpose two new criteria come into play: the measurement should have a *theoretical* foundation and it should be reasonably *isolatable*.

By being *theoretically* founded we mean that there should be some postulated *law* that is likely to describe the persistent object store's behaviour which the measurement may confirm or refute. More often the measurement shows that the law only holds under certain circumstances and the measurements are valuable in determining the limits of validity. This requirement is necessary for the measurement to be useful in predicting behaviour, more importantly the proposition of these laws and their verification by measurement drives and verifies the process of trying to understand the resultant behaviour of the store mechanisms that are built. Frequently the measurements also serve to determine parameters that are significant in these laws.

By requiring the properties be *isolatable* we seek to separate one set of measurements from another so that the results are more easily interpreted and combined. This requirement is often difficult to meet as the present store implementations are complex and there are interactions between many of the mechanisms.

The original four criteria remain important though their interpretation changes in this context. They will only be *relevant* if the store properties that are described by the measurement are useful in developing better engineered persistent stores. They can only be trusted if they attain *reliability* but some measures may well be context specific so that it is only the work-load parameters that need be precise in the first instance. *Feasibility* in this class of measurements is more concerned with Heisenberg-effects and with data volumes; some measurements are difficult or impossible to obtain because the necessary instrumentation distorts the store's performance and others require that a log of high frequency operations be kept for subsequent analysis. *Independence* here should be sufficient for different groups to test the same laws, measure the same parameters and usefully compare their values. These requirements suggest that the laws should satisfy gauge theory, that is the law (and the formula describing it) should be independent of the units and reference levels used for measuring each kind of value. For example the laws regarding stores will be the same whether the elapsed time is measured in seconds, clock-ticks or RAM-cycles. Units such as RAM-cycles are useful for comparison as they eliminate the variation resulting from changes in performance of the basic technology. But we can only sensibly use such a normalisation when we have sufficient measurements to show that the phenomena in stores which we wish to time are indeed proportional to RAM-cycle times.

3.1 The first law and its measurement

It is necessary that the simple behaviour should be characterised first. The first law therefore states a requirement for linear behaviour.

Any given operation takes the same time to execute however many times it has been performed

This law seems to be an obvious requirement on computing systems and it should lead to linear behaviour where execution time is proportional to the number of times an operation is applied as described by the following equation.

$$t = kn$$

where n is the number of times the operation is applied, t is the elapsed time and k is some constant for a given operation and a given implementation. Measurement was required to validate this law before investigating interesting questions such as how k varied with the parameters of the operation or the implementation. A harness for measuring various operations under the same conditions and processing the results was established [11]. Two issues were under investigation:

1. is linear behaviour observable for all operations, and
2. if so, under what circumstances does the law fail.

For the purposes of this investigation operations were divided into two categories:

benign those that do not require space to be allocated per operation, and

active those that require space to be allocated in the store at each operation.

3.1.1 Measuring linear behaviour in the absence of space allocation

Typical of the benign category are accessing and updating elements of stored objects, for example assignments to integer and string variables. The implementation of Napier88 would lead us to expect that all these operations had similar behaviour, similar values for k and should obey the first law. The law was measured by timing runs of repeated assignments to a variable, and averaging the results over several separate runs. The test was performed for a small selection of variables and bindings. The results are shown in Figure 3 and give a good adherence to the expected linear behaviour within the experimental error[8] and demonstrated no systematic differences for k.

Of course it would be surprising if these simple operations did not show linearity but it is important not to take this for granted and also to validate the measurement technology. The consistency between different operations demonstrated in this space means that later measurements need not sample as widely. The investigation of whether linearity holds is not satisfactory. We should measure for very small numbers of repetitions[9] (but don't have sufficiently sensitive clocks) and for very

[8]The errors occur for three different reasons: the times are short compared with clock quanta, the operations are short compared with the administrative overhead or the runs take sufficiently long that it is difficult to dedicate an isolated machine to them. The first two are the cause of the larger error for smaller numbers of repetitions.

[9]These would show speed-ups as câches became initialised. Only long-term and large-scale behaviour is of interest. However, Darwin spent much of his career establishing the significance of the accumulation of small effects: "The subject may appear an insignificant one, but we shall see that it possesses some interest; and the maxim *de minimus lex non curat* ('the law is not concerned with trifles') does not apply to science" [9]. Similar accumulations of small increments may occur in stores; an effect we would like to detect as early as possible.

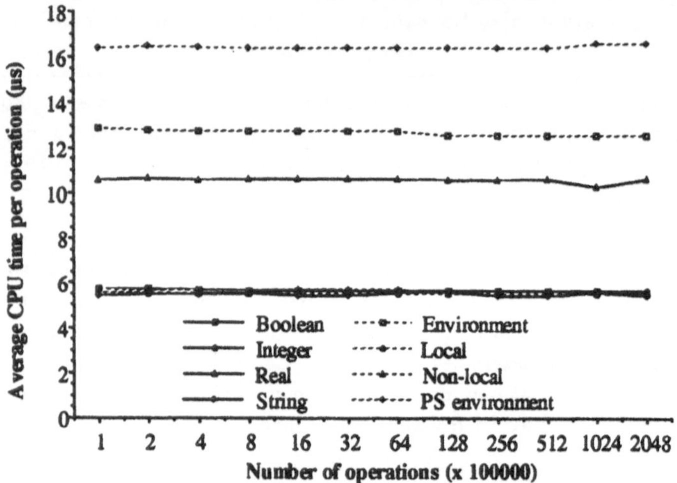

Figure 3: Average time per operation for benign operations at various repetitions

large numbers. Measurements for the larger samples will be made when resources are available.

Since this is an investigation of stores, measurements in the active category are of most interest. That category is further subdivided:

churning these operations keep requiring new space but on average release space at the same rate, and

expanding these operations keep churning space as above but on average progressively increase their total space occupied in the store.

3.1.2 Measuring space churning operations

Typical of a churning operation would be repeated generation of a string or repeated calls of a higher-order function. Typical of the expanding category are the operations that led to overload in the external measurements such as adding entries to a map giving the translation from English to French of the textual form of the 32-bit random number generated. As before, in investigating the first law simple operations were considered, one is described and reported here.

The first experiment is an example of a churning operation. The initialisation of the experiment involved the production of a vector of *size* entries each holding a list of random length distributed around a value given by the parameter *load*. The operation was to generate a new list element and prefix it to the list at a current position in the vector then traverse it and remove the last element. The current position was then changed by a step whose size was based on a distribution determined by a parameter called *locality*. Larger values of *locality* will scatter the changes more widely over the store and reduce the locality in the lists. This experiment is designed to allow the law to be tested as the values of *size*, *locality* and *load* are varied. The results of one run are shown in Figure 4 when these parameters had the values: 1 000, 50 and 10 respectively. It shows linearity holding for 10^7

operations, shows the initial noise of the experimenter checking the experiment was running and the noise of interference with the automatic dumper running in the middle of the night. There is also interesting fine structure here which may be due to there being 0, 1 or 2 garbage collections during each batch of 10 000 operations between timing points. Store creep (progressive loss of space), decay in the data structure used for space management, or decay in data structure locality would give this graph a positive gradient.

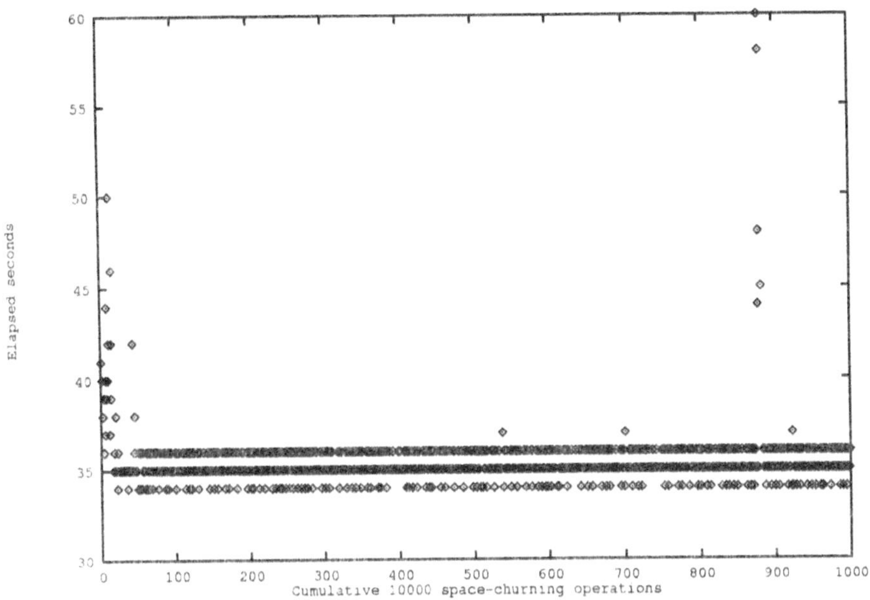

Figure 4: Measurements of list element replacement space churning operations

3.1.3 Deriving information from space churning measurements

Another operation that can be usefully used to evaluate linearity while space churning is the creation of new strings. The operation used was

dummyString := *sampleString* ++ *sampleString*

with the *sampleString* holding strings of length 1, 2, 4, 8, ..., 512 for different measurement runs. The copy operation was repeated 500 000 times for each sample string, so that the space allocator was well exercised. Linearity holds for these runs but an investigation of k against the string size s is interesting. As the operation has to allocate a new store to hold the string (which automatically makes the previous string constructed garbage) and then copy the characters in *sampleString* twice into this new store object, the expected relationship giving k is

$$k = g + ps$$

where g is the time required to allocate a new store object, including if necessary amortised garbage collection time, and p is a constant describing the cost of copying data from one object to another[10]. The graph in Figure 5 plots k/s against s, averaged over ten separate runs. It shows that the value of p is 2 μsecs and g is approximately 80 μsecs. These figures are clearly only approximate and, when more data has been collected, should be determined by curve fitting. Nevertheless, they show that by undertaking simple measurements quite specific properties of the store can be derived.

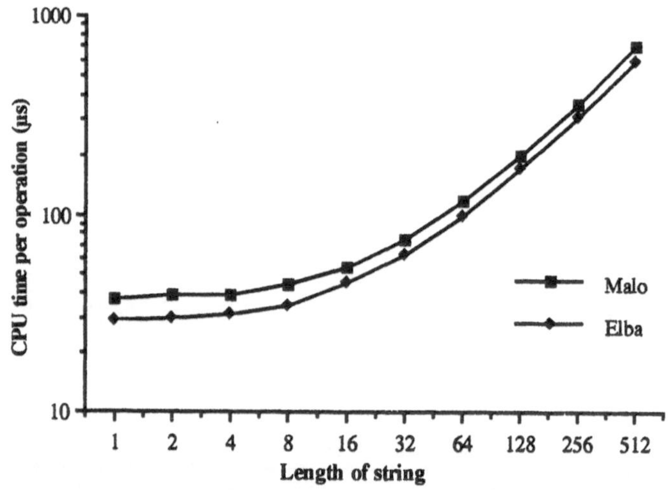

Figure 5: Measurements of average time per string concatenation

The elbow in this curve, between string lengths of 4 and 32 is probably a phase change (see below) due to the onset of garbage collection.

3.1.4 Measuring space expanding operations

The measurement of this category of operations can be illustrated by the following example. A new space churning operation is obtained by replacing the lists of the first space churning example by rings of doubly linked cells so that cyclic removal can be achieved without a traversal. A corresponding expanding operation adds to the ring but doesn't remove anything. These related churning and expanding operations can then be compared[11]. The initialised data structure occupies approximately 400 Kbytes in the example given in Figure 6 and each operation adds another 30 bytes on average to the accessible data. As the expansion continues space requirements grow inexorably so that here, for the first time, overload phenomena are expected.

---

[10]In reality the relationship will be a little more complex as the number of objects in the store at the start of a garbage collection will be inversely proportional to s and the frequency of garbage collections will be proportional to s. Similarly the number of page faults during copying will be proportional to s, so neither p nor g are entirely independent of s.

[11]There is also a benign category operation based on these rings involving the same initial data structure and traversal of the rings.

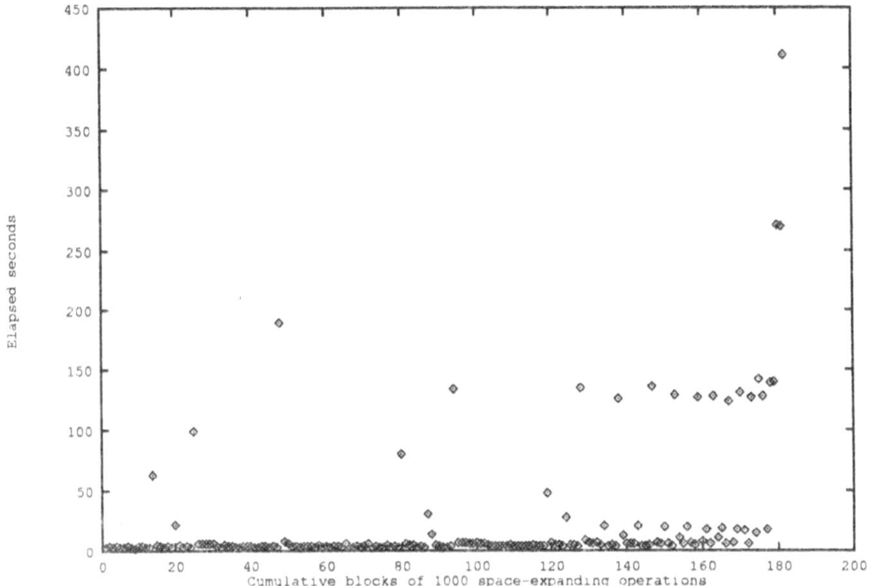

Figure 6: Measurements of expanding operations leading to overload

A phase change (see below) appears to occur at about 120 000 operations as the average time for 1 000 operations changes significantly here. Terminal overload sets in at 180 000 operations.

3.2 Phase changes, their laws and measurement

Typical stores are implemented from a number of storage technologies and can involve several space management techniques. As these come into play we can expect the value for k to change. These changes in behaviour we call phase changes and they will appear as elbows on the graph of time against number of operations, as shown schematically in Figure 7.

The first phase change might occur at the onset of garbage collection, the next at the onset of heap paging, the next at the onset of explicit disc usage by the store algorithms, the next at the onset of disc garbage collection, and so on. The onset of instability can be seen as such a phase change, since the transition may not be smooth as the extra mechanisms may have initialisation overheads or be required erratically at first. It is possible that some of the previous phenomena described as overload are in fact just transitions and that the system will stabilise for some time at a new rate of working. Eventually no new mechanism or media will be available and an impassable overload will have been observed. This final overload state will be considered as a phase change (to k becoming infinite) and subject to the phase change laws.

Determination of the phase change points and their dependence on store and measurement parameters effectively determines the limits of the regions where the

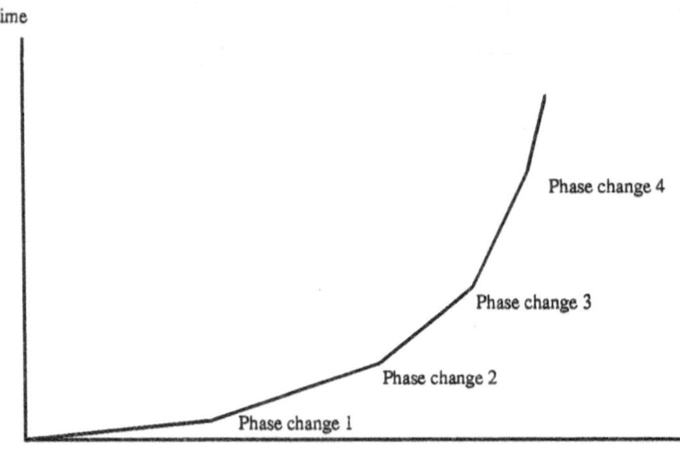

Figure 7: Phase changes occur as different store regimes come into play

actual behaviour approximates to linear behaviour.

> The point at which a phase change occurs should be predictable in terms of the store's and operation's parameters

For example, if the *additional* space required per operation doubles, it should be possible to predict that the phase change will occur after half as many operations. Similarly, if the physical store available doubles, it should be possible to predict that the phase change will occur after twice as many operations.

3.2.1 Benign operations

Phase changes should not occur for benign operations.

> Phase changes should not occur when benign operations are repeated

Laws of prohibition are impossible to confirm by measurement but so far no phase changes have been observed for these operations.

3.2.2 Space churning operations

With space churning operations the space so far used, v_u which is the sum of the reachable space and the released space, should determine when a phase change will occur. It would be an unusual store which continued to an additional medium when the operations were only space churning and so for these operations only one phase change should occur; which phase change will depend on the initial data structure volume, its persistence and the size of the individual operations.

> At most one phase change should occur when space churning operations are repeated

This has been observed at the early stages of space churning measurements as illustrated by the trace of the initial doubly-linked ring operation measurements shown in Figure 8.

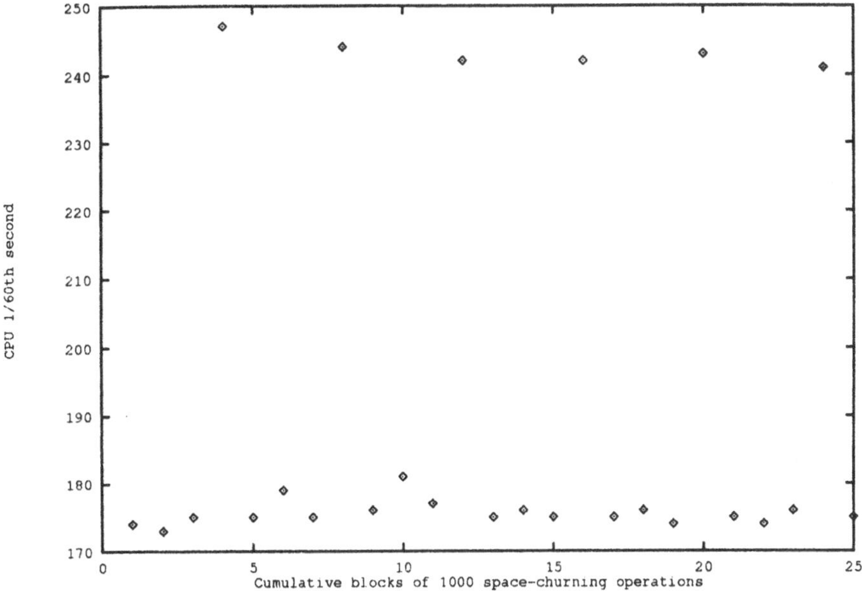

Figure 8: Initial measurements of cyclic replacement space churning operations

The phase change occurs after 4 000 operations as thereafter a new average operation cost appears. Note that the first high point (the first garbage collection) is higher than the subsequent high points, perhaps due to the garbage collector code being paged in, due to it initialising structures or due to structures left over from setting up the data structures for measurement.

So far multiple phase changes in the churning category have not been observed but we suspect that they may exist in store implementations where paging is allowed to set in and then garbage collection is later initiated, a situation recognised by Fenichel and Yochelson [10]. A formula such as the following should predict the onset of garbage collection:

$$m = ev_i + c_m + ev_o n_c$$

where m is the size of the medium, v_i is the store occupied before measurement begins, c_m is some overhead for this medium, e is an efficiency factor, v_o is the space churned per operation and n_c is the critical number of operations at which the phase change occurs. The experimentalist can know v_i, can control m and v_o and can measure n_c. Data is being collected to determine c_m and e and to verify that n_c is proportional to m and inversely proportional to v_o. It is desirable that e be small, as close to 1 as possible[12], and that c_m also be small.

[12]It could be less than 1 if the store automatically performed data compression.

3.2.3 Space expanding operations and their phase changes

The expanding operations will inevitably traverse the gamut of phase changes supported by the store. Of particular interest here is when the phase changes occur. It may be expected that the larger the storage medium the later the onset of the phase change. So a new law that we might wish to have hold is

> The onset of a phase change occurs after a number of expanding operations proportional to the size of the medium that becomes exhausted and inversely proportional to the average space required per operation

The previously stated formula should hold with v_o now being the extra space required. This is being explored for various operations and store parameters. The main focus of attention is to understand the factors controlling the point at which a phase change will occur, and hence be able to predict that occurrence.

3.3 Investigating the linear behaviour

In all the previous discussion the time t has been the elapsed time. During our experiments we are also collecting the cpu time and a few other system measures. So far the cpu times and elapsed times have had very similar behaviour until overload is encountered. Analysis of these other measures will be reported elsewhere.

The investigation will initially focus on the factors controlling the value of k, the time for one operation in the linear phase. In our experiments the size of the operation, for example the string length or the number of objects in a traversal, is determined by the parameter *load*. We expect to find that in all cases the value of k is proportional to *load*. This is simply a re-application of the first law at a finer scale. An example of the verification of this was given above for the string concatenating space churning operation.

The context of the operation will also affect the value of k. Here we are investigating several factors including the effect of the size and speed of the hardware and of the parameters available to control the Napier88 store. These particular correlations however take a considerable time to build up as the set up time for different parameters is considerable, for example we either have to take RAM out of machines or wait for other machines to be available. Consequently, for one set up of these parameters we explore the sensitivity to programmable parameters.

These are the sensitivity to two experimental parameters, *size* and *locality* and to the choice of persistence. The parameter *size* (in conjunction with *load*) control the initial volumes of data in the experiments. Both v_i, the initial volume of data, and o_i, the initial number of store objects are proportional to *load* $*$ *size*. The constants involved are known for each experiment. It is expected that the contextual volume of data will have little effect on benign category operations.

> The value of k for benign operations may depend on the size of the data read or written but should be independent of the contextual volume of data

Experiments have not, so far, revealed a refutation of this law. In contrast it is expected that as v_i and o_i increase the space churning and space expanding operations may show an increase in k for constant *load*. This may be expected as cost of space management will increase as these properties increase. It should be possible to devise stores for which k deteriorates at a rate no worse than linear in o_i and v_i. Such effects are currently not reliably measurable.

> The speed of active operations should not deteriorate at a rate worse than linear in measures of the total population of the store

The parameter *locality* is used to investigate the sensitivity of k to the locality of data accesses by the following method. Each element of a vector of length *size* has its own size determined by *makeRandom(load)*[13]. During data structure construction and during operation measurement there is a current position, *cp*, which determines which element of the vector to work on next. The position is changed by

cp := (*cp* + *makeRandom(locality)* - *locality* div 2) rem *size*

which results in a random walk around the data structures. If *locality* is 0 one data structure is completed before the next is begun. Otherwise data structures are intermingled with their neighbours, being more scattered for larger values of *locality*. For typical stores it is expected that k will increase as *locality* increases but as yet there is insufficient data or understanding of stores to propose what a reasonable relationship between k and *locality* should be.

When these general dependencies of k on various factors have been understood it may be appropriate to try to measure the contributing components of k such as the costs of garbage collection and space management and how these relate to the implementation strategies.

4 Summary and conclusions

Two classes of store measurement have been identified, the first, external behaviour measurement, is conducted to compare the total system and the second, internal behaviour measurement, is conducted to develop an understanding of the processes in stores.

The external behaviour measurement is typically conducted using benchmarks and two sets of such measurements were reported. One, the Object Operations benchmark specified by Cattell and Skeen, was run in Napier88 and the other, a benchmark based on a distribution of MAPS operations, was run in both Napier88 and C++. Four criteria for such external measurements were established: relevance, reliability, feasibility and independence. It was thought that the structure of the second of these two benchmarks offered reproducibility, relevance, and a systematic way of developing mixes of operations incrementally. However a note of caution was introduced when the task of interpreting external measurements was considered. For example they could have stopped just before some phase change or overload introduced much worse performance or total failure. Furthermore they gave little useful information for those wishing to improve store implementations and while the internal behaviour of stores is poorly understood it is difficult to correct measurements to take account of different experimental conditions.

[13]The function *makeRandom(limit)* returns *random()* rem *limit* where *random* returns the next integer in the specified pseudo-random sequence.

At present, because of the complexity of store implementations, internal behaviour measurements are likely to be the best path to better understanding of store processes and improved engineering of persistent object stores. A large number of arbitrary properties could be measured. This is not thought to be useful. Instead laws are proposed that correspond to the behaviour under specific circumstances that is expected of a well engineered store. Specific and reproducible measurement experiments are then devised to test the laws and to determine the associated parameters.

The laws proposed so far are

1. Any given operation takes the same time to execute however many times it has executed previously
2. The point at which a phase change occurs should be predictable in terms of the store's and operation's parameters
3. Phase changes should not occur when benign operations are repeated
4. At most one phase change should occur when space churning operations are repeated
5. The onset of a phase change occurs after a number of operations proportional to the size of the medium that becomes exhausted and inversely proportional to the average space required per operation
6. The rate at which benign operations are executed may depend on the size of data read or written but it should be independent of the contextual volume of data

To enable the measurement a standard approach to organising the collection of data has been prototyped. This includes a standard form of measurement program, in our case in Napier88[14], into which a pre-amble and a test-load operation are fitted. The behaviour for a given store is then investigated for that operation over a space explored via four parameters: *size*, *load*, *locality* and *repetitions*. The standard form then includes methods of processing the results, storing, tabulating and plotting them. A document describing this standard approach and giving some of the existing results is available [11].

An important feature of our measurement technique is that the programs used are small, less than a page, and simple. Furthermore, these programs only vary in the prelude setting up the initial data structure and in the measured operation. This makes them easy to understand and to discuss with a store designer.

A strategy of investigating laws has been adopted where the simplest possible laws are tested first. These are refined only if necessary, otherwise other laws that are independent or which describe the limits of the previous laws' validity are developed.

[14]This is also described in pseudo-code and may be available in other languages, so that the measurements may be produced in other contexts.

This was illustrated with laws concerned with three categories of store operation: benign operations that leave store unchanged, churning operations that claim store but on average return equal amounts and expanding operations that increase store usage. Some of the preliminary evidence concerning these laws is shown in the paper. It is desirable to develop laws that provide properties that may be relatively straightforwardly combined to predict composite behaviour.

It is important to describe the laws and the measurement techniques carefully and independently of the particular store and language so that the methods may be re-used as new stores are developed and so that comparisons can be made with measurements conducted by other groups.

4.1 Measurement problems

Some ingenuity is needed to conduct the measurements. There are several problems:

1. it is difficult to isolate one activity;
2. the measurement apparatus modifies behaviour; and
3. accurate timing information or other results of the operations such as disc traffic or page faults are not easily obtained.

4.2 Law formulation problems

Ideally the laws should be formulated to meet several properties:

1. they describe relevant behaviour in a way that is easily understood and is useful to persistent object store engineers;
2. they are intuitively sensible in that they describe the way it is believed a persistent object store ought to behave;
3. they are sufficiently independent that they can be used separately and can be combined; and
4. they are formulated so that they may be tested by experiment and if validated the relevant parameters may be determined.

It is not easy to formulate laws that meet these requirements. A particular difficulty is that there does not appear to be a comprehensive and consistent view of the way a store should behave.

4.3 The future of laws and measurement

One motive of this paper is to provoke discussion on the laws and on the validity and implications of the measurements. It is hoped that the initial laws will be challenged and tested, in particular it is intended that rival and additional laws will be proposed. The discussion about their desirability as a description of persistent object stores will sharpen the community's understanding of the behavioural goals for persistent object stores. Or, as Pareto remarked when considering Kepler's attempt to formulate laws, "Give me fruitful error any time, full of seeds, bursting with its own corrections. You can keep your sterile truth for yourself".

The laws and measurements should enable a more productive dialogue between store providers and other engineers building with these stores. They should sharpen the questions asked and enable more precise and verifiable replies. In particular important questions, such as those concerning the location of phase changes, particularly overload, will not be forgotten.

Phase changes are viewed as a crucial issue. They are probably inevitable. The important requirement is that store designers and store users should know about them. Ideally, the properties of stores should be sufficiently well-understood that phase changes can be predicted.

It is intended that others will repeat the measurements to better verify or modify the proposed laws and then to compare the specific performance properties of persistent store technologies.

Currently two additional areas of store characterisation are being pursued at Glasgow:

1. The capacity of stores, both the total data volumes that may be accommodated and limits on object size; and

2. The ageing of stores.

Laws 1, 3 and 4 indicate that a store should not show signs of ageing. The space churning measurements are designed to detect decay in the space allocation and reclamation methods. An additional agent for ageing, *tangling*, is the process which decreases the locality of references. The susceptibility of stores to tangling is being measured by a separate set of instruments.

Only when the laws concerning the simple behaviour of actual stores have been established and their parameters and limits of applicability determined will it be possible to return to benchmarks and interpret them as anything more than an indication of how the benchmark itself runs under certain measurement conditions. But if the laws are that well understood benchmarks will not be needed.

Acknowledgements

This work was supported by the EC ESPRIT II Basic Research Action FIDE, no. 3070. The C++ implementation was built at GIP Altaïr by Christophe Lécluse and run by Véronique Benzaken. Our colleague Phil Trinder was helpful in clarifying the categories of operation and Ron Morrison contributed by telling us to try again harder. The team at St Andrews provided the Napier88 system which proved robust and reliable, for example it supported continuous measurement for months with some individual runs taking several days to complete and still gave us repeatability.

References

[1] M.P. Atkinson, V. Benzaken, C. Lécluse, P.C. Philbrow, and P. Richard. Experiments with persistent map stores. Technical Report FIDE/91/22, ESPRIT Basic Research Action, Project Number 3070—FIDE, 1991. 22pp.

[2] M.P. Atkinson and O.P. Buneman. Types and persistence in database programming languages. *ACM Computing Surveys*, 19(2):105–190, June 1987.

[3] M.P. Atkinson, C. Lécluse, P.C. Philbrow, and P. Richard. Design issues in a map language. In P. Kanellakis and J.W. Schmidt, editors, *Proceedings of the Third International Workshop on Database Programming Languages (Nafplion, Greece, 27th-30th August 1991)*. San Mateo, CA: Morgan Kaufmann Publishers, 1991.

[4] M.P. Atkinson and D. Maier. Perspectives on persistent object systems. In A. Dearle, G.M. Shaw, and S.B. Zdonik, editors, *Implementing Persistent Object Bases, Principles and Practice. Proceedings of the Fourth International Workshop on Persistent Object Systems, Their Design, Implementation and Use (Martha's Vineyard, USA, September 1990)*, pages 425–426. San Mateo, CA: Morgan Kaufmann Publishers, 1990. Concluding remarks on Workshop.

[5] A.L. Brown. *Persistent Object Stores.* PhD thesis, Department of Computational Science, University of St Andrews, 1988.

[6] R.G.G. Cattell, editor. *Next Generation Database Systems.* October 1991. Special Issue of Communications of the ACM, 34, 10.

[7] R.G.G. Cattell and J. Skeen. Engineering database benchmark. Database Engineering Group, Sun Microsystems, March 1990.

[8] R.G.G. Cattell and J. Skeen. Object operations benchmark. *ACM Transactions on Database Systems*, 17(1):1–31, March 1992.

[9] C. Darwin. *The Formation of Vegetable Mould through the Action of Worms, with Observations on their Habits.* John Murray, London, 1881.

[10] R.R. Fenichel and J.C. Yochelson. A LISP garbage collector for virtual-memory systems. *Communications of the ACM*, 12(11):611–612, November 1969.

[11] N. Jackson. Persistent store behaviour: A measurement method. Technical report, Department of Computing Science, University of Glasgow, 1992. In preparation.

[12] R. Morrison, A.L. Brown, R.C.H. Connor, and A. Dearle. The Napier88 reference manual. Technical Report PPRR-77-89, Universities of Glasgow and St Andrews, 1989.

[13] J.R.B. Whittlesey. A comparison of the correlational behavior of random number generators for the IBM 36. *Communications of the ACM*, 11(9):641–644, 1968.

Persistent Hyper-Programs

G.N.C. Kirby, R.C.H. Connor, Q.I. Cutts and R. Morrison
Department of Mathematical and Computational Sciences, University of St Andrews
St Andrews, Scotland

A. Dearle and A.M. Farkas
Department of Computer Science, University of Adelaide
Adelaide, Australia

Abstract

The traditional representation of a program as a linear sequence of text forces a particular style of program construction to ensure good programming practice. Tools such as syntax directed editors, compilers, linkers and file managers are required to translate and execute these linear sequences of text. At some stage in the execution sequence the source text is checked for type correctness and its translated form linked to values in the environment. When this is performed early in the execution process confidence in the correctness of the program is raised, at the cost of some flexibility of use.

Persistent systems allow the persistent environment to participate in the program construction process. This raises the possibility of allowing the representations of source programs to include direct links to values that already exist in the environment. By analogy with hyper-text, where a piece of text contains links to other pieces of text, this source representation is called a hyper-program.

This paper outlines how hyper-programming facilities may be provided within a persistent system, discusses advantages of the technique and proposes some outstanding research areas. The advantages of hyper-programming over conventional systems include the following: it allows more convenient program composition mechanisms; it allows earlier checking; it provides more flexible linking mechanisms; it allows more succinct program representations; and it allows procedure closures to be represented at a source code level.

1 Introduction

This work is motivated by a belief that programming language systems could provide better support for the software engineering process than they do at present. Where the language is persistent, the persistent store can participate in the program construction process. The programmer composes programs interactively by navigating the persistent store and selecting data items to be incorporated into the programs. This requires direct links to the persistent data items to be represented in the program source. By analogy with hyper-text, where a piece of text contains links to other pieces of text, this source representation is called a hyper-program.

Figure 1 shows an example of a hyper-program. The hyper-program contains both text and a token that denotes a data item in the persistent store, a procedure to write out strings.

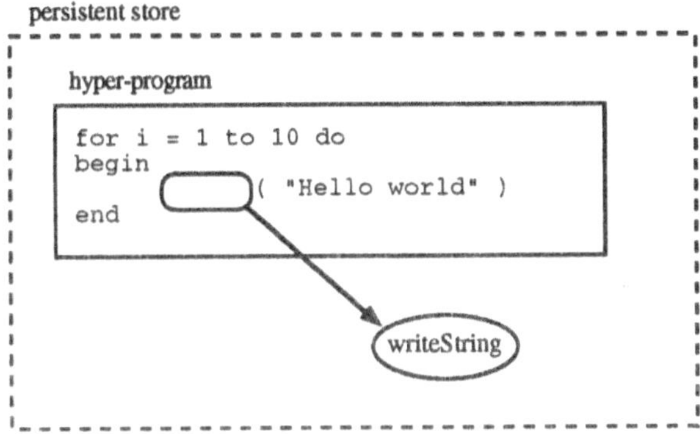

Figure 1: A hyper-program

Figure 2 shows how the hyper-program might appear to the programmer during editing. A more detailed description of a hyper-programming user interface can be found in [1].

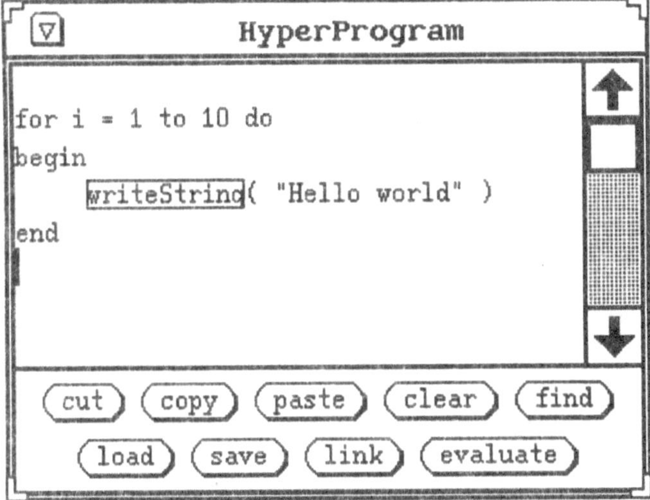

Figure 2: A hyper-program editor

The references to values are linked into the hyper-program by selecting each value with a store browsing tool and then pressing the *link* button. The system asks the programmer whether to link the program to the value itself or to the store location that currently contains the value. The editor then inserts a token at the current text position, represented by a light-button. The programmer can examine a value in a hyper-program by pressing the appropriate button in the text, which causes the browsing tool to display a representation of the value.

The benefits of hyper-programming include:

- increased ease of program composition;

- being able to perform program checking early;
- being able to enforce associations from executable programs to source programs;
- availability of an increased range of linking times;
- reduced program verbosity; and
- support for source representations of procedure closures.

The principal requirement for supporting a hyper-programming system is a persistent store to contain the program representations and the data items corresponding to the tokens in the programs. The assumption is made here that the store is stable and that it supports referential integrity. One consequence of this is that once a reference to a data item in the store has been established, the data item will remain accessible for as long as the reference exists.

Secondly, all hyper-program representations, both source and executable, must consist of denotable values within the persistent programming language environment. A further consequence is that the compilation process itself must also be supported within this same environment. One mechanism particularly well suited to realise this is known as type-safe linguistic reflection, as described in [2].

A third requirement is for tools that provide the programmer with a graphical representation of the persistent store. The representation shows the values, locations and types in the persistent store and the links between them. The programmer can point to the representations of specific data items and obtain tokens for them to be incorporated into hyper-programs.

To be useful in practice a hyper-programming system will also have to support additional facilities for 'programming in the large', that is, building large applications from smaller components. These include facilities for controlling the sharing of components between applications, for limiting the visibility of some components for protection reasons, and for imposing a degree of partitioning on the persistent store to aid intellectual manageability and execution efficiency. A model to support these facilities, the *hyper-world* model, is proposed.

2 Motivations and benefits

First some terms used in the following discussion will be defined:

data item: a value, or a location containing a value, in the persistent store;

access path: a description of the position of a data item relative to the root of the persistent store;

access specification: the access path of a data item together with a description of its expected type.

The principal benefits of hyper-programming are now described in more detail.

2.1 Program composition

The primary motivation for providing a hyper-programming system is to allow the programmer to compose programs interactively, navigating the persistent store and selecting data items to be incorporated into the programs. This removes the need to write access specifications for persistent data items that are accessed by a program.

Existing languages that allow a program to link to persistent data items at any time during its execution, such as PS-algol [3] and Napier88 [4], require it to contain code to specify the access path and type for each data item. The access path defines how the data is found by following a particular route through the persistent store starting from a root of persistence. The type specifies the expected type of the data at that store position. When a program is compiled the compiler checks that subsequent use of the data is compatible with its expected type. When the program is executed the run-time system checks that the data is present at the declared position and that it does have the expected type.

This mechanism gives flexibility because a program can link to data in the store at any time during its execution. However in many cases the programmer knows that a particular data item is present in the store at the time the program is written. Although the programming system could obtain all the information in the access specification by inspecting the data item at that time, the programmer must still write the access specification.

In a hyper-programming system the programmer has the option of linking existing data items into a program by pointing to graphical representations rather than writing access specifications. Note that the ability to link to data items at run-time is still required in the cases where data becomes available only after a program is written.

2.2 Early checking

Hyper-programming can provide improved safety in several ways. One of these is that it allows some program checks to be performed earlier than normal, subsequently giving increased assurance of program correctness. This is possible because data items accessed by a program may be available for checking before run-time. Referential integrity then ensures that the checked data remains available at run-time.

Checking can be performed at several stages in the program development process in existing systems. The principal opportunities are at compilation-time when a program is translated into an executable program, and at run-time when the executable program is executed. Categories of checking include checking programs for syntactic correctness and type consistency, and checking persistent data access. Usually the program checks are performed at compilation-time, although in some syntax directed programming systems [5] type consistency is verified as a program is constructed.

2.2.1 Checking persistent data access

In conventional strongly typed persistent systems a program contains an access specification for each persistent data item used. These access specifications are checked at run-time: at that time the system verifies that each data item is present in the store, with the previously declared access path and type. This is illustrated in Figure 3:

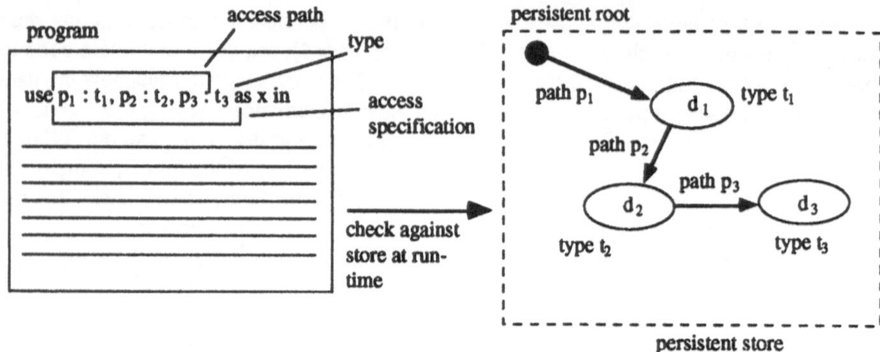

Figure 3: Access specification with run-time checking

In the program the identifier x is introduced to denote the data item obtained by traversing the access path $p_1 : t_1, p_2 : t_2, p_3$. In the diagram this data item is labelled d_3. The type of x is declared to be t_3. Each component of the path—p_1, p_2 and p_3— is a fragment of code that defines a route between two data items. p_1 is first applied to the persistent root to give data item d_1, then p_2 is applied to d_1 to give d_2, and finally p_3 to d_2 to give d_3. The types of the intermediate data items, t_1 and t_2, also form part of the access path. Note that there may be other routes to d_3 apart from the one shown. At compilation-time the system checks that the access specification is consistent with the rest of the program. At run-time it checks that the access specification is valid with respect to the current state of the store, i.e., that d_3 can be accessed along the given path at that time, and that it does have the declared type t_3.

A program execution will fail if the store does not contain a route to a data item corresponding to the access path specified in the program. Thus even if it is known at the time of writing that a particular program will execute correctly, it cannot be predicted when it may fail on some future execution.

The use of hyper-programs as source representations allows the checking of access specifications to be performed before run-time. Each token embedded in a hyper-program denotes a data item that exists in the store at the time the hyper-program is composed. The process of checking the access path is moved from run-time to program composition time. The access path is established incrementally as the programmer manipulates the graphical representations of the data in the store to locate the required data item. Once the path has been established the data item at the end of it is linked into the hyper-program and the path need not be followed again at execution time. This is illustrated in Figure 4. The hyper-program will be unaffected if the access path is then removed. This might occur, for example, due to the link from d_2 to d_3 being overwritten by a link to some other data item.

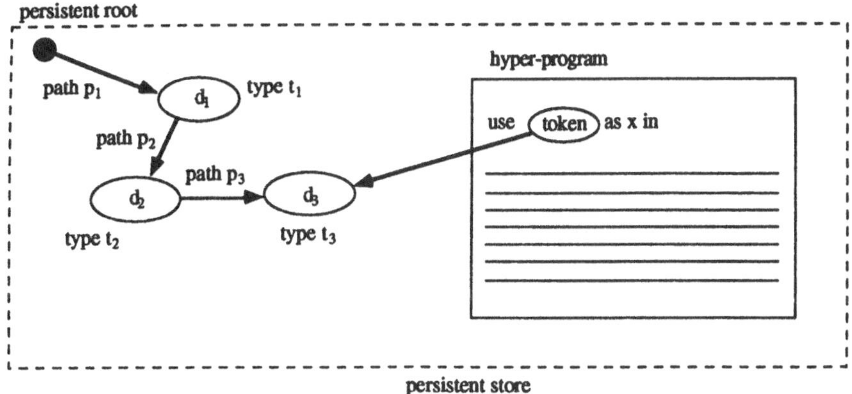

Figure 4: Access path with hyper-program

The access path part of the access specification is established during hyper-program composition. The other part, the type specification of the data item, is checked when the type consistency of the hyper-program is verified at or before compilation-time. The system checks that the type of the data item denoted by the token is compatible with the use of the token in the program.

Creating direct links from a hyper-program to values in the store, with the attendant safety benefits described above, is only applicable where values are present in the store at hyper-program composition time. Added flexibility can be gained by using tokens to denote mutable locations in the store. Linking a location into a hyper-program involves the same processes as for linking a value, with the difference that the value associated with the token changes when the location is updated. Updates to the location may occur at any time after the composition of the hyper-program. Strong typing ensures that the type of any value assigned to a location is compatible with the type of its original contents. This allows the type checking of persistent locations to be performed at compilation-time. The values in locations associated with the tokens in a hyper-program can vary but their types will always remain compatible. Where a token denotes a location, that location is linked directly into the executable program produced from the hyper-program, so that updates to the location also affect the executable program.

2.2.2 *Other kinds of checking*

Language systems also perform other kinds of checking at run-time, some of which can be performed earlier in a hyper-programming system. An example of this is dependent type checking.

A dependent type is a type that depends on a value. In general this requires dynamic type checking. To determine whether two dependent types are compatible, the language's type checker takes account of the associated values as well as their structure. An example of a dependent type is the generic type *map* [6], instances of which are associations between sets of values. The type of a particular map is dependent on the identity of the procedure which defines equality over the key set. Because of this it is not generally possible to type-check at compilation-time a program that contains map operations, as the map values themselves must be tested.

In a hyper-programming system the value on which a dependent type depends may be linked directly into a program, and may thus be available for checking at compilation-time. This makes it possible for the system to check operations on dependent types at compilation-time rather than planting code in the executable program to perform the checking at run-time. The system may also provide tools that allow the programmer to verify the type compatibility of selected values before they are linked into the hyper-program. Transmission of the results of such checks to the compilation system is a topic for future research.

More generally the programmer may perform arbitrary checks on data values before linking them into a hyper-program, by writing and executing other programs that compute over them. If the checks succeed, the code that performs the checking can then be omitted from the main hyper-program, since the links to the original values are guaranteed to remain intact.

2.3 Source code control

2.3.1 Relationships among program forms

Safety can also be improved with respect to the relationships between executable programs and source programs. In a programming system it is often desirable to maintain links between executable programs and their corresponding source code programs, to facilitate debugging and software evolution. These links enable the system to show the source code corresponding to the point where an error occurs in a running program, or to supply the source code for a given executable program so that it can be modified and a new version created.

In existing systems these links operate by conventions and can be corrupted by programmer actions that do not conform to those conventions. Given a language that supports executable programs as first class values—for example, procedures—a hyper-programming system can enforce links from executable code to source code. To illustrate this, the relationships between these different forms of code and other data values will be described, first in general and then with particular reference to file-based systems, persistent systems and finally hyper-programming systems.

Application development involves a number of activities including the following:

- constructing source code programs;
- compiling source code to give intermediate programs;
- linking intermediate programs to give executable programs;
- linking existing data items into executable programs; and
- executing linked programs in a run-time environment.

The software entities involved in these activities are:

- source programs;
- intermediate programs—these are not executable since the code in them contains unresolved references to other programs;
- executable programs—these can be executed directly; and
- data items that are manipulated during execution.

Language systems support several varieties of relationships between the software entities listed above. These are *causations*, *associations* and *direct links*.

Causations are one-way 'cause and effect' relationships. A causation from an entity *A* to another entity *B* is a relationship mediated by some process having *A* as input and *B* as output. This means that a change to *A* results in a corresponding but indirect change to *B*. An example of a causation is the relationship between a source program and the corresponding compiled version, mediated by the compiler which takes the source program as input and produces a compiled version. A modification to the source program causes a corresponding change in the compiled program but only after the process of compilation.

Associations are general relationships between entities. An example is an association between an executable program and the corresponding source program, maintained by a source level debugging system. This information is not intrinsic to the associated entities themselves but is maintained by an external mechanism. In general the accuracy of associations depends on adherence to conventions: if changes to the entities are made outside the control of the external mechanism the associations may become invalid. In the example the source program could be updated without notifying the debugging system, in which case its association with the executable program would become invalid.

Direct links are references between entities in the run-time environment. A direct link from an entity *A* to another entity *B* exists if a change to *B* results in a corresponding and immediate change to *A*. This could be implemented by storing the address of *B* inside *A*. The language systems considered here support identity, that is, a reference to a given entity is guaranteed to remain valid and to refer to the same entity for as long as the reference exists. Thus a direct link from *A* to *B* always remains valid regardless of the operations performed on *B*. A change to *B* has an immediate effect on *A* without the need for any intermediate process.

2.3.2 Languages with external storage systems

In languages such as Pascal [7], Ada [8] and C [9], the persistent data, that which survives for longer than the program execution that creates it, is manipulated differently from the transient data. It is held in a storage system, separate from the run-time environment, with which programs communicate through an interface. An example is the Unix file system [10].

The program entities listed earlier—source programs, intermediate programs and executable programs—all reside in the external storage system. Source programs are compiled to produce intermediate programs. Where necessary a linker is then used to link in existing intermediate and executable programs from a program library. This linking involves combining the intermediate program with copies of the library programs to produce a new executable program. At run-time the resulting executable program is itself copied into the data space of a run-time environment and evaluated in that context. The running program may create new data items (values and locations) with direct links between them. It may also access existing data in the external storage system. The run-time environment disappears at the end of execution, along with any new data items created in it.

The relationships are illustrated pictorially in Figure 5. Here solid rectangles represent source programs, rounded rectangles represent intermediate programs, diamonds represent executable programs and ellipses represent data items that can be denoted in the programming language.

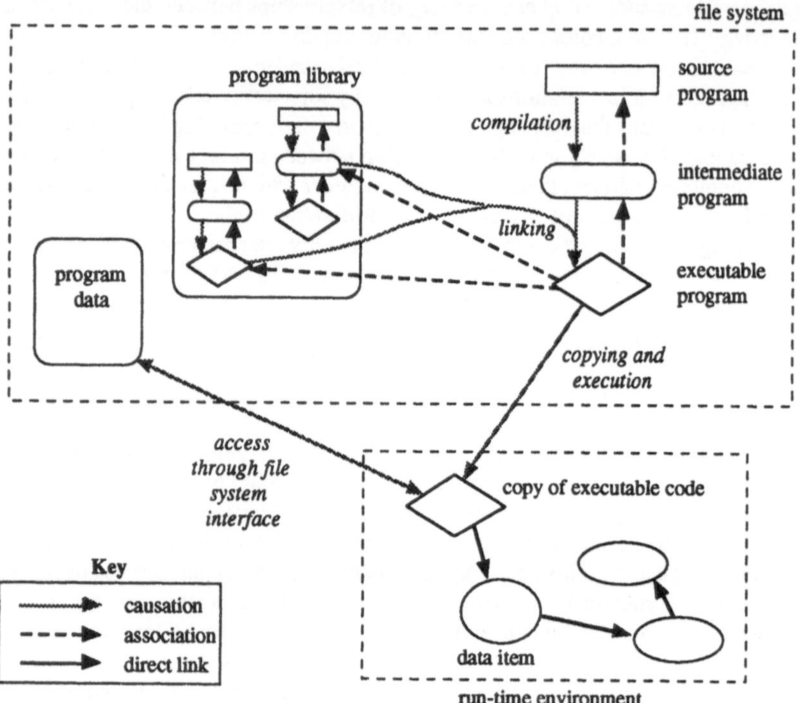

Figure 5: Relationships in a file-based system

2.3.3 *Persistent languages*

Persistent languages that support first class procedures are now considered. Examples of these are PS-algol, Napier88, Galileo [11, 12], P-Quest [13, 14] and STAPLE [15]. The model of persistence in these languages is persistence through reachability [16]: this means that a data item will persist at the end of a program's execution if and only if it is reachable from one or more persistent roots.

In these languages executable programs can be represented as first class procedures or functions and can thus be stored in a persistent store rather than a file system. Since each executable program is a language value it can contain direct links to other data items, and other values can contain direct links to it. A separate program library is not necessary since direct links to other executable programs in the store can be incorporated into an executable program when it is formed. Programming techniques to achieve the effects of incremental linking in this way are described in [17-20]. As executable programs are values, incremental linking of code and incremental loading of data reduce to the same problem and are handled by the run-time system.

Note that although the languages listed above use procedure closures to represent executable programs this is not essential to the schemes described in this section. All that is required is some mechanism to denote executable programs as values in the programming language.

The persistent store may subsume the functions of the file system, or the persistent store and file system may be used together. Figure 6 shows the relationships in a hybrid system in which source programs are kept in the file system and executable programs in the store. Here the program library contains only source programs; the corresponding executable programs reside in the store. The combined ellipses and diamonds in the diagram represent these procedure values. As the linking process can be achieved without a separate linker, no intermediate programs are required.

The figure shows causations and associations between source programs and executable programs as before. There is also a causation from the main executable program e_1 to the data item v_1 which is created by execution of that program. Data item v_1 contains a direct link to data item v_2, as does e_1, which also contains direct links to other executable programs; these direct links replace the associations between executable programs and library programs shown in Figure 5.

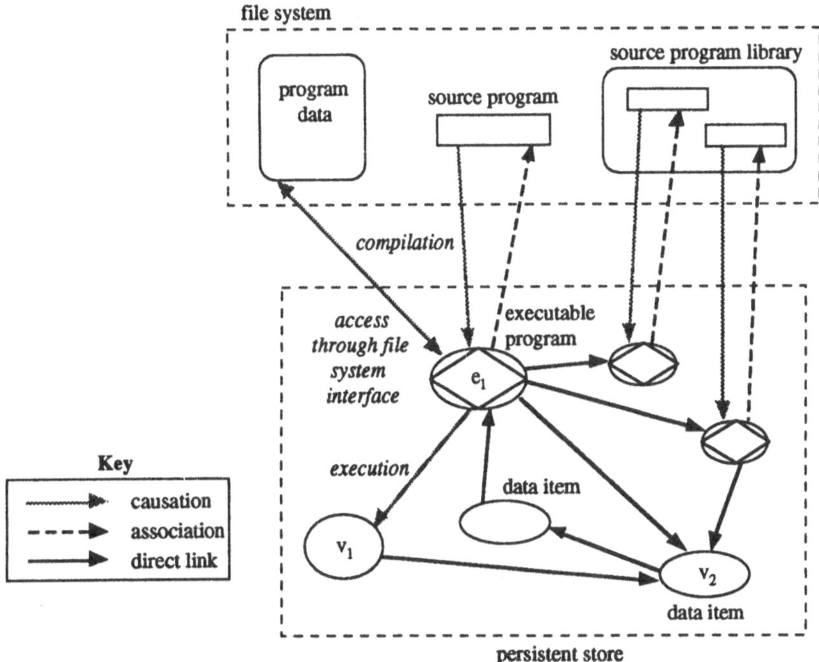

Figure 6: Relationships in a hybrid persistent / file-based system

Figure 7 shows the relationships in a persistent system where all components and data reside in the persistent store. The combined ellipses and rectangles represent source programs that are denotable values in the programming language. These values may be, for example, text strings or abstract syntax trees.

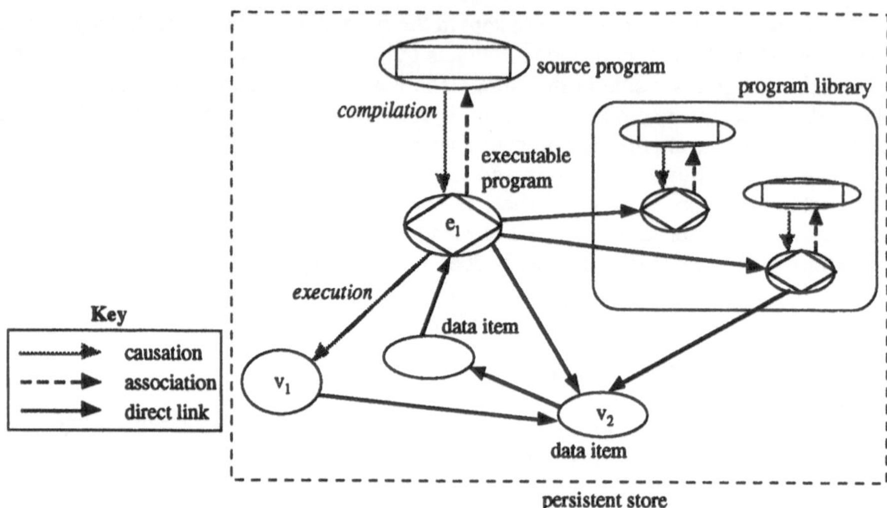

Figure 7: Relationships in a persistent system

Both schemes shown have the advantage that executable programs are associated with the others that they use by direct links. Once established these links are guaranteed to remain in place. In contrast, in a non-persistent system the integrity of the associations between executable programs that reside in the external storage system depends on the programmer following certain conventions. For example the deletion of an executable program from the program library might break these conventions.

The scheme shown in Figure 7 has the further advantage that the source programs, being in the persistent store, are brought under control of the language. This allows the system to be self-supporting: the environment in which programs are composed, compiled and executed can itself be implemented using the same programming language. Functions that are normally controlled by the operating system can then be integrated with the programming language. These include source code control and versioning, source level debugging, controlling the configuration of applications built from multiple components, documentation, etc. A number of workers are currently addressing the problems of supporting the whole software engineering process within an integrated persistent system [20-24]. Type-safe linguistic reflection is needed to implement such a system.

2.3.4 Hyper-programs

Bringing executable programs into the persistent store allows associations between them to be enforced by direct links. It would be beneficial for the associations between executable programs and source programs to be replaced by direct links also, for the same reason, i.e., they could not then be accidentally corrupted. Then each executable program would contain a direct link to its corresponding source program. As an executable program can also contain direct links to other data items in the persistent store, a source program must be able to denote those data items in order to represent the executable program accurately. This requires the use of hyper-programs as source representations.

Figure 8 shows the relationships in a hyper-programming system. Each executable program contains a direct link to its source hyper-program. Each of the other direct links contained in an executable program is duplicated in its corresponding hyper-program.

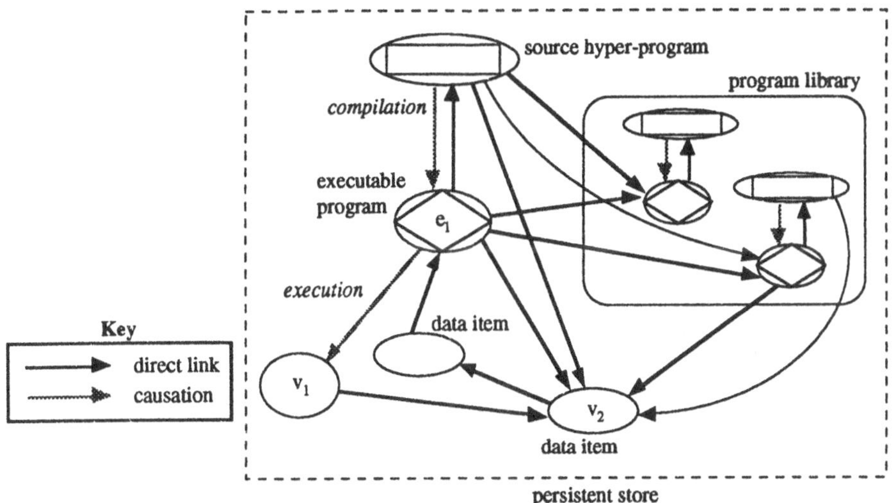

Figure 8: Relationships in a hyper-programming system

To illustrate the necessity of hyper-programs for providing accurate source representations of executable programs, consider the situation where multiple executable programs have direct links to a shared store location as illustrated in Figure 9:

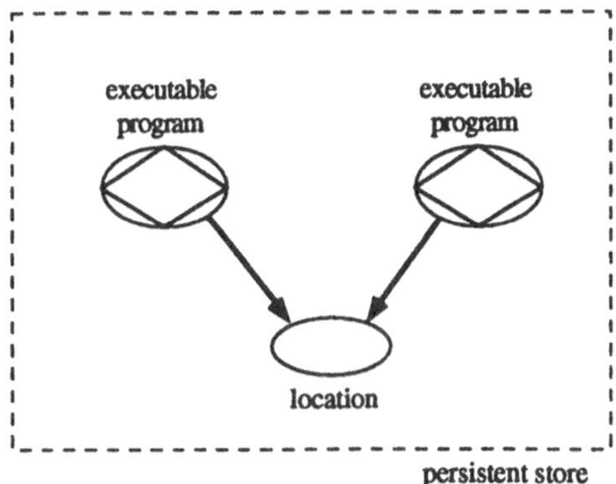

Figure 9: Executable programs sharing a location

The problem in conventional systems arises in supplying separate source programs for each of the executable programs. Unless there is a direct access path to the location from a persistent root, and in general there does not have to be one, conventional source representations do not provide any notation with which the location can be denoted in a source program.

A solution is to change the program notation by introducing hyper-programs as source representations. It is then possible to denote the shared location in the source programs by including tokens for the location. This makes it feasible for every executable program to contain a direct link to its own source hyper-program as illustrated in Figure 10. To preserve the association the source hyper-program is read-only although it can be copied and the copy edited.

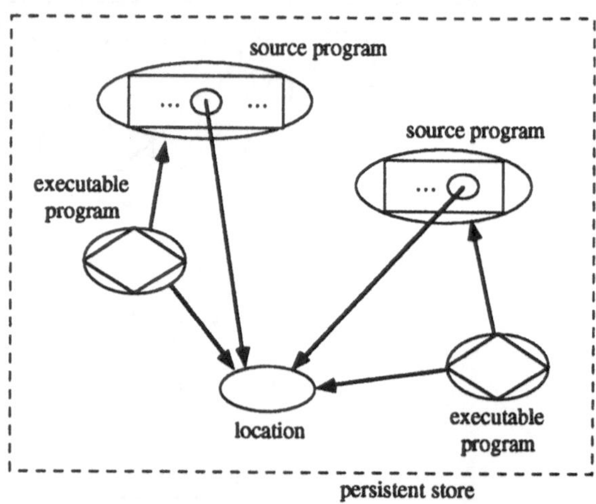

Figure 10: Executable programs with direct links to hyper-programs

Thus the use of hyper-programs as source representations allows associations from executable programs to source programs to be replaced by direct links, improving the robustness of the programming system by eliminating accidental changes to or deletions of source programs.

2.4 Flexible linking mechanisms

Programming languages support a number of different mechanisms for establishing direct links from programs to persistent values, locations and types. The degrees of freedom include constancy or variability, linking to L-values or R-values [25], and the time at which the linking takes place. The focus here is on the range of times available. Some possible times are during program composition, during compilation, during a separate linking phase, and during execution.

The principal varieties of programming system identified earlier were file-based, persistent and hyper-programming systems. Another possibility is a compile-time linking system in which the tokens embedded in a program are associated with data items in the persistent store when the program is compiled rather than when it is written. The linking times possible in each of these systems are shown in Figure 11. From here on it will be assumed that the hyper-programming systems under consideration incorporate facilities for compile-time linking as well as composition-time linking.

System	Linking Time							
	composition		compilation		linking phase		execution	
	program	data	program	data	program	data	program	data
file-based					•			•
persistent					•	•	•	•
compile-time linking			•	•	•	•	•	•
hyper-programming	•	•	•	•	•	•	•	•

Figure 11: Comparison of possible linking times in various systems

File-based systems allow links to existing data to be formed only at run-time. Links to existing programs are formed during a linking phase by copying library programs into the main program. In persistent systems a linking phase can be implemented using first class procedures. Since these executable programs are a form of data, linking to both programs and data can be performed either at link-time or run-time. Compile-time linking systems support these same linking times and also allow linking to programs and data at compilation-time.

A hyper-programming system supports all the linking times described. The programmer can specify various linking times as appropriate for different components of an application. Deciding when components should be linked into a main program involves trade-offs between program safety, flexibility and execution efficiency.

Run-time linking gives flexibility as the data (*data* will now be used to denote both programs and other kinds of data) accessed does not have to be present in the persistent store, file system or database before run-time. Indeed the access path to the data may not be known until run-time. Program safety is low since the data may not be present when the program is run, causing a run-time failure. Execution overheads are also higher, in strongly typed systems, since the type of the data must be checked dynamically. This kind of linking is possible in many systems, for example, C, Pascal, Ada, Smalltalk-80 [26], PS-algol, Napier88.

A distinct linking phase occurs between compilation and execution in some file-based systems, involving the copying of other executable or intermediate programs into the main executable program. A similar effect can also be achieved in persistent languages with higher-order procedures, where all types of data may be linked into an executable program before run-time. This provides improved safety and efficiency over run-time linking, since checks for the data's existence and type are performed before run-time. Flexibility is reduced since its use requires the data to be present earlier.

Linking at compilation-time increases safety and efficiency, bringing checks further forward in time, and reduces flexibility correspondingly. With this mechanism the data linked into an executable program is fixed.

Composition-time linking is the least flexible of the alternatives described as the data linked to must be present at the time that the program is written. It offers the most safety since access to the data is always maintained once it is linked into the source code, even if the source code is edited and re-compiled. This is not true of the other linking styles where editing of the source code requires all links to be re-established. Efficiency is slightly increased overall since the access path to the data, whether it is expressed by textual code or by user gesture, need be followed only once, at composition-time, and not on every re-compilation.

2.5 Program succinctness

Persistent systems offer significant savings over non-persistent systems regarding the data access code required. One empirical study concluded that 30% of the code in a large set of commercial non-persistent programs was dedicated to transferring data to and from an external storage system [27]. Recent measurements of Napier88 programs have suggested that these access specifications occupy around 13% of program code [28], a considerable reduction on 30%. The intellectual effort required to write the code is also significant: in writing access specifications in a persistent system the programmer is not concerned with programming transformations between structured and flattened formats.

Hyper-programming gives a further improvement in conciseness as the access specifications can in some cases be replaced by tokens that denote persistent data items. The information that was specified in the access specifications is provided through the interactive gesturing by which the programmer points out data items to be linked in. The measurements of Napier88 programs found around 20% of identifiers referring to persistent data. Further work is required to measure the proportion of this data that is available for linking at hyper-program composition time.

Figure 12 summarises the nature of the persistent data access code that appears in source programs in the various cases:

System	Access path code
non-persistent	file access + importing + exporting
persistent	access path + type description
hyper-programming (data present at composition time) (data not present at composition time)	 token access path + type description

Figure 12: Comparison of access path code

2.6 Procedure representations

Since hyper-programs can contain direct links to values and locations in the persistent store they can be used to represent executable programs, including those with links to shared locations. This provides a convenient representation format for procedure values.

As described earlier, associations between executable programs and source programs can be replaced by direct links. When a procedure value is created the compilation system can insert a direct link to its source hyper-program. Given referential integrity, the source code will then remain accessible for as long as the procedure value.

The use of hyper-program source representations allows browsing tools to display meaningful representations of procedure values, showing both source code and direct links to persistent data items. This may aid software reuse since documentation in the form of the original source code can be made available for every procedure value in the persistent store.

Hyper-programs allow separate procedure source representations since shared locations can be denoted by tokens. A further consequence is that one of a group of procedures that share values or locations can be replaced by a refined version without the need to replace the others. This reduces the cost of modifying applications that are composed of multiple procedures.

The use of hyper-programs to represent procedures with shared locations will be illustrated with an example. Figure 13 shows a Napier88 program that places in the persistent store two procedures that share an integer location:

```
let i := 0

in PS() let inc := proc() ; i := i + 1
in PS() let get := proc( → int ) ; i
```

Figure 13: Procedures with a shared location

The program first initialises an integer variable *i* with the value 0. It then creates two persistent procedures that operate on *i*, the first incrementing it by 1 and the second returning its current value. The procedures are made persistent by declaring them in the context of the persistent root environment, obtained by calling the pre-defined procedure *PS*. Although the store location corresponding to the variable *i* is not declared in the persistent environment, it will persist because it is reachable from the procedures *inc* and *get* which are themselves persistent. The result of executing this program is that the persistent store contains the two procedures and the shared integer location which is not directly accessible from the persistent root.

Figure 14 shows the links between the procedures, their hyper-program source representations and the shared location:

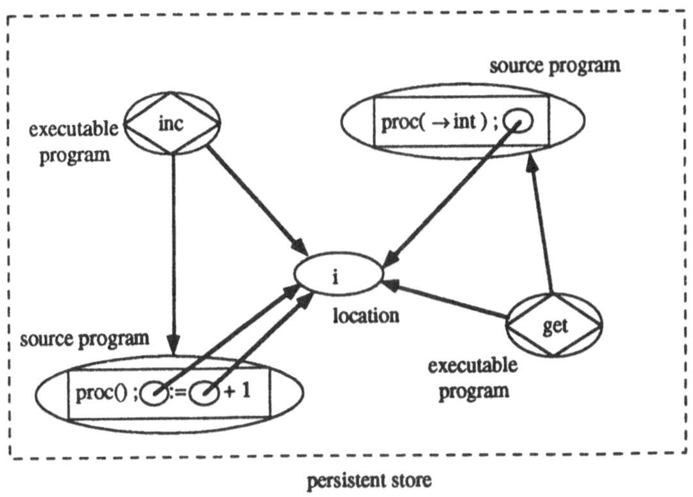

Figure 14: Hyper-programs with a shared location

The use of hyper-program source representations for procedures in this way avoids having to replace all procedures that share locations when a single one is changed. Another advantage is that the same shared locations are retained after the replacement of a procedure. Without hyper-program source representations not only do all the procedures have to be replaced in order to preserve sharing, but new shared locations must be created and the values that were previously shared copied into the new locations.

3 Hyper-worlds

There are a number of components that a persistent programming environment should support if it is to provide for the software engineering process as a whole. These include:

- program composition, compilation and execution;
- storing of source and compiled versions of programs;
- debugging;
- documentation;
- decomposition of large application programs into components, and organisation of those components;
- navigating the persistent store to locate programs and other data with given attributes;
- querying of the types of programs and data in the persistent store.

The model of hyper-programming as described so far allows source programs to contain links to any other data in the persistent store. In large scale systems this generality may lead to several problems. Firstly, the store may become intellectually unmanageable as the number of links increases. Secondly, evolution of application programs by substituting new versions of their components becomes difficult to manage if unrestricted linking to the components is permitted—it may be necessary to locate each data item linked to the component being substituted and determine whether a new version of the data item is required in turn. In addition the model described does not provide a uniform framework for storing meta-data about application components.

One research topic is the provision of additional structure over a basic hyper-programming system to address these needs. The *hyper-world* model offers the programmer a loose coupling mechanism to offset the disadvantages of the tight coupling made possible by hyper-programming. In this model, based in part on that described in [29], the persistent store is partitioned into a number of application spaces or hyper-worlds. Each hyper-world contains the program components and data used by an application, and a schema that describes their relationships. Each hyper-world has a single visible component which may be linked to from outside the hyper-world; no other components inside the hyper-world may be linked to from outside.

The schema includes documentation information, a type description and hyper-program source for each component. It also includes a representation of the component linking topology, and a list of type definitions local to the hyper-world. This allows the programmer to perform various queries over the components, and to determine the implications of replacing a component with a changed version.

The partitioning supported by hyper-worlds may reduce problems such as keeping track of inter-component links to a manageable scale, by restricting the region of interest from the entire persistent store to the hyper-world. It may also allow type-checking to be performed more efficiently.

Figure 15 shows a representation of a persistent store containing nested hyper-worlds and linked components:

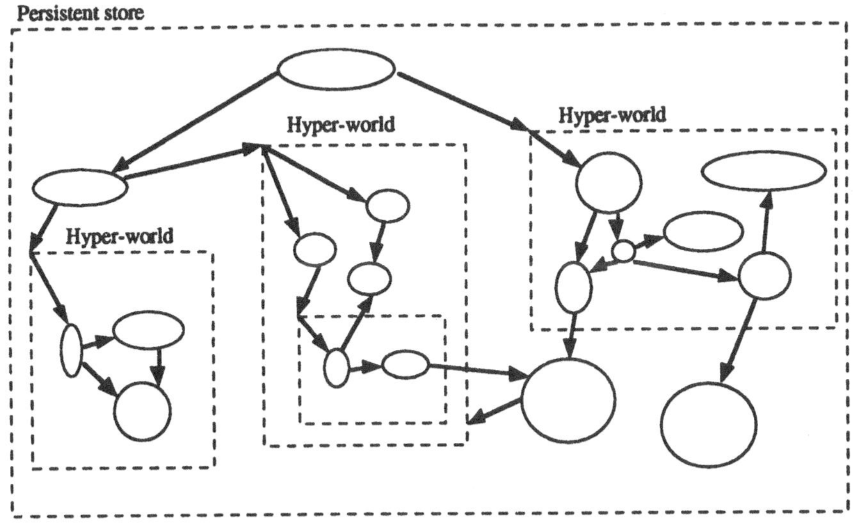

Figure 15: A store with hyper-worlds

4 Implementation status and further research

A prototype Napier88 hyper-programming system has been developed [30], building on earlier systems developed at St Andrews and Adelaide [22, 23].

Although the concept of hyper-programming has been illustrated using Napier88 it is not restricted to that language. It could be implemented for any language that supports first class procedures, orthogonal persistence, run-time linguistic reflection and graphical user interface tools.

There are several avenues for further research in hyper-programming:

Hyper-worlds: the model described above will be further developed and implemented.

Reflective programming: the implementation of the hyper-programming environment is founded on the reflective facilities of Napier88: the ability to write a program (the programming environment) that constructs another program (the code composed in the environment by the user) and compiles it dynamically. This is an implementation issue and one that the user need not be aware of. However, run-time reflection can be a more generally useful programming tool, and some current research addresses the problems of how the programmer can express in a comprehensible way the computations that produce new programs [31]. The possibilities of writing reflective programs that produce hyper-programs will be investigated.

Programming by gesture: in the existing systems values can be browsed by gesturing with the mouse but to achieve any updates to the store the user must write and evaluate new code. Another line of research is to investigate the possibilities of performing more general computation over the store via a 'direct manipulation' approach. It would not be hard to provide in an ad-hoc manner ways of performing specific pre-defined actions; the challenge is to develop some more general model.

5 Conclusions

There are many situations when the programmer writes code to access data items in the persistent store, knowing that those data items are present in the store at the time of writing. This paper has shown how data can be linked directly into a source program as opposed to the program containing instructions on how to link to it at run-time. This gives the benefits provided by interactive languages: greater program safety as there is no danger of losing access to the data during the time between writing and execution, and better efficiency as run-time type and access path checks are factored out. The flexibility of being able to link to the store dynamically when required is retained.

An analysis has been given of the program entities and their inter-relationships in a hyper-programming system, and compared to those found in file-based and existing persistent systems. A number of benefits of using hyper-programs have been described. These include being able to: perform program checking early; enforce associations from executable programs to source programs with direct links; support an increased range of linking times; reduce program verbosity; and provide source representations for procedure closures.

The user interface of a prototype hyper-programming system has been outlined. A store browser is used by the programmer to navigate the persistent store and identify data items. Tokens that denote these data items can then be incorporated into the hyper-program under construction. Facilities for viewing and editing hyper-programs are provided.

Finally a framework, called hyper-worlds, has been proposed for supporting 'programming in the large' in the context of a hyper-programming system. It allows the programmer to impose a degree of partitioning on the persistent store, in order to aid intellectual manageability and improve execution efficiency.

6 Acknowledgements

This work was supported by ESPRIT III Basic Research Action 6309 – FIDE 2 and SERC grant GR/F 02953. Richard Connor is supported by SERC Postdoctoral Fellowship B/91/RFH/9078. Alan Dearle and Alex Farkas are supported by ARC grants "Controlled Evolution" and "Browsing in Persistent Integrated Programming Environments", Adelaide University grant "Persistent Integrated Programming Environment" and by the DSTO. We thank Dave Stemple for his useful comments.

7 References

1. Farkas AM, Dearle A, Kirby GNC, Cutts QI, Morrison R, Connor RCH. Persistent Program Construction through Browsing and User Gesture with some Typing. In: Proc. 5th International Workshop on Persistent Object Systems, San Miniato, Italy, 1992

2. Stemple D, Stanton RB, Sheard T, Philbrow P, Morrison R, Kirby GNC, Fegaras L, Cooper RL, Connor RCH, Atkinson MP, Alagic S. Type-Safe Linguistic Reflection: A Generator Technology. University of St Andrews Report CS/92/6, 1992

3. PS-algol Reference Manual, 4th edition. Universities of Glasgow and St Andrews Report PPRR-12-88, 1988

4. Morrison R, Brown AL, Connor RCH, Dearle A. The Napier88 Reference Manual. University of St Andrews Report PPRR-77-89, 1989

5. Altmann RA, Hawke AN, Marlin CD. An Integrated Programming Environment Based on Multiple Concurrent Views. Australian Computer Journal 1988; 20,2:65-72

6. Atkinson MP, Lécluse C, Philbrow P, Richard P. Design Issues in a Map Language. In: P. Kanellakis and J. W. Schmidt (ed) Bulk Types & Persistent Data. Morgan Kaufmann, 1991, pp 20-32

7. Wirth N. The Programming Language Pascal. Acta Informatica 1971; 1,35-63

8. Reference Manual for the Ada Programming Language. U.S. Department of Defense Report ANSI/MIL-STD-1815A, 1983

9. Kernighan BW, Ritchie DM. The C programming language. Prentice-Hall, 1978

10. Ritchie DM, Thompson K. The UNIX Time-Sharing System. The Bell System Technical Journal 1978; 63,6:1905-1930

11. Albano A, Cardelli L, Orsini R. Galileo: a Strongly Typed, Interactive Conceptual Language. ACM ToDS 1985; 10,2:230-260

12. Albano A, Ghelli G, Orsini R. The Implementation of Galileo's Values Persistence. In: M. P. Atkinson, O. P. Buneman and R. Morrison (ed) Data Types and Persistence. Springer-Verlag, 1988, pp 253-263

13. Brown AL, Mainetto G, Matthes F, Müller R, McNally DJ. An Open System Architecture for a Persistent Object Store. In: Proc. 25th International Conference on Systems Sciences, Hawaii, 1992, pp 766-776

14. Matthes F, Müller R, Schmidt JW. Object Stores as Servers in Persistent Programming Environments—The P-Quest Experience. ESPRIT BRA Project 3070 FIDE Report, 1992

15. Davie AJT, McNally DJ. Statically Typed Applicative Persistent Language Environment (STAPLE) Reference Manual. University of St Andrews Report CS/90/14, 1990

16. Atkinson MP, Bailey PJ, Chisholm KJ, Cockshott WP, Morrison R. An Approach to Persistent Programming. Comp. J. 1983; 26,4:360-365

17. Atkinson MP, Morrison R. Persistent First Class Procedures are Enough. In: M. Joseph and R. Shyamasundar (ed) Lecture Notes in Computer Science 181. Springer-Verlag, 1984, pp 223-240

18. Atkinson MP, Morrison R. Procedures as Persistent Data Objects. ACM ToPLaS 1985; 7,4:539-559

19. Atkinson MP, Morrison R. Integrated Persistent Programming Systems. In: Proc. 19th International Conference on Systems Sciences, Hawaii, 1986, pp 842-854

20. Dearle A, Cutts QI, Connor RCH. An application architecture using type-safe incremental linking. Submitted for publication, 1992

21. Cooper RL. On The Utilisation of Persistent Programming Environments. Ph.D. thesis, University of Glasgow, 1990

22. Farkas AM. ABERDEEN: A Browser allowing intERactive DEclarations and Expressions in Napier88. University of Adelaide Report Honours Project, 1991

23. Kirby GNC, Cutts QI, Connor RCH, Dearle A, Morrison R. Programmers' Guide to the Napier88 Standard Library, Edition 2.1. University of St Andrews, 1992

24. Dearle A, Marlin CD, Dart P. A Hyperlinked Persistent Software Development Environment. In: Proc. Hyper-Oz '92: A Workshop on Hypertext Activities in Australia, Adelaide, Australia, 1992

25. Strachey C. Fundamental Concepts in Programming Languages. Oxford University Press, Oxford, 1967

26. Goldberg A, Robson D. Smalltalk-80: The Language and its Implementation. Addison Wesley, 1983

27. IBM Report on the Contents of a Sample of Programs Surveyed. IBM, San Jose, California, 1978

28. Sjøberg D. Measuring Name and Identifier Usage in Napier88 Applications. ESPRIT BRA Project 3070 FIDE Report FIDE/92/37, 1992

29. Wile DS, Allard DG. Worlds: An Organizing Structure for Object-Bases. In: Proc. 2nd ACM SIGSOFT/SIGPLAN Symposium on Practical Software Development Environments, Palo Alto, California, 1986

30. Kirby GNC. Reflection and Hyper-Programming in Persistent Programming Systems. Ph.D. thesis, University of St Andrews, 1992

31. Kirby GNC. Persistent Programming with Strongly Typed Linguistic Reflection. In: Proc. 25th International Conference on Systems Sciences, Hawaii, 1992, pp 820-831

Run-Time Support for Hierarchic Records in Persistent Languages*

Giorgio Ghelli
Dipartimento d'Informatica dell'Università di Pisa
Corso Italia 40, 56100 Pisa, Italy, e-mail: ghelli@di.unipi.it

Abstract

Subtyping among record types is a basic feature of typed database languages supporting the semantic or the object-oriented data-model. It is often supported by recording labels in records and implementing field access as a linear search. We study a more efficient approach, based on the idea of dividing records into an access structure and a label-free tuple, and of sharing and optimizing the access structures. For different records different access structures can be exploited, based on a linear, direct or hash organization, depending on the size and on the usage of the different records. We report experimental and analytic results on this approach.

1 Introduction

In recent years many languages have been defined which support the notion of type inclusion. In these languages a subtype relation is defined on types, such that any value of a subtype can be used in any context where a value of a supertype is expected. Subtyping is especially useful in connection with record types (unordered labelled cartesian products): if the only operation on records is field selection, any record with more fields can be used where a record with a subset of its fields is expected. This observation is at the basis of the subtype relation defined in systems like Galileo, Amber or Quest [1, 2, 3].

Type inclusion is of great benefit for the programmer, but makes it impossible to translate a field access operation *record.field* as an access to a cell at a fixed offset from the beginning of the *record* data structure. For this reason, the run-time support of languages with record subtyping often represents records as arrays of pairs "label-value", and each field access is interpreted by a search in this structure; consequently, field access is a costly operation in these systems.

In this paper we study efficient implementations of record field selection in presence of subtyping, based on the idea of separating the "search structure" associated with a record from the values contained in the record itself, centralizing and sharing these structures, and applying to them optimization efforts.

---

*This work has been partially supported by E.E.C., Esprit Basic Research Action 3070 FIDE, and by "Progetto Finalizzato Sistemi Informatici e Calcolo Parallelo" of CNR under grant n.91.00877.PF69

The paper is structured as follows. In section 2 we specify the problem. In section 3 we introduce our solution. In section 4 we introduce the cost model used to compare the different search structures which can be used to speed up record access. In section 5 we introduce a further optimization technique. In section 6 we discuss the hash functions used in our approach. In section 7 we discuss the possibility of dynamic reconfiguration of search structures, depending on collected information about their use. In section 8 we report the results of measures performed on a prototypical systems which implements our technique.

2 The problem

We want to study an efficient implementation of a strongly typed calculus supporting record substyping. We will denote records as $\langle\langle l_1 = a_1, \ldots, l_n = a_n \rangle\rangle$, record types as $\langle\langle$*label*: $T, \ldots,$ *label*: $T\rangle\rangle$ and record field access as $a.l$. Subtyping means that a subtyping relation $\leq$ is defined among types, such that if $T \leq U$ then a value of type T can be assigned to any identifier, formal parameter or data structure component which was declared of type U. In our terminology, a record type is a type which is characterized by the set of of its <label,type> pairs, but where the order of these pairs is immaterial. A record type T is a subtype of a record type U if and only if all the labels of U appear in T, and for each label appearing in both of them, its corresponding type in T is a subtype of its corresponding type in U.

In languages with subtyping we distinguish between the compile-time type of an expression and the run-time type of a value, where an *expression* is a syntactic unit whose type is computed by the compiler, while a *value* is the result obtained at run-time by a specific evaluation of an expression, and the type of a value describes its actual structure. The rule holds that if *val:T* is obtained by evaluating *expr:U*, then $T \leq U$. Consider for example a formal parameter: any value which could be associated to it, and so which could be the result of an evaluation of the parameter itself, has a run-time type which is a subtype of the compile-time type of the parameter.

In languages without subtyping, records are represented as blocks of consecutive cells, and a record access $r.l_i$, where the compile-time type of r is $\langle\langle l_1 : T_1, \ldots, l_n : T_n \rangle\rangle$, is translated as $\| r \| [i]$, where $\| r \|$ is the translation of the record expression, and $[i]$ is an operation to access directly to the i-th field of the resulting block. In our language this is not possible, since in the case above the result of the evaluation of $\| r \|$ could have more labels than just the labels $l_1 \ldots l_n$ of its compile-time type. For this reason, in languages with subtyping, records are often implemented as sequences of pairs <field-label,field-value>, and field selection is implemented by searching in this list. Since subtyping is expecially useful in record-intensive application fields, like data base languages or compiler construction for example, this high overhead on record storage and record access is not acceptable.

A partial solution to the problems above, adopted for example in the language Quest [3], can be achieved by adopting labelled tuples instead of records. Labelled tuples differ from records since their fields are ordered. Labelled tuple subtypes can be obtained only by adding fields at the end of the labelled tuple supertype, or by specializing the type of fields, while in record subtypes new fields can appear in any position. So, access to a field of a labelled tuple can be compiled as access at a fixed offset in the tuple and there is no need of storing field names of tuples. On the other side the subtyping relation between labelled tuples is very limited; in particular it forms just a tree, without any kind of so-called multiple inheritance. Combining labelled tuples and records in a language, to allow the programmer to choose between speed and flexibility, is dangerous since the programmer runs the risk of having to change is choice as the application evolve.[1]

Solutions to the problem of field access supporting multiple inheritance are presented in section 9, where are compared to the one described here.

3 The proposal

We propose to represent a record as the tuple of its field values plus a reference to a "search structure", used to retrieve the offset of the field associated to each label. In our proposal, labels are represented as small integers, where "small" means smaller than the maximum number of different labels used in the program. The centralized structure mapping labels to integers is maintained by the compiler, and more precisely by the linker-loader if separate compilation is allowed. For this reason, even if in the rest of the paper we will discuss generically about the compiler synthesizing the search structures, in case of separate compilation most of the tasks described are initiated by the compiler but are substantially accomplished by the linker-loader, or by later optimization phases, as discussed in section 7. Notice that, programs using new labels are added to a working system, the pre existent label-integer map needs just to be xtended, and not to be rebuilt. This implies that this mapping can be managed by an incremental linker-loader, i.e. by a loader which can link new code to an already running system, like the loaders used for persistent systems.

The "search structure" associated to each record is not devoted to it; the compiler sythesizes a search structure for each $\langle\langle \ldots \rangle\rangle$ expression in the text, and any record created by that expression will share that search structure, as shown in figure 1, where a graphical representation of a record $\langle\langle b = 20, a = 10, c = 30, d = 40 \rangle\rangle$.

This fact implies that:

- there is no need of minimizing the space used by each search structure, since their number is limited by the size of the program, so that, especially in big persistent applications, the number of different search structures is negligible with respect to the number of different records;
- since search structures are sythesized once for all at compile time, we can afford spending some time in preparing them.

[1] In this paper we will follow Quest terminology, and "record" will denote a value associating labels to fields where the order of labels is immaterial, while a "tuple" will be an ordered structure associating fixed positions to labels.

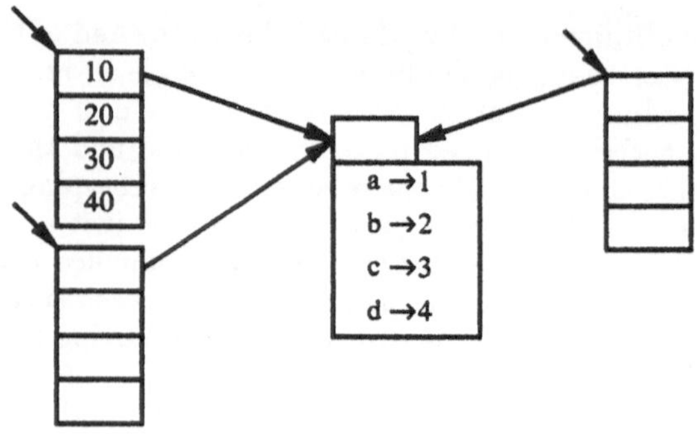

Figure 1: Different records share a unique access structure

A search structure is composed by an algorithm plus a data structure. In our implementation, we have chosen the following different types of search structure:

- a linear search structure, where the algorithm performs a linear search in the associated data structure, which is an array of pairs <label,offset>.
- a hash search structure, where the data structure contains the parameters of the hash function (like, e.g., the m parameter of the hash function $fun(x).(x \times x) \bmod m)$ and the hash table. Each entry of the hash table points to a linear search structure, called a bucket, containing all the <label,offset> pairs for all the labels colliding on that entry. The algorithm performs a hash search in the table followed by a linear search in the bucket. The size m of the hash table is equal to n/α, where n is the number of record fields and α is a loading factor, which in our approach is much smaller than one (0.1-0.5 in our experiments). We experimented different hash functions, as discussed in section 6.
- a perfect hash search structure, where the hash table directly contains the field offsets, rather than a reference to a bucket, and hashing is guaranteed collision-free.
- a direct access search structure, where the data structure is a (sparse) array of field offsets, and the algorithm accesses this array using the field name as an index. This is just a special case of perfect hashing, employing a very simple hash function.

Notice that hash structures can be heavily oversized, thanks to the observations above. For this reason, most of the hash structures have no collision.

A graphic representation of these three kinds of structures can be found in figure 2.

The compiler chooses a specific search structure for a given list of field names on the basis of two parameters:

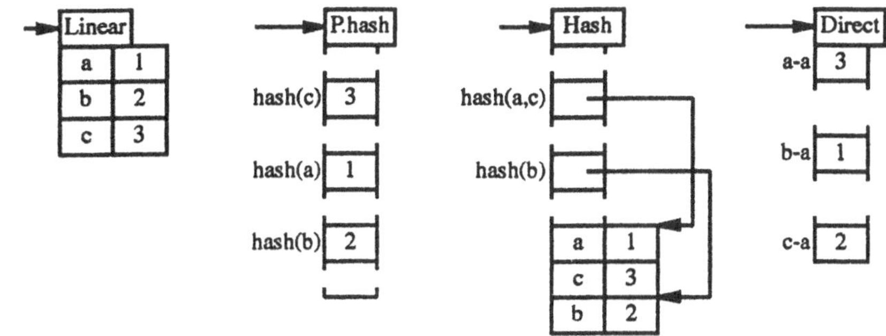

Figure 2: A graphic representation of a linear, hash, perfect hash and direct access structure

- Record size and "field density": if the ratio between the record size (number of fields) and the spanning of record labels (the integer difference between the maximum and the minimum record label) is greater than a "minimum loading factor" β, then direct access is used[2]. Otherwise, the compiler chooses between hashing or linear search depending on whether the record has respectively more or less than γ fields. γ is a threshold, depending on the machine and on the hash algorithm adopted, such that for records shorter than γ linear search is faster than perfect hashing.
- Requested compilation speed: during code generation, the compiler generates only linear and direct search structures. If optimization is required, and only in this case, the compiler tranforms the longest linear structures in hash structures, randomly generating the parameters for the hash function. Then a hash structure, or a perfect hash structure, is generated, depending on whether collision management is needed.[3] If further optimization time is left, the compiler randomly generates different parameter sets for some non-perfect tables, trying to transform them in perfect ones.

Note that the compiler can compute the field offsets for a record generated by the record expression $\langle\langle l_1 = a_1, \ldots, l_n = a_n \rangle\rangle$ only if it knows the space occupied in the data structure by $a_1 \ldots a_n$. Since the compiler does not know the run-time types of the values associated to $a_1 \ldots a_n$, but only their compile-time type, then our technique can be applied only if the space occupied by a record field can be determined on the basis of any supertype of its run-time type. In other words, if we say that two types belong to the same family when they have a common supertype, we need that all the values whose types are in the same family occupy the same space inside a record. Note that in languages where a global maximum type "Top" is defined, there is a unique family which covers all types, while, for example, in a language with record subtyping but

[2] β is a system parameter, smaller than α: since direct structures are faster than hash structure, we accept to use some more space

[3] In case of separate compilation, the compiler generates only the <label,offset> pairs, while everything else is accomplished at link time, or dynamically as discussed in section 7.

no "Top" type, the set of all the record types forms a family, disjoint from the other type families.

Observe that, if values in a subtype can occupy an amount of space in a record which is different from the space occupied by values of a supertype, then problems arise also when the value of a field is updated. In fact, if a field value is substituted by a value belonging to a subtype, the space allocated to contain the old value could not be enough to contain the new value. For this reason our requirement is usually satisfied in any language with subtyping, for example by putting in the record fields just pointers to the corresponding values, so that each record field occupies the same size.

4 Cost model

Each search structure has a bidimensional cost, in terms of time and space, modelled by the functions summarized in table 1.

	linear	hash	p. hash	direct
worst time	l_f+ $n \times l_p$	h_f+ $n \times l_p$	h_f	d_f
mean time[1]	l_f+ $l_p \times \sum_{i=1}^{n} \pi_{l_i} \times pos_{l_i}$	h_f+ $l_p \times \sum_{i=1}^{n} \pi_{l_i} \times pos_{l_i}$	h_f	d_f
mean time[2]	l_f+ $l_p \times (n+1)/2$	h_f+ $l_p \times \sum_{i=1}^{n} (c_{l_i}+1)/2n$	h_f	d_f
space	$2 \times n$	h_s+ $n/\alpha + 2 \times n$	h_s+ n/α	$1+$ $M-m$

Table 1: Time and space cost of the search structures

In the table we have distinguished between the mean access time which can be computed when the relative access frequence π_{l_i} of each label l_i is known (mean time[1]), and the time which can be computed if the π distribution is uniform or unknown (mean time[2]); for each search structure π_{l_i} is defined as the probability that an access to the structure is aimed to retrieve the l_i's offset.

In the table, n is the number of different labels in the search structure, while M and m (direct-space) are the maximum and minimum labels. pos_{l_i} is the position of the label l_i in a linear structure (linear-time) or in the bucket $hash(l_i)$ (hash-time). c_{l_i} is the length of the bucket $hash(l_i)$. For every kind of structure the access time is given by a formula $t_f + f_n \times t_p$, where t is either l, h or d, and stands for linear, hash or direct; t_f is the "fixed" component of the cost and t_p is the component of the cost which depends on the structure size and features.

A graphic representation of the relationships between the different mean-time-costs functions, in case of uniform distributions, can be found in Figure 3. It is based on the reasonable assumptions that $d_f \leq l_f + l_p \leq h_f$, and on the approximation that the mean access time to a hash access structure does not depend in a relevant way on its size but just on its α loading factor.

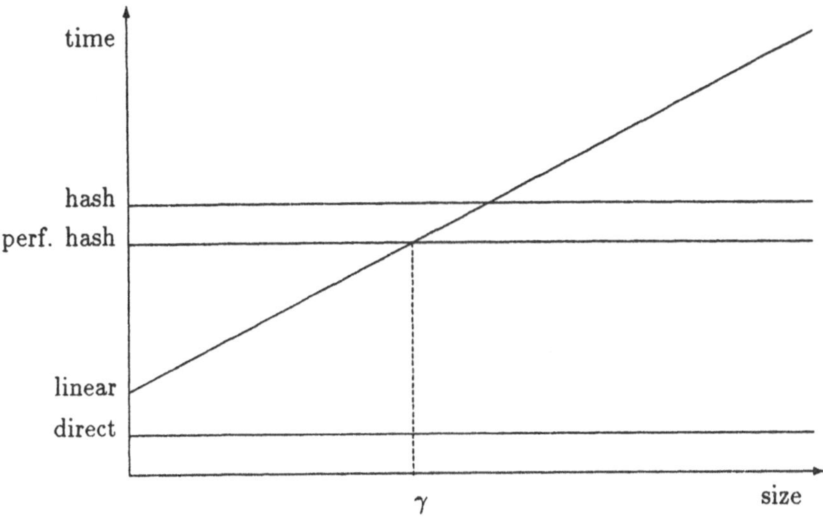

Figure 3: Time costs of the search structures

The formulas in the table are justified in the rest of the section, which can be safely skipped if the reader is not interested.

In the linear case, accessing label l_i requires an access to the table (l_f) plus pos_{l_i} accesses to all the labels up to l_i included, plus an equal number of comparisons ($pos_{l_i} \times l_p$, where l_p is the time required to access and compare one element of the linear table). The data structure must be big enough to contain n <label,offset> pairs.

In the hash case, accessing label l_i requires *(a)* retrieving from the table the hash parameters, computing the hash function and accessing the bucket (h_f) and *(b)* performing a linear search in the bucket, scanning pos_{l_i} entries, where pos_{l_i} is one in most cases if the table is almost perfect. The mean value of pos for the labels in a bucket of c elements is $(c+1)/2$, so the mean pos of a label is $\sum_{i=1}^{n}(c_{l_i}+1)/2$. A hash data structure contains h_s cells for the hash parameters ($0 \leq h_s \leq 3$ in our examples), n/α cells containing, for each i, a reference to the bucket of the labels whose hash value is i (with $\alpha < 1$ in our case), and a total of $2 \times n$ cells to hold all the buckets, which contain the n <label,index> pairs. Notice that, since our hash table are static structures, we can represent buckets as arrays rather than linked list, and since we perform only successful search we do not need storing the size, or a terminator, for each bucket (see figure 2).

In the perfect hash case, accessing label l_i requires retrieving from the table the hash parameters, computing the hash function and accessing the hash table to retrieve the corresponding offset. This operation requires the same time h_f needed in the hash case to retrieve the bucket. The space required is just $n/\alpha + h_s$, since buckets are not needed.

Direct access is a special case of perfect hash, but d_f is generally less than h_f, since in the direct case the "hash" function is trivial. The size of the table is $M-m+1$, which is always smaller than n/β, where β is a "minimum density factor", smaller than α, as explained above.

5 Merging sparse tables

5.1 Introduction

Our run-time support manages a lot of sparse tables, since we use low loading factors α and β; in this section we study how some space can be saved by merging these sparse tables and how much space can be saved in this way. Adopting techniques to save space allows adopting lower α and β factors, which results in bigger number of perfect hash tables and of direct tables, and in better performance.

We will consider three different kinds of table merging, *plain merging*, *overlap merging* and *shift merging*, which are graphically represented in figure 4

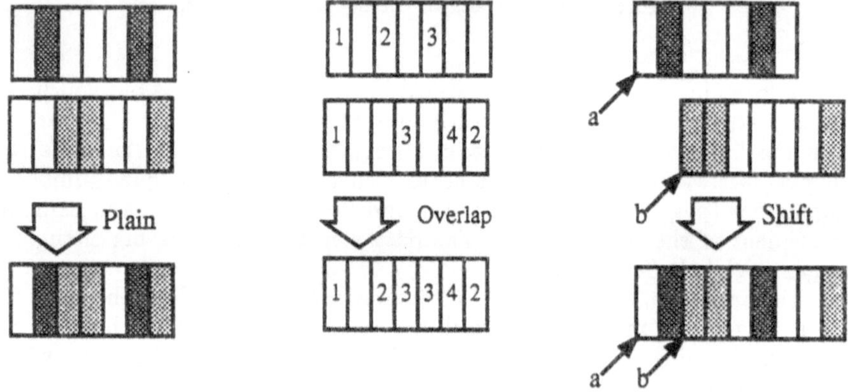

Figure 4: Plain merging, overlap merging and shift merging

5.1.1 *Plain merging*

If we consider two little hash tables with a low fill factor (say, two hash tables with 5 used entries and with a loading factor $\alpha = 0.1$) there is a reasonable probability (about 60% in this case, as we will see) that the two hash tables have no common used entry.

In this case, the two tables can be merged, and two different search structures can share the resulting table, since we are considering a problem of never failing search and empty positions in hash or direct tables convey no information. When the loading factor is suitably low, this process can be repeated many times, merging many tables in one (in this context we do not distinguish between hash tables and direct tables, which are just hash tables with a trivial hash function).

5.1.2 Overlap merging

Intersecting tables can be merged too, if they contain the same values in the conflicting entries; we call this situation "overlap merging". Two randomly generated structures have a negligible probability of being candidate for overlap merging. However overlap merging is possible with structures corresponding to record types which have a related structure.

Consider two record expressions r and R with label sets L_r and L_R, such that $L_r \subseteq L_R$ (say $L_r = \{a, c\}$ and $L_R = \{a, b, c, d\}$). The run-time representations of these records can share the same access structures, provided that the fields are ordered in a compatible way. More precisely, the L_r fields must be the initial fields in the R representation, and the order of these fields must be the same in r and in R (for example, we can order the fields as $\{a, c\}$ and $\{a, c, b, d\}$ in our example, and the two records can share a structure associating *abcd* to 1234[4].).

This is a very special case of overlap merging, where one of the two structures is contained in the other one; we call it *inclusion merging*. In the case of label lists related by inclusion, rather than just merging the hash tables of different hash structures, records with different label lists can share the full search structure. Moreover, this optimization is not limited to hash search structures, but a unique search structure can be employed for records which, without the optimization, would have been associated to different classes of structures.

However, there is sometime a space-time tradeoff in this sharing. For example, if we have two linear structures with a known, highly unbalanced, field access probability distribution, distinct structures could be used to obtain a lower mean access time, putting the most commonly accessed fields for each record in the first positions of its structure. A similar tradeoff is present when there is the possibility of "merging" structures which, if separate, would be represented using different techniques. In this case, we propose the following approach.

Given a sequence $\{s_i\}_{i=1...n}$ of structures such that s_j is included in s_{j+1}, define the following indexes:

$$\begin{aligned} d &= \max\{j \in 1 \ldots n \mid s_j \text{ direct}\} \\ l &= \max\{j \in 1 \ldots n \mid s_j \text{ linear}, j > d \text{ if } d \text{ is defined}\} \\ h &= \max\{j \in 1 \ldots n \mid s_j \text{ hash}, j > d \text{ if } d \text{ defined}, j > l \text{ if } l \text{ defined}\}. \end{aligned}$$

Structures $s_1 \ldots s_d$ are represented by the direct structure s_d, structures $s_{d+1} \ldots s_l$ are represented by the linear structure s_l, where the fields appearing first in the $s_{d+1} \ldots s_l$ list appear first in the linear table, and structures $s_{h+1} \ldots s_n$ are represented by the hash structure s_n; each of the three structure sequences could be empty (when the corresponding index d, l or h is undefined).

We now present a technique to detect lists of structures candidates for inclusion merging. Consider the "sublabel directed graph" of a program, i.e.

[4]Let us suppose that any field occupies space 1

the graph having as nodes the label sets used by all the $\langle\langle\rangle\rangle$ expressions[5] in the program, and an arc from L' to L when $L' \subseteq L$ but no other intermediate label-set is present in the graph. The sublabel graph of a program using the label sets $\{a\}, \{a,b,c\}, \{a,c,d\}, \{a,b,c,e\}, \{a,b,c,d\}$ and $\{a,b,f,g\}$ is reported in figure 5.

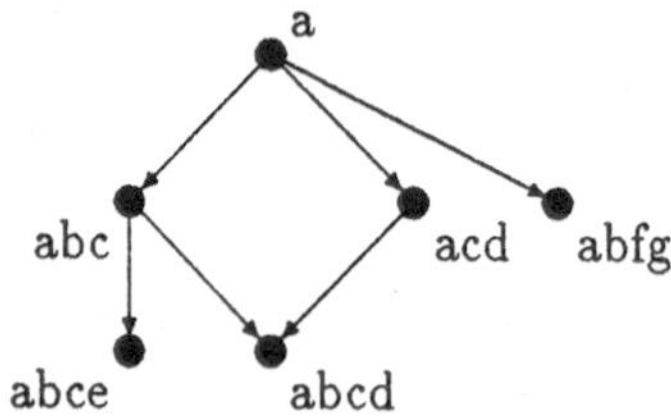

Figure 5: the "sublabel directed graph" of a program

The nodes in any direct path in the graph are candidate for inclusion merging.

Consider for example the graph in figure 5. It can be managed using only the structures of the two leaves a, b, c, e and a, b, c, d, reordering labels as shown in figure 6. In the same picture each set of nodes which are dealt with by a unique structure is joined by a thick line. Detecting a set of search structures which can cover an entire label graph with this technique amounts to detecting a set of disjoint directed paths whose nodes cover the entire graph; we call such a set of paths a "path cover".

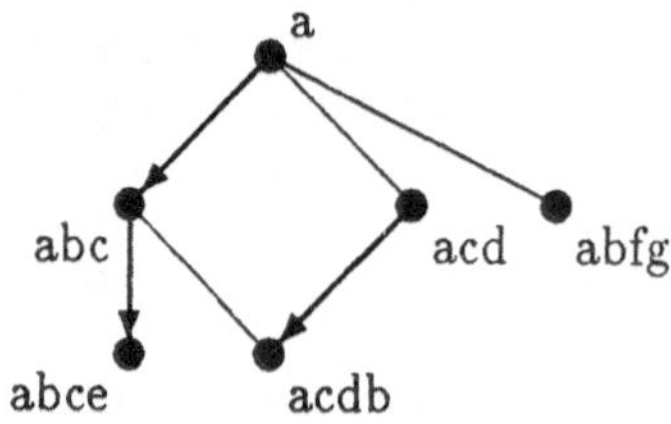

Figure 6: A path cover for a DAG

A path cover can be chosen by transforming the DAG in a forest, by keeping only one of the arcs entering each node and deleting all the other ones, and then by drawing a path for any leaf of the tree, starting from the leaf and going up until another path is met. Finally, in each path, labels are ordered starting with the ones which are first met coming from the root.

When we have defined the order of all the labels in the label search tree, we can search for candidates for true overlap merging by considering leaves having a common label prefix and a disjoint label suffix, like e.g. *abce* and

[5]This is correct only if all the record fields have the same sizes; otherwise we need one node in the graph for each set of label-type pairs.

abfg. The correspoding structures, associating *abce* to *1234* and *abfg* to *1234* can be realized by a unique structure associating *abcefg* to *123434*. Since this is true overlap merging (i.e. without inclusion) it is convenient only for direct and hash structures, but not for linear ones.

In the next subsection we try to analyze how much space we can spare by plain merging, and introduce shift merging. No mathematical analysis is attempted for overlap merging, since the performance of overlap merging depends critically on the inheritance mechanisms provided by the language and on the amount of inheritance exhibited by each program.

5.2 Analysis of plain and shift merge

The number of different sets of a elements chosen from a universe U of N elements is

$$\binom{N}{a} = \frac{N!}{a! \times (N-a)!}$$

So, if we consider two sets A and B with a and b elements randomly chosen form a universe of size N, with $a + b \leq N$, the probability that the two sets have an empty intersection can be computed as the ratio between the number of subsets of N with cardinality b which are included in $U \setminus A$ and the total number of subsets of N with cardinality b:

$$\begin{aligned}\pi^N_{a,b} &= \frac{\binom{N-a}{b}}{\binom{N}{b}} = \frac{(N-a)!}{(N-a-b)! \times b!} \times \frac{(N-b)! \times b!}{N!} \\ &= \frac{(N-a)! \times (N-b)!}{(N-a-b)! \times N!}\end{aligned}$$

Let $a = b$ and $\alpha = a/N$; then the formula above can be rewritten as:

$$\begin{aligned}\pi^N_{a,a} &= \frac{(N-a)! \times (N-a)!}{(N-2a)! \times N!} = \frac{(N-a) \times \cdots \times (N-2a+1)}{(N) \times \cdots \times (N-a+1)} \\ &= \prod_{i=0}^{a-1} \frac{N-a-i}{N-i} = \prod_{i=0}^{a-1} 1 - \frac{a}{N-i} = \prod_{i=0}^{a-1} 1 - \frac{\alpha}{1-i/N}\end{aligned}$$

Since i ranges from 0 to a, then $1 - \frac{\alpha}{1-i/N}$ ranges from $(1-\alpha)$ to $(1-\alpha^+)$, where α^+ is defined as $\alpha/(1-\alpha)$. Since we are interested only in low values for α, we can approximate α^+ with α, and the probability above with:

$$\pi^N_{a,a} \simeq (1-\alpha)^a$$

And more precisely we have:

$$(1-\alpha^+)^a < \pi^N_{a,a} < (1-\alpha)^a$$

If $a \times \alpha \ll 1$ (say $a\alpha \leq 1/2$) then $(1-\alpha)^a$ can be approximated as $1 - a\alpha$ (with an error $< 1 - (a\alpha)^2/2$), which means that there is a high probability of empty intersection. If $a\alpha \geq 1$ the probability of an empty intersection is low. It is lower than $1/e$, where e is the Napier constant, since the following inequalities hold:

$$\pi^N_{a,a} \;<\; (1-\alpha)^a \;=\; ((1-\alpha)^{\frac{1}{\alpha}})^{a\alpha} \;<\; (1/e)^{a\alpha}$$

So the probability of empty intersection does not depend on α, as could be expected, but rather on the $a\alpha$ product, and is high or low depending on whether this product is lower than 0.5 or greater than one. This means that a fixed α, say 0.1, allows merging small tables but does not allow merging big tables.

To gain a greater probability of being able of merging bigger tables, with $a \geq 1/2\alpha$, we must consider the possibility of shifting the tables of some positions before merging them; we call this process "shift merging".

Consider, like above, two tables A and B with a busy entries and $N-a$ empty entries. If we shift one of them by b positions, with $b = \beta N, \beta < 1$, the probability that there is no intersection between them can be approximated by $(1-\alpha)^{a(1-\beta)}$. The probability that it is not possible to merge two tables even if we accept to shift the first table of at most βN entries in either direction ($\beta < 1$) can then be approximated by the following formula:

$$\prod_{i=-\beta N}^{\beta N} 1 - (1-\alpha)^{a(1-i/N)}.$$

6 The hash functions

We have experimented many different hash functions; the most important ones are listed below. *size* is equal to n/α (rounded), while *sizeMask* is the smallest number shich can be written as $2^n - 1$ and is greater than *size*; d and m are randomly generated; & is bitwise conjunction.

hash(i) $= ((i \times d) \bmod m) \bmod size$
maskHash(i) $= (i \times i)\ \&\ sizeMask$
fastHash(i) $= i\ \&\ sizeMask$

The first hash function was chosen at the beginning since it guarantees high probability of perfect hash; however, as we will see in section 8, it is too slow, giving raise to very high values for the γ threshold. Function *fastHash*, on the other hand, guarantees a very high performance and acceptable γ values, which are even better when *sizeMask* is hardwired in the algorithm, so that no parameter must be retrieved from the search structure. *maskHash* has intermediate features.

Even if in general applications the *fastHash* function is not considered a good hash function since it does not scatter the input enough, in our situation it could give a better collision rate than the *hash* one. The *hash* function is very good in destroying any correlation between the input values, but in our case the most important correlation is given by the fact that new labels defined inside a module can be associated by the linker to consecutive integers. If the number of the new labels in a module is smaller than *sizeMask*, than all these new labels are guaranteed not to collide when *fastHash* is used.

7 Dynamic reconfiguration

While the system is running, it is always possible to substitute a search structure with a better one. To take the maximum advantage from this possibility, each search structure family can be implemented in a self-profiling way. Self-profiling search structures keep track of the total number of accesses and of the number of accesses at each field. Since access through self-profiling search structures is more costly than access through regular ones, self-profiling search structures are subtituted by regular ones when enough information has been collected.

Profiling information can be used in the following ways:

- Information about total accesses at a structure: for heavily used search structure we can relax the β factor, to give them a higher probability of enjoying a direct access table. If they are still accessed by a non-perfect hash table, we can adopt a lower α factor to increase the probability of achieving perfect hashing. The space required by this politics can be obtained by adopting higher values of γ, α and β for seldom accessed structures[6].

- Information about access probability of each item in a structure: can be used to reorder linear search structures and buckets of hash structures, putting more heavily accessed fields in the first positions. Perfect hash search structures whose fields are accessed in an unbalanced way can be conveniently transformed in linear structures when the following disequality holds, where labels are order by access probability, a_i is the number of accesses to l_i, and a is the total number of accesses:

$$l_f + l_p \times \sum_{i=1}^{n} \frac{a_i \times i}{a} \quad \leq \quad h_f + h_p.$$

  A similar disequation can be written for non-perfect hash structures.

In a more abstract way, each time a dynamic reorganization of the system is tried, the support should try to minimize the time-cost function without increasing the global space-cost function. Besides this, we can exploit reorganization time to let the optimizer generate new hash parameters for non-perfect hash structures, to get better or even perfect structures.

---

[6]Increasing γ, α and β trades some space for some time: a higher γ produces less hash structures and more linear structures, a higher α produces smaller hash structures and a higher β produces less direct structures and more hash or linear structures

8 Experimental results and measures

Our experiments have been run on the following machines: HP 9000/720, Sun 4 (Sparc II), VAX 8530; experiments on other machines should be soon completed.

Experiments have been run using a routine "OpField" which receives a search structure and a label and returns an offset. We set up a program randomly generating linear search structures, and then producing, for each linear structure, a set of three hash structures, one for each of the three hash functions described in section 6, and, when the appropriate, a direct structure. Actually, to have a reasonable amount of direct structures, in half of the "random" linear search structures we put a consecutive set of labels.

Then, to time the operation, we wrote a tight loop where the operation is called on a unique structure for a big number of times (say $10^5 - 10^6$ times). This is necessary since the clock granularity, on our machines, is about 10 milliseconds, while the OpField routines takes about 1 microsecond to execute. We wrote also a tight loop calling a no-operation routine, to try to understand how much time is spent actually by OpField and how much by the test bed, and a tight loop calling OpField on the first label on the first element of a linear structure in order to be able to compute both l_f and l_p (see section 4) and then to obtain the *gamma* threshold for the different hash functions.

This first experiment gave us very high values for γ. We then introduced faster hash functions, like *maskHash* and *fastHash* (see section 6), but we also decided to change slightly our test bed. Since linear structures use much less space than hash ones, if they are executed in a tight loop they have better possibilities of taking a big advantage from caching mechanisms, but this happens only in the test bed, while in the run-time support of a running system these structures would not enjoy this advantage. For this reason we filled, for each search structure, an array containing a big number (say 100-1000) of copies of that structure, and the test loop now circulates among these different copies, to prevent an effective use of caching mechanisms.

The output of this experiments are the l_f, l_p, h_f, d_f and γ parameters introduced in section 4; γ is the most interesting one, since it allows understanding whether the greater complexity of this approach, with respect to an approach based just on linear search, is justified. Some typical values for the *fastHash* function are reported in table 2, where times are expressed in microseconds.

machine	γ	l_f	l_p	d_f	h_f
HP 9000	17	1.2	0.11	1.5	2.2
Sun SPARC II	6	2.3	0.25	2.7	3.2
Vax 8530	5	8.2	1.2	16.2	11.3

Table 2: Experimental results

These results shows that our technique has some interest only with very fast hash functions (*fasthash* simply returns the $\log_2(\alpha n)$ lower order bits of the label); the other functions gave us γ values in the 15-200 range, and so have no practical interest for our purposes. They show also that the γ value is highly machine dependent. For this reason it should not be cabled in the linker, but should rather be computed, using a well designed test bed, by the linker itself once for each installation.

Another interesting result of these experiments is that the direct access technique resulted in many cases slower than linear search for short structures, resulting usually not convenient for structures with less than four fields. If this result were confirmed, we should revise some of the politics described in these paper. We are planning finer experiments to understand the reason of this unexpected behaviour.

These experiments are still in a very preliminary phase, they are still producing unstable results, and we expect to gain much more information from their prosecution.

9 Comparisons

A different solution to the problem of fast record field access has been proposed in [4]. In their approach every record expression is evaluated to a pair formed by a record and by a direct access search structure which maps every label in the compile time type of the expression to the corresponding position in the record. A label is encoded as its position in the compile time type of the record expression, and for this reason the access map for a record is simply a direct access structure with no holes, which allows any field access to be executed in constant time. Another advantage of this method is that there is no need of a centralized label-integer table. However the search structure associated to the result of a record expression has to be recomputed when the record is bound to an identifier associated to a supertype, since in this case the correspondence between labels and positions in the compile-time type changes. Besides this, when a record is accessible through paths associated to different types, different search structures have to be associated to these different paths. This second drawback can be rather serious in the context of a persistent system supporting the object oriented data model. In such a system, if a class A is a subclass of n different superclasses each record in A can be accesse through $n+1$ different paths usually associated to $n+1$ different types, so that it should be associated to $n+1$ different access maps. This is a problem since in this approach sharing the access maps is not easy, and requires a further overhead on the assignment operations to be accomplished. Nevertheless this approach is very interesting, since it makes record fields access almost as fast as tuple field access[7].

Another technique which guarantees the same performance on field access offered by [4], but without their space penalties and their overhead on assignments, is described in [5]. The basic idea is that labels are not represented by *different* small integers, but non-conflicting labels can be represented by the same integer, where two labels are non-conflicting when there is no record containing both. In this way we can use a very low number of different integers,

[7]Remember the technical meaning we have given to the terms *record* and *tuple* in the introduction.

which means that we can afford using direct tables for every record.

The integer associated to a label is called its *color*. The problem of assigning mutually different colors to all mutually conflicting labels while using a small number of different colors is an instance of the graph-coloring problem. The authors give a simple algorithm that should work reasonably well in most cases.

This approach is the best one, among those presented, for compiled "closed" systems, where closed means that no new code can be added to the compiled system. It is however not suited for persistent systems where new code can be incrementally added, since any time a new record expression (or a new record type) is introduced, some labels which did not conflict before can appear together in this new record expression. Then the color assignment must be modified for these labels, all the access structures referencing these labels must be rebuilt, and all the code containing field access operations must be, in principle, recompiled to substitute the old colors with the new one[8].

10 Conclusions

We have presented a technique for supporting record field access in the context of a strongly typed persistent language with record subtyping, where faster techniques available for non-persistent systems (like to one of [5]) cannot be exploited. The presented technique can be exploited, or adapted, in slightly different contexts, e.g. to perform method dispatch for objects, in the context of a language with name equivalence and name subtyping rules, or in the context of a language with weak typing.

Measurement on the performance of this technique are being carried on at Pisa University, in the context of the implementation of the new version of the Galileo persistent language.

References

[1] A. Albano, L. Cardelli, and R. Orsini. Galileo: A strongly typed, interactive conceptual language. *ACM Transactions on Database Systems*, 10(2):230–260, 1985.

[2] L. Cardelli. Amber. In *Combinators and Functional Programming Languages, Proc. of the 13th summer school of the LITP, Le Val D'Ajol, Vosges (France)*, number 242 in LNCS, Berlin, 1986. Springer-Verlag.

[3] L. Cardelli. Typeful programming. Research Report 45, Digital System Research Center, Palo Alto, CA, May 1989.

[4] R. C. H. Connor, A. Dearle, R. Morrison, and A. L. Brown. An object addressing mechanism for statically typed languages with multiple inheritance. In N. Meyrowitz, editor, *Proc. of Object Oriented Programming Systems Languages and Applications (OOPSLA) '89, New Orleans, Louisiana,*

[8] This last operation could be avoided, at some price.

number 24 (10) in Special Issue of SIGPLAN Notices, pages 279–285. ACM Press, 1989.

[5] R. Dixon and P. Schweizer. A fast method dispatcher for compiled languages with multiple inheritance. In N. Meyrowitz, editor, *Proc. of Object Oriented Programming Systems Languages and Applications (OOPSLA) '89, New Orleans, Louisiana*, number 24 (10) in Special Issue of SIGPLAN Notices, pages 211–214. ACM Press, 1989.

Transactions

M.S. Powell

Department of Computation, University of Manchester Institute of Science & Technology,
P.O.Box 88 - M60 IQD
Manchester, U.K.

The session on transaction mechanisms contained two papers, both addressing concurrency control issues. The first paper was presented by Luigi Mancini from the University of Pisa and proposed a linguistic mechanism to allow the degree of concurrency between transactions in an object-oriented language to be controlled by the programmer. The second paper was presented by Laurent Daynès from INRIA and presented an efficient implementation of nested locking derived from a formalisation of locking rules based on set and tree theory.

Transaction mechanisms must provide two primary means of maintaining the logical consistency of shared objects. Firstly, concurrency control must ensure that operations are scheduled so that the intermediate states of objects are hidden during updating. Secondly, recovery mechanisms must negate any state changes caused by failing operations. Efficient transaction implementation is complex, and the techniques which have been developed in the database world must be extended to cope adequately with persistent object systems in which the required access speeds and range of object lifetimes are much greater. Both of the papers in this section concentrate almost exclusively on the concurrency control aspects of transactions.

A challenge facing workers in the persistent object systems area is to develop suitable programming language mechanisms to allow transactions to be specified safely, flexibly and with reasonable efficiency. The first paper in this session describes a possible extension to the Nuovo Galileo language which allows the programmer to specify the degree of concurrency which should be permitted between operations on objects described by a particular type. Galileo is an object oriented database programming language, and it seems natural to augment the description of an object's type, specified in terms of the set of methods it supports, with details of which methods may be applied concurrently.

In the simplest case, any two transactions may be allowed to proceed concurrently if they apply two *mutually commutative* operations to an object, i.e. each of the two possible sequential applications of the operations are equivalent. In principle, the identification of such commutative operations might be based on a complete formal specification of the object's semantics. However, the approach presented here is based on providing a syntactic construct to allow the programmer to specify which operations may be regarded as mutually commutative. This provides the freedom to control the degree to which concurrent operations are applied to objects of a particular type, but places the responsibility on the programmer to avoid inconsistency. The paper extends the approach to allow the definition of mutually commutative operations to depend on an object's state, presents correctness criteria and outlines possible implementations.

In the second paper in the session Laurent Daynès presented a new interpretation of Moss's nested transaction model. This formalises nested locking rules so as to avoid hierarchical deadlocks and enhance concurrency between operations on different sub-trees in the data hierarchy. An implementation strategy was presented based on the structured data model of EOS. The EOS data model has two levels. The bottom level is made up of primitive objects called *quarks*. These provide the unit for recovery logging. The second level consists of arbitrary, single entry point graphs of quark objects called *nucleons*, which may themselves be organised into complex structures, but may not share quarks. The unit of locking is the nucleon. Performance figures are presented in terms of the slowdown factor for a C++ benchmark with and without nested locking extensions. The results indicate a substantially reduced overhead for nested locking based on the nucleon/quark data model.

Although not explicit in the discussion at the end of this session, the rôle of types in persistent object systems was questioned on a number of occasions in a way that is characteristic of the different approaches underlying the two presentations in this session. The first paper exploits the availability of static type information, and annotates it with semantic information to enhance and control concurrency between method invocations. The second paper relies only on the characteristics of a relatively low level data model and a dynamically applicable set of scheduling rules.

At the end of this session the participants retired for dinner. This was followed by a harpsichord recital in which the players achieved such high degrees of concurrency and synchronisation as to suggest the application of some theory of concurrency control, as yet, undiscovered by computer science.

Specification of Concurrency Control in Persistent Programming Languages[1]

N. De Francesco and G. Vaglini

Dipartimento di Ingegneria dell'Informazione
Via Diotisalvi 2, 56126 Pisa, Italy

L.V. Mancini

Dipartimento di Informatica
Corso Italia 40, 56100 Pisa, Italy

A. Pereira Paz

Engineering S.P.A.
Via Benedetto Croce 51, 56100 Pisa, Italy

Abstract

This paper proposes a mechanism for object-oriented database languages which allows the specification of as much concurrency among method executions as a user needs. This proposal goes towards the use of semantic information about methods and it allows a user to specify some kind of observational independence among methods by means of a construct called *concurrent behaviour*. It is shown that, as far as such method commutativity is concerned, there is no direct relation between super-types and sub-types, that is, a sub-type can be either "less concurrent" or "more concurrent" than its super-type. The notion of correctness for interleaved executions of transactions is presented taking into account the concurrent behaviour of objects, and a possible implementation of the proposed construct is outlined.

1 Introduction

The recent interest in new database applications, as CAD, office information systems, software development environments etc., has modified some of the traditional requirements about transactions [1]. For example, transaction length makes the serialisability requirement unsuitable for new applications: this requirement might lead to an unacceptable waiting time for locks or, alternatively, to an extensive use of aborts. Thus, transaction execution requires that more parallelism is allowed.

Many researchers [2, 3, 4, 5, 6] have suggested the use of the semantics of an application to increase concurrency. For example, two transactions that increment some kind of counter can proceed concurrently, because increments are commutative if considering that an *increment* operation does not read the value of the counter at a logical level, although, at a lower level, a *read* operation may be needed. Thus a transaction should be enabled to increment the counter even if a transaction, that previously incremented it, is still uncommitted.

The semantics-based concurrency control fits very well with the application of the object-oriented approach to database definition and management: the concurrency specification can be given as part of the object-type definition. Following this idea, in [5, 6,

[1]This work has been supported in part by grants from the C.E.C. under ESPRIT BRA No. 3070 (FIDE: Formally Integrated Data Environment), and the "Progetto Finalizzato Sistemi Informatici e Calcolo Parallelo" of C.N.R. under grant No. 91.00877.PF69.

7] an approach is investigated which considers objects to have both a *sequential* and a *concurrent* specification. The sequential specification resembles a traditional definition of the object methods, while the concurrent specification defines the allowed interleaving (denoted as *schedules*) of operations issued by the transactions and can be employed to monitor the behaviour of the transactions which share the same objects. The degree of parallelism defined by a concurrent specification is measured in terms of the number of the allowed schedules which are output by the *scheduler*. Two directions can be taken when following this approach: the first one, more formal, derives the concurrent specification from the sequential one; the other supplies the programmer the ability of defining concurrent specifications. A formal derivation of the concurrency properties from the object semantics guarantees the consistency between the two specifications, but it needs a formal sequential specification too and, moreover, it is not flexible. The second approach instead, at the price of possible inconsistencies, leaves more freedom to the programmer, which can specify the degree of parallelism she/he wants (for instance, lower than the maximum depending on recoverability and efficiency considerations). The first approach has been followed in [7, 8], while in the present paper we follow the other one.

We propose a linguistic construct by means of which the programmer specifies when, from her/his observational point of view, two (or more) methods can be executed in any order without producing appreciable differences in the expected result. In fact, it is responsibility of the specifier of the objects to assert what kind of results must be necessarily distinct and what are equivalent for his/her own purposes. For this purpose, we leave to the user the definition of the interesting *conflicts* for each particular object-type, as a consequence also the definition of commutativity, i.e. two methods commute if they do not conflict, results into being practically extended. The proposed construct allows us to define some kind of external behaviour of an object-type, which is, in general, determined both by the way the type is expected to be used (i.e., its semantics) and by its internal structure (i.e., its implementation); obviously, the converse may be not true, because objects with different internal structures may have the same external behaviour and thus belong to the same type.

In object-oriented systems based on a sound typing schema, the legal definitions of class hierarchy is constrained by the sub-typing rules of the language. The best known example of this situation is the *contravariance* of method redefinition. This rule states that a redefined method can specialise its result type, but not its arguments. The body of the method, however, can be rewritten with no constraint, but respecting the contravariance rule, and the actual code for a method is determined at run-time by late-binding. One of the issues addressed here is whether a sub-typing relation can be established between the concurrent specification of a sub-type and that of its super-type. It is shown that, unfortunately, there is no reasonable constraint at the type system level between the concurrency properties of an object-type and those of its super-type. That is, the properties of a sub-type may either strengthen or relax those of its super-type for the same (or for redefined) methods. Thus a sub-type can be "more concurrent" or "less concurrent" than its super-type, where by "more concurrent" we mean that conflicts, that are possible in the super-type for some methods, are not relevant in the sub-type; while by "less concurrent" we mean that the sub-type definition imposes some restrictions in the concurrency properties of its super-type. In conclusion, since it is typical of database applications to successively define sub-types by using existing types, and thus by inheriting code, the sub-type relation may result in an inclusion relation between values, but not necessarily in an inclusion of external behaviour. However, since it turns out to be useful in practical cases, essentially for hierarchically defined abstract data types, we also provide a mechanism to incrementally define concurrency properties of methods of an object-type by means of some kind of inheritance.

In the paper we present a formal transaction model and a correctness criterion, based on it, for possible implementations of the construct. Moreover, we sketch an implementation based on compatibility tables and prove that it is correct. The proposed implementation suggests that the rules about method commutativity can be considered in the same way as the code of a redefined method: they can be arbitrarily redefined, while the correctness of concurrency control is ensured by late-binding of compatibility tables.

Object-oriented concurrent languages provide the application programmer with at least two different concurrency control policies: transactions for concurrency control across multiple objects, and atomic blocks for critical sections on individual objects. The focus of this paper is mainly on the first kind of concurrency control. Transactions are considered sequences of method invocations, each method execution is regarded as atomic and the concurrent activities to be coordinated are represented only by transactions. However, the presented approach is also valid for objects with internal concurrency; in this case, the synchronisation mechanisms of the language should be employed in addition to the concurrency specification. In this paper we will not deal with the additional issues related to internal concurrency.

Section 2 presents the basic object mechanism. Section 3 defines the formal transaction model. Section 4 presents the construct to specify concurrency properties of an object. Section 5 outlines the implementation of such construct. Section 6 concludes.

2 The basic object mechanism

In this section, we present the basic object mechanism of the language, which will be later enriched to deal with conflict information. For the sake of concreteness, we present an object model in the style of Nuovo Galileo [9], although the ideas of this paper can be applied to many object-oriented languages.

An object is a software entity equipped with a set of local operations (*methods*) which manipulate its internal state. An object *encapsulates* its state, since the state can only be accessed and modified through the associated methods. The only way to interact with an object is to request it for executing a method (this is accomplished by *message sending*). The structure of an object state is modeled by a set of variables which can have values of arbitrary complexity, including other objects. Objects are denotable and expressible as "first-class" values of the language, i.e. they can be assigned as values of variables, and used as data structure components, as parameters, as results of functions. Finally, each object is distinct from any other object, i.e. has an *identity* that persists despite any changes to the value of its state. We present here only the mechanism to define object-types. The object creation mechanism is beyond the scope of this paper.

2.1 Object-types

An object-type is defined with the **Object** construct. The definition of the object-type must provide the name and the type of the operations (*methods*) that can be applied to an object instance. The invocation of a method takes zero or more values (*method parameters*), and produces a value, by executing the corresponding method body. Note that each object-type defines only the methods that can be applied to an object. The *instance variables* that constitute the internal state of an object are specified when the object is created, and are accessed only by message sending. The following example shows the definition of the object-type *Person*:

```
Let Person =
        Object With
                fiscal_Code : String
                name : String
                address : String
                modAddress(String): Null
                introduceYourself : Null
        End
```

It is worth noting that what are modelled by "attributes" in other object data-models, e.g., like *name* in the example above, are modelled employing only messages in the approach of the Nuovo Galileo.

2.2 Object sub-types

An object-type T' is a sub-type of another object-type T iff

a) T' offers more (or an equal number of) methods than T ;
b) for any method M, defined in both types, which is declared as $M(x_1{:}t_1, \ldots, x_n{:}t_n){:}t$ in the super-type *T*, and as $M(x'_1{:}t'_1, \ldots, x'_n{:}t'_n){:}t'$ in the sub-type *T'*, there is $t' \leq t$ and $t_i \leq t_i'$, for $1 \leq i \leq n$. Notice that n can be zero if the corresponding method has no argument.

The rules *a)* and *b)* above ensure the contravariance of the sub-type relation, in fact the sub-typing relation between the argument types goes in the opposite direction with respect to the sub-typing relation between result types.

The following example shows how a sub-type can be defined by inheritance from a super-type:

```
Let Student =
        Object Person With
                s_number: Int
                year: AcademicYear
        End;
```

The operator

Object *O* **With** *Methods* **End**

extends the object-type *O* with the specified *Methods*. If some method is defined both in *O* and in *Methods*, the resulting object-type exploits the definition in *Methods*. The operator is *well used* only if the resulting object-type is a sub-type of *O*; otherwise the compiler raises an error. This may happen when a method is redefined with an incorrect type. In what follows, we only consider single inheritance.

3 The model

In this section we introduce the formal model for a database, by which it is possible to define a notion of correctness for concurrent executions of transactions. The model which we refer to considers a *database* composed by a set of objects, $\mathbb{O}$ ={ A, B, C,.. }, each of which belongs to a defined object-type, and a set of transactions $\mathbb{T}=\{T_1,.., T_n\}$ defined as follows.

Transaction. A *transaction* $T_i \in \mathbb{T}$ is a sequence of steps, each of which is a triple

$$< i, M(\text{parameter-list}), O> \quad (O \in \mathbb{O}).$$

Each step of a transaction represents the request of executing a method *M*, belonging to an object *O*, with parameters *parameter-list*; such request is a message sent to *O* from transaction *i*. To describe the behaviour of an object we consider the possible sequences of methods (or *operations*) that can be performed on the object itself.

O-history. Given an object *O*, an *O-history* is a couple (m, s), where *m* is a sequence of methods of *O*, with some parameters, and *s* a state of *O* such that *m* can be applied to *O* starting from the state *s*.

Moreover, taking into account the transactions that issue the operations, we can define:

Schedule. A *schedule S* for a set $\mathbb{T}$ of transactions is whatever interleaving of the steps of the transactions of $\mathbb{T}$, such that the total order among the steps of each transaction is respected.

O-schedule. Given an object *O* and a set of transactions $\mathbb{T}$, an *O-schedule* is a schedule composed only by the transaction steps referring to *O*.

S/O. Given a schedule *S* and an object *O*, *S/O* is the O-schedule obtained by deleting from *S* all the transaction steps not naming *O* and maintaining the same order as in *S* among the transaction steps naming *O*.

Obviously, S/O is an O-schedule if it is not empty. On the one hand, any O-schedule can correspond to more than one O-history (m, s), for different *s*. On the other hand, a given O-history corresponds to more than one O-schedule for different set of transactions. Given an O-schedule *S*, we call h(S) the O-history obtained deleting the transaction names from *S*. As an example, consider the following schedule *S* acting on two objects A and B by means of the methods m1 and m2 issued by transactions I and J

S=< I, *m1*(parameter-list1), A> < J, *m1*(parameter-list1), B> < J, *m2*(parameter-list2), A> < I, *m2*(parameter-list2), B>

the sub-schedules S/A and S/B are the following

S/A = < I, *m1*(parameter-list1), A> < J, *m2*(parameter-list2), A>
S/B = < J, *m1*(parameter-list1), B> < I, *m2*(parameter-list2), B>

Moreover,

h(S/A) = *m1*(parameter-list1); *m2*(parameter-list2)
h(S/B) = *m1*(parameter-list1); *m2*(parameter-list2)

while a possible A-history is (h(S/A, s'), and B-history is (h(S/B, s"), where s' and s" are possible states of A and B, respectively.

Seriality. A schedule S of a set $\mathbb{T}$ of transactions is *serial* if the steps of each $T_i \in \mathbb{T}$ occur consecutively, that is the executions of the transactions in $\mathbb{T}$ are not interleaved.

A crucial problem in transaction processing is to establish the set of *correct* schedules. *Serialisability* [10, 11] is the most widely accepted interpretation of schedule correctness: a schedule is serialisable if it is *equivalent* to a serial one. The equivalence notion can be based on a very simple model, in which all that we know on an operation is if it is a *read* or a i operation (*read/write model*): so two schedules are equivalent if, in each interpretation, each *read* reads the same value in both of them and the final state of each database object is the same. However, since serialisability may results in a too restrictive requirement (see [3] for an exposition of the problem) for a lot of recent applications, it can be substituted by weaker correctness criteria which also take into account the semantics of the objects of the database. In the following section, a language construct to specify the concurrent behaviour of an object is introduced, allowing the user to exploit her/his semantic knowledge on the type of the object.

4 The language construct

This section introduces the linguistic mechanism used to express that certain methods of an object can be independently executed. Since the definition of this independence is responsibility of the application programmer, we supply her/him the facility of specifying also a *concurrent behaviour.* This concurrent behaviour is defined by a set of independent conditional rules, each of which states when a couple of methods can be executed in any order without affecting the resulting observation a user can made on the object state. A conditional rule has the form

m1(parameter-list11) | *m2*(parameter-list2) **when** *C*,

where the condition *C* is a boolean expression where the method parameters and any other procedure and variable, which are visible according to the language scoping rules, can be employed. Note that, since method calls can appear in the expression, as a consequence also the results of an operation can be employed to determine its possible conflicts. The parameter list of a method can be omitted in a rule definition if parameter values are not used in the condition. The **when** portion of a rule can also be omitted if the rule always holds.

Note that *m1* | *m2* does not mean that *m1* and *m2* necessarily run concurrently, but it specifies that they can be executed up to completion in any order and still lead to the same final observation. This specification is useful in a system with sequential objects where each method is regarded as atomic. Nevertheless, the approach is still valid if the objects have internal concurrency. In the last case, the proper synchronisation mechanisms of the language must be programmed in the method's body, independently from the concurrent specifications of the object-type.

4.1 Examples

Suppose that a user defines an object-type *Collection* equipped with the methods: *get*, which reads an element, *rem*, which removes an element, and *ins*, which inserts an element. The expected behaviour of an object with type *Collection* is such that an element among those previously inserted by *ins* is returned by *get* or removed by *rem*; moreover, each inserted element is removed after a finite time.

We can assert the following concurrent properties of *Collection*, taking into account the semantics of the methods; some of these properties are rejected by simpler models as the *read/write* one. First of all, two successive invocations of *get* always commute, because *get* is a read-only operation that does not affect the state of the object. We express this fact by the following rule:

get | *get*

whose meaning is that, even if a transaction T_i has been allowed to perform a *get* on an object, another transaction can be allowed to perform another *get* on the same object before T_i commits. Moreover, the removal of two elements can be executed in any order: the final state of the object will be the same. Also the insertion of a new element can be allowed concurrently with another insertion, since we are not interested to maintain the temporal ordering of the elements. We express these facts with the rules

rem | *rem*
ins | *ins*

If we consider now the interferences between *ins* and *get*, some care is needed: they are independent only if performed on a non-empty *Collection*. In fact, we shall obtain different results from *get* when it is executed before or after having inserted an element in an empty object; a similar thing happens for *ins* and *rem* if concurrently executed on an empty object. Thus we write

ins | *get* **when not** *empty*;
ins | *rem* **when not** *empty*

where the function *empty*, that does not belong to the type interface, returns a boolean that is **true** if the collection is empty. The sequential specification and the *concurrent behaviour* of the object-type **Collection** is given below.

Let Collection =
    Object
    ins(n:Int):Null;
    rem:Null;
    get:Int;
    ConcBehaviour
    get | get;
    rem | rem;
    ins | ins;
    get | rem **when not** *empty*;
    ins | get **when not** *empty*;
    ins | rem **when not** *empty*
    End.

Another example of object-type specification may be the type **Set** which will be used in a following section to discuss the implementation of the proposed construct. Note that method *member* is called in the condition of a rule: this condition expresses the fact that *member* can be allowed to be concurrently executed with *ins*, when the element to be inserted is already present in the set.

```
Let Set =
        Object
        ins(n:Int): Null;
        rem(n:Int): Null;
        member(n:Int):Bool;
        ConcBehaviour
        member | member;
        rem | rem;
        ins | ins;
        ins(n) | member(m)  when  (n≠m) or member(m);
        rem(n) | member(m)  when  (n≠m);
        ins(n) | rem(m)  when  (n≠m)
        End.
```

In the rest of the paper, we will use some abbreviations to write concurrent behaviours: for example, the rule

$$(m_1|m_2|m_3|\ldots|m_n)$$

stands for the following set of rules:

$m_1|m_1$; $m_1|m_2$; $m_1|m_3$;...$m_1|m_n$;
$m_2|m_2$; $m_2|m_3$;...$m_2|m_n$
...
$m_n|m_n$.

This abbreviation is useful, for instance, to concisely express that some read-only methods commute each other. In addition, we employ the following convention: if there is more than one rule involving a pair of methods, thus the last rule is the valid one. This convention helps to define concurrent behaviours by specifying the "complement", that is: one states that everything commutes and then one overwrites the rules for the methods that do not commute. When combined with the abbreviation, this is a very concise way to deal, for instance, with methods that read an object variable and methods that write it. For example, we have three methods *rx1*, *rx2* and *rx3* to retrieve the value of three variables and *modx1*, *modx2* and *modx3* to modify them, if their commutativity rules are

rx1 | rx1 ; rx1|x2; rx1|x3; rx2 | rx2 ; rx2|rx3; rx3 | rx3 ;
modx1|rx2; modx1|rx3; modx2|rx1; modx2|rx3; modx3|rx1; modx3|rx2;
modx1|modx2; modx1|modx3; modx2|modx3,

it is more convenient to specify an abbreviated behaviour as follows:

(rx1|rx2|rx3|modx1|modx2|modx3)
rx1|modx1 **when false**
rx2|modx2 **when false**
rx3|modx3 **when false**

4.2 Concurrent behaviour semantics

In this section, the formal semantics of concurrent behaviours is briefly given, for a more complete treatment see [7]. Since a concurrent behaviour defines under what condition two methods of a type *commute*, the rules of the concurrent behaviour of an object *O* can be interpreted as establishing a relation between any two O-histories which differ only by the ordering of two successive invocations of the methods involved in a rule. We define the relation $\leftrightarrow$ and its transitive closure $\equiv$, for a given concurrent behaviour, as follows:

$\leftrightarrow_B$ **Relation**. Given a concurrent behaviour *B* for an object *O* and two O-histories *h1* and *h2*, *h1* $\leftrightarrow_B$ *h2* holds if:

i) *h1*= (m,s) and *h2*= (m',s), i.e. the initial state of the two histories is the same;
ii) *m* = μ' m1(parameter-list1) m2(parameter-list2) μ",
iii) *m'*= μ' m2(parameter-list2) m1(parameter-list1) μ",
iv) a rule exists in *B* with the form
    m1 (parameter-list1) | *m2* (parameter-list2) **when** *cond*,
v) *cond* is *true*, when evaluated in the state obtained after having executed μ' and with the parameters of *parameter-list1* and *parameter-list2*.

The relation $\leftrightarrow_B$ holds between two histories which start from the same state of the object and which contain the same sequence of operations apart from the exchange of *m1* and *m2*. Nevertheless, since μ' is equal in both histories, the state of the object after μ' and the values retrieved by the read-only operations occurring in μ' are the same. As a consequence, the condition of the rule involving *m1* and *m2* is evaluated on the same values in *h1* and *h2*, so giving the same result. After the execution of both *m1* and *m2*, the operations in μ" find the object in states observationally equivalent and thus they produce an equivalent final state of the object.

B-equivalence of O-histories. The reflexive-transitive closure of $\leftrightarrow_B$ is called *B-equivalence*, denoted by $\equiv_B$.

It is easy to see that $\equiv_B$ is an equivalence relation on O-histories, since the reflexivity, symmetry, and transitivity properties hold. This relation partitions the histories themselves into equivalence classes employing the following assertion: two histories h=(m,s) and h'=(m',s') for the same object *O* belong to the same equivalence class if s=s' and a finite sequence of rules belonging to the concurrent behaviour of *O* can be applied to transform *m* into *m'*. The *concurrent semantics* of an object-type is defined just by such an equivalence relation.

In order to define our serialisability concept, we must consider O-schedules and not just histories. B-equivalence can be easily extended to O-schedules:

B-equivalence of O-schedules. Given the concurrent behaviour B of an object O, two O-schedules S and S' are *B-equivalent for a state s*, if and only if (h(S), s) $\equiv_B$ (h(S'), s).

Δ-serialisability. Given a set $\mathbb{T}$ of transactions acting on a set $\mathbb{O} = \{O_1, ..., O_n\}$ of objects, each in the state s_i, $1 \le i \le n$, a schedule S is *Δ-serialisable* if a serial schedule S_S of the transactions in $\mathbb{T}$ exists, such that, for each $O \in \mathbb{O}$, if B is the concurrent behaviour of O, then $S/O \equiv_B S_S/O$.

4.3 Subtypes

4.3.1 Motivations

In this section we argue that, with respect to method commutativity, there is no direct relation between an object-type and its sub-types. This means that a sub-type may be either more or less concurrent than its super-types.

For *less concurrent* sub-types, we intend that not all the valid (by its concurrent behaviour) interleaving of methods of the super-type are valid also for the sub-type. More precisely, a $\{B_1\}$-serialisable schedule may not be $\{B_2\}$-serialisable, where B_i is the concurrent behaviour specification of the object-type O_i, and O_1 is a super-type of O_2. This situation may happen when the sub-type drops some commutativity rule of the super-type, or when the sub-type strengthens the condition of a rule of the super-type, that is, it redefines

m1 | m2 when *C*

by

m1 | m2 when *C'*,

where *C'* logically implies *C*.

A classical example of this situation is when the sub-type adds an ordering requirement to the unordered structure of the super-type. For example, consider a type **OrderedCollection** which must behave as a FIFO queue. It is possible to specify it as a sub-type of the type **Collection** defined in section 4.1. The *ins* operation always commutes with itself for **Collection**, but it does not behave in the same way for **OrderedCollection**. In fact, in the latter type, the order in which elements are inserted is relevant, and must be observed by the *get* operation. Therefore, two *ins* operations can commute if they insert the same element in **OrderedCollection**. Moreover, the operations *get* and *rem* do not commute in **OrderedCollection** because they are always interested in the same element. So, the concurrent behaviour of the sub-type will be the same as **Collection**, except for the rule get | rem **when not** *empty* which is dropped, and for the rule ins | ins that will be modified in the following way:

ins(n) | *ins*(m) **when** n=m

Also the type **StackCollection**, which behaves as a LIFO Queue can be specified as a sub-type of **Collection**. No method must be added, but *ins* should be redefined; moreover, the concurrent behaviour of **Collection** must be substituted by the following set of rules:

get | *get*;
rem | *rem*;
ins(n) | *ins*(m) **when** n=m;

The examples above show that sub-types can be defined as 'ordered versions' of the super-types: such hierarchical organisation is typical in the libraries of object-oriented languages like Smalltalk [12].

As a further example of a "less concurrent" sub-type, consider the following definition of a type **Counter**. A counter has the *add* method to increment (by x) its contents and the *value* method to inspect its current value.

```
Let Counter =
        Object With
        add(x:Int):Null
        value:Int;
        ConcBehaviour
        add | add;
        value | value;
        value | add(x) when x=0
        End
```

We may define a sub-type **CounterWithMemory**, which, in addition to the **Counter** operations, is equipped with an operation *last_add* which remembers the value added by the last *add* operation. The commutativity rule *add|add* must be modified in the **CounterWithMemory** specification, since the new read-only operation *last_add* can observe the last value added and thus can notice the difference between the two possible interleavings.

```
Let CounterWithMemory =
        Object Counter With
        last_add:Int;
        ConcBehaviour
        (add | value | last_add);
        add(x) | add(y) when x=y;
        value | add(x) when x=0;
        last_add | add  when false;
        End
```

So far, we have shown that a sub-type can be 'less concurrent' than its super-type. It remains to show that there are cases where the opposite is also true, that is, the sub-type can be 'more concurrent' than the super-type. If we regard types as sets of values and sub-types as subsets, we can make an algebraic analogy: a certain operation of an algebra may be non-commutative in the general case, but it may commute for a certain sub-set of the elements of the algebra that satisfy some condition. If a sub-type happens to coincide with one of these subsets, we can exploit this property by adding the corresponding rule to its concurrent behaviour.

Consider the following example that defines **Matrix** (with simplified operations) and the sub-type **Diagonal Matrix**:

```
Let Matrix =
        Object With
        det:Int
        multiply(m:Matrix):Null
        transpose:Null
        square:Null
        ConcBehaviour
        det | det;
```

```
        det | transpose
        End
```

Matrices have a method for computing their *det*erminant, a *multiply* method, a method for *transpos*ing a matrix and a method *square* that multiplies a matrix by itself. The rule det | det is obvious since *det* is a read-only operation, whereas the commutativity of *det* and *transpose* is based on a well-known property of matrices. The definition of the **Diagonal Matrix** object-type as sub-type of **Matrix** is:

```
Let DiagonalMatrix =
        Object Matrix With
        ConcBehaviour
        det | det;
        det | transpose;
        transpose | square
        End
```

It does make sense to have a **DiagonalMatrix** sub-type, since its operations can be implemented much more efficiently, and a diagonal matrix can be stored saving space. The important point is that, when restricted to diagonal matrices, the *transpose* and *square* operations commute, so we can add the corresponding rule to the sub-type's concurrent specification. It may be argued that the same effect could be achieved by adding in **Matrix** definition the rule

transpose | square **when** diagonal

instead of forbidding any commutativity between these two methods. Recalling the algebraic analogy given above, adding this rule corresponds to specify in the concurrent behaviour of the type itself the sub-set of values for which a commutativity rule holds, instead of defining a more specific sub-type when needed. It seems that this approach contradicts the object-oriented methodology in two ways: (1) it is not reasonable to assume that the need of sub-types is known when the super-type is defined: a major reason for using object-orientation and inheritance is to allow the evolution of software systems; (2) it may be inefficient always to test if a certain object satisfies a certain condition. It is precisely the use of sub-types that makes unnecessary such tests.

Now we present another example, whose flavour is closer to typical database applications. An employee has a name, an employee number and a hierarchical level. Moreover, a record of how many hours he has worked in the current month is maintained. There is a method *addHours* to increment this variable and a method *computeSalary*, that computes the salary of an employee as a function of his level and the hours he has worked. Below, the concurrent behaviour of an employee is given using the abbreviation introduced at the end of Section 4.1; it specifies that concurrency is allowed among the following methods: (1) the read-only methods for accessing the object state, and (2) the methods which update a part of the state with the methods that read other parts of the state. In particular, *addHours* and *computeSalary* do not commute, since there is a conflict between the increment of the worked hours of an employee and the read of this value to compute the salary. The definition of the object-type **Employee** follows:

```
Let Employee =
        Object With
```

```
name:String
eNumber:Int
level:Int
workedHours:Int
addHours(h:Int):Null
computeSalary:Int
ConcBehaviour
name | eNumber | level | workedHours | addHours | computeSalary;
workedhours | addHours when false
computeSalary | addHours when false
End
```

We now define **Salesman** to be a sub-type of **Employee**. A salesman has, in addition to the methods and the variables of **Employee**, a record of the amount of his sales in the current month, and a method to update it. The interesting point is that a salesman is no more paid in function of the hours he worked, but only in function of how much he sells. So, the *computeSalary* method redefined in **Salesman** can commute with *addHours*. Note that it could makes sense to maintain the hours record for a salesman; since it might be used for purposes other than computing his salary.

```
Let SalesMan =
    Object Employee With
    sales:Int
    addSales(s:Int):Null
    ConcBehaviour
    (name | eNumber | level | workedHours | addHours | computeSalary | sales |
addSales);
    workedhours | addHours when false
    sales | addSales when false
    End
```

This example shows that some conflicts that forbid the commutativity of two methods of the super-type may disappear in the sub-type, when some methods is redefined, thus producing a more concurrent sub-type.

4.3.2 Definition of the concurrent behaviour of sub-types

The last section argued that a sub-type can be either more or less concurrent than the super-type: more precisely, the concurrent specification of a sub-type can be *unrelated* to that of its super-type, because some commutativity rules may be dropped while others may be added. However, in the most common situations the differences between concurrent specifications are not large. For conciseness reasons, while in the previous section we have repeated the rules in each subtype specification, it is useful to inherit the concurrent specification of the super-type in the sub-type as if they were methods not redefined. We choose to inherit all the rules of the super-type and to redefine them only when necessary. The effect of the redefinition of a rule is to override the corresponding super-type rule. The redefinition can either strengthen or weaken the previous condition. A rule

m1 | m2 **when** *C*

is dropped by redefining it as

m1 | m2 **when false**.

For example, the sub-type **CounterWithMemory** can be defined by inheriting the concurrent specification of the **Counter** as follows:

Let CounterWithMemory=
    Object Counter **With**
    last_add:Int;
    ConcBehaviour
    add(x) | add(y) **when** x=y;
    last_add | last_add
    last_add | value
    End

It should be noted that, with respect to the definition given in Section 4.3.1, the condition add(x) | add(y) **when** x=y overwrites the condition add | add of the **Counter** object, and the condition value | add(x) **when** x=0 is not needed being inherited from the super-type.

In addition, a new abbreviation can be introduced to specify concisely the commutativity of the new methods added in the sub-type with the existing ones. This abbreviation specifies the commutativity of a set of methods with another set of methods. For example,

(m1, m2) | (m3, m4, m5)   is equivalent to

m1|m3; m1|m4; m1|m5; m2|m3; m2|m4; m2|m5.

5 Implementation

5.1 Compatibility table

In this section we outline the implementation of the concurrent behaviour of an object and prove that it defines a scheduler which outputs Δ-serialisable schedules only. We associate each object with a *compatibility table*. This table has as many rows and columns as the number of methods: each position (m1, m2) of the matrix contains the condition under which the methods *m1* and *m2* commute. Compatibility tables to define methods commutativity were introduced in [13] and used also in [4, 5] in the context of different semantic models.

The compatibility table can be directly derived from the concurrent behaviour of an object-type as follows:

- For each rule
  m1 (parameter-list) | m2 (parameter-list) **when** *cond*,
  cond is present in the position (mth1, mth2).
- For each rule
  m1 (parameter-list) | m2 (parameter-list),
  a **true** condition is present in the position (m1, m2).
- A **false** condition occurs in all the positions of the table corresponding to methods for which a rule does not exist.

As an example, the compatibility table derived from the concurrent behaviour of **Set** is shown below.

	ins(n)	rem(m)	member(p)
ins(n)	**true**	**not n=m**	**(not n=p) or member(n)=true**
rem(m)	**not m=n**	**true**	**not m=p**
member(p)	**(not p=n) or member(n)=true**	**not p=m**	**true**

5.2 Data manager functionality

Compatibility tables are exploited by the so-called Data Manager, one for each object O in the database (we call it DM(O)) and to which are sent all the requests for executing a method. DM(O) maintains a copy of the object in a consistent state, and stores the modifications to the object state at transactions commit time only. Moreover, it maintains the sequence of the enabled methods and the list of the active transactions. The behaviour of DM(O) is the following, starting from a situation in which no transaction is active and the object is in the initial state *s0*.

If a generic T_i requires the execution of a method *m1*, T_i is allowed to initiate such an execution. Moreover, in order to manage future conflicts, DM(O) tries to evaluate the conditions of each element (m1,m2), taking into account the state *s0* of the object and the value of the parameters of *m1*. In general, a complete evaluation of the condition is not possible, since the actual values of the parameters of *m2* are not available at this time. Our choice is to use partial evaluation, that is, DM(O) evaluates as far as possible the conditions. To verify the conflicts, the evaluation will be completed when a successive request of method execution comes. From these evaluations, DM(O) derives what methods possibly conflict with *m1*. A structure, associated with each T_i is created, called $conflict_i$, with as many entries as the methods of O, each entry $conflict_i[m]$ may hold:

- **false**, when *m* conflicts with no method until now executed by T_i;
- **true**, when *m* can no more be allowed to be executed because it conflicts with at least one method executed by T_i; or
- the condition under which *m* may conflict with a method previously executed by T_i; such a condition may be not completely evaluated, because of the lack, at the time $conflict_i[m]$ was written, of the value of the actual parameters of *m*.

Initially, when $conflict_i[m]$ is created, it contains **false** in each entry.

Consider, for example, an empty object *I* of type **Set** as defined before, and a transaction T_i which executes *m1* = ins(3). After the invocation of ins(3), $conflict_i$ will contain:

ins(n)	**false**
rem(m)	**m=3**
member(p)	**p=3**

When a transaction T_j requires the execution of a method *m2* = member(p), each existing $conflict_h$, $h \neq j$, is examined to check if *m2* is specified in the rows of some previously enabled method. This check may require an evaluation (using the parameters of *m2*) of some partially evaluated condition, in this case, T_i and T_j conflict if p=3. If the method cannot be executed (i.e., it is specified in some row of some structure a **true** value or a condition which results to **true**), then the method joins a queue from which it will be successively resumed following a discipline explained below, so halting the T_j execution. If the method can be executed, T_j is allowed to go on, while DM(O) partially evaluates the conditions under which some future methods may conflict with *m2* and possibly modifies $conflict_j$ by adding the new conditions in each row in logical disjunction. Obviously, the modified conditions can only be more restrictive. For example, if m2=ins(4) and $T_j = T_i$, the row of *member* in $conflict_i$ is modified and now holds the value **p=3 or p=4**.

Note that the evaluation of the conditions must not modify the state of *O* in any way. This means, for example, that, if a condition requires the invocation of some other method of the object itself, it is evaluated on a copy of the state obtained after the execution of the methods previously enabled by DM(O) (such copy is subsequently discarded).

Transaction T_i, upon its successful termination, sends a *commit* message to each object it has affected during its own execution; when each DataManager receives such a message from T_i it simply discards $conflict_i$, and updates the consistent state *of the object* to take into account the results of T_i. Successively each Data Manager inspects its waiting queue to verify if some method can now proceed because of the termination of conflicting methods. The Data Manager behaviour when a transaction aborts is explained in a following sub-section, where it will be also shown as transactions execution is guaranteed to be *recoverable*, i.e, the order in which transactions start is the same in which transactions commit.

The principal characteristics of the above implementation are the following:

i) Concurrency control is not centralised, but distributed in each object of the database.
ii) The code of the Data Manager is produced on compilation of each object and is standard, apart from the compatibility table which is derived from the object concurrent behaviour. If the concurrent behaviour of an object is empty, a default compatibility table is derived in which the non-conflicting methods are only the *read* methods. The distinction between *read* and *write* methods can be easily made by the compiler exploiting the method's code to see when instance variables are never assigned.
iii) Evaluations of conditions and methods executions can occur concurrently.

In the next sub-section, it will be shown that the Data Managers practically follow a 2PL protocol, and therefore that they correctly output only Δ-serialisable schedules.

5.3 Implementation correctness

With the previous implementation of the Data Manager, each transaction respects the following rules.

Compatibility Rule. A method *m*, required by a transaction T_i, can be executed on an object O iff, for each j≠i, $conflict(O)_j[m]$ evaluates to **false**.

Commitment Rule. For each transaction T_i and for each object O, $conflict\ (O)_i$ is created at the first method execution required on O from T_i, and is discarded only when T_i aborts or commits.

Thus a transaction, upon its successful termination, sends a *commit* message to each object it affected during its execution, and the Data Managers consider such a message as the termination of all the methods issued by the transaction. Only after its termination a transaction is considered to *release* the objects (more precisely the parts of the objects) which it *acquired* for its operations. This behaviour of transactions and Data Managers corresponds to two-phase transactions, and thus it can be proved to correctly output serialisable schedules in the context stated by the concurrent behaviour B, which is implemented by the compatibility tables of the objects.

Theorem 5.1. Each accepted output by the Data Managers is Δ-serialisable.

Proof sketch. Given a schedule S, a total order < on the transactions occurring in S can be defined, such that $T_i < T_j$ only if T_i commits before T_j : let us call S_S the serial schedule which respects such total order. We prove that, for each object O, S/O is B-equivalent to S_S/O, where B is the concurrent behaviour of O. S_S/O can be obtained from S/O by a sequence of intermediate schedules S_0 S_1..S_m, such that S_0=S/O, S_m= S_S/O and S_i is obtained from S_{i+1} by exchanging two near steps. We can prove that, because of the Commitment and Compatibility rules, $S_i \equiv_B S_{i+1}$ for each $0 \leq i \leq m-1$. By the transitive property of equivalence, we have S/O $\equiv_B$ S_S/O. Since this reasoning can be repeated for each object O, by definition of Δ-serialisability we have that S is Δ-serialisable.

The compatibility table of a type T', which is a sub-type of T, can be obtained by *inheriting* that of the super-type and by adding new rows and columns for the new methods of T'. The conditions of methods of T which are modified in the sub-type are substituted in the corresponding positions of the table. In some sense, the compatibility tables can be regarded as the code of methods and their actual values are determined at run-time depending on the most specific type of the object.

5.4 Recovery

We pay in this work less attention to recovery than to concurrency control, because of the philosophy of the approach which delegates to the user the responsibility to define her/his concept of correctness and of concurrency degree. As a consequence, it is again responsibility of the user to limit concurrency among methods with the purpose of avoiding an extensive use of cascading aborts. The system ensures only that transactions are *recoverable.* To obtain this result it must be guaranteed that transactions commit in the same order they initiate; this can be easily accomplished by interpreting the *commit* messages sent by the transactions as a *request* of commitment, so giving to the Data Managers the capability of allowing transactions to terminate in the correct ordering.

For what regard system failures, each transaction, when an error raises, sends an *abort* message to the Data Managers of all objects it has affected. Each DM(O), when it receives an *abort* message, restores a consistent state of *O* referred to the committed transactions only. Moreover, each DM(O) sends a message to all non-committed transactions which have read or written *O* to force them to abort.

6 Conclusions

We have proposed a linguistic mechanism to increase the degree of concurrency among transactions in an object-oriented language with inheritance and sub-typing. The proposal is based on the specification of the method commutativity in an object-type. We have shown that, with respect to this commutativity, there is no relation at the type system level between an object-type and its sub-types. Moreover, we have defined a formal model of correctness for our proposal. An implementation based on compatibility tables has been sketched, in which concurrency control of objects of a sub-type is done by late-binding of compatibility tables.

7 References

1. Skarra A.H., Zdonik S.B., "Concurrency Control and Object-Oriented Databases", in Object Oriented Concepts, Databases, and Applications, Kim W. and Lochovsky F.H. eds., ACM Press, (1989), pp.395-421.

2. Garcia-Molina H., "Using Semantic Knowledge for Transaction Processing in a Distributed Database", ACM Trans. on Database Systems, 8, 2 (June 1983), pp.186-213.

3. Korth, H. F., Speegle, G. D., "Formal model of correctness without Serialisability", SIGMOD-ACM, June 1-3, 1988, pp. 379-386.

4. Schwarz P.M. and Spector A.Z., "Synchronizing Shared Abstract Types", ACM ToCS, 2, 3 (Aug. 1984), pp. 223-250.

5. Weihl W.E., "Local Atomicity Properties: Modular Concurrency Control for Abstract Data Types", ACM ToPLaS, 11, 2 (April 1989), pp.249-283.

6. Herlihy, M.P., Weihl, W.E., "Hybrid Concurrency Control for Abstract Data Types", Journal of Computer and System Science 43, 25-61, 1991.

7. De Francesco, N., Vaglini, G.,"An axiomatic approach to Concurrency Control", submitted for publication.

8. Bondavalli, A., De Francesco, N., Latella, D., Vaglini, G., "Shared abstract data types: an algebraic methodology for their specification", MFDBS-89, LNCS 364, Budapest, June 26-July 1, 1989, pp.53-67.

9. Albano, A., Ghelli, G. and Orsini, R. "Objects for a database programming language", 3rd International Workshop on Database Programming Languages, Napflion, Greece, August 1991.

10. Papadimitriou C.H., "The Theory of Database Concurrency Control", Computer Science Press, Oakville, Maryland, 1986.

11. Bernstein P.A., Hadzilacos V. and Goodman N., "Concurrency Control and Recovery in Database Systems", Addison-Wesley, Reading, Mass 1987.

12. Goldberg A. and Robson D., "Smalltalk-80: the language and its implementation", Addison-Wesley, 1983.

13. Korth, H. F., "Locking primitives in a Database System", Journal ACM, 30, 1 (Jan. 1983), pp. 55-79.

Nested Actions in Eos

Laurent Daynès, Olivier Gruber
Projet Rodin, INRIA
Rocquencôurt 78153 Le Chesnay Cedex, France
{daynes,gruber}@rodin.inria.fr

Abstract

Persistent and distributed object systems have to cope with chaos resulting of concurrent accesses and failures. This suggests the properties of atomicity, isolation and persistence of effects. This paper presents the Eos action model which is an interpretation of Moss's model. We focus on Eos's efficient support for nested isolation which upholds an adaptive granule of locking based on complex objects. In particular, we formalize nested isolation based on set and tree theory. This approach leads to an efficient implementation in the context of a distributed single-level store. First measurements showed encouraging performance of Eos that seems to outperform largely existing systems providing nested actions. Finally, we propose a simple criterion to order conflicting actions, avoiding false conflicts and therefore enhancing parallelism.

1 Introduction

Persistent object systems have to deal with chaos resulting from uncontrolled sharing of data and failures. Nested transactions are advocated for this purpose [9, 18, 19, 2]. However, nested transactions are said to be expensive.

The overhead has two origins. One is inherent to nested models which provide several levels of atomicity and isolation. In other words, nesting may yield repetitive locking and logging costs on the same data item. This overhead is structural, i.e., it is dependent upon the way data items are manipulated within a hierarchy of actions. Therefore, it is application-dependent.

The other overhead is an added complexity of the internal management of locks and logs. This is an implementation-dependent overhead which decomposes as follows.

- More complex conflict detection.
- Complexified awaking condition of actions.
- Increased complexity of log structure (multi-level undoability).
- Repetitive inheritance and anti-inheritance[1].

[1] Inheritance and anti-inheritance, also called downward and upward inheritance in literatures, name the lock and log flows going up or downward the action tree. This is detailed later in this paper.

In this paper, we propose a new implementation of traditional nested transaction models. Our purpose is **not** to propose a new model of transactions. On the contrary, we only interpret the Moss or Argus models somewhat differently in order to come up with an efficient implementation. The first contribution is an expression of the rules of lock inheritance and anti-inheritance which is based on set theory. The second contribution is an efficient implementation in a distributed environment.

Our implementation supports a model of nested actions with sibling parallelism as in [10]. Therefore, it permits to take advantage of distributed architecture abilities for function shipping parallelism.

This work is part of the Eos system [4] which is a general-purpose programming environment for building multi-user softwares that need sharing, persistence and distribution capabilities. Our fast implementation is particularly adapted to such environments by reducing to a minimum the locking and logging overhead in single-level distributed stores. This paper focuses on locking overhead only due to space limitation.

The paper is structured as follows. Section 2 presents our new understanding of nested transaction model. Section 3 introduces the new set of rules for nested isolation. Section 4 details Eos's implementation of nested isolation. Section 5 presents performance measurements and Section 6 concludes.

2 Eos Model

This section presents our data model and our nested action model. Our interpretation of the Moss model distinguishes the properties of transactions : persistence of effects, atomicity, and isolation as advocated in [14]. This distinction permits to treat each property independently and enables a modular design. This section further introduces our terminology.

2.1 Store and Data Model

The Eos system provides a distributed persistent store over a distributed architecture. The hardware platform is a local area network (LAN) of workstations, called nodes. The store is fragmented over the nodes, i.e., each of them has a disjoint part of it. A function shipping paradigm is applied to access remote data.

Locally, on each node, Eos uses a single-level store approach to provide access to the local part of the store. The rationale is efficiency [1]. The store is implemented using a micro-kernel technology. Mach 3.0 from CMU [20] has been chosen, but Chorus would have been as well adapted [17]. The corner stone is of the implementation is the Mach memory object abstraction [21].

Today, systems which manipulate persistent data through a single-level store [7, 6] support page-based locking. The rationale is the little overhead induced by a page-based locking. However, locking at a coarser granule than the unit of sharing (e.g page locking wrt object sharing) causes false conflicts, which in turn may degenerate in false deadlocks. In this context, the correctness of a program with respect to deadlocks is related to the actual grouping of objects within pages. Correctness is therefore non deterministic if objects can be moved. This is illustrated in Figure 1. If one program (A) reads the white objects and another (B) writes the black ones, a deadlock occurs if both access their first object and then access the other one.

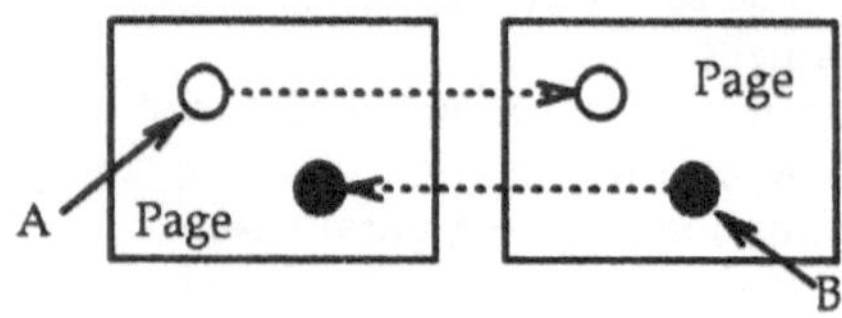

Figure 1: False Deadlock

This non-determinism makes page-based locking unsuitable for persistent object systems. Persistent object systems are general-purpose platforms for the development of complex concurrent applications such as CAD/CAM systems which requires a predictable concurrency control. We therefore advocate that grouping and locking issues should be kept orthogonal.

Orthogonality suggests an object locking granularity where object refers to programming language entities. However, such a fine grain locking may increase significantly and unnecessarily the concurrency control overhead. Therefore, we advocate for a hierarchical locking based on the following data model.

The store manages *quark objects*. Quark objects are the unit of allocation and access. The store further imposes that quark objects be smaller than a page size. Quark objects are aggregated into disjoint complex graphs. Each graph is called a *nucleon objects* and has a single entry point called a root object. Nucleon objects can be themselves aggregated into arbitrarily complex structures. Nucleon objects never share quark objects, but only their root object. Our data model is depicted in Figure 2.

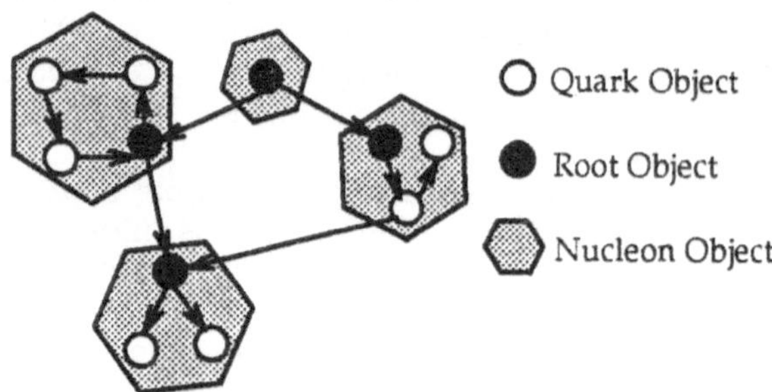

Figure 2: Eos Data Model.

The store supports different granules for locking and logging while retaining a concurrency control which is deterministic. Nucleon objects are the granule of locking while the quark objects are the granule of logging. The rationale is that a coarse granule of locking is needed to reduce concurrency control overhead, while a fine granule of logging is necessary for reducing logging overhead. Logging overhead is reduced by a small granule because large objects are often scarcely modified. Moreover, a fine granule of allocation and aggregation upholds the necessary flexibility of the store.

2.2 Nested Model

Our nested model includes the notion of actions which can be nested to arbitrarily depth. An action is a sequential thread of execution, executed on a single node. A node is defined as an entity composed of one or more processors sharing primary memory and disks. Nodes are interconnected through a local area network. Actions are the basic unit of concurrent execution.

Actions are isolated and atomic. Isolated means serializable. Atomic means an action either completes successfully or has no effect at all, even in presence of failures and deadlocks. Atomicity and isolation are traditionally ensured through locking and logging. Note that node-local actions provide node independency with respect to failures.

Actions can be nested in two ways. An action may call **synchronously** (resp. **asynchronously**) one or more subactions in parallel using specific constructs like co-begin [10]. A call is said synchronous (resp. asynchronous) when the caller waits (resp. does not wait) until the completion of all callees. Synchronously called subactions are termed *concurrent actions*.

Hierarchies of concurrent actions are termed action hierarchies. An *action hierarchy* is a sphere of isolation and atomicity. In other words, action hierarchies introduce a recursive nesting of spheres of isolation and atomicity based on synchronous calls of actions. Asynchronous calls create new action hierarchies. Action model is depicted in Figure 3.

Our model distinguishes atomicity from persistence of effects. We define an *activity* as the unit of durability with respect to failure. An activity contains a single action hierarchy and is durable. In other words, activity effects are resilient to failure once the activity is committed.

Our model is equivalent to Moss's nested model extended with the top-level call of Argus. An activity with its enclosed action hierarchy is equivalent in effect to a transaction, i.e., it is ACID[2][5]. Actions of an action hierarchy are equivalent to subtransactions in Moss model which are allowed to execute in parallel, their parent awaiting their completion. Asynchronous calls of actions are equivalent to top-level calls of Argus [10].

3 Support of Nested Isolation

Actions are isolated entities which can be nested, thereby introducing nested isolation and atomicity. This section presents our support for such nesting of

[2]The C property (consistent) requires a user-supplied meaning though, and is rather a responsibility of the client of the system, not of the system itself.

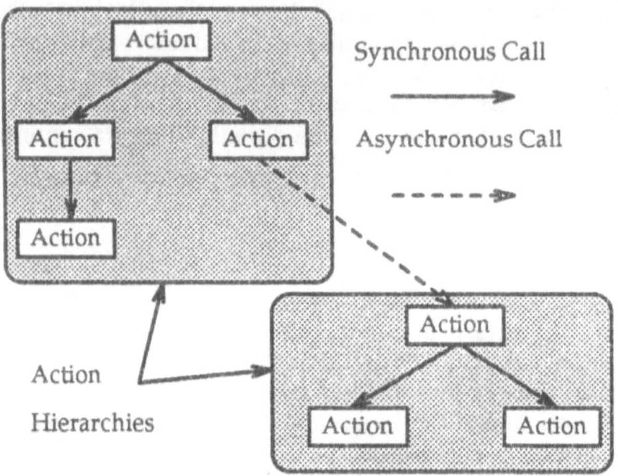

Figure 3: Action Model

isolation properties. It is based on inheritance and anti-inheritance of locks along the hierarchy of synchronous calls of actions. Our rules of inheritance and anti-inheritance derive from [13].

In the following, we use the classical tree terminology to describe action relationship within action hierarchies. Actions having called concurrent actions are termed parents, and the callee actions are called children. We will also speak of ancestors and superiors. The ancestor (resp. superior) of a given action is the reflexive (resp. non-reflexive) transitive closure of parent.

We formalize lock management based on tree and set theories. Lock management includes conflict detection, commit, and rescheduling of pending actions. This formalization aims at permitting a fast implementation.

Here is some more terminology about locks and actions. When a lock is granted to an action, the action is said to be a *holder*. Later, when a holder action commits, it releases all its locks which are *anti-inherited* by its parent action, if any. The parent is said to *retain the lock*. Locks may be granted in some cases to an action albeit they are currently held or retained in incompatible mode by its superiors. This is called inheritance of locks. If a lock is inherited, its requester becomes a holder and the current retainers/holders actions remain so.

3.1 Action Information

Each action is uniquely identified throughout the system. The immediate parent identity is returned by the function $Parent()$. The complete ancestor set is returned by $Ancestors()$. The complete superior set is returned by $Superiors()$.

We further define the concept of *leaf-active actions* on a given object. An *active action* for a given object is an action which is not suspended on the lock of that object. A leaf-active action is a running active action which has currently no children (concurrent actions).

3.2 Lock Information

Lock management can be expressed using simple information associated to objects. For each object, we keep a couple of *owner action* sets. We define a *owner action* as either a holder or a retainer action. One owner set corresponds to owners in a read mode (noted R_{owners}) and the other to owners in a write mode (noted W_{owners}). In those two sets, retainers and holders are not differentiated.

The $leafSet()$ notation indicates for a given lock which set of owner actions holds leaf-active actions. One can remark that all leaf-active actions upon an object belong to only one owner set at a given instant. In other words, an object is accessed concurrently by leaf actions in a single mode: read or write.

3.3 Conflict Detection

We now give the rules for the detection of conflicts between concurrent actions. Note that these rules work only in the case of no parent/child parallelism.

- **Conflict detection on a read lock request.**

  An action which requests a read lock, noted requester, does not conflict with the current lock settings if all write holders and write retainers of the lock are ancestors of the requester.

  $$W_{owners} \subset Ancestors(requester)$$

- **Conflict detection on a write lock request (including the upgrade case).**

  An action requesting a write lock does not conflict with the current lock settings if all holders and retainers of the lock are ancestors of the requesting action.

  $$(W_{owners} \bigcup R_{owners}) \subset Ancestors(requester)$$

3.4 Scheduling of Actions

Nested actions with sibling parallelism introduce a more complex scheduling of actions than flat models. In a flat model, transactions are granted a lock in their order of arrival. The goal pursued is fairness and that simple policy copes because all transactions are equivalent. However, actions are not all equivalent in a nested model because of inheritance and anti-inheritance of locks. Treating all actions as equivalent would lead to hierarchical deadlocks.

Hierarchical deadlocks might appear upon a single object. A hierarchical deadlock exist if all the owners of a lock are retainers and suspended, awaiting the completion of one or more of their child actions. However, these child actions are pending down the queue of this same locks after some actions that cannot be granted the lock because they conflict. This is depicted in Figure 4, where the action A retains the lock, and the action B conflicts and is first in the queue.

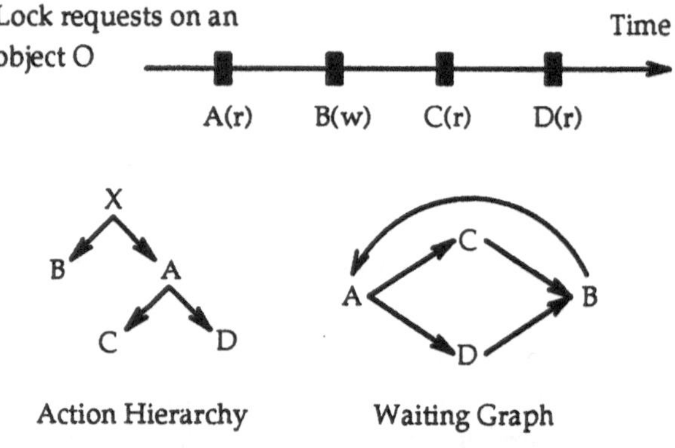

Figure 4: Hierarchical Deadlock

The solution to hierarchical deadlocks is to order the queue based on the hierarchical relationship between actions. Each action requesting a lock inserts itself correctly in the ordered queue of that lock based on the following criterion. This criterion involves the actual owner actions of the lock, the requesting action noted A_r, and a pending one noted A_p, and is based on the path of superiors which are common between action A_i ($i \in \{p, r\}$) and actual owners. These paths are denoted SA_i. The formal definition of SA_i is given below, following by an example of such SA_i given in Figure 5.

$$Owners = W_{owners} \bigcup R_{owners}$$

$$SA_i = \{Superiors(A_i) \bigcap (\bigcup_{\forall O \in Owners} Superiors(O))\}$$

The criterion for queue ordering is based on the comparison of SA_r with each SA_p. For each couple (A_r, A_p) there are five cases.

1. Both A_r and A_p request read locks, A_r should jump to check the next pending writer.

2. $SA_r \subset SA_p$

   The action A_p should be first in the queue.

3. $SA_p \subset SA_r$

   The action A_r should be first in the queue.

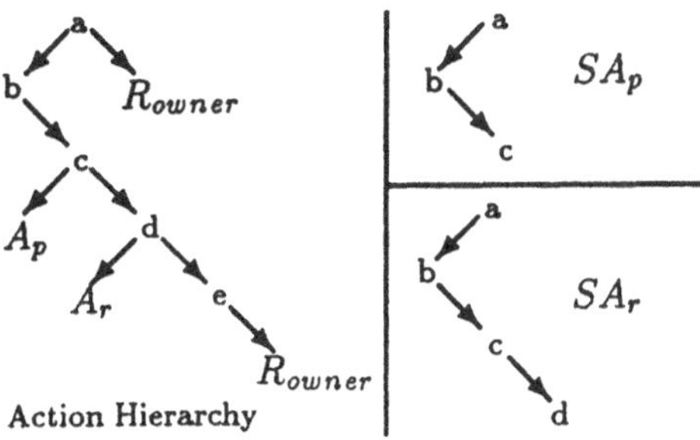

Figure 5: Example of SA

4. $SA_r = SA_p$

   There is no special order imposed by the hierarchy of actions, therefore, the order of arrival should be used to have a fair behavior.

5. $SA_r \neg \subset SA_p \; and \; SA_r \neg \subset SA_p$

   This case suggests a read state for the lock since two concurrent actions have to be owners and the read state is the only state permitting parallelism.

   - Write/write. This corresponds to the case of a true deadlock when a double upgrade occur.
   - Read/write. The read action should be first.

Once the queue is ordered, there is no longer the possibility of a hierarchical deadlock. The first in the queue is the first that can be granted the lock. Due to space limitation, we do not include the proof of the ordering criterion. Intuitively, the SA_i express how close to actual owners actions A_i are. The closer among two actions will be the first structurally able to inherit the lock, i.e the first schedulable and therefore should appear before in the queue.

3.5 Action Commit/Abort

We now present a second set of rules which describe the effect on locks of the completion of an action. An action completes either by aborting or committing. Only leaf-active action can complete, since non-leaf actions have to wait for the completion of their children before they can themselve complete.

- **Action commit (anti-inheritance of locks).**

  When an action, denoted by A_c, commits, its parent, if any, anti-inherits all its locks, both retained and hold ones. The code to anti-inherit a lock follows. The $\ominus$ sign denotes the set substraction.

if ($leafSet()$ is W_{owners})

$$W_{owners} = (W_{owners} \ominus A_c) \bigcup Parent(A_c)$$
$$R_{owners} = R_{owners} \ominus Parent(A_c)$$

else if ($Parent(A_c) \subset W_{owners}$)

$$R_{owners} = R_{owners} \ominus A_c$$

else

$$R_{owners} = (R_{owners} \ominus A_c) \bigcup Parent(A_c)$$

endif

This code works under the following assumption:

$A_c \in W_{owners} \Rightarrow A_c \notin R_{owners}$

$A_c \in R_{owners} \Rightarrow A_c \notin W_{owners}$

- **Action abort.**

  When an action, denoted by A_a, aborts, it releases all its locks. I.e., for each lock it own, the aborting action withdraws itself from the owner sets.

$$leafSet() = leafSet() \ominus A_a$$

Recall that $leafSet()$ notation denotes for a lock which set of owner actions holds leaf-active actions.

4 Implementation of Nested Isolation

This section presents our implementation of nested isolation. An implementation of nested isolation has to answer the following issues.

- Localization of the lock of an object.
- Mutual exclusion between actions to avoid concurrent manipulation locks.
- Conflict detection in a nested model.
- Action Completion (abort/commit).

Following subsections cover each of these issues.

4.1 Lock Localization

Objects are directly manipulated by actions in their virtual space. Moreover, object reference is supported through a single-level addressing scheme which means the use of virtual memory addresses plus a forwarding mechanism [3]. Hence, the lock of an object has to be located given the virtual address of that object.

Speed is crucial for several reasons. The number of locks manipulated by an Eos program is likely to be greater than in existing systems which use page locking because Eos locking granule is likely to be smaller than a page. Remark though that it can be also wider than a page since nucleon objects are not bounded to a page size. Moreover, the number of lock manipulations per lock is also likely to be greater within a store which interface is a general-purpose programming language [16].

The speed constraint is to be as close as possible to native non concurrent programming languages. Indeed, locking overhead should not spoil the advantages of single-level store and single-level addressing schemes. Therefore, this forbids complex access structures to locate a lock. A simple solution would be to include the lock within the object itself. However, this solution is out of consideration. Locks are always updated regardless of the access mode (read or write). Hence, if locks were stored along with objects, read-only actions would dirty all object pages. Dirty pages reduce system throughput since they have to be written back on secondary storage.

Our solution is to access object locks via a simple indirection. This is implemented as follows. A virtual page is associated with a lock table. This table has one entry (lock) per root object within the page. Furthermore, each root object has a sequence number in its page. The lock of a root object is accessed as follows. The address of the lock table is red from the page header. Then, the sequence number of the object is used as an index within the table.

The lock tables and sequence numbers are managed by the Eos external pager which supports the mapped object store. Each mapped region of a virtual space in the Mach 3.0 may be associated an external pager. An external pager provides the kernel with pages needed to service page faults in the associated region, and also takes care of pages which are flushed out from the cache. This external pager is a user-defined process in Mach 3.0 which enables Eos to have a certain control.

Upon the first fault on a page, the external pager reads the page from the disk in a buffer, allocates a lock table in the kernel region, and sets the address of this table within the page header. The kernel region holds system data needed to manage user ones. The page is finally provided to the micro-kernel so it can install it in the cache and resume the faulting threads.

Later, the micro-kernel will flush the page out of the cache. The micro-kernel is forced to notify[3] flushed pages to the external pager so that lock table deallocation can take place. Upon the notification of a flushed page, the state of the lock table of that page is tested. If no lock is actually owned, the lock table is deallocated.

---

[3]This is done using Mach 3.0 *precious pages* [15].

The sequence number of root objects are managed in order to avoid internal fragmentation of lock tables. I.e., the size of lock tables matches the exact number of root objects within the corresponding page. Numbers of root objects within a page are re-sequenced when the page is flushed out, if some of them have been collected. Therefore, lock tables are never created with holes.

4.2 Mutual Exclusion

Mutual exclusion is necessary to control concurrent manipulations of locks by different actions. Again, speed is crucial since this mutual exclusion is around each lock manipulation which are themselves in the critical path of most object accesses. Moreover, the solution has to work in a multi-processor environment since small-scale multi-processors are likely to be the next generation of workstations.

Mutual exclusion yields two questions. The first one is which granularity of mutual exclusion? The page sounds a natural granule in a small-scale multiprocessors because the loss of parallelism should not be noticeable since the mutual exclusion is very short. The second question is how is mutual exclusion achieved?

Test and set is now a common assembler instruction in a wide variety of processor, it is fast and requires only one machine word of storage. For long, test-and-set instruction has been known to have poor performance in multiprocessors. This is no longer true though [12, 11].

However, test-and-set operations may significantly increase paging in persistent systems. Each test-and-set operation upon a memory word dirties the page it is in. Hence, if test-and-set operations are applied directly on store pages, paging is drastically increased. Similarly to locks, test-and-set words should be outside data pages. A natural location which still enables a fast access is in the lock table.

However, this location introduces a critical section between locking code and lock table deallocation in the external pager. The problem is the following. The address of the lock is red from the page header, but the couple (page,lock table) is not pinned in memory. Hence, the page can be flushed out by the cache replacement policy. This is unlikely, but possible. When the external pager is notified of this flush, it may decide to deallocated the lock table if it is empty. In such an event, the address red from the page header is now a dangling address.

Our current solution is to introduce a cooperation between the locking code and the lock table management. First of all, we split lock tables into headers and arrays of locks. The header is a small fixed-size structure composed of the test-and-set word, the virtual address of its associated page, and the address of the lock array. Headers have a specific allocator using a free list approach for keeping track of deallocated header. Place holders are used in place of deallocated headers with their page virtual address set to nil. Hence, an address of a header is never dangling, but at least always points to a place holder that can be identified as so.

In this context, the cooperation required is the following. The locking code,

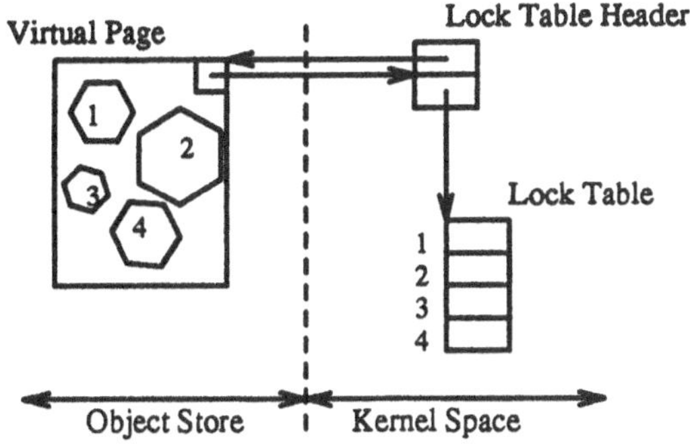

Figure 6: Locking Environment

once it red the lock table address and took the mutual exclusion around that table, tests the page address stored in the table header against the one it thinks it should be. If there is a mismatch, it means the page has been flushed out and the table deallocated. Therefore, the locking code loops and attempts to re-read the table address in the virtual page. Since the page is flushed out, a page fault occurs which is forwarded to the Eos external pager. It then re-allocates a new lock table (header and lock array), sets the table header address in the page header, and provides the page. Then, normal execution resumes. The external pager for itself has to obtain the mutual exclusion upon a lock table before it can deallocated it. The pseudo-code is given in Section 7.

4.3 Lock Information

The implementation of locks subsumes in an efficient support of action sets based on the formalization of Section 3. Efficient in terms of space but primarily with respect to operations: $\cup, \cap, \subset$, which are needed for the conflict detection, inheritance, and anti-inheritance of locks.

Bitmaps support efficiently small sets and the above operations. Each element of a set is assigned a bit number. If the bitmap is small, this bit allocation is fast. Moreover, the aforementioned operations are respectively implemented with the simple logical operations: $OR, AND, (\alpha OR \beta) = \beta$.

However, bitmaps are unable to support large system-wide sets of actions. Indeed, if a bit is reserved per action, the bitmap size will soon induce an unacceptable space and time overhead per lock since the bitmap size should be equal to the maximum number of possible actions. This is unrealistic.

A solution is to use bitmaps to only support sets of actions known locally at a single node. This approach reduces greatly the number of bits necessary within a large-scale distributed systems. This works as follows. Each node manages a local mapping between system-wide identifiers of actions it is aware of and bit numbers. In other words, only actions known locally on a node are assigned a bit number. The bit number of an action is called the mapping of that action. This is depicted in Figure 7 where an action has "j" as its identifier and "i" as its mapping and also holds a lock on objects one and three.

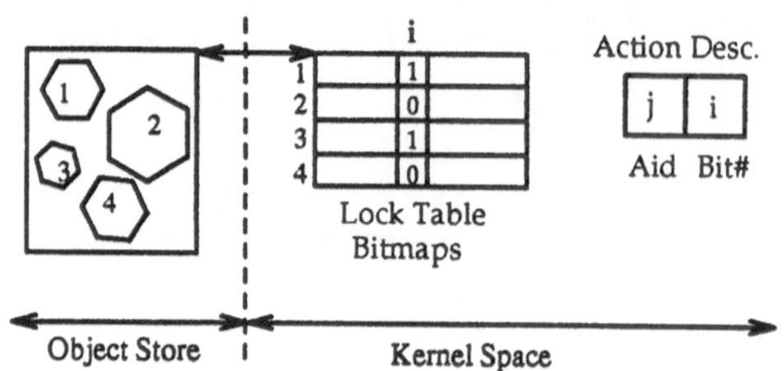

Figure 7: Action Mapping

System-wide action identifiers are integer. Their allocation scheme is derived from the one used for page allocation in the IVY system [8]. That is, each node has a reserved range of integers from which it can allocate identifier without involving any distributed protocol.

Given that action sets are represented by bitmaps using local mappings, we now presents the necessary information to achieve concurrency control. Recall that a lock is a couple of owner action sets: R_{Owners}, W_{Owners}. Therefore, each lock has two bitmaps, one for each set. To detect conflicts based on the rules given in Section 3, actions should store the knowledge of their ancestors. Therefore, each action keeps the identity and local mapping of all its ancestors.

4.4 Conflict Detection

The general sketch of a conflict detection is the following. An action which desire a lock on an object has to run the algorithm given in Section 7.

The major costs in conflict detection are in the manipulation of owner sets. Therefore, efficiency calls for small bitmaps upon which the $\cup, \cap, \subset$ operations are fast. However, the bitmap size limits the maximum number of mapping allowed on a node. These two objectives clearly conflicts. We propose a solution which enables fast manipulations of small bitmaps but enables them to grow when needed. In other words, locking supplies a pay-as-you-go behavior.

The idea is to adapt the C++ virtual method mechanism to be able to dynamically change the representation of bitmaps. Two representations for bitmaps are provided. A small one that fits into the lock array when few mappings are needed. It only takes one or two couple of words and further permits very fast manipulations. And an extended representation, allocated outside the lock array, which copes with wider mappings but with reduced performance.

Lock manipulations are encapsulated in methods. There is a virtual table per method which points to both version of the codes: for small or overflowed bitmaps. Moreover, each lock has a state byte that indicates if its bitmap is overflowed or not. This lock state is used as an index in virtual tables to apply the correct code.

This approach is adapted to load balanced systems where all nodes have an average number of actions. In that case, nodes will have all their lock in compact representation and will run full speed. Although, overloaded nodes will degrade nicely since only locks effectively manipulated by too much actions will overflow.

4.5 Commit

The completion of an action necessitates the knowledge of all its locks. To commit, an action has to make its locks anti-inherited by its parent, or to release them if it has no parent. To abort, an action has to undo all its effects both on objects and lock settings.

Each action maintain this knowledge of all its locks. This set of locks is called the *locking set* of an action. For space and time reasons, each action maintains only a stack of the addresses of lock tables where it has locks. This stack of table addresses will be subsequently called the locking set of an action by assimilation.

The locking set is kept without double so that each lock table is processed only once when the action completes. This is easily achieved by maintaining in each lock table a set of actions which have at least one lock in that table. This set is called the *locker set*. Hence, when an action gets a lock, it checks if it appears in the locker set. If it does not, it adds the table address to its locking set and adds itself to the locker set of that table. The locking set of an action is depicted in Figure 8.

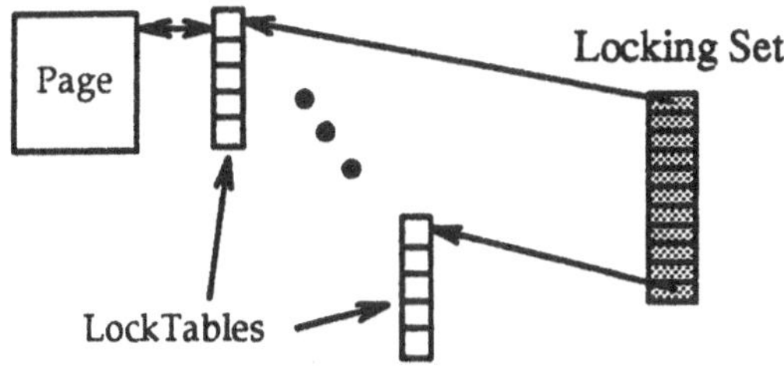

Figure 8: Locking Set

An action completes by scanning all the lock tables of its locking set. For each lock of these tables, the action checks if it is in one of the owner sets. If it appears to be in one of the sets, the correct action is undertaken: anti-inheritance of the lock or undo.

When a lock is anti-inherited by a parent action from a child one, two things have to be done.

- The setting of the lock has to be changed.
- The locking set of the parent has to be maintained up-to-date.

The setting of the lock has to be changed to reflect that the lock is now retained by the parent and released by the child. Hence, the bitmaps representing the owner sets have to be modified: removing the bit of the child and setting the bit of the parent.

The second point was to maintain up-to-date the locking set of the parent. The invariant of the locking set of an action is that it should contains all the table addresses where that action has at least one lock. Hence, when a parent action anti-inherits a lock, this lock may be in a new lock table which does not appear in its locking set. Hence, this has to be checked and the table address added if necessary. The check is easy using locker sets of lock tables.

One can remark that having separated lock tables from data pages enables actions to commit without accessing data pages. Hence, data pages can be replaced freely in the cache based on any replacement policy without endangering faults at commit time.

Eos system is distributed which complexifies commit. Actions are local to a node, but a hierarchy can be distributed. Therefore, the parent and the child might be running on two different nodes. This raises two problems.

- The parent has no local mapping.
- The locking set has to be maintained.

Since the parent action does not run on the child node, it is unknown and has no mapping. However, the anti-inheritance of locks necessitates the parent mapping. Our solution is to give the parent the mapping of the committing child. Hence, there is nothing to do to anti-inherit locks: the commit is free with respect to lock anti-inheritance! This may be impossible if the parent has already a mapping locally because another of its child action has already committed on that node. In which case, the normal anti-inheritance rule is applied.

The locking set of an action is now distributed. A parent action which has remote child actions will anti-inherit their locks on their remote nodes. Hence, its locking set is fragmented onto these nodes. This is depicted in Figure 9. The first time a remote parent anti-inherits locks from a child on a node, the locking set of the child is simply given to its parent by a pointer play. Next times, a merge has to take place to eliminate double which requires to check the locker sets of all the tables as stated above.

To summarize, our mechanism provides a free anti-inheritance of locks in the case of a distributed action hierarchy with no more than one action per node. Otherwise, a scan of the lock tables for a bit play is necessary.

5 Performance Measurements

This section presents some measurements we made to evaluate the overhead of nested locking within an object-oriented programming language. All objects

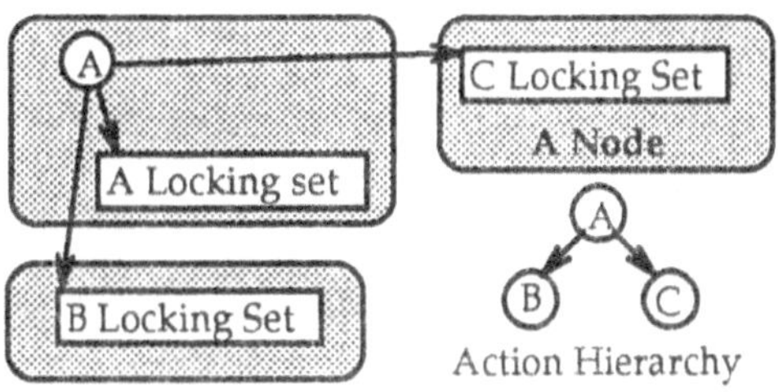

Figure 9: Distributed Locking Set

are in memory and logging is turned off. We made two different sets of measurements. The first set permits to compare Eos with other object-oriented programming systems that include nested actions like Argus [9] and Camelot [2]. The second set of measures show a comparison between Eos and native C++ in order to evaluate the locking negative effect on performance that we will term from now *slowdown*.

5.1 Argus/Camelot Comparison

We compare Eos to Argus and Camelot which are two programming environments that provide nested atomicity. These two systems provides equal functionalities and therefore a comparison basis for Eos. The comparison is around the locking and commit costs. Measurements show that Eos is faster on slightly slower hardware (sun3/60 compared to MicroVax and IBM RT).

The results of pure locking are given in the Table below along with Argus and Camelot results. There are four basic measures in nested locking scheme: acquiring, inheriting, anti-inheriting, and releasing a lock. The time for each measure is decomposed into the localization and Test-and-Set time for a lock table (LTAS), the update of the lock owner set (LOU), the update of the set of touched lock tables (TLT).

	LTAS	LOU	TLT	Global Time	Argus	Camelot[a]
Acquiring	0.7 μ	22.4μ	22.9μ	46μ	200μ	210μ
Inheriting	0.7 μ	44.6μ	22.9μ	67μ	-	330μ
Anti-Inheriting	-	41.8μ	-	41.8μ	290μ	330μ
Release	-	23.5μ	-	23.5μ	210μ	180μ

[a]Performance of local locking, no communication across the network with a lock server.

5.2 C++ Comparison

The idea here is to modelize a "standard" C++ program and to evaluate the slowdown due to locking. By standard, we mean that object sizes and method number of instructions correspond to most class and method definitions. Based

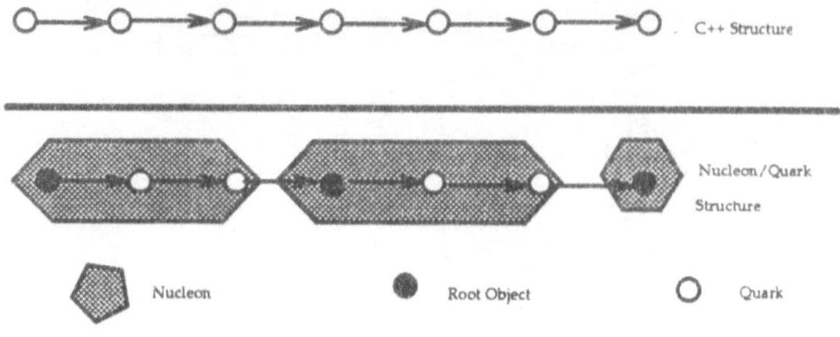

Figure 10: Structuring Using Nucleons and Quarks

on Smalltalk statistics we adopted a granule of 32 Bytes for objects. Based on the R. Cattel benchmark for object-oriented databases we adopted an empty method call per object.

The benchmarks we used is rather simple. Objects are structured in a list which is scanned. On each object of the list, the scan invokes an empty method. Table below presents the execution time of the corresponding program in pure C++ and the same program including nested locking.

	# of Objects	Exec Time	Commit Time	Total Time
Pure C++	40000	240000μ	none	240000μ
Eos	40000	2341000μ	1223000μ	3564000μ
Ratio	1	9.75	∞	14.85

The slowdown due to nested locking is 14.85. This is a significant slowdown but not unacceptable though. The slowdown can be drastically reduced through Eos dual data model. Basically the idea is the following. By structuring his or her objects into nucleons and quarks, a programmer can reduce the number of locks taken and therefore reduce the overhead of locking. The counter part is a potential loss of parallelism.

To show the benefit of nucleon/quark structuring, we made the following measurements. The pure C++ program was kept untouched. Its version with locking was modified to introduce nucleons and quarks. The total number of objects scanned and invoked was unchanged, so the program essence was unchanged. However, we created nucleons made of a varying number of quarks which reduced the number of locks by increasing the granule of locking. The structuration in nucleons and quarks is depicted in Figure 10. The Table below shows the evolution of the slowdown when the number of quark objects per nucleon is increased. Each quark is an object of 32 Bytes as before.

# of Quarks	1	2	4	8	16
Nucleon Size	32	64	128	256	512
# of Nucleon	40000	20000	10000	5000	2500
Slowdown	14.85	8.51	4.84	2.93	1.95

The above slowdown measures are made without taking into account the locality of locking within pages. They have been made with one hundred percent of object locked per page.

The above measurements are quite encouraging. The ratios between pure C++ and locking-extended C++ are significant but quite acceptable. Of course, these measurements only aim at providing a first insight of performance that can be obtained. More complex applications have to be made concurrent and slowdown evaluated. The impact of the locking locality, i.e. the ratio of locked objects by the total number of objects per page, has to be taken into account. However, we believe the order of magnitude is correct.

6 Conclusion

This paper presented an interpretation of Moss's model of nested transactions. We focused on nested isolation only with the following contributions. A formalization of locking rules based on set and tree theory. This formalization further permitted to propose for the first time an ordering criterion for actions awaiting in a lock pending queue. The consequence is that hierarchical deadlocks are avoided and therefore intra-hierarchy parallelism is enhanced. Finally, our formalization allowed an efficient implementation.

Nested locking in Eos outperforms existing programming languages which provide nested actions like Argus [9] or Camelot [2]. Furthermore, Eos performance are even comparable to pure C++ through the benefits of its dual data model. The duality of nucleon and quark objects enables adaptive granularity of locking without the problems of physical hierarchical locking. Performance measurements suggest that the nucleon/quark data model is a promising way to integrate nested locking in traditional programming languages with minimal performance loss. We are currently working in that direction.

7 Pseudo Code

```
object::Acquire_Table_TAS()
{
  // Pointer on the page header.
  Page_Header_t * page_hdr;

  // Deduce page virtual address from
  // object address.
  page_hdr = mask(this);
  table_hdr = page_hdr→table_hdr;

  // Acquire the Test_And_Set in the table
  // header.
  test_and_set(table_hdr→TAS_word);

  // Check mismatch bewteen page addresses.
  while(table_hdr→page_hdr != page_hdr) {

  // Release Test_And_Set.
  release_TAS(table_header→TAS_word);

  // Re-read : fault : re-acquire Test_And_Set.
  table_hdr = page_hdr→table_hdr;
  test_and_set(table_header→TAS_word);
  }
}
```

```
IFthere are pending actions
  Insert myself correctly in the ordered
  queue.
  IFI am on the top of the queue
    Check if I conflict with the lock
    setting.
    IF there are no conflicts
    Adds myself in the correct owner set
    with respect to the requested mode
    for the lock.
  ELSE
    Get asleep.
  FI
  ELSE
    Get asleep.
  FI
ELSE check conflict
  IF there are no conflicts
    Add myself in the correct owner set
    with respect to the lock mode
    requested
  ELSE
    Inserts myself on top of the queue,
    and go to sleep.
  FI
FI
```

Acknowledgements We are especially grateful to Eric Amiel for its interest in our work, wise comments, and efforts in measuring the system. We also thank Laurent Amsaleg for its useful comments. Finally, we would like to acknowledge the continous encouragements of Patrick Valduriez in regards of Eos becoming.

References

[1] G. Copeland, M. Franklin, and G. Weikum. Uniform Object Management. In *Proc. of the Int. Conf. on Extended Database Technology*, Venice, Italy, 1990.

[2] J. Eppinger, L. Mummert, and A. Spector. *Camelot and Avalon*. Morgan Kaufmann, 1991.

[3] R. J. Fowler. The complexity of using forwarding addresses for decentralized object finding. In *Proc. of the Fifth SIGACT/SIGOPS Conf. on the Principles of Distributed Computation*. SIGACT/SIGOPS, August 1986.

[4] O. Gruber, L. Amsaleg, L. Daynès, and P. Valduriez. Eos, An Environment for Object-Based Systems. In *Proc. of the 25th Hawaii International Conference on System Sciences*, volume 1, pages 757–768, January 1992.

[5] T. Haerder and A. Reuter. Principles of transaction oriented database recovery. *ACM Computing Surveys*, 15, 1983.

[6] B. Koch and al. Cache coherence and storage management in a persistent object system. In *Fourth International Workshop on Persistent Object System*, 1990.

[7] C. Lamb, G. Landis, J. Orenstein, and D. Weinreb. The Object Store Database system. *In Communications of the ACM*, 34(10):51, October 1991.

[8] K. Li. IVY : a shared virtual memory system for parallel computing. *In Proc. of the Int. Conf. on Parallel Processing*, August 1988.

[9] B. Liskov, D. Curtis, P. Johnson, and R. Scheifler. Implementation of Argus. In *ACM Transactions on Programming Languages and Systems*, Cambridge, Ma, 1987.

[10] B. Liskov and R. Scheifler. Guardians and Actions : Linguistic support for robust, distributed programs. In *ACM Transactions on Programming Languages and Systems*. ACM, July 1983.

[11] J. M. Mellor-Crummey and M. L. Scott. Algorithms for scalable synchronization on shared-memory multiprocessors. *ACM Trans. Comput. Syst.*, 9(1):21–65, February 1991.

[12] J. M. Mellor-Crummey and M. L. Scott. Synchronization without contention. In *ASPLOS, International Conf. on Architectural Support for Programming Languages and Operating Systems*, pages 269–278, Santa Clara, CA (USA), April 1991.

[13] J. Moss. *Nested Transactions : An Approach to Reliable Distributed Computing.* MIT Press, 1985.

[14] S. Nettles and J. Wing. Persistance + Undoability = Transactions. In *Proc. of the 25th Hawaii International Conference on System Sciences*, volume 2, pages 832–843, January 1992.

[15] R. Rashid, A. Tevanian, M. Young, D. Young, R. Baron, D. Black, W. Bolosky, and J. Chew. Machine-independent virtual memory management for paged uniprocessor and multiprocessor architectures. *IEEE Trans. Comput.*, 37(8):896–908, August 1988.

[16] J. E. Richardson and M. J. Carey. Implementing persistence in E. In J. Rosenberg, editor, *Proc. Workshop on persistent object systems*, pages 302–319, Newcastle NSW (Australia), January 1989.

[17] M. Rozier and J. Martins. The CHORUS distributed operating system : some design issues. *Distributed operating systems. Theory and practice*, 1987.

[18] S. Shrivastava, G. Dixon, and G. Parrington. An overview of the Arjuna Distributed Programming System. *IEEE Software*, January 1991.

[19] V. Technology. *Versant in Brief.* Prentice-Hall, 1991.

[20] L. Walmer and M. Thompson. MACH documents. Technical report, Department of Computer Science, Carnegie-Mellon University, Pittsburg, January 1988.

[21] M. Young, A. Tevanian, R. Rashid, D. Golub, J. Eppinger, J. Chew, W. Bolosky, D. Black, and R. Baron. The duality of memory and communication in the implementation of a multiprocessor operating system. In *In Proc. of the 11th ACM Symp. on Operating Systems Principles*, pages 63–76, Austin TX (USA), November 1987. ACM.

OBJECT STORE IMPLEMENTATION

Fausto Rabitti
IEI-CNR, Via S.Maria 46, 56100 Pisa, Italy.

In this Session, three papers were presented. The first, "μDatabase: a toolkit for constructing memory mapped databases", by P. Buhr, A. Goel and A. Wai, and the third, "The Papyrus object library", by T. Connors and M.A. Neimat, deal with the problem of building efficient database functions on a persistent storage. The third paper, "Coherence in distributed persistent object systems", by M. Livesey and C. Allison, argues about the possibility of having a unifying principle (i.e., rollback) for enforcing "coherence" (i.e., stability, fault-tolerance, recovery, concurrency control, etc.) in distributed persistence system. We introduce the first and third paper together because they tackle the same basic problem in the implementation of object stores, proposing two different approaches (and relative implementations). The third paper remains at a more general level, concerning the principles of distributed object store implementations, with possible long-term implications but still to be validated with experiments, and so it will be discussed separately.

One of the fundamental decisions in building low-level database functions, both for database systems and persistent programming languages is the interface to the I/O subsystem, i.e., explicit I/O versus mapped files. With the first solution, a database programmer has the problem of dealing with two different views of structured data, i.e., the data in primary storage and the data on secondary storage. These two views of data tend to be incompatible with each other: considerable programming effort is necessary to transform data structures from one view to another (i.e., necessity to convert pointers and sometimes the entire data structure) when they are stored or read from secondary storage. With the second solution, a single-level view of the store gives the programmer the illusion that the data on disk (secondary storage) is accessible in the same way as the data in main memory (primary storage). The uniform view of data eliminates the need for complex conversions at execution-time of structured data between primary and secondary storage. For complex structures, a single-level store offers substantial implementation advantages over conventional file access. This is crucial to such database applications as CAD/CAM systems, text document management and GIS.

Although a single-level store is an old idea (the usage of memory mapping techniques can be traced back 20 years to the MULTICS system), it has seen only limited use inside operating systems, and no real use inside database management systems. During the last few years, however, is being receiving new attention, mainly for the implementation of the object stores in advanced database systems and persistent programming languages.

The two papers, "μDatabase: a toolkit for constructing memory mapped databases", and "The Papyrus object library", present systems adopting two different approaches in implementing the persistent object store: the first is based on a single-level store, while the second is based on a two-level store.

The first paper argues that the use of memory mapping, eliminating the need to convert programming language data structures to a secondary storage format, results in code more reliable and easier to maintain. Moreover, the need of explicit buffer management is reduced, and access methods can be rapidly prototyped, since a contiguous address space is defined. Experimental results, shown in the paper, also demonstrates that the performance of access structures implemented on the single-level store are comparable with the performance of access structures implemented on traditional two-level stores.

In the second of these two papers (the third in the Session), the more traditional approach of a two-level store is adopted. Here the disadvantages of a single-level store are stressed, such as non-uniform access speed (when a non-resident page is referenced, a long delay occurs for a I/O operation), the fact that a database must always be mapped at the same address in virtual memory (implying that multiple database access is disallowed or that each database is assigned a unique virtual memory address), and, more important, implementing recovery is difficult in memory mapping and a satisfactory solution is still a research issue. Therefore, in order to avoid to the programmer the difficulty of directly accessing the file system interface, an object library is proposed to build highly-tuned customized data managers.

The last paper (second in the Session), "Coherence in distributed persistent object systems", proposes an approach to coherency control over a variety of requirements faced by the distributed system builders (such as stability, fault-tolerance, failure recovery, concurrency control, commitment, and consistency of replication). It is argued that the existing operating system services do not provide an adequate platform for addressing coherence in distributed persistent object systems. In the design, rollback is used as the agent to solve the violations of coherence and in this sense, the approach is optimistic. Specifically, the design is based on a transaction service supported by a uniform rollback mechanism and integrated communication services.

Several requirements for distributed coherence mechanisms are considered: locality (not demanding the global view of the system), adaptivity (the coherence premium depending only on the actual incoherence potential of a given computation and not on some statically predicted worst case scenario), homogeneity (not requiring or expecting any particular topology), deadlock prevention.

The paper emphasises the system design at conceptual level, presenting more the requirements and ideas rather than the real theoretical and technical solutions pertinent to the coherence problem. The authors correctly mention the performance problem of the rollback technology which has lead to its controlled and limited use in the database environment and state as a major goal of their paper to demonstrate that coherency control in distributed persistent object systems can be done economically, if based on their approach. However, this goal is not yet reached in the paper, where no proof of efficiency is given and no detailed comparison with other approaches can be found. This is also due to the "generality" of the aims and the discussion and the certainly preliminary stage of the work. A more convincing proof on the feasibility of this approach would require much a more detailed and theoretically sound design and/or extensive experimentations with prototype systems.

μDatabase : A Toolkit for Constructing Memory Mapped Databases

Peter A. Buhr, Anil K. Goel and Anderson Wai
Dept. of Computer Science, University of Waterloo
Waterloo, Ontario, Canada, N2L 3G1

Abstract

The main objective of this work was an efficient methodology for constructing low-level database tools that are built around a single-level store implemented using memory mapping. The methodology allowed normal programming pointers to be stored directly onto secondary storage, and subsequently retrieved and manipulated by other programs without the need for relocation, pointer swizzling or reading all the data. File structures for a database, e.g. a B-Tree, built using this approach are significantly simpler to build, test, and maintain than traditional file structures. All access methods to the file structure are statically type-safe and file structure definitions can be generic in the type of the record and possibly key(s) stored in the file structure, which affords significant code reuse. An additional design requirement is that multiple file structures may be simultaneously accessible by an application. Concurrency at both the front end (multiple accessors) and the back end (file structure partitioned over multiple disks) are possible. Finally, experimental results between traditional and memory mapped files structures show that performance of a memory mapped file structure is as good or better than the traditional approach.

1 Introduction

The main objective of this work was an efficient methodology for constructing low-level database tools that are built around a single-level store. A *single-level store* gives the illusion that data on disk (*secondary storage*) is accessible in the same way as data in main memory (*primary storage*), which is analogous to the goals of virtual memory. This uniform view of data eliminates the need for complex and expensive execution-time conversions of structured data between primary and secondary storage. A uniform view of data also allows the expressive power and the data structuring capabilities of a general purpose programming language to be used in creating and manipulating data structures stored on secondary storage. Although a single-level store is an old idea [1, 2], it has seen only limited use inside of operating systems, and it is only during the last few years that this idea has begun to receive new attention and approval from researchers in the database and programming language communities [3, 4, 5]. For complex structures, a single-level store offers substantial performance advantages over conventional file access, which is crucial to database applications such as CAD/CAM systems, text management and GIS [6]. We argue that the performance advantage of a single-level store is lost if the pointers within it have to be relocated or swizzled [7, 8, 9].

One way of efficiently implementing a single-level store is by means of memory mapped files. Memory mapping is the use of virtual memory to map files stored on secondary storage into primary storage so that the data is directly accessible by the processor's instructions. Therefore, explicit read and write routine calls are not used to access data on disk. All read and write operations are done implicitly by the operating system during execution of a program. When the working set of the data structure can be kept in memory, performance begins to approach that of memory-resident databases.

To show the efficiency of memory mapping, a memory mapped implementation was constructed, which allowed file access experiments to be performed between traditional and memory mapped schemes. A tool kit approach was adopted for the implementation because it allows programmers to participate in some of the design activity; the tool kit is called μDatabase. Persistence in μDatabase is orthogonal because creating and manipulating data structures in a persistent area is the same as in a program. μDatabase is intented to provide easy-to-use and efficient tools for developing new databases, and for maintaining existing databases. While μDatabase shares the underlying principles of a single-level store with other recent proposals [3, 4, 5, 10], it offers features that make it unique and an attractive alternative. μDatabase is *not* an object store but it could be used to implement one.

In this paper, a *file structure* is defined to be a data structure that is a container for user records on secondary storage; a file structure relates the records in a particular way, for example, maintaining the records in order by one or more keys. An *access method* is defined to be a particular way that records are accessed. Examples of different access methods are: initial loading of records, sequential access of records, keyed access of records.

2 Motivation

A database programmer is faced with the problem of dealing with two different views of structured data, viz. the data in primary storage and the data on secondary storage. Traditionally, these two views of data tend to be incompatible with each other. It is extremely difficult and cumbersome to construct complex relationships among different objects without the help of direct pointers. However, it is generally impossible to store and retrieve data structures containing pointers from disk without converting at least the pointers and at worst the entire data structure into a different format. Considerable efforts, both in terms of programming and execution time, have to be made in such systems to transform data from one view to the other. In general, these transformations are data structure specific and must be executed each time the data structure is stored or read from secondary storage. Furthermore, the powerful and flexible data structuring capabilities of modern programming languages are not directly available for building data structures on secondary storage.

In spite of these rather taxing difficulties, database implementors have traditionally rejected the use of mapped files and have chosen to implement the lower-level support for databases themselves using traditional approaches. This rejection is not totally based on the lack of memory mapping facilities. The earliest use of memory mapping techniques can be traced back 20 years to the Multics system. However Multics provided these facilities in a framework that was very rigid and difficult to work with. More recent operating systems have begun to provide means for implementing the idea of a single-level store. See [4, p. 90] for other reasons why mapped files have not been popular with database designers. All of these reasons are now addressed by new operating systems [11, 12], which provide extended access to the virtual memory, and new hardware, which provides large address spaces (64 bits) and N-level paging [13, 14].

3 Memory Mapping

3.1 Disadvantages of Memory Mapping

Larger Pointers Memory pointers may be larger than disk offsets, which increases the size of the file structure marginally increasing access cost.

Non-Uniform Access Speed The apparent direct access of data can give a false sense of control to the file structure designer. While a file's contents are directly accessible to the processor, the access speed is non-uniform—when a non-resident page is referenced, a long delay occurs as for a traditional I/O operation; otherwise the reference is direct and occurs at normal memory speed. When programming a file structure using memory mapping, certain data structures will be inappropriate because of their access patterns.

3.2 Advantages of Memory Mapping

Common Data Structure in Primary and Secondary Memory Use of programming-language data structures to organize the contents of a file eliminates the need to convert to a secondary storage format, which results in code that is substantially more reliable and easier to maintain. Also, for complex data structures, like an object in a CAD/CAM system, there is a significant performance advantage.

Reduced Need for Explicit Buffer Management A sophisticated buffer manager is crucial for the performance of a traditional database system. Furthermore, a file structure designer must be skilled in its use, explicitly invoking its facilities and pinning/unpinning buffers. On systems without pinning support, double paging is a serious drawback. A memory mapped access method is less complex because I/O management is largely transparent and is handled at the lowest possible level (instruction fetch and store).

Simple Localization While locality of references is crucial for all data structures where access is non-uniform, memory-mapped access methods can easily take advantage of it by controlling memory layout. Because the data structures on secondary storage can be manipulated directly by the programming language, tuning for localization is straightforward.

Rapid Prototyping of Access Methods Because a file structure designer works with a uniform view of data, a file structure can be reliably constructed in a short period of time, using all the available programming-language tools. Polymorphism, interactive debuggers, execution and storage profilers, and visualization tools are some examples of directly usable aids.

Memory Mapping on a Loaded System It is our contention that memory-mapped access methods can potentially achieve better performance than traditional database systems, particularly on a shared system. A buffer manager is often in conflict with other applications, in particular, holding storage that it is not using. On the other hand, memory-mapped access methods can immediately take advantage of available storage to reduce I/O operations.

Contiguous Address Space Memory mapping provides the file structure designer with a contiguous address space even when the data on secondary storage is not contiguous. A single object within a given file structure may be split into several extents on one disk or across multiple disks, and a file structure designer may see nothing difference or only a sparse address space.

4 μDatabase Design Methodology

Instead of using reachability [15, 16], μDatabase uses the notion of a persistent area, in which data objects can be built or copied if they are to persist [17, 18]. A persistent area is currently implemented by an operating system file. If data is to be transferred from one persistent area to another, the data must be copied through an intermediate area. Alternatively, persistent data can be manipulated directly by migrating an application task to the persistent area and perform the operations directly on the data. The amount of task migration and/or copying depends on the size of the data and the amount of work performed when manipulating the data. In all cases, the user interface to the file structure provides encapsulation to ensure its integrity.

An application may need to access several persistent areas simultaneously. Our design requirements mandate that support for multiple accessible file structures in a single application be provided, while allowing each file structure to use conventional pointers without having to adjust them. To accomplish this requirement, each persistent area is mapped into its own segment. This approach is in contrast to systems that provide simultaneous access by mapping multiple persistent areas into the same segment. In these systems, all pointers are relocated when portions of an area are mapped. In general, this requires access to the type information of the file structure at runtime, which is not usually possible in programming languages that do not have runtime type-checking. Also, significant execution overhead is incurred in relocating pointers.

Currently, μDatabase does *not* cover pointers among persistent areas (see [18] for a possible solution). Nor does it deal with distributed persistent areas; we believe that distributed shared memory [19, 20] will allow our current design to scale up to a distributed environment. Object-oriented programming techniques are employed in the implementation of μDatabase, but are not essential. μC++ [21] is used as the implementation language, which is a superset of C++ with concurrency extensions, because it allows immediate technology transfer.

The following two properties evolved during the design and implementation of μDatabase. First, data associated with accessing a file structure, such as current location in the file, concurrency data or transient recovery information are not mapped in the file structure. Second, a deliberate attempt is made to retain the conventional semantics of *opening* and *closing* a file. Implicit schemes, like pointer-swizzling, have problems detecting the first access but the most difficult problem is knowing when the access can be terminated (garbage collectors are too slow). The properties involve several levels, each performing a particular aspect of the storage or access management of the file structure (see Figure 1).

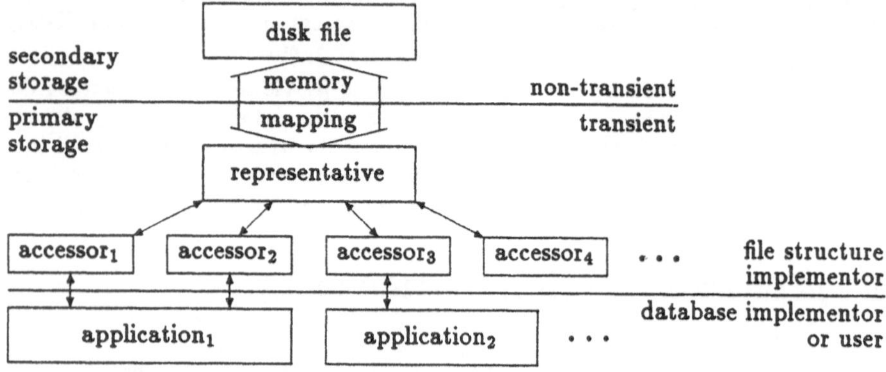

Figure 1: Basic Structure of the Design Methodology

4.1 Representative

A *representative* is responsible for creation and initialization of the file structure for the storage management of access method data in primary storage, for concurrent accesses to the file's contents, and for recovery. Each file structure has a unique representative. In μDatabase, the representative is a UNIX process, which has its own virtual address space in which transient information is maintained and the file is mapped, and its own thread of control. The representative process is created on demand, during creation of a file and for subsequent access by a user, and exists only as long as required by either of these operations.

A representative's memory is divided into two sections: private and shared (see Figure 2). Private memory can only be accessed by the thread of control associated with the UNIX process that created it, i.e. the representative. The disk file is mapped into the private memory while all data associated with concurrent access to the file is contained in the representative's shared memory; such data is always transient. Shared memory is accessible by multiple threads associated with UNIX processes that interact with the representative. There is no implicit concurrency control among threads accessing shared memory; mutual exclusion must be explicitly programmed by the file structure designer using the facilities in μC++.

To allow addresses to be stored directly into the file and subsequently used, the following convention is observed by all representatives: the disk file must be mapped into memory starting at a fixed memory location, called the *Segment Base Address.* The file base address is conceptually the *virtual zero* of a separate segment; this is how μDatabase uses a UNIX process as a separate segment. In μDatabase, the value 16M has been chosen for the Segment Base Address as the starting location of all mapped files; this leaves a sufficiently large space for the application and the representative(s).

An application in μDatabase can have multiple file structures accessible simultaneously. This capability is possible because each representative has its own

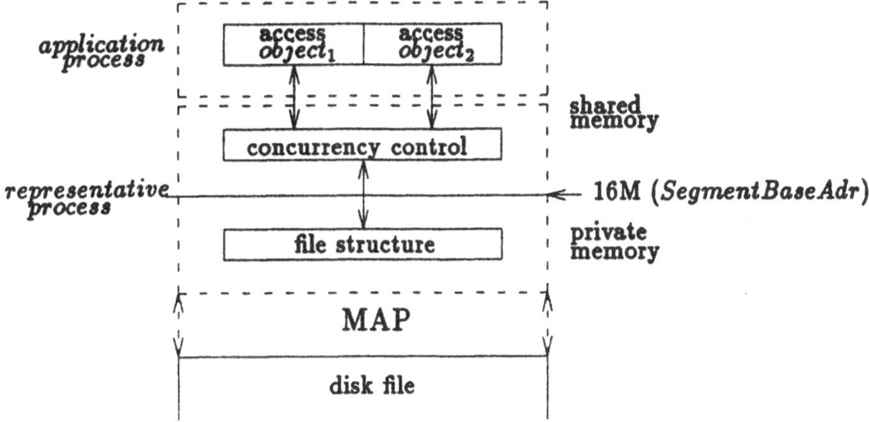

Figure 2: Storage Model for Representative

private mapping area. Figure 3 shows the memory organization of an application using 3 file structures simultaneously. Since each representative has its own segment, relocation of pointers in a file structure is never required. The disadvantage of this approach is that there can never be pointers from the shared area to any of the private mapped areas and vice versa. However, addresses from one file structure can be stored in another file structure, but such addresses can only be dereferenced in the file structure they come from. Hence, either data must be copied out of a file structure to be manipulated by the application and copied back again, or an application light-weight task must migrate to the representatives to perform a series of operations.

4.2 B-Tree Example

To define a file structure, e.g. BTreeFile, an abstract data-type is defined with two operations that are implicitly performed: initialization and termination; no other operations are available. A B-Tree is defined as follows:

```
class BTreeFile {
  public:
    BTreeFile( char *DiskFileName, ... ) { initialization code };
    ~BTreeFile( void ) { termination code };
};
```

The initialization routine BTreeFile and the termination routine ~BTreeFile are invoked automatically whenever an instance of BTreeFile is created and deleted, respectively. An instance of a B-Tree file structure is created using type BTreeFile, as in: BTreeFile f("StudentData", *other arguments*), where StudentData is the name of the UNIX file in which the data are stored and retrieved from. There are no user visible routines, which ensures that after the declaration of an instance of BTreeFile, the corresponding file structure is not accessible to the user/application program.

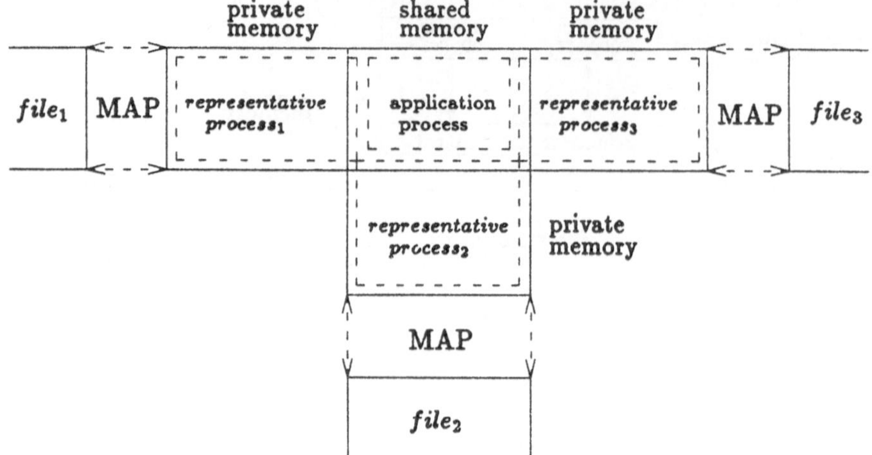

Figure 3: Accessing Multiple File Structures

4.3 Access

The mechanisms for requesting and providing access to a file structure are provided in the form of another abstract data-type, which is implemented as a class called an *access* class. Declaration of an access class instance, called an *access object*, constitutes the explicit action required to gain access to a file's contents (i.e. create the mapping). Creating an access object corresponds to opening a file in traditional systems but it is tied into the programming-language block structure. As well, the access object contains any transient data associated with a particular access (e.g. the current record pointer), while the representative contains global transient information (e.g. the type of access for each accessor). Because the access object is in the application process, communication between it and the representative process is done by synchronous calls passing data through shared memory. At least one access class must be provided for each file definition. It is possible to have multiple access classes, each providing a distinct form of access (e.g. initial loading, sequential, keyed). It is also possible to have multiple access objects communicating with the same representative. This capability allows an application to have multiple simultaneous views of the data (see Figure 1).

For BTreeFile, the access object is called BTreeFileAcc.

```
class BTreeFileAcc {
  public:
    BTreeFileAcc( BTreeFile *f, char *access ) { initialization code };
    ~BTreeFileAcc() { termination code };
    read( ... ) { ... };
    ... { other appropriate access routines };
};
```

To gain read access to a file structure object f, an application program declares an instance of BTreeFileAcc, as follows: BTreeFileAcc pf(&f, "r"). The pointer to f specifies the file structure that is to be accessed through pf, and "r" specifies the kind of access for concurrency control purposes. Depending on the particular kind of concurrency control, the declaration of the access object may block until it is safe to access the file contents and/or individual access routine calls may block. Once instantiated, the access object can be used by an application to perform operations on the file structure by invoking the public member routines of BTreeFileAcc. For example, in order to read from f, a call is made to the member routine read of BTreeFileAcc, as in pf.read(...). The routine read communicates with the representative to perform the desired operation.

4.4 Generic B-Tree

The polymorphic facilities of a programming language can be applied to generalize the definitions of file structures and to allow reuse of the file structure's implementation by other file structures. A generic B-Tree file structure is presented to demonstrate the basic concept. The template facilities of C++ allow the creation of generic file structures (as in E [22]). The generic B-Tree definition has 2 type parameters and 1 conventional parameter. The type parameters provide the type of the key and the type of the record for the B-Tree. The optional conventional parameter provides the size of the B-Tree nodes in bytes. Each B-Tree instance generated from a generic B-Tree type has 3 conventional parameters: the backing-store UNIX file name, the routine used to compare the keys and the initial space allocated for the B-Tree in bytes. The following creates two specialized B-Trees:

```
BTree<int, Record, 4 Kb> db1( "db1BTree", less ),  // default initial size
      db2( "db2BTree", greater, 30 Kb );          // 30 K initial size
```

Both B-Trees have int keys, Record records and a 4K node size. One instance is sorted in ascending order (less) and the other one in descending order (greater). Unfortunately, this B-Tree instantiation requires the UNIX file name and the name of the comparison routine be re-specified at each subsequent usage of the file structure, which is type unsafe. However, once these two aspects of a file structure are specified correctly, all subsequent access to the database file structure can be statically type-checked.

There are several requirements on the key type, the record type and the comparison routine. As well, some additional routines must be supplied. For example, the type of the key and the record must provide an assignment operator, among other things, and the comparison routine must have a specific type. A complete example showing the creation of a B-Tree and insertion and retrieval of records is presented in Figure 4.

In μDatabase, each file structure can provide range queries using a generator or iterator [22, 23], e.g. BTreeGen. The *generator* is an object whose arguments define the kind of range query and it returns one record at a time from the set of records that satisfy the requirements denoted by the information provided to the generator. The operator >> returns a pointer to some record within the specified range, but successive records are not normally ordered. If all records in the range have been returned, the NULL pointer is returned. By iteratively invoking the operator >>, the individual records of the range query are obtained.

```
class Record {                                    // data record
  public:
    float field1, field2;
    Record &operator=( const Record &rhs ) { // define assignment
        field1 = rhs.field1;
        field2 = rhs.field2;
        return( *this ); }
};
int greater( const int &op1, const int &op2 ) { // key ordering routine
    return op1 > op2;
}
void uMain::main() {                              // uMain uC++ artifact
    BTree<int, Record, 4 Kb> db( "testdb", greater, 30 Kb );
    BTreeAccess<int, Record, 4 Kb> dbacc( db ); // open B-Tree
    int key;
    Record rec, *recp;
    // insert records
    for ( key = 1; key <= 1000; key += 1 ) {
        rec.field1 = key / 10.0;
        rec.field2 = key / 100.0;
        dbacc.insert( key, &rec ); }              // static type-checking
    // retrieve records
    for ( BTreeGen<int, Record, 4 Kb> gen(dbacc); gen >> recp; ) {
            uCout << recp->field1 << " " << recp->field2 << endl; }
}
```

Figure 4: Example Program using a Generic B-Tree

4.5 Storage Management

In μDatabase, memory is divided into three major levels for storage management: an address space, which is a set of addresses from 0 to N used to refer to bytes or words of memory; a segment, which is a contiguous portion of an address space; and a heap, which is a contiguous portion of a segment. All segments are nested in an address space and all heaps are nested in a segment. Further, since a heap is simply a block of storage, it is possible for heaps to be nested within one another. The form of the address for each level may depend on the storage management scheme at that level.

While there are a large number of storage management schemes possible at each level of nesting, the following three basic schemes are provided in μDatabase: uniform management, the allocation size is the same for the duration of the heap; variable management, the allocation size can vary but each allocation remains that size for its duration (like C's malloc and free routines); dynamic management, the allocation size can vary in size and each allocated area can expand and contract in size after its allocation.

A heap may be accessed in two ways: by the file structure implementor and by a nested heap. For example, the storage management for a B-Tree has 3 levels: the segment, within which uniform-size B-Tree nodes are allocated, within which uniform or variable sized records are allocated. Depending on the particular implementation of the storage manager at each level, different capabilities will be provided. A file structure implementor makes calls to the lowest level (variable storage manager) to allocate records. An expansion object can be passed to the uniform storage manager to deal with node splitting and other application-specific requirements. If the segment fills with uniform-size nodes, the representative storage manager is called by the uniform storage manager to extend the segment.

The criterion used to judge the general storage management approach is whether it can provide performance that is close to traditional schemes that amalgamate storage management directly with the data structure. Both an independent and integrated storage management B-Tree were constructed and creation tests were run. The results were virtually identical, with timings varying by ± 2%.

5 Experimental Proof

A number of compelling arguments have been made in [3] and other publications for the use of single-level stores for implementing databases. In spite of these arguments, it is clear there is still resistance and skepticism in the database community. Furthermore, our contention is that mapped files can be used advantageously for building databases not only in the new single-store environment but also in the traditional environment. Traditional databases can be accessed using memory-mapped access methods without requiring any changes to the file structure. In all cases, the mapped access methods should provide performance comparable to traditional approaches while making it much easier to augment the access methods of the file structure in the future by greatly reducing program complexity.

At the start of our work, there was little published experimental evidence available to support the view that memory-mapped file structures could perform as well as or better than traditional file structures. Therefore, it was necessary to implement a number of different memory-mapped file structures and to compare their performance against equivalent traditional ones.

5.1 Experimental Structure

To demonstrate the benefits of memory mapping, different experiments were constructed. The general form of an experiment was to implement a file structure in the traditional and memory-mapped styles, perform retrievals from a file, which is the most common form of access in a database, and compare the results. While every effort was made to keep the two file structures as similar as possible, some system problems precluded absolutely identical execution environments. In particular, the traditional file structures were stored on disk as character-special UNIX files and an LRU buffer manager was used. The memory-mapped files could not be mapped from a character-special file and had to be accessed from the UNIX file system, which performs all I/O in 8K blocks even though the system page size is 4K. Therefore, to make the comparisons equal, all of the file structures had 8K node sizes and all I/O was done in 8K blocks.

All experiments were run on a Sequent Symmetry with 10 i386 processors, which uses a simple page-replacement algorithm. The page-replacement algorithm is FIFO per page table plus a global LRU cache of replaced pages so there is a second chance to recover a page before it is reallocated. The maximum total size of the resident pages for a program is determined by the user and upon exceeding that size, pages are removed from the resident set on a FIFO basis. Upon removal, a page is put into the global cache where it can be reinstated to the resident set if a fault occurs for the page before the page is reused. This page replacement algorithm was matched against an LRU buffer-manager used by the traditional databases.

The execution environment was strictly controlled so that results between traditional and memory-mapped access methods were comparable. First, all experiments were run stand-alone to preclude external interference, except for those experiments that needed a loaded system. Second, the amount of memory for the experiment's address space and the global cache were tightly controlled so that both kinds of file structures had exactly the same amount of buffer space or virtual memory, respectively. The test files varied in size from 6-32 megabytes. The amount of primary storage available for buffer management or paging was restricted so that the ratio of primary to secondary storage was approximately 1:10 and 1:20. These ratios are believed to be common in the current generation of computers, supporting medium (0.1G-.5G) to large databases (1G-4G) but not very large databases.

The following experiments were implemented:

Prefix B^+Tree In this experiment, 100,000 uniformly distributed records were generated whose keys were taken from the unit interval. A record had a variable length with an average of 27 bytes. These records were inserted into a prefix B^+Tree [24]. For this B-Tree, 4 query files were generated, where the queries followed a uniform distribution. Each file is described by the tuple (n,m) where n is the number of queries and m is the number of records sequentially read from the B-Tree (range query). For example, (10,1000) means executing 10 queries with each query reading a set of 1000 records sequentially. A 5th query file contained 10,000 exact match queries that follow a normal distribution with mean 0.5 and variance 0.1.

R-Tree The R-Tree [25] is an access method for multidimensional rectangles. It supports *point* queries and different types of *window* queries. A point query asks for all rectangles that cover a given query point whereas a window query asks for all rectangles which enclose, intersect or are contained in a given query rectangle. The window queries are similar to a range query in an ordinary B-Tree. However, there is one basic difference: index pages (internal nodes) are accessed more frequently in the case of the R-Tree than in the B-Tree case.

For this experiment, 2-dimensional data (100,000 rectangles) and queries from a standardized test bed [26] were taken. The maximum number of data rectangles was limited to 450 in the data pages, and to 455 in the directory pages. The query file consisted of 1000 point queries and 400 each of the three different types of window queries.

Graph To simulate the access patterns found in other data intensive applications (e.g. hypertext or object-oriented databases), a large directed graph was constructed consisting of 64,000 nodes, each of which was 512 bytes. The nodes were grouped into clusters of 64 where nodes in a cluster were physically localized. An edge out from a node had a high probability (85%, 90%, 95%) of referencing a node within the same cluster. Edges leaving a cluster went to a uniformly random selected node. Each experiment consisted of 40 concurrent random walks within the graph, consisting of 500 edge traversals each.

The results of the experiments are presented in Table 1. For each query file, three performance measures were gathered: the CPU time, the elapsed time, and number of pages or buffers read. The CPU time is the total time spend by all processors in a given test run, and hence, the CPU time may be greater than the elapsed time. Multiple processors were used in both traditional and memory mapped experiments. The retrieval application ran on one processor while the access method for the particular file structure ran on another processor. The elapsed time is the real clock time from the beginning to the end of the test run. Both times include any system overhead.

Primary Memory Size 10% of Database Size

		Memory Mapped			Traditional		
Access Method	Query Distr.	CPU* Time (secs)	Elapse Time (secs)	Page Reads	CPU Time (secs)	Elapse Time (secs)	Disk Reads
Prefix B-Tree	1x10,000	35.7	19.7	61	32.2	32.9	53
	10x1,000	35.7	19.5	56	32.5	32.6	58
	100x100	37.5	22.4	147	35.4	35.7	150
	10,000x1	98.1	217.6	8789	240.5	223.6	8746
	normal	91.8	181.0	6777	202.3	183.6	6638
R-Tree	non-point	154.0	174.5	1414	330.4	334.1	1462
	point	109.4	124.1	934	230.5	234.4	896
Network Graph	85% local	318.1	476.1	15294	526.7	458.8	15004
	90% local	271.6	375.5	11278	449.0	370.7	11368
	95% local	207.0	243.8	6584	337.7	254.7	6539

Primary Memory Size 5% of Database Size

		Memory Mapped			Traditional		
Access Method	Query Distr.	CPU* Time (secs)	Elapse Time (secs)	Page Reads	CPU Time (secs)	Elapse Time (secs)	Disk Reads
Prefix B-Tree	1x10,000	35.5	19.5	61	35.3	35.5	117
	10x1,000	35.2	19.6	66	34.2	33.5	131
	100x100	37.0	22.1	155	37.4	36.6	216
	10,000x1	127.8	255.6	9415	260.7	224.1	9723
	normal	126.6	235.8	8250	253.8	217.6	9313
R-Tree	non-point	181.3	227.8	2913	367.1	374.5	3396
	point	136.8	184.5	2647	279.5	289.6	3491
Network Graph	85% local	383.3	565.8	17772	563.4	495.8	16550
	90% local	330.3	462.1	13602	484.0	403.9	12781
	95% local	264.9	316.6	8338	361.9	276.1	7400

* CPU times may be greater than elapse time because multiple CPUs are used.

Table 1: Access Method Comparison : Node Size 8K

The results of the experiments confirm the conjecture that performance of memory-mapped file structures is equivalent or better than traditional file structures. For the read operations, the memory-mapped access methods are comparable (± 10%) to their traditional counterparts. An exception occurs when the LRU buffer space is only 5% of the file size for sequential reads because the LRU algorithm is suboptimal in this case while the FIFO page-replacement algorithm is near optimal. For the CPU times, the memory-mapped access methods are generally better than the traditional ones because there is less time spent doing buffer management. For the elapsed times, the memory-mapped access methods are comparable (± 10%) to their traditional counterparts. An exception occurs when memory-mapped access methods perform small sequential reads because the FIFO page-replacement algorithm is near optimal in this case. All of the results show that the Sequent page replacement scheme performed comparably to the LRU buffer-manager.

To verify the conjecture on the expected behavior of mapped access methods on a loaded machine, the previous B-Tree experiments were run during a peak-load period of 20-30 time-sharing users on the Sequent. The memory mapped and traditional B-Tree retrievals were started at the same time (3:00pm) and so were competing with each other as well as all other users on the system. The two file structures were on different disks accessed through different controllers so the OS could not share pages and retrievals were not interacting at the hardware I/O level. However, the amount of global cache could not be restricted during the day, so if there was free memory available, the memory-mapped access method would use it indirectly. Table 2 shows the averages of 5 trials. As can be seen, there was a difference only when there were a significant number of reads. In those cases, the memory-mapped access methods make use of any extra free memory to buffer data. This is particularly noticeable for the normal distribution because any extra memory significantly reduced the pages read, and hence, the elapse time. Clearly, the LRU buffer manager could be extended to dynamically increase and decrease buffer space depending on system load, but that further complicates the buffer manager and duplicates code in the operating system.

Primary Memory Size 10% of Database Size

		Memory Mapped			Traditional		
Access Method	Query Distr.	CPU* Time (secs)	Elapse Time (secs)	Page Reads	CPU Time (secs)	Elapse Time (secs)	Disk Reads
Prefix B-Tree	1x10,000	35.8	21.6	60	34.0	35.7	53
	10x1,000	36.1	21.8	56	34.8	36.8	58
	100x100	37.4	25.24	143	37.0	38.68	150
	10,000x1	111.2	277.0	6677	263.4	263.3	8746
	normal	97.82	134.5	2063	221.5	217.0	6638

Table 2: Peak Load Retrievals : Node Size 8K

6 Parallelism

Currently, μDatabase allows a file structure designer to build whatever form of concurrency control is appropriate. Concurrency control can be specified at a low-level, where semaphores are used to protect data, or at a high-level, where light-weight server tasks control access to data. While concurrency control is often tied into a particular data structure, we believe it is possible to provide some general concurrency abstractions to the file structure designer to aid in this process. A number of different concurrency techniques are being studied that provide two different forms of parallelism. *Backend concurrency* deals with the I/O bottleneck, a file structure is partitioned across multiple disks and access is performed in parallel. *Frontend concurrency* allow a number of requests to execute in parallel if the requests access data in different areas of the database. The question to be addressed is how to use memory mapping with both backend and frontend concurrency.

6.1 Backend Concurrency

Backend concurrency attempts to deal with the CPU-I/O bottleneck by partitioning data across multiple disks and then accessing the data in parallel [27]. Exact match queries usually cannot take advantage of parallelism possible from partitioning because there is usually only one disk access to service the request. Range queries can take advantage of the parallelism possible from partitioning if the data is distributed so that portions of the range can be accessed in parallel. A range query may be broken down into a number of smaller range queries so that each can be executed in parallel. Similarly, if the file structure is aware of the access pattern of different blocks, it can employ pre-reading techniques to increase the parallelism in reading blocks of data from the disk. In general, the records returned from a range query are unordered. If records must be returned in a specific order, that can significantly reduce the amount of parallelism. In μDatabase, the generator types for each file structure can manage all concurrent retrieval of records implicitly (see Figure 4)

In the following discussion, the general concern is not about access to the index portion of the file structure. Normally the index is relatively small so that most of it remains resident in main memory, and consequently, does not play a significant role as far as disk accesses are concerned.

6.1.1 Generic Backend Concurrency Algorithm

Once a file structure is partitioned, a retrieval algorithm can take advantage of the potential parallelism, but only if sufficient hardware is available. First, the disks must be able to be accessed in parallel, which implies that there must be multiple disk controllers. Second, if multiple processors are available, they must be able to be used to perform any file-structure administration in parallel with the application processing the records from the range query. Both of these hardware requirements were satisfied by our Sequent computer.

The algorithm used for backend concurrency is as follows. For a file structure partitioned across N disks, the N disk files are memory mapped into one contiguous segment. Then M (a control variable) kernel threads (UNIX processes) are created that all share the data segment containing the mapped file. $N+1$

light-weight tasks are created to perform the retrieval requests and they execute on the M kernel threads. N of the tasks are retrievers and the $(N+1)^{th}$ task is the *leaf retrieval administrator* (LRA). For each generator created, a buffer is allocated by the generator, which is shared between the application and the file structure. As well, another task, the *file structure traverser*, is generated, which partitions the range query. The size of the buffer can be specified as an optional parameter when creating the generator. The default buffer size is 32K bytes. The traverser task assumes the responsibility of organizing the buffer space in the form of a sharable buffer pool in some suitable manner. Then the traverser task searches the index structure finding the leaf nodes that contain records in the range. For each leaf node, the traverser communicates with the LRA specifying the leaf, number of records in the leaf, and the buffer pool. The LRA farms out the generator requests to its retrieval tasks. A retrieval task accesses the specified leaf page, allocates a buffer from the buffer pool, and copies as many records as will fit from the leaf page to the buffer. The last step is repeated until all the records have been copied into buffers and then the retriever task gets more work from the LRA. The structure of this algorithm is illustrated in Figure 5. This structure ensures that the only bottleneck in the retrieval is the speed that the buffer can be filled or emptied. In general, an application program can keep ahead of a small number of disks (1-7 disks). This generic backend concurrency algorithm can be used for different file structures by specializing the file structure traverser and the component responsible for processing of individual leaves to extract information.

6.1.2 Experimental Analysis of Partitioned B-Tree

The machine used for these experiments was the same Sequent Symmetry with 8 disk drives, of which 4 were used. There were 2 disk controllers, each with 2 channels. The drives were equally divided between the controllers. The experiment was 1000 range queries with each query consisted of reading a random number of sequential records starting at a randomly selected initial key. The average query size was 2000 records. Two partitioned B-Trees were tested, one created using a round-robin partitioning (each block is created on the next disk) and one created using the Larson-Seeger algorithm [28]. The partitioned experiments were performed with 1–4 partitions and the application program received each record but did no processing on the record. The results of the experiments appear in the graphs of Figure 6. The largest decrease in elapsed time is from 1 to 2 partitions because there are 2 controllers. After that, the elapse time increases because of contention on the two controllers.

6.2 Frontend concurrency

Here the concern is with allowing multiple client accessors to simultaneously traverse and manipulate the file structure. Currently, μC++ provides a number of language mechanisms for a file designer to build concurrency control. Many options will be built, tested and provided as part of μDatabase tool kit, however these will be used to build file-structure specific concurrency control. It is also our intention to study and develop a general purpose low-level concurrency control facility that will be automatically available to applications written in μDatabase.

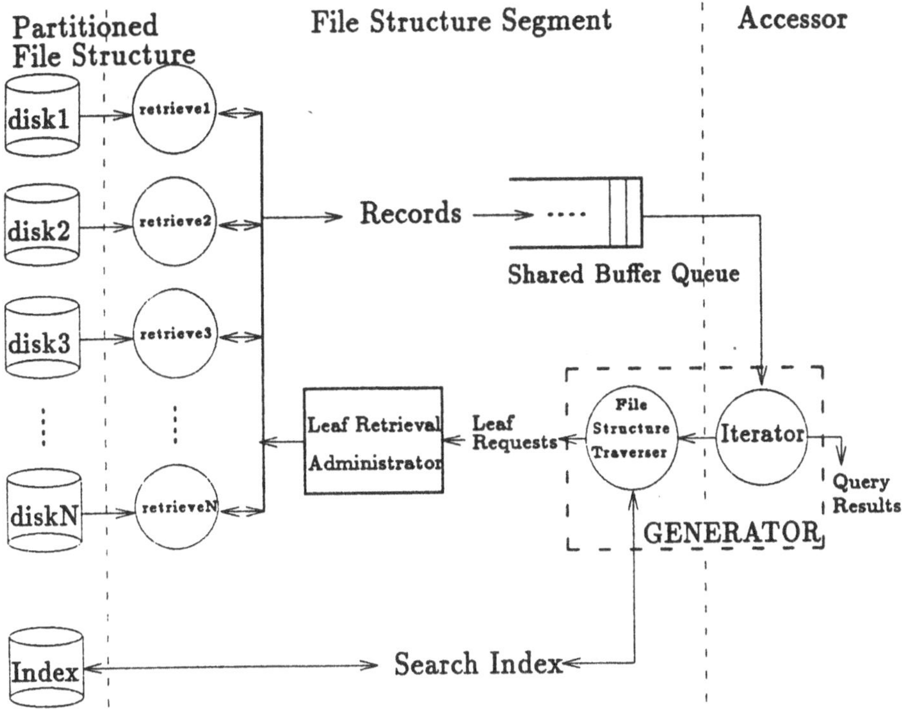

Figure 5: Backend Concurrency Structure

For example, allowing multiple versions of data to co-exist allows a high degree of concurrent and can be implemented in a general way.

7 Recovery Control

Implementing recovery is difficult in memory mapping and a satisfactory solution is still a research issue. If there is operating-system support to pin pages, traditional schemes can be used (however, with all the associated disadvantages). With no operating-system support, new techniques must be developed. We will be examining the use of dual memory maps to allow shadow write pages. One mapping represents the consistent database, which can be read at any time. The shadow mapping is for pages that are currently being modified. By precisely controlling when the shadow pages are copied back to the consistent mapping, it is possible to mimic traditional recovery schemes without operating-system support. The main problem to overcome is premature writing of modified pages by the operating system.

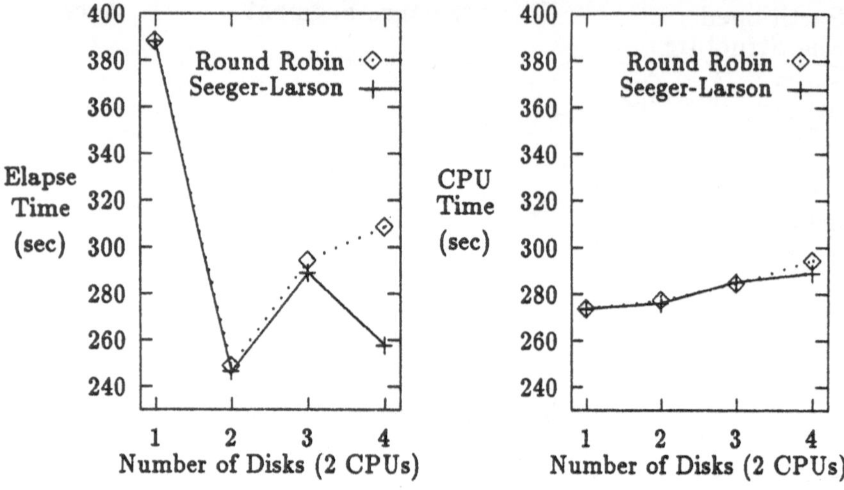

Figure 6: Backend Concurrency with B-Trees

8 Related Work

The earliest use of memory mapping techniques (or a single-level store) can be found in the Multics system [29]. In recent times a number of efforts have been made to use memory mapping. The systems described below are most closely related to μDatabase.

Objectstore Database System Objectstore shares a number of goals and objectives with μDatabase. However, Objectstore differs significantly from μDatabase in how the goals and objectives are achieved. In Objectstore, only the currently accessed pages used by a given transaction are mapped into the address space of the application. This approach introduces a limit on the number of different data pages that can be used simultaneously by any single transaction; large operations may have to be broken into a series of smaller transactions. In μDatabase, an entire file structure is mapped into an individual segment. This approach limits the size of any single file structure to be less than the virtual space supported by the available hardware; large file structures have to be split into smaller ones. There is, however, no restriction on how much data a single transaction can access simultaneously.

The approach used in Objectstore results in an inferior solution to the problem of accessing multiple file structures. Objectstore maps pages of all the databases used in an application into the same address space. Each page to be used is dynamically allocated a virtual address where it is mapped; pointers have to be dynamically relocated, which requires some portion of the type system to be available at runtime. Also, the need to relocate pointers has the potential of degrading performance of the database.

Cricket: A Mapped, Persistent Object Store Cricket uses the memory management primitives of the Mach operating system to provide the abstraction of a "shared, transactional single-level store that can be directly accessed by user applications" [4, p. 89]. Cricket follows a client/server paradigm and, upon an explicit request, maps the database directly into the virtual space of the client application. The fundamental difference from μDatabase is that the mapping takes place in the address space of the application, and hence, only one database at a time can be used by an application. Indeed, the concept of a disk file to group related objects in one collection is not a basic entity in Cricket and it takes the view that everything that an application needs to use is placed in a single large persistent store. We feel that this will lead to a certain amount of awkwardness in organizing various components of data and in sharing pieces of data across different projects. More importantly, this approach will not be able to handle partitioning of data across multiple disks adequately.

Paul Wilson's work In [9], Paul Wilson describes a scheme that uses pointer swizzling at page fault time to support huge address spaces. The basic scheme is very similar to the one employed by Objectstore except that in Wilson's scheme pointers on secondary store can have a format different from the pointers in primary storage. Wilson's scheme requires a special page fault handler for translating (swizzling) persistent pointers into transient pointers at execution time, which requires runtime type information. Since some of the pointers in a page can refer to pages that have not yet been made available, the translation of these pointers requires that all the referent pages be *faulted* as well. To prevent a cascade of I/O operations, Wilson's scheme only reserves the addresses for these extra pages in the page table instead of actually mapping them to primary storage. However, this solution underutilizes the address space and an application can potentially run out of addresses. Wilson suggests periodically invalidating all the mappings and rebuilding them to deal with this problem. Furthermore, objects that cross page boundaries require additional language support. Wilson's scheme is a clear winner for applications that require extremely large persistent address spaces using existing virtual memory hardware. However, the scheme is complex and may result in significant overhead, especially for applications with poor locality of references. Finally, Wilson's approach has the same problems as Objectstore with regard to dynamic relocation and multiple accessible databases.

The Bubba database system The designers of Bubba [30, 3], a highly parallel database system developed at MCC, exploited the concept of a single-level store to represent objects uniformly in a large virtual address space. The focus of Bubba was on developing a scalable *shared-nothing* architecture which could scale up to thousands of hardware nodes and the implementation of a single-level store was only a small, though important, portion of the overall project. The current design of μDatabase is based on a multiprocessor shared-memory architecture and is not intended to be used in a distributed environment. In Bubba, the Flex/32 version of AT&T UNIX System V Release 2.2 was extensively modified to build a single-level store, which makes their store highly unportable.

9 Conclusion

We have shown that memory mapping is an attractive alternative for implementing file structures for databases. Memory-mapped file structures are simpler to code, debug and maintain, while giving comparable performance when used stand-alone or on a loaded system than for traditional databases. Further, buffer management supplied through the page-replacement scheme of the operating system seems to provide excellent performance for many different access patterns. Our design for structuring the low-level portions of a DBMS for memory mapping provides the necessary environment to implement concurrency control and recovery. Finally, these benefits can be made available in tool kit form on any UNIX system that supports the mmap system call. Currently, μDatabase is only missing recovery facilities and these will be added in the near future.

References

[1] E. I. Organick. *The Multics System.* The MIT Press, Ma, USA, 1972.

[2] *System/38 Services Overview.* IBM, 1978.

[3] G. Copeland, M. Franklin, and G. Weikum. Uniform Object Management. In *EDBT'90*, pages 253–268, Venice, Italy, March 1990. Springer-Verlag.

[4] E. Shekita and M. Zwilling. Cricket: A Mapped, Persistent Object Store. In A. Dearle, G. Shaw, and S. Zdonik, editors, *Implementing Persistent Object Bases: Principles and Practise*, pages 89–102. Morgan Kaufmann, 1990.

[5] C. Lamb, G. Landis, J. Orenstein, and D. Weinreb. Objectstore Database System. *Communications of the ACM*, 34(10):50–63, October 1991.

[6] Peter van Oosterom. *Reactive Data Structures for Geographic Information Systems.* Ph.D. Thesis, Dept. of CS, Leiden University, December 1990.

[7] W. P. Cockshott, M. P. Atkinson, K. J. Chisholm, P. J. Bailey, and R. Morrison. Persistent Object Management System. *S-P&E*, 14(1):49–71, 1984.

[8] J. Moss. Working with Persistent Objects: To Swizzle or Not to Swizzle. Technical Report CS 90-38, University of Massachusetts, May 1990.

[9] Paul R. Wilson. Pointer Swizzling at Page Fault Time: Efficiently Supporting Huge Adrress Spaces on Standard Hardware. *Computer Architecture News*, 19(4):6–13, June 1991.

[10] Alfred Z. Spector, D. Thompson, R. F. Pausch, et al. Camelot: A Distributed Transaction Facility for Mach and the Internet. Technical Report CMU-CS-87-129, Carnegie Mellon University, 1987.

[11] A. Tevanian, Jr., R. F. Rashid, M. W. Young, et al. A Unix Interface for Shared Memory and Memory Mapped Files Under Mach. In *Summer 1987 USENIX Conference*, pages 53–67. USENIX Association, June 1987.

[12] *System Services Overview.* Sun Microsystems, 1990.

[13] *MIPS R4000 Microprocessor User's Manual.* MIPS Computer Systems, 91.

[14] J. Rosenberg, J. L. Keedy, and D. A. Abramson. Addressing Mechanisms for Large Virtual Memories. *The Computer Journal*, 35(4):369–375, August 1992.

[15] The PS-Algol Reference Manual, 4th Ed. Technical Report PPRR 12, University of Glasgow and St. Andrews, Scotland, June 1987.

[16] R. Morrison, A. Brown, R. Carrick, et al. The Napier Type System. In *Persistent Object Systems*, pages 3–18. Springer-Verlag, January 1989.

[17] P. A. Buhr and C. R. Zarnke. A Design for Integration of Files into a Strongly Typed Programming Language. In *International Conference on Computer Languages*, pages 190–200, Miami, Florida, U.S.A, October 1986.

[18] P. A. Buhr and C. R. Zarnke. Addressing in a Persistent Environment. In J. Rosenburg and D. Koch, editors, *Persistent Object Systems*, pages 200–217, University of Newcastle, Australia, January 1989. Springer-Verlag.

[19] M. Stumm and S. Zhou. Algorithms Implementing Distributed Shared Memory. *IEEE Computer*, 23(5):54–64, May 1990.

[20] K.L. Wu and W.K. Fuchs. Recoverable Distributed Shared Virtual Memory. *IEEE Transactions on Computers*, 39(4):460–469, April 1990.

[21] P. A. Buhr, G. Ditchfield, R. A. Stroobosscher, B. M. Younger, and C. R. Zarnke. μC++: Concurrency in the Object-Oriented Language C++. *Software–Practice and Experience*, 22(2):137–172, February 1992.

[22] J. E. Richardson, M. J. Carey, and D. T. Schuh. The Design of the E Programming Language. Technical Report CS-TR-824, Computer Science Department, University of Wisconsin-Madison, February 1989.

[23] B. Liskov, R. Atkinson, T. Bloom, et al. *CLU Reference Manual*, volume 114 of *Lecture Notes in Computer Science*. Springer-Verlag, 1981.

[24] R. Bayer and K. Unterauer. Prefix B-Trees. *ACM Transactions on Database Systems*, 2(1):11–26, March 1977.

[25] A. Guttman. R-trees: a dynamic index structure for spatial searching. In *Proceedings of the ACM SIGMOD Conference*, pages 47–57, 1984.

[26] N. Beckmann, H. P. Kriegel, R. Schneider, and B. Seeger. The R*-Tree: An Efficient and Robust Access Method for Points and Rectangles. In *Proceedings of SIGMOD Conference*, pages 322–331, 1990.

[27] D. A. Patterson, G. Gibson, and R. H. Katz. A Case for Redundant Arrays of Inexpensive Disks(RAID). In *Proceedings of SIGMOD'88*, June 1988.

[28] Bernhard Seeger and Per-Ake Larson. Multi-Disk B-trees. In *Proceedings of SIGMOD'91*, pages 436–445, Denver, Colorado, USA, June 1991. ACM.

[29] A. Bensoussan, C. T. Clingen, and R. C. Daley. The Multics Virtual Memory: Concepts and Design. *CACM*, 15(5):308–318, May 1972.

[30] H. Boral, W. Alexender, L. Clay, et al. Prototying Bubba, A Highly Parallel Database System. *IEEE Trans. on Knowledge and Data Eng.*, 2(1):4–24, March 1990.

Coherence in Distributed Persistent Object Systems

Mike Livesey and Colin Allison

mjl, colin@cs.st-andrews.ac.uk
Division of Computational Science, University of St Andrews
North Haugh, St Andrews
Scotland KY16 9SS

Abstract

Distributed system builders are faced with the task of meeting a variety of requirements on the global behaviour of the target system, such as stability, fault-tolerance and failure recovery, concurrency control, commitment, and consistency of replicated data. Coherence means satisfying these types of requirements, although the subset may vary from system from to system.

This paper describes an approach to coherence enforcement in distributed persistent object systems based upon system-wide backtracking. The approach is optimistic in the sense that violations of coherence are resolved rather than prevented—backtracking is the agent of this resolution. The coherence support is realised as a transaction service, supported by the backtrack capability.

1 Introduction

It is important that persistent object systems support distribution and concurrency. We take the view that a good model of distribution and concurrency in persistent object systems should provide three particular properties:

- conceptual uniformity and distribution transparency;
- efficient realisation;
- a protocol for maintaining global *coherence*, by which we understand some model of distributed computation that involves constraints on the view of the global system state visible to a user or running program.

This paper presents a distribution model based on processes which communicate by asynchronous message-passing. The model is realisable by OS kernel functions that interface directly with device drivers and basic memory management, although implementation details will be discussed elsewhere. The paper then concentrates on a coherence protocol and one particular coherence model. The protocol is based upon a universal *backtrack* mechanism, and provides a system of stable processes. Coherence is modelled by the notion of a *transaction*—an atomic disseminating computation. The transaction model of coherence is not new (c.f. [13]); the novelty lies in the protocol, which provides a flexible kind of transaction and is also able to support a variety of different coherence models.

2 Background

The work described here is an attempt to apply the concept of backtracking to the maintenance of coherence in distributed systems, and distributed persistent object systems in particular. The term "backtracking" carries the connotation of search—in our context a search for a coherent computation path. The term also implies a fundamentally optimistic approach. A computation is allowed to proceed eagerly, relying on backtracking to remedy the effects of over-eagerness.

A primary component of backtracking in a distributed system is *rollback*—finding and (effectively) returning to a consistent global *snapshot* [3,11]. Any form of rollback must obviously be supported by state checkpointing. In a distributed system the checkpoints would ideally be made locally, yet a snapshot implies a global constraint on such local checkpoints. The information in a global snapshot resides in transit messages as well as local state. If transit messages are lost, the system loses guaranteed message delivery. So rollback based on local checkpointing alone is prey to the *domino* effect, where a rollback avalanches back to the initial state because no other combination of local checkpoints constitutes a complete snapshot. The only defence against the domino effect is to log inputs as they are consumed, so that they can be made to reappear as transit messages when rollback occurs.

However, there still remains the problem of how to return to a particular snapshot—the *rollback protocol*. This combines with the *retry protocol*—how to run forward again—to give the complete backtrack protocol. In our system this protocol is maximally optimistic. Not only is the checkpointing performed locally and asynchronously, but also the rollback. Each separate process in the system rolls back to its own local checkpoint and retries independently. Every "wave" of backtracking is triggered from a single process, which defines a local state that the "goal" snapshot must contain. The rollback protocol, which derives from the Time Warp distributed simulation system [7], forces the rest of the system back to a snapshot by sending *antimessages* corresponding to all the messages it has originally sent during computation (we say that it "unsends" its messages). An antimessage rolls its target process back to the state in which it consumed the original "positive" message—the target process then unsends all its messages since that point, thereby propagating the rollback. When the rollback wave has finished, the resulting local states form a snapshot: no process has rolled back further than necessary, and any event causally dependent (in the sense of Lamport [8]) on the initial backtrack point is connected to it by a chain of communications and will therefore also have been undone by the wave.

However, propagation is only one of three issues concerning backtracking. The other two are:

- triggering backtrack
- immunity from backtrack (*commitment*)

Eagerness is limited by the outside world. Messages to print a page or launch a missile cannot be unsent. A process that represents a driver for some real device must therefore always operate with maximal pessimism, or *conservatism*—it can do nothing until it is guaranteed to be immune from further backtrack. Such a guarantee is called *commitment.*

In the light of our experience with an earlier version of the backtrack protocol [9], this paper describes a revised architecture aimed at a lower level of implementation, though the main emphasis is on the model. Because the backtrack protocol is the "atemporal" part of Time Warp, we call the architecture "Warp".

3 The Warp Architecture

The primary components of the Warp architecture are shown in Fig. 1. A major design decision has been to base the Warp architecture on the notion of stable process rather than stable data structures (as in [2,4]). Processes do not share address space or clocks. They communicate by asynchronous message passing, and all data resides in the virtual address spaces of processes. The process is therefore the unit of:

- stability and recovery
- backtrack
- logical storage
- persistence and global naming—the unit to which persistent IDs (PIDs) attach.

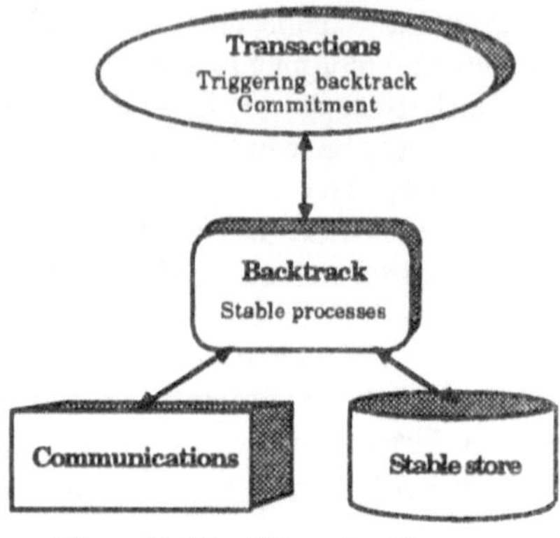

Figure 1: The Warp Architecture

Each process in the system consists logically of two components: the *client*, representing the application computation, and the *server*, implementing the generic features of the Warp architecture. Each operates in its own region of the process virtual address space, the client running at user level and the server as part of the operating system kernel.

The communication behaviour of a process is controlled by three message repositories (see Fig. 2(a)): the *input pool* contains waiting messages; the *input log* contains consumed messages; and the *output log* contains those messages already generated by the process, whether sent or not. Notice that the input and output logs are necessarily sequences because a process is a single locus of control. The logs together with state checkpoints constitute a complete record of the process history. The queues are managed by the server, and client communication is via system calls to the server. The effect of a client input is to move some message from the pool to the input log. The means by which this message is determined from the input instruction issued by the client is called the *selection* protocol.

3.1 Backtracking

We have already described how backtrack is propagated by means of antimessages. Fig. 2 shows a schematic representation of backtrack at a typical process. Fig. 2(a) is the situation before backtrack occurs. Fig. 2(b) shows the *rollback* caused by the receipt of the antimessage ¬M corresponding to the positive message M. Fig. 2(c) shows how backtrack results in a tree-structured computation over time, because generally a different *retry* computation ensues after each rollback.

Notice that in Fig. 2(a) the message M is already in the recipient's past. Were M still in the input pool, it would simply be cancelled out by ¬M without causing rollback.

For subsequent retry to take place, the

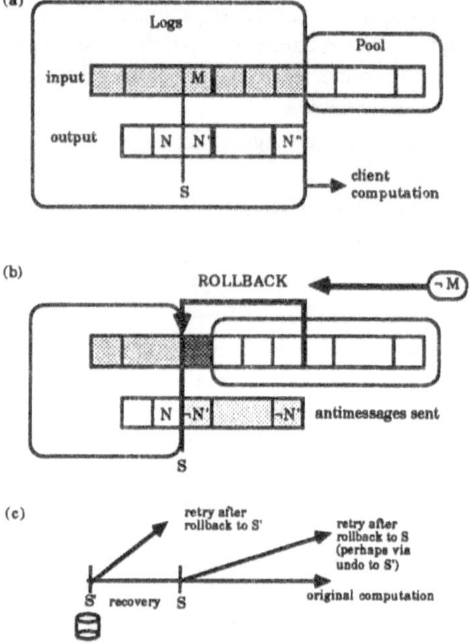

Figure 2: The Backtrack Protocol

client state S at the backtrack point must be restored. It may happen that S itself was not checkpointed, in which case the nearest previous checkpoint (e.g. S' in Fig. 2(c)) must be restored and the client run forward using the appropriate past inputs to reconstruct S—we say that the process *undoes* to S', and that S is *recovered* from S'. Notice that this scenario does not require the output messages between S' and S to be unsent, and also that for recovery to be an exact replica of the original computation, the selection protocol must be deterministic.

4 Transactions

Transactions are a global mutual exclusion primitive, and as such constitute a fundamental coherence mechanism. They are identifiable units of computation which disseminate through the system from process to process. Transactions are orthogonal to processes, in the sense that one transaction may touch many processes and many transactions may be hosted at a single process at any given time.

The purpose of mutual exclusion is to guarantee that all the computation that disseminates round the system associated with a particular transaction is atomic, i.e. not interleaved causally with the computation from any other transaction. This is equivalent to the database concept of serialisability. Transactions thus operate *competitively*, coming into conflict with each other when they try to communicate with the same process. Whenever conflict occurs, one of the competitor transactions must lose. Two of the primary functions of the transaction protocol are to prevent deadlocks and to ensure *liveness*—that a transaction does not keep backtracking indefinitely but will eventually commit (provided its computation is actually finite).

Transactions are identified by unique totally-ordered transaction IDs (TIDs). The ordering of TIDs is used to ensure liveness, by treating the TID of a transaction as its age, with oldest having highest priority. Moreover, every message in the system carries a unique TID stamp. A distributed mechanism for generating TIDs from local clocks in an unbounded system is described in [9].

4.1 The Computational Model

A process can host many *visiting* transactions, all executing simultaneously. However, when more than one transaction is present, the thread of each visitor T executes on its own private *clone* of the process (the T-clone), which lives only for the duration of its *parent* transaction T. To distinguish it from its clones, the original copy of the process is called the *master*. When a process originates a transaction, it is the *root* of that transaction.

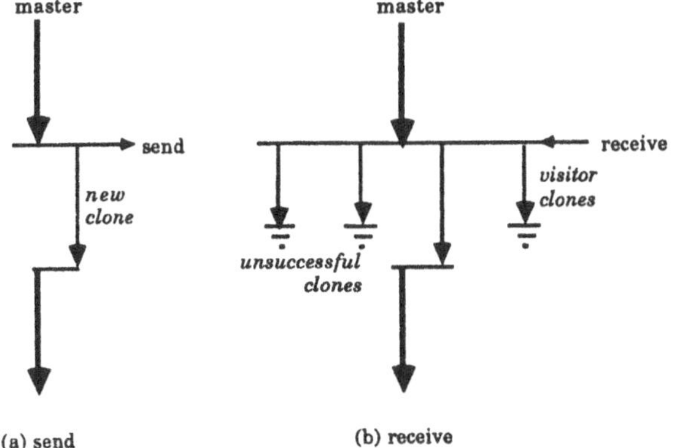

Figure 3: Clone creation

Only a T-clone can execute on behalf of T, i.e. send or consume messages stamped with the TID T. Also, the commitment protocol described below forbids the T-clone of any process other than the root of T spontaneously to send messages on behalf of T. It follows that a master cannot itself perform communications; it must create a clone, or clones, to do so. If the master is attempting input, it must create a clone for every transaction represented in its input pool; if it is attempting output, it must create a clone for a new TID. The two scenarios are shown in Fig. 3.

Only when one of its visitors commits will the master resume execution, from the point where the visitor clone terminates. A clone cannot terminate until it executes a special *end of transaction* (ETX) system call. It is worth noting that ETX is the only manifestation of the transaction mechanism at the program level.

4.2 Commitment

When a transaction commits, each of its clones replaces the master of the corresponding host process. Commitment is obviously impossible without some coordination amongst all the component computational threads of a transaction. To this end, each process keeps track of every transaction that visits it, until the transaction commits. At any given time, the visitors to a process are competing for its attention, so are in conflict; precisely one of the visitors *owns* the process. If a process has no visitors, the next visitor becomes the owner. Thereafter, ownership may change in one of two ways: the current owner either deliberately relinquishes ownership (which does not necessarily entail rollback) or ceases to be visitor, in one of two ways: by rollback, triggered elsewhere in the transaction, or by commitment. If the latter, the current owner clone becomes the master and the clones of all the other visitors must be rolled back to their starts and re-cloned (this is the only way in which backtrack can be triggered). In every case, ownership passes to the oldest of the remaining visitors.

Commitment uses a stable property detection protocol (SPDP) derived from the termination detection algorithm of [5], which is a form of reference count garbage collector. Specifically, the protocol detects that all the processes involved in a transaction have some *locally stable* property P. A locally stable property will never fail spontaneously at any process, but only by virtue of the process receiving another message from within the transaction.

To use the SPDP to detect transaction termination suggests taking P to be local termination. However, the local stability requirement means that P must also guarantee immunity from backtrack as the result of another transaction committing. This is the role of ownership. We guarantee that no clone belonging to the owning transaction of its host process is ever subject to backtrack from outside that transaction, and ownership is never confiscated. The SPDP will then detect termination if we take the property P to be local termination plus ownership.

To avoid deadlock, an owner which is unable to attain P must eventually back off and release its ownership. Moreover, the backoff must be transmitted to every clone of the transaction to allow the possibility of backtrack wherever other transactions may be waiting for ownership. This is accomplished by the originator of the backoff sending a special *backoff* message to all its acquaintance clones. Since these are the only messages that can invalidate P, they must also be SPDP messages.

Once termination has been detected by the transaction root, it disseminates a "second wave" of *commit* messages, following the paths of the original computation messages.

On receipt of the commit message, a process commits the relevant transaction and transfers ownership as described above.

4.3 An Example

Fig. 4 shows active processes which are engaged in two transactions, with TIDs $T_1 < T_2$. Transaction T_1 and T_2 have been independently initiated by processes A and E respectively. Recall that each process is owned by exactly one transaction, although it may be hosting many, and each clone belongs to its parent transaction. Initial ownership of a process goes to the first visitor, and the transaction initiator always clones itself. In this example process C is hosting both T_1 and T_2. T_1 has reached process C before T_2, so owns C, which has cloned of itself for each transaction.

We consider some possible outcomes in the above scenario.

- T_1 completes before T_2. Process A, the root of T_1, knows this when its SPDP reference count falls to 0. The clones $A|T_1$, $B|T_1$ and $C|T_1$ replace their masters. This invalidates clone $C|T_2$ and it must roll back to its start and be re-cloned from the updated C. Ownership of C then transfers to T_2, which runs to completion. Recall that a transaction cannot commit unless it owns all the processes it visits, but liveness ensures that all transactions commit eventually.

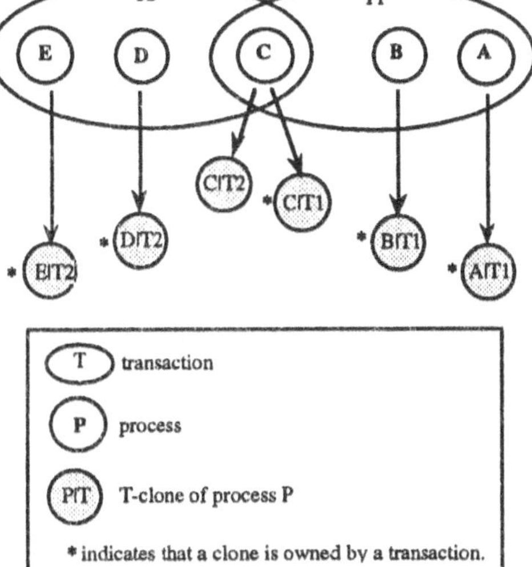

Figure 4: A snapshot of two transactions T_1 and T_2

- T_1 has visited, prior to C, a process F already owned by another transaction that eventually commits. T_1 rolls back and ceases to be a visitor at C, whence ownership of C passes to T_2. T_2 then owns all its hosts and is able to commit. This outcome shows that even though T_2 is initially waiting on an older transaction at C, the eagerness of its clone may still be beneficial, although how beneficial is a decision that must depend on some suitable heuristics.
- T_1 backtracks to its start (i.e. aborts itself) and commits by not changing C, thus releasing ownership. In this case ownership transfers to T_2 and there is no need for the work done by $C|T_2$ to be invalidated because the state of C is unchanged. This shows that backtrack can be optimised in certain special cases.

Finally, we illustrate how the TID (age) ordering avoids deadlock and ensures liveness. Suppose T_2 later visits another process F, acquiring the ownership, and that subsequently T_1 also visits F before T_2 has committed. Then T_1 and T_2 wait on each other: T_2 for ownership of C and T_1 for ownership of F. Eventually, one or both of the transactions will start to back off and release ownership of all their host processes. However, T_1, being the older transaction, will retain its ownership of C and acquire ownership of F. T_1 will therefore be able to commit.

5 Implementation Issues

5.1 Communications

In message-based computational models, it is usual to consider the communications layer as a black box that provides a channel with the desired properties—probably unique delivery, and perhaps monotonic (FIFO). Unfortunately, this may not be the most efficient approach where backtrack is involved. During the recovery that follows an undo, messages may be resent. These repeats should be effectively lost, otherwise they may be processed twice by the recipient. Similarly, the obvious way to tie an antimessage to its positive counterpart is to make the antimessage look like a "negative" repeat of the original. Messages must therefore contain sufficient information to distinguish repeats, and the backtrack protocol must act upon it.

Now consider how the channel service has been constructed in the first place. It will almost certainly be built upon an assumed unreliable and non-monotonic link, obtaining unique delivery by some sort of "repeat-until-ACKed" protocol. One effect of this is the possibility of copies of old messages suddenly popping out of the ether at a particular target process. So the channel protocol must be able to distinguish such repetitions from bona fide new messages, and it exercises this ability in providing the at-most-once part of its unique delivery service.

Thus, the channel protocol labels messages in order to separate them, whereupon the backtrack protocol relabels them in order to conflate them! This is just an example of the down side of modularity, but must be addressed by any system that claims good performance.

We therefore intend to prototype our channel protocol on top of a datagram service (e.g. UDP) to incorporate the specific needs of backtrack. Moreover, the problem just described is not the only drawback with off-the-shelf unique delivery protocols. They tend to interpret a "channel" as a virtual circuit, with all the overhead of connection and disconnection. Our channels need to be logical entities with a minimum of physical baggage.

5.2 Stability

The stable process model provides two distinct functions:

- checkpointing
- recovery

Checkpointing needs the underlying stable store to provide failure-atomic transfer of the client and/or server virtual address regions to the stable storage medium. Although the process is the unit of stability, we shall see below that failure recovery requires the client and server components to be stabilisable separately. Retry requires that a checkpointed state can be reloaded as the current state.

5.2.1 Failure Recovery

In principle, recovery from a failure—by which we mean a loss of information in volatile store—is just the recovery associated with a null backtrack. A process which temporarily fails is effectively undone back to its latest checkpoint, from which it recovers its current state. What complicates failure recovery is the fact that the log and input pool may also have been lost. In order to handle recovery by the backtrack mechanism, these backtrack data structures—in effect the server state—must be properly stabilised. We now derive two rules of recovery which make this precise.

- Once an incoming message has been ACKed, it is possible that no more copies of it will ever arrive again. Therefore an ACKed message in volatile store may be completely lost in the event of a failure. Furthermore, should a client run ahead into volatile input, even though this is unACKed and hence "stored in the ether", it might appear in a different order to a recovery computation, making this differ from the original. So the first rule of recovery must be ("consume" here means either ACK or act upon):

  R1: Never consume any message until it is stable.

Given this rule, a sender can stabilise an output message in two ways: by writing it explicitly to stable storage, or by getting an ACK for it. Whenever we refer below to stabilising an output message, we allow either of these possibilities.

- It is possible that a process might create a volatile section of output log—the *overrun*. Once an antimessage is consumed by a process, no more copies of the obsolete outputs will be generated. Should a failure strike during backtrack, those outputs may never be unsent. So we formulate the second rule of recovery as:

  R2: Never consume an antimessage until the overrun has been stabilised.

A traditional problem with failure recovery is the domino effect [14], whereby a cascade of backtrack throughout the system is triggered by one or more failures. The domino effect can only arise if global state information is destroyed by a failure, otherwise recovery is inevitable. The only potential source of information loss is an overrun, which could vanish in a failure. However, the rules specifically exclude any "information gaps", so the information persists somewhere in the system. An equivalent argument would be to observe that processes can always avoid overrunning without ever blocking.

6 Other Properties of the Warp Model

6.1 Autonomous Backtracking and Abort

During the course of its computation, a transaction may find it necessary to backtrack to some point and take an alternative computational path. The archetypal example involves booking a series of airline flights for a multi-stage journey, where the flight for the last stage turns out to be full. The only reasonable course open to the transaction may then be to backtrack to the beginning and commit a "noop". This is a form of abort, but a "user abort" in contrast to an automatic abort arising out of concurrency conflict—the latter variety does not exist in our model, because backoff and retry are simply part of a transaction's ongoing attempt to commit.

This kind of *autonomous* backtracking differs from the kind described so far in one crucial respect. Ordinary backtracking is controlled by the inputs—if these repeat, so will the computation path. In contrast, autonomous backtracking requires the new path to differ right from the backtrack point. Nevertheless, the autonomy can be achieved by means of *self-targeted* messages (see Fig. 5). When a process P identifies a possible autonomous backtrack point, it sends a message (M) to itself then checkpoints its state

(S). This is shown in Fig. 5(a). The content of M will determine the subsequent computation path. P then immediately inputs a message from itself, and proceeds accordingly. If P later perceives a need to backtrack, it simply sends itself the antimessage ¬M, which will undo it back to the backtrack point S. Actually, this is not quite sufficient. P must also be able to piggy-back a new version M' of M onto ¬M (giving the combined message M"), otherwise it has lost the opportunity to redirect its computation from the backtrack point. It is also crucial that S itself, and not some earlier state, be checkpointed, otherwise the undo will overshoot, recovery will resend the original M, and the computation will follow the first path again.

This mechanism provides completely general autonomous backtracking, sufficient to support any search strategy. User abort is simply the special case of a failed search. Returning to the example, the transaction might be aware of alternative flight combinations, backtracking over some stages to try other routes. Only ultimate complete failure will result in a user abort.

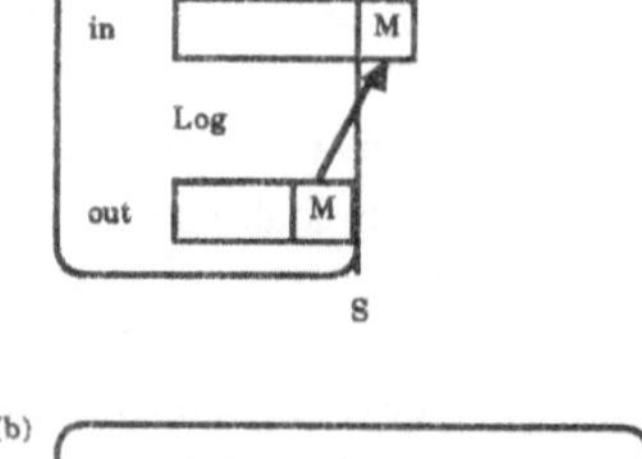

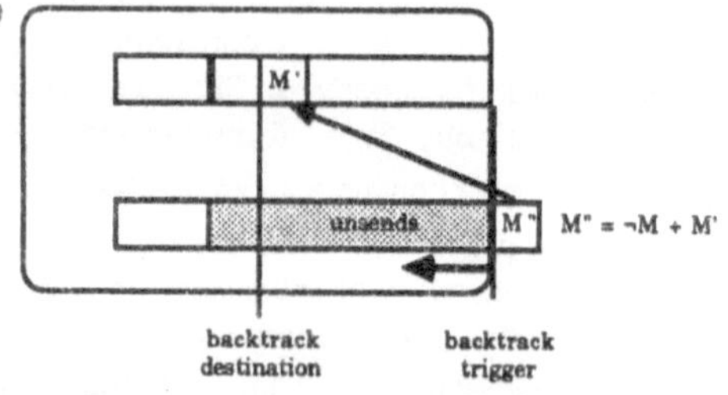

Figure 5: Autonomous Backtrack

6.2 Anchoring

As well as detecting termination, we would like to be able to detect *anchoring* of a transaction—immunity from further backtrack—irrespective of whether the computation has actually terminated. For interactive transactions, it can be important to get such a guarantee as soon as possible. The SPDP will detect anchoring if we take the property P to be simply ownership. It is still necessary to detect termination as well, in order that other ownership can be passed to other transactions. However, half the messages in each use of the SPDP are identical, so only 50% more messages are needed to add the anchoring detection.

6.3 Varimism

One of the novel features of the model of [9] is its "varimism". Tunable parameters of the system provide a spectrum between optimism and pessimism. This feature is retained by the present model. Although we have implied above that clone computation is eager, making the whole approach optimistic, this need not be the case. Since the commitment protocol detects anchoring rather than computational termination, it is possible for a clone to be fully pessimistic by not executing until its parent transaction owns the host process. Allowing behaviours between these extremes (particularly with regard to how much a clone disseminates its parent before awaiting ownership) gives the spectrum of varimism.

6.4 Nesting

Exactly the same commitment protocol can be applied at lower levels to perform intra-transaction concurrency control via transaction nesting. The only additional requirement is the ability to generate tree-structured TIDs. One issue that nesting raises is: how does a parent transaction interact with its children? (we call this *vertical* interaction—what we have considered so far is *horizontal* interaction amongst peer transactions). We take the view that while horizontal interaction is about competition, vertical interaction should be about cooperation. Such a view implies that a parent and a child clone cannot be allowed to execute simultaneously. Since the basic model makes masters wait on clones, we generalise this to the nested case by allowing only "leaf" clones to execute. Thus a message to a non-leaf clone at a process is forced to wait for all descendent clones to vanish. No deadlock possibility is thereby introduced, because waiting is only ever down the tree. Similarly, ownership of a process will attach directly to a leaf clone of that process, although the ownership must extend back up the corresponding branch of the ancestor tree—it is impossible to give a guarantee of local immunity from backtrack to a child clone yet not to its parent.

This semantics allows ancestor transactions to be active along with their descendants. In particular, it allows an overall ancestor computation, whose messages are outwith any transaction, that coexists with the top-level transactions. Notice that we refer to it as the ancestor "computation" rather than "transaction". This is because, having no peers, it is not in competition so need never commit. The ancestor therefore has a special status, with three particular implications: it is not concerned with ownership; it need never terminate; and it need have no single root—any process can spontaneously send an ancestor message (although only processes with special privileges would be permitted to do so).

6.5 Hard Commit

We have mentioned above that processes representing real-world effectors must always be pessimistic. Indeed, in terms of the transaction model, they must be "super-pessimistic" because they must not allow any clone to execute until its parent transaction is anchored. This is only possible if the clone can terminate without doing any computation, which requires it to know that it will never send any invocations. In other words, a device driver must satisfy the very reasonable assumption that it be a final node in the computation graph of any transaction that uses it.

6.6 Cooperation

Transactions are considered to be an inappropriate model for some applications. The main reasons are that they impose too much restriction on concurrency, particularly in cases of coarse granularity when they tend to become long, and being intrinsically competitive do not adequately support cooperative work.

We saw in section 6.4 that our model allows unrestricted computation outside transactions, and within a transaction at any level the interactions are also unrestricted. Nevertheless, because a transaction has a unique root it is not clear how distinct users of a database, for example, can ever have their own computations participating in the same transaction. This kind of "transaction sharing" would seem to be necessary to support cooperative work, and is impossible without more dynamic control over transaction boundaries. For example, suppose that a long transaction (T) has been initiated on a database by one user (A), and a second user (B) wishes to perform computations that could exist cooperatively with T. This can only come about if B can "join in" or "subscribe to" T in some way.

Our model supports this capability very straightforwardly, by what we call *reverse invocation*. User B joins in the transaction, but to fit the model this action is made to look as thought the transaction invoked B. The mechanism is as follows. B sends an enquiry message (E) to some process P that is known to be participating in T (perhaps but not necessarily the root of T). If the T-clone of P has not yet terminated locally, E can be viewed as an invocation by T of B, even though E flows from B to P. So A and B now have a joint participation in T, asymmetrical only in that overall termination control and responsibility lies with the transaction originator, A.

7 Status

Work to date has proceeded on two fronts.

7.1 Design

This includes formal verification of the model and the algorithms employed. We have formal proofs of the communication protocol, and the design of the detection algorithm is proceeding jointly with the development of a general proof of correctness of the interaction between the two time axes.

7.2 Implementation and Evaluation

The implementation platform consists of four autonomous Unix workstations connected by a dedicated 10Mb/s ethernet and 9.6K X25 links, providing both LAN and WAN operating conditions. The first phase began with an implementation of Time Warp [10], and evaluation of backtrack performance in this context (using distributed simulations) is currently under way, so far with favourable results. Starting with Time Warp has a dual benefit: it implements the core of the backtrack engine, and also provides a platform for any simulation required during evaluation. Current work is focused on implementing the Warp protocol on the above platform and refinement of the evaluation framework.

Recent micro-kernels such as Mach 3.0 [1] and Chorus [12] have removed many of the conventional OS obstacles and have been designed to support distributed environments. Although they do not provide direct support for persistent object systems or coherence in highly concurrent object environments they would appear to provide better implementation platforms than mainstream Unix systems and we are currently investigating their feasibility for this project.

8 Summary

In this paper, we have approached the problem of coherence in distributed persistent object systems with the aim of finding a model which supports conceptual uniformity and distribution transparency. To this end, we have presented the Warp architecture. The interface appears as an optimistic but safe transaction service which supports nested and cooperating transactions as well as simple atomic transactions. The central mechanism of Warp is of a system-wide backtrack protocol based upon stable processes communicating by asynchronous message-passing. This protocol has a number of important properties: it is deadlock-free, live, fair, highly distributed, scalable and fault tolerant to volatile storage failures.

9 References

1. BLACK D.L., Scheduling support for concurrency and parallelism in the Mach operating system, CMU Department of Computer Science Research Report, April 1990.

2. BROWN A.L. & ROSENBERG J., Persistent object stores: an implementation technique in *Implementing Persistent Object Bases: Principles and Practice*, Morgan-Kaufmann (1991) 199–212.

3. CHANDY K.M. & LAMPORT L., Distributed snapshots: determining global states of distributed systems, *ACM TOCS* **3**, *1* (February 1985) 63–75.

4. DASGUPTA P. & CHEN R.C., Memory semantics in large grained persistent objects in *Implementing Persistent Object Bases: Principles and Practice*, Morgan-Kaufmann (1991) 226–238.

5. DIJKSTRA E.W. & SCHOLTEN C.S., Termination detection for diffusing computations, *Info. Proc. Letters* **11**, *1* (August 1980) 1–4.

6. HÉLARY J-M. & RAYNAL M., Towards the construction of distributed detection programs, with an application to distributed termination, INRIA Research Report 1460, June 1991.

7. JEFFERSON D.R., Virtual time, *ACM TOPLAS* **73** (July 1985) 404–425.

8. LAMPORT L., Time, clocks, and the ordering of events in a distributed system, *Commun. ACM* **21**, *7* (July 1975) 558–565.

9. LIVESEY M.J., Distributed varimistic concurrency control in a persistent object store in *Implementing Persistent Object Bases: Principles and Practice*, Morgan-Kaufmann (1991) 293-304.

10. LIVESEY M.J. & ALLISON C., A general purpose Time Warp toolkit *Research Report CS/92/1*, University of St. Andrews, 1992.

11. MATTERN F., Efficient distributed snapshots and global virtual time algorithms for non-FIFO systems (private communication), March 1990.

12. ROZIER M. *et al.* Overview of the CHORUS distributed operating system, Chorus systemes, 1990.

13. SCHMUCK F. & WYLIE J., Experience with transactions in Quicksilver, *Proc. 13th ACM SIGOPS Symp. on Operating Systems Principles*, Pacific Grove, CA (October 1991) 239–253.

14. STROM R.E. & YEMINI S., Optimistic recovery in distributed systems, *ACM TOCS* **3**, *3* (August 1985) 204–226.

The Papyrus Object Library

Tim Connors Marie-Anne Neimat
Hewlett-Packard Laboratories
1501, Page Mill Road, Palo Alto, CA 94305, U.S.A
email: `lastname@hpl.hp.com`

Abstract

The Papyrus Object Library is a set of routines that provide simple access to persistent recoverable storage. It is intended to be used as one of several tools for implementing Data Managers in Papyrus. Three primary goals have shaped the design of the Object Library. The first is flexibility in adapting to Data Manager needs. The Object Library can be used to implement traditional storage managers as well as to provide persistence to programming languages. The second goal is to insulate Data Manager implementors from operating system and file system details without sacrificing performance. Simple localized modifications to one module of the Library can be easily made to take advantage of operating system features that can improve performance such as mapped files or raw I/O. The last goal is to provide high performance. The system is designed to provide very fast access to objects and very efficient allocation and deallocation of objects.

1 Introduction

The Papyrus project [6] at HP Labs is investigating ways of integrating and parallelizing highly-tuned customized Data Manager. Data Managers may be built using Papyrus services, or may be built independently of Papyrus. The Object Library is one of the services provided by Papyrus to construct Data Managers.

In Papyrus terminology, a *Data Manager* is a set of specialized methods that manage persistent data. Examples of specialized Data Managers are CAD systems or spatial data managers as found in Geographic Information Systems. Through specialization, Data Managers can provide specific functionality that is often absent from general purpose Database Management Systems (DBMSs). They can also provide better performance by focusing only on the functionality that is required. A collection of operators defines the interface to a Data Manager. A Data Manager has exclusive access to its data and permits access to its data only through the operators that define its interface. Thus Data Managers encapsulate persistent data and operators on the data.

Papyrus provides a number of services that are deemed useful for the construction of Data Managers. One of these services is the management and access of persistent recoverable storage. It is provided by the Object Library. Three primary goals have shaped the design of the Object Library. The first is flexibility in adapting to Data Manager needs. The Object Library can be used to implement traditional storage managers as well as to provide persistence to programming languages.

Several alternatives were considered in the design of the Object Library and the paradigm presented to its users. At the interface to the I/O subsystem, we considered explicit I/O versus mapped files. At the user level, we considered the single-level store model versus the object surrogate model. With the single-level store model, an object's identifier is synonymous to its virtual memory address and hence a user can directly access an object by using its identifier as an address. With the surrogate model, a user may request access to the object by supplying its identifier to an underlying storage manager. The storage manager uses the identifier to retrieve the object and gives back to the user either a copy of the object or the virtual memory address of the object.

The idea of mapped files if fairly old [2]. Mapped files take advantage of available virtual memory hardware support to bring desired file pages into memory. A mapped file must first be mapped into an application's virtual address space. After the initial request to map a file, the application references the portion of virtual memory allocated to the mapped file in exactly the same way it references any other portion of virtual memory. If the application references an address that has not been loaded into memory, the reference causes a page fault. The operating system services the page fault and resumes the execution of the application unbeknownst to the application. Mapped files are attractive because they relieve applications from the burden of issuing explicit I/O and of being cognizant of page boundaries. They can be very efficient because they take advantage of the typically highly-optimized virtual memory system. By bypassing the file system, they also avoid the potential copying and double buffering that can take place when using a file system. However, mapped files have not been popular with DBMSs because it is not easy to make them recoverable, they limit the size of databases to the size of virtual memory and they leave page replacement policies to the operating system [17, 18, 20].

The single-level store presents to its users a model where persistent and volatile objects are indistinguishable. Under this model, an object identifier (OID) and its virtual memory address are one and the same. Methods that need an object just reference it. This requires a database to be always loaded at the same address in virtual memory. The advantage of the single-level store model is that it simplifies programming since applications do not have to distinguish between persistent and volatile objects. It is also very efficient since object accesses do not have to go through any levels of indirection.

The single-level store model is somewhat orthogonal to the method used for bringing the database into memory. The database can be brought into memory in its entirety prior to any object accesses by the application. Alternatively, if a mapped file mechanism is used for doing I/O, then page faults cause desired pages to be brought into memory on demand. The first approach cannot be realistically used for large databases as it imposes an enormous initial loading overhead, but it has been used in some prototypes. The second approach is more realistic but still presents some disadvantages, the major one being that the database must always be mapped at the same address in virtual memory. This either means that access to multiple databases is disallowed or that each database is assigned a unique virtual memory address. We deemed the first choice unacceptable and the second choice unrealistic on today's hardware platforms.

Another disadvantage of the single-level store model is that since object identifiers are synonymous with object addresses, moving an object in memory means changing its OID. Moving objects may be required because of updates to the objects or to reorganize memory. This can represent a high overhead for the users of the single-level store as all references to a moved object must be replaced with its new identifier. To guarantee atomicity of transactions, the underlying system must be able to detect updates and to guarantee their recoverability. Yet with the single-level store, recoverability must be handled at the page level, which is the finest granularity at which updates can be detected. This is yet another disadvantage of the single-level store.

Many systems have chosen to swizzle pointers as a compromise to the single-level store model. Under this scheme, OIDs are not synonymous to virtual memory addresses but appear as such to applications. An initial conversion, or *swizzle* [12, 22], replaces an OID by its corresponding virtual memory address. Like the single-level store model, swizzling pointers does relieve the application from distinguishing between persistent and volatile objects. However, the supporting software must distinguish between a first reference to an object and subsequent references to the object. Upon detecting the first reference or prior to the first reference, the supporting software replaces the OID with the virtual memory address of the object. After this initial overhead, object accesses are executed as rapidly as virtual memory accesses.

We voted early on against the single-level store model because of the disadvantages listed above. We designed the interface to the Object Library to support the implementation of pointer swizzling as well as to support traditional data access. For interface to the I/O subsystem, we were interested in exploring the mapped file approach, especially if some of the problems listed with mapped files could be resolved. Section 2 describes the design of the Object Library and the motivation behind various design decisions. Section 3 describes how the Object Library can be used in a recoverable environment and under different concurrency control policies. Section 4 shows how efficient access methods can be implemented in an environment where details about pages are hidden from the method writer. Section 5 measures the performance of a number of operations supported by the Object Library. Finally, Section 6 compares the Object Library with other persistent object stores and we conclude in Section 7.

2 Design of the Object Library

The goal of the Papyrus Object Library is to provide Data Manager implementors with easy and efficient access to persistent recoverable storage. Data Managers are expected to have different requirements. Some may be implemented using a persistent programming language, others may want a more traditional approach to programming. Some may want to be cognizant of page boundaries and be in control of page layout, others may not want to bother with such detail. Some Data Managers may be single-user systems and hence have no need for concurrency control, while others may have different concurrency control requirements. We designed the Object Library to simplify the management of persistent data while being flexible and efficient.

As stated in the Introduction, we were interested in exploring the mapped file approach to disk I/O especially if some of the problems associated with mapped files could be resolved. The Mach operating system [1] overcomes what we consider to be the major problem with mapped files, namely that of making them recoverable. Mach also allows user programs to influence its page replacement policy through prefetching. With new architectures, the size of virtual memory is no longer an issue.

When the Object Library was being designed, mapped files were not available in HP-UX, but indications were that Mach-like mapped files would be made available. We were interested in experimenting with recoverable mapped files and comparing their performance to that of explicit I/O. Hence we designed the Object Library to localize the dependency on the file system in one module. The rest of the Object Library is oblivious to the choice of file system. This has resulted in a library that can be easily ported to other operating systems and file systems.

Data Managers request an object by OID and get back a pointer to the object. ¿From that point on, they can use the pointer to access the object as many times as they wish. Thus pointer swizzling may be easily implemented on top of the Object Library. The Object Library makes the fundamental assumption that each Data Manager has exclusive access to its data and that any external access to that data can only be made by invoking the data manager's interface. Thus, handing a pointer to an object back to a Data Manager does not represent a breach in security. Through that pointer, the Data Manager has access only to data that belongs to it.

Persistent data is organized in *Storage Segments* that are uniquely associated with a Data Manager. The Object Library allocates and deallocates objects in a Storage Segment, provides access to objects in a Segment, and handles updates to objects. Updating an object may make the object larger, thus requiring that it move to a different location in the Segment. The Object Library handles such movement of objects if necessary.

A Data Manager executes in its own address space, separately from all other Data Managers. It may choose to be multi-threaded to support multiple users. The Object Library is linked with each Data Manager and executes in a Data Manager's address space. It assumes that it may be used in multi-user mode. Thus, all accesses to the Object Library meta data are synchronized by semaphores (or latches). The Object Library does not handle the concurrency control of the real data. It assumes that a Data Manager will handle concurrency control if it requires it. This was a deliberate choice in order to allow Data Managers to adopt the concurrency control policy of their choice.

Objects are uniquely identified by their OID. The OID encodes the Segment identifier as well as the location of the object within the segment. Storage Segments are logically divided into 4K byte pages. In addition to the Segment identifier, an object's OID encodes the Segment-relative page number of the

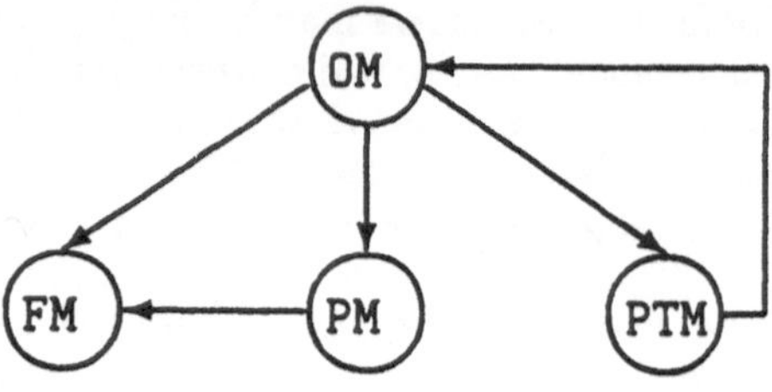

Figure 1: *Object Library Modules*

page containing the object. It also encodes the slot number of the object within the page (see Section 2.3). An OID is 64 bits long with 32 bits reserved for the Segment identifier, 26 bits for the page number and 6 bits for the slot number. Data Managers do not have to understand the encoding of OIDs.

The Object Library consists of four modules (Figure 1). The *Frame Manager* (FM) keeps track of Segments and Segment ownership, and provides the direct interface to the file system. It is currently implemented using Unix raw I/O and manages the Object Library's buffer pool. Its implementation would be simplified if explicit-access files were replaced by mapped files. The *Page Table Manager* (PTM) partitions each Segment into equal size pages that are the unit of I/O. It keeps track of various information about the pages of a Storage Segment in the Page Table (PT). The *Page Manager* (PM) manages individual pages. It is in control of page layout and object management within a page. The *Object Manager* (OM) is the only module whose interface is visible to users of the Object Library. It is also the only module with a global understanding of the different components in the Object Library. It manages small and big objects and invokes the other modules as necessary.

2.1 Frame Manager

The *Frame Manager* (FM) manages Segments and provides the direct interface to the file system. All file system dependencies are localized in the FM. In order to understand its design, we first discuss the different ways in which the interface to the file system can be managed. As discussed earlier, it may be an explicit-access interface or a mapped-file interface. The space allocated for a file in the requesting process' address space may be equal to the size of the file or may be smaller. DBMSs have traditionally used explicit-access interfaces to the file system and have allocated fixed-size buffer pools in their address space that are smaller than the databases they access. The main reason for that is to enable access to databases that are larger than virtual memory and to control page replacement. The merits of controlling page replacement of a buffer pool that resides in virtual memory are dubious because of the double paging that can take place. Furthermore, new computer architectures with large address spaces are becoming more common. Hence it is not unreasonable to allocate for a file an amount of virtual memory equal to its size.

In the case of mapped files, the typical approach is to allocate, in virtual memory, an amount of space equal to the size of the file. Allocating a smaller amount could be done but defeats the purpose of using mapped files.

The current implementation of the FM uses an explicit-access interface to the file system and allocates, for each open file, an amount of virtual memory equal to its size. The implementation contains "hooks" to move easily to a fixed size buffer pool or to a mapped file approach. Our intent was to compare the performance of these three approaches once recoverable mapped files became available in HP-UX.

The allocation of Storage Segments and their association with Data Managers is managed by the FM. Segments are identified by a 32-bit identifier. When a Data Manager requests the creation of a Storage Segment, it must specify the level of recoverability to be used for the Segment. There are three possible choices: *none*, *redo* and *undo/redo*. On updates to objects, the Object Library will do the logging necessary to guarantee the level of recoverability requested for the Segment. It is to be noted that logging is not currently implemented in the Object Library.

Before accessing any object in a Segment, the FM ensures that the appropriate file system or operating system call is issued. In our current implementation, this means that the FM issues an "open file" request. When we convert to a mapped-file implementation, this will have to be replaced with an operating system request to map the file in the Data Manager's virtual address space.

Meta data associated with a Segment is not stored in the Segment itself. The FM stores it outside the Segment and controls access to it through latches. It thus guarantees that access to meta data can be safely manipulated in a multiuser environment. Access to the real data in the Segment is not synchronized by the Object Library. It is expected that Data Managers will synchronize access to data stored in a Segment through a concurrency control algorithm of their choice and will enforce it outside the Object Library.

The FM encapsulates the operations required to convert a page number within a Segment into a virtual memory address for the corresponding page frame, and to ensure that the page is in memory. It is invoked by the OM whenever such a conversion is required.

With each open Segment is associated a Frame Buffer Control Block. It is an array with as many entries as the number of pages in the Segment. Each entry is 1 byte long. The entry contains the state of the corresponding page frame (*empty*, *full*, or *in transit*), a latch bit and a frame pin count. Latches are used to synchronize page meta data access and to ensure atomicity of object updates. They are of page granularity and are used only by the PM since it is the only module to read or write objects. The frame pin count is not used but has been reserved for the case of the fixed-size buffer pool where page replacement must be used to make room for newly-read pages. A pin on a page indicates that the page is not a candidate for replacement because at least one object on the page is in use.

In the current implementation, converting a Segment page number to a virtual memory address for the page frame involves the address conversion as well as issuing a read request to the file system if the corresponding page frame is *empty*. When we move to mapped files, only the address conversion will be required. A subsequent access to an object on the page will cause a page fault and will bring the page in memory.

There is a problem with the explicit-access interface to the file system. When a big object (an object that requires more than one page) is requested, the entire object must be read from the Segment into the buffer pool. This happens even if only a small portion of the object is accessed. This problem will be avoided when the FM is converted to a mapped file implementation. In this case, only the parts of the object that are referenced will cause page faults and will be read into memory. The Object Library could have circumvented this problem by providing an interface for requesting big objects not only by OID but also by byte offset and range of bytes. We chose to keep the interface transparent to the size of objects.

2.2 Page Table Manager

The *Page Table Manager* (PTM) partitions each Segment into equal size pages that are the unit of I/O, and keeps track of various information about the pages of a Storage Segment in the *Page Table* (PT). The main function of the PT is to simplify the management of free space within a Segment by keeping track of the amount of free space in each page of the Segment.

With each Storage Segment is associated a pre-assigned object with a hard-wired OID. This object contains Segment-related meta data such as Segment size and log method. It also contains an array of OIDs for the objects that hold the Segment's PT. The PT contains information about all the pages in a Storage Segment. It is broken up into several objects so that only the required entries of the PT must be memory resident. The partitioning of the PT into objects is such that each object occupies exactly one page.

A Segment's meta data and PT are implemented as objects so they can be accessed and updated using the regular Object Manager interface to objects. We thus avoid dual mechanisms for storing and retrieving information in a Segment. Of course this approach requires a bootstrapping process for initiating a Segment. Since creating an object requires reading the PT, creating the first PT object is a special case handled by the Object Manager.

Each page in a Segment has a corresponding entry in the PT. Each PT entry is one byte long. It contains a latch bit, a big object bit, and the number of free object slots available on the page. Section 2.3 contains a description of how pages are divided into 64-byte object slots and how "big objects" are allocated. When the big object bit is on, it indicates that the entire page is allocated to a portion of a big object.

To allocate an object of size n, the PTM searches sequentially through the PT entries looking for a page with at least $\lceil n/64 \rceil$ free object slots. When found, the PT entry for that page is latched and the page number is returned. Note that each PT entry has its own latch. This allows high contention on the PT. Allocating a new object requires searching the PT only, it does not require

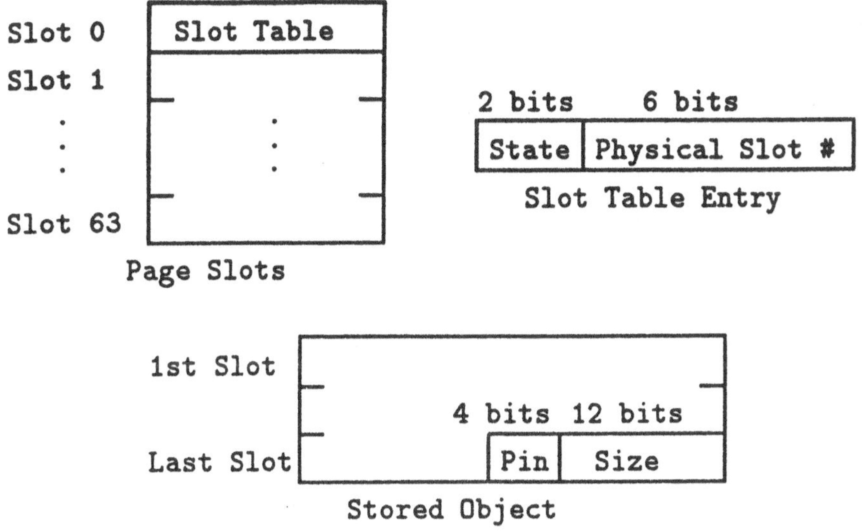

Figure 2: *Page Layout*

searching the pages themselves for free space. Moreover, the search of the PT is optimized to test several entries at a time.

2.3 Page Manager

The Page Manager (PM) is the only module that knows the layout of pages. Each 4K-byte page is divided into 64 slots with the first slot reserved for the slot table (see Figure 2). The slot table contains 64 1-byte entries describing the 64 slots on the page. One of the encodings in an OID is a 6-bit quantity called the slot table index or slot number. Its corresponding entry in the slot table contains the physical address of the object and the state of the slot (*free*, *small object*, *big object*, *tombstone*). This allows objects to move around on a page without changing OIDs. In fact, if an update to an object causes the object to require additional space that exceeds the size of the free space available on the page, the object is moved to a different page and a tombstone with forward reference is left on the old page. Thus the object's OID does not change even if the object must be moved to another page. It is a permanent identifier for the object, and the number of indirections required to reach the object never exceeds one.

As shown in Figure 2, an object can occupy more than one slot on a page. The physical address of an object, as it appears in the slot table, is really the physical slot number of the last slot occupied by the object on the page. This takes the PM directly to an entry containing the size of the object and a pin count for the object. Computing the beginning address of the object is an inexpensive shift and subtract operation using the size of the object. A pin on an object indicates that a pointer to the object has been returned to some user of the Object Library and hence the object cannot be moved around. Although pin counts are only needed at runtime, they are stored with objects for efficient access. This extra information is not kept at the beginning of the object so that the object itself can start on a boundary that is likely to satisfy the alignment requirements of RISC processors.

Although somewhat wastful of space, we decided to go with the fixed partitioning of pages into slots in order to simplify space management in general. The fixed partitions make it easier and faster to keep track of free space, to allocate objects, to reduce fragmentation, and to guarantee safe alignment for the beginning of objects.

2.4 Object Manager

All entry points to the Object Library are handled by the Object Manager (OM). It is the only module with a global idea of what is going on. It invokes the other modules as needed to support the operations of the Object Library. The OM manages objects and hides the notion of pages from its users. Objects may be big or small, they may or may not span page boundaries. Users of the OM do not need to know these details. For Data Managers that need to format their own pages, a facility is provided as will be shown in Section 4.

The OM's interface supports the allocation and deallocation of objects, the fetching of objects, and the update of objects. In addition, the OM supports the scanning of all objects in a Segment. This done by opening a scan on a Segment, and by repeatedly requesting the next object in the Segment until all objects have been returned.

The OM classifies objects that fit on a page as *small objects*, and objects that cannot fit on a page as *big objects. Big objects* require more than 63 slots to store them. They are broken up into two components, the object descriptor and the body. The object descriptor is handled as a small object and contains information about the big object including where it starts in the Segment and how large it is. The body is stored on contiguous pages within the Segment. The body of a big object does not share pages with any other objects big or small. A big object's OID is the ID of its descriptor.

Users of the Object Library request objects by OID. The OM returns to them a virtual memory pointer to the object. In the case of a big object, the pointer is to the body of the object. The object is automatically pinned by the Object Library. Similarly, Segment scans return virtual memory pointers to objects in a Segment.

Users of the Object Library are not supposed to update objects themselves even though they hold pointers to the objects. Instead, they must call an OM object update method. This method handles the object update, object relocation, if necessary, and invocation to the log manager if the Segment is recoverable. Since big objects are stored contiguously, the update of a big object may require copying a large portion of the object. In spite of this disadvantage, we felt strongly about keeping large objects contiguous so that their access could be as efficient as possible. In [3], the authors describe the way EXODUS handles big objects. A tree structure is used to index into big objects. This structure allows efficient updates to big objects. However, under their scheme, the mapping of big objects into contiguous space in virtual memory represents a very high overhead. We shyed away from such an approach because we believe that updates to big objects are infrequent and their efficient access is much more important.

3 Transaction Management

The Papyrus Object Library is designed to guarantee, for each Segment, the level of recoverability that was requested for it. Although not implemented yet, write ahead logging will be used to support the atomicity and durability of transactions. Depending on the level of recoverability required (*none*, *redo*, *undo/redo*), no images, after images, or before and after images of updated objects will be logged. For big objects, we will explore a combination of logging and shadow pages to guarantee atomicity and durability.

The Object Library assumes that concurrency control is handled by the Data Managers that invoke it. Data Managers may choose to do no concurrency control, if for example they are intended as single-user systems. They may choose to implement semantic locks, or to lock objects based on their OID. They may choose traditional two-phase locking or other protocols such as optimistic concurrency control. Using the Object Library does not prevent Data Managers from using any of these concurrency control models.

One of the more common variations on locking is the addition of intention lock modes to support hierarchical locking [7]. Hierarchical locking means that an explicit lock on an object implicitly locks the descendants of that object in the hierarchy. This substantially reduces the number of locks that must be held (e.g. only one lock is required to read all the objects in a Segment). Intention lock modes permit higher degrees of concurrency for transactions that only access a small number of items in a hierarchy. For correctness, there are specific protocols that must be followed to explicitly acquire or release a lock. For example, locks must be acquired from the root of the hierarchy down to the requested object.

Hierarchical locks can be easily implemented outside the Object Library. As seen earlier, an object's OID encodes the entire hierarchy of the object: segment, page and slot within page. Furthermore, OIDs are immutable. Hence, although isolated from the Object Library internals, Data Managers can benefit from this encoded hierarchy to use intention lock modes if they so wish.

4 Access Methods

We have seen so far that the user of the Object Library is insulated from page boundaries and page layout. Objects are requested by OID, and virtual memory pointers to the objects are returned. This is a nice simplified model that can serve a large number of users. One can easily implement a variety of access methods for the content-based retrieval of objects using this model. In fact, the access methods themselves can be implemented using the Object Library.

There are cases however where the user wants to be in control of page layout and wants to be cognizant of page boundaries to have a better handle on performance. One of these cases is in the implementation of tree-structured access methods that were designed specifically for retrieving data stored on block-oriented secondary storage devices.

To support this class of users, we have provided a function that allocates page-size objects. An invocation of this function allocates an object that occupies exactly one page after leaving room for the page header and object trailer information required by the Object Library. The function returns a pointer to the object as well as its size. This object can then be used by the caller as a page in a tree-structured access method. The caller can format it in any way that is appropriate for the application for which it was intended. Thus the isolation from page structures and page boundaries at the object level does not preclude implementations that must really know about them.

5 Performance

We ran a number of experiments to measure the performance of what we assumed would be the most frequently used operations of the Object Library. All experiments were run on an HP 9000 Series 800 Model 835 workstation with 32 MBytes of memory, and running the HP-UX operating system. The 835 has a 15 peak MIPS and 9.5 SPECmark processor. All experiments were run while the workstation was connected to the network, and although no other processes were explicitly run, the system was not brought to single-user mode so that the results of the experiment would be close to what one would expect in a running system. Average numbers are reported for all experiments where the number of runs was large enough to reduce the variance to an insignificant number.

The first set of experiments were to measure the time it takes to fetch an object. The caller of the Object Library requests an object by OID and gets back a virtual memory pointer to the object. This pointer may be used to swizzle the OID or just to get access to the object. To fetch an object, the Object Library must compute the virtual memory address of the object and must check if the page containing the object is in its buffer pool. If it is not in the buffer pool, it must initiate an I/O request to read it in memory. Finally, before it can return the pointer to the object, it must pin the object so that it remains at the same address while the object is in use.

The first set of experiments were run for various I/O requirements. Table 1 summarizes their results. In the first case, the pages containing the requested objects were not in the Object Library's buffer pool. Hence an explicit I/O request was required to bring them into the buffer pool. The amount of time to fetch an object was dominated by the I/O time and was fairly consistent at around 20 msecs. This turns out to be a side-effect of the HP-UX kernel

Table 1: *Time required to fetch one object*

Type of Object	I/O Requirement	Time in μsecs
Small Object	Object Library initiated I/O	20000
	No I/O	70
Big Object	No I/O	91
Object with Tombstone	No I/O	140

configuration. The quantum time allocated to a process is set at 10 msec. When an I/O completes, the operating system services the I/O completion interrupt but continues to execute the process that was running at the time the I/O completed until its quantum is exhausted. Since the process running the Object Library was the major process running during the experiment, it got scheduled immediately afterwards. Hence the 20 msec represents two quanta and indicates that the I/O time took somewhere between 10 and 20 msecs.

In the second case, the objects were memory resident and their access was guaranteed not to cause any page faults. We measured the time to fetch an object for small objects, big objects, and objects that had to move to another page, thus leaving a tombstone behind. For small objects, the time required to fetch an object was 70 μsecs and is fairly indicative of the expected cost of swizzling an OID. This roughly corresponds to 700 RISC instructions on the 835. We did not measure the time to fetch big objects or objects with a tombstone when I/O is required since the fetch time becomes dominated by the I/O time. For big objects, of course, the I/O time should be proportional to the size of the object. Fetching a big object is only slightly more costly than fetching a small object if the big object is already in memory. Fetching an object with a tombstone is equivalent to fetching 2 objects.

In the second set of experiment, we measured the time it takes to fetch an object when scanning a Segment. Recall that one can request to scan a Segment and then repeatedly request the next object in the Segment until all objects have been returned. In this case, the objects are not requested by OID, but are requested in the context of the scan. The numbers returned under this experiment fall into one of two categories. The first one is when the first object on a page is requested, thus causing the page to be brought into memory. The second one is when objects are requested on a page that has already been brought into memory.

We report these two numbers separately in Table 2. The time to get the next object in a scan when the page containing the object must be read from disk is dominated by the 20 msec I/O service time. Note, however, that the cost of getting the next object in a scan from a memory resident page is twice the cost of fetching an object by OID as shown in Table 1. This is because the scan operation has to first find the next valid OID in the Segment and then fetch it. It finds the next valid OID by inspecting the slot table. The amount of time it takes to scan a whole Segment can be easily derived from the

Table 2: *Time required to fetch one object in scan mode*

Object	Time in μsecs
First object on a page	20000
Other objects on a page	140

Table 3: *Time required to allocate and deallocate one object*

Operation	Time in μsecs
Object Library first *allocation* on a page	20000
Object Library other *allocations* on a page	279
HP-UX *malloc*	354
Object Library first *free* on a page	21000
Object Library other *frees* on a page	304

numbers listed in Table 2 and from the number of objects in a Segment and their average size. Similarly the average time to access an object in scan mode can be derived from the results of the experiment and the number of objects in the Segment and their average size.

In the last set of experiments, we measured the time it takes to allocate and deallocate an object. Table 3 summarizes the results of the experiments. As can be observed, if the allocation of an object happens to find free space in a page that is not memory resident, the cost of the allocation becomes dominated by the I/O service time. If the page is already in memory, the time required is roughly 279 μsecs. To calibrate the meaning of this number, we measured the time required by the HP-UX supported *malloc* function. The 354 μsecs reported are the result of performing *mallocs* in unfragmented space. We expect this time to get larger as space becomes fragmented after many HP-UX *malloc* and *free* calls are executed. Note that the time to perform an Object Library *free* operation is slightly higher that the time required to perform an *allocation* operation. This is due to the free space coalescing that must take place.

In summary, the results of our experiments show that once data becomes memory resident, the cost of fetching a small object that has not moved around is roughly 700 instructions, the cost of accessing an object in scan mode is roughly 1400 instructions, and the cost of allocating objects is comparable to performing HP-UX malloc functions. The Object Library can easily support the demanding performance requirements of persistent programming languages while still providing much of the basic functionality required by traditional storage managers.

6 Related Work

Several new storage managers have been recently implemented to meet the demands of new applications [3, 8, 9, 10, 14, 16, 19, 21]. Some are extended relational storage managers, others support persistent programming languages, while others provide a single-level store model. We discuss some of them below.

EXODUS [4] is an extensible DBMS developed at the University of Wisconsin. While the interface of the Storage Object Manager [3] is similar to that of the Papyrus Object Library, some differences exist in how they are implemented and used. The major difference is in the extent of modularity supported by the two systems. EXODUS incorporates concurrency control within the Storage Object Manager while the Papyrus Object Library does not. Both systems use a buffer pool scheme to cache disk pages. EXODUS implements a fixed-size buffer pool with traditional page replacement. The Papyrus Object Library allocates, for each open file, an amount of virtual memory equal to its size and hence does not implement any page replacement.

In their intended use, the EXODUS Storage Object Manager and the Papyrus Object Library are very different. The EXODUS system includes the E persistent programming language [13, 15]. References to persistent variables cause the E compiler to generate code which contains calls to the EXODUS Storage Object Manager. Thus, the major user of the Storage Object Manager is the E code generator. EXODUS DBMS implementors program in E. In Papyrus, implementors program in whatever language seems appropriate to the task. They use the Papyrus Object Library routines directly.

The ObServer [8] storage manager is used to implement an object-oriented DBMS and an object-oriented programming environment. It manages chunks that resemble what the Papyrus Ojbect Library refers to as objects. Much of the emphasis in ObServer is in providing transaction support for groups of users who share designs and must share modifications of transactions that are in progress. ObServer uses the traditional Unix file system and objects are requested by OID through a procedural interface. Copies of objects are handed back to the user. ObServer supports an intricate update mechanism as objects can be cached by clients and multiple copies must be kept consistent.

The Starburst [9] and POSTGRES [19] storage managers are examples of extensible relational storage manager. The table is the primary data type supported. User defined data types can be specified for table attributes and user defined access methods are permitted for those types. Both storage managers adhere to the traditional explicit-access interface to the file system and fixed-size buffer pool with DBMS controlled page replacement. Access to data is through a procedural interface.

The O2 object manager [21] is implemented using the Wisconsin Storage System [5] (WiSS). Like Starburst and POSTGRES, WiSS adheres to the traditional explicit-access interface for I/O, fixed-size buffer pool with controlled page replacement, and data access through a procedural interface.

The Mneme Persistent Object Store [10, 11] is a system under development at the University of Massachusetts, Amherst. It is intended to support the integration of programming languages and DBMS functionality. It focuses on object-oriented languages such as Smalltalk. For this reason, Mneme objects incorporate higher level semantics than do Papyrus objects. These semantics cost in reduced generality. Objects are expected to be small. As in the Object Library, the body of an object is an uninterpreted sequence of bytes but it has some state and flag bits associated with it. Mneme objects also include an attached list of references to other objects to support the typical internal data representation of object-oriented languages. The size of a Mneme object and the number of slots are fixed when the object is created and cannot be changed afterward. Mneme objects could be easily implemented on top of Papyrus objects.

Mneme objects are segregated in a complex hierarchy which includes files, pools, logical segments and physical segments. For all this classification, search or scan mechanisms are missing, but applications can "pointer chase" through object slots. The initial reference using a Mneme OID requires the use of three lookup tables to find the object. Subsequent references use a handle. Thus, a read of a cached object requires the invocation of a Mneme subroutine followed by access through one level of indirection. Experiments with swizzling objects were conducted in the context of Mneme [12] and they showed that swizzling is worthwhile when objects are accessed many times within a session.

Mneme allows flexibility in locking and logging. This is accomplished through strategy routines associated with pools of objects. Additionally, these routines may affect placement of objects in persistent store, replacement policy in the volatile buffers and pre-fetching.

Cricket [16] is an experiment in using operating system memory management primitives for implementing a persistent object store. It uses primitives of the Mach operating system to provide a shared, transactional, single-level store. In scope, it compares more closely to the Frame Manager component of the Papyrus Object Library. The entire database is mapped into the application address space and is manipulated with normal memory reference instructions. In contrast, the Papyrus Object Library maps one object at a time, and only reads are performed with normal instructions. Locking, protection and logging in Cricket are all at the page level and are implemented using the Mach external exception and page handling mechanisms. Locks are *shared* or *exclusive* and recovery uses a form of page shadowing. Hence users of Cricket are given no choice of concurrency control algorithm or of granularing of locking and logging.

The Cricket runtime environment includes routines for Object manipulation. Creation and deletion mimic the Unix *alloc* and *free* functions. Cricket objects may be small or large, but cannot grow in size. Since it provides a single-level store model, an OID is the address of the object.

There is no formal grouping mechanism in Cricket. However, objects created at the same time have a good chance of being close on disk and in the address space. Object creation takes a "near" hint. No access methods are provided by Cricket, but they can be implemented on top of it. Buffer management is provided by Mach.

7 Conclusion

We have presented the design of the Papyrus Object Library, the motivation behind many design decisions, and the performance of what we expect to be the most commonly used operations in the Object Library. The design of the Library had been driven by the desire to provide simple and efficient access to persistent recoverable storage for implementors of specialized Data Managers, by the desire to accommodate the varied requirements of Data Managers and by our own interest in experimenting with various options for implementing I/O. While providing a very simple model, the Object Library can be easily used to support pointer swizzling as well as to support the basic functionality required by traditional storage managers such as intention lock modes and access methods for block-oriented secondary storage devices.

Our current implementation is based on explicit-access to the file system through Unix raw I/O and on the allocation of enough space in virtual memory to hold all open files without doing any page replacement. Users of the Object Library are insulated from the specific I/O implementation. The Object Library has localized all file system dependencies in one module, the Frame Manager. Simple modifications to the Frame Manager can be easily made to move to other I/O implementations. The current Object Library implementation has proven to be very efficient. In the future, we will compare it with the performance of recoverable mapped files. We will also compare it with the performance of a fixed-size buffer pool that is locked in main memory and where the Object Library is in control of page replacement.

Based on the performance figures reported in [16], we expect that recoverable mapped files will have some overhead associated with them. They do however simplify programming. In our case, most of the Frame Manager would no longer be needed. On the other hand, the Frame Manager is not a complex piece of code (it is only 1100 lines of C code). The allocation of enough space in virtual memory to hold all open files is a reasonable compromise if recoverable mapped files are not available or do not provide adequate performance.

In its current implementation, the Object Library provides excellent performance for fetching objects, scanning Storage Segments and allocating and freeing objects. It can easily support the demanding performance requirements of persistent programming languages while still providing much of the basic functionality required by traditional storage managers.

Acknowledgments: We gratefully acknowledge the contributions of Waqar Hasan, Curt Kolovson and Donovan Schneider.

References

[1] M. Accetta et al. Mach: A New Kernel Foundation for UNIX Development. *Proc. of the Summer Usenix Conference*, June 1986.

[2] A. Bensoussan, C. Clingen, R. Daley. The Multics Virtual Memory. *Proc. of the 2nd Symposium on Operating Systems Principles*, Princeton University, New York, October 1969.

[3] M. Carey, D. DeWitt, J. Richardson, E. Shekita. Object and File Management in the EXODUS Extensible Database System. *VLDB*, Kyoto, Japan, August 1986.

[4] M. Carey, D. DeWitt, G. Graefe, D. Haight, J. Richardson, D. Schuh, E. Shekita, S. Vandenberg. *The EXODUS Extensible DBMS Project: An Overview*, University of Wisconsin-Madison, Computer Sciences Technical Report #808, November 1988.

[5] H.-T. Chou, D.J. DeWitt, R.H. Katz, and A.C. Klug. Design and Implementation of the Wisconsin Storage System. *Software - Practice and Experience*, vol. 15, no. 10, October 1985.

[6] T. Connors, W. Hasan, C. Kolovson, M.-A. Neimat, D. Schneider, K. Wilkinson. The Papyrus Integrated Data Server. *Proc 1st International Conference on Parallel and Distributed Information Systems*, December 1991.

[7] J. Gray. Notes on a Database Operating System. In *Operating Systems: An Advanced Course*, Springler-Verlag, 1979.

[8] M. Hornick and S. Zdonick. A Shared, Segmented Memory System for an Object-Oriented Database. *ACM Transactions on Office Information Systems*, vol. 5, no. 1, January 1987.

[9] B. Lindsay, J. McPherson, H. Pirahesh. A Data Management Extension Architecture. *ACM SIGMOD Conference*, San Francisco, California, May 1987.

[10] J.E.B. Moss and S. Sinofsky. Managing Persistent Data with Mneme: Designing a Reliable, Shared Object Interface. In *Advances in Object-Oriented Database Systems*, vol. 334 of *Lecture Notes in Computer Science*, Springer-Verlag, 1988.

[11] J.E.B. Moss Design of the Mneme Persistent Object Store. *ACM Transactions on Office Information Systems*, vol. 8, no. 2, April 1990.

[12] J.E.B. Moss Working with Persistent Objects: To Swizzle or not to Swizzle. *IEEE Transactions on Computers*, 1992. To appear.

[13] J. Richardson. *E: A Persistent Systems Implementation Language*. Ph.D. thesis, University of Wisconsin-Madison, Computer Sciences Technical Report #868, August 1989.

[14] H. Schek et al. The DASDBS Project: Objectives, Experiences, and Future Perspectives. *IEEE Transactions on Data and Knowledge Engineering*, vol. 2, no. 1, 1990.

[15] D. Schuh et al. Persistence in E Revisited - Implementation Experiences. *Proc. 4th Intl. Workshop on Persistent Object Systems Design, Implementation and Use*, 1990.

[16] E. Shekita and M. Zwilling. Cricket: a Mapped Persistent Object Store. *Proc. 4th Intl. Workshop on Persistent Object Systems Design, Implementation and Use*, 1990.

[17] M. Stonebraker. Operating System Support for Database Management. *CACM*, vol. 24, no. 7, 1981.

[18] M. Stonebraker. Virtual Memory Transaction Management. *ACM Operating Systems Review*, vol. 18, no. 2, 1984.

[19] M. Stonebraker et al. The Implementation of POSTGRES. *IEEE Transactions on Data and Knowledge Engineering*, vol. 2, no. 1, 1990.

[20] I. Traiger. Virtual Memory Management for Database Systems. *ACM Operating Systems Review*, vol. 16, no. 4, 1982.

[21] F. Velez, G. Bernard, and V. Darnis. The O2 Object Manager: an Overview. *VLDB*, Amsterdam, The Netherlands, August 1989.

[22] P. Wilson. *Pointer Swizzling at Page Fault Time: Efficiently Supporting Huge Address Spaces on Standard Hardware*. Technical Report UIC-EECS-90-a6, University of Illinois at Chicago, December 1990.

Keynote Discussion Session on Persistent Type Systems

Richard Connor

Department of Mathematical and Computational Sciences, University of St Andrews
St Andrews, KY19 9SS, Scotland

Malcolm Atkinson

Department of Computational Sciences, University of Glasgow
Glasgow, G12 8QQ, Scotland

Giorgio Ghelli

Dipartimento di Informatica, Università di Pisa, Corso Italia 40,
Pisa, Italy

Atsushi Ohori

Kansai Laboratory, OKI Electric Industry, Crystal Tower,
1-2-27 Shiromi, Chuo-ku, Osaka 540, Japan

1 Introduction

The idea for this session was prompted by the observation that there has been a decline in the number of papers on the subject of type systems research in the persistent object system community over recent years. In 1985 the first Persistent Object Systems workshop took place in Appin, Scotland, wholly on the theme of persistent data types. Since then the number of presentations in this workshop on the subject of type systems has steadily reduced, this year reaching zero. Does this signify such an increase in understanding that that there is little research left to be achieved? Or does the community no longer perceive such importance for the subject? Or perhaps the outstanding problems are either intractable, or at least too difficult for significant progress to be made.

In the light of this observation the panel, all of whom believe strongly in the importance of type systems research, was called to justify the continuation of research into persistent type systems. In the ensuing lively debate, in which some elements of the audience were perceived as distinctly "type-unfriendly", this justification may be summed up by two points for which good evidence was given:

- the type systems of languages such as C and C^{++}, although currently being used for many experiments in persistent object store design, may not be considered sufficiently good for the requirements of persistent systems

- the use of static persistent type systems, such as those which have resulted from recent research, help to produce demonstrably more reliable code than strong dynamic systems

The key issues of the debate will be presented under these headings. In retrospect it is difficult to assign statements, agreements and disagreements accurately to individual members of the panel and audience. What is presented here is believed to be a summary of the consensus of opinion which prevailed during the debate, and all of the opinions expressed here should not necessarily be believed to be held by all the audience or indeed all of the panel members!

2 Why isn't the C++ type system good enough?

The question was asked to the panel: "Does anyone believe that type systems of languages such as C++ are actually good enough?" They were unanimous in the strong conviction that such type systems are simply not acceptable; when the question was opened to the audience nobody was prepared to admit to a belief that such type systems are viable in the persistent context. Three main reasons were given by members of the panel for this conviction.

2.1 Unnecessary dynamic errors

There is at least anecdotal evidence, which everyone present seemed to have experienced, that programming in languages with such type systems leads to a great number of annoying run-time errors which could easily have been discovered statically with a more sophisticated type system. The consequences of such errors occuring in long-lived applications are significantly more serious than in short-lived applications. One such anecdote involves the AT&T telephone network, which failed in 1990 for some time due to a C programming error. This failure was later attributed to a type error which was undetected by the C compiler. This failure eventually resulted in a restructuring of Bell Labs, to give a greater commitment to the ML project there!

2.2 Pointer integrity not guaranteed

The inherently weak nature of these type systems means that pointer integrity can not be guaranteed. It was pointed out that, while persistent object systems are expected to contain all the data of large and long-lived applications, they have frighteningly little centralised information about this data. Much of the semantics of the data is contained implicitly in the topology of graphs of persistent objects and pointers. If any kind of failure should occur then there is a very serious chance of not being able to interpret whatever is left in the persistent store if the type integrity is not guaranteed. Therefore any persistent type system must be strongly enforced, at least to the extent of disallowing arbitrary address arithmetic.

2.3 No support for code as persistent data objects

One last point, which again all the panel and the majority of the audience were in agreement with, is that a persistent type system must be able to support persistent code, that is code must be representable as persistent data objects. This requires a type system with support for first class procedures. There is no real hope of being able to build an integrated persistent system if the executable code and the data are forced to exist in separate universes.

3 Why are static systems better than dynamic?

Given that weak type systems are insufficient, the question still remains as to whether the kind of type systems proposed by recent research are an improvement over previous persistent type systems. For example, the first persistent language, PS-algol, has a type system which although largely dynamic is strongly enforced and supports first class procedures. Subsequent type systems have greater modelling power and are more statically enforceable, but at what cost? A number of possible criticisms were raised about more modern and sophisticated type systems.

3.1 Are modern type systems too complex?

Type systems are fundamentally built in at the bottom layer of the persistent technology. Is there not a danger of providing complex type systems which are not perfectly suited to the applications designers' needs, in which case a simpler less sophisticated type system would be a better thing to provide?

The panel were unanimous in agreement that one of the most important tasks for type systems researchers is to simplify type systems, rather than complicate them. It is not always clear how to achieve this, or even that it is always possible, but it is always the aim.

Type systems are becoming more powerful in that they can describe more structures rather than less. One danger of this of course is that they may become incomprehensible. This however should be mainly a matter of patient language design, as things which start off incomprehensible generally become more understandable after some language design work.

It was stated that language designers had gone through a bad phase in type systems, where there have been good reasons to include many different type concepts into their languages. Much of the best work which has been done recently in type systems however actually simplifies and unifies these concepts. It was believed that it is possible to achieve a very powerful and very simple type system, and that this would become apparent in the next few years.

There was some argument from the audience that the use of static type systems makes it significantly more difficult to write good software, due to the writing of much redundant information, which also hinders the reuse of software. This was accepted as possibly true for some existing static type systems, but it was pointed out that fundamentally there was no reason why the task of writing correct programs should be made more difficult by a mechanism which prevents the writing of incorrect programs.

3.2 Are there any demonstrable advantages?

Does anyone know of any real engineering evidence that static typing results in better engineered, more reliable systems?

There was at least some anecdotal evidence of this. The difficulty of collecting such evidence is that it requires a sizable piece of code to have been hand-coded from a dynamically typed language into a similar statically typed language. The dynamically typed code should then be extensively used so that a number of the dynamic errors come to light, and then the statically typed code should be inspected to see if these errors have been factored out statically by the type system. Clearly such an experiment would be extremely costly to perform.

This situation had arisen accidentally, however, during the construction of the Napier88 language system. The Napier88 compiler was originally written in PS-algol, and then hand-coded from PS-algol into Napier88 as part of the bootstrap process. The compiler used in the release system was the PS-algol version. Subsequently, a number of errors have come to light in the release compiler which have turned out not to exist in the Napier88 version as the code had to be changed to comply with the type system. In all cases correct code had resulted through this process, even although the errors in the original code had not been noticed.

How much evidence do we have that the class of errors which type systems avoid is actually a serious class of errors? Maybe we should be moving to a stronger technology which may be able to catch real errors, instead of the trivial ones that typecheckers can find.

It was accepted that type systems may be able to find only trivial bugs, but that trivial bugs are not necessarily less important that non-trivial ones: even a very trivial bug can cause an aeroplane to crash! The degree of importance of an error is a difficult thing to assess until after it has occurred.

Of course there is a large class of errors in programs which can not be detected by type systems. However the hypothesis is only that there is a class of errors in programs which can be detected by type systems. It is hard to understand the argument that we shouldn't bother checking for a particular class of errors just because these errors are trivial. In the experience with the Napier88 compiler, there were three errors in the dynamically typed system which didn't come to light for three years after the software was released. These are perhaps examples of the most potentially devastating class of errors which exists in software systems.

3.3 Is polymorphism ever used?

Is there any evidence to support the belief that all the polymorphism features in recent languages are contributing significantly to code reuse? Are programmers prepared to take the extra time to write a polymorphic routine rather than a monomorphic routine so that someone else can use their code in the future?

The panel were first keen to dispel the myth that it must necessarily the more difficult to write a polymorphic routine, which would have exactly the same code as the equivalent monomorphic routine. Some current systems may make it more difficult, but there is no fundamental reason for this to be the case. The only difference should be the way in which the code is typed. If the type system works by inference then the programmer wouldn't even be aware of the difference.

In answer to the first question, the answer is yes: there is evidence of a great deal of polymorphic code reuse among programmers who have been given a statically typed polymorphic persistent environment in which to program. Unfortunately it is not widespread as such systems are relatively uncommon.

There is also much anecdotal evidence of people who have switched from using C to C++ and have immediately started to use template types, parameterised collection types and so on. These type abstractions have been found to greatly reduce the difficulty of programming and sharing code. (Not that anyone present was advocating the use of C++ - but it was admitted to being an advance over C! The point was that the polymorphic features provided were heavily used by programmers.)

There is also an amount of evidence in the object oriented community. It was proposed that one of the major reasons for the great popularity of object orientation is to do with the subtype polymorphism that object oriented languages provide.

3.4 Are static systems too restrictive?

Is there not a serious danger that there are many useful programs which cannot be written in most static type systems?

The difficulty here is that when we impose a type system on a language we restrict the class of computations that we can describe. With a good type system, most of the disallowed computations are undesirable ones; however any such generalised restriction necessarily also disallows a class of desirable computations. Some well-identified classes of correct programs can be re-introduced by special mechanisms, polymorphism being a good example of this. However these classes are re-introduced at risk of complicating the type system of the language and even to the point of starting to lose the static checking capability.

One example of a function that can't be described in most statically checked type systems is natural join, which fact should worry the database programming community. This is not to say that it is impossible to design a type system that can check this statically; indeed the language Machiavelli does this. The point is that it has to be allowed for explicitly, and this involves not only complicating the type system for each such function, but also knowing in advance the set of such required functions, which is clearly impossible.

One hope in this area is the recently emerged technology of strongly typed linguistic reflection, which allows a programmer to write generator functions which effectively contain the generic abstractions normally associated with type systems. This allows a way of defining functions which are not statically typeable, by effectively allowing the programmer to provide a higher-order type abstraction which is checked at the time of function call. It is believed that this technology may be used to outmanoeuvre the type system in places where it is found to be overrestrictive, but without compromising its safety.

3.5 What is the performance overhead?

It should be the case that enhanced static type information may be exploited to improve the performance of language processors and stores. Why is it most programmers perceive that it is possible to write programs with better performance in weakly typed languages like C?

The main reason for this perception is because of the difference in the investment in compiler and in particular optimisation technology. Certainly in principle the compiler can do a better job with better type information. However the performance comparisons are being made between well-established systems which have large amounts of industrial investment and very new systems in the research domain with very little investment in performance.

Another factor is a confusion between the language processor performance itself and the memory management strategy. As C has no memory management overhead it will always execute faster until the memory runs out. Many persistent systems however will actually out-perform C systems for data-intensive applications, according to the patterns of memory usage.

3.6 Are type systems a distraction from salvation?

On the correctness and safety issue: is there a danger that, by a concentration on types, there is a neglect of other methods of statically analysing the correctness and safety of programs. There are significantly different ways of doing this; is type systems research a cul-de-sac in which you can get so far and no further?

This may quite possibly be the case. The original concern, however, is that people aren't even concentrating on type systems, never mind other static methods! It is difficult to say whether people put their faith into type systems at the expense of these other methods, which are very valid and dangerously neglected areas of research.

4 Conclusions

The overall mood of the debate was encouraging. The audience on the whole seemed to be very much in sympathy with most of the panelists' less outrageous statements, and the importance of type systems research in the persistent context seemed to be generally agreed upon. The reason for the lack of such research being presented at the workshop was not however forthcoming!

5 Acknowledgements

As well as the panelists, many members of the audience contributed to the ideas presented here. In particular, Fred Brown, Peter Buhr, Elliot Kolodner, Mike Livesey, Ron Morrison, John Rosenberg, Ray Welland and Paul Wilson are to be thanked for their illuminating insights and questions, along with many others who remain anonymous.

Schema Manipulation and Optimisation

Véronique Benzaken

Universite de Paris I
Sorbonne,12 place du Pantheon, 75005 Paris, France

Schema manipulation and (query) optimisation have been topics of increasing interest in the last few years. While the former usually addresses the problems of supporting evolution in databases, the latter addresses the problem of efficiently performing queries.

This session contained three different papers. The first one, presented by Eric Amiel from France, discussed the need for a model independent schema manager. The second paper by Elisa Bertino from Italy, presented by Danilo Montesi, deals with cost-based optimisation techniques for object models. Lastly, the third paper, presented by Waqar Hasan from USA, addressed the problem of defining an intermediate language providing optimisable and parallelisable language features.

The paper presented by E. Amiel proposes an interesting way of handling schema evolution in the context of object-oriented databases. The paper asserts that most of existing schema managers fail to ensure consistency between classes and their instances as soon as changes in the schema occur. The main reason is that the object manager knows very little about the type's semantics. Even if object managers are provided with the right information, they are bound to a particular object-model. As there is no consensus on a standard model such a solution prevents the system from supporting different models. The approach proposes the definition of a generic schema manager (OMNIS). This is achieved through full exploitation of reflexivity and object-oriented features. The core schema manager is designed (in C++) with a few classes which when specialised capture the essence of a given object model.

The second paper, by E. Bertino, proposes an analytical cost model for object-oriented queries. The model is suited for four distinct strategies combining two different query graph traversals and two different access methods for instances. The cost model captures specific aspects of object-oriented models such as complex objects and class hierarchies. The main contribution consists in defining those parameters which precisely characterise an object-oriented database and in expressing cost formulas which will be useful as basic blocks for a general query optimiser.

The third paper by W. Hasan, is devoted to the design of an intermediate language, PIL, dedicated as a target language for end-users languages such as OSQL. The aim is to provide PIL with a set of optimisable and parallelisable features. It is argued that such an intermediate language should not be object-oriented. The main reason is that object-oriented features while enhancing programmer's productivity prevent optimisation. PIL supports a functional model of computation thus providing declarative semantics allowing for optimisations. In order to cope with data intensive applications adequate data type constructors as bags, sets, tuples are incorporated to PIL. Offering different abstractions for iterations over bags and sequences is the focus of some discussion. Such different abstractions are expected to reflect usual databases operations and to be optimisable.

The first part of the discussion concerned the first paper and it was pointed out that having semantics in the object manager prevents it from performing further optimisation. Concerning the first paper, a second question about comparisons between OMNIS and ENCORE was asked and more generally an actual implementation of different object models such as O_2, Gemstone, etc... should be of valuable interest.

The second part of the discussion addressed optimisation issues. A first question was about how well the cost model fitted. It was answered that yet no measurements have been performed. Nevertheless, while in the deductive database field, optimisations are syntactic and well understood, in the object-oriented field, due to a lack of theoretical framework, it is not yet the case. Formal studies should therefore be encouraged. The last questions concerned the PIL paper, the first one pointed out that the choices made are dedicated to a particular optimisation technique. Is it a good choice? It was answered that not much experience was collected at the present time. The second question asked for a comparison between PIL and other relational or general purpose languages (like Modula, etc...). The aim of designing PIL was not to build yet another user programming language but an intermediate language with almost all features provided in any language.

Then, everbody went to the cloister to enjoy an actual italian expresso...

A Model-Independent Object Schema Manager*

Eric Amiel, Marie-Jo Bellosta and Patrick Valduriez

INRIA-Rocquencourt
78153 Le Chesnay Cedex, France

Abstract

In this paper, we propose an object management interface system (OMNIS) intended for use by OO tools, e.g., compilers, interpreters or CAD/CAM programs, which require support for managing persistent objects. Through extensibility, it achieves a high degree of independence with respect to both the object models of the client OO tools and the underlying object managers. To this end, we use a reflexive object model allowing the dynamic creation of meta-description levels to capture new object models. Implementing this model implies being able to create objects whose type, i.e. structure and behavior, is dynamically defined, a kind of genericity normally impossible in a typed and compiled language like C++. The idea is then to build our own type layer on top of C++ type system to describe the structure and behavior of objects. To build this layer, we use polymorphic structures and abstract function invocation. Finally, we define the notion of a manager to capture each aspect of an object model such as instantiation, inheritance or aggregation.

1 Introduction

Most object-oriented database systems (OODBMS) like Exodus [1,2], Ode [3,4], Ontos [5] and ObjectStore, extend an existing OOP language to make it persistent [6]. This approach makes it possible to rely on the compiler of the host language but with two problems : the blindness of the object manager and the amnesia of the compiler. The object manager is typically blind with respect to the types of the objects it stores : a persistent object looses its type when put in the object manager and recovers it only when copied in memory. Since all typing information is lost after compiling, the compiler is unable to remember the data dictionary.

However, information on types, meta-information, is central for database schema evolution, i.e. making consistent changes to the structure and methods of classes and instances. Consistency between objects and their types is essential for guaranteeing the integrity of the database. Programs cannot safely manipulate objects whose type definition has changed. Therefore, the objects must be deleted and reconstructed with the new type or conversion routines must be written.

Some systems like Orion [7] and GemStone [8] use a persistent data dictionary in an interpreted environment. If the amnesia is cured, the object manager is still blind. Schema evolution remains the responsibility of the higher-level layers of the system that maintain the consistency between classes and their instances.

The O2 system [O291, O2B92] incorporates the notion of class within the object manager, thereby opening its eyes. It offers a higher-level interface to the compiler, building classes and managing instances according to their classes. The object manager becomes a *schema manager*, since it is able to handle both instances and classes through schema evolution operations. However, a problem arises : how do the schema manager's

---

* This work has been partially funded by a grant from the CNET, Lannion.

object model and that of the host language coexist ? In O2, the problem is solved by having the schema manager and the language share the same object model. Nevertheless, this solution hinders the connexion of the schema manager to languages with different object models. This is a particularly acute problem as no consensus whatsoever exists on object models.

The originality of OMNIS [11] is to tackle the above problem of amnesia and blindness *independently of a particular object model* : it is a generic schema manager that can be adapted to different object models via its models'analysis and its extensibility. OMNIS'fundamental assumption for analyzing object models is that any object model may be decomposed into at least five submodels : instantiation, inheritance, aggregation, composition and client. The semantics of each of these submodels is defined by a set of invariants and a set of operations. To capture a new object model starting from an existing one involves determining for each submodel which invariants and which operations differ. In this sense, a specialization relation may be established between submodels. Thus, capturing a new model amounts to specializing existing submodels if needed. Indeed, a model may only differ in one of its submodels and thus wish to reuse some others.

The fundamental assumption for extensibility in OMNIS is that any object model may be captured using two meta-description objects : the *instantiation root* to describe the common structure and behavior of classes, and the *inheritance root* to describe the instances. Together, these roots have the ability to create new roots describing new models. Such an extensible approach is particularly relevant in the OODBMS world where existing object models are augmented to serve database requirements : for example, Ode adds integrity constraints and triggers to the C++ model. Beyond the traditional benefits of reusability and extensibility, this approach is a step towards interoperability between systems based on different object models by providing uniformity in schema management protocols, object representation and access. This approach to interoperability can be found in the ENCORE database[12], but OMNIS uses an object-oriented data model and its extensibility aims at bridging the gap between its default model and the specific semantics of any object-oriented model. By extending its model to directly support the semantics of a given language data model, OMNIS eliminates any impedance mismatch.

In this paper, the focus is on the implementation of OMNIS'model. Implementing OMNIS'model implies being able to create objects whose type, i.e. structure and behavior, is dynamically defined. One of the challenges of OMNIS was to integrate the dynamicity required by its reflexive model into compiled, static C++. The idea is to build our own interpretative type layer on top of C++ type system to describe objects structure and behavior. To build this layer, we use polymorphic structures and abstract function invocation.

The paper is organized as follows. Section 2 presents the objectives and architecture. The primary objective is to manage meta-information regarding the persistent objects stored in the object manager without being tied to a particular object model as advocated in [11]. Section 3 presents OMNIS reflexive object model and shows how this model allows capturing the semantics of various object models thereby achieving genericity. Section 4 describes the implementation of OMNIS'reflexive model in C++. In Section 5, we introduce the notion of a manager. A manager is a class which supplies all the operations defining the semantics of the model restricted to one of its dimensions such as instantiation, aggregation or inheritance. The integration of managers with OMNIS objects and their specialization is shown to help in capturing a new model.

2 Objectives and Architecture of OMNIS

2.1 Objectives

OMNIS is intended to connect various *user tools* such as compilers, interpreters, or CAD/CAM tools, to an object manager that supports persistent and shared objects (see Figure 1). OMNIS aims at providing these different persistent object systems with full schema management services. The primary objective is to manage the meta-information regarding the persistent objects stored in the object manager. This translates into two dimensions : management and evolution of the schema. Moreover, these are to be achieved according to the semantics of different object models, as a unique object model is still lacking.

Persistent objects are described in a schema which may be dynamically changed. However, some update operations may violate the database consistency. For instance, the deletion of an instance variable can invalidate the methods referring to it. To maintain database consistency under updates, a number of invariants and restructuring rules need to be enforced [7,13]. For example, an instance variable may not be deleted if it is still referred to by a method. OMNIS supports consistent schema evolution over all operations on database schemas.

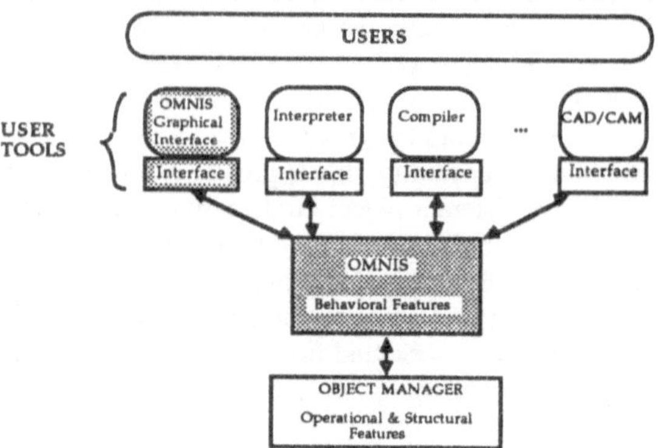

Figure 1: OMNIS Users

The design of OMNIS is motivated by four important considerations : OO methodology, extensibility, interoperability and object manager independence. OO *methodology* is chosen for gaining the engineering advantages of OOP. OMNIS is organized as a C++ class library, in which each class describes an important component with its behavior in terms of methods. *Extensibility* is the solution to the lack of unique OO model. OMNIS classes and methods capture general OO concepts, and can be specialized or redefined to match the requirements of OO systems (OOS). *Interoperability* allows different systems to share object and thus relies on the uniformity of schema management protocols, object representation and access. *Independence* from the underlying object manager makes OMNIS portable to various object managers such as Geode [14], Exodus or a more complete system like Ontos. The object manager supplies all the capabilities of a DBS kernel, e.g., cache and transaction management, as well as data structures with their associated operations.

2.2 Architecture

OMNIS is a class library intended for any user tool which needs to manipulate persistent entities defined using a specific OO model. Each user tool can choose the relevant subset of OMNIS facilities and build its own interface for dealing with any operation on persistent data: definition, access and update.

OMNIS'architecture is shown in Figure 2. It is composed of two main components: conceptual and physical. The conceptual component represents all the OO aspects; it is a meta-model which can be made equivalent to another model by the addition of constraints. The physical component is responsible for the connection with the underlying object manager and provides facilities to design the clustering of persistent objects.

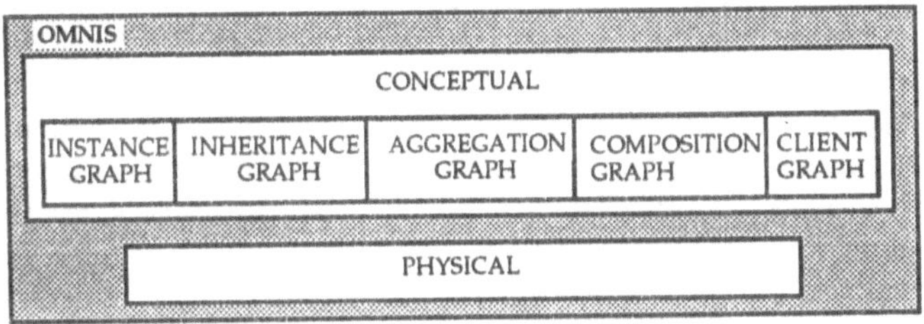

Figure 2: OMNIS Architecture

The conceptual component manages five submodels represented as graphs. The instantiation graph defines the entities of the model and the mechanism to create new objects. The inheritance graph defines the mechanisms for class specialization and generalization. The aggregation graph defines the structural composition of the classes. The composition graph defines the references between instances and is only needed to support composition constraints, such as cardinality or exclusivity [15]. Finally, the client graph defines the behavioral aspects of the classes, i.e., the inter-class relationships in terms of messages. These five graphs model the five aspects of OMNIS'object model. As OMNIS'extensibility relies on instantiation and inheritance, we'll only detail these two.

3 Generating Object Models : the Reflexive OMNIS Model

OMNIS defines a default object model whose invariants are common to the vast majority of object models. This model is then to be specialized to capture other object models. Its OO concepts are those necessary for object creation, class inheritance, object structure and class behavior. Each of them has a corresponding graph whose types of nodes, edges, invariants and evolution rules define the model semantics. As OMNIS is reflexive, its model is expressed using its own representation, that is by describing its graphs. These concepts are obtained by generalizing the OO concepts of the most representative OOS, e.g., Smalltalk [16], Eiffel [17], C++ [18] and Clos [19] as well as OODBS, e.g., Orion and O2.

In order to illustrate these concepts, we use a common example taken from [20] which models a publishing company. A publication is either a journal, a conference paper, or a book; it has a title, a set of authors, a set of figures and a set of pages. A publication can be printed, sold, reedited, and distributed; to each of these actions corresponds a particular method. A journal is referenced by a name, a date and a number. A book is referenced by an editor, a prefacePage, a titlePage, and a price. A page is referenced by a character policy, a length, a width and a set of paragraphs. TitlePage and PrefacePage are specializations of Page.

3.1 Instantiation

The instantiation mechanism deals with the way objects are created. The schema management facilities of OMNIS imply maintaining meta-information on instances as well as on classes. To capture object models, another level of meta-description is required. For this reason, OMNIS uses the ObjVLisp instantiation model [21] which considers three entities: instance, class and metaclass. An *instance* is the terminal element; it has a structure, its *instance variables*, and a behavior, the instance methods; it is the only entity which cannot perform creation. A *class* can create instances; it maintains the common structure and behavior of its instances, i.e. the definition of their instance variables and their methods. In the same manner, a *metaclass* can create other classes *or metaclasses*; it maintains the common structure and behavior of the objects it creates. When the instance is a class, the instance variables are called *class variables*, as they describe a class or metaclass. Metaclasses and classes are *generators* as they have the ability to create objects, unlike instances.

Instantiation defines an *Is-A* relationship from a class to a metaclass and from an instance to a class. These relationships can be captured by the instantiation graph. The instantiation graph is a directed connected graph with a unique root, the metaclass OmMetaclass. To break the infinite recursion on meta-level of description, OmMetaclass is its own metaclass and thus its own instance as illustrated in Figure 3. This is the basis for OMNIS reflexivity. OmMetaclass is predefined and all other metaclasses are generated by and must inherit from it. As it captures the default structure and behavior of all other classes, it is the *instantiation root*. of the OMNIS model.

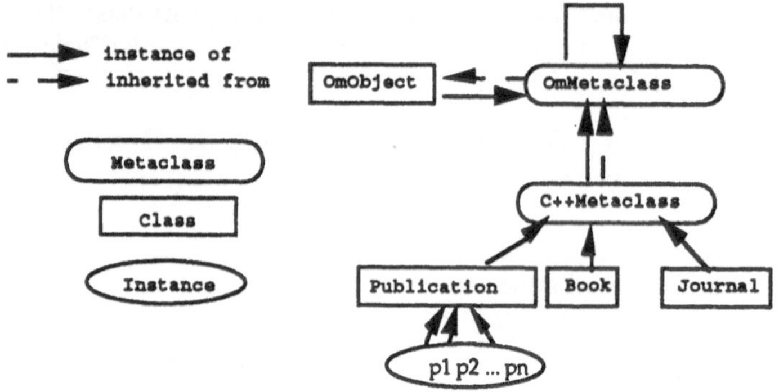

Figure 3: Instantiation Graph

As OmMetaclass is its own instance, its structure must be defined by its own instance variables stored in class variable *instVars*. OmMetaclass structure is composed of the following class variables defining relevant information on each OMNIS graph : *name*, *generator*[1] and *instances* for the instantiation graph, *superclasses* and *subclassess* for the inheritance graph, *instVars* for the aggregation graph and *instMethods* for the client graph.

[1]references the generator of the current schema object.

OmMetaclass methods include creation and schema management methods like *New*, *AddSuperclass* and *AddMethod* that are specific to class behavior.

As the metaclass defines the common structure and behavior of its classes, it may be used as the instantiation root of the model, i.e., the generator of the model's classes. Thus, the metaclass is the first meta-object needed to capture an object model. This contrasts with the Encore data model [12] or Smalltalk which offers a fixed number of meta-description levels and in which each metaclass is used to describe only one class. Therefore, the ability of a metaclass to create other metaclasses is the key of OMNIS'extensibility.

The evolution of an instantiation graph involves only actions on the nodes, i.e., addition or deletion of instances, classes, and metaclasses. The consistency of the graph is regulated by the two following invariants:

Node Semantics Invariant. A class cannot become a metaclass and vice-versa.

Uniqueness Invariant. A metaclass is an instance of either OmMetaclass or another metaclass. A class is an instance of only one metaclass and cannot become an instance of a different metaclass.

3.2 Inheritance

Inheritance defines an Is-Kind-Of relationship between two classes, one being the superclass and the other the subclass. A subclass inherits all the instance variables and the behavior (the methods) from its superclass(es). Therefore, inheritance is a complement to instantiation : the definition of an object is determined both by its generator and by its generator's superclasses. Inheritance can thus be used to define the structure and behavior common to the instances of *all* classes of a model : this common definition is embodied in a class that is the superclass of all the model's classes. This superclass is our second meta-object needed to capture an object model : the inheritance root.

Combining inheritance with instantiation is the key to the creation of metaclasses. The only difference between metaclasses and classes lies indeed in the ability of their instances to still be generators, i.e. create other objects. Such ability is granted by inheriting from OmMetaclass as it defines the structure and methods of generators, and most importantly the creation and schema management methods : by inheriting from a metaclass, a generator ensures that its instances also have the structure and behavior of a generator.

The inheritance graph is a directed acyclic connected graph. It has a single root, the OmObject class, which has the same structure as the OmMetaclass class. The OmObject methods, from which all OMNIS classes inherit, defines access to the object's structure, method invocation and error management. As it captures the common structure and behavior of all OMNIS objects, including classes and metaclasses, it is the *inheritance root*. of the OMNIS model. Note that OmMetaclass also inherits from OmObject. Moreover, the OMNIS model supports multiple inheritance with explicit conflict resolution. To be general, inheritance of instance variables is static (done at creation-time) while method inheritance is resolved dynamically.

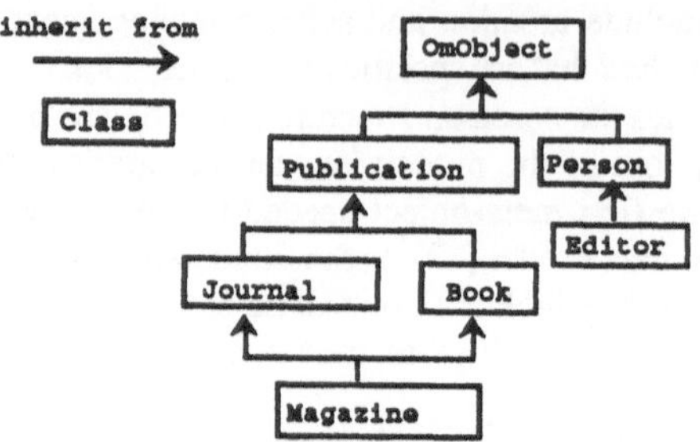

Figure 4: Inheritance Graph

The inheritance graph can be changed using operations on the nodes and edges. These are the addition of a new class, the addition of an edge (addition of a superclass or a subclass), the deletion of a class, the deletion of an edge, and the modification of an edge (change in the superclass ordering). The consistency of the graph can be maintained using the following invariants :

Inheritance Graph Invariant. The inheritance graph is a directed acyclic connected graph whose unique root is the OmObject class.

Full Inheritance Invariant. A class inherits all instance variables and methods from its superclasses.

Metaclass Inheritance Invariant. All the direct superclasses of a metaclass must be themselves metaclasses, except for the root of the instantiation graph which inherits from the OmObject class.

3.3 OMNIS'Extensibility : Building New Roots

The fundamental assumption of OMNIS is that the definition of a new model is achieved by creating a new instantiation root and a new inheritance root. The new instantiation root metaclass describes the common behavior of the model's classes and the new inheritance root class specifies the behavior shared by the instances. Specializing OmMetaclass is the way to redefine the schema creation and management methods of the classes. By contrast, the access and invocation methods have to be redefined by specializing OmObject. The new inheritance root class is itself an instance of the new instantiation root, as it is a class of the new model.

We illustrate this central idea with an example. Figure 5 represents an OMNIS schema combining instantiation and inheritance which shows how the C++ model can be generated by OMNIS. C++Metaclass represents the metaclass defining the structure and behavior of C++ classes. For it to be a metaclass, it inherits from OmMetaclass. But C++Metaclass has also additional instance variables, e.g., *friends* to capture C++ friend classes that are allowed to access the private instance variables. Moreover, its methods are specialized versions of OmMetaclass'methods. Thus, its instances, the C++ classes, will behave according to the C++ model semantics. For example, method addSuperclass takes a new parameter specifying whether the superclass is virtual or not.

Moreover, in C++, access to the structure and method invocation is restricted by different levels of visibility : *private*, *protected* and *public*. In order for all C++ instances to obey to these rules, a new root superclass, C++Object, is created. It is an instance of C++Metaclass as it is a regular C++ class. C++Object specializes the access and invocation methods. C++Metaclass inheritance management methods check that all C++ classes ultimately derive from C++Object. Thus, C++metaclass and C++Object capture the C++ model, in the same way OmMetaclass and OmObject define OMNIS'default model. Note that C++Object creation was only motivated by the redefinition of the object access protocol. A model having the same protocol as OMNIS, only needs to create a new metaclass.

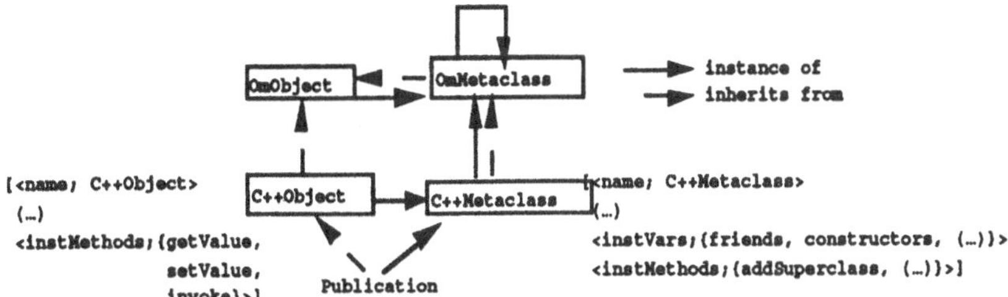

Figure 5 : C++Metaclass and C++Object for Capturing the C++ model

The structure of a class being defined by the instance variables stored in the *instVars* class variable of its metaclass, its creation amounts to valuating them either in the parameters of the New method, or using their default value. Thus, to create the C++ Publication class, the New method defined in OmMetaclass is invoked with parameters valuating C++Metaclass instVars. These instance variables become Publication's class variables : *name* gets the value 'Publication', *instVars* gets [figure, editor][2] , *methods* gets [print()] and *friends* gets (Editor). The remaining class variables are valuated by the instantiation method : *generator* gets C++Metaclass, *instances* gets { }, *superclasses* gets (C++Object), *subclasses* gets { }. As no superclass is initially specified, the C++Metaclass instantiation method assigns C++Object as the default superclass of Publication. The schema of OMNIS now contains five persistent objects : OmMetaclass, OmObject, C++Metaclass, C++Object and Publication. C++Metaclass represents the meta-information on the C++ model classes, C++Object describes C++ instances and Publication, class Publication.

4 The OMNIS Model and C++

Existing implementations of OMNIS'reflexive model [21] are based on interpreted, weakly typed languages like Lisp. Metaclasses, classes and instances are dynamically created via message sending, with various structures and behaviors. In statically typed languages, a type is normally used to define structure and behavior. In OMNIS, this role is played by metaclasses and classes that describe their instances. As they are dynamically created, we would need to dynamically create types if we were to rely on the type system of host language to describe OMNIS objects. For example, C++Metaclass is the type of Publication, which is itself the type of its instances. While this dynamicity is easily achieved in Lisp, it is impossible in typed languages in which the types of all objects must

[2] { } denotes a set, () denotes a list and [] a dictionary.

be statically defined. One challenge was to integrate the dynamicity required by OMNIS'model into a typed language like C++.

The way to solve the dynamic typing problem is to build a layer on top of C++'s type system allowing the dynamic definition of any structure and any behavior. As the OO methodology is the guideline of our design, we implement this layer as a class hierarchy (see figure 6) addressing two requirements : one essential, genericity, and the other, closeness to the OMNIS model. Genericity, both structural and behavioral, makes it possible for objects to be parameterizable in their instance variables and methods. Thus, all objects may be uniformly represented as instances of a unique class. This class is *AnyObject.*

Being close to OMNIS allows to offer a more specific interface than the one provided by AnyObject's genericity. By exploiting the semantics of the OMNIS model, we factorize the structure and the interface common to all OMNIS objects by defining class OMNISObject. Using the instance versus generator distinction, we further specialize OMNISObject into two classes : Instance and Generator.

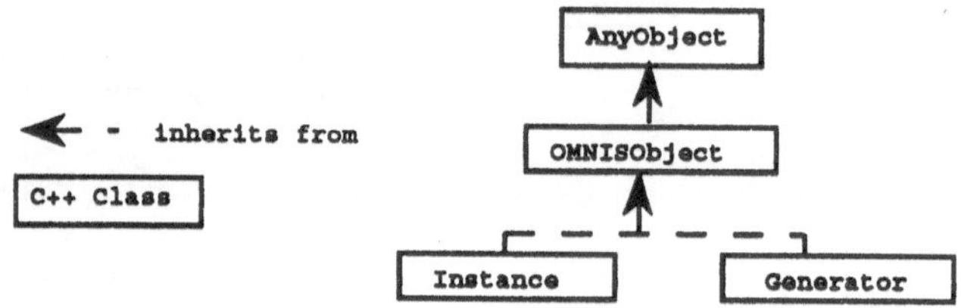

Figure 6 : OMNIS Implementation Classes Hierarchy

4.1 AnyObject

4.1.1 Providing AnyObject with Structural Genericity

To achieve structural genericity, class AnyObject (see Figure 7) is provided with methods to manage the logical abstraction of an associative collection of member variables, *memberVars.* Depending on the objects represented by AnyObject, memberVars contains either class or instance variables. The associations are composed by the name of the member variable as the logical key, and the value of the member variable as the association value. As the values may be of different types, the associations must be polymorphic. For this purpose, the untyped pointer void* is used together with type coercion.

```
class AnyObject {
   AssociativeColl* memberVars;
public:
   AnyObject( AssociativeColl* valuedMemberVars);
// observers
   void* getValue( char* memberVarName);
   void* setValue( char* memberVarName, void* memberVarValue);
   Result invoke(char* functName, Dictionary* args);
// modifiers
   void addMemberVar( char* memberVarName, void* memberVarValue);
   void removeMemberVar( char* memberVarName);
};
```

Figure 7 : AnyObject definition

4.1.2 Providing AnyObject with Behavioral Genericity

To add behavioral genericity, AnyObject objects must be able to receive messages. As methods are ultimately implemented with functions, AnyObject must be provided with the ability to be attached functions and invoke them. To this end, class AnyObject has an invoke method relying on a dictionary of functions, with function names for key and function addresses for value. The function name must uniquely identify a method, possibly by encoding its signature. This dictionary is stored as a member variable "functDict" in memberVars.

As the functions produced by the C++ preprocessor, cfront[3], to implement methods, the functions of the dictionary have a distinguished argument, "this", that is the receiver of the message. They take various numbers and types of arguments. Now, to be able to call a function, one must know its signature. To allow these functions to take any number and any type of arguments while still being able to uniformly invoke them, they all take a dictionary as single argument and return void*. The dictionary, passed at invocation, contains the actual arguments of the function call as pairs of <formal argument name ; actual argument value> : the actual values are retrieved from the dictionary in the function prologue[4] as shown in Figure 8 and coerced to the appropriate type.

```
void* addSuperclass(Dictionary arguments)
{
   AnyObject* subclass = (AnyObject*) arguments->getValue("this");
   AnyObject* superclass = (AnyObject*) arguments-
>getValue("superclass");
   // code to add the superclass to the subclass
   (...) }
```

Figure 8 : Schema Management Function Example

Method invocation is achieved by the *invoke* method which first adds the receiver object as the "this" argument to the parameters dictionary. It then gets the function with matching signature from the dictionary "functDict" and applies it to the parameters dictionary.

4.1.3 Representation of OMNIS Objects using AnyObject

The creation of an OMNIS object is achieved by creating an instance of AnyObject using the object's description. To this end, an associative collection, e.g., a dictionary, is filled with the object's member variable names, as described in the generator's *instVars* dictionary, together with their values. Next, if the object is a generator, class variable *instMethods* is valuated with a dictionary of functions defining the behavior of its instances. Conversely, the *instMethods* dictionary of its generator is stored as its *functDict* class variable. In this way, all OMNIS objects are uniformly represented as instances of a single class, AnyObject, solving the problem of dynamic type creation. Figure 9 illustrates the creation of the instantiation root OmMetaclass. As OmMetaclass is the instantiation root, it is not generated by another object but using the C++ instantiation mechanism. Note how OmMetaclassFuncts is at the same time the instMethods of OmMetaclass and the functDict of its instances. In the same manner, instVars contains

[3] with a pointer to the receiver added as the first argument.

[4] In the paper, we use this non-positional variation on the C var args functions for clarity purposes, but an array of arguments is more efficient.

OmMetaclass'member variables. This reflects the fact that OmMetaclass is its own instance.

```
// behavior creation
OmMetaclassFuncts =[< "addSuperclass" ; descriptionofAddSuperclass >
                    < "addInstVar" ; descriptionofAddInstVar >
                    (...) ]
// creation of the structure with associated behavior
OmMetaclassValuedMemberVars = [        < "name" ; "OmMetaclass" >
                              < "generator" ; OmMetaclass >
                              < "instances" ; OmMetaclass >
                              < "superclasses" ; {OmObject} >
                              < "subclasses" ; {} >
                              < "functDict"; OmMetaclassFuncts >
                              < "instVars"; [<"name";
descriptionOfName>...] >
                              < "instMethods"; OmMetaclassFuncts > ...]
AnyObject* OmMetaclass = new AnyObject(OmMetaclassValuedMemberVars);
```

Figure 9 : OmMetaclass Creation

To retrieve the value of *superclasses*, the *getValue* method is used :

```
OmMetaclass->getValue("superclasses");  // instead of ->superclasses
```

To add OmObject as OmMetaclass superclass, an addSuperclass message is sent to OmMetaclass through the invoke method :

```
parameters = [  < "superclass" ; OmObject > ]
OmMetaclass->invoke("addSuperclass", parameters);
```

Note that while this implementation offers a maximal degree of genericity, it incurs the cost of its interpretative character due to the desired ignorance of the type of objects to represent. With more semantics, it is possible to hardwire part of the structure and behavior of some OMNIS objects to match more closely OMNIS'model.

4.2 Hardwiring AnyObject : OMNISObject, Generator & Instance

4.2.1 OMNISObject

The notion of generator and the dynamic inheritance of methods are common to all objects of the default model. Thus, instead of getting the functions dictionary from the object itself, method invocation gets it from the object's generator. To support dynamic inheritance of methods, invoke must be specialized to search the inheritance hierarchy, generator's superclasses, for the method. To specialize invoke and to promote generator as a member variable, we derive AnyObject into class OMNISObject. OMNISObject represents all OMNIS objects. Deriving from AnyObject preserves genericity and thus the possibility of extending the structure and the interface.

To take further into account the semantics of the OMNIS model, we note that, as shown in Section 3.3, all generators share a minimal structure and interface defined in OmMetaclass. This knowledge allows us to derive OMNISObject and explicitly put their common member variables and methods. Moreover, as instances are far more numerous than generators, we want to represent them differently, using a space-saving associative collection for their member variables We then end up with two new classes, Generator and Instance.

4.2.2 Generator

Hardwiring member variables allows to access them faster. Note that this shunts the inheritance mechanism between generators. Indeed, generators need not inherit the explicit member variables and methods as usual, from a generator: they simply get them by typing, as they are instances of class Generator. To support the extension of a generator's description, *memberVars* references a dictionary as it is a standard associative collection. The new class has member variables such as name and superclasses, as well as methods such as addSuperclass, addInstVar, etc...

Class Generator's methods implement the behavior of OmMetaclass, i.e. the default OMNIS model, as it is the root generator. But they also have to provide for specialization via invocation. Indeed, to capture a new model, a generator has to specialize some of these methods. Figure 10 illustrates this dual management for method New : as all Generator's methods, it has to start by trying to invoke the function to see if a specialized version of it exists. If it is the case, the function is invoked using OMNISObject's invoke. Otherwise the Generator's method body is executed.

```
void* Generator::New(Dictionary* args)
{
   Result* result = (Result*) invoke("New");
   if (result->valid)   // a specialized version of New exists
      return result->value;

   // hardwired method body

   OMNISObject* schemaObject;
   bool ok = TRUE;
   if (isMetaclass())
   {
      if (*(bool*)checkGenerator(args) == FALSE)
                return NULL;
      Generator* generator = (Generator*) GeneratorAllocation(args);
      char* instVars = (List*) args.get("instVars");
      (...)
      foreach iv in instVars do
      ok = ok && *(bool*)generator->addInstVar(&Dictionary("iv",iv));
      foreach super in superclasses do
      (...)
      schemaObject = generator;
   }
   else
   {  // generator is a class, thus it creates an instance
      if (*(bool*)checkInstance(args) == FALSE)
            return NULL;
      Instance* instance = InstanceAllocation(args);
      foreach (memberVarName,memberVarValue) in args do
            ok = ok && *(bool*)instance->setValue(memberVarName,
                                                  memberVarValue);
      schemaObject = instance;
   }
   if (ok)
      return schemaObject;
   schemaObject->delete();
   return NULL; }
```

Figure 10 : Generator's New

Generator's instantiation method New needs to determine whether the receiver is a metaclass or not, in order to create an object of the appropriate class : Generator or Instance. Creating generators or instances involves valuating the object's member variables. But while this is straightforward for instances, it is not for generators since this valuation has to follow the semantics of the different submodels, as expressed by checkGenerator, addInstVar, etc.... For example, valuating the ***superclasses*** member variables implies applying the inheritance rules of the model. Persistent allocation and addition to the schema of the appropriate type of object is achieved by GeneratorAllocation and InstanceAllocation.

4.2.3 Instance

As instances are far more numerous than generators, representing them using dictionaries is too expensive in term of memory space. The logical keys of the associative collection of member variables, the names, are indeed already stored in the class of the instances. Only the value part of the collection is needed : thus a new class, ***Instance***, is derived from AnyObject and its memberVars points to a list. Class Instance redefines AnyObject's getValue and setValue methods to first look for the position of the member variable in the instVars dictionary of the class and then access the member variable in the list using this number.

5 Model Capturing Aid : the Graph Managers

Up to now, to capture a new model, operations specialization is achieved via abstract invocation. However, abstract invocation imposes a costly method look-up to search for a specialized version of it, even if the method has not been specialized. To reduce the cost of method specialization, we use the inheritance mechanism of our implementation language by introducing the notion of a manager. A manager groups as its methods all the operations defining the semantics of an object model restricted to one of its dimensions such as instantiation or inheritance. It has no structure.

As its default model is decomposed into five aspects, OMNIS has five managers, all deriving from the same abstract base class, Manager and shown on Figure 11 : InstMan, InhMan, AggregMan, ClientMan and CompositionMan. All managers have a method New and Delete that capture their specific contribution at creation or destruction of the object. Again, we will only deal with the instantiation and inheritance managers, as instantiation and inheritance are the core of this paper.

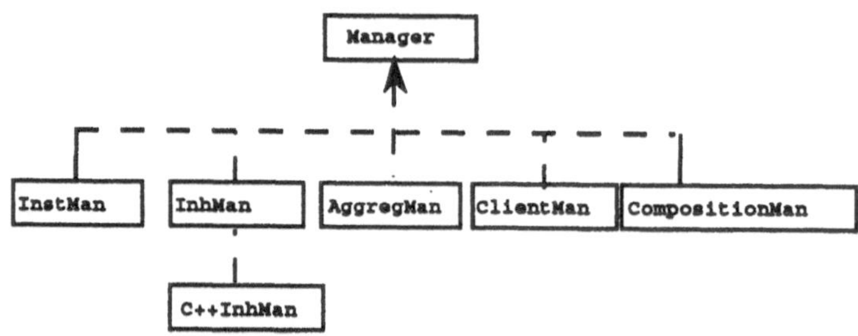

Figure 11 : OMNIS Managers Classes

As it is the case for methods, OMNIS objects own the managers for their instances in memberVars as a dictionary named *instManagers*. The managers are given to a generator when it is created in the instantiation parameters. As the first four managers are associated with the behavior of generators, they are owned by metaclasses. The access methods being defined on all objects, a composition manager has to be owned by a model's inheritance root like OmObject. For example, C++ adds visibility constraints on instance variables and methods. Thus a new inheritance root, C++Object, has to be defined to own a specific composition manager.

5.1 OMNIS and the Managers

Instead of invoking a function on their behavior object, OMNIS objects methods delegate the execution of their functionality to the appropriate manager. The manager is looked for in the *instManagers* of the object's generator, in the same way method *invoke* uses the *instMethods* of the object's generator. If the manager is not found in the generator's instManagers, it is looked for in the generator's superclasses. Typically, Generator's method New looks like this:

```
void* Generator::New(Dictionary* args)
{  return getInstMan()->New(this, args);  }
```

The New method of the instantiation manager is illustrated in Figure 12. The parts of the method dealing with aspects of other submodels are delegated to the relevant managers.

```
void* InstMan::New(Generator* receiver, Dictionary* args)
{
if (*(bool*)check(args) == FALSE)  // check instantiation invariants
   return NULL;

bool ok = TRUE;
OMNISObject* schemaObject;

if (receiver->isMetaclass())
{  // create a generator
Generator* generator=(Generator*)persistentGeneratorAlloc(receiver,
args);
ok = ok && *(bool*)schemaObject->getAggregMan()->New(schemaObject,
                                                         args);
ok = ok && *(bool*)schemaObject->getInhMan()->New(schemaObject, args);
ok = ok && *(bool*)schemaObject->getClientMan()->New(schemaObject,
                                                         args);
schemaObject = generator;
}
else
{  // create an instance
Instance* instance =(Instance*)persistentInstanceAlloc(receiver,
args);
ok = ok&& *(bool*)schemaObject
                   ->getCompositionMan()->New(schemaObject,args);
schemaObject = instance;
}
if (ok)
   return schemaObject;
schemaObject->delete();
return NULL;
}
```

Figure 12 : Instantiation Manager's New Method

5.2 The Managers for Method Specialization

By relying on manager class specialization for redefining schema management methods, abstract function invocation can be optimized. For example, to capture C++ inheritance semantics, the default inheritance manager, InhMan, is derived into class C++InhMan, redefining methods such as New, addSuperclass, etc... These methods may actually even take different parameters from their superclass'equivalent. For example, C++InhMan's addSuperclass has two additional arguments : whether the inheritance is virtual or not and whether it is public or private. This is masked by the variable arguments mechanism.

The new manager is given at instantiation. Method invocation now amounts to finding the appropriate manager and calling the management method. As the managers use C++ inheritance, checking that no specialized version of the methods exists before using the default version, is not necessary anymore. Moreover, using C++ dynamic binding for Manager methods, the body of Generator's methods may stay unchanged : the code that gets executed only depends on the actual type of Manager the generator uses. This is why all managers methods are defined as virtual.

6 Conclusion

In this paper, we proposed an object management interface system (OMNIS) intended for use by OO tools, e.g., compilers, interpreters or CAD/CAM programs, which require support for persistent objects. OMNIS supplements a type-free object manager with class and schema management facilities. Its salient features include independence through extensibility, independence with respect to both the object models of the client OO tools and the underlying object managers. OMNIS achieves extensibility through its object model and its object-oriented design. It is designed as a library of classes which can be either constrained or specialized to adapt to the specific requirements of the user tools.

OMNIS does not support a particular object model but generalizes the OO behavioral concepts in terms of five submodels, represented as graphs: instantiation, inheritance, aggregation, composition and client relations. Generality is achieved by minimizing the constraints on these graphs. Thus, OMNIS supports metaclasses in the instantiation graph, multiple inheritance in the inheritance graph. For each graph, schema evolution invariants maintain the consistency of the persistent objects.

OMNIS reflexive object model allows to represent the meta-information on persistent objects of different models by capturing their semantics. We showed a way to introduce type dynamicity in a compiled, strongly-typed language like C++. The idea is to build a type layer on top of C++'s type system to describe objects structure and behavior. This layer uses polymorphic structures and abstract function invocation. Finally, we also added the notion of manager as an optimization for specializing management methods when building new models.

Future work on OMNIS is on-going. We are currently using OMNIS to capture the object model of O2, C++ and Ode. This will demonstrate the fundamental assumption of OMNIS : that it can be used to easily capture a variety of object models. This will also show how to prototype persistence and schema management for an existing OOP language. Another direction into validating our approach is the design of OVI, an object CASE tools with advanced schema evolution capabilities [22]. Ultimately, OMNIS will be extended to enable the interoperability of various OOS.

7 References

1. J.E. Richardson, M. Carey, "Persistence in the E Language: Issues and Implementation", *Software-Practice and Experience*, Vol. 19(12), December 1989.

2. J.E. Richardson, "Compiled Item Faulting", Int. *Workshop on Persistence Object Systems*, Martha's Vineyard, MA, September 1990.

3. R. Agrawal, N.H. Gehani,"ODE (Object Database Environment): The Language and the Data Model", *ACM SIGMOD* Int. Conf., Portland, Oregon, Vol. 18(2), June 89.

4. R. Agrawal, S. Dar, N.H. Gehani, "The O++ Database Programming Language : Implementation and Experience", AT&T Internal Report, 1991.

5. "The Ontos Reference Manual", Ontologic Inc., Burlington, MA, December 1989.

6. E. Amiel, M.J. Bellosta, P. Valduriez, F. Viallet, "Persistence in OODBMS", Technical Report INRIA-1592, INRIA, Rocquencourt, France, 1992.

7. W.Kim, F.H. Lochovsky, eds "Object-Oriented Concepts, Databases, and Applications", ACM Press/Addison-Wesley, Reading, Massachusetts, 1989.

8. P. Butterworth, A. Otis, J. Stein, "The GemStone Object Database Management System", *Comm. of the ACM*, Vol. 34(10), October 1991.

9. O2 and al., "The O2 System", *Comm. of the ACM*, Vol. 34(10), October 1991.

10. F. Bancilhon, C. Delobel, P. Kannelakis, "The O2 Book", Morgan Kaufman (eds), 1992.

11. M.J. Bellosta, P. Valduriez, F. Viallet, "Design Considerations for OMNIS, an Object Management Interface System", Int. Conf. *TOOLS*, Paris, France, March 1991.

12. G. Mitchell-Shaw, S.Zdonik, "A Query Algebra for Object-Oriented Databases", in *Proc. of the 6th Int'l Conf. on Data Engineering*, pp.154-162, 1990.

13. Roberto Zicari , "A Framework For O2 Schema Updates", in [02B92].

14. M.J. Bellosta-Tourtier, A. Bessede, C. Darrieumerlou, O. Gruber, P. Pucheral, J.M. Thévenin, H. Steffen, "GEODE: Concepts and Facilities", *Sixièmes Journées Bases de Données Avancées* , September 1990.

15. W. Kim, E. Bertino, J.F. Garza, "Composite Objects Revisited", on Int. Conf. *SIGMOD*, Portland, Oregon, Vol. 18(2) , June 89.

16. A. Goldberg and D. Robson, "Smalltalk-80, the Language and its Implementation", Addison-Wesley, Reading, Massachusetts, 1983.

17. B. Meyer, "Object-Oriented Software Construction", Prentice Hall, 1988.

18. B. Stroustrup, "The C++ Programming Language", Addison Wesley, 1986.

19. L.G. DeMichiel and R.P. Gabriel, "The Common Lisp Object System: An Overwiew", *In Proceedings ECOOP*, special issue of Bigre n°54, Paris, 1987.

20. Perkham J., Maryanski F., "Semantic Data Models", *ACM Computing Surveys*, Vol.20(3), September 1988.

21. P.Cointe, "Metaclasses are First Class: The ObjVlisp Model", Int. Conf. *OOPSLA*, SIGPLAN Notices, Vol 22 (12), December 1987.

22. M.J. Bellosta, P. Valduriez, F. Viallet, "Reusing Engineering Components in OODB", Int. Conf. *DKSME*, Lyon, France, March 1992.

An Analytical Model of Object-Oriented Query Costs

Elisa Bertino and Paola Foscoli
Dipartimento di Informatica e Scienze dell'Informazione
Università di Genova
Via L.B. Alberti 4, 16132 Genova (Italy)
e-mail: bertino@igecuniv.bitnet

Abstract

In this paper we present a model of costs for object-oriented queries. These costs are based on a set of parameters able to exactly model topologies of object references in object-oriented databases. The model we present considers also the cases of multi-valued attributes and null references. Moreover, the usage of reverse references among objects is considered. The query strategies considered are based on different methods for visiting the query graph. We consider both forward and reverse traversal methods. Those visiting strategies are then combined with two different approaches for retrieving instances from the visited classes. Those approaches are the nested-loop technique and the merge-join technique. Therefore, four possible basic strategies are considered.

1 Introduction

Object centered database systems represent one of the most promising directions in the area of database towards providing appropriate support for advanced applications [3, 9, 17]. However, while several experimental and commercial systems already exist, theoretical foundations concerning object-oriented data models and architectures have not been largely investigated. Lately, researches aiming at establishing theoretical foundations for object-oriented database systems are being reported. The main efforts are concentrated around formal definitions of object-oriented data models, mainly based on logics [1, 12, 21, 22, 37] and query languages [15, 19, 27, 29, 36].

An important issue related to query languages concerns optimization techniques and access structures able to reduce query processing costs. This issue is a central one in data management architectures, since performance is a key factor. In particular, while there has been a lot of research for new query languages, no comparable amount of research has been reported concerning the foundations of optimization techniques for object-oriented databases. In particular while research on selectivity estimation techniques for relational systems is still continuing [23], for object-oriented database systems it is still in its infancy. An important aspect of that research is determining all parameters that affect query cost functions. These parameters can then be used in devising analytical cost models to be used by query optimizers to select the most efficient execution strategy among a set of possible strategies for a given query.

A parameter model is presented in [11]. The model precisely characterizes topologies of object references. It takes into account multi-valued attributes as well as null references. Previous works found in the literature [6, 8, 25] consider simpler cases, such as only single-valued attributes or no null references, or do not take into account both aggregation and inheritance hierarchies. Moreover, a number of important derived parameters have been devised allowing the evaluation of nested predicate selectivities. The parameter model has been used in [10] to derive cost formulas for three different indexing organizations tailored for object-oriented databases.

In the present paper we re-visit cost formulas for processing strategies of object-oriented queries on the basis of the parameter model defined in [11]. Cost formulas have been defined in [7, 24]. However, those formulas are based on a number of limiting assumptions such as single-valued attributes. In this paper we remove those limiting assumptions by considering the cases of multi-valued attributes and null references. Moreover, the usage of reverse references [30] among objects is also considered.

The remainder of this paper is organized as follows. Section 2 presents some preliminary definitions and provides a brief overview of query processing in object-oriented databases. Section 3 presents the query cost model. Finally Section 4 outlines some conclusions and presents future work.

2 A Reference Object-Oriented Data Model and Query Execution Strategies

In this section the main features of object-oriented data models are summarized by a reference model which will be used in the rest of the paper for the discussion. This reference model should not be interpreted as a new model. Rather it is similar to the *core model* described in [31], in that has most features commonly found in various object-oriented data models.

In this model, a class is defined by specifying its name, its attributes, and the name of its superclass(es). Multiple inheritance and the existence of a default class, called TOP_CLASS, root of an aggregation hierarchy encompassing the entire database is assumed. An attribute is defined by specifying its name and its domain. If the domain is a primitive class, the attribute is called simple attribute. Classes have both the intensional and extensional meaning and an object can be instance of only one class. An object, however, can be *member* of several classes through the inheritance hierarchy.

Attributes of the same class must have different names. However, no such constraint is imposed on their domains. Attributes can be single-valued or multi-valued. In defining multi-valued attributes, the various object-oriented data models use different constructors such as set, list, tree, array. In the reference model we will abstract from specific constructors, and we assume that multi-valued attributes are defined by using a constructor denoted as C (collection).

The following definitions $1 \div 4$ specify a notation for the Reference Model.

Definition 1.
(a) An attribute name is a string.
(b) A method name is a string.
(c) A class name is a string.□
Definition 2.
If a_i is an attribute name and C_i is a class name then:
(1) $P_i = a_i : C_i$ is the definition of a single-valued attribute;
(2) $P_i = a_i : \mathcal{C}(C_i)$ is the definition of a multi-valued attribute.
Class C_i is the *domain* of attribute P_i.□

A method definition consists of a *signature* and a *body*. The signature specifies the method name, and the classes of the objects that are input and output parameters for the method. The body provides the implementation of the method and consists of a sequence of statements written in some programming language.
Definition 3.
If M is a method name, In_i $(1 \leq i \leq n)$ is an input parameter specification and Out is an output parameter specification,

$$M(In_1, In_2, \ldots, In_n) \rightarrow Out$$

is a method signature definition.
An input parameter specification consists of the parameter name and of the parameter domain. The parameter domain is a class name or can be defined as a collection of instances of a class, in the same manner as attributes are specified (cf. Definition 2). An output parameter is a class name, or a collection of instances of a class.□

Note that, in addition, the method has an implicit input parameter, represented by the class of the object receiver. In our reference model, methods are always associated with some class. The class with which a method is associated with represents the class of the object receiver.

The invocation of a method M on an object O has the form

$$O.M(O_1, O_2, ..., O_n)$$

where $O_1, O_2, ..., O_n$ are objects that are passed as input parameters.
Definition 4.
Classes are recursively defined as follows:

- Integers, floats, strings and boolean are classes (called primitive classes)
- There is a special class, called TOP_CLASS, which has no superclass; it is default for superclass, if no superclasses are specified
- If $P_1, P_2, \ldots, P_n$ $(n \geq 1)$ are attribute definitions, with distinct names, if $M_1, M_2, \ldots, M_k$ $(k \geq 0)$ are method definitions, with distinct names, and $C, C_1, C_2, \ldots C_h$ $(h \geq 0)$ are distinct class names then
  Class C
  Attributes $(P_1, P_2, \ldots, P_n)$
  Methods $(M_1, M_2, \ldots, M_k)$
  Superclasses $(C_1, C_2, \ldots C_h)$
  is a class. □

- **Class** $C_{1,1}$
  Attributes (A_1: C_P, A_2: C'_P, A_3: C_P,A_4: $\mathcal{C}(C_{2,1})$)
  Superclasses TOP_CLASS

- **Class** $C_{1,2}$
  Attributes (A_5: C_P)
  Superclasses $C_{1,1}$

- **Class** $C_{2,1}$
  Attributes (A'_1: C_P, A'_2: C'_P, A'_3: $\mathcal{C}(C_{3,1})$)
  Superclasses TOP_CLASS

- **Class** $C_{2,2}$
  Attributes (A'_4: $\mathcal{C}(C_P)$)
  Superclasses $C_{2,1}$

- **Class** $C_{2,3}$
  Attributes (A'_5: C_P)
  Superclasses $C_{2,1}$

- **Class** $C_{3,1}$
  Attributes (A''_1: C_P, A''_2: C'_P, A''_3: $\mathcal{C}(C_{3,1})$, A''_4:$\mathcal{C}(C_{4,1})$, A''_5: $\mathcal{C}(C_{4,1})$)
  Superclasses TOP_CLASS

- **Class** $C_{4,1}$
  Attributes (A'''_1: C_P, A'''_2: C'_P, A'''_3: C_P, A'''_4: C'_P)
  Superclasses TOP_CLASS

Figure 1: Object-oriented database schema example

Figure 1 presents some examples of class definitions according to the reference model. In the example, $C_{i,j}$ denotes the $j-th$ class in the $i-th$ class inheritance hierarchy. Therefore, two classes $C_{k,i}$ and $C_{k,h}$ belong to the same class inheritance hierarchy. In particular, if a class has the value 1 for the second subscript, it is the root of the hierarchy. For example, in the database schema of Figure 1, class $C_{2,1}$ is the root of a class inheritance hierarchy; classes $C_{2,2}$ and $C_{2,3}$ are subclasses of $C_{2,1}$.

A common way of reasoning about query execution strategies is to consider object-oriented database schema as a graph. In such graph there is a node for each class in the schema; an arc from a node N_i to a node N_j indicates that the class represented by node N_j is the domain of an attribute of the class represented by node N_i. Query execution strategies often consist of different ways of traversing the graph representing the database schema for a given query. Therefore, an accurate modeling of reference topologies among instances of the various classes is crucial in estimating query execution strategy costs. In the remainder of this section we introduce definitions that characterize the concepts of *path* (a branch in the graph representing a database schema), and *path instantiation* (a sequence of objects found instantiating a path on a specific database extension).

Definition 5.
A *path* $\mathcal{P}$ is defined as $C_1.A_1.A_2.\ldots.A_n$ $(n \geq 1)$ where:

- C_1 is class in the database schema
- A_1 is an attribute of class C_1
- A_i is an attribute of a class C_i such that C_i is the domain of the attribute A_{i-1} of class C_{i-1}, $1 < i \leq n$.

Moreover

- len($\mathcal{P}$) = n denotes the length of the path
- class($\mathcal{P}$) $= C_1 \bigcup \{C_i | C_i$ is domain of attribute A_{i-1} of class C_{i-1}, $1 < i \leq n\}$
- dom($\mathcal{P}$) denotes the class C domain of attribute A_n of class C_n
- scope($\mathcal{P}$) $= \bigcup_{C_i \in class(\mathcal{P})} C_i^*$ where C_i^* is the set of the classes of the inheritance hierarchy rooted at the class C_i the class C_1 is the root of the scope
- given a class C in the scope of $\mathcal{P}$, the *position* (shortly pos) of C is given by an integer i, such that C belongs to the inheritance hierarchy rooted at class C_i, where $C_i \in$ class($\mathcal{P}$).

The scope of a path simply represents the set of all classes along the path and all their subclasses. The following is an example path for the schema in Figure 1:
$\mathcal{P} = C_{1,1}.A_4.A'_3.A''_5.A'''_2$ len($\mathcal{P}$)=4
$C_{1,1}$ is the class root of the scope
class($\mathcal{P}$)=$\{C_{1,1}, C_{2,1}, C_{3,1}, C_{4,1}\}$
dom($\mathcal{P}$)=C'_P
scope($\mathcal{P}$)=$\{C_{1,1}, C_{1,2}, C_{2,1}, C_{2,2}, C_{2,3}, C_{3,1}, C_{4,1}\}$
pos($C_{1,1}$)=pos($C_{1,2}$)=1
pos($C_{2,1}$)=pos($C_{2,2}$)=pos($C_{2,3}$)=2
pos($C_{3,1}$)=3
pos($C_{4,1}$)=4

Given a class C root of an inheritance hierarchy, an object is *instance* of C if C is the most specialized class associated with the object in the inheritance hierarchy. An object is *member* of a class C if it is an instance of C or of some subclasses of C. Therefore, the instances of a class C are all objects that do not belong to any of the subclasses of C.

Definition 6.
Given a path $\mathcal{P} = C_1.A_1.A_2 \ldots A_n$, an *instantiation* of $\mathcal{P}$ is defined as a sequence of $n+1$ objects, denoted as $O_1.O_2 \ldots O_{n+1}$, where:

- O_1 is an instance of class C_1
- O_i is the value of the attribute A_{i-1} of object O_{i-1}, $1 < i \leq n+1$. In particular
  - $O_{i-1}.A_{i-1} = O_i$ if A_{i-1} is a single-valued attribute;

- Members of class $C_{1,1}$:
  $O^1_{1,1}$: (A_1: V_1, A_2: V'_1, A_3: V_2, A_4: $O^2_{2,1}$)
  $O^2_{1,1}$: (A_1: V_2, A_2: V'_4, A_3: V_2, A_4: $O^1_{2,2}$)
  $O^1_{1,2}$: (A_1: V_2, A_2: V'_4, A_3: V_2, A_4: $O^1_{2,3}$, A_5: V_1)
- Members of class $C_{2,1}$:
  $O^1_{2,1}$: (A'_1: V_1, A'_2: V'_1, A'_3: $\{O^3_{3,1}\}$)
  $O^2_{2,1}$: (A'_1: V_2, A'_2: V'_4, A'_3: $\{O^1_{3,1}\}$)
  $O^1_{2,2}$: (A'_1: V_2, A'_2: V'_3, A'_3: $\{O^2_{3,1}, O^1_{3,1}\}$, A'_4: $\{V_1, V_2\}$)
  $O^1_{2,3}$: (A'_1: V_1, A'_2: V'_4, A'_3: NULL, A'_5: V_1)
- Members of the class $C_{3,1}$:
  $O^1_{3,1}$: (A''_1: V_1, A''_2: V'_1, A''_3: $\{O^2_{3,1}\}$, A''_4: $\{O^3_{4,1}\}$, A''_5: $\{O^1_{4,1}\}$)
  $O^2_{3,1}$: (A''_1: V_1, A''_2: V'_4, A''_3: $\{O^1_{3,1}\}$, A''_4: $\{O^1_{4,1}\}$, A''_5: $\{O^2_{4,1}\}$)
  $O^3_{3,1}$: (A''_1: V_2, A''_2: V'_3, A''_3: $\{O^2_{3,1}, O^1_{3,1}\}$, A''_4: $\{O^1_{4,1}, O^2_{4,1}\}$, A''_5: $\{O^3_{4,1}\}$)
  $O^4_{3,1}$: (A''_1: V_3, A''_2: V'_1, A''_3: $\{O^1_{3,1}, O^3_{3,1}\}$, A''_4: $\{O^1_{4,1}, O^3_{4,1}\}$, A''_5: NULL)
- Members of the class $C_{4,1}$:
  $O^1_{4,1}$: (A'''_1: V_1, A'''_2: V'_1, A'''_3: V_{10}, A'''_4: V'_1)
  $O^2_{4,1}$: (A'''_1: V_2, A'''_2: V'_9, A'''_3: V_3, A'''_4: V'_{10})
  $O^3_{4,1}$: (A'''_1: V_7, A'''_2: V'_4, A'''_3: V_2, A'''_4: V'_8)

Figure 2: An hypothetical database

  - $O_i \in O_{i-1}.A_{i-1}$ if A_{i-1} is a multi-valued attribute.

In the remainder of the discussion, we will consider some example from the hypothetical database of Figure 2 based on the schema of Figure 1. In such database, V_i and V'_i are values of the primitive classes C_P and C'_P, while $O^k_{i,j}$ is instance of class $C_{i,j}$. If an attribute A_j holds no value, then A_j =NULL.

An example of instantiation of $\mathcal{P} = C_{1,1}.A_4.A'_3.A''_5.A'''_2$ with respect to the database in Figure 2 is $O^1_{1,1}.O^2_{2,1}.O^1_{3,1}.O^1_{4,1}.V'_1$.

2.1 Object-Oriented Query Languages

Most OODBMSs provide an associative query language [19, 29, 36]. In general such languages are similar to relational ones; often, the former are defined as an evolution of the latter. Moreover, nested relational languages [32, 33, 34, 35] have many similarities with object-oriented query languages. However, there are some differences between relational and object-oriented query languages. A discussion can be found in [15].

Here we summarize the aspects that most influence query processing:

- Nested predicates
  Because of object's nested structures, most object-oriented query languages allow objects to be restricted by predicates on both nested and non-nested attributes of objects. An example of a query against the

database schema of Figure 1 is:
Retrieve all instances of class $C_{1,1}$ *such that their nested attribute* A''_1 *contains a value equal to a given constant a* (Q1)
This query contains the nested predicate. Nested predicates are often expressed using path-expressions. For example the nested predicate in the above query can be expressed as $C_{1,1}.A_4.A'_3.A''_1$

- Inheritance
A query may apply only to a class, or to a class and to all its subclasses. An example of a query against the database schema of Figure 1 is:
Retrieve all members of class $C_{1,1}$ *such that their nested attribute* A''_1 *contains a value equal to a given constant a*

- Methods
Methods can used in queries as *derived attribute method* and *predicate method.* A derived attribute method has a function comparable to that of a attribute, in that it returns an object (or a value) to which comparisons can be applied. A predicate method returns the logical constants True or False. The value returned by a predicate method can then participate in the evaluation of the Boolean expression which determines whether the object satisfies the query.

A common distinction often made in object-oriented query languages in between *implicit join* (called *functional joins* by other by other authors, e.g. [18]), deriving from the hierarchical nesting of objects, and the *explicit join,* similar to the relational join where two objects are explicitly compared on the values of their attributes. Note that some query languages, for example [4], only support implicit joins. The motivation for this is based on the argument that in relational systems joins are mostly used to recompose entities that were decomposed for normalization [16] and to support relationships among entities. In object-oriented data models there is no need of normalizing objects, since these models directly support complex objects. Moreover, relationships among entities are supported through object references; thus the same function of joins as used in the relational model to support relationships is provided more naturally by path-expressions. It, therefore, appears that in OODBMSs there is no strong need for explicit joins, especially if path-expressions are provided. The evaluation of a query with nested predicates may cause the traversal of objects along aggregation graphs. Examples of strategies for evaluations of these queries can be found in [7, 24, 28].

2.2 Query Execution Strategies

Here we present basic query execution strategies to exemplify our discussion and cost formulas. The queries that we consider for the purpose of this paper are single-target queries. A single-target query retrieves members or instances from only one class (called *target class*). Other classes, however, may be used in the query based on their relationships with the target class. Therefore, only implicit joins (i.e. joins based on the aggregation hierarchy) may occur in the qualification part of the query. An example of query on aggregation hierarchy of Figure 1 is query Q1.

As discussed in [28], a query can be conveniently represented by a *query graph*. A detailed description of query graphs is presented in [28]. The query execution strategies described in [28] vary along two dimensions. The first dimension concerns the method used to traverse the query graph. The second dimension is the technique used to retrieve data from the classes that are traversed for the evaluation of nested predicates. We consider two traversal methods:

- *Forward traversal*: the first class visited is the target class of the query (root of the query graph). The remaining classes are traversed starting from the target class in any depth-first order. The forward traversal strategy for query Q1 is $(C_{1,1}C_{2,1}C_{2,2}C_{2,3}C_{3,1})$.

- *Reverse traversal*: the traversal of the query graph begins at the leaves and proceeds bottom-up along the graph. The reverse traversal strategy for query Q1 is $(C_{3,1}C_{2,1}C_{2,2}C_{2,3}C_{1,1})$.

Note that if the query Q1 were to retrieve the members of class $C_{1,1}$ (that is, not only the instances) also the class $C_{1,2}$ would have been accessed.

In [28] two methods are considered for retrieving data from a visited class. The first method is called *nested-loop* and consists of instantiating separately each qualified instance of a class. The instance attributes are examined for qualification, if there are simple predicates on the instance attributes. If the instance qualifies, it is passed to its parent node (in the case of reverse traversal) or to its child node (in case of forward traversal). The second method is called *sort-domain* and consists of instantiating all qualified instances of a class at once. Then all qualifying instances are passed to their parent or child node (depending on the traversal strategy used).

Reverse traversal may be particularly efficient when reverse references among objects are allocated. An object O references an object O', if the OID of O' is stored in some attribute of O. There is a reverse reference between O and O' if O' also contains a reference to O. Reverse references have been used for supporting referential integrity and enforcing certain types of constraint (see [30]). In the analysis of reverse traversal strategies we also consider the case when reverse references are allocated.

By combining the graph traversal strategies with the retrieval strategies, we obtain four basic query execution strategies, namely nested-loop forward traversal (NLFT), nested-loop reverse traversal (NLRT), sort-domain forward traversal (SDFT), sort-domain reverse traversal (SDRT). When complex queries are concerned these strategies can be combined giving place to more complex strategies.

A query execution strategy is the decomposition of a query into a set of basic operations: index scan (I), nested-loop join (NJ), sort-merge join (SJ), intersection (∩), selection (S), projection (P), sort-order (O) all with the straightforward semantics.

To further illustrate the decomposition of a query, we consider the database schema of Figure 3 and the query *Find all red vehicles with 2 doors manufactured by Fiat*, whose graph is displayed in Figure 4. The database schema is

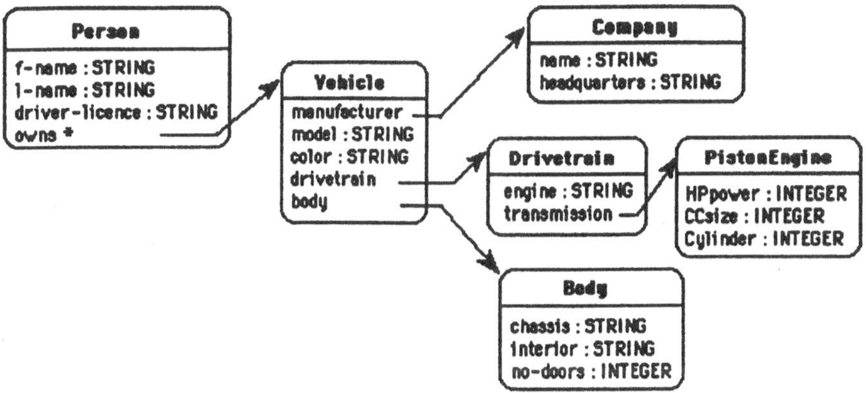

Figure 3: An example of database schema

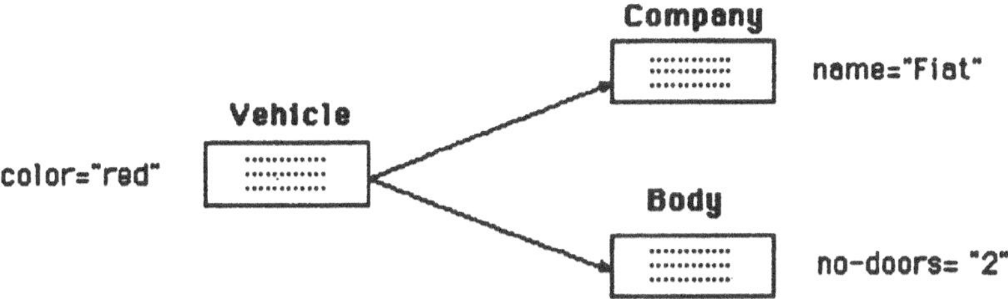

Figure 4: Query graph example

represented by using a graphical notation where each box represents a class. A box contains, in addition to the class name, the names of all attributes of the class. An arc from a class C to a class C' denotes that C' is the domain of an attribute of C.

In order to represent a query execution strategy we introduce the notion of *query execution graph* (QEG), revisiting the notation for relational queries presented in [39]. A node in a QEG represents one of the basic operations described above and is labeled by the name of the operation together with additional information that specify the operation. Nodes can also denote the classes on which the query is executed. In this case the label is the name of the class. Arcs in a QEG are oriented. An arc from N to N' means that the result of the operation denoted by N is given as input to the one denoted by N'. A description of the graphical notation is presented in [7]. Figure 5 shows some execution strategies for the query whose graph is presented in Figure 4.

Given a QEG, the execution of the query consists of the linearization of the QEG; that is giving a topological sort on the QEG. More than one linearization can exist. The spectrum of possible strategies increases when indexing techniques are also considered. Some preliminary discussions on the usage of nested indexing techniques in queries can be found in [7] and [13].

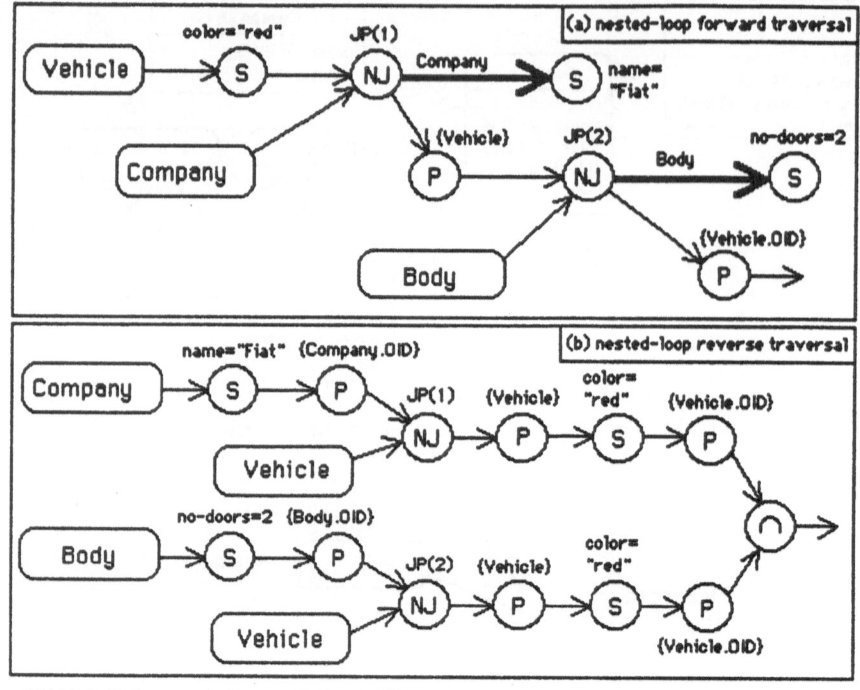

Figure 5: Examples of query execution graphs for a query

3 Cost Model

In this section we first introduce parameters and assumptions of the model. Then we present cost formulations for traversal and retrieval strategies described previously.

3.1 Parameters

Logical data parameters
Given a path $\mathcal{P} = C_1.A_1.A_2...A_n$, the parameters, listed in the following, describe the characteristics of the classes of such path. Most of parameters are introduced to characterize precisely the *topology* of references among objects, instances of the given classes.

- nc_i Number of classes in the inheritance hierarchy rooted at class $C_{i,1}$, $1 \leq i \leq n$.
- $D_{i,j}$ Number of distinct values for attribute A_i of class $C_{i,j}$, $1 \leq i \leq n$, $1 \leq j \leq nc_i$.

- D_i Number of distinct values for attribute A_i for all instances in the inheritance hierarchy rooted at class $C_{i,1}$.
- $N_{i,j}$ Cardinality of class $C_{i,j}$, $1 \leq i \leq n$, $1 \leq j \leq nc_i$.
- Nh_i Number of members of class $C_{i,1}$, $1 \leq i \leq n$; $Nh_i = \sum_{j=1}^{nc_i} N_{i,j}$.
- $fan_{i,j}$ Average number of references to members of class $C_{i+1,1}$, contained in the attribute A_i for an instance of class $C_{i,j}$, $1 \leq i \leq n$ and $1 \leq j \leq nc_i$.
- fan_i Average number of references to members of class $C_{i+1,1}$, contained in the attribute A_i of a member of class $C_{i,1}$, $1 \leq i \leq n$. The difference of this parameter with the previous is that this parameter is obtained as the average evaluated on all members of a class hierarchy, while in the previous the average is for each class.
- $d_{i,j}$ Average number of instances of class $C_{i,j}$, having a value different than NULL for attribute A_i, $1 \leq i \leq n$ and $1 \leq j \leq nc_i$.
- d_i Average number of members of class $C_{i,1}$, having a value different than NULL for attribute A_i, $1 \leq i \leq n$; $d_i = \sum_{j=1}^{nc_i} d_{i,j}$
- $k_{i,j}$ Average number of instances of class $C_{i,j}$, having the same value for attribute A_i, $1 \leq i \leq n$ and $1 \leq j \leq nc_i$; $k_{i,j} = \lceil (d_{i,j} * fan_{i,j})/D_{i,j} \rceil$
- kh_i Average number of members of class $C_{i,1}$, having the same value for attribute A_i, $1 \leq i \leq n$.

Physical data parameters

- $P_{i,j}$ Number of pages containing instances of the class $C_{i,j}$ for $1 \leq i \leq n$, $1 \leq j \leq nc_i$.
- Ph_i Number of pages containing members of the class $C_{i,1}$ for $1 \leq i \leq n$.
- r_i A binary variable assuming value equal to 1 if members of class $C_{i,1}$ have reverse references to members of class $C_{i-1,1}$ in the path, equal to 0 otherwise for $2 \leq i \leq n$.

Query parameters

- NI_i Number of members of class $C_{i,1}$ to be searched for, $1 \leq i \leq n$. (Note that for a query containing a single nested predicate, NI_i has the same value of the number of instances (or members) of class $C_{i,1}$. However, when dealing with complex queries, the number of instances (or members) of class $C_{i,1}$ may have been reduced due to the resolution of other predicates.)
- AP_i Number of accessed pages containing members of the class $C_{i,1}$ for $1 \leq i \leq n$.

Derived parameters.
These parameters are derived from the input ones and are particularly important since they precisely characterize the topology of the database. Because of space restriction, we cannot present here the derivations for these parameters (they can be found in [11]). A summary is presented in Appendix A.

- $RefBy(i,s,y,k)$ Average number of values contained in the nested attribute A_y for a set of k instances of the class $C_{i,s}$, $1 \leq i \leq y \leq n$.
- $RefByh(i,y,k)$ Average number of values contained in the nested attribute A_y for a set of k members of class $C_{i,1}$, $1 \leq i \leq y \leq n$.
- $\overline{k}_{i,j}$ Average number of instances of class $C_{i,j}$ having the same value for the nested attribute A_n $(1 \leq i \leq n, 1 \leq j \leq nc_i)$
- $\overline{kh}_i$ Average number of members of class $C_{i,1}$ having the same value for the nested attribute A_n $(1 \leq i \leq n)$
- $Ref(i,s,y,k)$ Average number of instances of class $C_{i,s}$ having as value of the nested attribute A_y a value in a set of k elements for $1 \leq i \leq y \leq n$. Also in this case, as for $RefBy(i,s,y,k)$, s determines the position of the class in the inheritance hierarchy supposing that the classes are sorted in the hierarchy.
- $Refh(i,y,k)$ Average number of members of class $C_{i,1}$ having as value of the nested attribute A_y a value in a set of k elements for $1 \leq i \leq y \leq n$.

Assumptions
Most of the assumptions made are commonly found in analytical models for database access structures. In particular, we make that assumption that the cardinality of instances of a class is not correlated with cardinalities of instances of other classes belonging to the same inheritance hierarchy.

3.2 Cost functions

We now present the cost functions for evaluating a nested predicate of the form

$$C_1.A_1 \ldots A_n \; op \; exp$$

where *op* is a relational comparison operator, while *exp* is an expression. According to the query execution strategies described in the previous section, this predicate can be evaluated by either performing a forward traversal, or a reverse traversal.

Costs are estimated in terms of disk page accesses. There are two categories for which cost are computed.

Category 1: The first category is to compute the cost of accessing the class $C_{n,1}$ (as well as its subclasses if applicable) from just the class $C_{1,1}$ or from $C_{1,1}$ and its subclasses according to the type of query (forward traversal strategy).

Category 2: The second category is to compute the cost of accessing a class $C_{1,1}$ (as well as its subclasses if applicable) from the class $C_{n,1}$ and its subclasses (reverse traversal strategy).

The evaluation of parameters D_i and kh_i depends on the type of distribution of the key-values among the classes of the inheritance hierarchy rooted at $C_{i,1}$, for $1 \leq i \leq n$. There are two extreme cases for such distributions:

the *disjunctive distribution* and the *inclusive distribution*. In the former, each key-value of attribute A_i appears in only one class and then the total number of distinct key-values in the domain of A_i, D_i, is given by the sum of D_i of all classes of the hierarchy. For this distribution, moreover, we have that the parameter kh_i corresponds to the highest k_i between all k_i's of the classes of the hierarchy rooted at $C_{i,1}$. In an inclusive distribution, instead, D_i assumes the highest value between the D_i of the classes of the inheritance hierarchy rooted at $C_{i,1}$ while the value of kh_i is given by the sum of the k_i of all classes of the hierarchy.

Category 1

First, we consider the retrieval strategy called nested-loop. The value for the parameter NI_1 is determined as follows:

- $NI_1 = N_{1,1}$ if class $C_{1,1}$ has not subclasses or the considered query has just $C_{1,1}$ as target class
- $NI_1 = Nh_1$ if class $C_{1,1}$ has some subclasses and the given query has the inheritance hierarchy with root $C_{1,1}$ as target class.

Note that in this case we have considered queries with simple predicates. If we consider also complex predicates then NI_1 is given by a subset S of $N_{1,1}$ or of Nh_1. Now we determine the value of the parameter NI_k for $1 < k \leq n$:

$$NI_k = \begin{cases} NI_{k-1} * fan_{k-1,1} & \text{if } k = 2 \text{ and the given query has the class } C_{1,1} \\ & \text{as target class} \\ NI_{k-1} * fan_{k-1} & \text{otherwise} \end{cases}$$

Suppose that the total number of accessed instances is equal to the number of accessed pages. Therefore, we have that $AP_k = NI_k$. The total cost is given by the following expression:

$$C = \sum_{k=1}^{n} AP_k$$

If we consider the sort-domain retrieval method, we obtain other formulas described subsequently. The parameter NI_1 is determined as before while the parameter NI_k for $1 < k \leq n$ is determined as follows:

$$NI_k = \begin{cases} D_{1,1} & \text{if } k = 2 \text{ and the target of the query} \\ & \text{is the class } C_{1,1} \\ D_1 & \text{if } k = 2 \text{ and the target of the query is} \\ & \text{the inheritance hierarchy rooted at the} \\ & \text{class } C_{1,1} \\ RefBy(1, 1, k-1, NI_1) & \text{if } k > 2 \text{ and the target of the query} \\ & \text{is the class } C_{1,1} \\ RefByh(1, k-1, NI_1) & \text{otherwise} \end{cases}$$

Suppose that the instances of the same class are clustered. Then, using the function of Yao formulated in [38], we obtain that the number of pages, AP_k, for $1 \leq k \leq n$ containing the NI_k accessed objects is

$$AP_k = \begin{cases} H(NI_k, Ph_k, Nh_k) & \text{if } k > 1 \\ P_{k,1} & \text{if } k = 1 \text{ and the query has the class } C_{1,1} \\ & \text{as target class} \\ Ph_k & \text{otherwise} \end{cases}$$

If $NI_1 = S$ then also for $k = 1$ must be applied the function of Yao [38] because the number of accessed pages is lower than $P_{1,1}$ or than Ph_1. Therefore, the total cost is given by the following expression:

$$C = \sum_{k=2}^{n} SORT(NI_k) + \sum_{k=1}^{n} AP_k$$

The number of disk page accesses needed to sort a list of instance OIDs can be determined as follows. Let the number of instance OIDs be n, the size of each OID be s and the size of a disk page be d. The unit of s and d are in bytes. The number of disk page accesses needed to sort a list of n instance OIDs is $D_p * (log_2 D_p)$ where D_p, the number of disk page accesses needed to accommodate the list of instance OIDs, is $(n/(d/s))$. We are assuming that two-way sorting is performed.

Category 2

We consider the retrieval strategy called nested-loop. The value for the parameter NI_n is determined as follows:

$$NI_n = Nh_n$$

Indeed, initially, all objects of the classes of position n must be accessed. Then, among those objects only the ones containing in the attribute A_n the value or the set of values fixed in the query are considered in the reverse traversal. The average number of accesses to these objects is kh_n if the predicate of the query is of the type "attribute=value" or $c * kh_n$ if the predicate is of the type "attribute op value" where op $\in \{<, >, \leq, \geq\}$ and c is the cardinality of the range of values that resolve the predicate and that may be contained in the attribute A_n. Note that the same object may be accessed several times in the nested-loop strategy . The value of the parameter NI_k for $1 \leq k \leq n-1$ is determined as follows:

$$NI_k = c * \prod_{j=k+1}^{n} kh_j * (r_k * V1_k + (1 - r_k) * V2_k)$$

where $V1_k$ and $V2_k$ are two auxiliary parameters whose values are the following:

$$V1_k = \begin{cases} k_{k,1} & \text{if } k = 1 \text{ and the query has the class } C_{1,1} \text{ as target class} \\ kh_k & \text{otherwise} \end{cases}$$

$$V2_k = \begin{cases} N_{k,1} & \text{if } k = 1 \text{ and the query has the class } C_{1,1} \text{ as target class} \\ Nh_k & \text{otherwise} \end{cases}$$

We may note that if the objects, members of a class $C_{i,1}$, have reverse pointers to the members of the previous class in the path $C_{i-1,1}$, it is not necessary to access all instances of the classes of position $i-1$ but only the objects containing in the nested attribute A_n the value given in the query.

The average number of accessed pages is equal to the number of accessed objects and for this reason we obtain that

$$AP_k = NI_k$$

The total cost is the following:

$$C = (1 - r_1) * AP_1 + \sum_{k=2}^{n} AP_k$$

Note that if the members of class $C_{2,1}$ have reverse pointers to the members of the class $C_{1,1}$, it is not necessary to access the classes of position 1 in the path because the reverse pointers, that are given by OIDs, of the objects members of class $C_{2,1}$ form the solution of the query.

We now consider the method sort-domain. The parameter NI_n is determined as before while the parameter NI_k for $1 \leq k < n$ is given by the following expression:

$$NI_k = r_k * V3_k + (1 - r_k) * V2_k$$

where $V2_k$ is an auxiliary variable defined previously. $V3_k$ is determined as follows:

$$V3_k = \begin{cases} \overline{k}_{k,1} & \text{if } k = 1 \text{ and the query has the class } C_{1,1} \text{ as target class} \\ \overline{kh}_k & \text{otherwise} \end{cases}$$

The definition of $V3_k$ is valid for queries with predicates of the type "attribute = value". But if the predicate is based on a range of values of length c then in the definition of $V3_k$ we substitute $Ref(k,1,n,c)$ to $\overline{k}_{k,1}$ and $Refh(k,n,c)$ to $\overline{kh}_k$. We make the assumption that instances of the same class are clustered. Then, we use the function of Yao [38] to obtain the number of pages containing a given number of objects to be accessed.

$$AP_k = r_k * H(NI_k, Ph_k, Nh_k) + (1 - r_k) * V4_k$$

where $V4_k$ is a binary variable whose value is the following:

$$V4_k = \begin{cases} P_{k,1} & \text{if } k = 1 \text{ and the query has the class } C_{1,1} \text{ as target class} \\ Ph_k & \text{otherwise} \end{cases}$$

Therefore, the total cost is given by

$$C = (1 - r_1) * (AP_1 + SORT(NI_2)) + \sum_{k=2}^{n} AP_k + \sum_{k=3}^{n} SORT(NI_k)$$

3.3 Discussion

The cost model we have presented in this section is based on a large number of parameters. Maintaining statistics for all those parameters may be quite expensive and, therefore, unrealistic in some cases. However, the first goal of the work reported in this paper was to define a complete set of parameters able to precisely characterize an object-oriented databases. Our next step is to identify a suitable subset of those parameters that would allow to determine optimal (or sub-optimal) query execution strategies, without requiring the maintenance of the entire set of parameters. It is, however, important to stress that the most appropriate subset may depend on the data and query characteristics. Moreover, note that in a real system various approaches could be used for parameter evaluation. For example, statistics could be collected and updated only upon database administrator requests, as it is done in some relational systems. In addition, the administrator could request statistics gathering and updating only for some specific classes and/or on limited samples of instances.

Another important issue concerns how to extend the previous model when dealing with queries containing method invocations. As discussed previously, methods can be used as predicate methods, when returning a Boolean value, or as attribute methods, when returning an object, or a set of objects. Moreover, a query may contain a path-expression having a method invocation instead of a nested attribute. As an example consider the class Vehicle and suppose that a method Value is defined for this class. The purpose of this method is to determine the current value of a vehicle. A query retrieving all persons owning a vehicle whose value is greater than 2,000 could be formulated using a predicate 'Vehicle.owns.value > 2000'. This predicate contains a path-expression having a method invocation as one of the elements. The parameter model can be easily extended to the case of a method if the cardinality of the set of possible results of the method invocations is known. In practice, a method could be seen as a derived attribute and therefore the parameters D_i, $1 \leq i \leq n$ (representing the number of distinct values for attribute A_i), would have the meaning of the possible results for the derived attribute A_i. However, determining the set of possible results of a method invocations may be quite complex. Moreover, methods may have input parameters, and therefore the statistics about possible results should take into account possible values of input parameters. One approach is based on pre-computing or caching the method results, as proposed in [14] and in [26]. Other approaches could be based on periodic samples. The problem of optimizing queries with method is still, however, an open problem which has not been much investigated.

4 Conclusions and Future Work

In this paper we have presented a cost model for execution strategies of object-oriented queries. We considered two methods for traversing the query-graph and two methods for accessing instances of the visited classes. Therefore, four different basic strategies have been considered. The cost model takes into account several specific aspects of object-oriented databases, such as complex objects with multi-valued attributes and class inheritance hierarchies. Therefore, the cost formulas presented in this paper can be used as building blocks to derive costs for complex queries.

The work presented in this paper is being extended in three directions. The first is to consider alternative techniques for fast traversal of object aggregation hierarchies. In particular, we are considering the use of *simple continued fractions* [20] to generate compressed codes able to materialize the transitive closure of objects. This mechanism associates with an object a number (or set of numbers) from which the OIDs of ancestors can be efficiently obtained. We are also investigating mechanisms such as the one presented in [2]. A second direction concerns the extension of query cost formulas when object clustering [5] is also taken into account. A third direction concerns the investigation of heuristics to limit the number of strategies to be examined in the optimization of queries and to determine a suitable subset of the parameters, in order to reduce the costs of collecting and maintaining statistics. Finally, the model is now being validated through an implementation.

A Formulation of derived parameters

We first evaluate $RefBy(i,s,y,k)$ $(0 \leq i \leq y \leq n,\ 1 \leq s \leq nc_i \text{ e } 1 \leq k \leq D_y)$ that denotes the number of values contained in the nested attribute A_y for a set of k instances of class $C_{i,s}$. Recall that the average number of members of class $C_{i,1}$ $(i > 1)$ referenced by at least a member of a class $C_{i-1,1}$ is given by parameter D_{i-1}; similarly, the number of members of class $C_{i,1}$ $i > 1$ referenced by at least an instance of class $C_{i-1,j}$, is given by parameter $D_{i-1,j}$. The probability P_{A_i} that an object O_i, member of class $C_{i,1}$, has as value of attribute A_i a value different from null is:

$$P_{A_i} = \frac{d_i}{Nh_i}$$

We now determine the probability that given an object O_i, instance of class $C_{i,j}$, none of the $fan_{i,j}$ references values of attribute A_i references a given object O_{i+1}, member of class $C_{i+1,1}$. This probability is obtained by first determining the number of possible subsets of $fan_{i,j}$ elements taken from a set of $D_{i,j}$ objects, members of class $C_{i+1,1}$. The number of possible subsets is given by the binomial coefficient

$$\binom{D_{i,j}}{fan_{i,j}} = \frac{D_{i,j}!}{fan_{i,j}! * (D_{i,j} - fan_{i,j})!}$$

Therefore, the probability that a given object O_{i+1}, member of class $C_{i+1,1}$ and belonging to the definition domain of attribute A_i of cardinality $D_{i,j}$, is not referenced by a given instance of class $C_{i,j}$ is:

$$\frac{\binom{D_{i,j}-1}{fan_{i,j}}}{\binom{D_{i,j}}{fan_{i,j}}} = \frac{D_{i,j} - fan_{i,j}}{D_{i,j}} = 1 - \frac{fan_{i,j}}{D_{i,j}}$$

By extending the previous derivation we have that if $k_{i,j} > 1$, the probability that O_{i+1} is not referenced by any object belonging to a set of instances of class $C_{i,j}$, with attribute A_i having a set of values $\{O^1_{i,j}, O^2_{i,j}, ..., O^k_{i,j}\}$ all different from null value, is the following:

$$Pr(i,j,k) = \left(1 - \frac{fan_{i,j}}{D_{i,j}}\right)^k$$

If $k_{i,j} = 1$, the formulation is obtained as a probability without repetitions as follows

$$Pr'(i,j,k) = \prod_{y=0}^{k-1} \left(1 - \frac{fan_{i,j}}{D_{i,j} - y * fan_{i,j}}\right)$$

This is explained by observing that when $k_{i,j} = 1$, any object among the ones belonging to the set of $D_{i,j}$ elements is referenced by only one object. Therefore, given an object of class $C_{i,j}$, the objects referenced by it must be considered only once and must be eliminated from the set of $D_{i,j}$ elements. Then, we have that

$$RefBy(i,s,y,k) = \begin{cases} D_{i,s} * (1 - v(i,s) * Pr(i,s,k) - \\ (1 - v(i,s)) * Pr'(i,s,k)) & \text{if } y = i \\ \\ D_y * (1 - v(i,s) * Pr(i,s,E'(i,s,y-1,k)) - \\ (1 - v(i,s)) * Pr'(i,s,E'(i,s,y-1,k))) & \text{if } y > i \end{cases}$$

where

$$v(i,s) = \begin{cases} 1 & \text{se } k_{i,s} > 1 \\ 0 & \text{otherwise} \end{cases}$$

where

$$E'(i,s,y,k) = RefBy(i,s,y,k) * P_{A_y}$$

The parameter $RefByh(i,y,k)$ is evaluated by a similar approach. This parameter gives the average number of values contained in the nested attribute A_y for a set of k member of the inheritance hierarchy with position i-th in the path. The expression for $RefByh(i,y,k)$ is obtained by substituting in the expressions that value $RefByh(i,y,k)$ the parameter D_i to $D_{i,j}$, kh_i to $k_{i,j}$ and fan_i to $fan_{i,j}$.

The evaluation of $\overline{k}_{i,j}$ and of $\overline{kh}_i$ is based on the determination of other two parameters $Ref(i,j,y,k)$ and $Refh(i,y,k)$. They determine respectively the average number of instances of class $C_{i,j}$ having as value of the nested attribute A_y a value in a set of k elements for $1 \leq i \leq y \leq n$ and $1 \leq j \leq nc_i$ and the average number of members of class $C_{i,1}$ having as value of the nested attribute A_y a value in a set of k elements for $1 \leq i \leq y \leq n$. The evaluation of such parameters has the same style of the evaluation of $RefBy(i,j,y,k)$ and of $RefByh(i,y,k)$ and for this reason it will not be here reported. We say only that the parameters k and d will substitute respectively fan and D. A deeper evaluation of such parameters is presented in [11]. Then we have that $\overline{k}_{i,j} = Ref(i,j,n,1)$ while $\overline{kh}_i = RefByh(i,n,1)$ for $1 \leq i \leq n$ and $1 \leq j \leq nc_i$.

References

[1] Abiteboul, S., and Kanellakis, P. Object identity as a query language primitive. *Proc. of ACM-SIGMOD Conference on Management of Data*, Portland (Oreg.), 1989.

[2] Agrawal, R., Borgida, A., Jagadish, H.V. Efficient management of transitive relationships in large data and knowledge bases. *Proc. ACM-SIGMOD Conference on Management of Data*, Portland (Oreg.), June 1989.

[3] Atkinson, M., Bancilhon, F., DeWitt, D., Dittrich., K., Maier, D., Zdonik, S. The object-oriented database system manifesto. *Proc. of First*

International Conference on Deductive and Object-Oriented Databases (DOOD), Kyoto (Japan), Dec. 4-6, 1989.

[4] Banerjee, J., et Al. Queries in object-oriented databases. *Proc. Fourth IEEE Int. Conference on Data Engineering Conf.*, Los Angeles, Feb. 1988.

[5] Benzaken, S. An evaluation model for clustering strategies in the O_2 object-oriented database system. *Proc. Third Int. Conference on Database Theory (ICDT)*, Paris, Dec.1990.

[6] Bertino, E., Kim, W. Indexing techniques for queries on nested objects. *IEEE Trans. on Knowledge and Data Engineering*, Vol.1, No.2 (1989),196-214.

[7] Bertino, E. Query optimization using nested indices. *Proc. of 2nd Int. Conference on Extending Database Technology (EDBT)*, Venice (Italy), March 26-30,1990, Lecture Notes in Computer Sciences 416, Springer-Verlag.

[8] Bertino, E. An indexing technique for object-oriented databases. *Proc. of Seventh IEEE Int. Conference on Data Engineering*, Kobe (Japan), April 8-12, 1991.

[9] Bertino, E., Martino, L. Object-oriented database management systems: concepts and issues. *Computer* (IEEE Computer Society), Vol.24, No.4 (1991), 33-47.

[10] Bertino, E., Foscoli, P. Index organizations for object-oriented database systems. Submitted for publication, Nov. 1991.

[11] Bertino, E., Foscoli, P. On modeling cost functions for object-oriented databases. Submitted for publication, Dec. 1991.

[12] Bertino, E., and Montesi, D. Towards a logical-object oriented programming language for databases. *Proc. of Third Int. Conference on Extending Database Technology (EDBT)*, Vienna, March 23-27, 1992.

[13] Bertino, E., and Guglielmina, C. Optimization of Object-Oriented Queries Using Path Indices. *Proc. Research Issues in Data Engineering: Transaction and Query Processing (RIDE-TQP) Workshop*, Phoenix (Ariz.), Febr. 2-3, 1992.

[14] Bertino, E., and Quarati, A. An approach to support method invocations in object-oriented queries *Proc. Research Issues in Data Engineering: Transaction and Query Processing (RIDE-TQP) Workshop*, Phoenix (Ariz.), Febr. 2-3, 1992.

[15] Bertino, E., Negri,M., Pelagatti,G., Sbattella, L. Object-oriented query languages: the notion and the issues. *IEEE Trans. on Knowledge and Data Engineering*, June 1992.

[16] Breitl, R., et Al. The GemStone data management system. *Object-Oriented Concepts, Databases, and Applications*, W. Kim, and F. Lochovsky, eds., Addison-Wesley (1989), 283-308.

[17] Special section on next-generation database systems, *Comm. of ACM*, Vol.34, N. 10, October 1991.

[18] Carey, M., DeWitt, D. An overview of the EXODUS project. *Proc. of ACM-SIGMOD Conference on Management of Data*, Chicago (Ill.), June 1988.

[19] Cluet, S., et Al. Reloop, an algebra based query language for an object-oriented database system. *Proc. of First International Conference on Deductive and Object Oriented Databases (DOOD)*, Kyoto (Japan), Dec. 6-8, 1989.

[20] Gagliardi, R. An encoding technique for clustered objects. To appear, 1992.

[21] Gyssen, M., Paradaens, J., and Van Gucht, D. A graph-oriented object database model. *Proc. SIGACT-SIGMOD-SIGART Symposium on Principles of Database Systems*, 1990.

[22] Lou, Y., and Ozsoyoglu, Z.M. LLO: an object-oriented deductive language with methods and method inheritance. *Proc. of ACM-SIGMOD Conference on Management of Data*, Denver (Color.), 1991.

[23] Ioannidis, Y.E., and Al. On the propagation of errors in the size of join results. *Proc. of ACM-SIGMOD Conference on Management of Data*, Denver (Col.), May 1991.

[24] Jenq, P., Woelk, D., Kim, W., Lee, W.L. Query processing in distributed ORION. MCC Technical Report, No. ACA-ST-035-89, January 1989.

[25] Kemper, A., and Moerkotte, G. Access support in object bases. *Proc. of ACM-SIGMOD Conference on Management of Data*, Atlantic City (N.J.), May 1990.

[26] Kemper, A., Kilger, C., and Moerkotte, G., Function materialization in object bases. *Proc. of ACM-SIGMOD Conference on Management of Data*, Denver (Colorado), 1991.

[27] Kifer M., Lausen G. F-Logic: A higher-Order Language for Reasoning about Objects, Inheritance, and Scheme., *Proc. of ACM-SIGMOD Conference on Management of Data*, Portland (Oreg.), 1989.

[28] Kim, K.C., Kim, W., Woelk, D., Dale, A. Acyclic query processing in object-oriented databases. *Proc. ER Conference*, Rome, Nov. 1988, also MCC Technical Report, No. ACA-ST-287-88, September 1988.

[29] Kim, W. A model of queries for object-oriented databases. *Proc.of 15th International Conference on Very Large Data Bases (VLDB)*, Amsterdam, Aug. 1989.

[30] Kim, W., Bertino, E., Garza, J. Composite object revisited. *Proc. ACM-SIGMOD Conference on Management of Data*, Portland (Oreg.), June 1989.

[31] Kim, W. Object-oriented databases: definition and research directions. *IEEE Trans. on Knowledge and Data Engineering*, Vol. 2, No. 3 (1990), 327-341.

[32] Ozsoyoglu, M., et Al. Extending relational algebra and relational calculus with set-valued attributes and aggregate functions. *ACM Trans. on Database Systems*, Vol.12, No.4 (1987).

[33] Pistor, P., and Traunmuller, R. A database language for sets, lists, and tables. *Information Systems*, Vol.11, No. 4 (1986).

[34] Roth, M.A., Korth, H.F., Silberschatz, A. Extended algebra and calculus for nested relational databases. *ACM Trans. on Database Systems*, Vol.13, No.4 (1988).

[35] Schek, H.J., and Scholl, M.H. The relational model with relational-valued attributes. *Information Systems*, Vol.11, No.2 (1986).

[36] Shaw, G.B., and Zdonik, S. An object oriented query algebra. *Proc. 2nd Int. Workshop on Database Programming Languages*, Portland (Oreg.), June 1989.

[37] Zaniolo, C. Object identity and inheritance in deductive databases - an evolutionary approach. *Proc. of the First International Conference on Deductive and Object-Oriented Databases (DOOD)*, Kyoto (Japan), Dec. 4-6, 1989.

[38] Yao, S.B. Approximating block accesses in database organizations. *ACM Comm.*, Vol. 20, N. 4 (1977), 260-261.

[39] Yao, S.B. Optimization of query evaluation algorithms. *ACM Trans. on Database Systems*, Vol.4, No.10 (1979).

PIL : An Optimizable Functional Language for Data Intensive Applications

Waqar Hasan Ravi Krishnamurthy
Hewlett-Packard Laboratories
1501, Page Mill Road, Palo Alto, CA 94305, U.S.A
email: lastname@hpl.hp.com

Abstract

The Papyrus Interface Language (PIL) has the design goal of providing *optimizable and parallelizable* language features. Analogous to the design philosophy of RISC instruction sets, the design of PIL is motivated by the desire to exploit query optimization and parallelization techniques. In contrast, most proposals of database programming language provide features to directly match user needs irrespective of the implementation problems, analogous to the CISC instruction set proposals. We have combined a functional model of computation with data types suitable for data intensive applications. A functional model gives a *declarative semantics* to all expressions including "procedural" constructs such as if-then-else, while and function calls provided the expression is without side-effects. We also provide specialized constructs for iteration over bags and sequences in order to facilitate optimization. The semantics of data types and computational abstractions are carefully chosen to retain the capability to parallelize programs. We have chosen to only *partially define the order of evaluation* for programs. This opens up more opportunities for reordering and for parallel execution. Just as in RISC instruction sets — what is not included will be a factor in dictating the performance of the system — we argue the need to exclude features such as object identity, semantic types and inheritance that are popularly included in most database programming languages.

1 Introduction

Database programming languages (DBPLs) provide increased functionality by the provision of features such as if-then-else, while loops, object-identity, type inheritance and overloading. These designs have been traditionally motivated by the goal of directly reflecting the needs of an end-user as features in the language. This is much like the design of instruction sets for CISC [1] architectures which had the similar intention of removing impedance mismatch. In contrast the design of instruction sets for RISC[2] architectures is primarily motivated by what can be efficiently implemented on the underlying hardware.

The design goal of PIL (Papyrus Interface Language) is to provide a set of *optimizable and parallelizable* language features. Analogous to the RISC design

[1] Complex Instruction Set Computers
[2] Reduced Instruction Set Computers

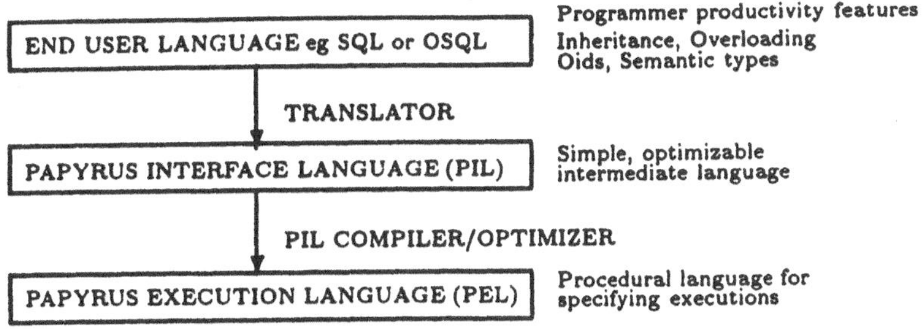

Figure 1: Language Levels in Papyrus

philosophy, the design of PIL is motivated by the desire to exploit query optimization techniques, and parallelization capabilities such as cloning — wherein clones of code are executed in parallel on disjoint partitions of data.

PIL is designed to be an *intermediate* language. Unlike most DBPLs such as OSQL[FAC+89, WLH90] (the language supported by Iris/OpenOdb), FAD[BBKV87], Napier[MBCD89], Galileo[ACO85] and Algres[CCRLZ89] PIL is *not* object-oriented. However, as shown in Figure 1, it is intended that several end-user database languages such as OSQL and SQL be supported on top of PIL. This reflects the belief that while object-oriented features such as object-identity, semantic types, inheritance and overloading enhance programmer productivity, the picture for optimization should be simplified by "pre-processing" away such features.

In keeping with the RISC design philosophy, we believe that gains from excluding features that hinder optimization will offset losses stemming from losing some of the semantics (and therefore some possible optimizations) of the features that are pre-processed away.

PIL combines a functional model of computation[BW88, AS85] with data types suitable for data intensive applications. A functional model gives a *declarative semantics* to all expressions including "procedural" constructs such as if-then-else, while and function calls provided the expression is without side-effects. A pure functional model can be extended to incorporate assignment without destroying the declarative reading of side-effect free (sub)expressions. We have adopted the environment model of expression evaluation as defined in the Scheme language[A+91].

We have chosen to only *partially define the order of evaluation* for programs. This opens up more opportunities for reordering and for parallel execution. For example we provide two constructs for iteration over bags, one with a parallel semantics (simple iteration) and the other with a serial-commutative semantics (reduction). Such constructs provide more degrees of freedom to the compiler in optimizing and parallelizing programs. Such constructs also make it possible to express that the order of eveluation is unimportant. This is important since compilers cannot always make such inferences. These and other such judicious choices for language semantics are elaborated in this paper.

This work is part of the Papyrus project[CHK+91] at HP Labs which is investigating ways of integrating highly-tuned, customized data managers while preserving their requirements for performance. Sources of high performance include optimization and parallel execution.

The next section gives a brief overview of PIL, Section 3 discusses the model of data and computation. Section 4 discusses the abstractions for iteration and opportunities for their parallelization.

2 PIL in a Nutshell

PIL provides several abstractions for iteration at different levels of generality. The *while* abstraction provides a very general form of iteration with a serial semantics. Reduction is a special case of while in which the domain of iteration is a bag and the body of the loop is executed once per bag element. Variables may be shared across iterations. Reduction is defined to have a serial-commutative semantics. In other words the execution must be equivalent to some serial ordering of the iterations. Simple iteration is a special case of reduction in which each iteration is independent (no variables are shared). Simple iteration has a parallel semantics.

Simple iteration is a generalization of Select-Project-Join queries while reduction is a generalization of queries with aggregation. The pre-existing body of knowledge on relational query optimization and execution may be applied to these abstractions.

Arguments to functions are passed by value. The only restriction on the order of evaluation of arguments is that it must be equivalent to some serial order of evaluation of arguments. This freedom allows a compiler to choose the best amongst alternate execution strategies.

Types are associated with values or in other words data is self describing. Types are also be stated as constraints on variables. Since PIL is an intermediate language, there is no type checking. However types serve the role of providing useful information to the compiler. The PIL compiler uses type inference to facilitate the generation of efficient code.

PIL provides the *type constructors* bag, tuple, labeled tuple and sequence for modeling aggregate data common in database applications. Direct support for sequences not only makes certain queries such as the k-day moving average of HP stock easier to express but also facilitates their efficient implementation. A disadvantage of not providing sequences in SQL is that queries with *order by* clauses do not produce relations and therefore have to be disallowed in SQL views.

PIL permits aggregate objects to be arbitrarily nested. A nested model is not as simple as a flat model. However, it provides modeling and processing advantages for domains where nested objects occur naturally.

PIL programs are block-structured like those in Algol or Pascal. Each use of a variable is associated with a lexically apparent binding of that variable.

A *database schema* is a named set of declarations of types and variables. Note that in our model functions are thought of as variables. An *environment* is a mapping of variables to values.

A *database* is a named persistent environment. A database is an instance of a database schema if it has the same name and provides bindings for exactly the variables and functions in the schema. A variable is persistent if it is defined in a database schema. A value becomes persistent if it is assigned to a persistent variable.

type *Cell*; /* A foreign type */
type *RoadSeg* = $\langle\langle name : String, segment : Cell\rangle\rangle$;
var *Roads*: {*RoadSeg*};
function *shape(Cell)* $\longrightarrow$ $[\langle\langle latitude : Float, longitude : Float\rangle\rangle]$);
function *length*($[\langle\langle latitude : Float, longitude : Float\rangle\rangle]$) $\longrightarrow$ *Float*;
function *plus(Float, Float)*$\longrightarrow$*Float*;

Figure 2: Logical Schema for the SimpleGIS database

Roads = { ⟨⟨ "El Camino", cell1 ⟩⟩
⟨⟨ "El Camino", cell2 ⟩⟩
⟨⟨ "Page Mill Road", cell3 ⟩⟩};
shape = `a function object`;
length = `a function object`;
plus = `a function object`;

Figure 3: The SimpleGIS database

2.1 Examples

Figure 2 shows the schema for a database of geographic information. The logical schema defines the names and types of the functions and variables in the database. Figure 3 shows the contents of the GIS database.

A road has a name and consists of a number of *segments*. A new segment starts each time the road intersects with a cross street or crosses a political boundary such as a county boundary. A segment is a continuous, but not necessarily straight, line. Segments are stored as geometrical objects of type *cell*. *Roads* is a bag of tuples with one tuple per segment of a road. The function *shape(cell)* returns the shape of the segment as a sequence of two or more points with each point represented as a tuple consisting of the *latitude* and *longitude* of the point. The *length* function computes the length of a sequence of points and *plus* adds two floating point numbers.

Example 1 The following query returns the shape of all segments that make up the road named "El Camino". The result of the query is a bag of sequences and may be used to graphically display the shape of El Camino on a map. The *simple iteration* construct used below is a generalization of select-project-join queries. One way of processing the query is to first select all road segments named "El Camino", then pipe the selected road segments to *m clones* of the shape function. The decision of which clone a particular road segments goes to may be made based on a hash function. The stream of results produced by each clone may then be merged to form the result.
for r:RoadSeg in Roads
where r.name="El Camino"
apply shape(r.segment) ∎

Example 2 The following query computes the length of El Camino. It uses a *reduction* construct which has a serial-commutative semantics. First the variable *len* is initialized to zero and then we iterate over all tuples in *Roads* which satisfy *r.name = "El Camino"* in an *arbitrarily* chosen order. For each such tuple the body of the loop, which accumulates the length of the road in the variable *len*, is executed.

with len:Float := 0
for r: RoadSeg **in** Roads
where r.name="El Camino"
reduceby len := plus(len, length(shape(r.segment)))

One way of executing the query is to partition the road segments amongst several clones. Each clone can compute the sum of the lengths of its segments and then the lengths produced by each clone may be summed up.

■

3 Model of Data and Computation

Our model consists of a functional model of computation and some chosen set of *built-in* data types and *built-in* functions defined on the types.

Persistence is provided through the notion of a database as a named persistent environment.

The choice of data types is orthogonal to the model of computation and may be easily extended to incorporate *foreign* types and functions in addition to the those that are built-in. A discussion of how foreign types and functions are implemented is beyond the scope of this paper.

Section 3.1 describes the built-in data types and Section 3.2 discusses the primitives out of which expressions are constructed and the model of expression evaluation. Lastly, in Section 3.3 we describe how type declarations (viewed as constraints on values for variables) may be added to the notion of expressions.

3.1 Data Types

All data objects in PIL are literal objects[FAC+89]. A literal object is a *value*. For example integers, bags and functions are literals but pointers and object identifiers are not.

Both built-in and foreign data types can be categorized into atomic and aggregate types. Data types such as *Integer*, *String*, and *Float* are *atomic*. Atomic objects have no structure visible in the language. *Aggregate* objects, on the other hand, are made up of components. This structure is made visible in the language by the provision of functions to pick out components, iterate over components and construct aggregate objects from components.

PIL provides *type constructors* for four kinds of aggregates: *bag* to model unordered collections with duplicates, *sequence* to model ordered collections and *tuple* and *labeled tuple* to model records. An additional type constructor, *function*, is provided to model functions.

Figure 4 shows the types provided in PIL and how they are related by a subtype relationship. Types constructed using the type constructors are not shown since there are an infinite number of such types. Types constructed

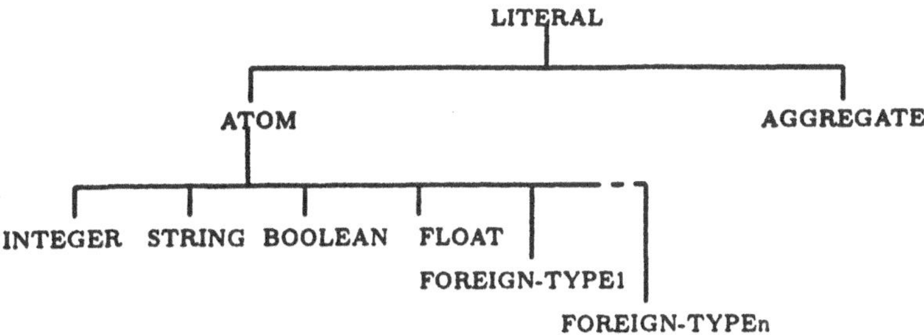

Figure 4: The PIL type graph

using the aggregate type constructors are subtypes of *Aggregate* while types constructed using the function type constructor are subtypes of *Atom*.

Kent[Ken] provides a general approach for characterizing a large variety of aggregate objects by giving dimensions along which they may be characterized. We have chosen specific kinds of aggregate objects which we describe along some of the suggested dimensions. Table 1 summarizes some of the characteristics and [Has92] provides precise definitions of the functions described informally below.

Each aggregate type has an associated *constructor* function. The symbol $\{\}$ is used to denote an empty bag, $\langle\langle\rangle\rangle$ for an empty tuple and $[]$ for an empty sequence. Given components $e_1, \ldots, e_n$ $[e_1, \ldots, e_n]$ constructs a sequence, $\langle\langle e_1, \ldots, e_n\rangle\rangle$ constructs a tuple, $\langle\langle l_1 : e_1, \ldots, l_n : e_n\rangle\rangle$ constructs a labeled tuple with labels $l_1, \ldots, l_n$, and $\{e_1, \ldots, e_n\}$ constructs a bag[3]. Null components are permitted for tuples and sequences but not for bags.

Functions are provided to access components of an aggregate object. Tuples and sequences are ordered collections. The function *tuple_pick(t, i)*, where i is a positive integer returns the ith component of tuple t. Similarly *seq_pick(s, i)* (which is alternatively written as $s[i]$) returns the ith component of sequence s. Bags are unordered collections. Therefore, for a bag, b, *bag_pick(b)* returns an arbitrarily chosen component or *Null* if the bag is empty.

The *equality* of aggregate objects is based on the equality of their components. Two sequences are equal if corresponding components are equal. Tuple equality is similar to that for sequences. Two bags are equal if the multiplicity of each member element is the same in each bag.

Bags and sequences are *homogeneous* in the sense that all components are of the same type. Tuples and labeled tuples are *heterogeneous* and a different type may be specified for each component.

3.1.1 Discussion

Inclusion of sequences: PIL provides sequences to model ordered collections of data. Having sequences permits the direct modeling of ordered domains such as time. For example the complexity of writing a query to compute the k-day moving average of stock prices changes considerably depending on whether

[3] Constructors are no different from ordinary functions. For example $\{e_1, \ldots, e_n\}$ is simply a different notation for *bag_construct*$(e_1, \ldots, e_n)$.

	Access to Components	*Iter. over Compnts.*	*Null Compnts.*	*Form of type expression*
Bag	*bag_pick*(*b*)	Yes	No	$\{T\}$
Sequence	*s*[*i*]	Yes	Yes	$[T]$
Tuple	*tuple_pick*(*t*, *i*)	No	Yes	$\langle\langle T_1, \ldots, T_n \rangle\rangle$
Labeled Tuple	*tuple_pick*(*t*, *i*) *t*.l_i	No	Yes	$\langle\langle l_1 : T_1, \ldots, l_n T_n \rangle\rangle$

Table 1: Characteristics of Aggregate Types

the daily stock quotes are represented as a sequence or as a bag. Sequences naturally provide the notion of the "next" element. If sequences are simulated using bags, the "next" element has to be computed as the minimum of all elements which are greater than the given element. We believe direct support for sequences is essential for their efficient implementation.

Another advantage of providing sequences is to remove the restriction of disallowing SORT to occur in view definitions in languages such as SQL.

Nested Model: Forcing a flat representation for objects that are naturally nested has some disadvantages. Flattening leads to the introduction of of artificial identifiers. It also leads to a loss of certain uniqueness constraints that are implemented by the very structure of a nested representation. Another advantage that is lost is the granularity of manipulation.

The disadvantages of the nested model stems primarily from sacrificing the simplicity of the flat model and the poor state of the art in effective query processing and optimization techniques (how do you estimate selectivities or implement pipelining for example).

Exclusion of Pointer: The *pointer* type constructor has been deliberately excluded from PIL. The presence of pointers increases the complexity of optimization. For example, in the absence of pointers it is easy to see that any two variable are disjoint and therefore may be operated upon in parallel. In the presence of pointers, any inference procedure for disjointness is likely to be highly pessimistic in order to ensure correctness. The intuitive reason is that the procedure would only have type information available to it. Therefore if the type of any component of one variable is "*pointer*(*t*)" where type *t* is the type of some component of the other variable, then we would not be able to infer the two variables to be disjoint.

Exclusion of Inheritance and Overloading: We believe that inheritance and overloading are end-user language features that increase programmer productivity but can easily be pre-processed in the translation to PIL. An overloaded function can either be resolved at translation time or an if-statement can be generated if the resolution is to be postponed to run-time.

Another reason for the exclusion of such features is that PIL is an intermediate language intended to support *multiple* end-user languages. Since end-user languages differ in their model of such features, we felt it would not make much sense to build yet another model of these features into PIL.

3.2 Expressions and Evaluation

We summarize below the syntax and semantics of the *primitive* expressions in PIL. More useful derived expressions such as abstractions for iteration may be constructed from the primitive expressions.

1. A constant c is an expression which evaluates to itself.
2. A variable v is an expression. A variable evaluates to its binding.
3. A conditional expression has the form **if** p **then** e_1 **else** e_2. First p is evaluated and after that if p was *True*, e_1 is evaluated, otherwise e_2 is evaluated. The else part is optional.
4. A lambda expression **lambda**$(v_1, \ldots, v_n)e$ consists of a list of formal parameters (variables) and a body. It evaluates to a function object.
5. A function call $f(e_1, \ldots, e_n)$ is an expression. It is evaluated by first evaluating the parameters in an arbitrarily chosen order. Then the body of the function is evaluated.
6. An assignment $v := e$ is an expression. The expression e is evaluated and v is bound to the resulting value. The result value of an assignment expression is undefined.

We also introduce the following *derived* constructs:

1. **begin** $expr_1; \ldots; expr_n$ **end** explicitly sequences the evaluation of the expressions and returns the value of $expr_n$ as the result[4].
2. **function** $f(v_1, \ldots, v_n)$ as e defines f as a function[5].

Example 3 The following expression evaluates to *False* in the environment of the SimpleGIS database shown in Figure 3.

```
begin
   function empty(b) as is_null(bag_pick(b));
   empty(Roads)
end
```

■

3.3 Typed Expressions

The primary intention of a type system in PIL is to increase the information available to the PIL compiler. More specific type information permits the generation of better code in the translation of PIL to PEL[CS92, SC92].

The PIL compiler uses type inferencing to derive information on the types of expressions. Since PIL is an intermediate language, we decided that the compiler should desist from type checking. It is assumed that the type-correctness of programs is guaranteed by translator from the end-user language.

---

[4]For example **begin** $expr_1; expr_2$ **end** is equivalent to $(lambda(x)expr_2)expr_1$. $(lambda(x)expr_2)$ evaluates to a function which takes one parameter. $expr_1$ is the parameter which is evaluated *before* the body of the function, consisting of $expr_2$ is evaluated.

[5]This construct is equivalent to $f :=$ **lambda** $(v_1, \ldots, v_n)$ e.

In PIL programs, a type must be declared for each variable. A type declaration is simply a *constraint* on the set of values considered legal for a variable. In addition to type constraints, it is also possible to specify a variable to be a *constant*. In other words the variable is assigned to exactly once.

Example 4 The expression of Example 3 must now be written as:

```
begin
   function empty(b:{Literal}) → Boolean
   as is_null(bag_pick(b));
   empty(Roads)
end
```

■

We require that types be declared for the parameters and the result of a lambda expression. Consider T or T_i to be type expressions. The syntax for a lambda expression becomes as follows:
T **lambda**$(v_1 : T_1, \ldots, v_n : T_n)e$

The derived construct for function definition is also extended to be of the following form[6]
function $f(v_1 : T_1, \ldots, v_n : T_n) \rightarrow T$ **as** e

4 Abstractions for Iteration

We provide several abstractions for iteration over bags and sequences. The intention of providing these built-in constructs is to capture the operations *common* in database applications in such a way as to facilitate their optimization and parallelization. The choice of abstractions takes into consideration the capabilities that can be reasonably expected from a compiler.

A *while* loop construct is provided as a general means of iteration. We also provide *simple iteration*, *reduction* and *grouping* as special cases. These special cases represent forms of iteration common in database applications and for which we can expect to develop optimization and parallelization techniques.

Simple iteration is a generalization of select-project-join queries. It provides opportunities for cloned parallel and the design facilitates the reuse of relational optimization techniques. Reduction provides the ability to compute aggregate properties such as sum or standard deviation. The semantics of reduction is defined so as to facilitate cloned parallel execution. The *groupBy* function divides a bag into equivalence classes and thus provides a natural granularity for the cloning of subsequent operations.

Clearly our philosophy is not to have the minimal set of abstractions but to provide optimizable constructs in a declarative language framework. For example, simple iteration is a special case of reduction and reduction is a special case of the while loop.

[6] This construct is equivalent to *Const* $f : (T_1, \ldots, T_n) \rightarrow T :=$ **lambda** $(v_1 : T_1, \ldots, v_n : T_n)\ e$

4.1 Simple Iteration Over Bags

Simple iteration is modeled as the higher order function

$$filter(f, p, b_1, \ldots, b_n)$$

which is a generalization of select-project-join queries. It takes n bags $b_1, \ldots, b_n$ and two n-ary functions f and g as parameters. The arbitrary predicate, p, may be used for selection and the arbitrary function, f, for projection. It is equivalent to

$$\Pi_f(\sigma_p((b_1 \times \ldots \times b_n)))$$

In other words, the *filter* function takes each element x in the cartesian product of the bags, tests whether $p(x)$ is true, and if so computes $f(x)$. The result is the bag of all such $f(x)$s.

Simple iteration offers the opportunity for parallel execution through cloning. Cloning is essentially based on the fact that it is possible to view a bag as the union (merge) of m partitions (split) based on some hash function.

$$b = Merge(Split(b, 1), \ldots, Split(b, m))$$

Operations such as Π_f and σ_p commute with Split and Merge. Join methods also offer opportunities for commuting since we can use the following rewrite rule.

$$\begin{aligned} Join(b_1, b_2) = Merge(&Join(Split(b_1, 1), Split(b_2, 1)), \ldots, \\ &Join(Split(b_1, m), Split(b_2, m)))) \end{aligned}$$

These rewrite rules open up a large space of parallel executions from which an optimizer can be expected to choose the cheapest plan. Several parallel join algorithms based on such rewrites are discussed in [SD89].

The FAD language provides a similar filter function but combines the selection (p) and projection (f) into a single function (g). The abstraction $filter_{FAD}(g, b_1, \ldots, b_n)$ creates two complications. Firstly the semantic complication is that g must be allowed to return *Null* and set insertion must be defined so that inserting a *Null* into a set returns the original set. Second, and more importantly, optimization becomes harder since selections, which are important to predict the cardinality of results, are "mixed" with projections. For example an expensive but highly selective selection should be done early while expensive projections should be delayed.

We will use the following syntax for the *filter* function in order to make PIL programs more readable ($expr(v_1, \ldots, v_n)$ represents an expression containing $v_1, \ldots, v_n$ as free variables). A type T_i is declared for each variable v_i.

for $v_1 : T_1$ **in** $b_1, \ldots, v_n : T_n$ **in** b_n
where $p(v_1, \ldots, v_n)$
apply $f(v_1, \ldots, v_n)$

Example 5 (Generalized Selection): The following query retrieves the shape of all roads in the Cupertino area. The Cupertino region is approximated by a rectangle and specified by giving the end-points of a diagonal of the rectangle. The $intersect(Cell, \{\langle\langle Float, Float\rangle\rangle\} \rightarrow Boolean$ function determines whether a cell intersects a rectangular window.

```
begin
   var Cupertino: {⟨⟨Float, Float⟩⟩};
   Cupertino:= {⟨⟨37.1500, 122.0000⟩⟩, ⟨⟨372230,1220730⟩⟩};
   for r: RoadSeg in Roads
   where intersect(r.segment, Cupertino)
   apply shape(r.segment)
end
```

■

Example 6 (Generalized Projection): The following query smooths the shape of Page Mill Road. Short curved segments are approximated by straight lines.

```
begin
   for r: RoadSeg in Roads
   where r.name = "Page Mill"
   apply
      begin
         var s:{⟨⟨Float, Float⟩⟩};
         s := shape(r.segment);
         if (length(s) < 10.0) then [s[1], s[card[s]]
         else s
      end
end
```

■

4.2 Reduction Over Bags

Reduction is a form of iteration which permits communication between iterations. It is intended to model queries which compute aggregate properties of bags such as averages and standard deviations of elements.

Reduction is modeled a higher order function of the following form

$$reduce(f, c, b)$$

where f is an binary function, c is a constant, b is a bag.

$$reduce(f, c, \{\}) = c$$
$$reduce(f, c, insert(e, b)) = f(e, reduce(f, c, b))$$

reduce iterates over all elements e of the bag b. The function $f(e, v)$ is evaluated in each iteration where v is the value returned by $f(e', v')$ in the previous iteration. The first iteration uses c as the value returned by the previous iteration.

Example 7 $reduce(+, 10, \{2, 4\})$ evaluates to 16. ■

Reduction also offers the opportunity for cloned execution provided that compiler knows the identity element, *id*, for f. The bag may be partitioned and clones of f may be used to reduce each partition as follows:

$$reduce(f, c, b) = reduce(f, c, \{r_1, \ldots, r_m\}))$$

where $r_i = reduce(f, id, Split(b, i))$

We will use the following syntax for reduction to make PIL programs more readable.

with $v_2 : T_2 := c$;
for $v_1 : T_1$ **in** b
reduceby $v_2 := f(v_1, v_2)$

Example 8 (Average): The following query returns the average length of road segments. The sum and count of the road segments is computed into the variable *sc* and then the average is computed by division.

```
begin
   var sc:⟨⟨ Float,Integer ⟩⟩;
   sc :=
      with sum:Float := 0; count:Integer := 0
      for r: RoadSeg in Roads
      reduceby
         begin
            sum := plus(sum, length(shape(r.segment)));
            count := plus(count, 1)
         end;
   divide(sc[1], sc[2])
end
```

■

Reduction iterates over bag elements in an arbitrary order. This leaves open a degree of freedom for exploitation by the compiler. Note that it is possible for the result of an expression to depend on the order of evaluation.

Example 9 The expression
with v_2:Integer:= c;
for v_1*:Integer* **in** $\{2, 4\}$
reduceby $v_2 := minus(v_1, v_2)$
evaluates to either $4 - (2 - 1) = 3$ or to $2 - (4 - 1) = -1$ depending on the order of iteration. ■

Such "ambiguity" is avoided if f is a *commutatively reducible* function.

Definition: A function f is termed *commutatively reducible* if for an arbitrary bag b and constant c,

$$reduce(f, c, b)$$

produces the same result for any order of iteration.

Lemma: A function f is *commutatively reducible* if and only if for arbitrary c, e_1 and e_2

$$f(e_1, f(e_2, c)) = f(e_2, f(e_1, c))$$

The following lemma follows easily. Note that this lemma is a sufficient condition but is not necessary. A counter example is $v - e$ which is commutatively reducible though minus is neither associative nor commutative.

Lemma: If f is an associative and commutative function then f is a commutatively reducible function.

4.3 Grouping over Bags

The higher order function

$$groupBy(f, b)$$

partitions the bag, b, into equivalence classes based on the result of applying the function, f, to each of its elements. The result is a bag of bags.

$groupBy(f,b) = \{p_1, \ldots, p_k\}$ where $p_1, \ldots, p_k$ is a partition of b (that is, $p_1 \cup \ldots \cup p_k = b$ and $i \neq j \Rightarrow p_i \cap p_j = \emptyset$); the elements in each partition, p_i, return the same value when f is applied to them ($c_1, c_2 \in p_i \Rightarrow f(c_1) = f(c_2)$); and elements from different partitions return different values ($c_1 \in p_i \wedge c_2 \in p_j \wedge i \neq j \Rightarrow f(c_1) \neq (c_2)$).

Grouping provides a natural granularity for cloning of subsequent operations.

Example 10 The following query computes a bag in which each tuple contains the name of a road and its length.

```
begin
    function roadLength(R:{roadSeg}) → Float as
        with len:Float := 0
        for  r: roadSeg in R
        reduceby len := plus(len, length(shape(r.segment)));

    function roadName(r:⟨⟨ name:String, segment:Cell⟩⟩) → String as r.name;

    for  p: roadSeg in groupBy(Roads, roadName)
    apply ⟨⟨ bag_pick(p).name, roadLength(p)⟩⟩
end
```

■

groupBy is also useful for creating nested objects. For example we could replace the second last line in the above program by

```
    apply  ⟨⟨ bag_pick(p).name,
              for r:roadSeg in p
              apply r.2
           ⟩⟩
```

4.4 Simple Iteration, Reduction, and Grouping Over Sequences

In this section, we extend the definitions of filter, reduce and groupby for sequences. We also show that directly supporting sequences not also makes some queries easier to write but also makes it easier for a compiler to obtain efficient execution plans.

Opportunities for cloned parallelism while iterating over sequences are similar to the opportunities available in iteration over bags.

Each element of a sequence has an associated index value. For example in the sequence [5, 7], the element 7 has the associated index value 2. The abstractions for iteration and reduction over sequences are similar to those for

stockOpen : $[\langle\langle name : String, date : Integer, price : Integer\rangle\rangle]$
stockClose : $[\langle\langle name : String, date : Integer, price : Integer\rangle\rangle]$

Figure 5: Logical Schema for the StockMarket Database

bags with two differences. Firstly, in addition to the value of an element, the index value of the element may also be used in the iteration. Secondly, the order of iteration is well defined.

The function

$$filter(f, p, s_1, \ldots, s_n)$$

is used for pure iteration over sequences. It takes n bags $s_1, \ldots, s_n$ and two $2n$-ary functions f and g as parameters. The functions are $2n$-ary since both the element and its index are passed as arguments to the functions. The *filter* function iterates over the elements of the sequence in the well defined order. If i_j is the index for an element of s_j, the index values $i_1, \ldots, i_n$ are traversed with i_n changing the fastest and i_1 the slowest [7]. In each iteration, it is tested whether $p(s_1[i_1], i_1, s_2[i_2], i_2, \ldots, s_n[i_n], i_n)$ is true and if so then $f(s_1[i_1], i_1, s_2[i_2], i_2, \ldots, s_n[i_n], i_n)$ is computed. The result is the sequence of all such results of computing $f()$.

The syntax for simple iteration over sequences is the same as for bags.

The examples below use the logical schema for the Stock Market database (Figure 5). We assume that bags are ordered by name as the primary sort key and date as the secondary key.

Example 11 (Merge) The following query computes, for each stock, the change in price for each day.

for o:⟨⟨ name:String, date:Integer, price:Integer ⟩⟩ **in** stockOpen,
c: ⟨⟨ name:String, date:Integer, price:Integer ⟩⟩ **in** stockClose
where o.index = c.index
apply $\langle\langle o.name, o.date, (c.price - o.price)\rangle\rangle$

This query may also be posed fairly easily even if *stockOpen* and *stockClose* were modeled as bags,by using the predicate $o.date = e.date$ *and* $o.name = e.name$. The next example illustrates how sequences are useful as compared to bags. ∎

Example 12 (Shifted Merge) The following query computes the change in stock price between the closing price on one day and the opening price on the *next* day. Sequences make the notion of *next* quite simple since the next element after an element with index i is the element with index $i + 1$.

for o:⟨⟨ name:String, date:Integer, price:Integer ⟩⟩ **in** stockOpen,
c: ⟨⟨ name:String, date:Integer, price:Integer ⟩⟩ **in** stockClose
where o.index = c.index+1
apply $\langle\langle o.name, o.date, (c.price - o.price)\rangle\rangle$

[7] More precisely the index values $i_1, \ldots, i_n$ are traversed in the order defined by $i_n + card(e_{n-1}) * (i_{n-1} + \ldots + (card(e_2) * (i_2 + card(e_1) * i_1)) \ldots)$.

Defining the next date without using index is quite complex since the Stock Market is closed on weekends and some other holidays. Therefore the next date has to be computed as the minimum of all dates which are greater than the given date. ■

Reduction over a sequence is similar to reduction over a bag with the difference that the iteration is ordered. It is a higher order function of the following form

$$reduce(f, c, s)$$

where f is a binary function, c is a constant, s is a sequence.

$$reduce(f, c, []) = c$$
$$reduce(f, c, insert(e, 1, s)) = f(e, reduce(f, c, s))$$

The syntax for reduction over sequences is the same as for bags.

Example 13 (Moving Average) The following query computes the k-day moving average of the closing price of HP stock.

```
begin
var hpstock:[⟨⟨name : String, date : Integer, price : Integer⟩⟩];
hpstock :=
    for c:⟨⟨ name:String, date:Integer, price:Integer ⟩⟩ in stockClose
    where c.name = hp
    apply c;
for c2:⟨⟨ name:String, date:Integer, price:Integer ⟩⟩ in hpstock
where c2.index >= k
apply ⟨⟨c2.date,
    divide( with sum : Integer := 0
            for c3: ⟨⟨ price:Integer ⟩⟩ in
                for c1:⟨⟨ name:String, date:Integer, price:Integer ⟩⟩ in hpstock
                where c1.index <= i and c1.index > i - k
                apply c1.price
            reduceby sum := sum + c3,
            k)⟩⟩
end
```

■

Grouping over sequences is similar to grouping over bags. The difference is that the result is a bag of sequences with the elements of a sequence being ordered in the same relative order as in the original (input) sequence.

4.5 While Loop

The higher order function, $while(c, p, f)$, provides a general iteration construct. The generality lies in the fact that the domain of iteration is arbitrary. We will use the following syntax for while loops in PIL programs.

```
with v : T := c
while p(v)
v := f(v)
```

The *while* function is defined as:

$$while(c,p,f) = c \quad \text{if p(c) is false}$$
$$while(c,p,f) = while(f(c),p,f) \quad \text{otherwise}$$

Example 14 The following program finds all road segments within a radius of distance 10 miles from a starting point such that it is possible to drive to the road segment without getting more than 10 miles from the starting point at any time during the drive.

```
begin
    var startPoint:[⟨⟨ latitude:Float, longitude:Float⟩⟩];
    var nearByRoads: {Cell};
    var connectedRoad: {Cell};
    startPoint:= [ 37.5, 122.0 ];

    nearByRoads :=
        for  r: RoadSeg in Roads
        where distance(r.segment,startPoint ) < 10
        apply r.segment;

    connectedRoads :=
        with new :=
            for  r:Cell in nearByRoads
                where pointInCell(startPoint, r.segment )
                apply r.segment
        while not(empty(minus(new, connectedRoads)))
            begin
                connectedRoads:= union(connectedRoads, new);
                new :=
                    for  r1: Cell in new, r2:Cell in nearByRoads
                    where intersect(r1.segment, r2.segment)
                    apply r.segment
            end
end
```

■

5 Conclusion

We have used a RISC design philosophy in choosing optimizable and parallelizable language features. We have shown how these features facilitate optimization and parallel execution through cloning.

We have combined a functional model of computation with a data model that directly supports sequences in addition to bags and tuples. Our choice of a functional model permits side-effect free (sub)expressions to have a declarative reading. We have also chosen a language semantics in which, even in the presence of updates, the order of evaluation is only partially defined in order to increase the space of possible executions.

An implementation of PIL is almost complete and is expected to be ready before the workshop. We are also implementing a translator from OSQL to PIL to validate our belief that "pre-processing" of object-oriented features is a good idea.

We are investigating mechanisms for the integration of foreign types, variables and functions in PIL. This feature is important towards achieving goal of integrating pre-existing data managers in the Papyrus. The semantics of updates to aggregate objects is also a subject of current research.

The investigation of optimization techniques for parallel execution is another important area of current work. Some preliminary results which provide a theoretical framework for the problem are reported in [GHK92].

Acknowledgements: We thank Marie-Anne Neimat for her advice, encouragement and support from the early stages of this research. We are particularly grateful to Bill Kent for several enlightening discussions. Thanks are also due to Stefano Ceri, Surajit Chaudhuri, Michael Heytens, Curtis Kolovson, Spyridon Potamianos, and Donovan Schneider. Comments from Surajit Chaudhuri, Michael Heytens, and Marie-Anne Neimat helped in substantially improving an earlier draft of the paper.

References

[A+91] H. Abelson et al. Revised[4] report on the algorithmic language scheme, November 1991.

[ABD+89] M.P. Atkinson, F. Bancilhon, D. DeWitt, K. Dittrich, D. Maier, and S. Zdonik. The Object-Oriented Database Manifesto. In *Proceedings of DOOD*, December 1989.

[ACO85] A. Albano, L. Cardelli, and R. Orsini. Galileo: A Strongly Typed, Interactive Conceptual Language. *Transactions on Database Systems*, 10(2):230–260, 1985.

[AGO90] A. Albano, G. Ghelli, and R. Orsini. Objects and Classes for a Database Programming Language. Technical report, Progetto Finalizzato Sistemi Informatici E Calcolo Parallelo, October 1990. Report n. 5/24.

[AS85] H. Abelson and G.J. Sussman. *Structure and Interpretation of Computer Programs.* The MIT Press, 1985.

[BBKV87] F. Bancilhon, T. Briggs, S. Khoshafian, and P. Valduriez. FAD, A Simple and Powerful Database Language. In *Proceedings of the Thirteenth International Conference on Very Large Data Bases*, 1987.

[BW88] R. Bird and P. Wadler. *Introduction to Functional Programming.* Prentice Hall, 1988.

[CCRLZ89] S. Ceri, S. Crespi-Reghizzi, G. Lamperti, and R. Zicari. ALGRES: An Advanced Database System for Complex Applications. Technical report, Dipartmento di Elettronica, Politecnico di Milano, 1989. Report n. 89-010.

[CHK+91] T. Connors, W. Hasan, C. Kolovson, M.-A. Neimat, D. Schneider, and K. Wilkinson. The papyrus integrated data server. In *Proceedings of the First International Conference on Parallel and Distributed Information Systems*, December 1991.

[CS92] T. Connors and D. Schneider. The Papyrus Query Processing Engine. In *Proceedings of the Second International Workshop on Research Issues on Data Engineering: Transactions and Query Processing*, February 1992.

[FAC+89] D. H. Fishman, J. Annevelink, E. Chow, T. Connors, J. W. Davis, W. Hasan, C. G. Hoch, W. Kent, S.Leichner, P. Lyngbaek, B. Mahbod, M. A. Neimat, T. Risch, M.C. Shan, and W. K. Wilkinson. Overview of the Iris DBMS. In W. Kim and F. H. Lochovsky, editors, *Object-Oriented Concepts, Languages, and Applications.* Addison-Wesley Publishing Company, 1989.

[GHK92] S. Ganguly, W. Hasan, and R. Krishnamurthy. Query Optimization for Parallel Execution. In *Proceedings of ACM-SIGMOD International Conference on Management of Data*, June 1992. To Appear.

[Has92] W. Hasan. Papyrus Interface Language. Technical report, HP Laboratories, 1992. HPL-DTD-92-4.

[Ken] W. Kent. Personal Communication and Several Unpublished Memos.

[MBCD89] R. Morrison, A.L. Brown, R.C.H. Connor, and A. Dearle. Napier88 Reference Manual. Technical report, Department of Computational Science, University of St. Andrews, 1989.

[PJ87] S.L. Peyton-Jones. *The Implementation of Functional Programming Languages.* Prentice Hall, 1987.

[SC92] D. Schneider and T. Connors. Managing query execution for an advanced database programming language, 1992. Submitted for publication.

[SD89] D. A. Schneider and D. J. DeWitt. A performance evaluation of four parallel join algorithms in a shared-nothing multiprocessor environment. In *ACM SIGMOD*, Portland, Oregon, June 1989.

[WLH90] K. Wilkinson, P. Lyngbaek, and W. Hasan. The Iris Architecture and Implementation. *IEEE Transactions on Knowledge and Data Engineering*, 2(1):63–75, March 1990.

Integrity Constraints and Methodology

Alan Dearle

Department of Computer Science, University of Adelaide
Adelaide, Australia

Two papers were presented in this session: "Enforcing Integrity Constraints in Database Programming Languages" presented by Veronique Benzaken and "Semantic Constructs for a Persistent Programming Language" presented by Shane Sparg. The papers were followed by a lively debate on many aspects of integrity constraints.

1 The Papers

The first paper focused on the difficult problem of enforcement of integrity constraints. Some database programming languages permit constraints of arbitrary complexity to be expressed. The enforcement of such constraints is sometimes intractable. This paper describes how checking may be optimised by statically calculating which parts of a database may be affected by some transaction. This leads to enforcement algorithms that are more efficient and should provide checking algorithms for problems that were previously intractable.

The second paper presented described language level constructs for expressing integrity constraints. The language described in the paper is based on the Semantic Data Model and is implemented using Napier88. This paper was one of several in the conference where the use of persistent systems to support themselves was evident. In this case, integrity enforcement procedures are placed in the store along with the data that they are protecting.

2 The Discussion

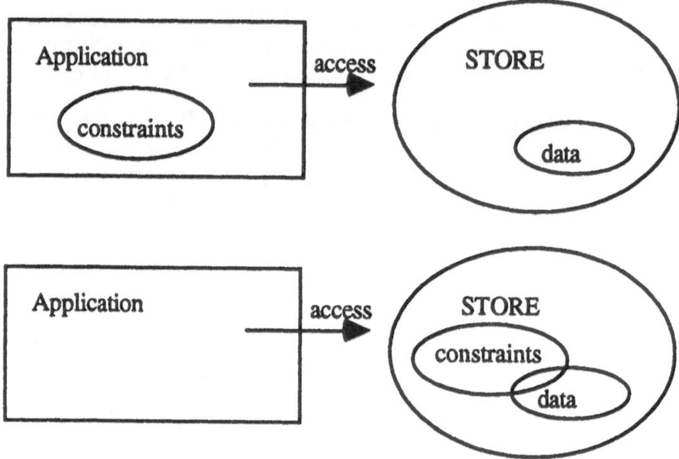

Some researchers in the audience felt that constraints should be encoded in the application program in some manner. This is shown in the first diagram above. For example, Malcolm Atkinson argued that integrity constraints could be placed within the definition of Abstract Data Types. It would be the responsibility of the application programmer to ensure that the access routines within the ADT enforced the appropriate constraints. In such a model constraints would be implicit in the code of the application program.

This technique was likened by some to programming in Common Lisp. The Lisp language provides little in the way of a type system to support the application programmer. However Lisp devotees argue that the programmer knows what he/she is doing and such an approach gives maximal flexibility.

Other researchers asserted that such an approach could never work since the programmer of a single Abstract Data Type did not have enough information about the entire database. It was the belief of these researchers that constraints were related to the database schema and not a single type within it. They argued that integrity constraints should be part of the database schema which should encode as much information about the database as possible. They advocated having no integrity checking within the application program as shown in the second diagram above. This approach was reinforced by the database programming language community who felt that database programming languages are higher level tools than ordinary programming languages and should provide special purpose abstractions.

Following this discussion was a vigorous debate on the difference between types and constraints. Some held the view that types and constraints were orthogonal to each other. Proponents of this view asserted that a constraint described a set of values. Of course, this fuelled further discussion (argument) since many in the room believed this to be exactly what a type is. This discussion led to the idea that the difference between constraints and types were related to what could be described statically. For example, most were happy with the type description of a person being a record with two fields, name and age. However, most were unhappy with the idea that if that person's age reached 71 his type would change. In contrast, most participants were happy specifying a constraint that a person must be in a given age range as in p: person, p.age > 18 and p.age < 70.

During this debate it was suggested by Giorgio Ghelli that the notion of class could help bridge the gap between the notions of type and constraint. In the database field a class is considered to be a type (an intent) plus a set of values (an extent). It would seem reasonable to extend the notion of class with some predicates placing constraints on the values in the set. However, this technique associates constraints with a single type of value. As described above, some researchers in the room objected to this approach.

It was suggested by Mike Livesey that it was a mistake to associate constraints with types at all. One example that was given to support this view was the constraint between two integers that one was bigger than the other. Such constraints describe a relationship between values and has little to do with types.

The session ended on a bright note with Atsushi Ohori suggesting that the technique described by Veronique in her talk may be further extended by analysing transactions at the semantic level. He suggested that the techniques of abstract interpretation and partial evaluation used by the functional programming community may be applied to the problem of constraint enforcement. This hypothesis remains for us to ponder.

Enforcing Integrity Constraints in Database Programming Languages

Véronique Benzaken
Université de Paris I - Sorbonne,
12 place du Panthéon,
75005 Paris, France
e-mail: benzaken@lri.lri.fr
Christophe Lécluse*
BL/AIS,
34 avenue du Roule,
92100 Neuilly sur seine, France.
e-mail: clec@AIS.Berger-Levrault.fr
Philippe Richard†
Alcatel-Alsthom Recherche,
Route de Nozay, 91460 Marcoussis, France.
e-mail: prichard@aar.alcatel-alsthom.fr

Abstract

This paper is concerned with the problem of efficiently checking of integrity constraints in data base programming languages supporting subtyping and class hierarchies. More specifically, we consider two different problems: (1) statically reduce the number of constraints to be checked, and (2) generate an efficient run time checker. Using simple strategies, one can significantly improve the efficiency of the verification. We show how to reduce the number of constraints to be checked by characterising the portions of the database that are concerned by the constraints and involved in a transaction. We also show how to generate efficient algorithms for checking a large class of constraints (universally quantified conjunctive constraints). Last, we show how all the techniques presented took great advantage of the underlying type system which provide a significant help both in solving (1) and (2).

---

*On leave from INRIA, BP 105, 78153 Rocquencourt le Chesnay cedex, since June 1991

†On leave from INRIA, BP 105, 78153 Rocquencourt le Chesnay cedex, since April 1991

1 Introduction

Efforts on database programming languages have mainly been devoted to the definition of elaborated type systems and persistence mechanisms for those languages. In particular, the problems of polymorphism, static typing and inference, and object identity were the main topics of [7]. On the other hand, database programming languages are in general not able to express integrity constraints in a global and declarative way although some interesting works are done in the context of object-oriented databases [11].

On the contrary, extended relational systems take integrity constraints and views into consideration, mainly in the relational way [15, 5, 16]. Those systems are mainly relational systems in which relations attributes domains are not necessarily atomic but can be constructed using abstract types. The associated query language can also be extended to manipulate these user defined types instances. However, extended relational systems are not integrated in the sense of database programming languages. In these systems, relations are a very special kind of data type that cannot be used orthogonally to the others. In most systems, sets cannot be constructed independently of relations, and the query languages are not integrated within the language used to define the new attributes domains.

In the deductive database field, the problem of integrity constraint checking has been fully investigated [6, 3, 8, 2]. A first technique consists in determining without accessing the database whether a transaction may violate an integrity constraint. Such a technique relies on theorem proving mechanism [13]. A second approach assumes transactions to be provided with the *atomicity* property and consists in restricting the constraints to be enforced and in avoiding to retest the portion of the database that was consistent before the transaction [15, 12].

Although the methods proposed in this paper rely on the same ideas, we would like to emphasize the benefits gained when relying on a type system in order to cope with object-oriented complexity.

We consider two different problems: (1) statically reduce the number of constraints to be checked, and (2) generate an efficient run time checker. Of course, in the general case the problem is very complicate and finding an optimal solution to (1), for instance, is undecidable. What we want to show is that, using simple strategies, we can significantly improve the efficiency of the verification. In this paper, we shall suppose that transactions can neither be nested nor call other transactions or functions, and that constraint specification does not involve method calls, in order to avoid interprocedural analysis. This general case will be the topic of a forthcoming study.

Our main goal is to fully exploit the type information in order to simplify constraint violation detection and to speed up constraint checking. Not only classes are partially ordered according to an inheritance hierachy but we also have to face the problem of constraint checking in an environment that allows updates to be propagated among several distinct paths among objects. A first part of the paper consist in using simple compilation techniques to statically determine which constraints might be violated by a transaction. The originality of this static analysis is that it captures the notion of inheritance. A second contribution consists, given a transaction and a constraint, in generating a checking algorithm which will operate on the smallest portion of the database involved by the transaction. Unlike in deductive databases, objects are much more structured and they can be accessed through several different paths in the database. We show how to significantly reduce the number of checking operations to be performed, relying on the underlying typing information.

In Section 2, we give an overview of the framework of [10] and show how to define integrity constraints in this framework. In Section 3, we consider the first problem, that is the reduction of the number of constraints. In Section 4, we show how the constraints can be transformed in order to be more efficiently checked. Section 5 contains some concluding remarks.

2 Overview of the Schema Definition Language

We study the constraints definition and maintenance problem in the framework proposed in [10] which we briefly recall here. We also give several examples that will be used in Section 3 and 4.

2.1 Types

We consider a framework in which all database manipulations are strongly and statically typed. Types can be atomic types like **integer**, **string** or **boolean**. Types can also be concrete structures like tuple and set types:

```
[name: string, children: { string }]
{ Person }, { integer }
```

Subtyping of concrete types is structural and inferred following the classical rules of Cardelli [4]. We have, for instance:

```
[name: string, age: integer] ≺ [name: string]
{ [name: string, age: integer] } ≺ { [name: string] }
```

Concrete type instances are *non shared*, *non mutable* values. Abstract types have a name and a list of features which model attributes and operations, as follows:

```
type Person is abstract
    name: string,
    age: integer,
    children: { Person },
    spouse: Person,
    licences: { string },
    changeAge(integer), /* an operation */
end
```

```
type Vehicle is abstract
    type: string,
    agev: integer,
    colour: string,
    number: integer,
    owner: Person,
end
```

The definition of the Person type states that a person has a name, an age, a set of children, a spouse and is equipped with an operation to update the age feature. Instances of an abstract type are "objects" in the sense that they have an identity which is independent of the value of their features (name, age, etc.). Instances of an abstract type are *mutable* and *shared* values.

2.2 Names and Classes

Types are used to describe the components of a database. The database can be seen as a graph of interconnected objects and values. The roots of this graph are names defined at the schema level:

```
let aSetofInts : { integer } := { 1, 2, 3 }
let Licences : { string } := { "truck", "car", "bike" }
```

The **let** keyword defines a new name with an associated type and binds an initial value to it. The value can be updated as for any variable.

The notion of class is an extensional notion which is not captured by the type definitions. A class represents a collection of objects of one type (abstract or not) and is characterised by a name and the type of its elements as follows:

```
class Persons of type Person
class Vehicles of type Vehicle
    key self.number
class Drivers of type [driver: Person, car: Vehicle]
```

Class names are special kinds of identifiers as they can be considered as set value names but classes can be organised in a subclass hierarchy. We can write, for example:

```
class Planes subclass of Vehicles
class BadDrivers subclass of Drivers
```

The class Planes is declared as a subclass of the class Vehicles. The associated types are the same, that is type Vehicle. The semantics of this subclass relationship is an inclusion semantics [9]. For instance, the class Planes is a subset of the class Vehicles.

2.3 Integrity Constraints

In our framework, integrity constraints are well-typed boolean expressions built using the names and classes of the schema, and general operators. We detail these operators in the following:

- Constants: **true, false, nil.**
- Variables: x, y, etc.
- Arithmetical operators: +, -, *, /
- Comparators: $=, \neq, <, >, \leq, \geq$
- Boolean operators: **and, or, not.**
- Tuple field or object feature extraction: x.a (where a is not a method).
- Set manipulations: **isin, in, inter, union**
- Aggregates: **card**

The equality operator can be applied on values of any type. The other comparators can be applied to numbers and sets.

While such expressions could also be built over tuple methods extraction, we first restrict our analysis to simple (non computable) field extraction.

A constraint has the following generic form:

C = Q x_1 **in** S_1, ..., Q x_k **in** S_k P(x_1, ..., x_k)

where Q denotes a quantifier (**all** or **exists**), the S_j's are set expressions, and P(x_1, ...,x_k) is a boolean expression with the x_j's as free variables.

The expression "Q x_1 **in** S_1, ..., Q x_k **in** S_k" will be referred as the *head* of the constraint while the predicate will be referred as its *tail*.

More precisely, the predicate P(x_1, ...,x_k) is of the form:

P(x_1, ..., x_k) = r_1 Co r_2, ... Co r_n

where Co denotes a logical connector (**or** or **and**), each r_i denotes a comparison expression of the form (x_j θ x_i) or (x_j θ c_i), where θ is one of the comparators (<, >, **isin**, etc.), and c_j are constants.

The following section gives some example of constraints.

2.3.1 Examples of constraints

The following are examples of constraints that can be constructed in our framework. They will be used as running examples in Sections 3 and 4.

(C_1) **all** p **in** Persons, p.**age** $\leq$ 130 **and** p.**age** $\geq$ 0;
(C_2) **all** d **in** Drivers, d.**driver.age** $\geq$ 18
(C_3) **all** i **in** aSetofInts, i $\leq$ 100

These constraints are range constraints. The reader should notice that they are different from a domain restriction in a type specification. A domain restriction is valid for every instance of a type and does not depend on the collection to which this instance belongs. A range constraint is local to a class (here Persons) and does not mean that *every* instance of the type Person has to satisfy this restriction. This is one example of what cannot be expressed only by means of type systems.

(C_4) **card**(Licences) $\geq$ 6;
(C_5) **all** p **in** Persons, **card**(p.children) < 20;
(C_6) **all** p **in** Persons, p.licences $\leq$ Licences;
(C_7) **all** d **in** Drivers, **card**(d.driver.licences) $\geq$ 1

These constraints put cardinality constraints on the named value Licences and on the attribute children of class Persons.

(C_8) **all** d **in** Drivers, d.car.type $\neq$ "truck"
or "truck-licence" **in** d.driver.licences
(C_9) **all** c_1, c_2 **in** Vehicles, c_1.number $\neq$ c_2.number **or** $c_1 = c_2$;
(C_{10}) **all** p **in** Persons, **card**(p.children) $\leq$ 12 **or** p.age $\geq$ 35;
(C_{11}) **all** p **in** Persons, p.spouse.spouse = p **or** p.spouse = **nil**;
(C_{12}) **all** c **in** Vehicles, **exist** d **in** Drivers, d.car = c **and** c.agev = d.driver.age

The constraint C_8 expresses that each driver in the Drivers class which drives a truck has the corresponding licence. The constraint C_9 states that the number attribute in class Vehicles is a key for this class. The constraint C_{10} expresses that if a person has more than 12 children then he (she) is older than 35. The constraint C_{11} expresses that a person is either single or is the spouse of his (her) spouse. The dummy constraint C_{12}imposes that for each vehicle there exists a driver whose age is the same as the age of his car.

(C_{13}) **all** x **in** { 3, 5, 7, 9 }, **exists** n **in** MyInts, x - n **isin** aSetofInts
(C_{14}) **all** x **in** aSetofInts **union** MyInts, x $\leq$ 15

The first of these last constraints shows the ability to express constraints on (set-structured) values without any need to assign them a name while the other one is expressed on the union of two populations.

2.4 Transactions

A transaction is a function which has the atomicity property. The following are examples of transactions:

let T_1 = **trans**(t, c: **string**, p: Person, a, n: **integer**)
insert Vehicle[**type**: t, **agev**: a, **colour**: c, **number**: n, **owner**: p]
into Vehicles
/* this transaction inserts a new vehicle in the class Vehicles */

```
let T2 = trans(p1, p2: Person):
            p1.spouse := p2;
            p2.spouse := p1;
            /* this transaction performs a marriage between two persons */

let T3 = trans(p: Person, l: string)
            p.licences += l;
            /* this transaction adds a new licence for a given person */

let T4 = trans()
            for p in Persons when (today = p.birthday)
                print("Happy Birthday ", p.name);
                p.age := p.age + 1
            /* this transaction updates the age of all Persons
            born on the current day */
```

3 Static Characterisation of a Set of Constraints

In order to avoid checking unnecessary constraints, we want to be able to statically characterise the integrity constraints that *may be* violated by a given transaction. As the problem of finding the exact solution is undecidable (because this depends on input data), we are only looking for a necessary condition, that is for a superset of the solution.

In order to characterise this superset of constraints, for a given transaction, we shall consider the parts of the database that are dealt with in a given constraint and/or involved in a given transaction. In the following subsections, we thus define *characterisations* of constraints and transactions.

Such characterisations consist, informally, in a set of *paths* into the database. A path starts from a schema name or a type name, which can be followed by one or several attribute names. For example, if the path "Person.**age**" is in the characterisation of a constraint, this means that the constraint refers to the age of an object of type Person. If the same path is in the characterisation of a transaction, this means that this transaction may update the age of a Person. Therefore, the transaction may violate the given constraint, and it will be checked at the end of the transaction.

One of the characteristics of this static analysis is the use we make of the underlying type system. As we said before, abstract types instances are mutable and shared values, whereas concrete types instances are non shared non mutable values. This concept of mutability and sharing is crucial when dealing with constraints checking. Indeed, an object may be referred to by several other objects and, as a consequence, updated through different database paths. The only information that can be statically manipulated for those objects is their type.

3.1 Characterisation of constraints

A constraint has the following generic form:

$C = Q\ x_1$ **in** $S_1, \ldots, Q\ x_k$ **in** $S_k\ P(x_1, \ldots, x_k)$

where Q denotes a quantifier (**all** or **exists**), the S_j's are set expressions, and $P(x_1, \ldots, x_k)$ is a boolean expression with the x_j's as free variables.

We illustrate this notation with some of the above constraint examples:

C_1 : **all** p **in** Persons, p.**age** $\leq$ 130 **and** p.**age** $\geq$ 0

S = Persons
P(p) = p.**age** $\leq$ 130 **and** p.**age** $\geq$ 0;
r_1 = p.**age** $\leq$ 130
r_2 = p.**age** $\geq$ 0

C_4 : **card**(Licences) $\geq$ 1

S = $\emptyset$
P = **card**(Licences) $\geq$ 1
r = P

C_8 : **all** d **in** Drivers, d.`car.type` $\neq$ "truck"
or "truck-licence" **isin** d.`driver.licences`

S = Drivers
P(d) = d.`car.type` $\neq$ "truck"
or "truck-licence" **isin** d.`driver.licences`
r_1 = d.`car.type` $\neq$ "truck"
r_2 = "truck-licence" **isin** d.`driver.licences`

C_{13} : **all** x **in** { 3, 5, 7, 9 }, **exists** n **in** MyInts, x - n **isin** aSetofInts

S_1 = { 3, 5, 7, 9 }
S_2 = MyInts
P(x, n) = x - n **isin** aSetofInts
r = P(x, n)

As we said before, the characterisation of a constraint is a set of paths into the database. For a constraint C, we shall note $\Upsilon(C)$ its characterisation. The set of paths $\Upsilon(C)$ is recursively constructed as follows:

Υ(expl θ exp2) = Υ(expl) $\cup$ Υ(exp2),
where θ denotes any comparator or set operation
and where expl and exp2 denote either a variable
or a tuple field extraction;
Υ(**card**(exp)) = Υ(exp);
Υ(**<name>**) = **<name>**, if name is a schema name and not a class name;
= the set of all subclasses of **<name>**, including itself,
if **<name>** is a class name.

Υ(exp.a) = {type(exp).a} ∪ Υ(exp), if type(exp) is an abstract type
(type() is a function which given an expression returns its corresponding type);
= Υ(exp) otherwise.
Υ(x) = Υ(S),
where x represents a quantified variable in the constraint ranging over
the set expression S;
Υ(P **and** P') = Υ(P) ∪ Υ(P'), where P and P' are two literals;
Υ(P **or** P') = Υ(P) ∪ Υ(P'), where P and P' are two literals;

The construction of "Υ(exp.a)" deserves some comments. Such an expression can be either the extraction of a *tuple field (non mutable non shared value)*, or the extraction of an *object feature (mutable and shared value).* If the type of the expression is an *abstract type*, this means that the corresponding value is an object that can be shared. Every update of an object of the same type may violate the constraint. For tuples that are not shared nor mutable, the expression "exp.a" may change only if the expression "exp" changes.

The characterisations for the constraint examples are listed in Figure 1. BadDrivers appears in the characterisation of constraints C_2, C_7, C_8 and C_{12} because it is a *subclass* of Drivers. The same is true for Planes.

Constraint	Characterisation
C_1	Persons, Person.age
C_2	Drivers, BadDrivers
C_3	aSetofInts
C_4	Licences
C_5	Persons, Person.children
C_6	Persons, Person.licences, Licences
C_7	Drivers, BadDrivers, Person.licences
C_8	Drivers, BadDrivers, Vehicle.type, Person.licences
C_9	Vehicles, Planes, Vehicle.number
C_{10}	Persons, Person.children, Person.age
C_{11}	Persons, Person.spouse
C_{12}	Vehicles, Planes, Drivers, BadDrivers, Vehicle.agev, Person.age
C_{13}	MyInts, aSetofInts
C_{14}	MyInts, aSetofInts

Figure 1: Characterisation of constraints

The characterisation of the constraint C_1 is made of the paths "Persons" and "Person.age". Indeed, there are two ways to violate the constraint : we can modify the class Persons (add a new person in it, for example) or we can modify the age of an existing person. The two paths in $\Upsilon(C_1)$ correspond to these two possibilities. For the constraint C_8, we obtain three paths. The first one expresses that a modification of the class Drivers may violate the constraint. The last two paths express that the constraint may also be violated if the feature **type** of a Vehicle or the feature **licences** of a Person is updated.

3.2 Characterisation of transactions

In this subsection, we characterise the transactions that can be run on the database. Our goal is to build, for every transaction T, the set $\psi(T)$ of all paths involved in the transaction. Such a path leads to data that the transaction might modify.

We first list the operations performed by a transaction. The set $\mathcal{B}$ of elementary statements is defined as follows:

$e_1 := e_2 \in \mathcal{B}$
$e_1.a := e_2 \in \mathcal{B}$
insert e_1 **into** $e_2 \in \mathcal{B}$
drop e_1 **from** $e_2 \in \mathcal{B}$

The set $\mathcal{I}$ of transactions is recursively constructed as follows:

$\forall\, s \in \mathcal{B},\, s \in \mathcal{I}$
$\forall\, s_1, s_2 \in \mathcal{I},\, s_1 \;;\; s_2 \in \mathcal{I}$
$\forall\, s_1, s_2 \in \mathcal{I}$, **if** (b) s_1 **else** $s_2 \in \mathcal{I}$
where b is a boolean expression with no side effect.
$\forall\, s \in \mathcal{I}$, **for** (o **in** x) $s \in \mathcal{I}$

In this paper, we suppose that transactions do not call other transactions or functions, so we shall do no interprocedural analysis. The characterisation ψ of a transaction is then defined as follows:

$\psi(s_1 \;;\; \ldots \;;\; s_n) = \psi(s_1) \cup \ldots \cup \psi(s_n)$;
$\psi($**if** (b) s_1 **else** $s_2) = \psi(s_1) \cup \psi(s_2)$;
$\psi($**for** (o **in** x) $s) = \psi(s)$;
$\psi(e_1 := e_2) = \Upsilon(e_1)$;
= the set of all subclasses of <name>, including itself,
if <name> is a class name.
$\psi($**insert** e_1 **into** $e_2) = \Upsilon(e_2)$;
$\psi($**drop** e_1 **from** $e_2) = \Upsilon(e_2)$;

This definition means that the characterisation of a transaction is the union of the characterisations of all the elementary statements involved in it. For an assignment operation like "$e_1 := e_2$", the data that can be modified is the data corresponding to the expression e_1, and it is characterised by $\Upsilon(e_1)$. We exemplify this definition with the examples of transactions above.

We have characterised both transactions and constraints as a set of paths into the database that are used by the constraint or involved in the transaction. The characterisation of the constraints which may be violated by a given transaction is then very simple, as stated by the following property:

Transaction	Characterisation
T_1	Vehicles
T_2	Person.spouse
T_3	Person.licences
T_4	Persons, Person.age

Figure 2: Characterisation of transactions

Property 1 Let T be a transaction and C be a constraint; the transaction T may violate the constraint C only if $\Upsilon(C) \cap \psi(T)$ is non empty.

As we said before, this property is only a sufficient condition. If we use this property on the running examples, we obtain the following table:

Transaction	Constraints
T_1	C_9, C_{12}
T_2	C_{11}
T_3	C_6, C_8
T_4	C_1, C_5, C_6, C_{10}, C_{11}, C_{12}

Figure 3: Constraints hit by a transaction

4 Enforcement Tests Generation

In the previous section, we characterised, for each transaction, a set of constraints that have to be checked at the end of the transaction. We now consider the problem of checking these constraints. Our proposal is based on the idea that all these constraints are satisfied when the transaction begins, and still have to be satisfied after the end of the transaction. The checking mechanism have to take this into account.

Informally, we propose to characterise the changes that are made by a transaction and collect (dynamically) some data that represent these changes; at the end of the transaction, these data are used to incrementally check the constraints.

4.1 Restriction of the constraint language

Incremental checking is not possible for every constraint. Existential quantifiers, for example, cannot be simply incrementally checked as illustrated by the following example:

exist x **in** aSet, Pred(x)

If a transaction removes an element α from aSet and Pred(α) is true, then there is no simple and cheap way to ensure that there is still another element that satisfies the predicate. In the remaining of this section, we shall thus consider only universally quantified and conjunctive constraints.

4.2 Collecting information at runtime

The problem of efficiently checking a constraint at the end of a transaction consists in finding the minimal set of objects involved in the process of checking. Then, the constraint will be checked only on this set which guarantees that data consistency is ensured at the end of checking. However, in general, collecting such a set (at run time) is not always possible. In order to illustrate this we use three constraints C_1, C_{11} and C_{15} and two transactions T_2 and T_4. For the first constraint, the minimal set is easily collected at run time (when executing T_4). For the second one, the minimal set could be obtained less easily (when executing T_2). In the last case, the minimal set cannot be collected (when executing T_4)[1].

(C_1) **all** p **in** Persons, p.**age** $\leq$ 130 **and** p.**age** $\geq$ 0;
(C_{11}) **all** p **in** Persons, p.**spouse**.**spouse** = p **or** p.**spouse** = **nil**;
(C_{15}) **all** p **in** Persons, **all** c **in** p.**children**, p.**age** > c.**age**

```
let T2 = trans(p1, p2: Person):
        p1.spouse = p2;
        p2.spouse = p1;
        /* this transaction performs a marriage between to persons */

let T4 = trans()
        for p in Persons when (today = p.birthday)
            p.age = p.age + 1
        /* this transaction updates the age of all Persons born
        on the current day */
```

If we consider T_4, for the first constraint, we just have to collect the identifiers of every person whose age is modified. The objects collected by this process correspond to the minimal set of objects on which C_1 has to be checked. For the second constraint, the minimal set consists of the identifiers of p_1 and p_2 as well as the identifiers of p_1.**spouse** and p_2.**spouse** *before* the assignment. Of course, collecting the latter identifiers requires the checker manager to be provided with some kind of "intelligence". Unfortunately, for the third constraint, the strategies adopted previously don't work, due to the fact that we don't have backward pointers and thus given an element of Persons, we are unable to retrieve its father directly.

As a consequence, we will not attempt to obtain the minimal set. At the same time, we will not assume the existence of special access structures like indexes or backward pointers. We rather address the problem of finding an efficient checking

[1] Unless indices are available, but we choose to ignore this issue.

algorithm which can be applied to all constraints. For constraints such as C_1, the algorithm will operate on the minimal set of objects; for other constraints, we shall show that the checking algorithm improves the trivial approach which consists in performing a whole scan on the populations involved in the constraints.

4.3 Constraints Transformation

Let T be a transaction, let C be a constraint. We are looking for an algorithm $\Delta_T(C)$ satisfying the following properties:

- The evaluation of $\Delta_T(C)$ at the end of the transaction ensures that the constraint C is still satisfied.
- The evaluation of $\Delta_T(C)$ is more efficient (smaller iteration domain) than the direct evaluation of C.

In order to build $\Delta_T(C)$ for each constraint C, we will collect the following data during the transaction:

Definition 1 Given a class name "n", we posit Δ^n the set of elements which have been inserted into n during the execution of T. Given an abstract type t, and a feature `f` of t, we posit Δ^t_f the set of all instances of t whose feature `f` has been modified during the execution of T.

These sets represent information on the changes that the transaction T has made on the database. Δ^n typically represents new objects, and Δ^t_f represents objects that have been updated. Following the restriction described in Section 4.1, a constraint now has the following general form:

C: **all** x_1 **in** $S_1, \ldots$, **all** x_n **in** S_n, $P(x_1 \ldots x_n)$

The expressions S_i can be any set expressions involving schema names and iteration variables $x_1 \ldots x_{i-1}$ as in constraint C_{15}. We first assume that only S_1 is a class name, such that the predicate P involves paths $x_1.a_{1,1}...a_{1,k_1}, \ldots, x_n.a_{n,1}...a_{n,k_n}$. We define $\Delta(P)$ by:

Definition 2 $\Delta(P)$:

> **all** α **in** $\Delta^{type<x_1>}_{a_{1,1}}$, **if** $(\alpha = x_1)$ **then check**$(P(\alpha))$
> **all** α **in** $\Delta^{type<x_1.a_{1,1}>}_{a_{1,2}}$, **if** $(\alpha = x_1.a_{1,1})$ **then check**$(P(\alpha))$
> ...
> **all** α **in** $\Delta^{type<x_1.a_{1,1}....a_{1,k_1-1}>}_{a_{1,k_1}}$, **if** $(\alpha = x_1.a_{1,1}....a_{1,k_1-1})$ **then check**$(P(\alpha))$
> ...
> **all** α **in** $\Delta^{type<x_n.a_{n,1}....a_{n,k_n-1}>}_{a_{n,k_n}}$, **if** $(\alpha = x_1.a_{n,1}....a_{n,k_n-1})$ **then check**$(P(\alpha))$

For example assume the following constraint has been defined:

C = John.**car**.**age** < 12.

Δ(P) = **all** α **in** $\Delta^{\text{Person}}_{\text{car}}$, **if** ($\alpha$ = John) **then check**(α.**car**.**age** < 12)
all α **in** $\Delta^{\text{Car}}_{\text{age}}$, **if** ($\alpha$ = John.**car**) **then check**(α.**age** < 12)

For any constraint C we define Δ(C) by:

Definition 3 Δ(C):

all x **in** $\Delta^{<S_1>}$ **check**(P(x))
all x **in** S_1 Δ(P).

We illustrate the checking algorithm generated for the constraints:

(C_1) **all** p **in** Persons, p.**age** $\leq$ 130 **and** p.**age** $\geq$ 0;
(C_{11}) **all** p **in** Persons, p.**spouse**.**spouse** = p **or** p.**spouse** = **nil**;
(C_{15}) **all** p **in** Persons, **all** c **in** p.**children**, p.**age** > c.**age**

$\Delta(C_1)$: {
all x **in** Δ^{Persons} **check**(C_1(x))
all x **in** Persons,
all α **in** $\Delta^{\text{Person}}_{\text{age}}$
if (α = x)
then check($C_1(\alpha)$)}

This can be simply rewritten in:

$\Delta(C_1)$: {
all x **in** Δ^{Persons} **check**(C_1(x))
all α **in** $\Delta^{\text{Person}}_{\text{age}}$
if (α **in** Persons)
then check($C_1(\alpha)$) }

This algorithm leads to check the constraint on the set $\Delta^{\text{Person}}_{\text{age}}$ testing for each element if it belongs to the population Persons. We thus perform as many check operations as the minimal algorithm does. Moreover, we iterate on the set $\Delta^{\text{Person}}_{\text{age}}$ which is, actually, the minimal set of objects involved in the process of checking. This algorithm is thus equivalent to the minimal checking algorithm. Note that the trivial algorithm would have performed as many checks as the number of elements in the class Persons.

$\Delta(C_{11})$: {
all x **in** Δ^{Persons} **check**(C_{11}(x))
all x **in** Persons,
all α **in** $\Delta^{\text{Person}}_{\text{spouse}}$
if (α = x)
then check(α.**spouse**.**spouse** = α **or** α.**spouse** = **nil**)
if (α.**spouse** = x)
then check($C_{11}(\alpha)$) }

Again this can be rewritten in:

```
Δ(C_11): {
        all x in Δ^Persons check(C_11(x))
        all α in Δ^Person_spouse
            if (α in Persons)
            then check(C_11(α))
        all x in Persons
            if (x.spouse in Δ^Person_spouse)
            then check(C_11(x)) }
```

For this algorithm we have to scan the whole population Persons and test whether an element of $\Delta^{\text{Person}}_{\text{spouse}}$ corresponds to the **spouse** feature of a given instance of Persons. Again, this algorithm performs as many check operations as the minimal algorithm does.

```
Δ(C_15): {
        all x in Δ^Persons check(C_15(x))
        all x in Persons,
            all α in Δ^Person_age
                if (α = x)
                then check(C_15(α))
                if (α in x.children)
                then check(C_15(x, α))
            all α in Δ^Person_children
                if (α = x)
                then check(C_15(α)) }
```

This can be rewritten in:

```
Δ(C_15): {
        all x in Δ^Persons check(C_15(x))
        all α in Δ^Person_age
            if (α in Persons)
            then check(C_15(α))
        all x in Persons
            all α in Δ^Person_age
                if (α in x.children)
                then check(C_15(α))
        all α in Δ^Person_children
            if (α in Persons)
            then check(C_15(α)) }
```

This algorithm iterates over three sets: Persons, $\Delta^{\text{Person}}_{\text{age}}$ and $\Delta^{\text{Person}}_{\text{children}}$. For each element x of Persons whose age has been modified we have to check the constraint C_{15}. For each element x of Persons, if one of his/her children's age has been modified we have to check if the above constraint is still valid. Last, for each element of Persons whose set of children has been modified, we also have to check the constraint. This algorithm performs as many check operations as the minimal algorithm does. However, the set of scanned objects is larger than the minimal set of objects.

As we said in Section 4.2, in the general case, such minimal sets cannot be obtained unless indices are available.

5 Conclusion

In this paper, we have considered the problem of efficiently checking integrity constraints in database programming languages. We have shown how to reduce the number of constraints to be checked by characterising the portions of the database that are concerned by the constraints and involved in a transaction. We then have shown a way to generate efficient algorithms for checking a large class of constraints (universally quantified conjunctive constraints).

This work is a preliminary work on the specification of a compiler for the language proposed in [10]. In order to get complete specifications, we will extend our techniques in the following directions.

In Section 3, we assumed that characterisations were attached to transactions and that transactions did not contain calls to functions and/or other transactions. We did not consider methods (that is n-ary features). The techniques described in Section 3 can be extended to deal with functions and methods in a straightforward manner by associating characterisations to functions and methods. Our work on static characterisation can also be extended by considering some theorem proving techniques [14, 13, 1], thus refining the set of constraints to be checked. Such techniques, however, are outside the scope of this work.

For the optimisation of constraint checking, we shall work in three different directions. First, we will try to extend our result in the case of quantifiers over general set expressions (not only class names). In the present work, we do not optimise such complex iterations. Then, we will consider the case of constraints with negation and/or existential quantifiers. Finally, the data collected during the execution of a transaction is somehow rough in our work. We will consider some more sophisticated ways of collecting informations during the execution of the transactions that could give more information on constraints and thus speed up their checking.

In order to be able to estimate the impact of such extensions, we will try, at the same time, to formalise the cost (in time and space) of constraints verifications. Such a formalisation would allow, for example, to make some trade-off between time (verification at the end of a transaction) and space (amount of data collected during the transaction).

Finally, in order to get more results on constraint optimisation, we will continue to compare our work with the more general domain of logic programs compilation. We think that, although the underlying data models and type systems are very different, there are enough commonalities between these two problems to get some more results. It is, however, interesting to note that we already got significant optimisations for a large class of constraints with only simple compilation techniques.

6 Aknowledgements

We are thankful to C. Collet for helpful comments and careful reading of the paper and to E. Simon and J. M. Larchevêque for helpful suggestions.

References

[1] P.A. Bernstein and B.T. Blaustein. Fast methods for testing quantified relational calculus expressions. In *ACM SIGMOD International Conference*, Orlando, Florida, June 1982.

[2] F. Bry, H. Decker, and R. Manthey. A Uniform Approach to Constraint Satisfaction and Constraint Satisfiability in Deductive Databases. In *EDBT International Conference*, 1988.

[3] F. Bry and R. Manthey. Checking Consistency of Database Constraints: A Logical Basis. In *VLDB International Conference*, 1986.

[4] L. Cardelli. A Semantics of Multiple Inheritance. In *Semantics of Data Types*. Springer-Verlag, 1984.

[5] G. Gardarin and M. Melkanoff. Proving the Consistency of Database Transactions. In *VLDB International Conference*, Rio, Brasil, October 1979.

[6] A. Hsu and T. Imielinski. Integrity Checking for Multiple Updates. In *ACM SIGMOD International Conference*, 1985.

[7] R. Hull, R. Morrison, and D. Stemple, editors. *International Workshop on Database Programming Languages*. Morgan Kaufmann, 1989.

[8] R. Kowalski, F. Sadri, and P. Soper. Integrity Checking in Deductive Databases. In *VLDB International Conference*, 1987.

[9] C. Lécluse and P. Richard. Modeling Complex Structures in Object-Oriented Databases. In *ACM PODS International Conference*, March 1989.

[10] C. Lécluse and P. Richard. Data Base Schemas and Types Systems for DBPLs, a Definition and its Applications. Technical Report, GIP Altaïr, June 1990.

[11] H. Martin. *Contrôle de la cohérence dans les bases objects : Une approche par le comportement.* PhD thesis, Université Joseph-Fourier - Grenoble I,1991.

[12] J.M. Nicolas. Logic for Improving Integrity Checking in Relational Databases. Technical Report, ONERA-CERT, 1979.

[13] T. Sheard and D. Stemple. Automatic Verification of Database Transaction Safety. *ACM Transactions on Database Systems,* 14(3), September 1989.

[14] E. Simon and P. Valduriez. Design and Analysis of a Relational Integrity System. Technical Report, DB-015-87, MCC, 1987.

[15] M. Stonebraker. Implementation of Integrity Constraints and Views by Query Modification. In *ACM SIGMOD International Conference,* San Jose, California, May 1975.

[16] W. Weber, W. Stugky, and J. Karzt. Integrity Checking in database systems. *Information Systems,* 8(2), 1983.

Semantic Constructs for a Persistent Programming Language

Shane B. Sparg and Sonia Berman
Department of Computer Science, University of Cape Town
Cape Town, South Africa

Abstract

One objective of persistent languages is to permit the structure and semantics of data to be expressed precisely and simply. As a result programs are easier to write and the integrity of the data is less likely to be compromised. This paper presents a persistent programming language which includes a constraint definition and checking system. The language uses a semantic data model to define the structure and operations on data. The paper begins with a description of the features of semantic data models and constraint enforcement systems. The constraint definition aspects of the language PERCI are then explained, along with an outline of the implementation of the constraint handling system. PERCI is compared with existing persistent languages and the advantages of the new language are indicated.

1 Introduction

Existing persistent languages lack adequate features for the accurate modelling of real world concepts. The structure and semantics of the data cannot be expressed precisely and simply. This makes programs more difficult to write and understand, as well as compromising the integrity of the data.

When a program operates on data which is not accurately described, the data may take on an invalid state or undergo an invalid transition. Traditional type systems cannot adequately express these invalid states. When the type system cannot cope, the programmer is forced to make up for this deficiency by including checks for correctness in the program. This is undesirable because [10]:

- The programmer has to remember to include these checks at all the appropriate points in the program, making the coding process more complicated and less natural.

- Programs become more difficult to comprehend because of the integrity checks in the code.

- The procedure is prone to error. The programmer may forget to include some checks, especially in large programs or when modifying programs written by someone else.

- It is inefficient. The integrity checks can only be executed at run time since they are part of the program. There is no way to statically check any of the constraints.
- It is unsuitable for a persistent programming language since data may easily outlive a program, and there is no guarantee that another program will enforce all the required integrity conditions.

PERCI was developed by the authors at the University of Cape Town. It is a persistent programming language which includes a constraint definition and checking system. The objective of PERCI is to provide a mechanism for describing the constraints on data, and a subsystem to monitor these constraints and ensure that they are not violated. The data definition language of PERCI is based on a semantic data model similar to SDM [6]. Existing persistent languages such as PS-algol [12], Napier88 [7] and DBPL [13] do not provide adequately for semantic modelling features and constraint enforcement. TAXIS [8] and Galileo [1] do provide semantic constructs, but TAXIS does not have any means of enforcing constraints. Galileo provides only static integrity constraints which are checked when objects are created, but not on updates.

The major contribution of PERCI is the provision of a simple and consistent constraint handling system in a persistent language which allows the programmer to specify the stage at which constraints are to be checked. This paper focuses on the constraint specification parts of the language and their implementation.

2 Outline of Paper

Section 3 introduces the basic concepts of semantic data modelling and integrity constraints. Section 4 briefly describes the syntax of PERCI and shows how the constraints on data are specified. Section 5 explains how the constraint handling system is implemented. In conclusion, PERCI is compared with the existing persistent languages, and the benefits of the new language are indicated. Future areas of work are also described. A small example program is outlined in Appendix A.

3 Background

Persistent languages [2] process database information using the same data types and operations as for transient data; there is no need for a mapping from one representation to another. A persistent programming language can be defined as [2]: a language which provides for the longevity of values of all types and does not require explicit movement of data to and from disk. Persistence should be orthogonal to type: the code used to manipulate a value does not depend on its persistence.

A data model consists of rules for defining the logical structure of data and the operations available. A data model should be simple, provide expressive power, and not be dependent on implementation details. A major weakness of the relational model is a lack of semantic expressive power. Concepts must be fragmented and distorted to fit the model, thus losing their simplicity and naturalness.

A semantic data model like SDM [6] is based on abstract entities (or objects) rather than tuples. There is also the provision for structural constraints and relationships between objects.

3.1 Semantic Data Models

In a semantic data model a database is viewed as a collection of *entities* which correspond to the actual objects in the application environment [6]. These entities are arranged into *classes*, which are meaningful collections of entities. Classes are in general not independent, but are logically related by means of *interclass connections*. Entities and classes have *attributes* which describe their characteristics and relate them to other entities. The value of an attribute may be derived from other values in the database. Attributes may be single-valued or multi-valued.

SDM [11] is a high-level semantics-based database model based on classification, aggregation and generalization. *Classification* refers to the member-class relationship. It is a form of abstraction in which a collection of objects is considered a higher level object class. This is essentially an instance-of relationship. *Aggregation* allows the relationship between entities to be treated as an entity itself at a higher level [14]. *Generalization* allows the differences between similar objects to be ignored to form a higher level type in which the similarities are emphasised. This results in a type hierarchy, with the more generalized types at the top and more specialized ones at the bottom.

Data types and attribute options are used to specify constraints in SDM. Attribute options such as unique, distinct, and maximum and minimum cardinality specify the structural constraints on the data.

4 The PERCI Language

PERCI is a persistent language which provides features for defining classes, class hierarchies, associations between classes and permissable operations on class members. This section contains a brief description of the data modelling and constraint handling features of the language. A more detailed description of PERCI may be found in [15].

4.1 Example database

An example data structure for a parts database is shown in Appendix A. This example will be used to illustrate the descriptions which follow.

4.2 Types

The type system serves to give the data a structure and to enforce constraints on the way the data is used. The type system supports structural equivalence between types. Functions are first class objects: they can be used in any context where a value is permitted, i.e. they can be bound to identifiers, stored in memory locations, and passed as function parameters.

The basic data types are: integers, reals, boolean, char, subranges and enumerations. Simple variables are declared as follows:

number : **integer**;

character : **char**;

test : **boolean**;

The following statement defines an enumerated type *days* along with its allowed values:

days = (Mon, Tues, Wed, Thur, Fri, Sat, Sun);

A subrange type consisting of only the first five of the allowed values of *days* is defined as follows:

week_days = days[Mon ... Fri];

4.3 Structures

Structures are constructed from base types and other structured types to model aggregation. Structures are generally the type over which classes are defined. A structure has a name and one or more attributes. Attributes consist of name-type pairs and may be constrained by attribute modifiers such as **unique** or **const**.

Figure 1 contains a structure definition for the data type *PartStructure*. *P#* is defined as a key attribute, which means that it will serve as the key for any class defined over *PartStructure* (as described below).

4.4 Subtypes

A type T_1 is a subtype of a type T_2 when all the values of type T_1 are also values of T_2. Subtypes must be explicitly declared using the **isa** construct. T_1 **isa** T_2 implies that T_1 is a subtype of T_2, its supertype. Subtypes can only be defined from a single supertype (simple inheritance).

Subtypes inherit the features of their supertypes which are added to their own. A subtype thus has at least the properties of its supertype, and may have

```
struct PartStructure with
  keys
    P#: Pnum, const;
  attributes
    Type: PartType;
    Name: String[25];
  end;

Part: class of PartStructure;

PartType = (BASE, COMPOSITE);
```

Figure 1: Structure and class definition

```
struct BasePartStructure isa PartStructure with
  attributes
    Cost: Rands;
    Mass: Grams;
  end;

BasePart: class of BasePartStructure
  subclass of Part
  where Type == BASE;
```

Figure 2: A subtype and subclass definition

additional properties. A value of type T_1 can be used wherever a value of type T_2 could be used, when T_1 is a subtype of T_2.

Figure 2 shows the definition of a subtype and a subclass. *BasePartStructure* is defined to be a subtype of *PartStructure*, inheriting all its supertype's attributes and adding two new attributes to the subtype.

4.5 Classes and Subclasses

The main abstract data type is the class, which represents some meaningful collection of entities of the same type. A class can be either a base class or a subclass. A base class is defined independently of all other classes in the database. A subclass does not exist independently; it is defined in terms of other classes. A subclass is a class which contains some, but not necessarily all, the members of its parent class. A subclass inherits all the attributes of its ancestor classes in the generalization hierarchy.

A class is a variable which denotes a particular set of objects, all of the

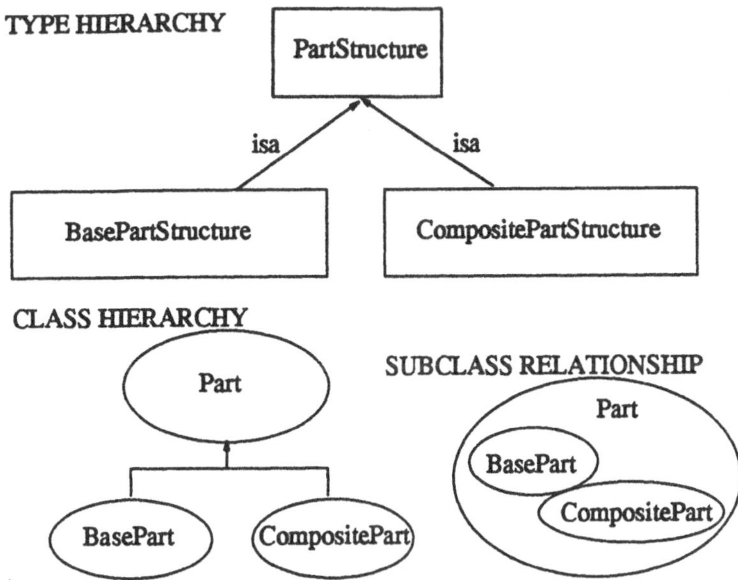

Figure 3: Type and class hierarchies

type over which the class is defined. Being a set, its elements are distinct and unordered. It is possible to define multiple classes over the same type.

Figure 1 defines a class called *Part* over the type *PartStructure*. This class has three member attributes: *P#*, *Type*, and *Name*. The attribute *P#* is a key attribute, which means that it must be unique for each member of a particular class over the type *PartStructure*. A class can be defined over any type, but usually structured types are used. When a class is defined over a simple data type, it is effectively defining a set over the type.

Figure 2 defines a class called *BasePart* which is a class over the type *BasePartStructure*, and a subclass of *Part*. The **where** clause specifies that the *Type* attribute of an object must be **BASE** for it to qualify as a *BasePart*. If the clause **where specified** is used instead, it indicates that an object has to be explicitly placed in the subclass [6]. An object placed in a subclass automatically becomes a member of the parent class. The type of a subclass must be a subtype of the type of its parent class.

Figure 3 shows the relationship between types, subtypes, classes and subclasses. An instance of the class *BasePart* is also an instance of the class *Part*, since the class *BasePart* is a subset of the class *Part*. We could define another class over the type *BasePartStructure*, call it *SomePart*. These two classes, *BasePart* and *SomePart*, have the same type, but contain different objects i.e. they provide different sets of *BasePartStructure*'s.

Attributes of a class may be either data-valued (DVA) or entity-valued (EVA) [6]. A DVA attribute describes some property of each element in a class by associating the element with a value or set of values from some domain. An

EVA describes a property of each class member by relating it to a member or set of members of another or the same class. EVA's serve to relate classes to each other.

The modifiers **req** (required), **uniq** (unique), **const** (unchangeable) and **inv** (inverse) may be applied to any attribute. Multi-valued relationships are indicated by defining an attribute as a class variable over some type. For example: the attribute *Uses* of the structure *CompositePartStructure* defines a multi-valued relationship with *UsesStructure*

A pair of attributes can be related by means of inversion. Attribute A_1 of class C_1 can be specified as the inverse of attribute A_2 of class C_2. This means that the value of A_1 for member M_1 of C_1 consists of those members of C_2 whose value of A_2 is M_1.

An attribute may be derived from other data, either in the same structure or in related entities (EVA's).

4.6 Constraints

Integrity constraints are rules which limit the allowed values of a data type and the transitions which may take place between different values [9], [4], [3]. Constraints can be grouped into a number of categories:

- Attribute constraints
- Entity constraints
- Constraints on collections of entities
- Types
- Dependencies
- Preconditions and postconditions

The first four can be found in PERCI . Constraints can be either implicit or explicit. Implicit constraints arise out of the constructs of the data model itself. An example of this type of constraint is that of type hierarchies. Explicit constraints are defined using constructors such as single-valued or multi-valued attributes.

Explicit constraints consist of static and dynamic constraints. Static integrity constraints serve to restrict the possible values of class members. Dynamic integrity constraints place restrictions on the way data values may be changed.

In PERCI a structure's allowed values can be specified by means of a constraint expression. This expression may be a simple expression involving only constants, or it may refer to other values in the database. Constraints are classified as initial, final or always, depending on when they are to be checked. Initial constraints are checked when an object is added to the class, final constraints

```
struct Customer with
  attributes
    name: string[25];
    address: Address;
    amountDue: Rands;
    creditLimit: Rands;
    creditRating: Rands;
  initially
    startClean: (amountDue == 0);
  finally
    noDebt: (amountDue == 0);
  always
    underLimit: (amountDue <= creditLimit);
end;
```

Figure 4: Structure with initial, final, and always constraints

must be true when an object is removed from the class. Always constraints must be true at all times for any object in the class.

In the structure in Figure 4 three constraints are defined. The first is an initial constraint and says that the value of *amountDue* must be 0 when an object is added to any class of type *Customer*. The second constraint will not allow an object to be removed from a class of this type unless it has a value of 0 for *amountDue*. The third constraint specifies that at all times the value of *amountDue* must be less than or equal to the value of *creditLimit*. An assignment which attempts to violate this constraint will not be allowed.

A function may suspend a particular constraint while it modifies the data, reinstating the constraint when it returns to the calling function. This allows a function to temporarily place the data in an inconsistent state. This is necessary because certain data transformations between consistent states requires the data to be temporarily inconsistent. The function *DebitAccount* in Figure 5 suspends the constraint *inBalance*. This allows the function to debit a value to the account without causing a constraint violation.

The function *DebitAccount* has two parameters: *acc* of type *AccountStruct* and *amount* of type *Rands*. The **suspend** section allows the constraint *inBalance* for the variable *acc* to be violated within the function. The **actions** section contains the body of the function.

A set of constraints is contradictory if they cannot be simultaneously satisfied. It is, in general, not possible to statically detect contradictory constraints, since they can be arbitrarily complex and may depend on data values which cannot be statically determined. There are two types of contradictory constraints: always contradictory (which are always contradictory for any data values), and intermittently contradictory (only contradictory for some sets of data values).

```
struct AccountStruct with
  attributes
    credit: Rands;
    debit: Rands;
    balance: Rands;
  always
    inBalance: (balance == credit - debit);
end;

Account: class of AccountStruct;

function DebitAccount (acc, amount ) with
var
  acc: AccountStruct;
  amount: Rands;
suspend
  acc.inBalance
actions
  acc.debit := acc.debit + amount;
  acc.balance := acc.balance - amount;
end;
```

Figure 5: Suspending a constraint

The constraint verification system should ensure that the data are never allowed to achieve a state which violates any declared constraint. The system must verify all constraints and must do so at the earliest possible time. If constraint checks are not factored out as soon as possible, the overhead of making all the checks may cause great inefficiency. Run-time checks must only be produced for those checks which could not be performed at compile-time.

Constraint verification may be necessary in the following cases:

- After a constraint is declared, to ensure that there is no violation of the constraint at the point of its creation.

- After an assignment the new value must be checked.

- When a new instance of a class is created or an existing member deleted.

- When returning from a function call. A function may temporarily suspend a constraint until after the function has executed.

5 Implementation of Constraints

In order to implement constraint checking a method is needed to produce and store a function which will check that the data obeys the constraint definitions. The ideal solution is to store the constraint function in executable form.

The PERCI compiler makes use of a (dynamically) callable compiler to construct the constraint checking functions. (See Figure 6.)

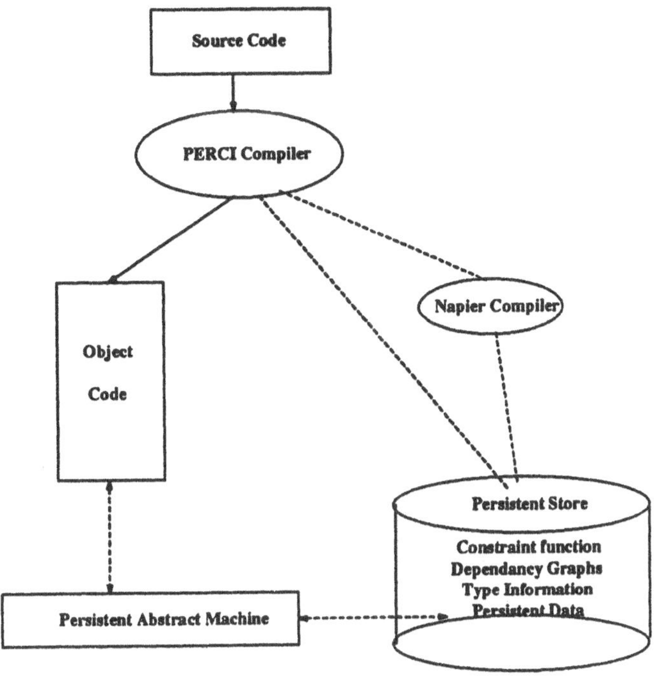

Figure 6: The compiler and constraint subsystem

It is written in Napier88 and produces code which runs on the Napier Persistent Abstract Machine (PAM) [5]. The Napier88 [7] system consists of the language and its persistent store. The Persistent Abstract Machine executes Napier88 programs and accesses the persistent store. The persistent store contains the Napier88 compiler as a procedure. This means that a program can generate another program by supplying the compiler with a string on which to act.

The advantage of using Napier88 to implement the PERCI system is that we can use its callable compiler to create an executable function for each constraint which is then placed in the persistent store. It is for this reason that Napier88 was chosen as the implementation language.

When the compiler encounters a constraint declaration it parses the declaration to check its validity. The compiler then constructs a function which will be used to verify the constraint. This function is compiled by the Napier88 callable compiler and stored in the persistent store.

The compiler constructs a dependency graph (Figure 7) of the type hierarchies and constraints so that dependencies between types can be checked and inherited constraints enforced. This dependency graph is also placed in the persistent store so that it is available while compiling and when running the compiled program.

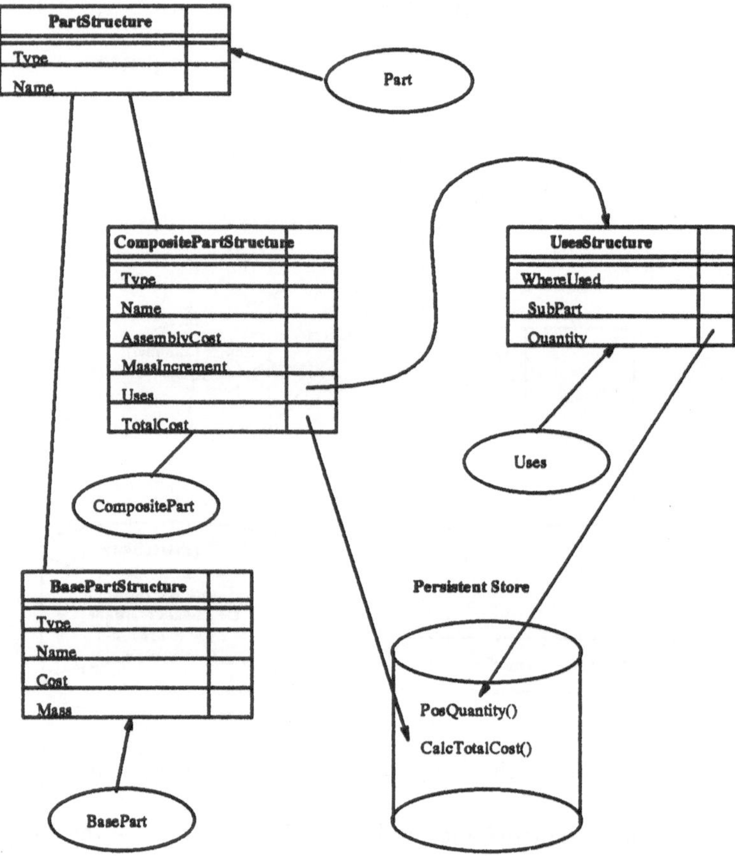

Figure 7: Dependency graph for the example program

Each class object has a pointer to its type object. The type object is part of the dependency graph and also contains references to any constraint functions acting on variables of that type. When a variable is assigned a value, the constraint management system checks whether the variable is constrained by consulting its type object in the dependency graph. The appropriate constraint functions are retrieved from the persistent store and called to check whether the changes about to be made to the variables will violate any of the declared constraints. If a violation is detected, the update is abandoned and an error condition is generated. Figure 8 shows the life-cycle of a typical constraint.

The following example outlines the creation and execution of a simple constraint on the values of *Quantity* in the class *Uses*. The value of *Quantity* is constrained to be greater than 0.

Creating the constraint:

```
constraint:
  PosQuantity: (Quantity > 0);

compiler:
  parses constraint PosQuantity
  creates function PosQuantity()
  compiles function PosQuantity() using Napier88 callable compiler
  stores PosQuantity() on Persistent Store in dependency graph
```

Executing the constraint:

```
program:
  X.Quantity := X.Quantity - 999;

compiler:
  looks up UsesStructure in the dependency graph
  creates object code:

    tmp := X.Quantity - 999;
    if (not PosQuantity(tmp)) ABORT;
    X.Quantity := tmp;
```

6 Conclusion

The PERCI system provides a persistent programming language with a semantic integrity constraint handling system. It allows programmers to concentrate on the program without being concerned about the validation, translation and storage of data. The constraint system allows the semantic information to be placed where the data is defined, making for a safer, more secure system.

The use of Napier88 to implement the PERCI system has a number of advantages, the most important being the availability of the callable compiler. This allows the compiler to automatically generate the constraint checking functions.

PERCI provides semantic data modeling features that are similar to those provided by Galileo and TAXIS. However, PERCI obeys the principles established for persistent programming languages which the other two do not. It is also a true programming language: TAXIS and Galileo were intended to be database design languages.

Persistence in PERCI is provided by classes. Since any type may be placed in a class, any type may persist. Since functions are first-class, they may placed

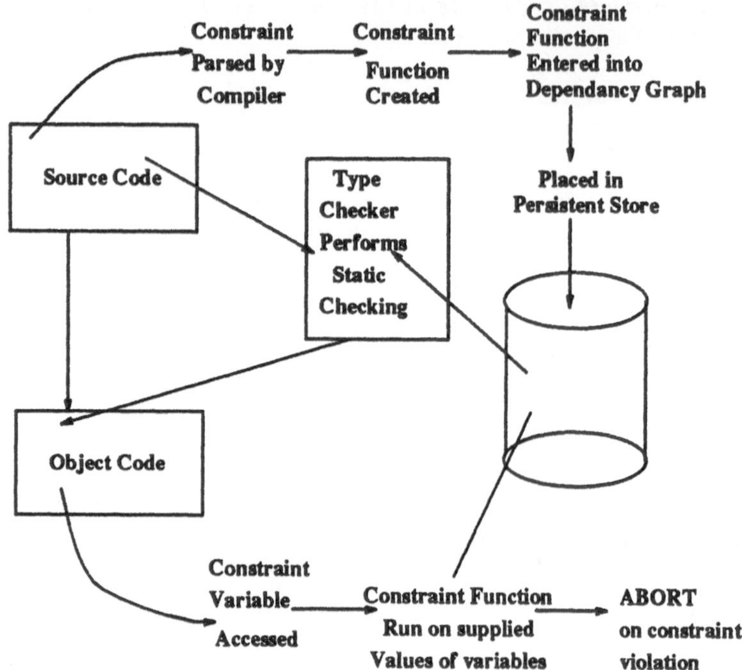

Figure 8: The life-cycle of a constraint

in classes and made to persist as well. This allows data and the operations allowed on the data to be stored together. Types and extents are separate, as in Galileo, but PERCI also allows multiple extents over the same type.

PERCI provides a more generalised constraint handling system than Galileo. Galileo provides for only static constraint checks which are made when data is created. PERCI can enforce constraints at any stage: at initialisation, deletion, or throughout the life of the data.

PERCI provides the bulk data modeling features which PS-algol and Napier lack. This means that less detail is required when modeling complex data, and the representation of the data is closer to the real system.

Possible areas for future work include performance analysis of programming languages with constraint features, query enhancement using the constraint subsystem and optimisation of the stage at which constraint are enforced. Currently the compiler does not perform any optimisation of constraint-time enforcement. An investigation into the performance of the constraint handling system will indicate whether the advantages of the constraint system outweigh the costs of the extra processing required.

References

[1] Antonio Albano, Luca Cardelli, and Renzo Orsini. Galileo: A Strongly-

Typed, Interactive Conceptual Language. *ACM Transactions on Database Systems*, 10(2):230–260, June 1985.

[2] Malcolm Atkinson and O. Peter Buneman. Types and Persistence in Database Programming Languages. *ACM Computing Surveys*, 19(2):105–190, June 1987.

[3] Francois Bancilhon and Peter Buneman. *Advances in Database Programming Languages*, chapter 12, pages 187–217. Addison-Wesley, 1990.

[4] C. J. Date. *An Introduction to Database Systems*, volume 2 of *The Systems Programming Series*, chapter 2, pages 35–81. Addison-Wesley, 1984.

[5] Alan Dearle. On the Construction of Persistent Programming Environments. Technical Report 65, University of St. Andrews, March 1988.

[6] Michael Hammer and Dennis McLeod. Database Description with SDM: A Semantic Database Model. *ACM Transactions on Database Systems*, 6(3):351–386, September 1981.

[7] R. Morrison, F. Brown, R. Connor, and A. Dearle. The Napier88 Reference Manual. Persistent Programming Research Report 77, Universities of Glasgow and St Andrews, July 1989. PPRR-77-89.

[8] John Mylopoulos, Philip A. Bernstein, and Harry K. T. Wong. A Language Facility for Designing Database-Intensive Applications. *ACM Transactions on Database Systems*, 5(2):185–207, June 1980.

[9] Shan-Hwei Nienhuys-Cheng. Classification and Syntax of Constraints in Binary Semantical Networks. *Information Systems*, 15(5):497–513, 1990.

[10] Gabriel Olusegun Owoso. *Data Descripton and Manipulation in Persistent Programming Languages*. PhD thesis, University of Edinburgh, Department of Computer Science, December 1984. CST-32-84.

[11] Joan Peckham and Fred Maryanski. Semantic Data Models. *ACM Computing Surveys*, 20(3):153–189, September 1988.

[12] Persistent Programming Research Group. *PS-algol Reference Manual*, 2nd edition, 1985. PPRR-12-85.

[13] J. W. Schmidt, H. Eckhardt, and F. Matthes. *DBPL Report*. Fachbereigh Informatik, Johann Wolfgang Goethe-Universitat, draft edition, November 1988.

[14] John Miles Smith and Diane C. P. Smith. Database abstractions: Aggregation and generalization. *ACM Transactions on Database Systems*, 2(2):105–133, June 1977.

[15] Shane B Sparg. Syntax of the language Perci. Technical Report, March 1992.

A Example Database

```
struct PartStructure with
   keys
      P#: Pnum, const;
   attributes
      Type: PartType;
      Name: String[25];
end;

struct BasePartStructure isa PartStructure with
   attributes
      Cost: Rands;
      Mass: Grams;
end;

struct CompositePartStructure isa PartStructure with
   attributes
      AssemblyCost: Rands;
      MassIncrement: Grams;
      Uses: class of UsesStructure;
      TotalCost: CalcTotalCost(this);
end;

struct UsesStructure with
   attributes
      WhereUsed: CompositePartStructure inv of Uses;
      SubPart: Part;
      Quantity: integer;
   constraint
      PosQuantity: (Quantity > 0);
end;

struct CostAndMassStructure with
   attributes
      Cost: Rands;
      Mass: Grams;
end;

struct Customer with
   attributes
      name: string[25];
      address: Address;
      amountDue: Rands;
      creditLimit: Rands;
      credtRating: Rands;
```

```
    initially
        startClean: (amountDue == 0);
    finally
        noDebt: (amountDue == 0);
    always
        underLimit: (amountDue <= creditLimit);
end;

struct AccountStruct with
    attributes
        credit: Rands;
        debit: Rands;
        balance: Rands;
    always
        inBalance: (balance == credit - debit);
end;


Account: class of AccountStruct;


function DebitAccount (acc, amount ) with
    var
        acc: AccountStruct;
        amount: Rands;
    suspend
        acc.inBalance
    actions
        acc.debit := acc.debit + amount;
        acc.balance := acc.balance - amount;
end;

Pnum = integer[0..100000];
PartType = (BASE, COMPOSITE);
Rands = integer[0..10000];
Grams = integer[0..100000];

TempParts: PartStructure;
TempBaseParts: BasePartStructure;

Part: class of PartStructure;

BasePart: class of BasePartStructure
    subclass of Part
    where Type == BASE;
```

```
CompositePart: class of CompositePartStructure
    subclass of Part
        where (Type == COMPOSITE);

Uses: class of UsesStructure;

CostAndMass: class of CostAndMassStructure;

function CalcTotalCost(thisPart) with
    var
        thisPart: Part;
        usedPart: Part;
        cost: Rands;
    actions
        if thisPart.Type == BASE then
            cost := thisPart.Cost;
        else
            begin
                cost := 0;
                foreach usedPart in thisPart.Uses do
                    cost := cost + CalcTotalCost(usedPart);
                    cost := cost + thisPart.AssemblyCost;
            end
    return
        cost;
end;
```

Applications

Fred Brown

Department of Mathematical and Computational Sciences, University of St Andrews
St Andrews, Scotland

This session presented two hardware based architectures that can support persistent systems, Monads and ACOM. A major goal of both architectures is to provide security. In the case of Monads the issue of security is addressed via capabilities in contrast to ACOM which attempts to provide read/write/execute protection to small areas of memory. Both architectures rely on some specialised hardware support in the interests of efficient implementation.

The Monads paper gives an overview of the Monads architecture with its capabilities, large objects known as modules, small objects known as segments and its uniform, distributed, virtual memory architecture. A transaction implementation based on two-phase locking and before looks is then presented. It makes use of the modules as the basis for individual databases that are fully protected by the capability mechanisms. This immediately provides for a distributed database system since the uniform virtual memory in which modules reside is distributed.

The transaction mechanism also takes advantage of constraints on distributing capabilities to accommodate garbage collection within modules. By controlling the distribution of inter module pointers the scope for garbage collection can be restricted to small numbers of related modules thereby avoiding the need to garbage collect an entire distributed network of databases in one step. The end result is an architecture capable of efficiently supporting a distributed database system whilst providing a high level of security.

The ACOM approach to protection is based on protecting small areas of memory within objects. The novel aspect of this work is an object cache that can be used with existing processor technology as an add-on either between processor and memory management unit or between the memory manager and memory. ACOM operates by monitoring bus traffic and pre-empting memory references on a cache hit. This allows the full performance of the virtual memory hardware to be realised and presents no execution overhead if ACOM is not required.

Clearly the ACOM architecture has considerable advantages in the cost of building hardware since the most up to date processor technology can be easily used. In contrast the Monads architecture requires one-off dedicated hardware which is expensive to reimplement each time new hardware technology becomes available.

ACOM's hardware object cache was designed with a view to supporting Smalltalk systems. As such it caches the first few words of an object, which is enough to hold most Smalltalk objects in their entirety. All memory accesses to objects are intercepted and processed by the cache. In effect the cache operates in the same way as local heaps used in systems such as PS-algol and Napier88. It supports the same sorts of algorithms including the ability to perform garbage collection over objects in the cache. Thus, many very short lived objects can be created, manipulated and subsequently discarded by ACOM without ever being written to memory. Experience with systems such as PS-algol suggest that this ability should significanlty enhance overall system performance.

Neither of the architectures has been fully implemented. In the case of Monads a stability mechanism is yet to be realised but the transaction mechanism presented is in place. The ACOM design is yet to be realised in hardware but it shows a great deal of potential and is eagerly awaited.

Implementing Databases in the MONADS Virtual Memory

J. Leslie Keedy Peter Brössler
Faculty of Computer Science, University of Bremen
Bibliothekstr. 1
D–2800 Bremen, FRG
Email: {keedy,pb}@informatik.uni-Bremen.de

Abstract

The MONADS computer architecture has been designed in order to support software engineering principles such as modularisation, information hiding and persistent programming, but it also strongly aims at appropriate support for security and protection. The paper describes how the architecture can be used to support databases and database-oriented applications. It also refers to current research issues such as paging strategies tailored to the need of database systems and transaction support within the computer architecture.

1 Introduction

This paper describes and discusses those aspects of the MONADS computer architecture which can be used to good advantage to support database applications. This architecture has evolved from research carried out in the late 1970s and throughout the 1980s primarily in the areas of operating systems, software engineering, local area networks and programming language design. Up to the present time the architecture has been only marginally influenced by database research (other than by file system considerations viewed primarily through the eyes of operating system designers). Nevertheless it is a very unconventional architecture which in our view provide a considerably improved base upon which database applications can be built compared with conventional computer architectures and operating systems.

The main features of the architecture of interest to database systems are

- a persistent virtual memory with very large virtual addresses,
- a combination of segmentation and paging which uses capability based addressing and efficiently supports both very small and very large objects in a uniform manner,
- a distributed shared virtual memory,

- support for modules designed according to the information-hiding principle and protection of such modules using module capabilities,
- a process architecture based on the procedure-oriented rather than the message-oriented paradigm.

The MONADS architecture is still evolving and we are currently actively interested in improving it by integrating concepts developed in the context of database systems, for example by transaction oriented concurrency control and recovery techniques and by page fetching and replacement strategies developed to support rapid access to large databases. Since we attach considerable importance to the aims of simplicity and elegance, we are concerned to ensure that any extensions and modifications which we make to the architecture inspired by database research can be applied orthogonally for the benefit of other users of the system. Thus the extensions proposed below to support transactions, for example, can be used in the execution of all programs, not just those which would be conventionally classified as "database applications". In this way we hope to make the benefits of database research available to a wider class of users than is presently the case.

Various (operating system oriented) descriptions of the MONADS architecture have appeared in the literature (e.g. [1, 2, 3, 4]) and can be consulted by readers interested in further detail than is possible in the present context. The new material in this paper includes a discussion of the relevance of the architecture to database applications and a description of extensions and modifications which we propose to make to accommodate such applications.

2 What is a Database in MONADS?

A conventional database management system (DBMS), developed on top of an operating system, has a variety of functions and properties, including at least the following:

- *physical memory management*, which is concerned with the physical organisation of information on disc and in main memory buffers;
- *logical information management*, which is concerned with accessing information based on its content and logical structure;
- *linguistic representation of the database*, e.g. in relational terms;
- *query language interpretation*;
- *query evaluation*, including for example query optimisation;
- *transaction management*, including concurrency control and recovery functions.

In the MONADS system structure there is no single entity which has responsibility for all database-oriented functions. Rather some functions are supported by the system architecture (i.e. the hardware, microcode and kernel software), some in the operating system, and some in application modules, whereby the distinction between the latter two categories is arbitrary and rather fluid.

The MONADS system architecture supports an environment in which *all* higher level software resources (code and data), including operating system modules, application modules and *files* are held in information hiding modules with entirely procedural interfaces. Thus the architecture naturally leads one to consider a database as an information hiding module, and our software engineering approach, which is basically object-oriented, would lead us to define the interface of such a module in terms of the operations semantically appropriate to the information content of the database. Suppose for example we want to store information about bank accounts, then we might define a module (or class of modules) along the lines shown in Figure 1. Such a module can be regarded as a basic form of an object-oriented database. Since the underlying virtual memory is persistent, modules and the information which they contain continue to exist when not in use (e.g. over system shutdowns). On the other hand the interface procedures can (subject to security requirements discussed in section 6) be invoked directly from other modules without indirectly using the services of an operating system file system or a database system.

```
class bank_acounts
  proc open_account(IN customer: string; OUT account: int)
  proc close_account(IN account: int)
    returns invalid_account
  proc deposit(IN account: int; IN amount: int)
    returns invalid_account
  proc withdraw(IN account: int; IN amount: int)
    returns invalid_account, amount_not_available
  proc transfer(IN account, destination: int;  IN amount: int)
    returns invalid_account, invalid_destination, not_available
  proc add_interest(IN account: int; IN percent: real)
    returns invalid_account, percent_unrealistic
  proc authorise_overdraft(IN account: int; IN limit: int)
    returns invalid_account
  enq  customer_name(IN account: int): string
    returns invalid_account
  enq  overdraft_limit(IN account: int): int
    returns invalid_account
  enq  current_balance(IN account: int): int
    returns invalid_account
end bank_accounts
```

Figure 1: An Interface for a Bank Accounts Module

Such a database may be directly implemented using the data structuring facilities provided by an appropriate programming language, or indirectly via inter-module calls to some other "container" module, which might for example offer sequential access to records or keyed access implemented via an indexing mechanism. The software of such container modules can provide services roughly equivalent to those provided by many current file systems, but using this technique in the MONADS environment has the advantage over conventional file systems that users or database experts can develop their own container modules. Nevertheless, the preferred approach by the MONADS designers is a direct implementation of database modules using an appropriate persistent programming language, and for this purpose the LEIBNIZ programming language has been developed with data structuring facilities based on sets and sequences with an expressive power roughly equivalent to that of relational calculus [5]. This is complemented by a compiler mechanism which allows system-provided or user-written modules for implementing sets and sequences to be bound into compiled programs [6]. However, since the technique used to implement data structures in database modules has only marginal influence on the issues to be discussed in this paper, further discussion of LEIBNIZ is avoided.

3 Virtual Memory as a Basis for Databases

One of the key features which makes the MONADS architecture interesting from a database viewpoint is its persistent virtual memory. There have of course been earlier proposals for implementing files and databases in virtual memory (e.g. [7, 8, 9]) and systems have been built with virtual memory hardware support of interest from a database viewpoint (e.g. Multics [10], IBM System/38 [11], IBM 801 [12]). The MONADS virtual memory has some features not found in any of these proposals or systems, which will be discussed in the following sections. In this section we restrict the discussion to general issues relevant to implementing databases in a virtual memory.

Because traditional virtual memory does not meet all the database requirements many database management systems (DBMS) continue to use a buffer pool into which database pages are read. The main problem with this approach is that it effectively duplicates the work of the virtual memory page manager. However, such an arrangement has several other disadvantages. Traiger [9] provides examples of anomalies which can arise when a buffer pool manager and a virtual memory paging manager are at work in the same system. Copeland et al [7] have pointed out that the advantages of mapping databases directly into virtual memory include processing speed considerations in traversing objects, a single format for objects on disk and in main memory, a reduction in the amount of copying, and reduced disk I/O. To these we could add, for example, the elimination of buffer-relative addressing constraints and of buffer-determined size limits for objects, as further points in favour of eliminating the buffer pool approach. Furthermore the persistent programming approach to database design [13], which is receiving increasing attention, is much more attractive and easier to implement if coupled with virtual memory databases.

There are however three general areas in which inadequate virtual memory design has caused many database researchers to remain sceptical about its use.

1. *Addressing capability and support:* Virtual memory addresses, often 32 bits or less, are too small to adequately address large databases, and the overhead of the virtual memory tables is too great. Perhaps the most unusual feature of MONADS systems is their very large virtual addresses (60 bits in the MONADS-PC, 128 bits in the MONADS-MM[1]). With 128 bit addresses it is possible to provide not only system- and networkwide unique addressing but even worldwide unique addressing for every piece of information held on computers. At the same time the code size is kept relatively small by using short addresses for local references (which are automatically extended to long addresses) and by loading addresses into a set of registers and using short register numbers in most machine instructions. Furthermore, as we shall see shortly, the fixed overhead for virtual memory tables is small, being proportional to the size of main memory rather than the size of the virtual space, as is the case with conventional virtual memory systems.

2. *Buffer management:* The normal virtual memory algorithms, such as demand paging and LRU, do not necessarily provide suitable support for database use. We shall discuss in the next section how this problem can be solved in MONADS.

3. *Recovery support:* Virtual memory is usually not persistent nor stable and usually does not give any control over transfers between volatile and non-volatile memory. It also falls well short of adequate in terms of transaction management. However, the MONADS virtual memory is persistent in the sense that the information which it contains survives between system shutdowns and across system crashes. In later sections we shall also explain our proposals for supporting database transactions.

The remaining sections of this paper present a more detailed discussion of the MONADS architecture and explain its relevance to database systems.

4 Managing Pages

Transfers between disc and main memory in MONADS are based on pages, which in the current system have a size of 4K-bytes. However, in view of the very large virtual addresses in MONADS, conventional page tables are not used. Instead the address translation unit uses a hash table[2] which is proportional in length to the main memory size[3]. This has several advantages for database applications compared with the conventional virtual memory mapping technique.

[1]MONADS-MM refers to the MONADS massive memory architecture, see Section 10

[2]This is comparable in principle to the IBM System/38 but the MONADS hash table is implemented directly in a very fast memory rather than in main memory with a supplementary cache.

[3]The following description applies to the MONADS-PC. Because of its massive main memory size a modified scheme is used in the MONADS-MM [14].

As Stonebraker has pointed out [15], virtual memory systems typically have a page table overhead of 4 bytes per page (e.g. 100K for a 100M-byte file). This substantial overhead does not exist in MONADS, since the address translation unit (ATU) contains entries only for pages currently in main memory [16]. Since the mapping from page number to disc address appears in tables used only by software it is not necessary to have a single fixed format, but a multitude of different page table organisations is possible. . For a large file accessed sequentially, disc space can be allocated in contiguous disc blocks, which has the advantage that its "page table" can consist merely of a starting block address and a length field. This has the further advantage enjoyed by database systems, that head movements are minimised for sequential access (assuming no interference from other processes). On the other hand lazy allocation of disc space, e.g. one page at a time, is implemented for say hashed random files as well as for the many small files needed in operating system and database environments. Thus in contrast with conventional virtual memory schemes, MONADS can offer an environment as efficient and as flexible as a conventional database system.

An important requirement for the efficient implementation of database systems is the use of appropriate algorithms to ensure that the "right" pages are in main memory at the right time. Normal paging strategies performed by the operating system can have harmful effects on the performance of a database system operating above a virtual memory operating system. For example, if the database system has a buffer pool, the discarding of pages in this pool by the operating system on an LRU basis will often be counterproductive. The situation is even worse if the operating system discards a buffer page and this then has to be paged back into main memory to allow the DBMS buffer manager to write a modified database page back to disk.

The problem of having the right pages in memory is not improved simply by mapping files directly into virtual memory, if their pages are subject to the normal discard rules. For example, pure demand paging and discarding following an LRU algorithm perform extremely unsatisfactorily for sequential access to large files. But a clever implementation of a database system can take advantage of its knowledge of the structure of files, access patterns to files, query evaluation plans, etc. to provide a much better buffer management strategy (e.g. double buffering for sequential files or set oriented I/O [17] for consecutive pages on disc).

MONADS currently uses the second chance page replacement algorithm originally designed for Multics, and like other virtual memory systems makes no use of prefetching. It is clear to us, however, that this is inadequate for database applications and we are investigating some alternative strategies, including the following.

Stonebraker has pointed out [15] that a database system is often in a position to know, when it begins accessing one page, which page (not necessarily a contiguous page) will be accessed next. This can therefore be immediately prefetched. To allow database software to signal in advance the use of a page we are considering adding a "probe" instruction (or kernel call) which has as an operand a virtual address; if the corresponding page is not in main memory a "non waiting" page fault will result. Another possible extension is the introduction of a further instruction or call allowing a module to indicate to the kernel that it no longer has interest in a page, thus increasing the kernel's interest in giving it high discard priority[4].

Another, recently implemented, extension is prefetching for sequential files in a form equivalent to "double buffering". Whenever consecutive page faults are detected by the page fault handler, the following page is read in advance (if it is not in the main memory already) and the last page is given a high discard priority. This scheme does not require any support from higher-level software, but the performance is improved only for strict sequential access to large files.

There are three areas of page management which give MONADS a potential advantage over conventional systems. The first is that the concept of a buffer pool is superfluous – a page of database information has the same status as any other page in the system. Consequently they need not be fixed in number and can therefore occupy as many page frames as is reasonable for the current system load.

Second, the MONADS systemwide unique virtual addresses have many advantages: software becomes simpler, ambiguous addresses cannot lead to breaches of security, cache memories do not have to be cleared on process switches, etc.

Third, performance is not slowed down by the need for database software to invoke expensive system calls (cf. Stonebraker [15]) in order to initiate the reading in of data blocks (although there is of course the cost of page fault interrupts[5]).

5 Managing Small Objects

So far we have considered MONADS as possessing a paged virtual memory. In fact the architecture supports segmented virtual addressing on top of paging. A segment is a logical unit (e.g. a record, an array, a procedure) addressed via a *segment capability*, as shown in Figure 2. Since the segment address is a full length virtual address, a segment can start anywhere in the virtual space, not necessarily on a page boundary. Thus collections of segments can where appropriate be placed contiguously, avoiding the heavy internal fragmentation costs and excessive disc transfers arising in operating systems where segments are individually paged.

Although we have used the term "Small Objects" in the heading for this section, the length field of a MONADS-PC segment capability is 28 bits long, allowing segments to vary in size between 1 byte and 256M-bytes[6]. We use the term *small objects* in the sense that segments are regarded as components

[4]The only purpose of these instructions is to increase efficiency. They should not be confused with the "pin" and "unpin" instructions necessary in some DBMSs to keep buffer-relative addresses valid [18].

[5]If database applications are designed using direct data structuring facilities of an appropriate persistent programming language a system call from application to database software is also saved.

[6]In the MONADS-MM segments have a maximum length of 4G-bytes.

Unique Segment Address	Segment Length	Access Rights

Figure 2: A MONADS Segment Capability

of some larger independent object, e.g. records in a file. In contrast to the Bubba design [7] the MONADS architecture does not automatically decompose segments longer than a page into multiple parts, although higher level software can of course make such a decision.

The segment length field in a capability is used to carry out hardware bounds checking on accesses to segments (a facility which is usually not available for debugging of database management systems, e.g. on accesses to records or to indices).

Segment capabilities are the mechanism on which memory protection is based, since a memory access can only proceed if the computation presents a segment capability (in a capability register) as an operand to a memory accessing instruction. Moreover the kinds of access permitted (e.g. read or read-write[7]) are determined by the access rights field of the segment capability.

Since several small segments can be mapped into the same page, it is desirable that they are the objects which are typically accessed together. To a considerable extent this occurs naturally in MONADS as a consequence of the division of the virtual space into a set of *address spaces*. Address spaces, which in the MONADS-PC have a maximum size of 256M-bytes[8], are the unit of virtual space allocation for holding major entities. Address spaces may be as small as one page and vary in size up to the limit. They may be organised as heaps, as process stacks or as code address spaces, using facilities provided in microcode.

The first page of each address space contains the organisational information[9] associated with the address space (e.g. primary page table, segment capability lists, free space information, stack pointers) and there is space remaining in this page for the first segments of the address space. Thus it is possible that the entire information associated with an object (e.g. a small text file, a trivial code module or a database relation consisting of a small number of tuples) may be held in a single page.

Space allocation in address spaces is under the control of the architecture, in order to guarantee memory protection. In process stacks related segments tend naturally to be held contiguously in the same page(s), and code modules will usually have related procedures and constants together. The main locality problem, therefore, tends to be with heaps (temporary and persistent). This is significant in that a persistent database will typically be held in a heap address space.

[7] The architecture supports other kinds of access protection for special segment types. An example of this appears in Section 6.

[8] 4G-bytes in the MONADS-MM.

[9] Since user code does not have segment capabilities for this information it is safe from tampering.

Heap segments may contain both data and protected pointers, as is shown in Figure 3. A protected pointer consists of an offset value (relative to the beginning of the heap address space), which is combined with the segment length and access rights value (taken from the destination segment itself) and loaded into a capability register for addressing purposes. Thus suitable data structures for databases, e.g. indices, lists, trees and arbitrary networks, can be easily implemented.

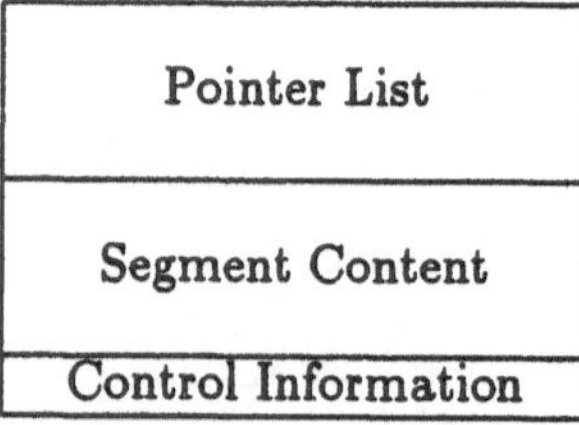

Figure 3: General structure of a heap segment

This organisation gives the database designer considerable freedom regarding the representation of database objects. At the one extreme a relation can be organised as an array of tuples without using pointers, or at the other extreme each attribute of the tuples can be addressed via pointers.

Copeland et al [7] have pointed out four performance dangers of ignoring page boundaries when allocating space for database objects in a persistent heap. Of these, two simply do not occur in the MONADS architecture. As we shall see later, locking is not on a page basis, so this is not an issue. Likewise MONADS does not maintain central object tables , so this too is irrelevant. However, the risk of excessive I/O operations and memory fragmentation which arise from ignoring page boundaries can be high[10].

At present the MONADS-PC system provides no special facilities to assist in clustering information into pages within heaps, but the issue is currently under consideration. Since the architecture can recognise pointers it would be possible to attempt to keep complex objects interconnected by pointers in a single page where possible, although to do this successfully would require the ability to distinguish between primary pointers within complex objects and secondary pointers used for example in indices. At present the architecture does not recognise such a distinction. Other mechanisms, including modifications to those proposed by Copeland et al, are currently under review. This is clearly an area which will benefit from further research.

[10] Actually these are only problems for the MONADS-PC; in the MONADS-MM databases will typically be held in main memory.

6 Managing Large Objects

As indicated in Section 2, in the MONADS context a database, like every other major software resource, is a module. For the *instance* segments of a particular database (i.e. the segments containing the information which constitutes the database) a persistent heap address space is used. The unique address space number of this *file* address space is used externally to identify the database. The organisational information associated with each file address space includes the unique address space number of its associated *code* address space (i.e. the address space containing the type manager which created it). The database segments can only be accessed directly from the procedures of the type manager, so that the protection and security of information reduces to the question: which subject(s) can invoke the interface procedures of a database (or other) module?

The MONADS architecture answers this question by ensuring that calls to the interface routines of modules can only proceed when the caller presents a *module capability* for the module it wishes to invoke. Module capabilities, which should not be confused with the *segment capabilities* described in Section 5, have three parts: a unique module number, some status indicators and an access rights field (Figure 4). In the case of a database module, the unique module number is in fact the number of the file address space containing the database. From this the file and associated code address spaces and their segment capability lists are located by the microcode when executing an inter-module call and the access rights field of the module capability is used to check whether the caller may invoke the required interface procedure[11].

Unique Module Number	Status Indicators	Access Rights

Figure 4: A MONADS Module Capability

Several users may possess different capabilities for the same module. If semantically appropriate interface routines are provided, as suggested in Section 2, this provides an extremely powerful basis for information security and data privacy. The matrix in Figure 5 provides an example of how different bank employees might be given access to a module of the class "Bank_Accounts" proposed in Figure 1. Notice first that the access rights are not hierarchically distributed (which would be inappropriate in this example) and second that protection is not based on database types or classes but that each database instance is separately protected.

This basic model of protection goes well beyond what is normally provided for database systems by operating systems. The main reason why most database systems are inadequate from the protection viewpoint (or are extremely complex as a result of their efforts to achieve protection) is of course

[11] For the present purpose the access rights field of a module capability can be regarded as a bit list of interface routine numbers, although in fact an indirection is involved in order to simplify the selective revocation of access rights.

	Teller	Manager	Accountant	Auditor
Open Accont	y	y	n	n
Close Account	y	y	n	n
Deposit	y	y	n	n
Withdraw	y	y	n	n
Transfer	y	y	y	n
Add Interest	n	n	y	n
Authorise Overdraft	n	y	n	n
Name and Address?	y	y	n	y
Overdraft Limit?	y	y	y	y
Balance?	y	y	y	y

Figure 5: Access Rights to Bank Accounts based on the Right to Invoke Operations

that they have to be built on top of operating systems which themselves are not secure and which provide hopelessly inadequate mechanisms for achieving protection at higher levels.

Whereas segment capabilities are stored in system-managed lists which can only be accessed indirectly, module capabilities may be stored in user segments and may be manipulated in ways determined by information in the status indicators (e.g. they may be copied, optionally with reduced access rights and optionally with the right to use the copy to produce further copies). The integrity of their content is guaranteed by the fact that they may only be stored in segments for which the corresponding *segment* capabilities have an access right setting "module capability", so that only acceptable operations are permitted by the architecture. Thus for example the value of the unique module number may be copied into an integer variable, but it may not be changed in the module capability itself.

An interesting and important result of this arrangement is that the management of file directories need no longer be regarded as the province of the operating system. A file directory under the MONADS architecture is in principle a mapping from symbolic names to module capabilities, and since module capabilities may be stored and appropriately manipulated in user segments, users can implement their own directories[12]. If directories are themselves implemented as modules (for example with an interface along the lines shown in Figure 6) these will be accessible in the normal way, via module capabilities which can themselves be stored in directory modules. In this way the user can develop his own tree- or network-structured directory system[13] using a naming structure of his own choice . Thus MONADS avoids the multiple operating

[12]For the convenience of users the MONADS operating system provides directory management software, but if this is ignored there is no performance or other penalty for the user.

[13]The architecture has a built in mechanism to ensure that objects remain reachable, as we shall see in the next section.

system tree structures of which Stonebraker has rightly complained [15] (since a directory entry containing a module capability is functionally equivalent, for example, to a Unix[14] *i-node*). Furthermore module capabilities can be stored in any module, not just in modules which are functionally equivalent to file directories, so that it is open to innovative database designers to store capabilities for databases in other databases, in transaction control modules, etc.

```
class directory
  proc create
  proc delete
  proc insert-entry(IN name: string; IN capability: modcap)
    returns entry-exists, invalid-modcap
  proc delete-entry(IN name: string)
    returns no-such-entry
  enq get-modcap(IN name: string): modcap
    returns no-such-entry
end directory
```

Figure 6: An Interface for a Directory Module

7 Managing Garbage

For "programming in the small" it is often convenient to have automatic system garbage collection, since this can considerably simplify the programmer's work. This widely used approach is also adopted in MONADS, in that the kernel is responsible for garbage collection at the *segment* level, at the user's discretion. This is a feasible activity since protected pointers, used to reference small objects and their components, can only interconnect segments within a single heap, which itself is in a single address space – a relatively small chunk of the entire virtual space. The proposals for clustering related objects into pages mentioned in section 5 could also be incorporated into a later version of the garbage collector whose functions include reorganising existing segments.

Researchers from backgrounds with a strong garbage collection tradition, e.g. from Lisp environments, sometimes propose that this technique should be scaled up for use in large persistent virtual memories. In such proposals all objects which can be reached from a persistent root are considered as persistent, while other objects are considered as transient and can be deleted as soon as they become unreachable [8]. However, the garbage collection of a large persistent virtual memory containing several substantial databases, measured in gigabytes or terabytes, is a quite different matter from collecting the garbage of a single program, even if it can be carried out in parallel with other computations. Suggestions have been made to alleviate this problem, e.g. by partitioning the memory into regions which have their own internal pointers

[14] Unix is a trademark of AT&T Bell Laboratories

and which can be referenced from outside the region by special inter-region pointers, thus allowing regions to be garbage collected individually [19]. While such an approach is an improvement over naive schemes, it is still based on the assumption, questioned by the MONADS designers, that garbage collection is desirable and possible in a large persistent virtual memory.

There is a compelling reason why the MONADS designers rejected a global garbage collection approach. While it is difficult to garbage collect over a large persistent virtual memory, it is even more difficult to do so over a network of computers which share a common virtual space, and it is impossible to do so when unconnected computers (and discs which are not on line) share a single virtual space. Since these conditions all hold for MONADS, global garbage collection simply does not come into question. Fortunately this is not a problem. The fact is that large commercial databases have survived happily without global garbage collection (or special pointers) for many years. The reason is simple: the many small objects which may reside in databases do not exist in unstructured isolation – they are components of recognisable larger objects (e.g. records in files, tuples in relations, etc). To view small objects in isolation is unrealistic. Garbage collection within a single large object (e.g. a file) is in some circumstances reasonable, but users naturally view large objects as units whose content can, for example, be deleted as a whole. Users normally have a semantic model of their files which includes concepts such as ownership, the right to delete, and so on. This means that they want the right to delete a file which they own even if some other user has a pointer to it, and on the other hand they do not necessarily want it to be deleted simply because it has become "unreachable". Rather they would prefer the system to ensure that it does not accidentally become unreachable.

For these reasons, and for others such as data privacy, MONADS, as already indicated, recognises two kinds of pointers: segment capabilities for small objects such as tuples, and module capabilities for persistent major objects such as files. In a sense the latter are special pointers interconnecting regions of the virtual space, but the important point is that they are semantically more than inter-region pointers: they reflect the same kinds of semantics which have served database systems well for many years. For each persistent major object there is one distinguished capability, the "owner" capability. The architecture guarantees that so long as an object exists, its owner capability is reachable by its owner. In particular it cannot by accident end up in a cycle of unreachable directories. Also, if the owner capability is deleted, the object is deleted, regardless of how many other module capabilities exist for the object[15]. Thus garbage collection is a technique which may be used within individual files, but it is not an issue for the virtual space in its entirety. Similar considerations can be found in [20].

---

[15] Since such "dangling pointers" contain unique non-reusable addresses (see section 6) attempts to use them after a module has been deleted result in a detectable error.

8 Managing Processes

It has never been a trivial problem for DBMS designers to map database activities onto operating system processes. Weikum discusses three basic approaches which have been used in practice [21].

The *symmetric server process* approach maps transactions individually onto operating system processes, either directly in the application processes (*in-process*) or for security reasons into separate DBMS processes dynamically created and deleted to execute individual transactions (*out-of-process*). In this model parallelism is potentially high, since individual transactions each have a process. In addition, scheduling is performed by the operating system, which is convenient for DBMS designers, avoids duplicating operating system functions and, perhaps most importantly, allows database software to take advantage of multiple CPUs in a natural manner. But most computer architectures and operating systems do not provide an adequate protection model to guarantee privacy of the database when using the in-process model. The many process switches and the management overhead for a doubled number of processes make the out-of-process approach undesirable.

The *single server process* method maps the DBMS onto a single operating system process. To achieve a reasonable level of parallelism this process must do asynchronous I/O operations and effectively schedule internal processes not visible to the operating system. Apart from the duplication of effort with the operating system to achieve parallelism this method suffers from the drawback that it cannot take advantage of multiple CPUs. On the other hand security of information is not a problem.

Multiple server processes are a statically created pool of processes which carry out transactions. Like symmetric server processes they need not carry out scheduling, they can take advantage of multiple CPUs and security is not a problem. However, since there are usually more transactions than processes, these become a resource which must themselves be allocated to transactions and may present a bottleneck.

Weikum's careful analysis of these models [21] confirms the intuition that the symmetric server process model is the most favourable. He points out that it is easy to implement, delegates all scheduling to the operating system and fits best with the concept of operating system transactions.

The main reason why the symmetric server process model is usually not used is that the facilities which an operating system must provide to support it are often not available, including for example appropriate communication and synchronisation facilities. It is especially significant that operating systems rarely provide the security facilities needed to support the more efficient version of the model, in which the DBMS code is actually executed in the application processes. This is undoubtedly the main reason why the other models are used, since creating and deleting processes dynamically on a per transaction basis to solve the security problem is extremely expensive.

The MONADS architecture provides explicit support for procedure-oriented process management [22], which is the model underlying the symmetric server process technique. This support includes its process stack structure, reentrant code, inter-module communication in the form of procedure calls and, most significantly from the database viewpoint, protection based on inter-module calls. This combination of techniques makes it a straightforward matter to implement symmetric server processes in a MONADS system.

Thanks to its persistent virtual memory, the MONADS operating system in fact supports *persistent user processes*, which are deactivated (but not deleted) when users log out and are reactivated when they log in again. This has convenience and protection advantages for users as well as performance advantages which are discussed in detail elsewhere [23]. In an appropriate database environment, for example with a regular group of users such as travel agents, this model could be adopted without modification. In an environment with a changing population of users (e.g. library users) it could be trivially modified by having a number of persistent processes which could be dynamically allocated to users (taking care to ensure that appropriate protection requirements are met). Such a scheme has the advantage of saving the overhead of creating even application processes for individual transactions or log-in sessions, but there is of course no difficulty in creating processes dynamically, as in conventional systems, if this is considered desirable.

Stonebraker [15] has argued that procedure-oriented operating systems can be expensive for database applications since a process switch is involved each time a disk I/O operation is required, causing the DBMS to suspend. But this argument applies only to systems where the database is not held in a persistent virtual memory. If prefetching is implemented successfully (as discussed in section 4) the problem scarcely arises, and even if a process is suspended to await a page fault another database process can be scheduled.

Stonebraker's other point, following Blasgen [24], is that in a procedure-oriented system the buffer pool has to be treated as a critical section and that descheduling of a process which has locked this can lead to a convoy with a devastating effect on performance. However, if there is no buffer pool, as in MONADS, this problem cannot arise. There may still be other critical sections in the DBMS leading to the convoy phenomena. As a solution to this problem we are considering a kernel call requesting a guaranteed amount of the remaining time slice or an immediate re-schedule.

Stonebraker's arguments against message-oriented systems, on the other hand, have general validity and strongly argue against the use of such systems in a database environment. We conclude that from this viewpoint the MONADS choice of a procedure-oriented system coupled with a persistent virtual memory is appropriate for a database environment.

9 Managing Transactions

The basic synchronisation mechanisms supported by MONADS is a collection of microcoded instructions which can be combined with process scheduler operations to provide efficient general semaphores , reader-writer semaphores [25] and priority semaphores [26]. However, we recognise that this does not provide support for transactions in a manner comparable to that found in database systems [27].

We are currently implementing a transaction extension to the system which has two major aspects. *Basic transactions* use a *segment based* two phase locking concurrency control and recovery mechanism [28], which is augmented by a higher level object-oriented transaction mechanism [29]. The object-oriented transaction mechanism uses semantic knowledge about objects to increase the possible degree of concurrency. It is tied to the basic transaction mechanism by a form of open nested transactions [30, 31], but will not be described further, as it does not affect the architecture. In this section we outline how the architecture is being modified to support the basic transactions.

Transactions are started by a "transactional procedure call"[16]. A normal return from this procedure corresponds to a commit and an exception corresponds to an abort of the transaction. Transactional procedure calls within transactions lead to nested transactions allowing for flexible error-handling strategies.

From the point that a transaction begins (by a "transactional procedure call") access to database segments is synchronised via reader-writer semaphores (locks) on a per segment basis. This is similar to the very efficient microcoded technique described in [25], thus avoiding the high overheads arising from (a) unnecessary system calls which arise when standard operating system locking techniques are used [21] and (b) the management of a central lock table, which is necessary in most DBMSs. Detection of deadlocks (cf. [32]) is integrated into the microcoded locking mechanism, causing a transaction to be aborted (see below). Fortunately it is possible to distinguish between read and write access cleanly when setting the reader-writer semaphore, in that the appropriate access can be deduced from the machine instruction.

When a write lock is set for a database segment a copy of it is made in a special heap address space associated with the process, know as its *transaction address space*. Associated with the segment copy is the address of the original segment and a pointer to the next log entry. When a read lock is set a dummy entry is made in the transaction address space to allow the segment lock to be located later. If the transaction commits, the list of recovery segments is discarded after unsetting the locks; if it aborts the log entries are used to restore the state of the original segments.

This is in principle the standard undo logging scheme for transaction management, but it has two significant differences from conventional implementations. First, all operations take place in the *virtual memory*, without regard for ensuring that hard copies exist on disc. This can be achieved either by a shadow paging mechanism, as described in [33] or by a safe RAM (cf. [34]). A significant advantage of this approach is that most copy operations will be main memory operations. Second, the operative unit is a segment rather than a page. Since segments are normally expected to be smaller than pages, this means that fewer bytes need to be copied for recovery, but it also means that logical units usually smaller than pages are locked, increasing the potential for parallel processing of transactions (cf. [35, 9]). On the other hand, huge segments, e.g. containing a bitmap, require one lock only, which can dramatically decrease the necessary locking overhead. As we indicated in section 5, the granularity of segments is not fixed by the architecture, but is determined

[16] A call of a routine in the form of a transaction can be requested by the implementors of either the called or the calling routine, or by the class specifier.

by the compiler, assembler programmer or DBMS programmer.

The absence of a buffer pool, the availability of efficient synchronisation operations and of fine granularity recovery units, which characterise the MONADS proposal, appear to remove the main drawbacks which database researchers (e.g. [21]) have brought forward against schemes to implement transactions at the operating system level.

10 Conclusion and Future Directions

The MONADS architecture was developed not with database aims but with operating system and software engineering aims in mind. Nevertheless, it is evident from the above survey and discussion that the architecture's unusual combination of basic features make it especially interesting for implementing databases. These include its persistent virtual memory with large unique virtual addresses, its address translation technique which allows flexible page table structures, its support for small objects in segments which may contain protected pointers, its module and file structures which lead to flexible protection mechanisms and its procedure-oriented process structures. We have attempted to show how these features can be effectively used to support the implementation of databases.

Recognising that the architecture contains deficiencies from a database viewpoint, we have also proposed, and are currently working on, appropriate solutions. These include the use of better virtual memory prefetching and discard algorithms, the addition of features to allow clustering of information in pages and a transaction-oriented concurrency and recovery scheme.

In focusing almost exclusively on the MONADS architecture we have inevitably presented a rather one-sided view of the project as a whole. As we have briefly indicated, the LEIBNIZ programming language supports object-oriented and persistent programming techniques. It also provides very high level data structuring facilities (sets, sequences, tuples) which have an expressive power comparable to relational calculus and also includes a pragma scheme which allows the programmer to influence implementations of programs, e.g. to improve efficiency.

We have occasionally referred to the MONADS-PC and MONADS-MM implementations of the architecture. The MONADS-PC is a "normal" minicomputer designed to support a main memory of up to 8M-bytes. Several prototypes of this design have been built and are currently in use at the University of Sydney and at the University of Bremen in West Germany as research vehicles.

The first prototype of the MONADS-MM is currently being constructed at the University of Sydney. This is a very unusual computer in that it is being designed to support a *main memory* of the order of 64 *gigabytes* [14]. The basic intention is to demonstrate that near-supercomputer speeds [36] can be achieved by the use of massive amounts of main memory (rather than massive numbers of microprocessors, although the two are not mutually exclusive). In contrast with most conventional virtual memory architectures the MONADS architecture is especially suitable to support such a development because of its very large virtual addresses. (The up to 32 bit virtual addresses found in most computers are already too small to address the amount of main memory which it is now feasible to configure computers with.) Apart from the cost benefits of achieving high speed by the use of massive amounts of memory, supercomputer applications are much easier to program for large amounts of memory rather than for large numbers of microprocessors. However, only applications which have large appetites for memory can gain from this approach (including, for example, many applications in theoretical physics and chemistry, in weather forecasting, in combinatorics, etc). Large databases with high demands for performance can benefit from such an architecture as with *main memory databases* [37], since discarding of database pages is very unlikely to occur with a huge main memory.

Finally we mention our work in the local area network area. The approach [38] is to share the virtual space across the network, with unique addressing network-wide (cf [39]). Basically this leads to the approach that nodes view other nodes as remote discs, with the unit of transfer being the virtual memory page. In this way there are virtually no changes needed to the software, except in the paging manager and the process manager. We hope to develop a local area network in which MONADS-PCs coexist with a MONADS-MM computer. This will provide a fruitful research basis for investigating distributed database systems.

Acknowledgements

Our thanks are especially due to our colleagues from the University of Sydney, especially John Rosenberg, David Koch and Frans Henskens. Their contributions to the project are too numerous to mention. We also thank the University of Newcastle, NSW, the Commonwealth Scientific and Industrial Research Organisation and the Australian Research Grants Committee for their contributions to the project in Australia and the University of Bremen for providing the funding to establish the project in Germany.

References

[1] D. A. Abramson and J. L. Keedy. Implementing a large virtual memory in a distributed computing system. In *Proc. of the 18th Hawaii Int. Conference on System Sciences*, pages 515–522, 1985.

[2] J. L. Keedy. Paging and small segments: A memory management model. In *Proc. of the 8th IFIP World Computer Congress*, pages 337–342, 1980.

[3] J. L. Keedy and J. Rosenberg. Support for objects in the MONADS architecture. In *Proc. of the Int. Workshop on Persistent Object Systems*, pages 202–213, 1989.

[4] J. Rosenberg and J. L. Keedy. Object management and addressing in the MONADS architecture. In *Proc. of the second Int. Workshop on Persistent Object Systems*, 1987.

[5] J. L. Keedy and J. Rosenberg. Data engineering with sets and sequences. In *Proc. of the third Australian Software Engineering Conference*, 1988.

[6] J. L. Keedy and J. Rosenberg. Uniform support for collections of objects in a persistent environment. In *Object-Oriented Databases*, pages 136–145. IEEE Computer Society Press, 1991.

[7] G. Copeland, M. Franklin, and G. Weikum. Uniform object management. In *Proc. of the Int. Conference on Extending Database Technology*, pages 253–268, 1990.

[8] S. M. Thatte. Persistent memory: A storage architecture for object-oriented database systems. In *Proc. of the IEEE Workshop on Object-Oriented Database Management Systems*, pages 148–159, 1986.

[9] I. L. Traiger. Virtual memory management for database systems. *ACM Operating Systems Review*, 16(4):26–48, 1982.

[10] A. Bensoussan, C. T. Clingen, and R. C. Daley. The multics virtual memory: Concepts and design. *Communications of the ACM*, 15(5):308–318, 1972.

[11] V. Berstis, C.D. Truxal, and J.G. Ranweiler. *System/38 Addressing and Authorization*. White Plains, New York, 1978.

[12] C. R. Attanasio. 801 architecture support for database – a case study. Technical Report RC 12416 REVISED, IBM T. J. Watson Research Center, Yorktown Heights, NY, 1987.

[13] M.P. Atkinson, P.J. Bailey, K.J. Chisholm, W.P. Cockshott, and R. Morrison. An approach to persistent programming. *The Computer Journal*, 26(4), 1983.

[14] J. Rosenberg, D.M. Koch, and J. L. Keedy. A massive memory supercomputer. In *Proc. of the 22nd Hawaii Int. Conference on System Sciences*, 1989.

[15] M. Stonebraker. Operating system support for database management. *Communications of the ACM*, 24(7):412–418, 1981.

[16] D. Abramson. Hardware management of a large virtual memory. In *Proc. of the fourth Australian Computer Science Conference*, pages 1–13, 1981.

[17] G. Weikum. Set-oriented access to large complex objects. In *Proc. of the fifth IEEE Int. Conference on Data Engineering*, pages 426–433, 1989.

[18] J. L. Eppinger and A. Z. Spector. Virtual memory management for recoverable objects in the tabs prototype. Technical Report CMU-CS-85-163, Carnegie-Mellon University, 1985.

[19] P. Bishop. *Computer Systems with a Very Large Address Space and Garbage Collection.* PhD thesis, Massachusetts Institute of Technology, 1977.

[20] O. Gruber, L. Amsaleg, L. Dayn'es, and P. Valduriez. Eos, an environment for oject-based systems. In *Proc. of the 25th Hawaii Int. Conference on System Sciences*, volume 1, pages 757–768, 1992.

[21] G. Weikum. Pros and cons of operating system transactions for data base systems. In *Proceedings of the ACM/IEEE CS Fall Joint Computer Conference*, 1986.

[22] H. Lauer and R. Needham. On the duality of operating system structures. *ACM Operating Systems Review*, 13(2):3–19, 1979.

[23] J. L. Keedy and K. Vosseberg. Persistent protected modules and persistent processes as the basis for a more secure operating system. In *Proc. of the Hawaii Int. Conference on System Sciences*, pages 747–756, 1992.

[24] M. Blasgen, J. Gray, M. Mitoma, and T. Price. The convoy phenomenon. *ACM Operating Systems Review*, 13(2):20–25, 1979.

[25] J. L. Keedy, J. Rosenberg, and K. Ramamohanarao. On synchronization readers and writers with semaphores. *The Computer Journal*, 25(1):121–125, 1982.

[26] B. Freisleben and J. L. Keedy. Priority semaphores. *The Computer Journal*, 32(1):24–28, 1989.

[27] J. Gray. The transaction concept: Virtues and limitations. In *Proc. of the seventh Int. Conference on Very Large Databases*, pages 144–154, 1981.

[28] P. Brössler and J. Rosenberg. Transactions in a segmented single level store architecture. In *Proc. of the Int. Workshop on Computer Architectures to Support Security and Persistence of Information*, Workshops in Computing, pages 319–332. Springer, 1990.

[29] P. Brössler and B. Freisleben. Transactions on persistent objects. In *Proc. of the third Int. Workshop on Persistent Object Systems*, Newcastle, Australia, 1989. Morgan Kaufmann Publishers.

[30] G. Weikum. Principles and realization strategies of multilevel transaction management. *ACM Transactions on Database Systems*, 16(1):132–180, 1991.

[31] G. Weikum, C. Hasse, P. Brössler, and P. Muth. Multi-level recovery. In *Proc. of the 9th ACM SIGACT-SIGMOD Symposium on Principles of Database Systems*, 1990.

[32] B. Jiang. Deadlock detection is really cheap. In *Proc. of the ACM SIGMOD Conference on Management of Data*, volume 17, 1988.

[33] J. Rosenberg, F.A. Henskens, A.L. Brown, R. Morrison, and D. Munro. Stability in a persistent store based on a large virtual memory. In *Proc. of the Int. Workshop on Computer Architectures to Support Security and Persistence of Information*, Workshops in Computing. Springer, 1990.

[34] G. Copeland, T. Keller, R. Krishnamurthy, and M. Smith. The case for safe ram. In *Proc. of the 15th Int. Conference on Very Large Databases*, pages 327–346. Microelectronics and Computer Technology Corporation, 1989.

[35] M. Stonebraker. Virtual memory transaction management. *ACM Operating Systems Review*, 18(2):8–16, 1984.

[36] H. Garcia-Molina, R. J. Lipton, and J. Valdes. "a massive memory machine. *IEEE Transactions on Computers*, C-33(5):391–399, 1984.

[37] D. J. DeWitt, R. H. Katz, F. Olken, L. D. Shapiro, M. R. Stonebraker, and D. Wood. Implementation techniques for main memory database systems. In *Proc. of the ACM SIGMOD Conference on Management of Data*, 1984.

[38] F. A. Henskens. *A Capability-Based Persistent Distributed Shared Memory*. PhD thesis, University of Newcastle, Australia, 1991.

[39] M. Hsu and Va-On Tam. Managing databases in distributed virtual memory. Technical Report TR-07-88, Harvard University, Aiken Computation Laboratory, 1988.

ACOM: An Access Control Monitor providing Protection in Persistent Object-Oriented Systems

J. Kaiser and K. Czaja
German National Research Center for Computer Science
5205 St. Augustin 1, Germany

Abstract

The paper describes ACOM (Access COntrol Monitor), a hardware device which we developed to enforce run time protection in an persistent object-oriented system. To obtain a wide acceptance, the efficiency of these systems must be comparable to conventional language systems. One of the key issues is to exploit the efficiency of virtual memory management of contemporary processors. We will argue that a careful analysis of the hardware-software trade-off will lead to a simple hardware device which can efficiently support encapsulation and protection of small objects in an object-oriented systems. The main idea is to separate encapsulation and protection from address translation issues. Since only the most basic functions of encapsulation and protection are incorporated into the design, leaving the more complex and language dependent issues to software, it can be seen as a RISC approach to object-oriented hardware support.

1 Introduction

The object-oriented programming paradigm maps real world problems into a universe of objects in a machine. Ideally, everything a user of an object-oriented system is concerned with are objects. The system should provide a uniform interface to objects and remove the classical distinction between program-variables, files, or database items. This view advocates that object-oriented and persistent programming go hand in hand. Actually, most object-oriented programming languages explicitly considered persistence in the language definition [1, 2, 3], or there are activities to subsequently add persistence [4, 5].

However, there are good reasons to provide objects not only at the language level but support them as a basic abstraction on the architectural or operating system level:

- Each language has its own specific object model and, particularly, its own object representation. Sharing or reuse of objects is hardly possible between different languages.
- If a persistent object-store is not provided by the system, each language has to reinvent the wheel by implementing persistence itself.
- In a multi-language shared-object environment, run-time protection of objects cannot efficiently be enforced at the language or runtime-system level by a pure software approach.

In recognising these problems much research effort has been expended in building systems which integrate persistent objects into the system level. The non compromise approach tackles the problem by building a completely new system from scratch, starting with processor design. The commercial iAPX432 [6], often called a silicon operating system, the Rekursiv machine [7], and a couple of research projects, most notably, the MONADS architecture [8], are well known examples following this direction. The non compromise approach is both, strength and weakness of these architectures. Strength, because many of the problems encountered with representing objects in persistent memory and providing protection, fast object creation and a uniform object invocation mechanism are embedded in the hardware level thus, providing a maximum of reliability and performance. The major problem of these approaches is that they cannot benefit from advances in performance and functionality of commercially available processor architectures and operating systems. Because of incompatibility with widespread operating systems they cannot use the software basis of conventional machines. Another problem is that languages tend to have widely different object models, type systems, and inheritance mechanisms which may be difficult to map on these architectures.

The MUTABOR [9] and Camoes [10] architectures tried to keep pace with the processor development by building a system around a standard microprocessor family supporting memory management and object invocation by a specially designed MMU and controlling hardware. However, our experience with MUTABOR showed that we encountered almost the same pros and cons as indicated above.

A number of research and commercial projects in the area of object-oriented operating systems tried to provide objects as a general abstraction at the user interface [11, 12, 13, 14, 15, 16, 17, 18, 19] without assuming any specially designed hardware platform. Of particular interest are those approaches which do not distinguish between the object model of the language and the system [16, 17, 18, 19, 20]. This has the following consequences on the support system:

- the entire application is structured in arbitrarily sized objects. This means that the size of the objects is determined by the application and not by artifacts of the system architecture. Particularly, the system must cope with a large number of small objects as well as with very large objects.
- individual objects should be the entities of protection and sharing. This implies that the architecture must recognise and protect those objects.
- the system should directly support generic functions only, i.e. the least common denominator of all languages in question. This means that the system basically provides the containers for language objects, maps and protects them.

In the following, we will concentrate on this basic functionality of an object support system. We will argue that a careful analysis of the hardware-software trade-off will lead to a simple hardware device which can efficiently support encapsulation and protection of small objects in an object-oriented operating systems. The main idea is to separate encapsulation and protection from address translation issues. The paper is organised as follows:

In the next section we briefly sketch two examples of systems supporting persistent objects to show how these systems implement the persistent store on a pure software basis. We will argue that basic protection issues cannot efficiently be solved in these systems. The rest of the paper describes ACOM (Access Control Monitor), a hardware device which we developed to enforce run time protection. It easily could complement object-oriented persistent systems shown in the examples. Since only the most basic functions of encapsulation and protection are incorporated into the design, leaving the more complex and language dependent issues to software, it can be seen as a RISC approach to object-oriented hardware support.

2 Representation of persistent objects

To exhibit the benefits of architectural support, we examine two example systems which provide basic support for persistent objects. We will concentrate on the Comandos system [18] and on an approach developed by [21], although many other language and database systems use similar techniques [22, 23, 24, 25]. We chose Comandos because it is a complete implementation of an object store addressing language and system aspects. Wilson's approach is sketched because he elegantly exploits available address mapping mechanisms to implement a persistent store. Both systems do not rely on special purpose hardware. The conceptual view of the persistent store in both systems is outlined in Fig.1. Both systems provide a shared persistent object store which includes all devices of a storage hierarchy. The system shields the programmer from the different addressing mechanisms found in the distinct storage media and allows a uniform location independent access to objects. The persistent object memory is constructed from a persistent passive space and a transient active space. The passive space is the long term object repository. Each persistent object has a representation in passive space. The active space constitutes a virtual address space where objects are directly accessible by a machine dependent address and where computations on objects are performed. However, for a programmer and even for a running program, the distinction is transparent and hence, conceptually, a single level store is provided. If a persistent object is referenced and it is not in the active space, it is automatically transferred from the passive to the active space by an appropriate manager.

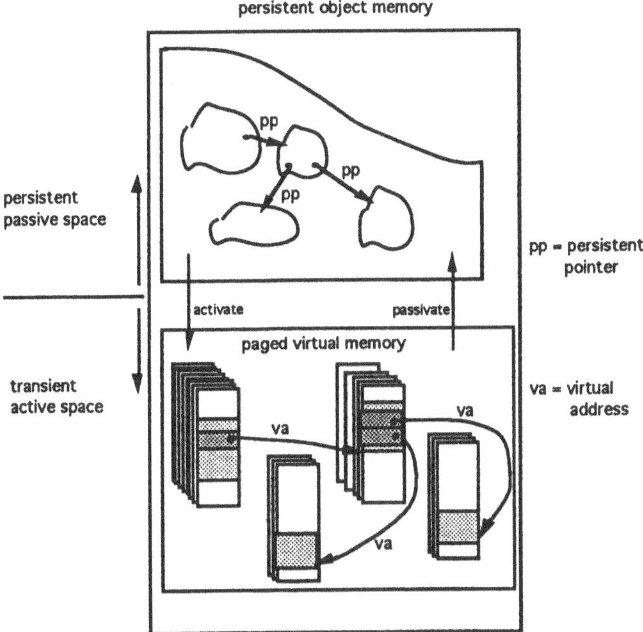

Figure 1: Structure of persistent object memory

Once in active space, it should be possible to operate on objects as conveniently and with the same performance as in the runtime environment of a language. This particularly means, that it is mandatory to fully exploit all the hardware facilities of the basic processor, especially, virtual memory management and address calculation. The overhead one has to pay for persistence should only occur on the activation and passivation of objects. With a sufficiently large (machine supported) virtual memory and a certain locality of computation, acceptable performance can be expected [21]. Therefore, we assume that the active space relies on a paged virtual memory because this is the standard supported by common address translation hardware and operating systems.

The following steps have to be performed to bring in an object from passive to active space. Firstly, the system must detect that a referenced object is not in active space. Secondly, the object has to be brought in, thereby converting its passive to an active representation. This conversion mainly affects persistent pointers which have to be transformed to virtual addresses, also termed transient pointers. This mapping is dynamic because the relationship between persistent and transient pointers is not fixed but determined at translation time and partial in that not all persistent pointers are mapped to virtual addresses. The technique of having multiple namespaces and translating pointers is known as pointer swizzling or pointer resolution and implementations exist in persistent languages e.g. [22] databases e.g. [23] on the OS-level and on the architectural level e.g. [24, 25]. Thirdly, the objects, now in virtual memory have to be protected according to their specified protection attributes.

Since the movement of individual small objects from passive to active space would be too expensive, objects are grouped to larger entities for activation. If locality of computations is assumed within these entities, this can also be viewed as a look-ahead technique for activation. In Comandos, the notion of a *cluster* [18] is introduced comprising objects which according to some grouping policy belong together. When an individual object is activated, all objects residing in the respective cluster are mapped into virtual memory, i.e. space is reserved in virtual memory for the entire cluster by updating the corresponding entries in the page translation tables. Copying of data to the active space then proceeds on demand in entities of pages. In Wilson´s approach, the entire persistent space is a huge linear paged address space. The entity which is transferred to active space on object activation is a page.

Starting with the detection of a reference to an object which is still in persistent memory, we can classify different approaches. In the Amadeus implementation [26] of the Comandos system it is assumed that an access to an object always takes place via an object invocation. If an object is brought to active space, all its persistent pointers are resolved. The object may contain pointers which address some other object not yet in active space. To cope with this situation, a so called *proxy* is inserted in place of the pointed-to object. When a subsequent invocation uses the address of the proxy, the code of the proxy is executed which initiates the transfer of the associated persistent object to active space. The important points are that an executing program never sees a persistent pointer and that a resolved pointer when used, really addresses the right object. It should be noticed that the detection of a proxy relies on the proper use of the invocation mechanism.

Another possibility, also developed in the Comandos project, is to replace a pointer to an object which is not in active space by an invalid address to cause a hardware trap if this pointer is used. The handler then has to determine which object should be addressed and subsequently move it to active space. This approach allows to access objects directly using normal pointer arithmetic additionally to the invocation mechanism (this is bad style but possible e.g. in C++). However, since the invalid address does not contain location information, effort has to be devoted to determine the respective object.

Wilson exploits the trap facility of the page translation mechanism to detect accesses to unmapped persistent objects in active space [19]. If a page holding one or more persistent objects is faulted into active space, all pointers of the page are resolved. As a consequence, all pointed-to pages have to be mapped in active space i.e. the corresponding space has to be reserved. Since these pages may contain persistent pointers they have to be access protected. This assures that a running program cannot see persistent pointers. If a program attempts to access a protected page, a trap handler is invoked which copies the page into active memory and translates all persistent pointers into transient pointers, again relocating the referred-to pages as needed.

These approaches show that the problem of detecting a reference to a persistent object in passive space and the resolution of pointers can be solved on a standard hardware platform with acceptable performance.

However, once in active space, there is no way in conventional, page-based systems to individually protect the subpage-objects from inadvertent accesses and hence, assuring the reliable and secure operation of the system [27]. In Comandos, protection of objects inside a cluster is enforced by a programming convention rather than by a mechanism provided by the system. It is possible to generate a virtual address without using the invocation mechanism properly, thus, compromising system integrity. Therefore, it is recommended that only those objects are grouped in a cluster which mutually trust each other. This restricts the freedom of grouping policies and may result in additional overhead to relocate objects. One of the great advantages of the Comandos system is that object sharing is supported. In the COOL-2 [17] kernel, which provides basic support for cluster objects and constitutes a lower level component of the Comandos system, an object can concurrently be mapped into many distinct virtual address spaces for efficiently sharing one object representation. This desirable feature however is questionable if it is not possible to map objects into distinct address spaces with different protection attributes. The current solution is that in cases where this is required, a critical object can only reside in a single address space. To access the object from another address space an invocation crossing address space boundaries has to be performed. This, of course is a workaround and an expensive solution.

Wilson proposes a solution for cases where sensitive objects happen to reside on the same page as non-sensitive objects. In this case the off-limit object should be replaced by a "bogus proxy" which is made unusable. This, of course, is no solution for controlled sharing where e.g. one process is allowed to read and write an object while others are only allowed to read it.

To summarise: while the addressing problem of persistent object systems seems to be acceptably solved by the above schemes, protection is still an open problem. Although the need for protecting individual objects may be obvious, the lack of it or the inadequate solutions are the price most designers are willing to pay in favour of running their software on a standard hardware platform. In the following sections we will present ACOM, a simple hardware device which addresses the protection problem. In its design, much emphasis has been placed on easy integration in existing hardware and software platforms.

3 Can existing address translation hardware be exploited ?

Typically, an object-oriented application is constructed from a large number of small objects. Existing hardware platforms like the Intel 386/486 [28] offer a segmentation mechanism which allows to specify and protect segments of arbitrary size up to 4 Gbyte. However, due to the size of the segment index, the number of segments which can be addressed in the protection domain of a task is restricted to 8k local and 8k global segments which may not be enough in object-oriented applications. Worse, the number of segments which can efficiently be accessed because they are maintained in hardware supported segment-registers is limited to 6 (six). When a large number of small objects has to be mapped to this architecture, the frequent loading of segment-registers causes an unacceptable overhead and slows down the overall system performance. Even the provision of a (much) larger number of segment registers would not be an adequate solution of the problem because (regardless of implementation problems) it would slow down the address translation mechanism and add a large maintenance penalty to process switching.

Another approach would be to provide small pages and place only one object on each page. This would trade space to gain protection. There are some MMUs (Memory Management Units) which support page sizes down to 256 byte (e.g. Motorola 68030 architectures [29]). This, of course, has a number of drawbacks starting with the larger number of pages which have to be maintained in a multi-level hierarchy of page tables (up to 5 levels using 256 byte pages in 68030 [29]). The hierarchy of page tables has to be traversed slowing down the address translation mechanism. Secondly, because of the still coarse granularity and the fixed size of a page, the internal fragmentation may be substantial.

Because of the insufficiencies of these approaches we propose an architecture which provides protection without touching the address translation mechanism. As a result, the most efficient address translation mechanism can be chosen, optimising page or segment size according to the need of the hardware devices. Objects can be arbitrarily grouped together on such entities for efficient memory management but they can be protected individually.

4 The conceptual view of ACOM

ACOM controls memory accesses without interfering with the address translation path of the processor, i.e. it checks memory accesses independently and concurrently to any existing address translation hardware. Because of this independence, ACOM can easily be integrated into any hardware platform. Only if an invalid access is detected by ACOM, an exception is generated to signal the violation. Since the detection of invalid addresses by ACOM is very fast in most processor systems, the memory access can be aborted before it overwrites or illicitly reads a memory location. If this is not possible, the trap handler has the responsibility of initiating corrective actions.

Fig. 2 shows a physical addressing path and indicates how ACOM is connected to the system. Today's processors exhibit a large variety of configurations concerning memory management units and caches. Most processors have these facilities on-chip. Therefore, to allow a universal application of ACOM, no assumptions about the physical structure of the processor should be made. In fact, ACOM can be integrated into a system regardless of the individual cache/MMU configurations. This topic is discussed in more detail in section 6. For the moment, it should be noted that any address, virtual or physical, applied to main memory uniquely selects a memory location.

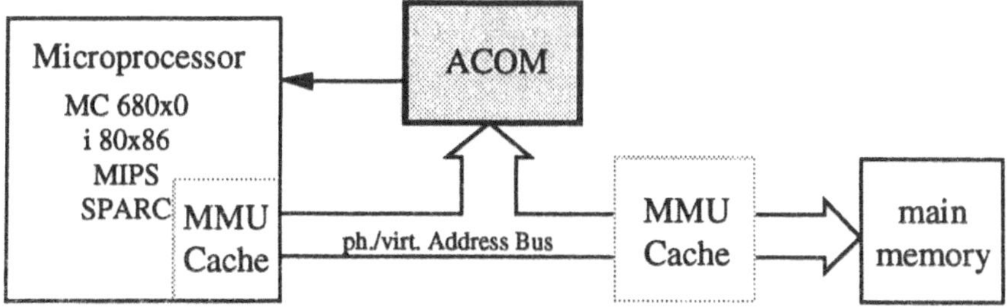

Figure 2: Physical integration of ACOM

The subpage segment structure is superimposed on linear memory by ACOM. These segments are the guarded containers for objects defined at a higher level. For each such segment ACOM provides the corresponding access rights. ACOM monitors the address bus and executes the necessary checks on the basis of the current address and the intended access (read/write/execute) of the processor which is also available during a memory access. A conceptual view of ACOM is presented in Fig. 3.

ACOM works much in the same way as a tagged memory [30] with the difference that ACOM logically defines the tagged architecture and substantially simplifies the management of tags. A tag comprising access rights is associated to the addressed memory location and evaluated with every access. This tag is stored in a separate memory the so called BMT (Block Map Table). For reasons of implementation efficiency, we assume small blocks of 8 or 16 words of 32 bits rather than provide a tag for each memory word. A segment then comprises a number of these blocks. For each block the specified access rights are derived from the protection state of the segment. It should be noted that the memory requirements for the BMT are very low. Assuming a block size of 64 byte and two bits per block to specify read/write/execute rights, a linear physical memory of up to 64 Mbyte can be supported by just two 1 Mbit memory chips. This is under 0.5% of the total memory hardware.

However, there are a couple of problems which cannot be solved in a straightforward implementation of a tagged memory concept. Firstly, the management overhead is unacceptable. Each tag in the memory has to be initialised and maintained. If we assume a standard page size of 4 kbyte, 64 entries have to be initialised when a new page is allocated, independent of whether sub-page structures are needed or not. Even worse, in a multiprogramming environment, where the address spaces of multiple processes have to be isolated from each other, this hardly can be achieved by modifying the tags for almost the entire memory on each process switch.

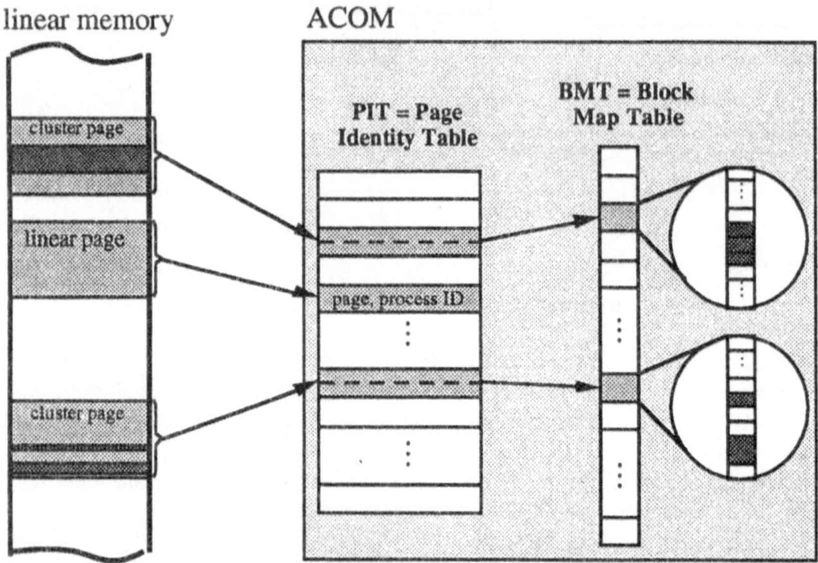

Figure 3: The conceptual view of ACOM

Therefore, we distinguish between two kinds of pages in linear memory. *Linear pages* are not subdivided into smaller entities. *Cluster pages* contain multiple segments and are specifically supported by ACOM. As a second improvement, ACOM supports multiple address spaces efficiently. To achieve this, it comprises an additional lookup table, the page identity table (PIT). The PIT and the BMT are concurrently accessed during a memory cycle. The PIT hardware is comparable to the hit/miss logic of a conventional direct mapped TLB [31, 9]. The PIT determines whether an address refers to a page for which it already contains a valid entry and whether this entry refers to an linear page or a cluster page. If an linear page is accessed, nothing more has to be done. In case of referring to a cluster page, the corresponding tag of the BMT containing access rights is evaluated. As an additional advantage over tagged memory, a hardware entry generator of ACOM creates the tags in the BMT for a segment automatically from the segment's base address and size. Thus, it eliminates the time consuming accesses by the main processor. The detailed description of the hardware architecture is beyond the scope of this paper. The reader is referred to [32].

5 Making the functionality of ACOM available to the application

The goal of ACOM is to provide encapsulation and protection for individual application level objects. Because of its generic functionality and its flexible design, ACOM can be embedded into an existing system in many different ways depending on the need of a specific application field. This may range from highly secure operation where intended malicious attacks to the system have to be considered, to a debugging aid which can detect wrong pointer operations. In the latter case ACOM could freely be controlled by user level procedures.

In a secure protection scheme, the procedures and data structures controlling ACOM must be protected. If it can be assured that the tables of ACOM are not modified deliberately, ACOM will provide the basic fine grain protection, necessary to enforce security. The straightforward way to achieve security would be the migration of functions controlling ACOM to the operating system kernel. All functions could be executed in system space which is assumed to be protected from malicious accesses. This however would require a considerable change in the operating system, particularly, the notion of small objects must be introduced on the kernel level.

A more adequate way in respect of flexibility and easy system integration is to control ACOM from user space. ACOM is maintained by trusted procedures which run in user space and may be executed during an object invocation. The architectural support of ACOM to guarantee that only a privileged procedure accesses ACOM is the provision of a *key*. A key is a number which is stored in an internal ACOM register. This key can only be modified and written into the internal ACOM register by the operating system kernel. When the trusted procedures are loaded into memory by the kernel, the kernel writes the key to a dedicated slot within the procedure code. Subsequently, these procedures are "execute only" protected by ACOM. Thus, they now hold the key as local data which is not accessible by regular read or write operations. In the operation which load ACOM, this key must be presented and ACOM raises an exception if it detects a wrong key. The use of the key and the ability to protect small segments enable ACOM to enforce security with minimal kernel support.

Referring to the systems described in section 2, object fault or page fault time, respectively, is the right place to perform the necessary updates on the tables inside ACOM. At this point, the persistent pointers in an object or inside a page have to be resolved. To perform the pointer swizzling, the internal layout of an object or a page must be known. Because now, this information is available anyway, there is no overhead to additionally retrieve this information for setting the ACOM entries. Since the pointer swizzling is achieved in user space, it is highly advantageous that ACOM can also be maintained without switching to system space. The overhead of updating the entries for a segment is then reduced to two dummy read accesses as described below plus the time to internally update the entries by the hardware entry generator. Depending on the technology used we assume an overhead of about 20ns/entry. If we assume a mean object size of 256 bytes, we need four cycles resulting in a total time of about 80ns which is in the order of a single memory access.

6 Physical Integration of ACOM

As mentioned earlier, we have to consider a large variety of processor/cache/MMU configurations to achieve a wide applicability of ACOM. This involves a detailed analysis of memory access cycles as well as cache algorithms of different processors. The optimal solution for placement would enable ACOM to directly observe the virtual addresses generated by the processor. However, the use of on-chip MMUs and caches makes this solution impossible. The following discussion will give a flavour of the problems encountered.

6.1 On-Chip MMU

If the MMU is on-chip, ACOM can only observe physical addresses on the external bus. In a straightforward solution, the procedure which is in charge of loading ACOM with the appropriate segment attributes must know the physical segment address. This, however, requires support from the operating system kernel which currently is not available. In our approach to cope with on-chip MMUs no kernel support is necessary. We exploit the address translation of the on-chip MMU to load ACOM. We issue two subsequent dummy read operations indicating that ACOM now will be loaded. The information issued with these accesses comprises the key, the lower and upper segment bounds, and the corresponding protection state. The procedure which issues the dummy reads must only know the virtual addresses of the lower and upper bound, respectively. The MMU translates these addresses and ACOM can take the proper physical values from the bus.

Whenever a page is swapped out, ACOM has to invalidate the corresponding entry in the PIT and the PIT is reloaded when a new page is swapped in. When the new cluster page is swapped into physical memory all tags in the BMT are set to their proper values. This is performed by the protected procedures described above providing the base addresses, size information and protection attributes for the subpage segments. The BMT hardware entry generator sets the internal tables according to these values. The low overhead of these operations is described above.

6.2 On-Chip Caches

A more serious problem is the existence of on-chip caches since individual accesses on memory locations are invisible for ACOM if the items are cached already. We looked at many different caching strategies. It is well beyond the scope of this paper to discuss them all in detail. Therefore, we will address the basic problems only. ACOM can only control memory accesses when loading or writing back the cache contents from or to main memory, respectively. The cache is usually loaded and written back in terms of so called *lines*. Lines are of fixed size of a power of 2 (typically 16 bytes). Therefore, lines always fit into a sub-page block defined by ACOM and do not cross block boundaries. Consequently, all items in a line belong to the same block and have common protection attributes. Hence, controlling accesses which load the cache can easily be achieved by ACOM. Writing back the cache contents to main memory can be distinguished in two basic strategies. The *write-through technique* immediately transfers the modified item to main memory and hence, ACOM can directly control the access. The *buffered write-through* and the *write-back* strategies delay the transfer of modified lines. As a result, the detection of a incorrect access by ACOM is also delayed. ACOM will indicate the access violation when eventually the cache contents is transferred to main memory. In this case, the damage may be more substantial and more complex recovery mechanisms [33] have to be applied. However, it should be noted that independent of detection latency, handling of a protection violation is difficult and needs assistance of higher system levels.

7 Conclusion

Persistent object systems try to hide the difference between language level objects and system objects. To obtain a wide acceptance, the efficiency of these systems must be comparable to conventional language systems. One of the key issues is to exploit the efficiency of virtual memory management of contemporary processors. We presented two approaches which follow this guideline and do not assume any specially designed hardware platform. Because, in these systems, controlled object sharing is highly desirable as an efficient mechanism for cooperation and communication, protection becomes a vital property. Since a fine grain protection scheme has to check individual accesses to objects, this can only be performed efficiently by hardware. However, the protection mechanisms of available high performance processors are tightly coupled with the address translation mechanism which, in these architectures is based on fixed size pages, inadequate to protect individual objects of arbitrary size.

We have developed ACOM, an architecture which provides protection for individual objects independently from any address translation issues. Separating protection from address translation results in a number of benefits:

- Exploitation of any high performance virtual memory implementation since ACOM does not interfere with the (critical) address translation path. Therefore, ACOM does not slow down memory accesses.
- ACOM can be securely controlled by user level trusted procedures. Hardware support is provided to check authority of these procedures.
- The overhead to maintain ACOM is very low. Updating ACOM is additionally supported by an entry generator.
- Easy integration in a conventional hardware platform. ACOM can be applied to systems with different hardware configurations, i.e. on-chip MMUs and caches.
- ACOM is a simple device in terms of hardware complexity. This will reduce hardware costs and make an implementation easy.
- Applications which do not need or want fine grain protection do not suffer from ACOM in terms of performance degradation or maintenance overhead. ACOM can be completely deactivated for these applications.

The paper sketches how ACOM can complement existing approaches to persistent object-oriented systems. The design of ACOM is ready to be frozen in silicon.

References

1. A. Goldberg, D. Robson. Smalltalk-80: The Language and its Implementation. Addison-Wesley, 1983

2. R. Morrison, A.L. Brown, R. Connor, A. Dearle. The Napier88 Reference Manual. Universities of Glasgow and St. Andrews PPRR-77, Scotland, 1989

3. M. Evered. Leibniz - A Language to Support Software Engineering. PhD thesis Technical University of Darmstadt, 1985

4. T. Atwood. Two Approaches to Adding Persistence to C++. Proc. 4th Int. Workshop on Persistent Object Systems, Martha's Vineyard, MA, 1990

5. C. Horn, V. Cahill. Supporting Distributed Applications in the Amadeus Environment. Conputer Communications Review 14(6), 1991

6. Intel iAPX432 General Data Processor Architecture Reference Manual, Intel Corp., Aloha, Oregon, 1981

7. D.M. Harland. REKURSIV - Object-Oriented Computer Architecture. Ellis Horwood Limited, Chichester, 1988

8. J.L. Keedy. The MONADS-PC System: A Programmer's Overview. Tech. Report No. 8/89, University Bremen, 1989

9. J. Kaiser. MUTABOR, A Coprocessor Supporting Memory Management in an Object-Oriented Architecture. IEEE Micro, Vol. 8, No. 5, October 1988, 30-46

10. A.R. Cunha, C.N. Ribeiro, J.A. Marques. The Architecture of a Memory Management Unit for Object-Oriented Systems. Technical Report RT 37-90, INESC, Sep. 1990, also in: Computer Architecture News, Vol. 19, No. 4, June 1991

11. P. Dasgupta, R.J. LeBlanc Jr., W.F. Appelbe. The Clouds Distributed Operating System, Functional Description, Implementation Details, and Related Work. Tech. Report: GIT-ICS-87/42, GIT, Georgia, 1987

12. G.T. Almes, A.P. Black, E.D. Lazowska, J.D. Noe. The Eden System: A Technical Review. University of Washington Department of Computer Science, Tech. Report 83-10-05, October 1983

13. W.E. Kühnhauser, H. Härtig, O.C. Kowalski, W. Lux, H. Streich. The Birlix Operating System Project. Proceedings of the 1991 ERCIM Workshop on Distributed Systems, Lisboa, Portugal

14. A.S. Tanenbaum, S.J. Mullender, R. van Renesse. Using Sparse Capabilities in a Distributed Operating System. Proc. 6th int. Conf. on Distr. Computer Systems, IEEE, 1986

15. M. Rozeir, V. Abrassimov, F. Armand, I. Boule, M. Gien, M. Guillemont, F. Herrmann, C. Kaiser, S. Langlois, P. Leonard, W. Neuhauser. CHORUS Distributed Operating Systems. Tech. Rep. CS/TR-88-7.8, Feb. 1989

16. Y. Yokote, A. Mitsuzawa, N. Fujinami, M. Tokoro. Reflective Object Management in the Muse Operating System. In Proc. of the 1991 International Workshop on Object Orientation in Operating Systems, October 1991, Pala Alto, California, IEEE Computer Society Press, Los Alamitos, California

17. R. Lea, P. Amaral, Ch. Jacquemot. COOL-2: an object oriented support platform built above the Chorus Micro-kernel. Proc. of the 1991 International Workshop on Object Orientation in Operating Systems, October 1991, Pala Alto, California, IEEE Computer Society Press, Los Alamitos, California

18. Comandos Consortium: A Guide to the Comandos Platform; Description of Comandos-2 Architecture. Esprit Project 2071 - Deliverable D1-T2.2, March 1991

19. P.R. Wilson. Operating System Support for Small Objects. In Proc. of the 1991 International Workshop on Object Orientation in Operating Systems, October 1991, Pala Alto, California, IEEE Computer Society Press, Los Alamitos, California

20. A. Black, N. Hutchinson, E. Jul, H. Levy. Object Structure in the Emerald System. Proc. 1986 ACM Conf. on Obj.-Oriented Progr. Systems, Languages and Applications, ACM, 1986

21. P.R. Wilson. Pointer swizzling at page fault time: Efficiently supporting huge address spaces on standard hardware. Computer Architecture News, June 1991

22. M.P. Atkinson, P.J. Bailey, K.J. Chisholm, W.P. Cockshott, R. Morrison. An Approach to Persistent Programming. The Computer Journal, Vol.26, No.4, November 1983, pp. 360-365.

23. T. Andrews, C. Harris, K. Sinkel. The Ontos Object Database. Tech. Report, Ontologic Inc., Burlington, Ma, 1989

24. W.P. Cockshott, M.P. Atkinson, K.J. Chisholm, P.J. Bailey, R. Morrison. POMPS: A Persistent Object Management System. Software Practice and Experience, Vol.14, No.1, January 1984, pp. 49-71.

25. A. Malhotra, S. J. Munroe. Support for Objects: Two Architectures. Proc. HICSS-25, Vol.1, Kauai, Hawaii, January 1992, pp. 737-746

26. Trinity College Dublin: Overview of the Amadeus Project, Tech. Report, Distributed Systems Group, May 1991, Trinity College Dublin

27. J. Kaiser. An Object-Oriented Approach to Support System Reliability and Security. In: J. Rosenberg, J.L. Keedy (eds): Security and Persistence, Bremen 1990 and: Workshops in Computing, Springer 1990

28. Intel: 80386 Hardware Reference Manual. Intel Corp., Santa Clara, California, 1986

29. Motorola: MC68030 Enhanced 32-Bit Microprocessor User´s Manual. Motorola Inc., 1987

30. G.J. Myers. Advances in Computer Architecture, 2nd Ed., John Wiley & Sons, 1982

31. K. Czaja. Entwurf eines Translation Lookaside Buffers für objektorientierte Architekturen. GMD-Studie Nr. 117, GMD, St. Augustin, 1987

32. K. Czaja, J. Kaiser, U. Kleinhans. Ein Hardware-Monitor zur Durchsetzung von Zugriffsschutz in objektorientierten Systemen. In: A Jammel (ed.), Architektur von Rechensystemen, 12. GI/ITG-Fachtagung, Kiel 1992, Springer 1992

33. J. Kaiser, E. Nett, R. Kröger. MUTABOR: A Coprocessor supporting Object-Oriented Memory Management and Error Recovery. Proc. HICSS-21, Vol. 1, 1988

Persistent Programming Practices

Malcolm Atkinson
Department of Computational Sciences, University of Glasgow
Glasgow, G12 8QQ, Scotland

This session involved two papers that develop improved methods of deploying the facilities of a persistent system. They are also both fine examples of international collaboration; the first paper having been built as a result of collaboration between the University of Newcastle-upon-Tyne, England and the University of Campinas, São Paulo, Brazil, the second being the fruits of a collaboration between the team developing persistence at the University of St Andrews, Scotland and a corresponding team from the University of Adelaide, Australia. Each paper shows how an existing persistent technology can be exploited to provide more conveniently engineered persistent application systems.

The first paper, Stabilis: A Case Study in Writing Fault-Tolerant Distributed Applications using Persistent Objects, by L.E. Buzato and A. Calsavara, starts with the facilities of Arjuna a distributed operating system providing support for fault tolerant programming. Arjuna presents its facilities as C++ objects that may be used via a remote procedure call mechanism. Its persistence is obtained via a relatively heavy weight protocol that depends on a name server and on object services that require frequent transmission of objects if the operations on objects are small and frequent. The authors show how the nested transaction mechanism of Arjuna and its basic persistence can be used to build an indexed database service with local câching. A systematic discipline is established so that if programmers prepare the application database as a set of specialisations of Stablis objects and provide for these objects certain methods essential to stability/persistence then the resulting population of objects can be managed as a fault-tolerant distributed database. A bibliographic database example is operational.

The second paper, Persistent Program Construction through Browsing and User Gesture with some Typing, A. Farkas, A. Dearle, G. Kirby, Q. Cutts, R. Morrison and R. Connor starts with the facilities of Napier88 a persistent programming language. This language already has rich mechanisms for incremental binding based on values called environments that hold updateable sets of bindings. When these are used purely via textual programming the programmer has to describe both types and persistent store navigation for every separate compilation unit. The paper presents three ways of avoiding this tedious housekeeping while retaining the precise enforcement of types. In the first, interaction with browsing facilities generates this interface description. In the second the navigation and some of the type specification is avoided by allowing the input to the compiler to contain textual references to items in the store and resolving these at compilation time via a map established during the browsing. In the third method the input to the compilation system includes non-textual references to objects and types in the store that have been resolved during the browsing session. This third form avoids navigation during execution and may in the future allow type checking to be performed before compilation perhaps restricting the items selected by browsing to those that are compatible.

The discussion on the first paper questioned whether the large number of subtransactions demanded from the nested transactional system of Arjuna were viable. There was not yet measurement data to support a positive answer but experience using the bibliographic database across five workstations suggested that this was not a cause of performance difficulties. It was noted that the locks were held exclusively for writes for the total duration of the outermost transaction. This was considered acceptable by the authors as their view of the use of this database methodology was that it was intended for small amounts of computation per use of the data. Some of the participants suggested that this was not a sustainable property of persistent programming, sooner or later larger or long running transactions would occur and be too greedy holding locks. For the present, the application programmer was expected to avoid this. The use of the word "persistent" to describe a system where the programmer had to provide operations to translate to and from persistent stored form was questioned. The authors pointed to the automated generation of this code but its restriction of attributes to the base types did not satisfy the purists.

The first observation about the second paper was its strong links with a paper given earlier in the workshop, Persistent Hyper-Programs by a permutation of the same authors[1]. These two papers were recognised as complementary and as signifying the introduction of a new technology for program production made possible by conducting the entire enterprise in the persistent context. Several speakers speculated on the potential this may have; for example, if values can be located and bound before compilation and hence before type checking a whole range of dependent types become possible. On a similar note, it might be expected that this pre-compile time binding would allow much improved optimisation since the compiler would have access to the full details of values; this might be exploited in constant folding and when in-lining procedure activations, and could yield new ways of efficiently compiling polymorphic code.

Some difficulties were also recognised. Browsing was not always the best way of finding things, particularly when you have a large number of them. It is common experience in hyper-text authoring that organising, constructing and maintaining the hypergraph is extremely difficult and laborious as the size of the information body increases. In the case of program construction much of the efforts of the software engineering research had been directed at trying to recognise and retain structure through methodologies and tools that support these methodologies. The greater flexibility of the hyper-programming world might exacerbate the difficulties for managing large construction. Certainly appropriate tools and methodologies would be needed to organise hyper-programming. The presenter did not disagree and was happy to be able to say "these are early days" for our technology.

---

[1]Thinly disguised by giving their full initials in the earlier paper

Stabilis*: A Case Study in Writing Fault-Tolerant Distributed Applications Using Persistent Objects

L.E.Buzato[†] A.Calsavara

l.e.buzato@newcastle.ac.uk a.calsavara@newcastle.ac.uk

Department of Computing Science, Computing Laboratory

The University, Newcastle upon Tyne, NE1 7RU, U.K.

Tel.: +44 91 222 8035

Abstract

This paper presents Stabilis, a fault-tolerant object-oriented distributed database management system that has been written as an exercise in persistent programming. Stabilis is implemented on top of Arjuna, an object-oriented programming system that provides the basic mechanisms for fault tolerance and distribution. The computational model used by Arjuna is based upon the concept of using atomic actions[1] to control operations upon persistent objects. Stabilis aims at experimenting with Arjuna to build large applications that use persistent objects. Such experiment has led us to extend some of the mechanisms for persistent programming already existent in Arjuna. Stabilis manages objects that are persistent, recoverable and can be accessed remotely and concurrently in a consistent manner. Objects with such properties have an important function in the overall operation of Stabilis. The database manager can be operated either through a visual database interface or a query interpreter; both translate commands into a series of operations of the database manager. All operations of the database manager make use of atomic actions and locks to structure and control accesses to objects. A flexible use of nested atomic actions permits objects to retrogress to previous consistent states. Stabilis has been developed using C++; dispensing with the use of any specifically designed language for persistent programming.

Key words:

Persistence, Atomic Actions, Type Inheritance, Fault Tolerance, Object-Oriented Databases

---

*Latin word synonymous with **stable**. This work has been partially funded by ESPRIT Project ISA (Project no. 2267), and CNPq (grants no. 200410/88-1 and 201905/91-4).

†On leave from the Department of Computing Science,University of Campinas, São Paulo, Brazil.

[1] Atomic transactions.

1 Introduction

As distributed systems become more widely used, there is an increasing need for effective ways of organising distributed applications. Distributed applications can be hard to design and write because of the problems of concurrency and partial failure inherent to distributed systems. Keeping data consistent in the presence of failures is another serious problem whose solution can rely on the use of persistent objects and atomic actions.

Distributed applications typically have a number of requirements, including reliability, reconfigurability, concurrency control, availability and consistency. An application domain that contains problems covering such a comprehensive set of requirements is that of distributed database management systems. In this paper we survey the experience we have had during the implementation of Stabilis, a fault-tolerant object-oriented distributed database management system. We have implemented Stabilis on top of Arjuna[1], an object-oriented distributed programming system.

Objects are instances of abstract data types. An *atomic object* is an object that is recoverable and can be used concurrently in a consistent way. Atomicity is achieved through the use of atomic actions controlling operations upon objects. The definition of robust object evolves naturally from the definition of atomic object [2, 3]. A *robust object* is an atomic object that is persistent and can be accessed remotely[2].

Stabilis uses robust objects as its database entries, henceforth denominated *database objects*. To construct a distributed database using Stabilis a user-defined object-oriented data model is converted into a set of classes from which database objects are generated. Nested atomic actions are used to allow a flexible management of the database objects, permitting it to undo operations.

Another interesting aspect of our work is that Arjuna and Stabilis make use of C++ [4] to implement all mechanisms necessary for persistent programming, dispensing with the use of any specifically designed language.

The next Section comments on those aspects of Arjuna that were relevant to the development of Stabilis. Some of the modules of Arjuna are analysed in more detail because they have been extended during the implementation of Stabilis. Section 3 shows how persistent programming is accomplished using Arjuna. Section 4 introduces a module developed to extend some of the programming facilities offered by Arjuna for persistent programming. Section 5 is built around the design and implementation of Stabilis, its use of Arjuna and the platform it offers to the development of distributed databases. Finally, Section 6 describes Dbib, a bibliography database implemented to assess Stabilis. The paper concludes with the discussion of possible improvements that could be made to both Arjuna and Stabilis as a result of our experience. It also evaluates the use made so far of robust objects and type inheritance, considering their appropriateness to persistent programming.

2 An Overview of Arjuna

Arjuna is an object-oriented programming system which provides a set of tools for constructing fault-tolerant distributed applications [1]. Arjuna supports nested

[2]Ideally, a robust object should also be replicated. Arjuna is being extended to include replication of objects.

atomic actions for structuring applications. Objects in Arjuna can be made either atomic objects or persistent atomic objects; they are the main repositories for holding system state. Operations upon them are invoked under the control of atomic actions. In Arjuna, operations on objects are of type *read* or *write*, following the locking rule that permits *multiple reads, single writes.* The well-known *strict two-phase* locking policy is adopted to ensure serialisability. Locks on objects are acquired inside an atomic action, and are released only when the outermost atomic action ends (or aborts) [5]. By ensuring that objects are persistent and only manipulated within an atomic action, it can be guaranteed that the integrity of objects - and hence the integrity of the system - is maintained in the presence of failures such as node crashes and the loss of network messages. This is the *object and action* model of computation - atomic actions controlling operations upon persistent objects.

2.1 Architecture

The main modules of the Arjuna system are shown in Figure 1. The RPC module is used to invoke operations on persistent objects. The **Name Server** module keeps identification and location information about persistent objects. The **Object Store** module encapsulates the stable representation of persistent objets. The **Atomic Action** module is the application-level interface. These modules are described further in the subsequent sections.

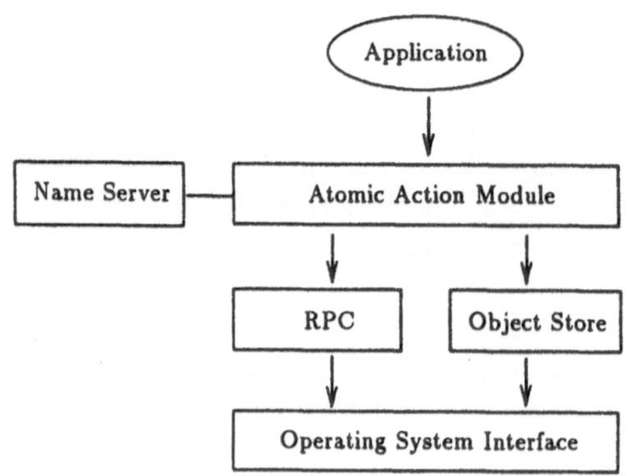

Figure 1: The architecture of Arjuna.

2.1.1 RPC Module

Arjuna adopts the client-server model for accessing persistent objects. A server manages an object state; it defines and executes operations that are exported to clients. Clients invoke these operations to manipulate the object state guarded by the server. Invocations of operations on persistent objects are implemented as *remote procedure calls* (RPC), which are supported by the RPC module.

The Arjuna programming environment provides a tool called **Stub Generator** [6] that processes definitions of C++ classes whose instances are persistent objects to be remotely accessed and, as a result, produces the corresponding client and server stub code. Transparency of location and access is obtained by making any invocation of an operation on the client stub object to trigger the same operation on the corresponding (remote) server stub object, using RPC.

2.1.2 Name Server Module

Names are used for several purposes in computer systems; one of the uses is to refer to objects. To name and find objects in a distributed system, *naming* and *binding* functions are usually provided through a *name server.* The naming function maps a user-suplied object name to a unique object identifier already assigned to the object. And, the binding function maps the unique identifier of an object to its location.

To further experiment with Arjuna and have a portable name server[7], we have decided to implement a naming and binding facility as an Arjuna application using persistent objects. In our version of the name server, two classes, `NameServer` and `NameServerManager`, implement a portable name server that relies solely on the mechanisms of the Atomic Action module of Arjuna. Instances of `NameServer` are robust objects, which act as servers, distributed among the nodes of the network, and instances of `NameServerManager` are clients that co-ordinate the operation of the servers. To a program, the Name Server module gives an illusion of a virtually centralised name server. All operations (for registering, unregistering and resolving names) invoked by a program are transfered by the Name Server client to the servers for execution. In the current implementation, all operations are sent to the servers using a round robin algorithm. In the future, other strategies for forwarding operations to the servers can be experimented. This issue has received lower priority since the main goal of the project was not to build a very complex name server but only to verify the possibility of building one based only on the services provided by the Atomic Action module of Arjuna.

2.1.3 Object Store Module

The Object Store provides an access service to the passive state of persistent objects. The stable representation of the passive state of a persistent object, usually stored in disk, has to be machine independent to permit its transmission between stable storage and volatile storage, and also its transmission as a message. The class `ObjectState` implements such a representation, providing operations for packing and unpacking the state of a persistent object into/from an instance of `ObjectState`. The function of the Object Store is to manage instances of the class `ObjectState`.

The set of operations provided by the Object Store include: **read_state**, which returns an instance of the `ObjectState` designated by a unique identifier, and **write_state**, which stores an instance of `ObjectState` identified by a given unique identifier. Figure 2 shows the lifetime and state transitions of a persistent object along with the operations that produce the transitions. The Atomic Action module activates a persistent object by first calling **read_state** and then **restore_state**, which unpacks the object state. The reverse operation comprises the execution of **save_state**, which packs the object state, and the invocation of **write_state**.

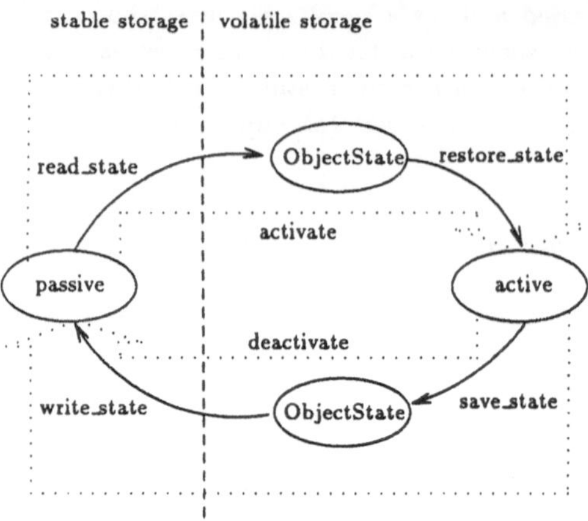

Figure 2: Object state transitions.

2.1.4 Atomic Action Module

The Atomic Action module provides the programming interface of Arjuna. The mechanisms necessary for concurrency control, persistence, recovery, and atomic action control are implemented by the classes of the class hierarchy depicted in Figure 3. These classes represent the internal structure of the Atomic Action module. To write an application that conforms to the *object and action* model of computation, a programmer declares instances of the class `AtomicAction` in his program; the operations provided by this class (**begin**, **end** and **abort**) can then be used to organise atomic actions. The only objects controlled by the resulting atomic actions are those objects that are either instances of Arjuna classes or user-defined classes derived from the class `LockManager` – type inheritance is used to make user-defined classes members of the hierarchy shown in Figure 3.

All Arjuna classes are derived from the base class `StateManager`, which provides the basic facilities needed for constructing persistent objects and atomic actions. The class `LockManager` uses the operations of the class `StateManager` to provide concurrency control. The other classes shown in Figure 3 implement most of the support operations of the Atomic Action module; further details about the class hierarchy of Arjuna can be found in [1].

2.2 Failure Assumptions

It is assumed that the hardware components of the system are workstations (nodes), connected by a communication sub-system (for example, a local area network). A node is assumed to work either as specified or simply to stop working (crash). After a crash a node is repaired within a finite amount of time and made active again. A node is assumed to have both stable and non-stable (volatile) storage. All of the data stored on volatile storage is assumed to be lost when a crash occurs; any data stored on stable storage, as stated earlier, remains unaffected by a crash. It is also

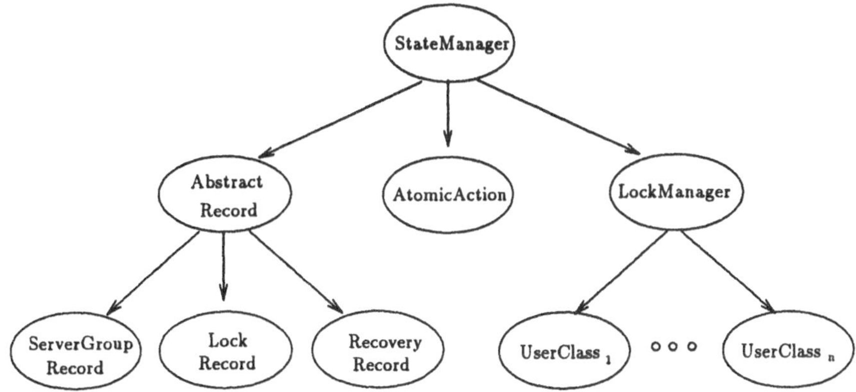

Figure 3: The Arjuna class hierarchy in the Atomic Action module.

assumed that faults in the communication sub-system are responsible for failures such as lost, duplicated or corrupted messages. The RPC system is assumed to be responsible for coping with such failures using well-known network protocol level techniques; it returns a failure exception to the caller if it suspects that the called server is not responding.

3 Persistent Programming in Arjuna

In this Section, a class denominated `Article` is used to explain the various steps involved in the conversion of a user-defined class into a class whose instances are robust objects using Arjuna. The programming procedure for the implementation of robust objects comprises the steps:

- Derive `Article` from the class `LockManager` provided by Arjuna (Figure 3);
- Implement the function to save the state of an `Article` instance into an `ObjectState` (**save_state**), and its reciprocal (**restore_state**);
- `Article` must have two constructors: one to be executed whenever a new persistent instance of `Article` is created; other to be executed every time an already existent instance of `Article` is reactivated;
- Every method of `Article` that modifies the state of the object has to be atomic.

At this stage instances of the class `Article` are persistent and recoverable but cannot be accessed remotely. To make them remotely accessible the class definition has to be submitted to the Stub Generator and the code for stub server has to be installed in each node of the distributed system where activations of `Article` occur.

The programming procedure described hitherto has some drawbacks. Let c be the number of classes an application (say A) controls, and n be the number of nodes where instances of these classes reside. If the procedure described is used to program the robust objects of the application A, then c classes will have to be submitted to the Stub Generator and $c \times n$ class-specific servers will have to be installed. Consequently, if c and n are large the development and management of a distributed application has its complexity considerably increased: more computational resources are used and more configuration errors can occur. Furthermore, the code obtained using this procedure does not intrinsically provide a caching scheme for robust objects.

An alternative procedure to implement robust objects can be based on the existence of a class (say `RobustObject`) that exempts the use of the Stub Generator and provides a caching mechanism. The programming procedure resulting from the adoption of this solution comprises steps very similar to those used by the procedure described earlier for Arjuna, except that:

- `Article` has now to be derived from `RobustObject`;

- it has not to be submitted to the Stub Generator.

A module, denominated Object Manager, described in the subsequent Section, has been implemented to provide the abstraction given by the class `RobustObject`.

4 Object Management

The Object Manager module provides an abstraction of robust objects that exempts the use of the Stub Generator while giving the possibility of caching objects to improve the efficiency of an application. Additionaly, a simple object migration mechanism can be developed using this module.

Several factors have to be considered before deciding on the use of the Object Manager: the size of the objects; the frequency of accesses made to the objects; the computational cost of the operations and the number of classes managed by the application. In particular, the Object Manager is very suited to the implementation of database managers because they control persistent objects that usually: have a small size, are frequently accessed, have no CPU-bound operations and are generated from a large number of classes.

4.1 Module Organisation

Figures 4a and 4b will be used to explain how the Object Manager module is organised. Figure 4a shows how persistent objects are remotely accessed in Arjuna: a Client invokes operations on a remote Server that uses the Object Store Manager to access the object. The dotted line shows the activation/deactivation of the persistent object, and the dashed line represents the communication between Client and Server. Figure 4b shows the configuration obtained when the Object Manager module is used. An extra client-server pair, the Object Manager and the Object Server, is interleaved between the Server and the Object Store Manager. In this case, the Server does not affect the persistent object directly because it is (potentially) remote: it works on a local *cache object*, a volatile copy of the robust object.

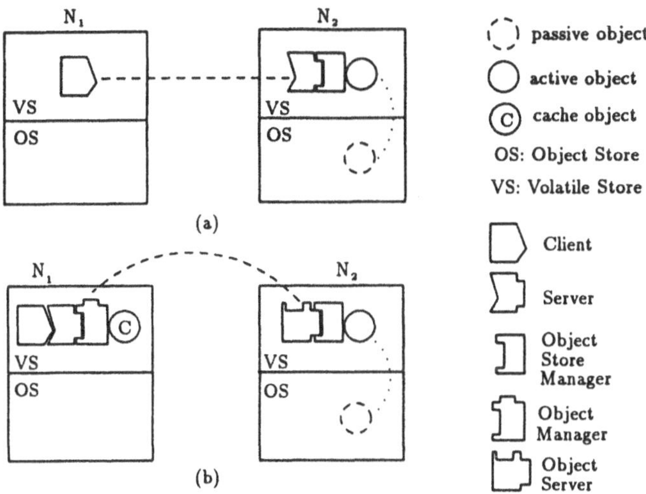

Figure 4: Organisation of the Object Manager.

4.2 Consistency of the Cache Object

The consistency of the robust object and cache object is guaranteed by the computational model of Arjuna. When a robust object is instantiated, the cache object is initiated with the state of the passive object. Subsequently, the server modifies the cache object and then its state is immediately copied to the passive object, i.e., the cache data is made permanent. If the update of the passive object fails then the state of the cache object has to be recovered. This implies that every server operation that modifies the cache object has to be atomic; its result (commit or abort) has to be the same of the update operation on the passive object. Depending on the type of lock (read/write) a client acquires on a robust object, the cache object behaves as a hint or as a proper cache[3]. When locked for read[4], the passive object can be modified by another client and, consequently, the cache object becomes stale. On the other hand, the write lock guarantees that the cache object will be always correct.

4.3 Implementation

The classes that implement the two components of the Object Manager module, Object Manager and Object Server, are respectively the classes `RobustObject` and `Package`.

The class `Package` is derived from the class `LockManager` of Arjuna. The atomic operations it exports are:

create ▷ stores a new object state on stable storage;

[3]An introduction about the use of hints, stashing and caching techniques can be found in [8].

[4]This read lock is released as soon as the object state has been read.

get ▷ reads an object state from stable storage using the specified access mode;

put ▷ overwrites the existing stable state of a designated object;

destroy ▷ removes an object state from stable storage.

The class `RobustObject` is also derived from `LockManager` to provide recoverability to the cache object. The operations it exports are:

create ▷ calls the **Package** operation **create** and registers the newly created object with the **Name Server**;

make_volatile ▷ locates the object (via **Name Server**) and calls **refresh_volatile**;

refresh_volatile ▷ calls the **Package** operation **get** with the designated access mode and restores the object state into the cache object;

make_permanent ▷ saves the cache object into an object state and calls the **Package** operation **put**;

destroy ▷ calls the **Package** operation **destroy**.

5 Stabilis

Stabilis is a fault-tolerant object-oriented distributed database management system built on top of Arjuna. Its design is based on the same principles that governed the design of Arjuna; type inheritance plays a key role in the development of classes that can be used by the database developer to add new qualities to his own classes.

The use of Stabilis entails the design of an object-oriented data model of the database from which database objects (robust objects) are obtained. Stabilis fully benefits from the functionality of the **Object Manager** module to simplify the implementation of distributed databases and the writing of application programs. In certain cases (Section 5.3), the distributed database can be automatically generated from a description of the object-oriented data model.

The installation and configuration of a new database is straightforward; the only measure that has to be taken is to register the database with the administration tool of Stabilis. All that this tool requires is the set of nodes where the database is to be made available.

In Stabilis, the database objects can have methods to implement services invoked on request, e.g., a database object could have a method (service) to write itself out in Postscript format.

Stabilis has two standard interfaces: a visual database interface [9] and a query interpreter. The visual database interface can mainly be used for short term queries involving small sets of objects. On the other hand, the query interpreter is proper for the processing of longer and more complex queries involving large sets of objects. New interfaces can be programmed as applications that access the database manager.

5.1 Object-Oriented Data Model

The object-oriented data model supported by Stabilis is represented as a *directed acyclic graph* where the nodes are classes, and the edges relationships between them.

A class defines the *domain* of all objects that share the same set of *attributes* and *methods*. The methods of a class are the implementation of the *services* provided by its instances. A relationship between two classes can be any of the following [5]:

- Generalisation/Specialisation: where one class (the *subclass*) inherits attributes and behaviour of another class (the *superclass*). A class with no superclass is called a *root class*. A class with no subclass is called a *leaf class*. *Multipe inheritance* exists when a class has more then one superclass.
- Association: where one class has an attribute whose domain is another class. Such attribute is called a *relational attribute*. It is implemented as a set of objects, whose lower-bound and upper-bound have to be defined.

A class can also be denominated *concrete* or *abstract*, depending on whether it can be instantiated or not [10]. The concrete classes define the classes whose instances are database objects.

5.2 Architecture

An application program interacts with the **Database Manager** (Figure 5) to manipulate objects of a database. This interaction comprehends calling operations of the database manager to access the database objects. A database object is accessed to have its state read and possibly modified by the application; it can be said that the application *edits* the object. The editing of a database object occurs with the help of an *interface object* that acts as a buffer that contains a volatile copy of the database object. This interface object is where an operation of the **Database Manager** fetches its arguments and returns its results. Database objects and interface objects are created by the Object Generator. The Index is used to resolve queries expedited by the applications.

5.2.1 Index Module

The Index module is responsible for evaluating queries formulated by an application program. A query is a declarative specification of a set of objects in the database that satisfy a set of conditions. The conditions are usually specified as a boolean combination of predicates of the form: $<$ *attribute_name operator value* $>$, for example, (*title* = "*Persistent*") **and** (*year* $>$ 1980).

The complexity of the query accepted determines the complexity of the algorithm and data structure used to resolve it. A query may be formulated against either a portion of the object-oriented data model or a single class. It may refer to attributes of a class, a superclass or a related class [11].

In the current version of Stabilis, the queries take as predicates the attributes of a single class. The attributes that can be used as predicates in a condition are denominated *key attributes*. Substrings of a key attribute can be used as values.

[5] A fully object-oriented data model should permit the representation of composite objects.

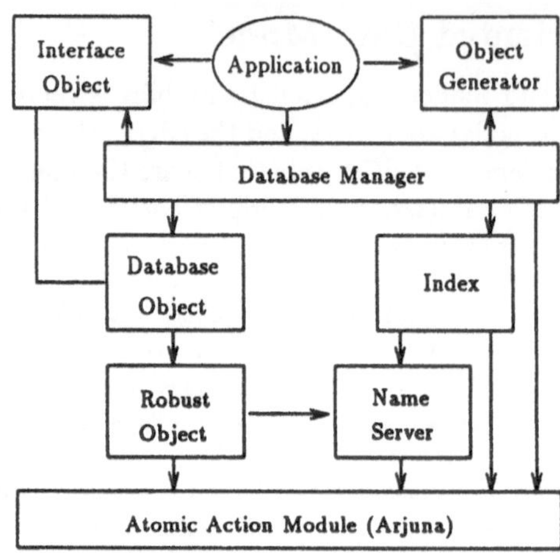

Figure 5: The architecture of Stabilis.

Two classes, **IndexManager** and **IndexServer**, implement the **Index** module. Instances of **IndexServer**, henceforth denominated *index servers*, are robust objects that implement autonomous servers for query processing. Instances of **IndexManager**, henceforth denominated *index managers*, are clients that co-ordinate the operation of the index servers. To the database manager the **Index** provides an illusion of a virtually centralised query processor.

The main problems that affect the organisation of the **Index** are:

- concurrency: several queries can be forwarded to an index server concurrently and a reasonable organisation should maximise the concurrency;
- fault tolerance: the data stored in the index servers should always be consistent in the ocurrence of failures. A graceful degradation of availability should occur even when some index servers stop their operation.

The current version of the **Index** is organised as a cluster of index managers that have references to disjoint sets of index servers. Each set of index servers keep the query data related to only one concrete class of the database. To further optimise the query processing, each index manager keeps a cache of the entries stored in the index servers.

Queries are resolved in the following way: the database manager accepts the query made by the application, e.g., the **Query Interpreter**, and sends the query expression to the **Index**. It is then transfered to the class-specific index manager for resolution. The index manager will only forward the query expression to the index servers if its resolution cannot be done using the local cache.

The present organisation of the **Index** has aimed at solving the problems listed above. The tree-like structure of this organisation permits a faster query processing, by allowing greater concurrency. The **Index** is well adapted to resolving queries based on attributes of a single class. Additionally, if an index server stops for some reason, only a fraction of the information related to a specific concrete class becomes unavailable.

5.2.2 Database Manager Module

The Database Manager module is the kernel of Stabilis. It provides all basic operations to access database objects.

Nested Atomic Actions Various degrees of operation rollbacks are offered by the database manager to an application program through the use of nested atomic actions. Two atomic actions are used to control the state transitions of the database objects: *outer* and *in-hand.* These transitions are shown in the Figure 6, where they are represented as a finite automaton with two states: *reading* and *writing.* The transitions are caused by the execution of the operations that are structured using both *outer* and *in-hand.*

The atomic action *outer* guarantees that a persistent object is kept locked for write. It is started in every transition from *reading* to *writing* (operations **create** and **mode**). And, it can be either ended (operation **mode**) or aborted (operation **abort**) in every transition from *writing* to *reading.* If it ends, all modifications made to the object are made permanent or else, if it aborts, the modifications are ignored and the states of the cache object and interface object retrogress to the previous state saved in the persistent object.

While in the *writing* state, an *in-hand* atomic action is kept running nested within the *outer.* It can be either ended (operation **save**) or aborted (operation **cancel**). If it ends all modifications made to the interface object are saved into the cache object or else, if it aborts, the modifications are ignored and the interface object is kept as it is. In both cases a new *in-hand* is started.

Figure 7 depicts a sequence of database operations and the corresponding atomic actions involved. In this sequence a new database object is created and subsequently modified. In the Figure 7, t_i $(0 \leq i \leq 13)$ marks the instants where relevant events occur; in any of the r_j marks $(1 \leq j \leq 3)$ the database application can either cause a commit or a rollback of the operation being executed.

At t_0, the operation **create** is started and as a consequence:

- *outer* is started;
- *in-hand* is started;
- *A* is started to ensure that the creation of the database object (atomic action *B*) and its registration with the Index (atomic action *E*) comprehend an atomic event (t_1 to t_4);
- *B* is started to guarantee that the persistent object is created (atomic action *C*) and registered with the Name Server (atomic action *D*) atomically (t_2 to t_3);

Between t_4 and t_5 the application makes alterations to the interface object. At t_5 the operation *save* is executed to confirm the alterations. At this point, *F* is started to ensure that the update of the object (atomic action *G*) and the update of the Index (atomic action *H*) are atomically executed. The present *in-hand* is committed but the changes are not made permanent yet because *outer* is still running. Another *in-hand* is started at t_8.

Between t_8 and t_9 the application modifies the interface object again. At t_9 the **cancel** operation is invoked to roll the state of the interface object back to the state it had at t_8. The present *in-hand* is aborted and a new one is started at t_{10}.

From t_{10} to t_{11} more alterations are made to the interface object. Finally, at t_{11}, the operation **mode** is executed to make permanent all modifications made since t_0. The same update process executed between t_5 and t_6 is repeated in the interval t_{11} to t_{12}. At t_{13} the *in-hand* and *outer* are ended.

Figure 6: Transition diagram for the finite automaton of Stabilis.

Operations The operation of the database manager is supported by an *operational context.* This operational context is defined by the selection of a class, the *current class*, and by the selection of an object of that class, the *current object.* Two operations, **select_class** and **select_object**, are defined to allow an application to traverse the database by changing the operational context. Some of the operations of the database manager are:

mode ▹ This operation allows the user to change the mode of access to the current object. The current object can be either in *writing* or in *reading* mode.

create ▹ Creates an instance of a database object in any of the object stores available. In the present implementation, an object store is selected at random. Other selection algorithms can consider factors such as: the space available in the object stores, frequency of access to a database object, etc, to decide where to create the database object. Every database object created is registered with the Name Server and has its key attributes entered in the Index.

remove ▹ All reference information related to the current object is removed from the modules Index and Name Server, and the current object is deleted from the database.

save ▹ All changes made up to this point to the current object are made permanent, including the corresponding Index entry.

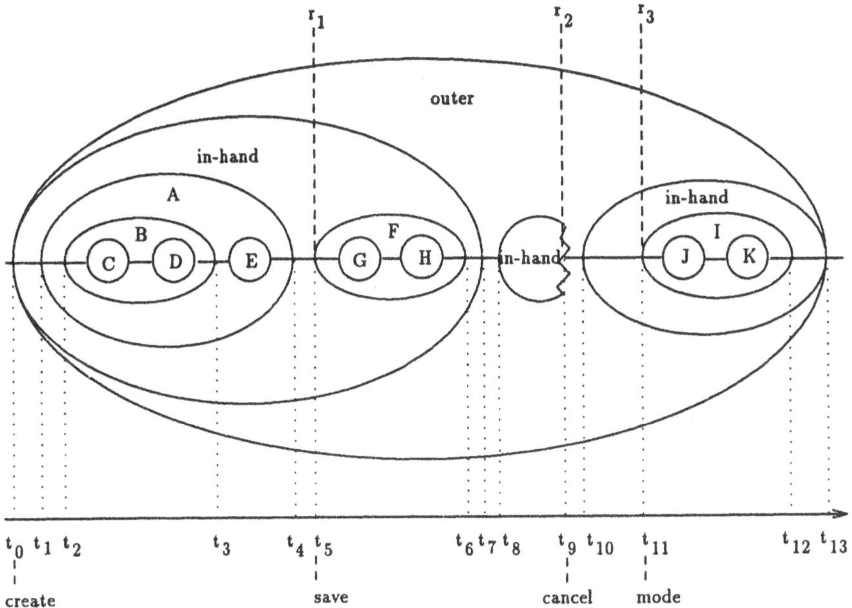

Figure 7: Nested atomic actions: a snapshot.

cancel ▹ All changes made to the current object since the last **save** operation are ignored; the state of the current object is retrogressed to the last saved state.

abort ▹ The state of the current object is retrogressed to the state it had before its last transition from *reading* to *writing* state; all changes made by operations executed during this interval are ignored.

search ▹ The search operation takes as input a query and returns the set of objects whose key attributes satisfy the query condition.

serve ▹ In Stabilis, database objects can have service operations that are executed on request. A request, triggered by an application program, causes the execution of a designated object method that implements that service operation. For example, a database object can have a method that implements the service operation *encrypt* to cryptograph its attributes.

relate ▹ In Stabilis, relations are always formed between a pair of objects, the current object, and another one, the *relational object*. When the **relate** operation is executed the current object becomes the relational object, and the current class the *relational class*. Subsequently, a new operational context is set. After the execution of a **relate** operation several link/unlink operations can be executed to do/undo relations between the relational object and the current object. Stabilis allows nesting of **relate** operations.

link ▹ Relations among database objects are expressed through links. A link is a reference to another database object. This operation always involves the current object and a relational object previously selected. When **link** is executed the unique identifiers of both objects are included as attribute values of their relational attributes. The reciprocal operation **unlink** is provided.

resume ▷ Concludes the process initiated by the execution of a **relate** command. The relational class becomes the current class, and the relational object the current object.

hibernate ▷ The current state of the database manager is saved as a persistent object. This operation can be used to migrate the state of the database manager among the nodes of the network.

reinstate ▷ The reciprocal of the operation **hibernate**. When a **reinstate** is executed the state of the database manager is set to exactly the same execution state it had when the corresponding **hibernate** was executed.

5.2.3 Standard Interfaces

A database user accesses the database either by issuing queries to the Query Interpreter or by using the visual database interface Object Editor.

Visual Database Interface The Object Editor is logically composed of two interactive interfaces: a main interface where all commands and query results are shown, and a set of application-specific interfaces corresponding to each concrete class of a particular database. An example is the interface for the class `Article`. When a user wants to change attribute values for instances of `Article` all that he has to do is to select this class, using a command available in the main interface, and the `Article` interface will be made available. At this point he can alter the attribute values for any instance of this class, create relations between objects, submit queries, etc.

Query Interpreter The Query Interpreter executes sequences of database operations coded as simple scripts. It is comparable to the command shell of an operating system. This interface is still under development.

5.3 Developing Databases and Application Programs

The development of a database for Stabilis starts with the creation of an object-oriented data model of the database, where all classes and its relationships are represented. Next, the concrete classes defined in the model have to be converted into classes whose instances are database objects. This conversion is achieved by making every root class a specialisation of the class `DatabaseObject`, a class derived from `RobustObject`.

The database manager will have to instantiate objects of the concrete classes. To enable it to instantiate such objects, a class called `DatabaseObjectGenerator`, which is capable of instantiating objects of the concrete classes, has to be programmed. An instance of `DatabaseObjectGenerator` will be used by the database manager.

At this stage the database manager is already prepared to manipulate any instance of the concrete classes of the database model internally. Another problem that has to be solved is how an application program will have access to the database objects. The solution is to create an interface object to convey information between the application program and the database manager. To permit the creation of the interface objects, the class `InterfaceObject` is provided; the same root classes that were made subclasses of `DatabaseObject` have to be made subclasses of `InterfaceObject`. Similarly, an `InterfaceObjectGenerator` class has to be programmed.

The programming steps above can be automated if all the attributes of the database classes are expressed in terms of C++ basic types (integers, strings, etc). In fact, we have implemented a tool called hgen that takes as input a description of an object-oriented data model and generates the corresponding C++ code for: the classes derived from `DatabaseObject`, the classes derived from `InterfaceObject`, the `DatabaseObjectGenerator` and the `InterfaceObjectGenerator`. As a consequence, applications that use Stabilis can be easily programmed since all classes needed to access the database have already been produced. An application has only to instantiate interface objects and operate on them according to its own algorithm. The application program will necessarily call operations of the database manager.

If the two standard interfaces, Object Editor and Query Interpreter are to be used then some extra work has to be done. The Object Editor uses InterViews [12] to implement the visual interfaces for editing database objects. Consequently, adapting the Object Editor requires the programming of a visual interface for each concrete class of the new database. Again, to automate the adaptation process of the Object Editor to different databases we have programmed a tool, denominated ivgen, to generate the C++ code necessary. This tool accepts as input the same description of an object-oriented data model that hgen accepts, generating the InterViews C++ code for the visual interfaces. The compilation and linking of the programs is all that needs to be done to obtain the new Object Editor version. The adaptation of the Query Interpreter is much simpler since there is no extra code that needs to be generated. It is only to compile and link the code produced by hgen to the code of the Query Interpreter.

In most cases, when the two standard interfaces to Stabilis satisfy the needs of the database user, the only real task the database developer faces is the design of an object-oriented database model.

6 Dbib - A Distributed Bibliography Database

This Section explains further, using an example, how databases and applications are developed using Stabilis. Lets suppose someone wants to design and implement a distributed bibliography database (Dbib) based on the types of entries for bibliography citation defined by Lamport in the LaTeX Manual [13]. Lamport's original definition has 14 types of entries, ranging from an entry for storing the bibliographic information about an *article* to an entry for *unpublished notes*. Each entry can have several fields. An article entry, for example, has fields for storing the article's authors, title, etc. Basically, in the object-oriented data model of Dbid (Figure 8) theses entries will be viewed as concrete classes. Later, when using Dbib, the user will be able to call object services to generate the file necessary to create bibliography lists for LaTeX.

The object-oriented data model (Figure 8) defines 18 concrete classes, five root classes and several associations between them. An example of association is found between `Article` and `Journal`; an article is present in one single journal and a journal can contain several articles. This association is implemented by the superclasses `Include` and `Group`.

Since all attributes defined in the data model are either strings or integers, the implementation of Dbib can be fully automated. First, the data model has to be coded using a graph description language. Second, this textual representation obtained is submitted to **hgen**. Figure 9a shows a description of the path

$$P =< Reference, Unit, Include, Article >$$

using the graph description language, which is self-explanatory.

Figures 9a and 9b juxtapose the representation of the path P using the graph description language (Figure 9a) with fragments of the corresponding C++ code generated by **hgen** (Figure 9b). In both Figures the lines are numbered to help explain the code. From now on we will refer to Figures 9a and 9b simply by stating line numbers followed by the the letter that identifies each Figure, e.g., 11b refers to the line 11 of the Figure 9b.

The code of the line 1a means that the root class `Reference` must be a class derived from the class `DatabaseObject` (line 1b).

The attributes defined in lines 3a to 6a generated the lines 3b to 6b and 13b to 16b. Line 5a is an example of the specification of a relational attribute: `libraries`, that is mapped to a variable of the type `SetOfObjects` (line 5b). This type is a set of unique identifiers of database objects used to implement the association relationship defined in the object-oriented data model. The parameters mean that: the class `Reference` is associated with the class `Library`, the corresponding relational attribute is `references` and an instance of the class `Reference` can be associated to several instances of the class `Library`. Line 9b shows the signature of the function that is used to initialise the data structures that keep the relations for the class `Reference`.

The code between the lines 1a to 22a are essential to specify the derivation path of the class `Article`, instructing **hgen** that the class `Article` inherits the attributes and association relationships of these superclasses.

The code in the lines 21a and 22a means that the class `Article` must be derived from the class `Include` and that it is a concrete class. The code of the line 18b implements this specialisation relationship. The fact that `Article` is a concrete class implies that the `DatabaseObjectGenerator` (not shown here) has to provide the code to instantiate objects of the class `Article`.

The functions **get** (lines 14b to 16b) and the function **put_attributes** (lines 23b to 26b, 28b to 42b) are called by an instance of the class `InterfaceObject` to read and write the state of the database object. For example, after modifying an `Article` interface object, the application program invokes the database manager operation **save**, which will then call the function **put_attributes** to update the database object.

The operation **put_attributes** must be atomic since it modifies the state of the database object. In the line 32b an atomic action A is declared. In the line 33b it is started. The attributes of the cache object are modified (lines 34b to 36b). Lines 38b to 40b have the code for making permanent these modifications. Line 38b shows the invocation of the operation **make_permanent** of the superclass `RobustObject`. If **make_permanent** commits then A can be committed otherwise it is aborted. This code guarantees the consistency of the cache object, as already discussed earlier (Section 4.2).

7 Concluding Remarks

This paper has presented Stabilis and described how its architecture has been realised using an object-oriented approach. This approach, already adopted by Arjuna, permits the properties of robust objects to be added to user-defined classes in a very flexible manner. Within this approach, type inheritance has also proved useful to simplify the automatic generation of code. The use of C++ in Arjuna and Stabilis has demonstrated to have both advantages and disadvantages. Since both systems make extensive use of inheritance and encapsulation, these features of the language have been of great use. A disadvantage is that the version of C++ used does not have automatic garbage collection of unreferenced objects.

The development of the Name Server, Object Manager and Index modules as portable applications has been possible since Arjuna encapsulates the essential functions for persistence, recoverability and atomicity in its Atomic Action module.

Although the *object and action* model adopted by Arjuna to structure programs has proved to be very adequate to the development of Stabilis as a whole, the provision of extra ways of structuring atomic actions could greatly improve the concurrency control. For example, the Name Server and Index modules would benefit if nested top-level atomic actions [14], currently being incorporated into Arjuna, were available.

The development of the database manager has been greatly simplified by the abstraction of robust object provided by the Object Manager module, since it exempts the database manager of the direct management of persistence, distribution, concurrency and recovery. Moreover, the use of caching has shown to be useful to the efficiency of Stabilis; the database manager can optimise the use of persistent objects by reducing the frequency of accesses to stable storage.

To evaluate Stabilis we have designed and implemented Dbib. At present, Dbib is installed in five nodes and holds aproximately three hundred bibliographic references. After having carried out several tests, we have realised that some improvements can be made to Stabilis. The query processing can be made more powerful, e.g., queries against a portion of the data model should be accepted. Stabilis should have mechanisms for the representation of aggregation of objects. An authorisation scheme should be implemented to improve security. On the other hand, Stabilis has shown that the development of fault-tolerant distributed databases can be made simple. Also, some of the tests involved forcing nodes to crash; in these situations Stabilis continued to operate consistently.

As far as this case study is concerned, the overall behaviour of Stabilis and Arjuna has been satisfactory; the concurrent use of Dbib has shown that the basic requirements set out initially have been fulfilled. In conclusion, the *object and action* model of computation has demonstrated to be a good framework for writing fault-tolerant distributed applications that use persistent objects.

Acknowledgements

Our thanks are due to Professor Santosh K. Shrivastava and Dr. Stuart M. Wheater for their critical comments on this paper. The Arjuna team also deserves our gratitude; they have been very supportive throughout the development of Stabilis.

References

[1] Shrivastava, S.K., Dixon, G.N., Parrington, G.D. "An Overview of the Arjuna Programming System", IEEE Software, **8**(1):66-73, Jan. 1991.

[2] Shrivastava, S.K. "Robust Distributed Programs" In Resilient Computing Systems, T. Anderson (editor), Collins, London, 1985, ch. 6, pp. 102-121.

[3] Weihl, W.E. "Using Transactions in Distributed Applications" In Distributed Systems, S. Mullender (editor), ACM Press, New York, 1989, ch. 11, pp. 215-235.

[4] Stroustrup, B. "The C++ Programming Language", Addison Wesley, Reading, Massachusetts, 1986.

[5] Shrivastava, S.K. and Wheater, S.M. "Implementing Fault-Tolerant Distributed Applications Using Objects and Multi-Coloured Actions", Proceedings of the Tenth International Conference on Distributed Computing Systems, Paris, France, May 1990, pp. 203-210.

[6] Parrington, G.D. "Reliable Distributed Programming in C++ : The Arjuna Approach", Second Usenix C++ Conference, San Francisco, USA, Apr. 1990, pp. 37-50.

[7] McCue, D.L. and Shrivastava, S.K. "Structuring Persistent Object-Oriented Systems for Portability in a Distributed Environment", Fourth ACM SIGOPT Workshop, Bologna, Italy, Sep. 1990.

[8] Mullender, S. "Introduction to Distributed Systems" In Distributed Systems, S. Mullender (editor), ACM Press, New York, 1989, pp. 3-18.

[9] Wu, C. T. "Benefits of Object-Oriented Programming in Implementing Visual Database Interfaces", Journal of Object-Oriented Programming, **2**(6):8-16, Mar./Apr. 1990.

[10] Rumbaugh, J., Blaha, M., Premerlani, W., Eddy, F. and Lorensen, W. "Object-Oriented Modeling and Design", Prentice-Hall, Englewood Cliffs, New Jersey, 1991.

[11] Kim, W. "Architectural Issues in Object-Oriented Databases", Journal of Object-Oriented Programming, **2**(6):29-38, Mar./Apr. 1990.

[12] Linton, M.A., Vlissides, J.M. and Calder, P.R. "Composing User Interfaces with InterViews", IEEE Computer, **22**(2):8-22, Feb. 1989.

[13] Lamport, L. "The Bibliography Database" In "LaTeX: User's Guide and Reference Manual", Addison Wesley, Reading, Massachusetts, 1986, pp. 140-147.

[14] Wheater, S. M. "Constructing Reliable Distributed Applications Using Actions and Objects", PhD thesis, The University, Computing Science Department, Newcastle upon Tyne, Jun. 1990 (Technical Report no. 316).

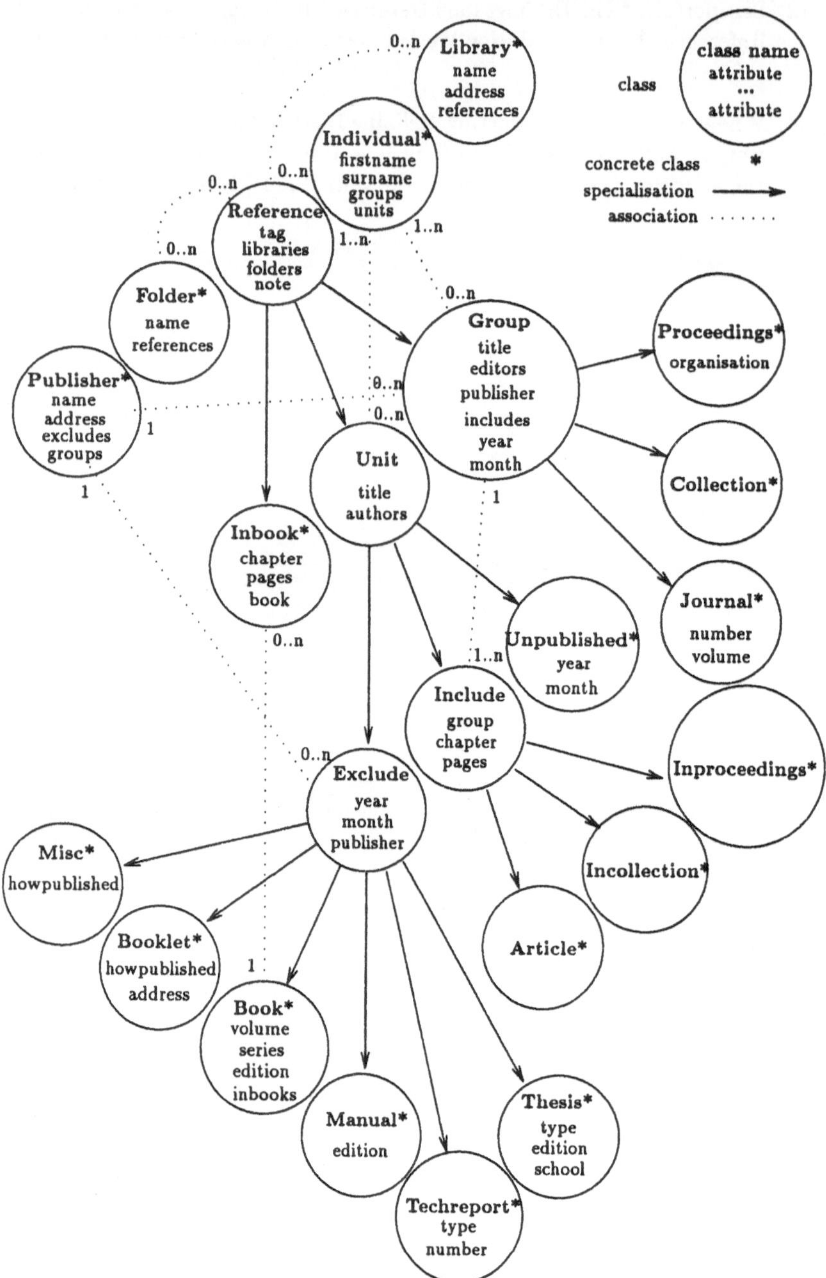

Figure 8: An object-oriented model for Dbib.

```
root class   Reference;
begin attributes
      tag:      SearchKey;
      note:     String;
      libraries: Relational
    (Library, references, 0, -1);
      folders:  Relational
    (Folder, references, 0, -1);
end attributes;

class   Unit;
parent   Reference;
begin attributes
      title:     String;
      authors: Relational
    (Individual, units, 1, -1);
end attributes;

class   Include;
parent   Unit;
begin attributes
      group:   Relational
    (Group, include, 1, 1);
      pages:   String;
      chapter: String;
end attributes;

concrete class   Article;
parent   Include;
begin attributes
end attributes;
```

(a)

```
class   Reference: public   DatabaseObject
{ protected:
    String tag;
    String note;
    SetOfObjects libraries("Library", "references", 0, -1);
    SetOfObjects folders("Folder", "references", 0, -1);
    virtual   bool restore_state(ObjectState&);
    virtual   bool save_state(ObjectState&);
    virtual   void relations(RelationTable&);
  public:
    Reference();
    ~Reference();
    virtual   String get_SearchKey();
    String get_tag();
    SetOfObjects get_libraries();
    SetOfObjects get_folders();
};
    ...
class   Article:   public   Include
{ public:
    Article(Uid&, bool&);  // constructor for creation
    Article(Uid, Lockmode, bool&);   // for access
    ~Article();
    bool put_attributes(String new_tag, ...
                  SetOfObjects new_libraries, ...
                  String new_title, ...
                  String new_chapter);
};  ...

bool Article::put_attributes(String new_tag, ...
              SetOfObjects new_libraries, ...
              String new_title, ...
              String new_chapter)
{ AtomicAction A;
  A.Begin();
     tag = new_tag; ...  libraries = new_libraries;...
     title = new_title; ...
     chapter = new_chapter;
  bool result = FALSE;
  if    (make_permanent() == COMMITTED)
       result = (A.End() == COMMITTED);
  else A.Abort();
  return result;
}  ...
```

(b)

Figure 9: (a) Path P coded in the graph description language. (b) C++ code for path P.

Persistent Program Construction through Browsing and User Gesture with some Typing

Alex Farkas, Alan Dearle

Department of Computer Science, University of Adelaide
Adelaide, Australia

Graham Kirby, Quintin Cutts, Ron Morrison, Richard Connor

Department of Mathematical and Computational Sciences, University of St. Andrews
St. Andrews, Scotland

Abstract

One method of evaluating programs is for them to be prepared as self contained pieces of source, then compiled, linked and executed. The last phase may involve binding to and manipulating persistent values. When the persistent store is supported by a user interface, the program construction can be augmented by the use of tokens as denotations for persistent values. That is, the manipulation of the persistent store by gesture, for example by an iconic interface linked to a mouse, can be used to provide tokens for persistent values. These tokens can be resolved to provide bindings at run-time, compile-time, program construction time or any mixture of these.

In this paper the main styles of token resolution are described in terms of their influence on the persistent program evaluation. This is done in tandem with a description of an example user interface required to support these new styles of persistent programming. We note that other modern user interfaces, such as OpenLook and the Macintosh Programming Environment also allow the manipulation of files by user programs and by gesture. The difference here is that the technique is uniform and that the persistent store is strongly typed with a greater variety of types.

Two prototype versions of these facilities have been implemented for the language Napier88.

1 Introduction

Most modern applications systems make use of an iconic interface linked to a mouse controller. This allows many operations on data to be described by user gesture rather than by the typing of a textual command. The advantages of this style of interface are well understood and documented.

One area this style of interaction has not generally pervaded is the activity of software construction. Some limited user gesture interaction may be possible, but in general programs consist of a flat textual representation of code. Mostly this code is typed by a programmer, although some systems provide support for a limited amount of automatic code production according to a programmer's description at a higher level of abstraction.

The advantages of user gesture can, however, be incorporated into the construction process for programs which make use of persistent data. Such programs normally contain textual code which describes an access path to data within the persistent store. As an alternative it may be envisaged that, rather than writing the textual form of this code, a programmer may be provided with iconic tools which allow the browsing of the persistent store, and then a particular value within the store may be indicated by some mouse gesture. This method of interaction is the topic of this paper.

The essence of the method is to include a persistent store browser, along with the notion of a token, as a part of the program construction environment. A value of interest encountered during browsing may be denoted or "tagged" by the use of a token. This token may then be used to construct a reference to the value it denotes.

The methodology of programming with tagged values is described in a practical manner, by the description of a program construction environment. The purpose of this is to make clear the potential use of such a mechanism in a practical context. Two prototype versions of such a program construction environment [1,4] have been constructed for the language Napier88 [6].

Three different schemes are described in this paper, the difference between them being the time at which persistent data is bound into the program being constructed. None of these schemes is intended to be used in isolation; indeed it is envisaged that a judicious mixture of the three different binding times will be of use in a complex application.

In the first scheme, programs contain code to locate data and the data is dynamically bound during the execution of the program in the normal fashion. In this scheme, the browser provides an interface to the programmer through which the data to be bound may be located. This in turn enables the programmer to construct an appropriate computation to locate the data.

The second scheme allows values from the persistent store to be bound during compilation, rather than execution. To achieve this the compiler must also be included in the execution environment. The meaning of a token within a program is not resolved by expansion into high-level code; instead when the program is compiled the value denoted by the token is resolved by the compiler and bound directly into the executable code. The meaning of a program in this system is dependent upon the environment in which it is compiled, and is no longer self-contained.

The last scheme is known as hyper-programming. Hyper-programs are constructed in a similar way to the other schemes described. Rather than the tokens being resolved by the compiler, however, the user may indicate that the tagged value itself should be included directly within the high-level program code. This requires a relatively sophisticated program editing tool, as programs may no longer be represented as flat textual structures. It may thus be seen that hyper-programs bear a similar relation to normal programs as hyper-text does to normal text.

Section 2 introduces an example Napier88 program which will be used throughout the rest of the description. Sections 3,4 and 5 describe the use of the three different binding styles to construct the example, and Sections 6 and 7 conclude with the possibilities of future research in this area.

2 An example

2.1 An example persistent store

A Napier88 persistent store consists of a graph of values connected by pointers and may be accessed from a single point known as the *persistent root*. The root of a persistent store may be accessed by executing the predefined Napier88 function *PS*, which returns a dynamically extensible collection of bindings known as an *environment* [2]. An important property of environments is that they enable the programmer to make bindings to typed locations as well as values.

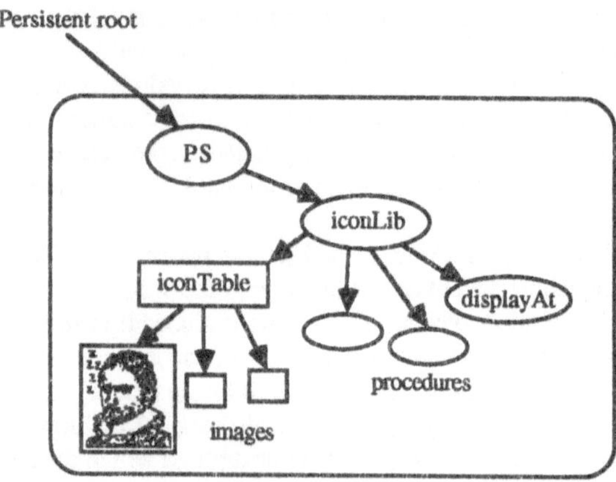

Figure 1: Conceptual view of a simple icon management system.

To illustrate the use of a persistent store, consider as an example a simple icon management facility structured as follows. In the root environment of the persistent store another environment called *iconLib* containing a table of icons, *iconTable*, and a number of procedures has been constructed. These procedures operate on icons which are of type **image**, a Napier88 data type which consists of a rectangular array of pixels. The *iconTable* consists of a table of icons indexed by a unique name in the form of a string. The structure of this store is shown in Figure 1.

In order to manipulate values in a persistent store, a Napier88 program must first bind to those values. In order for binding to occur, the value or values being bound must be located and type checking must take place to ensure that they have the type expected by the program. In the programming environment described in this paper, binding may take place at three different times during a program's life cycle:

- during program execution: the program binds to values at run-time,
- during compilation: binding takes place as the source code for a program is compiled, and
- during program construction: binding occurs as the source code for the program is constructed.

The sections which follow describe in more detail the manner in which each style of binding may be achieved in a persistent programming environment. First we describe an application that will be used as an example throughout the paper.

2.2 An example application

To demonstrate the different programming paradigms, the following application will be used as an example. A procedure called *wallPaper* shall be constructed which behaves as follows: when invoked, the procedure displays the icon associated with the name "John Napier" in the *iconTable*. The procedure displays the icon a number of times so that it "wallpapers", i.e. completely covers, the screen. In order to achieve this, the procedure makes use of a procedure known as *displayAt*, an application which causes an image to be displayed at a single location on the screen. The *wallPaper* procedure always accesses the most recent version of the *displayAt* procedure. It always uses the same icon to wallpaper the screen. Figure 2 shows the structure of the store as it would appear after the *wallPaper* application described above has been constructed. The double ellipse surrounding the *displayAt* procedure indicates that the *wallPaper* procedure contains a binding to a location containing the *displayAt* procedure. This enables the *wallPaper* application to make use of the most recent version of *displayAt* contained in that location.

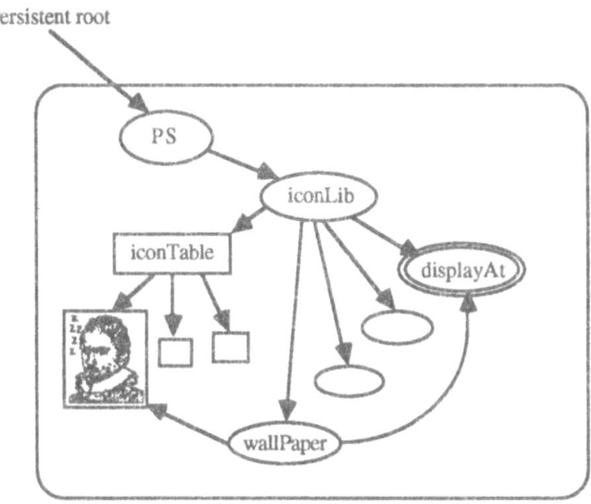

Figure 2: Conceptual view of the completed *wallPaper* application.

The following sections describe the way in which each of the various programming environment features may be used to implement the *wallPaper* application described above. For brevity, each section only describes the use of either run-time, compile-time or composition-time context in constructing the application, although in general, any combination of these programming styles may be used to construct a single application.

3 Run-time context

3.1 Programming using run-time binding

The first style of programming which shall be described is that in which a program binds to values at run-time. Programs which bind in this fashion must perform a computation which traverses the store to locate the values to be bound. Upon discovering the values in the store, type checking must take place to ensure that the discovered values are of the correct type. This requires the specification of the types in the program to be checked against the types of the values found in the persistent store. For example, in the case of the *wallPaper* application, a computation must be performed to locate the required icon and the *displayAt* procedure.

The programmer is able to construct source code by making use of a text editor known as an interaction window. This editor provides simple text editing features and allows existing source code to be stored or recalled. For example, the application described earlier to "wallpaper" an icon over the screen may be written as shown in the interaction window in Figure 3. The programmer is able to compile and execute this code by selecting the *exec* button.

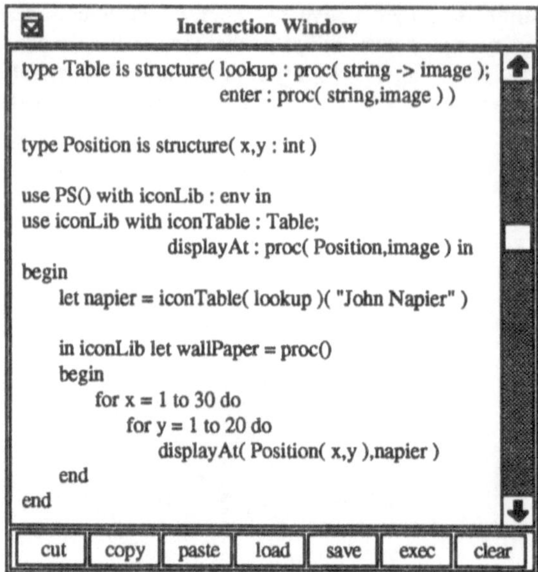

Figure 3: A window containing an expression to wallpaper an icon.

The first three lines of the program declare types; the first two lines define a record type called *Table*. This type contains two fields: *lookup* and *enter*, both of which are procedures. The second type, *Position*, which is a record type, is used to represent a point on the Cartesian plane. Following these declarations are two **use** clauses, which define the names and types of locations expected to be found in the persistent store at run-time. The block following the **use** clauses is statically type checked with respect to these **use** clauses. A once only check is required at run time to ensure that the values found in the store conform to the types specified in the **use** clauses. The bindings to the persistent store that are created when the **use** clauses are executed are bindings to locations. Next, the program declares an identifier called *napier* which is bound to the result of executing the *lookup* procedure from the *Table* structure in the store. The last declaration in the block declares a procedure called *wallPaper*. This declaration is made in the environment denoted by *iconLib* rather than the current scope. The procedure calls the procedure *displayAt* which has been found in the store with a *Position* record and an icon of John Napier as parameters.

The behaviour of the *wallPaper* procedure is such that whenever the procedure is invoked, the most recent version of the *displayAt* procedure is used to display the icon originally assigned to the identifier *napier*. This is due to the fact that the program binds to the location in the persistent store which contains the *displayAt* procedure but binds to the actual value of the image retrieved from the *iconTable*.

A program such as the one described above contains in the source code all of the information necessary to locate values and perform type checking. The process of compilation performs as much type checking as possible. However, correct execution relies on the expected values being present in the store and having the same type as specified by the program.

3.2 Inspecting values

One of the difficulties in constructing programs which bind to values at run-time is that the location and/or types of values in a persistent store may be unknown. For example, a programmer may be aware that a persistent store contains an icon library but may not know how to construct a computation which locates it. To assist the programmer, a tool known as a persistent store browser [3] may be used to inspect the contents of a persistent store in order to discover the location and types of the values in it.

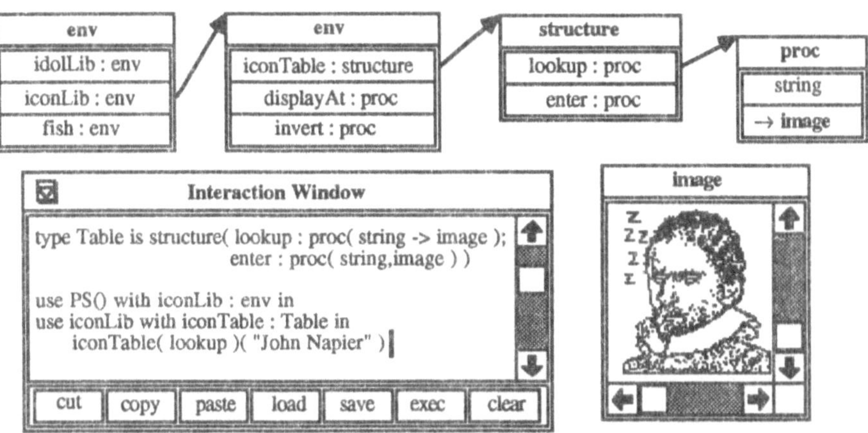

Figure 4: Finding values in a persistent store.

In the context of the icon manager example, the programmer may be unaware of the appearance of the icons in the icon table and may not know which icon manipulation procedures are available. A browsing tool may be used to discover the location and types of this data by traversing the store as shown in Figure 4. The browser allows the topology and content of the persistent store to be discovered, thus enabling the programmer to find the information necessary to construct the required program.

The browsing session shown in Figure 4 commences with the traversal of the persistent root displayed on the left hand side of the diagram. The user has selected the field labelled *iconLib* with the mouse resulting in the *iconLib* environment being displayed on the screen. Next, the field labelled *iconTable* was selected causing the table *iconTable* to be displayed. Similarly, the field representing the *lookup* procedure has been selected resulting in a representation of the procedure being displayed on the screen.

We will assume that the programmer knows the names of the icons in the *iconTable*. However, the icons in that table are encapsulated within the closure of the procedures *lookup* and *enter*. In order to examine one of these icons the *lookup* procedure from the table must be invoked with the name of the required icon as a parameter; in general, this requires a program to be written. This may be achieved by entering and executing a small program such as the one shown in the interaction window in Figure 4.

The programmer is required to enter code describing how the values used by the program are located. This is achieved with **use** clauses as described earlier. The result of executing the program is the icon associated with the name "John Napier" and is displayed by the browser as shown on the right hand side of the diagram. The result is displayed because in addition to viewing the contents of the store, the browser may be used to display values returned by expressions entered in an interaction window. In fact the content of the interaction window is treated as a single Napier88 expression which may or may not yield a result upon execution – if an expression yields a result, the result is passed to the browser to be displayed. Having discovered the icons and applications in the persistent store, the programmer is now able to construct a program such as the one shown earlier in Figure 3 which wallpapers the icon onto the screen.

The browser allows the topology of the store to be discovered and allows the programmer to discover information about the location and types of values in the persistent store. However, sometimes in order to manipulate the values and types encountered by the browser a program must be constructed. The code which must be written in order to perform the necessary computation becomes more verbose as the number of values to be bound and the complexity of the path from the root to those values increases.

3.3 Tagging browsed values

The browser supports a mechanism known as "tagging". This mechanism allows the programmer to select a value or location encountered by the browser and to associate a token, or tag, with that value or location. The effect of tagging a value or location is to create a mapping from the tag name to the value or location. Hence tagging represents a way in which tokens may be declared as denoting values or locations.

In order to tag a value, the programmer selects the title bar of the window representing that value with the mouse. This causes a dialogue box to be displayed prompting the user for a string to use as the name for the value. The user may enter any string provided it constitutes a valid Napier88 identifier and this string is displayed on the top left hand corner of the tagged value.

The method for tagging an environment location containing a value is similar to the method used for tagging a value but differs in two distinct ways. The first difference is that instead of selecting the title bar of the value, the programmer must select an environment entry containing the value. The second difference is that when a token has been supplied for the location, it is displayed on the top left hand corner of the value inside a box with a double line border.

In addition to values, the browser also allows types to be traversed. The tagging mechanism may also be used to tag the types encountered by the browser and is the same as the method used to tag values. However, in this case the tag is used to denote a type; in Napier88 there is never any ambiguity over the meaning of this since types are not values.

3.4 Using tags to effect run-time binding

One way to reduce the amount of programmer effort required to produce source code for programs which bind at run-time is to use the browser's tagging mechanism. For example, the two **use** clauses in Figure 4 may be automatically generated using the tagging mechanism as shown in Figure 5.

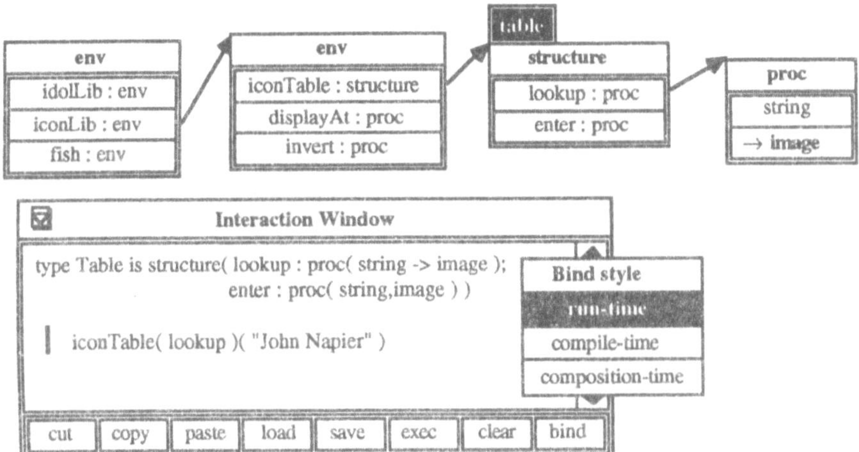

Figure 5: Tagging a value encountered by the browser.

Firstly, the programmer has tagged the environment location containing *iconTable* with the name *table*. This is indicated by the double line border surrounding the tag. Next, the programmer has selected the tag using the mouse and has pressed the *bind* button in the interaction window. This has caused the menu entitled *Bind style* to be displayed. At this point, the programmer is required to select which of the three styles of binding the tag is to be resolved into. In this example, selecting the field labelled *run-time* in the *Bind style* menu will cause the two **use** clauses shown earlier to be inserted into the source text at the text cursor's position.

In addition to constructing computations to locate values or locations in the store, the tagging mechanism may be used to construct a textual form for types encountered by the browser. A textual representation of a type may be inserted into source text using the same method as the method for inserting a computation to locate a value or location.

3.5 Reusing programs which bind at run-time

Programs which bind at run-time consist entirely of a textual source code representation. The text editing features provided by the interaction window permit sections of source code to manipulated using facilities such as *cut*, *copy* and *paste*. As with traditional systems, portions of existing code may be reused.

In addition to source code, values placed in the persistent store by one program may be used by other programs which bind to those values during execution. For example, the *wallPaper* procedure makes use of the *displayAt* procedure defined in another source code segment. Programs which bind at run-time provide the most flexibility in binding to persistent values as they do not require the values to be present at the time the program is compiled or constructed.

4 Compile-time context

4.1 Programming using compile-time binding

Programs that bind to values at compile-time may be constructed in a similar fashion to programs which bind at run-time: the source code for the program may be entered and manipulated through the interaction window text editor. However, the nature of the source code is different in that source code contains direct references to values in the form of tokens, which are to be resolved at compile-time. When such a program is compiled, the source code of the program is passed to the compiler along with a mapping from tokens to values. The compiler resolves the bindings so that the executable code produced contains references to values and locations. This reduces the verbosity of source code and ensures that referenced values are present at the time the source code is compiled rather than during program execution.

In the programming environment described in this paper there are two kinds of token which may appear in the source code of a program: tokens denoting values or locations and tokens denoting types.

4.1.1 Tokens denoting values or locations

As shown earlier, there is a tendency for the code which must be written in order to locate values to become verbose. Programs which bind to values or locations at compile-time reduce this verbosity by allowing direct references to values in the form of identifiers, or tokens. The mapping from tokens to values and locations generated through tagging is passed to the compiler each time a program is compiled, enabling the compiler to resolve these references.

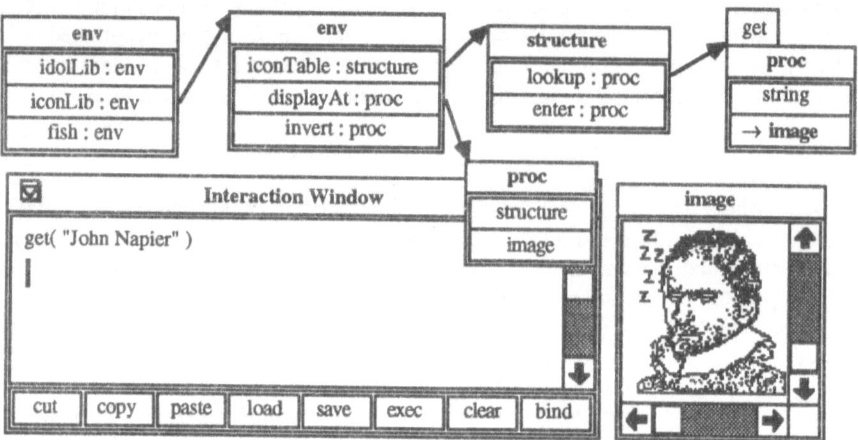

Figure 6: A session showing the application of a tagged procedure.

The programmer may create tokens using the tagging mechanism described earlier. In this case, however, the programmer must select the *compile-time* entry of the *Bind style* menu in order insert a compile-time reference to the value into the source text. The resulting reference is simply the name of the tag in the form of an identifier. To illustrate this mechanism, consider the programming environment session in Figure 6 showing a tag on the *lookup* procedure of the icon table *iconTable*. The procedure has been tagged with the name *get* indicating that the token *get* has been declared as a denotation for the procedure.

The programmer may now invoke the *lookup* procedure of the *iconTable* with the string "John Napier" as a parameter as shown in the interaction window of Figure 6. The expression binds to the *lookup* procedure at compile-time through the reference to the token *get*. The binding takes place when the programmer selects the *exec* button, which causes the expression to be compiled and executed. The icon returned by the expression is passed to the browser and displayed as shown on the right hand side of Figure 6.

The second method of tagging allows an environment location containing a value to be tagged. Using a combination of the two tagging methods, the programmer is able to construct the *wallPaper* procedure described in Section 2. This may be achieved by tagging the necessary values and locations and constructing the source code for the procedure as shown in the interaction window in Figure 7.

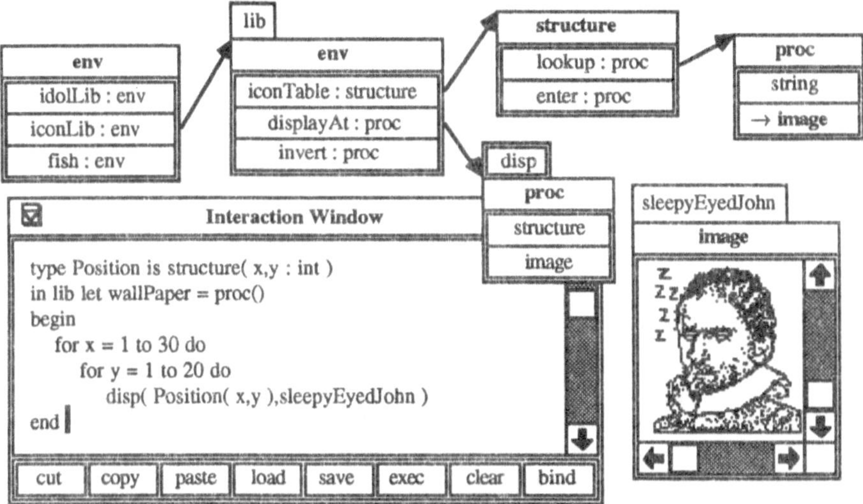

Figure 7: Constructing the *wallPaper* procedure using compile-time binding.

The procedure *displayAt* has been tagged with the name *disp* in a box with double line borders, indicating that the binding is to the location containing the *displayAt* procedure rather than its value. Next, the environment *iconLib* and the icon returned by the expression in Figure 6 have been tagged with the names *lib* and *sleepyEyedJohn* respectively. The plain boxes indicate that these tokens represent bindings to actual values rather than locations containing values. Lastly, the code entered in the interaction window declares the type *Position* and the procedure *wallPaper*. The program places the *wallPaper* procedure in the *iconLib* environment by declaring the procedure in the environment denoted by the token *lib*.

4.1.2 Tagging types

In the above example the program must declare the type *Position* because it is used to construct a value supplied as a parameter to the procedure *disp*. However, as the complexity and number of type declarations required by a program increases, the source code once again becomes verbose. Furthermore, an increasing proportion of the time taken by a programmer to construct a program is spent entering these type declarations.

By tagging the appropriate type and inserting a compile-time binding to that type, the code shown in Figure 7 may be rewritten as shown in Figure 8.

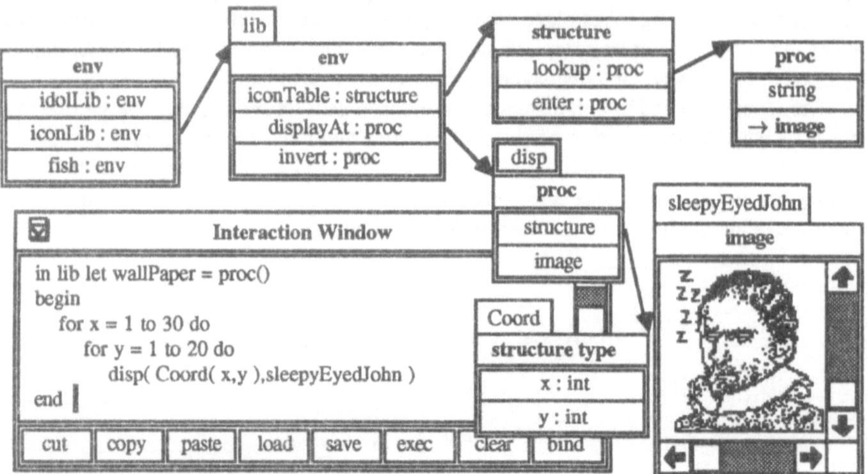

Figure 8: Using a tagged type in a program.

The programmer has selected the first entry of the *displayAt* procedure and this has caused the type of the first formal parameter of the procedure to be displayed. This type has been tagged with the name *Coord* and a compile-time reference to the type has been inserted in the source code in place of the first actual parameter supplied to the *disp* procedure. The declaration of the type *Position* has been omitted.

Thus, using compile-time references to tagged types, the verbosity of the code may be further reduced. Moreover, the process of compilation becomes more efficient since the need to recompile type declarations is reduced, or sometimes removed.

4.1.3 Tokens denoting types

An instance of a required type may not currently exist in the persistent store. Therefore some alternative method for creating tokens that represent types is required. The Napier88 programming environment supports a structure known as a type environment: a mapping from names to types which may be passed to the compiler to permit the use of types that have not been declared in the source program. This is achieved by the compiler resolving references to types contained in the type environment and used, but not declared, in the source program. The compiler is also used to create type environments, a string containing type declarations is passed to the compiler and a type environment is returned. This presents an alternative means by which tokens denoting types may be created and stored.

In the programming environment described in this paper, the following interface is provided to ease the creation of type environments. Types may be declared in a separate window known as the types window; this window is similar to the interaction window in that it consists of a text editor. However, rather than allowing arbitrary Napier88 programs to be entered, the types window only permits the declaration of types. Figure 9 shows the appearance of the type window when the types *Table* and *Position* are declared.

When the programmer presses the *comp* button, the text in the types window is compiled and a type environment is created. This type environment is implicitly part of the compilation environment of the interaction windows provided by the user interface. Therefore once a type environment is created, the programs do not need to declare the types being used. In this example this means that the types *Table* and *Position* may be used without declaring them in the source code.

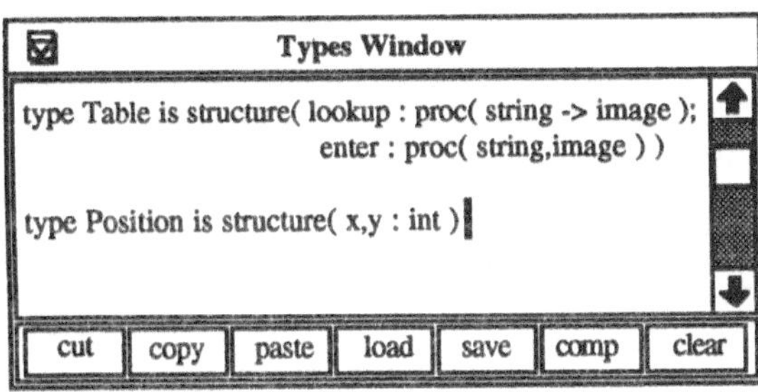

Figure 9: Declaring types in the type window.

In the example shown in this paper, we make two assumptions for simplicity, they are:

1. there is only one type environment in existence, and
2. the type environment implicitly forms part of the compilation context for interaction windows.

In practice, a programmer needs to use many different type environments – each tailored to the task in hand. Therefore the system needs to permit more than one type environment to exist and provide some mechanism to associate an arbitrary collection of type environments with an interaction window.

In addition to removing the need to recompile type declarations, type environments provide a means by which different programs may share type declarations as well as reducing the verbosity of programs which use a large number of types.

4.2 Editing compile-time context programs

The programmer is able to manipulate the source text of a program which binds at compile-time in the same ways as described in the previous section. However, by changing the mapping from tokens to values or types, the programmer is able to construct different applications using the same source text. For example, the programmer may bind the token *sleepyEyedJohn* shown in Figure 7 to a different icon in order to change the semantics of the application without having to alter the source text. More generally, the same source code may be used with different token mappings in order to produce a sequence of applications which vary depending on the values to which they are bound at compile-time. In this way, the nature of programs written using compile-time binding changes in comparison to programs which use only run-time binding.

5 Composition-time context

Binding to values at program composition-time is supported by *hyper-programming* [5]. A hyper-program is a source code representation that contains embedded bindings. This section outlines the main differences between this style of programming and the style described in the previous section.

5.1 Hyper-program source representations

In a hyper-program, the bindings embedded in a hyper-program are an integral part of the program. This contrasts with the compilation-time binding style where the source program and the mapping from tokens to values are distinct entities that are presented to the compiler separately. The physical realisation of that mapping depends on the interface provided to the programmer: with the tagging mechanism described earlier, the mapping is implicit in the tags that are present at the time of compilation. As described earlier, the source code of programs which make use of compile-time binding may be compiled with different mappings (by tagging different values) to give different executable programs. In a hyper-program, however, the bindings from tokens to values do not need to be resolved by the compiler as the resolution takes place earlier, at the time the program is constructed.

To provide flexibility, a hyper-programming system should support all three styles of binding and allow the programmer to choose the appropriate style for each application component. This would allow a source program to contain tokens that are already bound to values, tokens that will be matched with values at compilation-time, and expressions that will be evaluated to give values at run-time. As previously described, for brevity the example in the next section shows only composition-time binding.

5.2 Constructing hyper-programs

5.2.1 Method of construction

A hyper-program is constructed in a similar way to the construction of programs that contain compilation-time bindings. The programmer types textual code into an interaction window and uses browsing tools to navigate the persistent store to locate values to be bound into the program. The difference is in how the binding is effected; with compilation-time binding the programmer attaches a tag or token name to each value required and enters the corresponding token name at the appropriate point in the source text. The tokens in the code and the tokens attached to the value representations are matched by the compiler. To achieve composition-time binding, the programmer first tags the desired value and then selects the ***composition-time*** entry of the ***Bind style*** menu described earlier to bind that value into the program. The system inserts a button into the text to act as a place-holder and to allow the programmer to later examine the bound value. When that button is pressed subsequently, a representation of the value is displayed by the browsing tool.

The system allows the programmer to insert bindings to values themselves or to environment locations. As described earlier, the way in which a tag is effected will determine whether a binding is to a location or value.

It is also possible to bind a type into a program using the same method as the method for binding values into a program. This may also be achieved by selecting a type in the type environment window and pressing the *bind type* button. This mechanism reduces the number of type definitions that the programmer has to enter. As with values, a bound type can be examined by pressing the associated button

5.2.2 *An example*

This section illustrates how the *wallPaper* application described earlier may be constructed in a hyper-programming system. The first step is, as before, to tag the procedure that performs a look-up on the icon table and to execute some code to invoke the procedure in order to obtain the icon for John Napier. This process was illustrated earlier in Figure 6 of Section 4. Next, the programmer enters the textual part of the application, leaving gaps where values are to be bound into the code as shown in Figure 10. Note that the source code of the expression contained in the interaction window represents the declaration of a procedure – hence the result of evaluating the expression is the value of the procedure itself and not the execution of the body of the procedure.

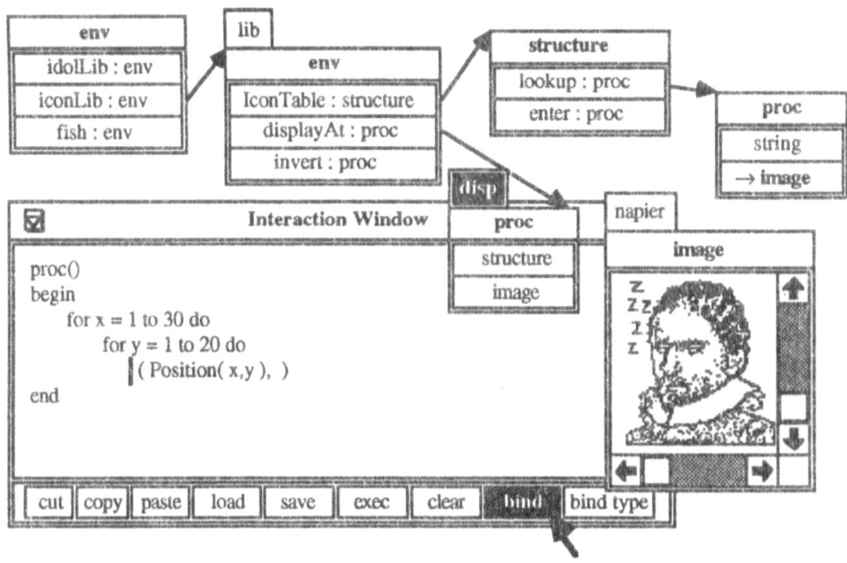

Figure 10: Binding a location into source code.

To bind the location of the *displayAt* procedure into the hyper-program the programmer uses the browsing tool to locate and tag a representation of the location and then presses the *bind* button in the interaction window. When the *Bind style* menu is displayed, the programmer selects the *composition-time* entry in order to insert a binding at the current text position. This is illustrated in Figure 10.

This inserts a button into the text to denote the binding to the selected environment location. The name displayed in the light button is the name of the tag. However, although a name for the button is not essential, we are accustomed to names in our programs so this probably makes the program easier to read.

A similar procedure is followed to bind the icon into the hyper-program but this time the programmer must tag the value of the icon in order to bind to the icon itself rather than its location. Note that in this case there is no corresponding environment location which may be bound to. The appearance of the interaction window at this stage is shown in Figure 11.

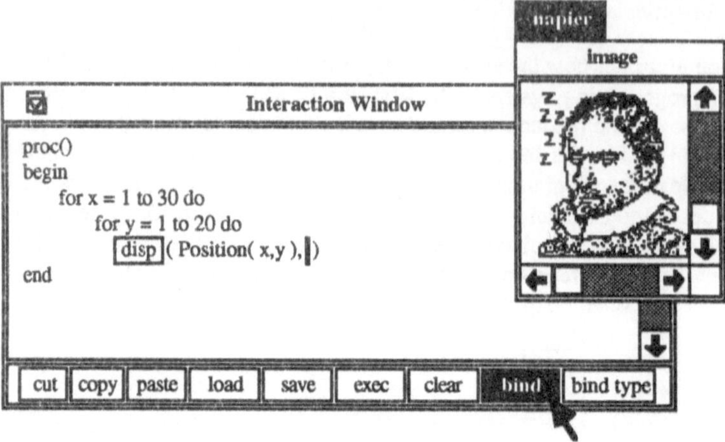

Figure 11: A light button in the source text indicating a binding to the location of the *displayAt* procedure.

The completed program is shown in Figure 12. To execute the program the programmer presses the *exec* button which will cause a representation of the resulting procedure to be displayed.

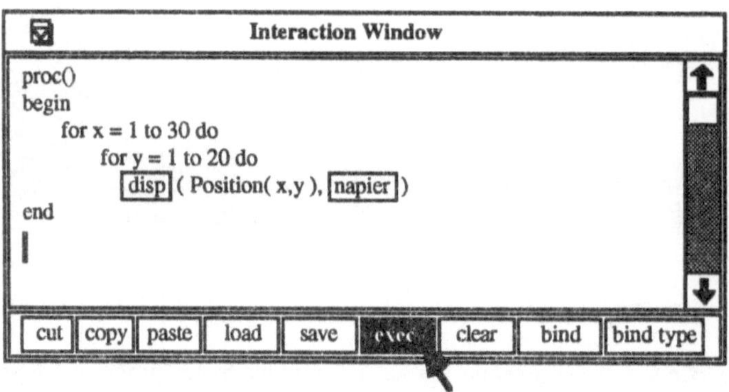

Figure 12: A complete hyper-program.

To make the procedure persist the programmer creates a binding to it in the environment *iconLib*. For example, one way to achieve this is by tagging the representations of the environment and the new procedure and executing some code to create the binding as shown in Figure 13.

The new application is now complete and may be accessed from the environment *iconLib*. In order to prevent the icon from being removed or corrupted by the actions of other programs, the value of the icon is bound into the application. Assignments to the environment location containing the *displayAt* procedure, however, will affect the *wallPaper* application: it will always use the procedure assigned to that location at the time the application is executed. The application's access to the *displayAt* procedure does not depend on the path that the programmer initially followed through the store when binding it into the hyper-program. For example, the binding to *displayAt* may be dropped from the *iconLib* environment without affecting the application or the hyper-program that represents it.

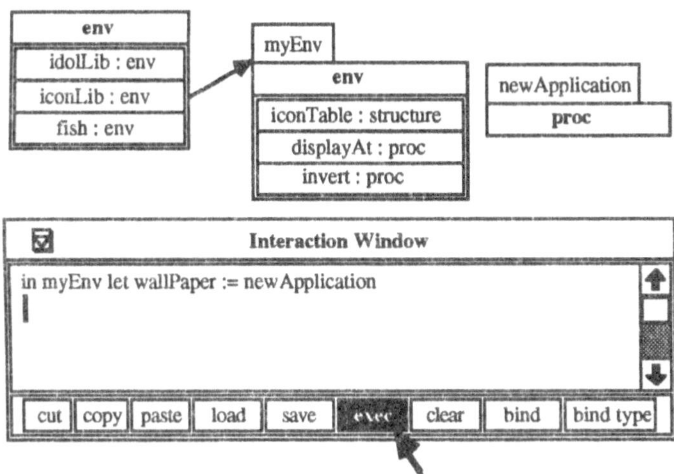

Figure 13: Placing the *wallPaper* application into the icon library.

5.3 Editing hyper-programs

The programmer can later refine the implementation of the application whilst leaving the bindings to its components intact. For example, the **for** loops may be changed so that the icon is drawn only around the edge of the screen rather than over the whole screen. To achieve this, the programmer selects the representation of the procedure and directs the system to supply its source code. This results in the display of a new interaction window containing a copy of the original hyper-program. Although a copy, it contains bindings to the same values and locations as the original source code. The programmer then edits the text of the new hyper-program and presses the *exec* button. If compilation is successful the representation of a new procedure is displayed by the browser.

This new procedure has different behaviour from the original application but contains the same bindings. Finally the programmer tags the new procedure and the location *wallPaper* in *iconLib* and executes some code to assign the procedure to the location as shown in Figure 14.

The technique of refining implementation whilst retaining state may be used in other cases. For example the programmer may discover that there is a bug in the implementation of the procedures that operate over the table of icons. By editing copies of the hyper-program source the programmer may correct the error and install a new version without losing the existing contents of the table. More generally, this provides a mechanism for repairing abstract data types without throwing away their state.

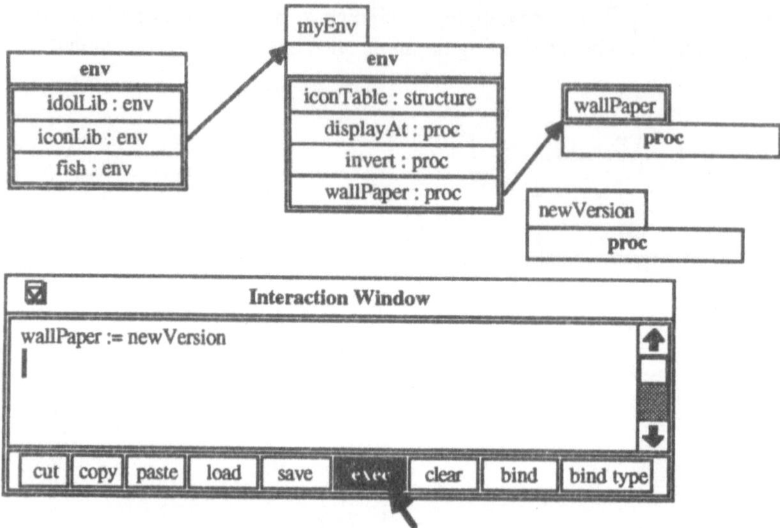

Figure 14: Updating the value in the location of the *wallPaper* procedure.

6 Current status and future work

To date two experimental systems [1,4] have been constructed to allow the exploration of the ideas described in this paper. Both the prototypes support the compile-time binding paradigm described in the paper. In addition, a system which permits composition-time binding has been constructed at the University of St. Andrews. Our plans for the future involve integrating the best features of these prototypes and we expect these facilities to manifest themselves in future releases of the Napier88 programming environment. A final field of research which remains untapped is the program development environment required to support this new kind of programming. This will be the subject of future research.

7 Conclusions

In this paper we have described a mechanism for program construction and manipulation using gesture. Such a paradigm differs greatly from conventional programs which consist of denotations which describe an algorithm and some values which may be constructed at run-time. The mechanisms described in this paper permit this conventional style of programming but augment it with the ability to describe values which exist at compilation- or construction-time. The new programming style allows programs to be constructed which are shorter than those previously expressible using persistent languages like Napier88. This brevity is not achieved without cost, the programs are more tightly bound than other Napier88 programs. We do not imagine that such a mechanism will be appropriate for all programming tasks. Instead, we assert that the new style of programming which emerges from this ability will augment techniques already at the disposal of the programmer.

Acknowledgments

This work is supported in part by ESPRIT III Basic Research Action 6309 – FIDE2, and SERC grant GR/F 02953. Richard Connor is supported by SERC Post Doctoral Fellowship B/91/RFH/9078.

We would also like to thank the Defence Science and Technology Organisation of Australia for their assistance through the PIPE project, The University of Adelaide through its University Grants Scheme and the Australian Research Council.

References

1. Kirby, G.N.C., Connor, R.C.H., Cutts, Q.I., Dearle, A. and Morrison, R., "Programmer's Guide to the Napier88 Standard Library (Edition 2)", Reference Manual, 1991, University of St. Andrews.

2. Dearle, A., "Environments: A Flexible Binding Mechanism to Support System Evolution", in Proceedings of the 22nd Hawaii International Conference on System Sciences, 1989.

3. Dearle, A. and Brown, A.L., "Safe Browsing in a Strongly Typed Persistent Environment", The Computer Journal, 1988. Vol. 31, No. 6: pp. 540-545.

4. Farkas, A.M., "ABERDEEN: A Browser allowing intERactive DEclarations and Expressions in Napier88", Honours Report, 1991, University of Adelaide.

5. Kirby, G.N.C., Connor, R.C.H., Cutts, Q.I., Dearle, A., Farkas, A.M. and Morrison, R., "Persistent Hyper-Programs", in Proceedings of the Fifth International Workshop on Persistent Object Systems, San Miniato, Italy, 1992.

6. Morrison, R., Brown, A.L., Connor, R. and Dearle, A., "The Napier88 Reference Manual", 1989, University of St. Andrews.

Garbage Collection and Reachability

Luigi V. Mancini
Dipartimento di Informatica, Corso Italia 40, 56100 Pisa, Italy

The two papers in this session discussed various issues in implementing persistent object systems where persistence is defined in terms of reachability from a persistent root.

An important issues is garbage collection which is used by such systems to achieve storage reclamation and reorganization The first paper by Mario Wolczko and Ifor Williams reports experience from the MUSHROOM Project at the University of Manchester that has designed an high-performance architecture for object-oriented computing.

They propose a garbage collection and a virtual memory system that cooperate in order to reduce the significant overhead due to garbage collecting a large object store. In particular, three levels of garbage collection are employed: the first level runs entirely within the data cache, and tries to reclaim the majority of garbage; the second level is an incremental collector operating in main memory, and uses information from the virtual memory system to collect garbage before it migrates to disk; and the third level performs a reference counting garbage collection in secondary storage. Moreover, to prevent the degradation of locality on the disk page, objects are relocate efficiently by the virtual memory system proposed.

Another issue related to the persistence model which is based on the notion of reachability is tackled by Elliot Kolodner who talked about Concurrent Tracking of Stable Objects. The problem here is in ensuring that any object reachable from a persistent or stable root is also stable. The algorithms described addressed two possible sources of instability: transaction aborts and system crashes; media failures were outside the scope of the paper.

When a transaction commits, a tracker needs to locate all objects that have become reachable from stable roots during the transaction, together with modified objects, and ensure they are written to stable storage. Two algorithms were presented, together with arguments for their correctness. The first, simple tracker was used as a construction to explain the correctness criteria and the basic requirements of a tracker. The simple tracker may exhibit undesirable behaviour (in locking out trackers for other transactions). The second algorithm, a concurrent tracker, overcomes this problem. Some of the issues concerning the implementation of a tracker were also discussed.

The final discussion session was very lively and mostly revolved around the following topics: the validity of the failure model commonly adopted for system crashes, the relevance of garbage collection on stock hardware, and the minimal changes needed to stock hardware in order to enable more efficient garbage collection.

In particular, Mario Wolczko raised the issue of the validity of the failure model used by Elliot Kolodner (and other researcher in this area), namely that the software should guard against system crashes, and that a system crash left the contents of disk intact, but lost the contents of main memory. The argument against the model was of this form. The extra software complexity could not be justified purely on the grounds of safeguarding against power failure: uninterruptible power supplies would be much more cost-effective, and exact no performance penalty. Therefore, the software was guarding against crashes due to either hardware failure or software failure. However, many failure modes of hardware cause unpredictable system behaviour, and it seems unlikely that any software can reliably counter this (e.g., if the processor or disk controller fails). Most appropriate solutions in hardware exist for this problem (e.g., the use of replicated hardware). This leaves only failures in software as a cause of crashes which the stable heap could guard against. But if the software does not behave as expected, i.e., is not correct, can we assume that the undesirable effects will be noticed before a transaction commits? And does not the extra complexity of the software itself invite further errors?

Multi-level Garbage Collection in a High-Performance Persistent Object System

Mario Wolczko*

Department of Computer Science, University of Manchester

Manchester, U.K.

mario@cs.man.ac.uk

Ifor Williams

Department of Computer Science, University of Manchester

Manchester, U.K.

ifor@cs.man.ac.uk

Abstract

Conventional garbage collectors exhibit poor virtual memory behaviour. This paper describes a novel garbage collection system that has been designed to co-operate with an object-based virtual memory system so that both their aims are satisfied. The garbage collection system has been separated into parts, each part tailored to the characteristics of one level in the memory hierarchy.

As the sizes of our persistent object systems increase, so do our garbage collection problems. Whereas for small systems it is acceptable to rely on fast memory access speeds in our garbage collectors, we cannot do this in large systems, where most of our objects are in secondary storage. The classic symptom of this problem is that *garbage collectors antagonise virtual memory systems.* They display the kind of behaviour that defeats virtual memory algorithms, and degrades system performance due to excessive paging.

We believe that many of the causes of these problems are removed if both the virtual memory and garbage collection systems are designed with persistent object storage in mind. In this paper we describe the garbage collection and virtual memory systems of the MUSHROOM object-based architecture, and show how they *cooperate* to their mutual benefit.

In the next section we outline the virtual memory problems of traditional garbage collectors. Next, we provide an overview of the MUSHROOM virtual memory system, and then describe the garbage collection system in detail. Finally, we compare our approach with previous work.

---

*To whom all correspondence should be addressed

1 Garbage collection problems in virtual memory systems

Garbage collection is still an important problem. Although some years ago it appeared that garbage collectors had become fast enough to be insignificant consumers of CPU time [1], it has now become apparent that garbage collection performance has not kept pace with improving performance in object-oriented languages [2]. Hence, garbage collection can be a significant overhead in an advanced implementation of an object-oriented language [3].

Furthermore, garbage collection poses severe problems for virtual memory systems. Simple garbage collectors access all live objects, many of which are inactive and hence paged out, causing large numbers of page faults and increased disk traffic. The page faults may also cause active objects to be ejected from memory, increasing access times. These problems are in addition to those caused by the mutation of fine-grained data structures, resulting in a loss of locality within pages over time.

Several schemes have been devised in an attempt to ameliorate these problems. The Baker collector [4] compacted virtual memory as it traversed the network of objects, in an attempt to regain lost locality. However, it still accessed all live objects. In order to counter these problems, generational collectors were developed which concentrated their activity on those parts of the system in which most garbage was created [5, 6, 7, 1, 8]. These collectors access the majority of data infrequently, attempting to avoid unnecessary paging, and also compact virtual memory in the more active areas.

However, these schemes do not address the degradation of locality in older generations of objects. The problem here is that objects are allocated to pages in an essentially arbitrary way. When a page is fetched from disk, very few objects on the page are of immediate use; many are there "by accident". This can result in excessive paging at changes of working set.

To address these problems, we have devised an architecture and virtual memory system which tries to prevent locality problems from arising, rather than attempting to cure them later. It does this by using a virtual memory system in which relocating an object is cheap, and hence an object need not be condemned to share a page with the same neighbours for its entire life. (Schemes with similar aims, but different approaches, are compared in Section 8 [9, 10].)

2 The MUSHROOM virtual memory system[1]

The MUSHROOM Project at the University of Manchester has designed a high-performance architecture for object-oriented computing, and is currently constructing a prototype implementation of this architecture. Amongst other innovations, the MUSHROOM architecture incorporates a virtual memory system that caters for the unusual demands of fine-grained object systems:

- Addressing is object-based, using a two-part address (object identifier and offset).
- Each memory word and register is tagged; primitive types (integers, reals, instructions, etc.) are distinguished from object identifiers.

[1]This section may be safely skipped by readers familiar with the architecture from [11, 12, 13, 14].

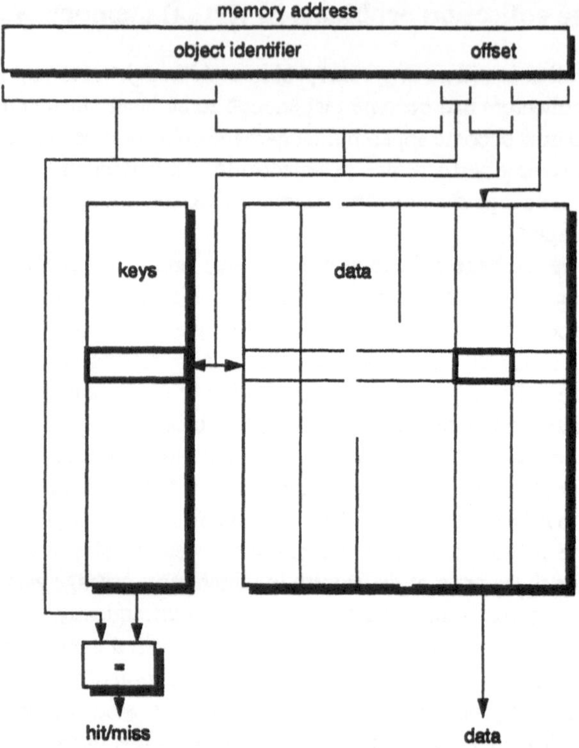

Figure 1: The structure of the MUSHROOM data cache

- A virtually-addressed object-level cache provides fast average access times, without constraining the arrangement of objects in memory or on disk.
- A dynamically-grouped virtual memory transfers collections of objects to and from secondary storage more effectively than conventional paging systems, by choosing the group of objects to place on a page based on recent system activity.

In the MUSHROOM architecture, all data accesses, due to LOAD and STORE operations, are first directed to a hardware data cache (see Fig. 1). A memory address, consisting of an object identifier and the offset within that object, is decomposed into three parts:

1. The row index selects a row from the cache (i.e., a cache line).
2. The column index selects a column from the row, (i.e., an individual data word).
3. The remainder is checked against a stored key to determine whether the cached value is truly associated with the address.

Each row of the cache stores part of a single object (or all, if the object will fit). This structure of cache, with a suitable number of rows and columns, and a pipelined

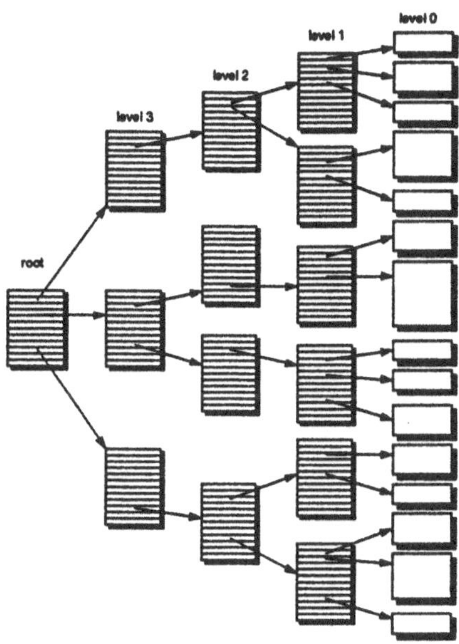

Figure 2: The structure of the MUSHROOM object table. Objects at level 0 are "user" objects; those at other levels are "object table objects". Each object table object can contain the addresses of up to 128 other objects.

implementation, has a very high hit rate and low average access time for Smalltalk programs [14, 13].

Should the cache miss, the appropriate cache line has to be filled by obtaining the data from main memory. This may also require the current contents of the cache line to be written back to memory. To perform both these operations, we need to know the main memory address of an object. This information is held in a data structure known as an *object table*. Conceptually, the object table is a huge array, indexed by object identifier, that holds the real address of an object, and some housekeeping information. Actually, the object table is itself broken into objects, known as object table objects, each of these having its address stored in an object table table object, etc., until a single root object table (with fixed address) is reached (see Fig. 2).

The combination of this cache structure, and the object table, means that the real address of an object is only stored in one place: in its object table entry. This enables us to relocate an object cheaply, as we do not have to search for occurrences of its address. In conventional systems without an object table, relocation is prohibitively expensive. Those that implement an object table entirely in software pay a high penalty for each object access. In the MUSHROOM architecture, object accesses are fast, but relocation is also cheap.

The ability to relocate objects cheaply is used by the virtual memory system. Rather than allocating an object to a particular page for its whole life, when the vir-

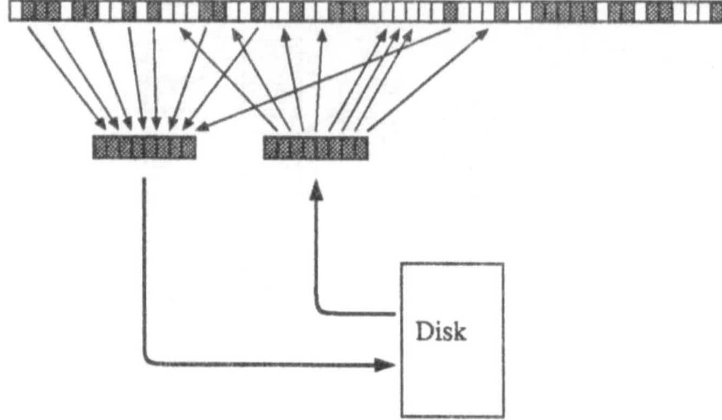

Figure 3: Dynamically grouping during paging. Objects being paged out are gathered from diverse parts of main memory. Objects being paged in are scattered into free areas.

tual memory system needs to eject objects to make room for others it chooses a group of objects sufficient to fill, or nearly fill, a page and ejects those (see Fig. 3). This choice is made dynamically, at the moment of ejection, in the hope that the group of objects is related. If they are related, when the page is later read back in (due to a page fault involving one of the objects on the page), many other useful objects will also be brought in at the same time. Earlier simulations of this technique, grouping objects by time of last access, suggest that it can substantially reduce the number of page faults in a system [11].

3 Design aims of the garbage collection system

The garbage collection system should reclaim the bulk of the garbage within the MUSHROOM virtual memory hierarchy. Allowing small amounts of garbage to remain on disk, uncollected, is acceptable. Small amounts of garbage in memory may be missed by any particular garbage collection cycle, but should be collected in the next cycle. To maintain the high performance of the system, the garbage collector must not negate the aims of the memory system:

- The garbage collector must have minimal impact on the performance of normal operations which change objects (so-called "mutator" operations). This excludes garbage collectors which substantially degrade the performance of elementary register or memory operations, or which increase the complexity of the hardware so much that the processor cycle time is significantly lengthened. Therefore, schemes which require a complex check or reference-count change for each mutator operation are unlikely to be acceptable.
- It must not adversely affect the performance of the storage hierarchy, e.g., by lowering cache hit rates or diluting main memory with inactive or garbage ob-

jects.

- It must not cause lengthy delays to users (i.e., it must be "non-disruptive"; real-time response is not required).

All of these criteria must be met in a high-performance system, i.e., one that is executing efficient codes emitted by an advanced compiler, with associated high rates of garbage creation.

4 Outline of the proposed solution

The MUSHROOM garbage collection system attempts to satisfy the above requirements by being integrated with the virtual memory system. Its parts are matched to the characteristics of the storage hierarchy, and it exchanges information with the virtual memory system.

The first level of garbage collection runs entirely within the data cache, in an attempt to reclaim the majority of garbage in the cheapest way. Confining the first phase to the cache has several benefits: the cache is relatively small (compared to main memory or virtual memory), fixed in size, and of constant, fast access time. This means that each phase of this collector has a small, fixed upper bound on the time it runs, and causes minimum disruption to the user.

The second level is an incremental collector operating in main memory. It too has a small, fixed upper bound on the time required for a garbage collection step, and uses information from the virtual memory system to avoid accessing disk, and to collect garbage before it migrates to disk.

The final level is used to reclaim garbage from disk, and is a reference counting system (with counts held separately from objects). Reference counting is a good choice for an area in which the death rate is low, and there are many live objects. Unlike marking collectors, it does not require a scan of live objects, but merely access to the data that change; these are present in main memory just before being written to disk.

5 The cache-based collector

In the MUSHROOM system, immediately after creation an object is resident only in the data cache. It is allocated an object identifier, but is not allocated a main memory address. Main memory space is allocated only when some part of the object leaves the cache. This speeds both object allocation, by saving unnecessary memory traffic loading data that will immediately be overwritten, and also reclamation, if the object never leaves the cache.

In-cache allocation is possible in the MUSHROOM architecture because the cache is *virtually-addressed*, *write-back* and *software-controlled*. By virtually-addressed, we mean that to access a word in an object the cache is probed using a function of only the object identifier and offset – no virtual-to-real address translation is performed. The cache is write-back because modifications to a cache line are propagated to memory only when the line is flushed. When a cache miss occurs, a *software* trap handler is invoked that writes back the current contents of the required cache line, if dirty, and

Table 1: Contents of an object's header

Size	8 bits
Local	1 bit
Marked	1 bit
Traced	1 bit
Tracing offset (see text)	8 bits
Free	1 bit

loads the cache line. For new objects, allocation of a real address is delayed until part of it is flushed from the cache, i.e., until the last possible moment.

The cache-based collector is generational in nature, reclaiming objects that die in the cache, so long as they have not been referenced from objects outside the cache. Previous studies have shown that most objects in Smalltalk or Lisp systems die relatively soon after their birth: "most objects die young." [1, 15]. Our own simulations, driven by lengthy memory traces from a Smalltalk-80 system, indicate that the majority of garbage, as much as 90%, can be reclaimed in this way [14]. Hence, most objects will be reclaimed by a fast, efficient collector. They will also benefit from having had no main memory image, saving on unnecessary fetches at allocation time, and unnecessary stores after they have been reclaimed; both problems can occur on conventional systems [16].

The collector can be triggered at any convenient time, performing a mark and sweep of the cache. The marking phase uses the contents of the registers as roots, as well as those objects that have been, and probably still are, referenced from main memory or disk. Clearly, determining the former of these is straightforward; the difficulty is knowing which objects in the cache may be referenced from outside. In order to achieve this, the objects are divided into those which are *local* to the cache, and those which are *non-local*. A bit in each object's header (the first word of the object, see Table 1) records whether or not it is local. When created, an object is marked as local. If its identifier is ever written into main memory (due to part of an object containing a reference to it being flushed from cache), or its header is flushed from the cache, then it is marked as non-local, and can never become local again. Hence, the test for locality is:

1. Probe the cache to see if the object's header is in cache; if not, it is not local.

2. If the header is in cache, examine its "local" bit.

Because the MUSHROOM cache is software-controlled, it is possible to probe the cache for the presence of an object without causing a cache-miss trap.

The in-cache collector uses the non-local objects in the cache as the roots for the marking phase; only local objects that are garbage are reclaimed by this collector.

Fig. 4 illustrates an example. At the top we see the state of the cache when the collector is triggered. For simplicity, we show only the objects in cache, paying no attention to the detailed structure of the cache, or to parts of the cache that are empty. Local objects are marked with an "L", non-local objects have no designation. Parts of

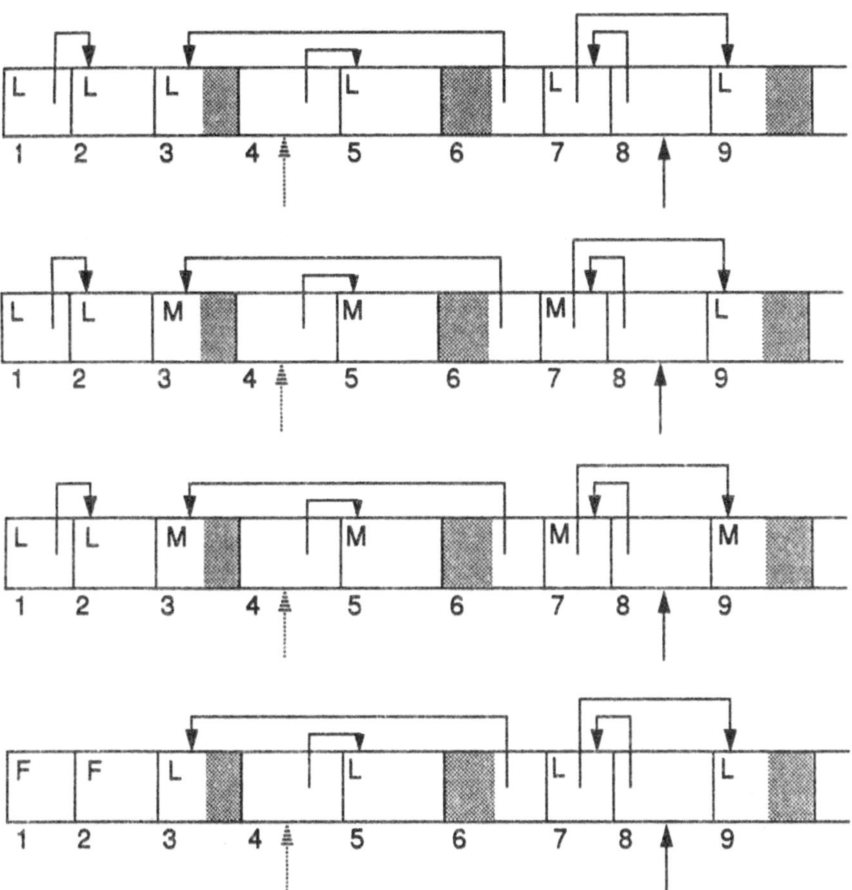

Figure 4: Four steps in the operation of the in-cache garbage collector (see text for explanation).

some objects (3, 6 and 9) are not in cache; these are indicated by shaded areas. Objects 4, 6 and 8 are not local, because:

- Object 8 has had a reference to it stored in memory.
- Object 4 has also had a reference to it stored in memory, but this has been subsequently overwritten. Despite the fact that object 4 is garbage, this collector will not reclaim it.
- Object 6 has had its header flushed from cache.

The marking phase starts by marking as live all local objects referenced from registers; the mark bit is also stored in the object header. Then it runs through all cache lines, and any cache line containing a portion of a non-local object is scanned; local objects referenced from such cache lines are marked as live. In the second part of Fig. 4, these objects (3, 5 and 7) have been marked with an "M". Finally, another pass through the cache uses the live, local objects marked in the previous phase as roots for a recursive trace of all live, local objects accessible from those roots. This picks up an additional object, 9, in the third part of the diagram.

The sweep phase runs through all cache lines, and reclaims those lines belonging to local objects that were not marked as live, i.e., objects 1 and 2, and resets the marks of other objects in preparation for the next scavenge (last part of Fig. 4). Thus, the primary garbage collector can reclaim all local garbage without a single access to main memory.

The local garbage objects are placed on a doubly-linked free list (actually, there is one free list for objects that will fit in a single cache line, one for objects that need two cache lines, etc.). When allocating an object, one is taken from the appropriate list if possible. If a cache line occupied by an object on a free list is required, it is immediately surrendered, the object is removed from the list, and its identifier added to a list of unused identifiers.

5.1 Handling the mark stack

One complication is due to the recursive nature of the tracing phase: storage is required for a stack. We could reserve some part of the cache for this, but in the worst case (in which every cache line contains an object, and all the objects form a single chain) this would be very expensive. Instead we use two properties of the system to make this phase more space-efficient:

1. This collector is uninterruptible, and therefore can manipulate the cache contents in any way it desires, so long as all live objects are restored to their initial states when it exits.
2. In the MUSHROOM architecture, objects are limited to being quite small (256 words in the prototype implementation) [12].[2] The size of an object is stored in its header.

[2]To recap the reason for this decision from [12], very few objects in a Smalltalk system are larger than 1 Kbyte. Rather than accommodating these objects in the architecture, and paying the price (wider buses, wasted memory, wider cache keys, etc.), we use the encapsulation mechanisms of object-oriented languages to build large objects from collections of smaller ones, rather like a file system provides the illusion of large contiguous files from assemblages of smaller blocks. The illusion of large objects can still be presented to the programmer by the use of suitable library classes, and a smart compiler.

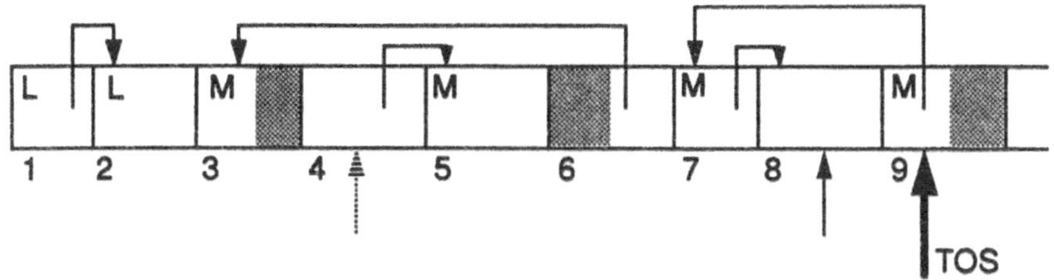

Figure 5: Reversing pointers while tracing

The recursive tracing process, when tracing a reference from object A to B to C, overwrites the reference to C that was previously in B with a reference to A so that it can "find its way back." That is, it reverses the chain of references it has traced, holding the identifier of the current and previous objects in registers. Fig. 5 (which logically goes between the second and third parts of Fig. 4) shows this at the time objects 8, 7 and 9 are on the stack.

Reversing pointers is sufficient to record *which* object was last traced, but we also need to know *how far* through the object we were, i.e., the offset of last word traversed in the last object. A solution to this problem is to reserve eight bits in each object's header to record the offset of traversal in the previous object (recall that every local object will have its header in cache).[3]

The storage overheads of the scavenger are:

- In each object's header, at least two bits are needed to represent the states: non-local; local and marked; local and traced; local garbage. To speed the inner loop of the collector it may be worthwhile encoding these alternatives using three bits (local, marked, traced).
- Eight bits in each object's header to record the traversal offset.
- A few registers during the garbage collection phase. These need not be dedicated to the collector, but can be saved when the collector starts, and restored when it exits.

The garbage collector operates in time proportional to the cache size.

6 The main memory collector

The second level of the garbage collection system reclaims garbage in main memory. Because main memory is large, this is done by an incremental mark/sweep collector, similar to that described in [17]. As with the cache-based system, this system relies on intimate knowledge of the memory structure to achieve good performance.

[3]Actually, we use less than eight bits. Because each item in the chain is an object reference, and not some primitive type, there are some tag bits in each word which can be overwritten while constructing the stack, and replaced when unwinding the stack.

To simplify the explanation, let us first consider the collector in abstract terms, devoid of any architecture-specific details. Using the terminology of [17], during the marking phase of the garbage collector each object is in one of three states:

White objects have not been examined by the garbage collector since its last sweep phase.

Grey objects have been examined by the garbage collector, and are therefore considered live, but their contents have not yet been scanned to see if they contain any references to white objects.

Black objects have also been examined by the garbage collector, and are also considered live, like grey objects. Additionally, they have been scanned and any white objects they referenced have been marked as grey.

At the start of the marking phase, the system roots are marked as grey; all other objects are white. The marking phase of the collector repeatedly performs the following actions: locate a grey object, mark it black, and mark any white objects it references as grey. When there are no more grey objects, the remaining white objects are known to be garbage, and the sweep phase can then begin; this will reclaim the white objects.

In order to assure the correct operation of this algorithm, the mutator must not be allowed to store a reference to a white object into a black object. If this is attempted, the white object is coloured grey before the store completes. As an optimisation, if the mutator accesses any white object, we can colour it grey immediately as it cannot be garbage (by virtue of being accessed).

In some ways this collector is also similar to a simple copying collector [4]. In a copying collector, an object's colour is encoded into its virtual address, and to change colour the object must either be copied from one virtual address space to another (when becoming grey), or the boundary between spaces shifted (when an object becomes black). The on-the-fly mark/sweep collector operates in a similar fashion, except that it does not need to copy objects. However, it cannot sweep up garbage by simply discarding a portion of virtual address space, but must search the object table for white objects.

6.1 Using a queue of grey objects

To locate grey objects, the garbage collector operates on a queue of object references, each object in the queue being grey. The queue is initialised with the system roots (e.g., contents of registers, and other root objects). In the marking phase, the collector proceeds in steps, each step taking one object from the queue, and tracing it. In tracing an object, its contents are scanned for references to white objects, and all such objects are added to the queue. Finally, the object is marked black. If, during the marking phase, the mutator attempts to store a reference to a white object into a black object, then the white object must be marked grey, and added to the queue.

When the queue is exhausted, the marking phase is complete, and all objects are either black or white. The white objects can be swept up and reclaimed. This can also be performed incrementally, as no white object can subsequently change state. Finally, all the black objects are marked as white, the queue is re-initialised, and the whole process repeats.

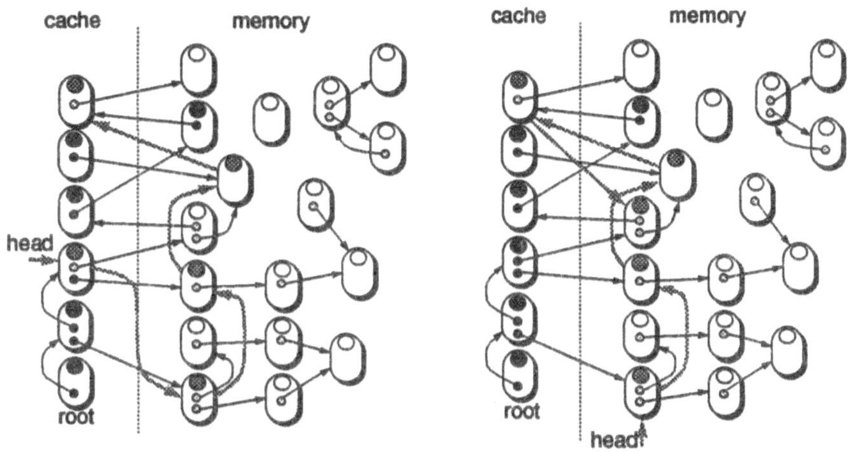

Figure 6: Colouring objects while marking, by traversing the "grey" queue

6.2 The MUSHROOM implementation

The MUSHROOM implementation of the collector described above is designed to co-operate with the virtual memory system as much as possible. It uses the movements of objects in the memory hierarchy to assist it in determining which objects are live. Occasionally it will mark an object as live when in fact it has recently become garbage, but all garbage present at the start of a collection cycle, resident in main memory and not referenced from in-cache garbage, will be reclaimed at the end of that cycle.

For the moment, let us ignore secondary (i.e., disk) storage, and consider only cache and main memory. The first assumption made by the collector is that all objects partially or wholly in cache are live. This is a reasonable assumption: an object must have been live when loaded into cache, and the normal cache turnover will tend to eject garbage from cache, to be reclaimed during the next cycle of garbage collection.[4] Thus, an object is marked as either black or grey when loaded into cache for the first time (depending on whether the whole object is loaded or not, respectively). If the newly-filled cache line contains any references to white objects, then these are added to the "grey" queue. The marking process consists of removing an item from the front of the queue, loading all parts of the object into the cache, scanning the parts for references to white objects, and then marking the object as black (see Fig. 6). By this process, all live objects will eventually pass through the cache and be marked black (Fig. 7, left). The sweep phase can then work through memory, scanning object-table objects for white objects, and reclaiming them (Fig. 7, right).

[4]Should this be a problem, due to large amounts of main memory garbage being retained by cached garbage, a background process could be run that cycled through the cache using a "clock" algorithm, ejecting objects from cache. If this were done slowly enough it would not degrade cache performance significantly, but would force all garbage out of cache. Early simulation results, however, suggest that such a process is unlikely to be necessary and cache turnover will be sufficient to achieve this.

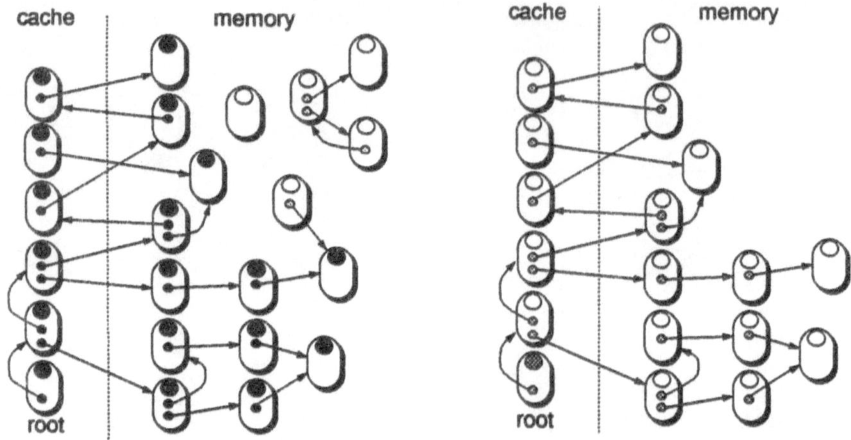

Figure 7: Final stage of marking (left) and after a "flip" (right)

6.3 Avoiding cache misses

Determining the colour of an object referenced from a newly-loaded cache line could be expensive. Each cache fill could result in a further series of cache fills, simply to examine the colour of each object referenced in the first fill. Clearly, we cannot store the colour with the object, as this could result in a potentially unbounded series of cache fills. To avoid this, the colour field is stored in the object table entry (see Table 6.3), along with the real address of the object. This entry has to be accessed whenever the object crosses a boundary in the memory hierarchy (e.g., is loaded into or flushed from cache, or is paged in or out), so is conveniently to hand at these times. Also, each object reference has a tag bit dedicated to the main memory garbage collector, and which is used as a hint to the colour of the object. The tag bit distinguishes between *possibly white* and *definitely non-white* objects (shown as grey and black references, resp., in the diagrams). If the tag bit is set to "non-white", then the referenced object has already been examined by the collector, and is considered live; if set to "possibly-white", then it may or may not have been examined – the object's colour field must be examined to ascertain the precise colour.

When a cache line is filled, only the object identifiers that are tagged "possibly-white" need be considered. If the object table entry for a "possibly-white" identifier happens to be in cache, then the true colour of the object can be directly ascertained. If not, the object is added to the "grey" queue (even though it may already be in the queue, or even black), so as to avoid further cache fills. The tags of the newly-loaded identifiers are set to "non-white" before the mutator is allowed to proceed.

Presence of an object's identifier in the queue implies that the object is non-white, and guarantees that eventually it will be marked black. It may or may not be marked grey when entered in the queue; this decision is based on local circumstances (such as whether marking it grey would require a cache-memory transfer or a disk access). Marking it grey immediately may save it from later being added to the queue again

Table 2: Contents of an object table entry

Field	State(s) when required	Size
State[a]	L,M,D^b	2 bits
Colour	L,M,D	2 bits
Address	L,M,D,F	24 bits[c]
Link (for free or local lists)	L,F	32 bits
LRU Link for grouping	M	32 bits
Disk reference count	M,D	8 bits
Size	L,M,D	8 bits

[a]Possible states are: local L; non-local, in main memory M; non-local, on disk D; free F.

[b]Free objects can be identified by their presence on a free list.

[c]This field is dependent of the size of memory and disk. Memory addresses are in units of words, disk addresses are in units of blocks.

(which is harmless, but inefficient). However, even this is not guaranteed, as determining the colour at that stage may also be inconvenient or expensive.[5]

6.4 Resuming marking after a sweep

One complication remains: when the collector has "flipped" state (i.e., black objects are now considered white), some objects, previously black and now white, and their references to other white objects, will still be in the cache (Fig. 7, second part). We must ensure that these references are accounted for in the next cycle of marking. A simple solution would be to add them to the "grey" queue immediately, but this could potentially result in an extremely long queue, and take a substantial period of time. Instead, we distribute this activity over the next mark/sweep cycle, by having the cache flush routine detect any attempts to store possibly-white references into main memory, convert them to non-white references, and add the referenced object to the "grey" queue. However, this does not guarantee that all such references are dealt with, so that when the queue has been exhausted, a single scan of the cache for any remaining possibly-white references is performed, and these are added to the queue. Further checks for possibly-white references in the cache flush routine are no longer required, as we can be certain that the cache has no more such references, and the cache fill routine will prevent them from entering cache. Therefore, the next time that the queue is empty, marking has finished and sweeping can begin.

6.5 Benefits

Chambers has identified store checks (e.g., when a reference to a white object is stored into a black object) as a significant obstacle to high performance in compiled systems [3]. In our scheme, the store checks are not performed on every store instruction (as in the SOAR architecture, Lisp Machine ephemeral collector, TI Explorer, or SELF system

[5]One might think that this would lead to much inefficiency, due to objects being entered into the queue many times. However, simple examination of a Smalltalk image shows that fewer than 30% of objects are referenced more than once, so at least 70% of objects cannot suffer this fate. Additionally, 90% of objects are referenced no more than four times, suggesting the probability of repeated enqueuing is low. Even fewer objects are multiply-referenced in Lisp systems [18].

[19, 6, 9, 3]) but only at cache misses - a much less frequent operation. Similarly, load checks (to ensure that the cache only contains references to non-white objects) are performed only at cache fills, and not at every load (as in the Baker collector or the i432 architecture [4, 20]). This means that normal memory operations can proceed at full speed. Stores into locations which never leave cache are not slowed at all.

Note also that the breadth-first approach used by the mark/sweep system does not have the same disastrous consequences on locality as observed in copying collectors [6], as no objects need to be relocated.

7 Disk-based garbage collection

As described, the garbage collection system would access all live objects on disk in every cycle. This can be avoided by having the main-memory collector cooperate with the virtual memory system, reducing the amount of garbage on disk to such an extent that it is not worth reclaiming by such brute-force techniques.

The first noteworthy gain can be made by observing that, by definition, garbage is never accessed. Hence, in MUSHROOM's dynamically-grouping virtual memory system (where grouping uses an LRU criterion, with ejection of an object header from cache being used as the time of last access), garbage will drift rapidly down the LRU chain. The paging system avoids paging out objects at the end of this LRU chain if they have not been marked as live by the garbage collector. When it can do this, then there is a good chance that such objects will be reclaimed in memory, where such reclamation is cheaper. Hayes has shown that for older garbage, there is strong tendency for garbage to form in clumps [21], explaining the "pig in a python" behaviour observed by Ungar and Jackson [22]. One possibility that we are exploring is to insert timestamps into the LRU chain so that we can detect such clumps, delay paging, and increase garbage collection activity (particularly if the collector is in the sweep phase, or thought to be near the end of the mark phase).

To avoid unnecessary disk accesses, we can go further. We confine the main memory garbage collector so that to reclaim in-memory garbage it does not access disk at all. Object references are partitioned between main memory and disk in a similar fashion to the partition between cache and main memory. To do this, every object referenced from disk is marked as such, and will not be reclaimed by the main memory collector (such objects are added to the "grey" queue when they are first referenced from disk). Objects in memory which are referenced from disk at the start of the marking phase can be located, scanned, and marked black by walking the in-memory object table objects.

Rather than use a single-bit mark to record when an object is referenced from disk, we use a reference count (of eight bits in the current implementation). The number of references to an object from disk is recorded in the reference count, and the counts are modified whenever a group of objects is read from, or written to, disk, by the paging routines (Fig. 8). The reference count is held in the object table entry.

An object on disk is only eligible for reclamation when its reference count has fallen to zero, and the main memory collector has not found a reference to the object during its mark phase. Any complete cycle of garbage on the disk, unreferenced from garbage in main memory, will not be reclaimed, but we expect this phenomenon to be rare. Similarly, objects referenced from disk 255 times or more will not be reclaimed,

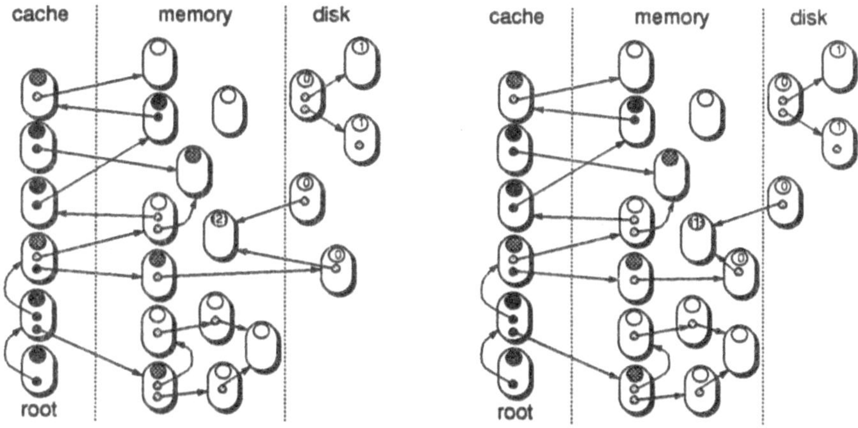

Figure 8: Using reference counts. Each object has a count of how many references to it are stored on disk (those not showing counts are zero). When an object is moved into memory (right) or out, any objects it refers to have their counts altered.

as their reference counts will stick at 255. To reclaim these objects, some other technique, possibly off-line, will be required. As we do not yet know the magnitude of this problem, this paper we have not considered possible solutions, and do not address the problem further in this paper.

In an attempt to reclaim cycles that are partially on disk, the marking part of the mark/sweep collector is split into two phases. In the first phase, marking starts from objects referenced from registers, and root objects that are in memory (Fig. 9, left). This phase is confined to main memory. In the second phase, objects in main memory with non-zero reference counts, that were not marked in the first phase, are used as the roots. These, and any objects reached from them that were not marked in the first phase, could be parts of garbage cycles. In this phase, if a reference is scanned to an object on disk, then that object may be fetched into memory for further scanning (Fig. 9, right). If the whole cycle is brought into memory, then it can be reclaimed by the next pass of the mark/sweep collector. Heuristics are used to limit the number of objects fetched into memory by this phase.

8 Comparison with other work

As mentioned in the introduction, all generation-based garbage collectors partition the object space so as to concentrate garbage collection activity in the most profitable way. However, few schemes have paid close attention to the interaction between garbage collection and the storage hierarchy. Those which have provided hardware support for cross-generational checks have usually made these checks on every fetch or store operation (depending on the particular scheme in use); ours checks only on cache fills

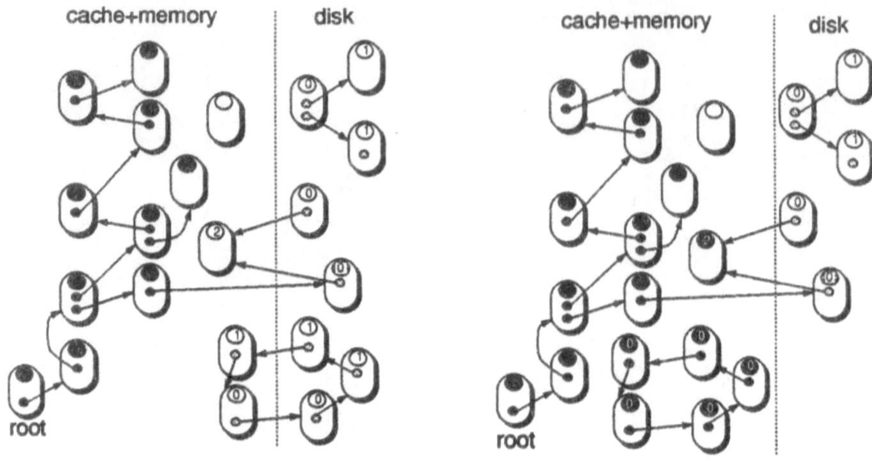

Figure 9: Reclaiming cycles partially on disk by bringing them into memory.

and flushes. Unlike previous schemes, our scavenger does not attempt to remember the locations of cross-generational references using a remembered set, page marking or card marking, or use indirection tables [1, 6, 8, 23, 24, 5, 9].

In conventional systems, garbage collection of older objects can disrupt the cache by causing newer, more active objects to be ejected [16]. Our incremental mark/sweep collector can make use of MUSHROOM's exposed cache structure to avoid ejecting active objects from cache, by ensuring that it always loads objects into a reserved cache area, unused by other objects.

An early description of the iMAX operating system for the iAPX-432 architecture suggested that garbage could be managed by being paged out rather than reclaimed [20], the complete opposite of our approach. Whether this was suggested because the garbage creation rate was expected to be much lower (the main programming language of the 432 was Ada), we do not know. Our view is that it is best to reclaim garbage sooner than later, and that reclaiming it in memory is better than letting it drift to disk. For systems with Lisp- or Smalltalk-like behaviour, it is essential that the reclamation rate match the allocation rate fairly closely over short time intervals (tens of seconds) if the system is not to run out of storage. We have been unable to locate any data as to the performance of the iMAX scheme.

In [25], Chiueh describes an in-cache garbage collector. This garbage collector runs during idle processor cycles at cache misses, and so requires a processor capable of switching to an alternate thread during these periods. The scheme is based on associating a three-bit reference count with each cached object, and performing reference count operations on objects that have been allocated but never left cache (similar to the local objects in the MUSHROOM scheme). To support this scheme, every store operation which may involve a reference to such an object (either as the value being stored, or the value being overwritten) must fetch the overwritten value, decrement its reference count, and increment the count of the stored value. Although the increments and decrements are deferred to the next cache miss, the extra fetch will undoubtedly slow store operations, even more than cross-generation checks. The MUSHROOM architecture has no provision for task switching during cache-memory transfers; this would complicate the architecture substantially.

Wilson describes using *opportunistic* garbage collection to hide garbage collection pauses from users [26]. Because our in-cache scavenger can be triggered at any time, and the mark/sweep collector is incremental, we can also exploit opportunism.

Our garbage collection scheme should also be well-suited to a shared-memory multiprocessor (the MUSHROOM architecture has provisions for multiple processors, but the prototype is a uniprocessor). The in-cache scavenger places no demands on main memory bandwidth. On a multiprocessor there would be no need to synchronise one processor's in-cache collection with any other processor's, unlike the scheme in [27]. Cache lines can even be invalidated during in-cache scavenging, to accommodate a cache coherency scheme, as other processors cannot possess references to local objects and can therefore only invalidate lines containing non-local objects.

Wilson *et al.* have pointed out that unless the data cache can contain the whole of the youngest generation, poor cache hit rates may result [16]. Our prototype implementation has a 512 Kword (2.5 Mbyte) cache. We realise this is large by current standards, but we wanted to have too much, rather than too little, for experimentation. The amount of cache actually in use can be controlled at system configuration time. It may also be that such cache sizes will be commonplace in a few years' time, especially using two-level structures. Our in-cache garbage collector needs no modification for a two-level cache in which the first level is not exposed but the second is.

8.1 Other systems that attempt to group objects

8.1.1 Courts' system

Courts has described a variety of techniques implemented on a TI Explorer system [9]:

- His temporal garbage collector divides objects into age-based address spaces, using indirections to locate cross-generational references. The Explorer has hardware support for the detection of cross-generation stores. A copying collector is used to move objects between spaces.
- The use of *training* to segregate active objects from inactive ones.
- An *adaptive training* system that attempts to segregate active objects from live but inactive ones (by delaying the action of the garbage collector after a flip).

The adaptive facility is of particular relevance, as it will perform a dynamic grouping function. However, the groupings so formed will be based not only on object activity (i.e., groups of objects accessed at approximately the same time will be placed together), as in the MUSHROOM system, but also on the ages of objects (i.e., a group will consist of objects of approximately the same age). Objects in the oldest age band are regrouped by being activated. Garbage in oldest age band is reclaimed by a scavenger that must copy all live objects – an expensive operation, as the ratio of live to garbage objects is likely to be high.

8.1.2 Static graph reorganisation

Initial attempts at static grouping showed disappointing improvements in paging activity [28], which led us to invent our dynamically grouped system. More recently Wilson *et al.* have suggested that alternative static grouping techniques could yield much better improvements [10].

As Courts has pointed out [9], any technique based on traversing graphs will group objects as to how they *can* be accessed, not how they *are* accessed. Whilst the suggestion that hierarchical groupings (rather than depth- or breadth-first groupings) may improve locality for Smalltalk is probably true, we are unsure as to how one might order the traversals of hash tables suggested in [10], given the lack of a "program" text. However, the techniques suggested in [10] are worthy of further investigation, particularly as they do not require special-purpose hardware.

8.1.3 The interaction between garbage collection and locality

Perhaps the best way of summarising our approach is that we do not attempt to make the garbage collector perform double-duty by both collecting garbage and improving locality. Responsibility for locality lies with the cache structure and the virtual memory system (in the way it manages memory and disk). The garbage collector merely has to collect garbage, while interfering with the activity of the virtual memory system as little as it can.

The only age-related collection that takes place is that done by the in-cache scavenger. The other two collection systems distinguish between garbage that was recently active (and hence in memory), or has been inactive (and hence is on disk). Neither is concerned with the age of an object. The division of labour between these two collectors will be based on the ratio of objects that become garbage having recently become active to objects that become garbage while inactive. To our knowledge, there have been no data published on this ratio for any system. We have attempted to estimate this ratio using traces from a Smalltalk system. A number of traces of object activity were taken, which included the times of every object creation, reclamation, and access (measuring time by ticks of a clock that advances with every memory reference). Plotting lifetimes, we obtained the familiar curve showing that 90% of objects lived less than 10^4 ticks; 50% live only for 100 ticks. If we assume that those with lifetimes less than 10^4 ticks are mostly reclaimed by the in-cache scavenger, then the remainder are eligible for collection by the other two techniques. For these objects, we measured the period of inactivity between the last access to each object, and it becoming garbage. Approximately 40% of objects become garbage within 10^4 ticks of their last access; this rises to 85%–90% within 10^5 ticks. Hence, most objects will become garbage within the period of 10 in-cache scavenge cycles since they were last active, and are therefore unlikely to be on disk. Increasing the scavenge cycle time by factors up to 100 had little effect on this ratio.

This would suggest the bulk of the garbage should be reclaimed by the in-memory collector, as hoped. The figures should be treated with caution, as the traces are not particularly long (between 10^8 and 10^9 ticks). Also, the traces came from a vintage Smalltalk system that dates from the era when reference-counting was the primary reclamation technique. Therefore, some of the code may explicitly break cycles to assist in reclamation, and this would skew the figures in favour of the in-memory collector. Nevertheless, the results are promising.

9 Summary and conclusions

We have described a garbage collection system which works hand-in-hand with a virtual memory system. The collector is split into three levels, to match the memory hierarchy: cache, main memory and disk. The in-cache collector is expected to reclaim most of the garbage (that due to young deaths), using no main memory bandwidth. An estimated time for the operation of the in-cache collector, on a 20 MHz machine, with a 128 Kword cache, is in the order of 20 ms; the worst case is around 100 ms (these figures are based on estimated timings using hand-coded inner loops). Of the remaining garbage, most will be reclaimed by the incremental in-memory collector. This assists the virtual memory system in determining which objects should be paged out, and tries to prevent garbage migrating to disk. Live, but inactive objects, should form the bulk of the traffic to disk. The main memory collector will only access disk in an attempt to reclaim cycles which are partially on disk.

10 Future work

This system is being implemented on the MUSHROOM prototype. Future work consists of measuring the performance of the various parts of the system, and examining the various time-space trade-offs we have described. Attempting to compare the performance of this scheme with a static-graph scheme looks particularly interesting.

We are also interesting in the use of compression techniques and "swizzling" to decrease disk bandwidth and increase the address space [29].

11 Acknowledgements

The authors would like to thank Trevor Hopkins and the referees for their comments on a draft of this paper. This work was supported by the Science and Engineering Research Council, under grants GR/E/65050 and GR/G/47568, and a SERC Research Fellowship.

References

[1] David Ungar. Generation scavenging: A non-disruptive, high performance storage reclamation algorithm. In *Proceedings of the Software Engineering Symposium on Practical Software Development Environments*, pages 157–167, Pittsburgh, PA, May 1984. ACM SIGSOFT/SIGPLAN.

[2] Craig Chambers. *The Design and Implementation of the* SELF *Compiler, an Optimizing Compiler for Object-Oriented Programming Languages*. PhD thesis, Department of Computer Science, Stanford University, March 1992.

[3] Craig Chambers. Cost of garbage collection in the SELF system. OOPSLA '91 Garbage Collection Workshop Position Paper, 1991.

[4] Henry G. Baker. List processing in real time on a serial computer. *Comm. ACM*, 21(4):280–294, April 1978.

[5] Henry Lieberman and Carl Hewitt. A real-time garbage collector based on the lifetimes of objects. *Comm. ACM*, 26(6):419–429, June 1981.

[6] David A. Moon. Garbage collection in a large Lisp system. In *Conference Record of the 1984 ACM Symposium on Lisp and Functional Programming*, pages 235–246, Austin, Texas, 1984. Association for Computing Machinery.

[7] S. Ballard and S. Shirron. The design and implementation of VAX/Smalltalk-80. In Glenn Krasner, editor, *Smalltalk-80: Bits of history, words of advice*, pages 127–150. Addison-Wesley, 1983.

[8] Robert A. Shaw. Improving garbage collector performance in virtual memory. Technical Report CSL-TR-87-323, Computer Systems Laboratory, Stanford University, March 1987.

[9] Robert Courts. Improving locality of reference in a garbage-collecting memory management system. *Comm. ACM*, 31(9):1128–1138, September 1988.

[10] Paul R. Wilson, Michael S. Lam, and Thomas G. Moher. Effective "static-graph" reorganization to improve locality in garbage-collected systems. In *Proceedings of the SIGPLAN '91 Conference on Programming Language Design and Implementation*, pages 177–191, Toronto, Canada, June 1991.

[11] Ifor Wyn Williams, Mario I. Wolczko, and Trevor P. Hopkins. Dynamic grouping in an object oriented virtual memory hierarchy. In J. Bézivin, J.-M. Hullot, P. Cointe, and H. Lieberman, editors, *Proceedings of the 1987 European Conference on Object-Oriented Programming, Lecture Notes in Computer Science*, volume 276, pages 79–88. Springer-Verlag, Paris, June 1987.

[12] Ifor Wyn Williams, Mario I. Wolczko, and Trevor P. Hopkins. Realisation of a dynamically grouped object-oriented virtual memory hierarchy. In *Proceedings of the Workshop on Persistent Object Systems: Their Design, Implementation and Use*, pages 298–308, August 1987. Persistent Programming Research Report, Universities of Glasgow and St. Andrews (PPRR-44-87).

[13] Ifor Williams and Mario Wolczko. An object-based memory architecture. In Alan Dearle, Gail M. Shaw, and Stanley B. Zdonik, editors, *Implementing Persistent Object Bases: Proceedings of the Fourth International Workshop on Persistent Object Systems*, pages 114–130. Morgan Kaufmann Publishers, Inc., 1991.

[14] Ifor W. Williams. *Object-Based Memory Architecture*. PhD thesis, Department of Computer Science, University of Manchester, May 1989.

[15] Robert A. Shaw. Empirical analysis of a Lisp system. Technical Report CSL-TR-88-351, Computer Systems Laboratory, Stanford University, February 1988.

[16] Paul R. Wilson, Michael S. Lam, and Thomas G. Moher. Caching considerations for generational garbage collection: a case for large and set-associative caches. Technical Report UIC-EECS-90-5, University of Illinois at Chicago, December 1990.

[17] Edsger W. Dijkstra, Leslie Lamport, A. J. Martin, C. S. Scholten, and E. F. M. Steffens. On-the-fly garbage collection: An exercise in cooperation. *Comm. ACM*, 21(11):966–975, November 1978.

[18] Douglas W. Clark and C. Cordell Green. An empirical study of list structure in LISP. *Comm. ACM*, 20(2):78–87, February 1977.

[19] David M. Ungar. *The Design and Evaluation of a High Performance Smalltalk System.* MIT Press, 1987.

[20] Fred J. Pollack, George W. Cox, Dan W. Hammerstrom, Kevin C. Kahn, Konrad K. Lai, and Justin R. Rattner. Supporting Ada memory management in the iAPX-432. In *Proceedings of the First International Conference on Architectural Support for Programming Languages and Operating Systems*, pages 117–131, March 1982.

[21] Barry Hayes. Using key object opportunism to collect old objects. In *Proceedings of the Conference on Object-Oriented Programming: Systems, Languages and Applications*, pages 33–46, Phoenix, Arizona, October 1991. Association for Computing Machinery, ACM Press.

[22] David Ungar and Frank Jackson. Tenuring policies for generation-based storage reclamation. In Norman Meyrowitz, editor, *Proceedings of the Conference on Object-Oriented Programming: Systems, Languages and Applications*, pages 1–17, San Diego, California, September 1988. Association for Computing Machinery, ACM Press.

[23] P. G. Sobalvarro. A lifetime-based garbage collector for LISP systems on general-purpose computers. Master's thesis, Dept. of Electrical Engineering and Computer Science, MIT, 1988.

[24] Paul R. Wilson and Thomas G. Moher. Design of the opportunistic garbage collector. In Norman Meyrowitz, editor, *Proceedings of the Conference on Object-Oriented Programming: Systems, Languages and Applications*, pages 23–35, New Orleans, Louisiana, October 1989. Association for Computing Machinery, ACM Press.

[25] Tzi-cker Chiueh. An architectural technique for cache-level garbage collection. In R. J. M. Hughes, editor, *Proceedings of the Fifth ACM Conference on Functional Languages and Computer Architecture*, volume 523 of *Lecture Notes in Computer Science*, pages 520–537, Cambridge, Massachusetts, August 1991. Springer-Verlag.

[26] Paul R. Wilson. Opportunistic garbage collection. *ACM SIGPLAN Notices*, 23(12):98–102, December 1988.

[27] Kazuhiro Ogata, Satoshi Kurihara, Mikio Inari, and Norihisa Doi. The design and implementation of HoME. In *Proceedings of the SIGPLAN '92 Conference on Programming Language Design and Implementation*, pages 44–54, San Francisco, California, June 1992.

[28] James W. Stamos. Static grouping of small objects to enhance performance of a paged virtual memory. *ACM Transactions on Computer Systems*, 2(2), May 1984.

[29] Paul R. Wilson. Pointer swizzling at page fault time: Efficiently supporting huge address spaces on standard hardware. *ACM Comp. Arch. News*, 19(4), June 1991.

Concurrent Tracking of Stable Objects

Elliot K. Kolodner
IBM Science and Technology
Technion City
Haifa 32000, Israel
kolodner@haifasc3.vnet.ibm.com

Abstract

A *stable heap* is storage that is managed automatically using garbage collection, manipulated using atomic transactions, and accessed using a uniform storage model. These features enhance reliability and simplify programming by preventing errors due to explicit deallocation, by masking failures and concurrency using transactions, and by eliminating the distinction between accessing temporary storage and permanent storage. Stable heap management is useful for programming languages for reliable distributed computing, programming languages with persistent storage, and object-oriented database systems.

In a stable heap, some programmer specified roots are stable; the rest are volatile. An object becomes stable when it becomes reachable from a stable root. A recovery system ensures that the stable objects survive failures. Many objects are volatile (e.g., objects local to a procedure invocation) and do not need to persist across failures. We would like to avoid recovery costs for these volatile objects, incurring the costs of recovery only for stable objects. To this end, the recovery system uses a tracking algorithm to find objects as they become stable and ensure that they survive failure. This paper presents a concurrent tracking algorithm: tracking runs concurrently with transactions and other trackers.

1 Introduction

A *stable heap* is storage that is managed automatically using garbage collection, manipulated using atomic transactions, and accessed using a uniform storage model. These features enhance reliability and simplify programming by preventing errors due to explicit deallocation, by masking failures and concurrency using transactions, and by eliminating the distinction between accessing temporary storage and permanent storage. Stable heap management is useful for programming languages for reliable distributed computing [6, 12], programming languages with persistent storage [1, 2], and object-oriented database systems [4, 14, 20, 21].

This paper reports on research done by the author at the Laboratory for Computer Science, Massachusetts Institute of Technology, Cambridge, MA 02139.
The research was supported by the National Science Foundation under grant CCR-8716884, by the Defense Advanced Research Projects Agency (DARPA) under Contract N00014-89-J-1988, and by an equipment grant from the Digital Equipment Corporation.

Many applications that could benefit from a stable heap (e.g., computer-aided design, computer-aided software engineering, and office information systems) require large amounts of storage, timely responses for transactions, and high availability. Our research [8, 10] has been concerned with the design of algorithms to support the large stable heaps necessary to support these applications.

In a stable heap, some programmer specified roots are stable; the rest are volatile. An object becomes stable when it becomes reachable from a stable root. Once stable a recovery system ensures that the object survives failures. Many objects are volatile (e.g., objects local to a procedure invocation) and do not need to persist across failures. We would like to avoid recovery costs for these volatile objects, so that we incur the costs of recovery only for stable objects.

To this end, the recovery system keeps track of the stable objects. It makes sure that the effects of a transaction on stable objects survive failures by writing information to a log on stable storage in conjunction with transaction commit. A volatile object becomes stable when a transaction modifies a pre-existing object and makes the volatile object reachable from it. Before allowing a transaction to commit, the recovery system invokes a *tracking algorithm* to find these *newly stable objects* and write their values to the log.

A newly stable object can be directly reachable from a modified object or reachable from some other newly stable object. Thus, a whole object sub-graph may become stable at once. The transaction that makes the sub-graph newly stable does not necessarily have locks on the objects in the graph. Since these objects are also reachable from a volatile root, they may be visible to other uncommitted transactions; these transactions may hold locks on the objects and may have modified them. Thus, the tracking algorithm must be coordinated correctly with the transaction system.

Furthermore, the sub-graph reachable from a newly stable object may be arbitrarily large. Thus, the time to track newly stable objects for any single transaction may be arbitrarily long. However, we do not want to delay other transactions or the commit of other transactions. Therefore, we require that the tracking algorithm be concurrent: that it run concurrently with transactions and other invocations of the algorithm.

Oki [16] described the first tracking algorithm suitable for a stable heap. His initial algorithm is correct, but it is not concurrent–it suspends all transactions while it processes a newly stable object graph. Later Oki [17] introduced concurrency into his algorithm; in the process he also introduced a subtle bug. A race condition in his concurrent algorithm allows a transaction to commit before all of the objects that the transaction made stable are recoverable. If a failure occurs after the transaction commits, but before the newly stable objects are recoverable; the results of the transaction will not be recoverable. Oki's concurrent algorithm was used in the implementation of Argus [13].

In this paper we present a correct concurrent tracking algorithm. In our dissertation [10] we show how the concurrent tracking algorithm fits together with other algorithms for managing a stable heap: an atomic incremental garbage collector [9, 8] for collecting stable garbage, a recovery system based on repeating history [15], and an algorithm that avoids the costs of atomic garbage collection for volatile objects by dividing the heap into areas.

Other research in persistence has also worked with a model where persistence is determined according to reachability from a persistent root [2, 3, 18].

PS-algol [2, 5] uses a weaker transaction model and restricts the sharing of objects; this simplifies its tracking of newly persistent objects. Transactions in PS-algol may only share persistent objects; they never share volatile objects. Thus, a newly persistent object is local to the transaction that created it and made it reachable from a persistent root until that transaction commits. At transaction commit a tracking algorithm traces the object graphs rooted at the objects read from the databases open for writing (a database is the unit of concurrency control and may contain an arbitrary object graph), and writes the modified and newly persistent objects in the graphs back to the database. Since no other transaction can access the object graphs being tracked, the algorithm does not have to coordinate itself with other transactions or other invocations of tracking.

Other approaches [3, 18] provide persistence for every object; thus, they pay the cost of persistence for every object rather than tracking newly persistent objects. These approaches also do not integrate transactions with persistence.

Here is an overview of the structure of this paper. Section 2 presents our model of a stable heap. Section 3 describes a simple implementation of a stable heap that provides a basis for describing our tracking algorithm. Section 4 describes a simple tracking algorithm that is correct but is not very concurrent. In Section 5 and Section 6 we present a series of refinements to the simple algorithm to increase its concurrency. In Section 7 we describe some implementation issues. In Section 8 we conclude.

2 Stable Heaps

In the model computations on shared state run as atomic transactions [7], and storage is organized as a heap. Transactions provide concurrency control and fault tolerance; they are *serializable* and *total*. Serializability means that when transactions are executed concurrently, the effect will be as if they were run sequentially in some order. Totality means that a transaction is all-or-nothing; i.e., either it completes entirely and *commits*, or it *aborts* and is guaranteed to have no effect.

Objects shared among transactions must be *atomic*. Atomic objects provide the synchronization and recovery mechanisms necessary to ensure that transactions are serializable and total. Atomic objects can be mutable or immutable. Immutable objects are always atomic because their values never change. For the purposes of this paper we assume that the heap synchronizes access to mutable atomic objects using standard read/write locking, and we describe appropriate recovery mechanisms. Using the built-in types, a programmer can build objects of user-defined atomic types [19] that exhibit greater concurrency than the built-in atomic types.

A transaction consists of a series of short low-level recoverable actions. Each action accesses a single object: a *read* action reads an object, an *update* action modifies an object, and an *allocate* action creates a new object.

In this paper we assume that transactions are not distributed; however, the changes to our algorithms necessary to support distribution and two-phase commit should be obvious.

A heap consists of a set of root objects and all the objects accessible from them. Objects vary in size and may contain pointers to other objects. In a stable heap, some programmer specified roots are stable; the rest are volatile. The stable roots are global. The *stable state* is the part of the heap that must survive crashes; it consists of all objects accessible from the stable roots. The objects in the stable state must be atomic. The *volatile state* does not necessarily survive crashes; it consists of all objects that are accessible from the volatile roots, but are not part of the stable state, e.g., objects local to a procedure invocation, objects created by a transaction that has not yet completed, and global objects that do not have to survive crashes.

The programmer sees one heap containing both stable and volatile objects. He can store pointers to stable objects in volatile objects, and can cause volatile objects to become stable by storing pointers to them in an object that is already stable. (A volatile object actually becomes stable when a transaction that makes it accessible from a stable object commits.) Transactions share a single address space that contains both shared global objects and objects local to a single transaction; the programmer does not need to move objects between secondary storage and a transaction's local memory, or distinguish between local and global objects.

3 Simple Stable Heap Implementation

Below we describe the storage architecture for a stable heap and the failure model. Then we sketch a simple implementation of a stable heap in order to provide a framework for describing our tracking algorithm. For concreteness we describe an approach to recovery based on versioning and a redo log. This approach is based on the recovery system of Argus [12, 17], except that we assume that disk storage survives a crash.

Our dissertation [10] describes two more realistic stable heap implementations: the recovery system of one is also based on versioning and a redo log; the recovery system of the other is based on repeating history and undo/redo logging. We show how to integrate the tracking algorithms into both systems.

3.1 Storage Architecture

A recovery system (often called recovery in the remainder of the paper) provides fault-tolerance by controlling the movement of data between the levels of a storage hierarchy. In a typical database there are four components in the hierarchy: (1) main memory, (2) disk, (3) log, and (4) archive. We assume a similar hierarchy for the design of our simple stable heap implementation.

A stable heap keeps its data on disk, which is non-volatile, and uses main memory, which is volatile, as a cache or buffer pool. Together the main memory and disk constitute a virtual memory and hold the current state of the stable heap. A buffer manager decides which pages to keep in the cache; it reads pages from disk into main memory and writes modified pages back to disk.

The log is a sequential file, kept on a stable storage device[1], to which the recovery system writes information that it needs in order to redo the effects of a committed transaction. The recovery system does not write directly to the log on stable storage; rather, it spools information to a log buffer. When a buffer fills, recovery writes it to disk asynchronously and begins spooling to the next buffer. The recovery system synchronously writes a buffer to stable storage, or *forces* the log, only at transaction commit when it must ensure that the effects of the transaction survive failure. In this paper when we say *write to the log*, we mean spool to the log buffer. If we want to describe a synchronous write, we use the phrase *force the log*.

The archive is an out-of-date copy of the database; it may be on disk or some cheaper non-volatile medium such as magnetic tape.

Separate from the hierarchy discussed above, the stable heap implementation also has other volatile memory at its disposal. It uses this volatile memory to store information that does not need to survive crashes such as locks and versions (discussed below in Section 3.3).

3.2 Failure Model

A recovery system deals with three kinds of failure: (1) transaction, (2) system, and (3) media. A transaction fails when it aborts; the recovery system ensures that the transaction has no effect.

A system failure can be caused by software (e.g., inconsistent data structures in the operating system) or hardware (e.g., power failure). When the system fails main memory is lost, but the disk and log survive. A system failure also aborts transactions that are active when it occurs. The recovery system uses information in the log and on the disk to recover the state of the heap. The recovered heap reflects the cumulative effects of all the transactions that committed before the failure, and none of the effects of aborted transactions. We also call a system failure a crash.

A media failure occurs when a page or several pages of the disk get corrupted. The recovery system uses the log together with the archive to recover the pages. In this paper we are concerned primarily with system failure. Our recovery system writes enough information to the log to recover from a media failure; but we do not discuss media failure further.

3.3 Stable Heap Implementation

To access an object, a transaction invokes a read or write operation. The transaction acquires a lock on the object in the mode appropriate to the operation and holds the lock until it commits or aborts. When a transaction obtains a write lock on an object for the first time, a copy of the object is made in volatile memory and the transaction operates on this copy, which is called the *current*

[1] With very high probability, a stable storage device [11] avoids the loss of information due to failure.

version. The previous version, called the *base version*, remains unchanged in the virtual memory.

To create a new object, a transaction allocates space for it in virtual memory, initializes its value, and obtains a read lock on the object (the lock is necessary since the object may become visible to other transactions before the allocating transaction commits).

To commit a transaction recovery writes new values to the log for the stable objects modified by the transaction and initial values to the log for the objects made stable by the transaction. We describe how recovery keeps track of the stable objects and finds the newly stable objects using a tracker in Section 4. Recovery writes new values for the modified stable objects in *data records*. A data record contains a transaction identifier and the value of the object's current version. It writes initial values for newly stable objects in *base-commit records*. A base-commit record contains the value of the object's base version. Then, recovery forces a *commit record* to the log. The commit record contains the transaction identifier of the transaction. Once the commit record is in the log, recovery overwrites the base versions of the modified objects in virtual memory with their respective current versions, and releases locks and storage for the current versions.

To abort a transaction, the recovery system releases locks and storage for the current versions of objects write locked by the transaction, and writes an *abort record* to the log. The abort record contains the transaction identifier of the transaction.

To recover from a crash, the recovery system makes a single forward pass through the log applying the information in the log records to restore the stable heap in virtual memory. It processes the log records as follows: for an object's data record it restores the value in the record as a tentative version for the object; for a transaction's commit record it installs the transaction's tentative versions as base versions; for an abort record it discards the transaction's tentative versions; and for an object's base-commit record it restores the value in the record as the object's base version.

An actual implementation would also employ a checkpointing mechanism to take advantage of information on disk and to reduce the amount of log processed after a system failure, an archiving mechanism to reduce the amount of log processed after a media failure and allow the log to be trimmed, and an atomic garbage collector [10] to reclaim storage and to reorganize storage for faster access.

4 The Simple Tracker

To keep track of the stable objects, the recovery system maintains the Accessibility Set (AS) [17], which is a superset of the stable objects, the objects accessible from the stable roots. An object becomes stable as a result of a modification to another object that is already stable. Recovery adds an object to the AS before the commit of the transaction whose modification made it stable.

The recovery system uses two additional sets when it writes to the log to make the effects of a transaction recoverable. The first set is the Modified Object Set (MOS), which is the set of objects modified by a transaction. The system keeps a MOS for each active transaction. An object is added to a transaction's MOS the first time it is modified by the transaction. The second set is the Newly Accessible Object Set (NAOS), which is the set of objects made stable by a transaction. An empty NAOS is created for a transaction before recovery begins writing to the log for it. Objects are added to a transaction's NAOS as described below.

To determine what to write to the log when it commits a transaction, the recovery system begins by scanning the transaction's MOS. For each object in the MOS that is also in the AS, i.e., potentially stable, recovery writes a data record to the log and checks the objects referenced by the object's current version for membership in the AS, inserting those objects not in the AS into the transaction's NAOS. Next, the recovery system invokes the stability tracker on each object in the transaction's NAOS. The tracker traverses the object's graph writing a base-commit record to the log for each object that is not yet in the AS, and inserting each such object in the AS.

Object B is said to be *commit-reachable* from object A, if it is directly reachable from A's base version or it is commit-reachable from another object which is directly reachable from A's base version. To be correct the recovery system must ensure the following correctness condition:

Correctness Condition 1 *If an object is commit-reachable from a stable root, then its value is recoverable from the log.*

Below we describe a simple tracker that is correct but allows no concurrency while it process a newly stable object graph.

4.1 Invariants

The recovery system and the simple tracker maintain three invariants on the AS:

Invariant 1 *If an object is commit-reachable from a stable root, it is in the AS.*

Invariant 2 *If an object is in the AS, then its value is recoverable from the log.*

Invariant 3 *If an object is in the AS, then all of the objects commit-reachable from it are in the AS, i.e., they are recoverable from the log.*

Taken together the first two invariants imply Correctness Condition 1. The third invariant allows the tracker to prune work from its search: if an object is in the AS, the tracker does not need to process it or the objects reachable from its base version.

4.2 Simple Tracker

The procedure for tracking newly stable objects takes a single argument, the object whose value should be tracked for newly stable objects.

Here is the code for **simple_track_newly_stable**(o), the simple stability tracker.

1. If o is in the AS, return.
2. In an atomic step, if o is not in AS, then
   (a) Log a base-commit record for o.
   (b) Insert o in the AS.
   (c) For each object p referenced directly by o's base version where p is not in the AS, **simple_track_newly_stable**(p).

To argue that the simple tracker is correct, we need to show that it maintains the three invariants. The tracker maintains Invariant 2 because it inserts an object in the AS and writes its base version to the log in a single atomic step. It maintains Invariant 3 because it tracks the object graph accessible from a newly stable object in a single atomic step. The recovery system and the tracker cooperate to maintain Invariant 1: before it commits a transaction, the recovery system calls the tracker to insert all of the objects made newly stable by the transaction in the AS.

Oki's concurrent algorithm [17] is similar to our simple algorithm, but it does not invoke itself recursively to track the whole object graph accessible from a newly stable object in a single atomic step. Therefore, it fails to maintain Invariant 3. As a result it incorrectly prunes work and allows a transaction to commit before all of its effects are recoverable. Section 5.2 describes an example that Oki's algorithm handles incorrectly.

5 The Concurrent Tracker

When the simple tracker described above is invoked on an object, it processes the whole sub-graph rooted at the object in a single atomic step by invoking itself recursively. If the sub-graph is large and contains many objects that were not previously in the AS, this may take a long time. Meanwhile, the recovery system cannot invoke tracking on behalf of other transactions and these transactions are prevented from committing.

The simple tracker invokes itself recursively within the atomic step in order to preserve Invariant 3. To increase concurrency we reduce the size of the atomic step by removing the recursive invocation from it. To do so we introduce another set called the Logged Set or LS, and use it (instead of the AS) to keep track of the objects whose graphs are recoverable from the log and to prune work from the tracker's search. We replace Invariant 3 with the following invariant.

Invariant 4 *If an object is in the LS, then all of the objects commit-reachable from it are in the AS, i.e., they are recoverable from the log.*

To track newly stable objects from an object o, the concurrent tracking algorithm does a depth-first traversal on the object graph rooted at o. On the way down the graph, it inserts newly stable objects (objects that are not yet in the AS) into the AS and it writes their initial values to the log. Inserting an object in the AS and recording its initial value in the log occur in an atomic step. When the downward traversal reaches an object in the LS, it does not search the sub-graph rooted at that object since membership in the LS indicates that the sub-graph is already recoverable from the log. On the way up from the traversal, the tracking algorithm inserts newly stable objects in the LS.

5.1 The Algorithm

The concurrent procedure takes two arguments. The first argument is the object whose value should be tracked for newly stable objects. The second argument is the set of objects that has already been visited by the traversal; it permits the tracking of cycles in the object graph. (The simple tracker does not need the visited set; while it is working it is the only tracker inserting objects in the AS so membership in the AS also indicates that it has already visited an object.)

Each invocation of the concurrent procedure uses its own local NAOS to take a snapshot of the roots of the sub-graphs that need to be searched recursively by the tracker. Without it, the commit of a concurrent transaction could interfere with the tracker.

Here is the code for the concurrent stability tracker, **track_newly_stable**(o, *visited*).

1. If o is in the LS, return.
2. In an atomic step, if o is not in AS, then
   (a) Log a base-commit record for o.
   (b) Insert o in the AS.
3. In an atomic step construct this invocation's local NAOS, i.e., for each object p referenced directly by o's committed value where p is not in *visited* and p is not in the LS, insert p in the local NAOS.
4. For each object p in the local NAOS invoke **track_newly_stable**(p, *visited* $\bigcup \{o\}$).
5. In an atomic step, insert o in the LS.

To argue that the concurrent tracker is correct, we need to show that it maintains Invariants 2 and 4. As with the simple tracker Invariant 2 holds because the tracker inserts an object in the AS and writes a base-commit record to the log for it in a single atomic step. The tracker does not insert an object A in the LS until all of the objects reachable from A are in the AS, so Invariant 4 also holds.

5.2 An Example

Figure 1 shows how the tracking algorithm works by example. It shows a sequence of six snapshots of the tracker, the log, and an object graph. At the beginning, objects A and B are stable, and objects C and D are volatile. In the first snapshot, a transaction has modified object A, inserting a pointer to object C. To commit the transaction the recovery system invokes **track_newly_stable**(C,{A}). In the second snapshot, A's tracker has added C to the AS, logged a base-commit record for C, and computed a local NAOS. In the third snapshot, a second transaction has modified object B and inserted a pointer to object C. To commit the second transaction the recovery system has has invoked **track_newly_stable**(C,{B}). The fourth snapshot shows that A's tracker has invoked **track_newly_stable**(D,{A,C}), which has added D to the AS and logged a base-commit record for D. By the fifth snapshot, A's tracker has completed, popped its stack, and inserted D and then C in the LS. In the last snapshot, B's tracker has noticed that D is in the LS and it completes.

The third snapshot illustrates the bug in Oki's algorithm [17]; his algorithm would have noticed that C is in the AS, would not have invoked B's tracker, and would have allowed the second transaction to commit before the graph rooted at C is recoverable.

6 Optimizations

Two optimizations of the concurrent procedure are possible. The first optimization saves work when two or more trackers that are running concurrently are tracking objects that share a common sub-graph. In step 3 of the concurrent tracker one tracker may insert an object in its local NAOS that is not in the LS or in *visited*, but is in the AS; if so, there must be a second tracker concurrent with the first that put the object in the AS. The second tracker may still be traversing the object's graph. The first tracker can save work by letting the second tracker finish the work of tracking the object's sub-graph or waiting to track that sub-graph until it has no other work to do.

To implement this strategy we introduce a second set called the NYLS, or *Not Yet in Logged Set*; each invocation of the tracker has its own local NYLS. When the tracker encounters an object that is not in the LS, *visited*, or the AS, it inserts the object in its local NAOS. When it encounters an object that is not in the LS or *visited*, but is in the AS, it inserts the object in its local NYLS. The tracker invokes itself recursively on all of the objects in its NAOS before invoking itself on the objects in its NYLS. By the time the tracker processes an object in its NYLS, another tracker may have inserted that object in the LS. Notice that the tracker must eventually process the objects in its NYLS; otherwise cyclical object structures could lead to deadlocks between concurrent trackers.

The concurrent tracker copies the visited set every time it invokes itself recursively. When tracking a large object graph the visited set may also grow large. The second optimization reduces the size and number of the visited sets; we keep just one copy of the visited set for each top-level invocation of the

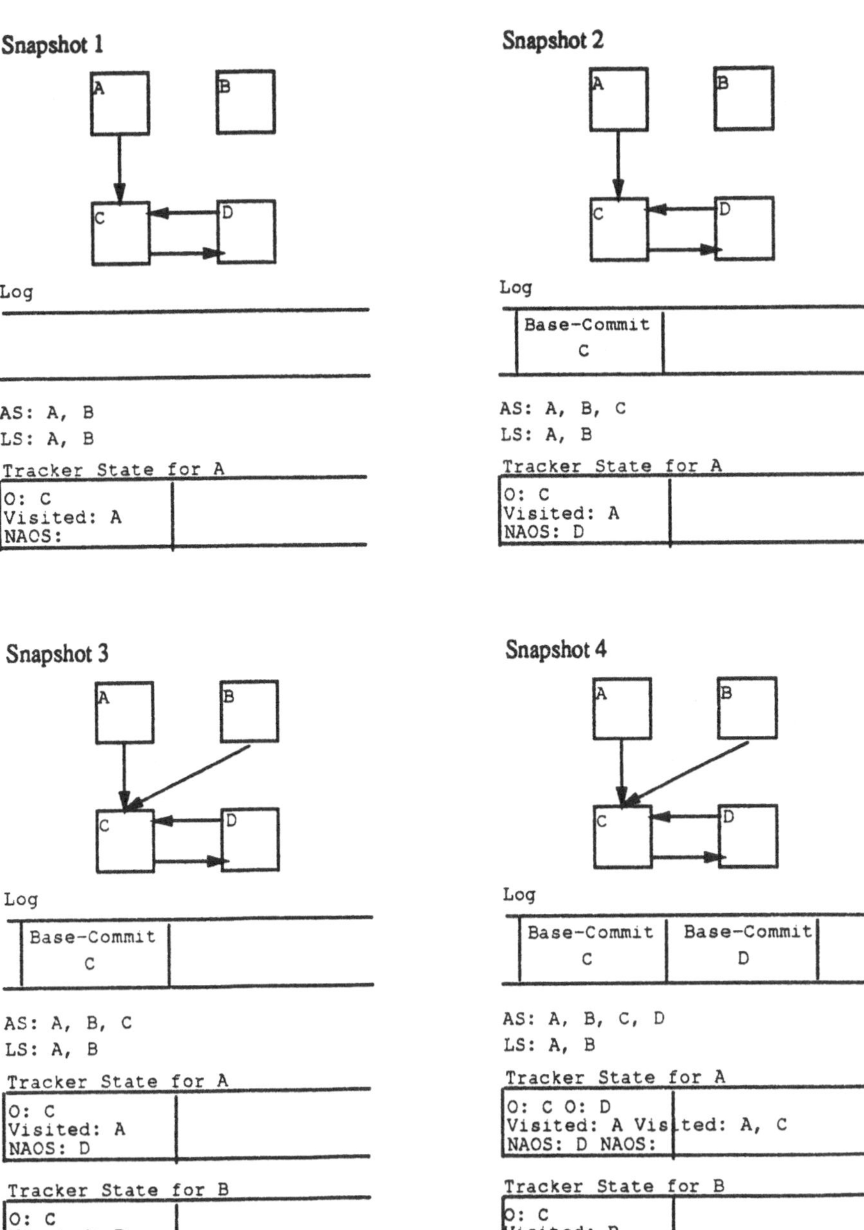

Figure 1: Concurrent Tracking

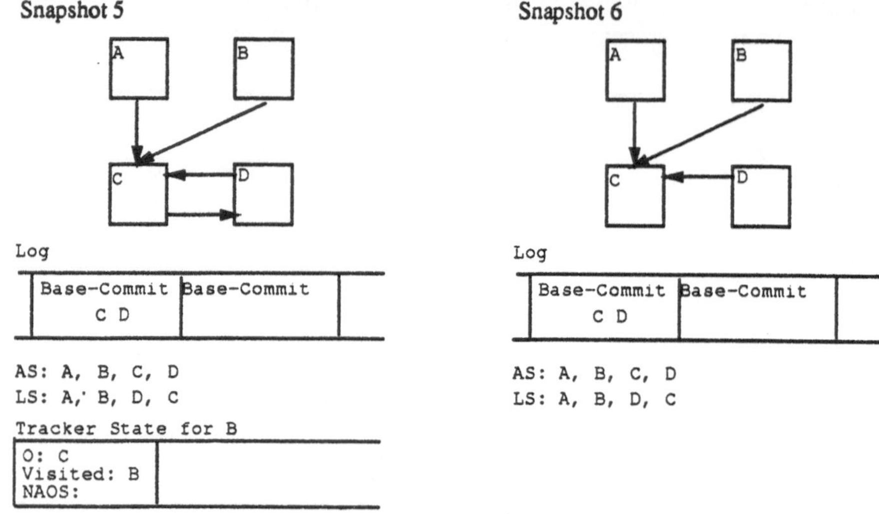

Figure 1: Concurrent Tracking (cont)

tracker and its recursions. We also delete an object from the visited set when it enters the LS.

The second optimization requires a top-level procedure that sets up the visited set for the top-level tracker, which we call **top_tracker_newly_stable**(o). It simply sets up an empty visited set, v, and calls the optimized recursive tracker, **opt_track_newly_stable**(o, v).

Here is the code for the optimized, **opt_track_newly_stable**(o, *visited*). We assume here that *visited* is passed by reference.

1. If o is in the LS, return.
2. In an atomic step, if o is not in AS, then
   (a) Log a base-commit record for o.
   (b) Insert o in the AS.
3. Insert o in *visited*.
4. In an atomic step construct the local NAOS and the local NYLS, i.e., for each object p referenced directly by o's committed value where p is not in *visited*:
   (a) if p is not in the AS, insert p in the local NAOS.
   (b) if p is in the AS but not the LS, insert p in the local NYLS.
5. For each object p in the local NAOS invoke **opt_track_newly_stable**(p, *visited*).

6. For each object p in the local NYLS invoke **opt_track_newly_stable(**p**,** ***visited*****)**.

7. In an atomic step, insert o in the LS.

8. Remove o from *visited*.

7 Implementation Issues

In order to implement our tracking algorithm we need an efficient representation for the AS and the LS, a way to recover the AS and the LS after a crash, and a way to delete objects from the AS and the LS when they are no longer stable. We discuss these problems below.

7.1 Representation of the AS and the LS

The AS and the LS could be represented as explicit sets using a hash table, but two other representations allow a faster membership check as well as simpler deletion and recovery. The two representations are: (1) two bits per object and (2) a single bit per object and an explicit set.

Using two bits per object, one bit would indicate membership in the AS and the second bit would indicate membership in the LS. These bits are placed in the object descriptor, which also holds the type and the size of the object. The current Argus system uses a similar representation for its AS [17].

To understand the single bit and explicit set representation, notice that there are only three states possible with respect to an object's membership in the AS and the LS: (1) not in either, (2) in the AS only, or (3) in both. The bit in each object would show whether the object is in both sets, while the explicit set would contain entries for objects that are in the AS but not the LS. Thus, an object is in the AS if its bit is set or if it is in the explicit set.

If two bits are available in object descriptors, it is clearly the best choice. If only one bit can be spared in the object descriptor, the single bit and an explicit set is a good alternative. The explicit set would be very small, so that the costs for storage and the cost for lookup could be very cheap. In the rest of this paper, we assume the representation using two bits.

7.2 Recovering the AS and the LS

We briefly discuss the requirements for recovery of the AS and the LS. The actual mechanics of recovery depend on details of the recovery algorithms that we have omitted from this paper for the sake of brevity. Our dissertation [10] describes the details.

Recovery must make sure that the AS bit is set for every object that is reachable from a stable root after a crash. If it misses an object, recovery will not record a new value for that object in the log the next time a transaction modifies it.

In contrast, it is permissible for recovery to fail to insert an object in the LS that really could be in the LS, i.e., the object is in the AS and every object reachable from it is in the AS. Notice that this is not incorrect, rather it just reduces the efficiency of the tracker. If an object belongs in the LS but the object's LS bit is not set, the tracker will just re-traverse the object's subgraph and re-insert the object in the LS the next time it reaches the object.

7.3 Deleting Objects from the AS and the LS

When an object is no longer accessible from any root, stable or volatile, the garbage collector frees its storage, which automatically deletes it from the AS and the LS. However, some objects in the AS and the LS may still be reachable from a volatile root, but no longer reachable from a stable root. Deleting these objects from the sets is strictly an efficiency problem, in that future modifications to the objects will be more expensive than necessary.

A stop-the-world algorithm to detect precisely which objects should no longer be in the AS and the LS is simple: first, trace from the stable roots and mark the reachable objects; second, trace from the volatile roots and delete objects from the AS and the LS that were not marked in the first step. However, a stop-the-world algorithm is not suitable for a large stable heap. Designing an incremental algorithm is more complex. Since we do not expect many stable objects to remain reachable from a volatile root after they have become unreachable from a stable root, we do not present a solution here. If the problem turns out to be troublesome in a real system, we will need to find an acceptable solution.

8 Conclusion

A stable heap is a persistent heap where updates to persistent objects run as atomic transactions. It is a model of computation that is appropriate for object-oriented databases, languages for persistent programming, and languages for reliable distributed computing. Our research has focused on the design of algorithms for storage management and recovery for a stable heap. This paper describes one such algorithm, a concurrent tracking algorithm that finds newly stable objects and ensures that they are recoverable. Many trackers can run concurrently with each other, and no tracker or transaction is held up because some other transaction has made a large object graph newly stable.

References

[1] A. Albano, L. Cardelli, and R. Orsini. A Strongly Typed Interactive Conceptual Language. *ACM Transactions on Database Systems*, 10(2):230–260, June 1985.

[2] M. P. Atkinson, P. J. Bailey, K. J. Chisholm, P. W. Cockshott, and R. Morrison. An Approach to Persistent Programming. *The Computer Journal*, 26(4):360–365, 1983.

[3] Alfred Brown and John Rosenberg. Persistent Object Stores: An Implementation Technique. In Alan Dearle, Gail M. Shaw, and Stanley B. Zdonik, editors, *Implementing Persistent Object Bases: Principles and Practice/ The Fourth International Workshop on Persistent Object Systems*, pages 199–212. Morgan-Kaufmann Publishers, San Mateo, California, 1990.

[4] M. Carey, D. DeWitt, J. Richardson, and E. Sheikta. Object and File Management in the EXODUS Extensible Database System. In *Proceedings of the 12th International Conference on Very Large Databases*, August 1986.

[5] W. P. Cockshott, M. P. Atkinson, K. J. Chisholm, P. J. Bailey, and R. Morrison. Persistent Object Management System. *Software–Practice and Experience*, 14:49–71, 1984.

[6] David Detlefs, Maurice Herlihy, and Jeannette Wing. Inheritance of Synchronization and Recovery Properties in Avalon/C++. *IEEE Computer*, 21(12), December 1988.

[7] James N. Gray. Notes on Database Operating Systems. In R. Bayer, R. M. Graham, and G. Seegmuller, editors, *Operating Systems–An Advanced Course*, volume 60 of *Lecture Notes in Computer Science*, pages 393–481. Springer-Verlag, New York, 1978.

[8] Elliot Kolodner. Atomic Incremental Garbage Collection and Recovery for a Large Stable Heap. In Alan Dearle, Gail M. Shaw, and Stanley B. Zdonik, editors, *Implementing Persistent Object Bases: Principles and Practice/ The Fourth International Workshop on Persistent Object Systems*, pages 185–198. Morgan-Kaufmann Publishers, San Mateo, California, 1990.

[9] Elliot Kolodner, Barbara Liskov, and William Weihl. Atomic Garbage Collection: Managing a Stable Heap. In *Proceedings of the 1989 ACM SIGMOD International Conference on the Management of Data*, pages 15–25, June 1989.

[10] Elliot K. Kolodner. Atomic Incremental Garbage Collection and Recovery for a Large Stable Heap. Technical Report MIT/LCS/TR-534, Laboratory for Computer Science, MIT, Cambridge, Ma., February 1992.

[11] Butler. W. Lampson. *Atomic Transactions*, volume 105 of *Lecture Notes in Computer Science*, pages 246–265. Springer-Verlag, New York, 1981. This is a revised version of Lampson and Sturgis's unpublished *Crash Recovery in a Distributed Data Storage System.*

[12] Barbara Liskov. Overview of the Argus Language and System. Programming Methodology Group Memo 40, Laboratory for Computer Science, MIT, Cambridge, Ma., February 1984.

[13] Barbara Liskov, Paul Johnson, and Robert Scheifler. Implementation of Argus. In *Proceedings of the Eleventh Symposium on Operating Systems Principles*, November 1987.

[14] David Maier, Jacob Stein, Allen Otis, and Alan Purdy. Development of an Object-Oriented DBMS. In *Proceedings of the Object-Oriented Programming Systems, Languages and Applications*, pages 472–482, November 1986.

[15] C. Mohan, D. Haderle, B. Lindsay, H. Pirahesh, and P. Schwarz. A Transaction Recovery Method Supporting Fine-Granularity Locking and Partial Rollbacks Using Write-Ahead Logging. Technical Report RJ6649, IBM Almaden Research Center, San Jose, Ca., January 1989.

[16] Brian Oki. Reliable Object Storage to Support Atomic Actions. Technical Report MIT/LCS/TR-308, Laboratory for Computer Science, MIT, Cambridge, Ma., May 1983.

[17] Brian Oki, Barbara Liskov, and Robert Scheifler. Reliable Object Storage to Support Atomic Actions. In *Proceedings of the Tenth Symposium on Operating Systems Principles*, pages 147–159, December 1985.

[18] Satish M. Thatte. Persistent Memory: A Storage Architecture for Object-Oriented Database Systems. In U. Dayal and K. Dittrich, editors, *Proceedings of the International Workshop on Object-Oriented Databases*, Pacific Grove, CA, September 1986.

[19] William Weihl and Barbara Liskov. Implementation of Resilient, Atomic Data Types. *ACM Transactions on Programming Languages and Systems*, 7(2):244–269, April 1985.

[20] Daniel Weinreb, Neal Feinberg, Dan Gerson, and Charles Lamb. An Object-Oriented Database System to Support an Integrated Programming Environment. Submitted for publication, 1988.

[21] Stanley Zdonik and Peter Wegner. Language and Methodology for Object-Oriented Database Environments. In *Proceedings of the 19th Annual Hawaiian Conference on Systems Science*, January 1986.

Keynote Discussion Session on Persistent Software Environments

Ray Welland

Computing Science Department, University of Glasgow
Glasgow G12 8QQ, Scotland

Abstract

The keynote discussion on Persistent Software Environments consisted of a series of presentations by invited contributors followed by a general discussion. The contributors identified issues on the construction and use of persistent software environments, and two of them described their experiences with Smalltalk and O_2.

The main research topics which emerged during the session were: how to support a variety of languages within a single environment; the need for change management in long-lived persistent systems; support for large-scale software development and building tools which take advantage of persistence.

1 Introduction

The first part of the keynote discussion consisted of five presentations by Ray Welland; Alan Dearle, University of Adelaide, Australia; Mario Wolczko, University of Manchester, UK; Anne Doucet, University of Paris Sud, France and Peter Buhr, University of Waterloo, Canada. This was followed by an open discussion with interaction between the audience and the contributors. The whole discussion was recorded and the main points are summarised below.

2 The Issues

Ray Welland opened the discussion by presenting a software engineer's view of environments and then posing some broad questions to provide a framework for discussion. Alan Dearle then focussed on the question of how persistent systems could provide more integration.

2.1 Software Engineering Issues

In the Software Engineering field, a great deal of research has focussed on the provision of methods and tools to support software development. This has progressed from individual programming tools, through groupings of tools into program development environments or workbenches, to considering the provision of Integrated Project Support Environments (IPSEs), also called Software Engineering Environments (SEEs). The ultimate aim of IPSEs is to integrate software development processes in a number of different ways: between tools (tool integration), between stages of software development (method integration), across the development team and between technical development and management. Much of the research in SEEs has been concerned with the integration of existing tools and methods into some coherent framework.

Research into Persistent Object Systems started from a different integration viewpoint, recognising the discontinuity between programming languages and the storage of long-lived data. However, now that the technology of persistence is maturing and the building of large-scale persistent application systems (PAS) is possible, it is necessary to consider the tools, workbenches or environments that are required to support PAS development. Since persistent application systems are by their nature long-lived these tools must support the long-term maintenance of systems as well as development.

The two main questions posed for this keynote discussion were:

- What are the features which characterise a good Persistent Software Environment? Is it possible to identify a set of general principles for supporting the development of PAS?
- What tools should be provided to support the development of large-scale persistent application systems? If it is too difficult to identify principles perhaps a consensus on (some of) the tools which should be included in a Persistent Software Environment can be reached.

Some of the sub-questions posed were:

- What is the current state of support for the development of persistent systems? Do these existing software architectures scale-up for large-scale software development?
- Are there special problems with the development of persistent application systems? How much of the general Software Engineering experience is applicable? Is Software Engineering experience being ignored because it is NIH?
- Are there features of the POS approach which make it easier to develop support environments? Persistence provides new technology for the building of tools (for example: linguistic reflection, different types of binding, handling of complex structures); how do these affect the approach to tool building? Current CASE tools and IPSEs usually consist of large tools with simple data interchange but POS may be better suited to smaller tool fragments.
- One of the characteristics of long-lived data is that both structure and applications change over time - how should long term change be managed by tools within a Persistent Software Environment? Is there a conflict between the constructs which are most suitable for increasing the efficiency of software development and those needed for change management? Are the type mechanisms being proposed by persistent language designers providing support for change management?
- Persistent systems are characterised by a close integration of the programming language and the object store, does this imply that persistent software environments must be mono-lingual?
- Re-use has long been recognised as desirable technology but software engineering has struggled for many years to find a suitable paradigm for re-use. Do POS provide a better route to re-usable software than conventional languages? If so, what tools could be provided to assist re-use?

2.2 Integration through persistence

Alan Dearle developed the theme of the integration which persistent systems could provide and identified a number of important issues for discussion. The first of these was the question of whether an environment should achieve close integration by supporting only a single language. If environments should be mono-lingual then which language? If multiple languages are supported then how is meaningful integration to be achieved?

The second question concerned bindings to values and locations in the store. In persistent systems it is possible to create sophisticated bindings between programs and data. How is it possible to take advantage of these mechanisms? How can the creation of a tangle of interactions which are incomprehensible to the programmer be avoided? How are values extracted from the store?

Alan then discussed the possibilities for re-use of system building components. The Lisp and Smalltalk communities have already demonstrated how re-use can be achieved by having programs in the store. Some of the persistent languages follow this approach but are there alternative models for re-use? What model is appropriate for C++, for example? There are also issues concerning the tight binding between the application being developed and the persistent store. Is it possible to have stand-alone applications or does the persistent store always have to be present? Is it possible to build embedded systems using persistent technology?

The final question Alan raised was a reiteration of the question of programs as data. Should programs be data items in the store? If procedures are not data objects, how can programs be stored? If programs are treated as data how does this affect the nature of programs and the process of program development?

3 The Smalltalk Experience

Mario Wolczko discussed how Smalltalk-80 could be viewed as a Persistent Software Environment. Although Smalltalk was not designed as a persistent programming language it does provide a very simple 'snapshot' model of persistence. In Smalltalk everything is an object and all non-garbage objects are saved to disk in a snapshot; this includes windows, the state of processes, etc.; there are no exceptions. There is no linguistic support for persistence, simply a primitive method for snapshots. Because snapshots are large, logging of source level changes is also provided. The main drawback of this model is that it is not multi-user.

One of the major strengths of Smalltalk is its support for incremental development; there is a large base image which provides a rich source of good examples and classes for development. Re-use of code is simplified because there are no type declarations in Smalltalk; the system depends on run-time typing via dynamic binding.

To consider Smalltalk as a model for a Persistent Software Environment it would be necessary to look at two major problems: protection and support for multi-user working. At present the system does not provide adequate mechanisms for the safe development of software by even a single user, improved modularity and some form of transaction mechanism would be useful. To support multi-user working the Manchester group are exploring the idea of extending the single space model to allow many users to inhabit the same space. The objective is to retain the single virtual space and distribute it across different machines, providing access and concurrency control.

Finally, Mario made the point that persistent systems should be simple for the programmer to use; at the moment the trend seems to be to add extra layers to the architecture, making the model more complex!

4 The O_2 Experience

Anne Doucet described the architecture of O_2, an object-oriented database system which has three main characteristics: database and programming language capabilities, a graphical user interface and a complete graphical programming environment. An O_2 application consists of a schema and a group of related programs. The code can be written in one of the O_2 languages: O_2C (extension of C), C or C++ and graphical user interfaces are constructed using O_2LOOK, a set of predefined high-level primitives.

The programming environment, O_2Tools, is graphical and includes a number of specialised graphical browsers (schema, classes, methods, documentation, data, etc.) and editors (for classes, methods, ...). However, there is also a mechanism to escape from the graphical environment to directly manipulate O_2 code and access Unix files. The system includes a source manager to provide version control, cross-referencing and automatic recompilation. There are incremental compilers to facilitate interactive testing of methods and programs, together with an object-oriented symbolic debugger. Other tools include integrated schema documentation and an O_2SQL query interface. O_2Tools is an O_2 application completely built using the O_2 languages.

Anne completed her talk by suggesting the following criteria for a good programming environment: adaptable user interface; integration and uniformity; persistence; extensibility (the ability to add new tools without changing existing tools); versioning; documentation tools; concurrency control and efficient interaction between users.

5 Provocation!

As the last contributor, **Peter Buhr** decided to be provocative and present a list of desirable and undesirable features in a Persistent Software Environment. He suggested that the following were undesirable features: - universal garbage collection, don't want to pay for it, don't understand it in distributed systems; - universal reachability, why can't I delete my own data even if somebody else has a pointer to it?; - strong type system, need to violate the type system for storage management; - universal transaction mechanisms, people don't understand them!; - programs writing programs are of doubtful use!

Peter's desirable features included: - single language; - static type checking wherever possible, distinguish static from strong type checking; - subtyping, parametric polymorphism, overloading and generics (for re-use); - browsers to find things to re-use; - visualisation tools for programs; - distributed capabilities and concurrency facilities; - performance monitoring tools; - support for teams of programmers building large systems; and all these things integrated into a coherent framework.

As Peter recognised himself, the above list is a mixture of language features and environment features; these are inevitably mixed together and the discussion which followed often strayed into questions concerning languages and types.

6 General Discussion

The first major topic to arise during the discussion was the management of change; how to build systems which will run for many years with changing requirements. It was suggested that languages and type systems constrain change rather than supporting evolution. It was stated that Smalltalk has managed to cope with change quite successfully because it has no static type system and so the generic code is easily modifiable. However, it was also pointed out that Smalltalk needs a more modular structure and better control of binding, information hiding and composition to be used for large-scale system development. Another point of view was that it is necessary to understand the process of building persistent programs before worrying about how to change them!

In existing systems, components can be changed (dynamic binding to changing schema); how is it possible to control the impact of change in persistent environments? It was suggested that the answer lies in developing methodologies and disciplines to establish structure. It was pointed out that when a store is populated with a large number of objects the main problem is not changing definitions but handling the instances in the store. It was suggested that the technique of hyper-programming could have an impact on this problem by allowing new bindings to existing data. It was obvious from this discussion that there is still plenty of research required in this area!

A second topic of discussion was how to make the best use of persistence to build tools? It was stated that the advantages of persistence should be emphasised as it is unlikely that persistence will be sold on performance. For example, existing systems for configuration management and source code control depend on naming conventions to encode associations between objects. Persistent environments allow these names to be replaced by links which can be maintained within the persistent store and enforced.

The question of single language versus multi-language environments was discussed extensively. Most people accepted the viewpoint that a single language would be nice but in practice it will be necessary to cope with a variety of languages for different types of applications. However, reservations were expressed about the safety of multi-lingual environments and also about whether enough is known to build them at the moment. The question of communication between languages was raised and it was agreed that something better than byte stream communication is required. Several people cited examples of other environments in which multi-lingual working had been investigated. In O_2 the three languages (O_2C, C and C++) are all type compatible; others cited work on heterogeneous databases and interoperation of C++ and Smalltalk. It was also suggested that the OMG work on object communication should provide solutions to the problem of inter-language communication.

7 Conclusions

The main principles for research into persistent software environments which emerged from this keynote discussion were:

- Environments need to support a variety of programming languages at some semantic level of interaction (not just byte streams!).

- Mechanisms for change management (schema evolution) are essential for applications in which the data may persist for many years.

- The problem of large scale software development needs to be addressed; how do teams of programmers build and maintain persistent application systems?

- Research should be focussed on tools which take advantage of persistence; tools which cannot be built in other environments.

Concluding Remarks

Gail Mitchell and John Rosenberg

What exactly is a persistent object system? Where are its boundaries? Does it include a type system? If so, what are the requirements of such a system? Does a POS include transactions? How does it relate to an operating system? What support is required of the hardware or an operating system to support a persistent object system? How do we evaluate persistent systems? What is needed to support programming in a persistent environment?

These questions illustrate just some of the issues discussed over the four days of the Fifth Persistent Object Systems Workshop. Although there are no clear cut answers to these questions, the paper presentations and discussions at the workshop helped all of us achieve an even better understanding of the issues.

The early POS workshops [1, 2, 3] concentrated on establishing appropriate theory and basic techniques for the design and construction of persistent object systems. In the Fourth POS workshop [4] there was a marked increase in the number of system implementations described. In this workshop we see even more working systems presented as well as more experience in using the technology. For example, μ Database (Buhr, Goel and Wai) provides a toolkit for implementing persistent object systems based on memory mapping. Texas (Singhal, Kakkad and Wilson) uses virtual memory combined with pointer swizzling for transparent and scalable access to transient and persistent objects and is implemented as a C++ library. The Papyrus Object Library (Connors and Neimat) is a tool for implementing managers which provide access to persistent storage.

Increased experience in using the technology is evident in the applications that are being built on persistent systems. Stabilis (Buzato and Calsavara) is a distributed object-oriented database implemented on an object-oriented programming system. Keedy and Brössler, on the other hand, explore the advantages of building databases on top of the MONADS architecture.

This experience also leads us to new ways to use the technology. For example, Kirby et al describe a new programming paradigm called *hyper-programming* which utilises the persistent store to assist with program construction. Hyper-programming is supported by a graphical, iconic programming environment that can browse the store and aid in program construction (Farkas et al).

The experience gained in developing and working with the many persistent object systems is encouraging in its implications for increased understanding of the problems that need to be addressed in the field.

At this workshop we continued to address issues involved with the implementation of efficient stores. These techniques range from the access level to the type level. New pointer swizzling techniques which are able to take advantage of the facilities provided by conventional paged virtual memory hardware were presented by Vaughan and Dearle, and by Wilson (the Texas system). The former paper contains a comparison of these techniques. Wolczko and Williams addressed the issue of garbage collection in persistent stores, and Kolodner presented an algorithm for tracking newly stable objects to ensure they can be recovered after a failure. Ghelli proposed a record structure that supports fast run-time access to subtypes. Hasan and Krishnamurthy proposed an intermediate language for data access that is optimisable and parallelisable. The issue of efficiency will continue to be of paramount importance if persistence technology is to move into the marketplace.

Data consistency and integrity is another issue that received considerable attention at this workshop. Kolodner's work supports the recovery system by ensuring that newly stable objects survive failure. Livesey and Allison addressed the enforcement of coherence in distributed systems through transaction rollback. Daynès and Gruber implemented nested transactions in a distributed environment. At the type level, DeFrancesco, Mancini et al presented a proposal for linguistic support for the definition of the semantics of concurrency, and Sparg and Berman discussed constraint definition and constraint checking in PERCI. Benzaken, Lécluse and Richard described the use of type information to generate run-time algorithms to verify that constraints over a database are maintained by transactions. Amiel, Bellosta and Valduriez presented an object management interface that supports schema evolution.

Kaiser and Czaja addressed the issue of security by providing a design for hardware to enforce run-time object-level protection. This raises the question of what support belongs in the hardware and what belongs in the software; a question that should spur further discussion at future workshops.

An encouraging trend at this workshop was the emphasis on measurement. A number of authors presented experimental results. For example, Buhr, Goel and Wai presented results of comparing memory-mapped with traditional file structures. Daynès and Gruber evaluated the overhead of nested locking in their system through comparisons with systems without locking. Ghelli presented results of a comparison of search structures used for access to record fields.

Other authors proposed models for evaluation. For example, Malhotra and Perry presented a strategy for evaluating object clustering heuristics. At the system evaluation level, Atkinson et al gave us a foundation for the design of benchmarks for the internal behaviour of persistent object systems and are promising to provide a persistent systems benchmark suite for use by other research groups.

We were also encouraged by the emphasis on providing a formal basis for persistent object systems. Atkinson et al presented us with criteria for formulating laws over the behaviour of persistent object systems. They also proposed some laws. Bertino and Foscoli's cost model for queries provides a formal basis for evaluating the execution of queries over persistent data.

A very positive feature of this meeting was the overall organisation of our 'formal' working time. Each paper session concluded with a discussion of the topics and issues raised during the paper presentations. These discussions are reported in the introductions to the different sections of this proceedings. We also had three keynote discussions, which were organised to focus on key areas in persistent object systems research. These discussions let us explore further some of the issues raised in the paper sessions, and introduced new questions to think about as well.

In the keynote session on operating systems support for persistence, for example, we further discussed some of the hardware and operating system features desired by builders of persistent object systems. What facilities should be provided by an operating system? What should be the features of hardware to support persistence? Where is the division between hardware, operating system and programming language support? Are there intrinsic costs in different decisions? Our increased experience with building persistent object systems offers insight into answers to these questions.

This experience also helps us formulate our requirements for environments for building persistent systems. In the keynote session on persistent environments the panelists described their requirements for programming environments and their experience with such environments. What tools are needed to support the development of persistent applications? What is needed to support change in such systems? Can the same tools support software development as well as methodologies for system modification? The discussion in this session indicated that these are some of the questions that still need to be addressed.

Our final keynote session centred around persistent type systems, a topic only peripherally addressed in some paper sessions. The major issues of discussion in the session were strong vs. weak typing, and static vs. dynamic type-checking. Are weakly typed languages at all useful for persistent systems? Are strong, static systems really necessary? Can we allow privileged access that can override the type system? Should objects that change structure over their lifetime be considered exceptional, or usual? We expect these issues to continue to be addressed at future workshops, as well as at the related Workshops on Database Programming Languages [5, 6, 7].

The progress made since even the last workshop in implementation and understanding of persistent object systems indicates a growing maturity of the field. With this maturity we can see a number of important issues that we expect will be further addressed in subsequent workshops. Implementation issues such as clustering, transactions and concurrency control should continue to receive attention. We also expect to see implementations of persistent type systems, and further work on issues such as schema evolution and integrity constraints.

We hope to see a continuing trend towards formulating a theoretical foundation for persistent systems. This should include a common framework for measuring the internal behaviour of such systems. This framework must also be accompanied by tools that can be used by system builders to measure and compare their systems.

An important complement to research into the issues involved with building persistent object systems is the need for implementations of large-scale applications using these systems. We hope that our increasing experience with the technology of persistent object systems will lead to reports of more applications using this technology. Such applications will not only test our theories but will enhance our understanding of the issues involved in building and using persistent object systems.

It is clear that there is much interest in persistent systems within the computer science community. There is now a growing number of workshops that overlap with the themes discussed at POS 5. This includes the Bremen Workshop on Security and Persistence, the IWOOOS series (International Workshop on Object Orientation in Operating Systems) and a number of workshops on distributed systems and memory management. These workshops are providing a larger forum for the dissemination of research results. However, this may mean that we need to carefully define the issues to be explored at future POS workshops in order to ensure that the high standard is maintained.

As we look forward to the next POS workshop, we'd like to thank everyone who was involved in this workshop for making it such a worthwhile learning experience for all. The program chairs, Antonio Albano and Ron Morrison, and the committee members did a great job of organising a challenging and interesting collection of papers and discussion topics.

Our 'informal' working time was at least as important as the organized sessions, and Luigi Mancini, Ettore Ricciardi, and Isabella Kardasz can't be thanked enough for the outstanding job they did in making the local arrangements. The Centro Studi "I Cappuccini" was an excellent place to work, and the staff there made our visit very easy and comfortable. The trip to Siena was a thoroughly enjoyable break. And the harpsichord concert with Annalaura Cavuoto and Chiara Tiboni was unforgettable.

We're already looking forward to meeting everyone again and exchanging our newest ideas and results at the next, Sixth, Persistent Object Systems Workshop.

References

1. "Datatypes and Persistence", *Proceedings of Data Types and Persistence Workshop Aug. 1985*, Appin, Scotland (ed M.P. Atkinson, P. Buneman and R. Morrison), Springer-Verlag, 1988.

2. *Proceedings of the 2nd International Workshop on Persistent Object Systems*, Appin, August 1987, (ed. M.P. Atkinson and R. Morrison), Universities of Glasgow and St Andrews PPRR-44, 1987.

3. "Persistent Object Systems", *Proceedings of the 3rd International Workshop on Persistent Object Systems*, Newcastle, Australia (ed J. Rosenberg and D.M. Koch), Springer-Verlag, 1989.

4. "Implementing Persistent Object Bases: Principles and Practice", *Proceedings of the 4th International Workshop on Persistent Object Systems*, Marthas Vineyard, USA (ed A. Dearle, G.M. Shaw and S.B. Zdonik), Morgan-Kaufmann, 1990.

5. "Advances in Database Programming Languages", *Proceedings of the International Workshop on Database Programming Languages*, Roscoff, France (ed F. Bancilhon and P. Buneman), Addison Wesley, 1987.

6. "Database Programming Languages", *Proceedings of the 2nd International Workshop on Database Programming Languages*, Salishan, Oregon, U.S.A., (ed R. Hull, R. Morrison and D. Stemple), Morgan Kaufmann, 1989.

7. "Database Programming Languages: Bulk Types and Persistent Data", *Proceedings of the 3rd International Workshop on Database Programming Languages*, Nafplion, Greece, (ed. P. Kanellakis and J.W. Schmidt), Morgan Kaufmann, 1991.

Author Index

Published in 1990–91

AI and Cognitive Science '89, Dublin City University, Eire, 14–15 September 1989
A. F. Smeaton and G. McDermott (Eds.)

Specification and Verification of Concurrent Systems, University of Stirling, Scotland, 6–8 July 1988
C. Rattray (Ed.)

Semantics for Concurrency, Proceedings of the International BCS-FACS Workshop, Sponsored by Logic for IT (S.E.R.C.), University of Leicester, UK, 23–25 July 1990
M. Z. Kwiatkowska, M. W. Shields and R. M. Thomas (Eds.)

Functional Programming, Glasgow 1989
Proceedings of the 1989 Glasgow Workshop, Fraserburgh, Scotland, 21–23 August 1989
K. Davis and J. Hughes (Eds.)

Persistent Object Systems, Proceedings of the Third International Workshop, Newcastle, Australia, 10–13 January 1989
J. Rosenberg and D. Koch (Eds.)

Z User Workshop, Oxford 1989, Proceedings of the Fourth Annual Z User Meeting, Oxford, 15 December 1989
J. E. Nicholls (Ed.)

Formal Methods for Trustworthy Computer Systems (FM89), Halifax, Canada, 23–27 July 1989
Dan Craigen (Editor) and Karen Summerskill (Assistant Editor)

Security and Persistence, Proceedings of the International Workshop on Computer Architecture to Support Security and Persistence of Information, Bremen, West Germany, 8–11 May 1990
John Rosenberg and J. Leslie Keedy (Eds.)

Women into Computing: Selected Papers 1988–1990
Gillian Lovegrove and Barbara Segal (Eds.)

3rd Refinement Workshop (organised by BCS-FACS, and sponsored by IBM UK Laboratories, Hursley Park and the Programming Research Group, University of Oxford), Hursley Park, 9–11 January 1990
Carroll Morgan and J. C. P. Woodcock (Eds.)

Designing Correct Circuits, Workshop jointly organised by the Universities of Oxford and Glasgow, Oxford, 26–28 September 1990
Geraint Jones and Mary Sheeran (Eds.)

Functional Programming, Glasgow 1990
Proceedings of the 1990 Glasgow Workshop on Functional Programming, Ullapool, Scotland, 13–15 August 1990
Simon L. Peyton Jones, Graham Hutton and Carsten Kehler Holst (Eds.)

4th Refinement Workshop, Proceedings of the 4th Refinement Workshop, organised by BCS-FACS, Cambridge, 9–11 January 1991
Joseph M. Morris and Roger C. Shaw (Eds.)

AI and Cognitive Science '90, University of Ulster at Jordanstown, 20–21 September 1990
Michael F. McTear and Norman Creaney (Eds.)

Software Re-use, Utrecht 1989, Proceedings of the Software Re-use Workshop, Utrecht, The Netherlands, 23–24 November 1989
Liesbeth Dusink and Patrick Hall (Eds.)

Z User Workshop, 1990, Proceedings of the Fifth Annual Z User Meeting, Oxford, 17–18 December 1990
J.E. Nicholls (Ed.)

IV Higher Order Workshop, Banff 1990
Proceedings of the IV Higher Order Workshop, Banff, Alberta, Canada, 10–14 September 1990
Graham Birtwistle (Ed.)